SOCIAL AND PERSONALITY DEVELOPMENT

Second Edition

SOCIAL AND PERSONALITY DEVELOPMENT

Second Edition

David R. Shaffer
University of Georgia

Brooks/Cole Publishing Company
Pacific Grove, California

Consulting Editor: Lawrence S. Wrightsman

Brooks/Cole Publishing Company
A Division of Wadsworth, Inc.

Printed in the United States of America

10   9   8   7   6   5   4   3   2   1

Library of Congress Cataloging-in-Publication Data

Shaffer, David.
   Social and personality development.

   Includes bibliographies and index.
   1. Personality development.   2. Socialization.
I. Title.   [DNLM: 1. Child Psychology.   2. Personality
Development.   3. Socialization.   WS 105.5.S6 S525s]
BF723.P4S48   1987   155.4'18   87-10958
ISBN 0-534-08412-5

Sponsoring Editor: *C. Deborah Laughton*
Marketing Representatives: *Jane Moulton and Tom Braden*
Editorial Assistant: *Amy Mayfield*
Production Coordinator: *Fiorella Ljunggren*
Manuscript Editor: *Rephah Berg*
Permissions Editor: *Carline Haga*
Interior and Cover Design: *Sharon L. Kinghan*
Art Coordinator: *Lisa Torri*
Interior Illustration: *Judith L. Macdonald and Lori Heckelman*
Photo Editor and Researcher: *Marquita Flemming*
Typesetting: *TypeLink, Inc., San Diego, California*
Printing and Binding: *Arcata Graphics/Fairfield, Fairfield, Pennsylvania*
(Credits continue on p. 513.)

PREFACE

In the preface to the first edition, I expressed the opinion that the study of social and personality development had come of age and the hope that my book reflected that fact. Clearly, the former premise turned out to be correct—so correct, in fact, that the information explosion that has occurred over the past nine years has rendered the earlier volume hopelessly obsolete.

My purpose in revising *Social and Personality Development* has been to produce a current and comprehensive overview of the discipline that reflects the best theories, research, and practical wisdom that social developmentalists have to offer. Throughout my many years of teaching, I have tried to select rigorous, research-based textbooks that are also interesting, accurate, up to date, and written in clear, concise language that my students can easily understand. I believe that a good text should talk to, rather than at, its readers, anticipating their interests, questions, and concerns and treating them as active participants in the learning process. A good "developmental" text should also stress the processes that underlie developmental change, so that students come away from the course with a firm understanding of the causes and complexities of whatever aspect(s) of development the text strives to present. Last but not least, a good text is a relevant text—one that shows how the theory and research that students are asked to digest can be applied to a number of real-life settings. The present volume represents my attempt to accomplish all these objectives.

Philosophy

Certain philosophical views are inherent in any systematic treatment of a discipline as broad as social and personality development. My philosophy can be summarized as follows:

• *I emphasize theory and believe in theoretical eclecticism.* And my reasons for doing so are straightforward: The study of social and personality development is now a well-established scientific discipline—one that has advanced because of the efforts of a large number of researchers who have taught us so much about developing children by formulating theory and systematically evaluating their theoretical hypotheses. This area of study has a very rich theoretical tradition, and all the theories we will review have contributed in important ways to our understanding of social and personality development. Consequently, this book will not attempt to convince its readers that any one theoretical viewpoint is "best." The psychoanalytic, behavioristic, cognitive-developmental, social information-processing, ethological, and behavior genetic viewpoints (as well as several less encompassing theories that address selected aspects of development) are all treated with respect.

• *The best information about human development comes from systematic research.* To teach this course effectively, I believe that one must convince students of the value of theory and systematic research. Although there are many ways to achieve these objectives, I have chosen to contrast modern developmental psychology with its "prescientific" origins and then to discuss and illustrate the many methodological approaches that developmentalists use to test their theories and answer important questions about developing children and adolescents. I've taken care to explain why there is no "best method" for studying social and personality development, and I've repeatedly stressed that our most reliable knowledge is based on outcomes that can be replicated using a variety of methods.

• *I favor a strong process orientation.* A major complaint with many developmental texts is that they describe human development without explaining why it occurs. My own "process orientation" is based on the belief that students are more likely to remember what develops and when if they know and understand the reasons that these developments take place.

• *Human development is a holistic process.* Although individual researchers may concentrate on particular topics such as physical development, cognitive development, emotional development, or the development of moral reasoning, development is not piecemeal but *holistic*: Human beings are at once physical, cognitive, social, and emotional creatures, and each of these components of self depends, in part, on changes that are taking place in other areas of development. Clearly, this is a "specialty" book that focuses primarily on the social and emotional aspects of development. However, I have striven to paint a holistic portrait of the developing person by stressing the fundamental interplay among biological, cognitive, social, and ecological influences in my coverage of each and every facet of social and personality development that we will discuss.

• *A developmental text should be a resource book for students—one that reflects current knowledge.* I have chosen to cite a fair number of very recent studies and reviews to ensure that my coverage (and any outside readings that students may undertake) will represent our current understanding of a topic or topics. However, I have tried to avoid the tendency, common in textbooks, to ignore older research simply because it is older. In fact, many of the "classics" of social and personality development are prominently displayed throughout the text to illustrate im-

portant breakthroughs and to show how our knowledge about developing persons gradually builds on earlier findings and insights.

Content

Though not formally divided into parts, the book can be viewed in that way. The first four chapters (which could be construed as Part One) present an orientation to the discipline and the tools of the trade, including a thorough discussion and illustration of research methodologies (in Chapter 1) and substantive reviews of psychoanalytic, ethological, and behavior genetic theories (in Chapter 2), the behavioristic and social information-processing viewpoints (in Chapter 3), and the cognitive-developmental perspective (in Chapter 4). An important feature of this coverage is its analyses of the contributions and limitations of each research method and each of the major theoretical traditions.

Chapters 5–12 (which could be labeled Part Two) focus on the "products," or outcomes, of social and personality development—that is, early social and emotional development (Chapter 5) and its implications for later development (Chapter 6); development of the self-concept, sociability, and social cognition (Chapter 7); achievement (Chapter 8); aggression (Chapter 9); altruism and prosocial development (Chapter 10); moral development (Chapter 11); and sex-typing and sex-role development (Chapter 12).

The final section (or Part Three) of the text explores the settings and contexts in which people develop, and it could be labeled the "ecology" of development. Here the focus is on the family as an agent of socialization (Chapter 13) and on three important extrafamilial influences: television, schools, and children's peer groups (Chapter 14).

New to This Edition

This second edition contains some important changes in the treatment of both theoretical and topical issues. These changes include expanded coverage of biological theories (ethology and behavior genetics) and a discussion of recent social information-processing approaches. The empirical literature has been extensively updated, with the result that now more than half the references date from the 1980s.

All chapters have been revised significantly to incorporate new topics and to better reflect recent developments in the field. The major alterations and additions from the first edition include the following:

- In Chapter 1, heavier emphasis has been placed on research methodology.
- Chapter 2 now also covers two biological approaches: ethology and behavior genetics.
- Chapter 3 includes an update of social-learning theory and a discussion of attribution theory.
- The topic of early emotional development in Chapters 5 and 6 has been expanded and now also covers the effects of maternal employment and daycare.
- There is an entirely new chapter (Chapter 7) on "The Self and Social Cognition."
- Chapters 8 through 12 present updated coverage of achievement, aggression, altruism, moral development, and sex typing. Included are Dodge's social information-processing theory of aggression and Martin and Halverson's social-information theory of sex typing, as well as a contemporary assessment of the literature on psychological androgyny.
- Chapter 13 is a new chapter entirely devoted to the family, with special emphasis on the role siblings play in the socialization process.
- Coverage of television and school as socializing agents has been added to Chapter 14.

Writing Style

My goal has been to write a book that talks directly to its readers and treats them as active participants in an ongoing discussion. I have tried to be relatively informal and down to earth in my writing style and to rely heavily on questions, thought problems, and a number of other exercises to stimulate student interest and involvement. Many of the chapters were pretested on my own students, who provided many useful ideas for clarification and suggested several of the analogies and occasional anecdotes that I've used when introducing and explaining complex ideas. So, with the valuable assistance of my student-critics, I have attempted to prepare a volume that is substantive and challenging but that reads more like a story than an encyclopedia.

Special Features

Among the features I've included to make the book more interesting and the material easier to learn are the following:

- *Boxes.* Each chapter contains boxes that call attention to important issues, ideas, or applications. The aim of the boxes is to permit a closer and more personal examination of selected topics, while stimulating the reader to reflect on the questions, controversies, and practices under scrutiny. All the boxes were carefully selected to reinforce central themes in the text.
- *Outlines and chapter summaries.* Outlines at the beginning of each chapter provide the student with a preview of what will be covered. Each chapter concludes with a succinct summary that allows the student to quickly review the chapter's major themes.
- *Subtitles.* Subtitles are employed very frequently to keep the material tightly organized and to divide the coverage into manageable bites.
- *Italics.* Italics are used liberally throughout the text to underscore central concepts and terminology and to emphasize important findings and conclusions.
- *Illustrations.* Photographs, figures, and tables appear frequently throughout the text. Although these features are designed, in part, to provide visual relief and to maintain student interest, they are not merely decorations. All visual aids, including the occasional cartoons, were selected to illustrate important principles and outcomes and thereby further the educational goals of the text.
- *Testing file* (for the instructor). An extensive testing file is available to all instructors who adopt *Social and Personality Development*. The test file for each chapter consists of 35 to 60 multiple-choice items, five to ten discussion questions, and page references for the answer to each question.

Acknowledgments

As is always the case with projects as large as this one, there are many individuals whose assistance was invaluable in the planning and production of this volume. I'll begin by expressing my gratitude to the following expert reviewers for their many, many constructive and insightful comments and suggestions: Leann Birch of the University of Illinois; David Lundgren of the University of Cincinnati; Suzanne Pallak of Georgetown University; Milton Rosenbaum of the University of Iowa (who perhaps deserves overtime pay, as he also shepherded me through the first edition of this text); Carol Sigelman of Eastern Kentucky University; Margi Stivers of Zonta Children's Center; and Colleen Surber of the University of Wisconsin.

Special thanks go to Geraldine Moon, who coordinated the efforts of the project's clerical staff, and to Marcia Edwards and Pat Smith, two true word pros who worked at least as diligently as I on this project, turning my nearly indecipherable handwriting into polished manuscript copy. It is difficult for me to express in words just how much their contributions have meant to me.

Last, but not least, the staff at Brooks/Cole has once again succeeded admirably in transforming an ugly caterpillar (my marked-up manuscript copy) into a beautiful monarch (the volume before you). Fiorella Ljunggren—a consummate professional, indeed—was the primary overseer of this epigenesis. She truly deserves a great deal of credit for the desirable attributes that this volume may possess. One of her wiser decisions was to select Rephah Berg as manuscript editor. Having now worked with Rephah on two projects, I am convinced that no one catches errors (in *logic* as well as syntax) any better than she. Carline Haga has been very helpful in securing permissions, and the art department has devoted many, many hours to the task of making this volume pleasing from a visual standpoint. I am indebted to all of them, especially designer Sharon Kinghan, art coordinator Lisa Torri, and photo editor Marquita Flemming. Finally, C. Deborah Laughton, my project editor, has once again succeeded in lifting my spirits and keeping me on track whenever I was beginning to suffer the ravages of burn-out. C. Deborah is a pleasure to work with, and I am indeed fortunate to have had her assistance and counsel.

David R. Shaffer

BRIEF CONTENTS

CONTENTS

7. THE SELF, SOCIAL COGNITION, AND SOCIABILITY   162

8. ACHIEVEMENT   195

9. AGGRESSION   233

SOCIAL AND PERSONALITY DEVELOPMENT

Second Edition

1

INTRODUCTION

To this day I can recall how I made the decision to become a psychologist. I was a first-quarter junior who had dabbled in premed, chemistry, zoology, and oceanography without firmly committing myself to any of these areas of investigation. Perhaps the single most important event that prompted me to walk over to the psychology table on that fateful fall registration day had actually occurred 18 months earlier. I am referring to the birth of my niece.

This little girl fascinated me. I found it quite remarkable that by the tender age of 18 months she was already reasonably proficient at communicating with others. I was also puzzled by the fact that, although she and I were pals when she was 5 months old, she seemed to fear me a few months later when I returned home for the summer. This toddler knew the names of a number of objects, animals, and people (mostly TV personalities), and she had already become very fond of certain individuals, particularly her mother and her grandmother. To my way of thinking she was well on her way to "becoming human," and the process intrigued me.

After studying developing children for nearly 20 years, I am more convinced than ever that the process of "becoming human," as I had called it, is remarkable in several respects. Consider the starting point. The newborn, or *neonate*, is often perceived as cute, cuddly, and lovable by its parents, but it is essentially an unknowing, dependent, demanding, and occasionally unreasonable little creature. Newborns have no prejudices or preconceptions; they speak no language; they have no idea of their sex and its implications; they obey no man-made laws; and they sometimes behave as if they were living for their next feeding. It is not hard to understand how John Locke (1690/1913) could describe the neonate as a *tabula rasa* (blank slate) who is receptive to any and all kinds of learning.

Irvin Child (1954, p. 655) has noted that, despite the enormous number of behavioral options available to the child, he is "led to develop actual behavior which is confined within a much narrower range— the range of what is customary and acceptable according to the standards of his group." Indeed, English children will learn to speak English while French children learn French. Jewish children will often develop an aversion to pork, Hindus will not eat the flesh of the sacred cow, and Christians learn that it is perfectly acceptable to consume either of these foodstuffs. American children are taught that they will someday play an active role in electing their leaders, while Jordanian and Saudi Arabian children learn that their rulers assume that role as a birthright. Children who grow up in certain areas of the United States are likely to prefer square dancing and country music, while those who live in other areas will prefer break dancing and Motown music. Some children are permitted to "sass" their parents, while others are taught to obey the commands of their elders without comment. In short, the child develops in a manner and direction prescribed by his or her society, community, and family.

What I had originally described as "becoming human" is more commonly labeled *socialization*. Socialization is the process through which the child acquires the beliefs, behaviors, and values deemed significant and appropriate by other members of society. The socialization of each succeeding generation serves society in at least three ways. First, it is a means of regulating behavior. I suspect that the penalties for rape, robbery, and murder are not the most important inhibitors of these heinous acts. Any one of us could probably walk outside, snatch someone's purse, and stand a reasonably good chance of making a few dollars without getting caught. Then why don't we mug little old ladies or commit several other low-risk but socially inappropriate behaviors? Probably because the control of antisocial acts is largely a personal matter that stems from the standards of morality—right and wrong—that we have acquired from our interactions with parents, teachers, peers, and many other agents of socialization. Second, the socialization process helps to promote the personal growth of the individual. As children interact with and become like other members of their culture, they acquire the knowledge, skills, motives, and aspirations that will enable them to function effectively within their communities. Finally, socialization perpetuates the social order. Socialized children become socialized adults who will impart what they have learned to their own children.

The study of socialization is truly an interdisciplinary science, for anthropologists, biologists, political scientists, psychologists, and sociologists have all contributed to our understanding of social and personality development. The sociologist concentrates on the *similarities* among children in their adjustment to society and its institutions. Sociologist Frederick Elkin (1960) notes:

> Although it is true that no two individuals are alike and that each person has a singular heredity, distinctive experiences, and a unique personality development, socialization focuses not on such individualizing patterns and processes but on similarities, on those aspects of development which concern the learning of, and adaptation to, the culture and society [p. 5].

Anthropologists share this interest in the products, or "common outcomes," of socialization but have proceeded a step further by studying the differences in socialization practices *across cultures* and the effects of these cultural variations on social and personality development.

Psychologists have emphasized the *processes* of socialization, or the means by which the child acquires socially approved beliefs, behaviors, and values. An important assumption of the psychological approach is that all children assimilate their social experiences in roughly the same fashion even though the content of this experience varies from family to family, community to community, and culture to culture.

One important difference between the psychological and the sociological perspectives concerns the emphasis placed on the similarities among children. Sociologists stress the common outcomes of socialization and pay little attention to individual differences. Psychologists also expect similarities among the children of any social group, but only to the extent that members of that group hold common beliefs about how their children should be raised. You can probably recall several occasions when you envied a friend who was allowed to do something or go somewhere that you couldn't. The point of this example is that each and every one of us faces a unique set of experiences while growing up, and therefore we should not be expected to emerge as carbon copies of our parents, our peers, or the child next door. In sum,

psychological theorists believe that individual personalities are an inevitable consequence of the socialization process.

THE UNIVERSAL PARENTING MACHINE—A THOUGHT EXPERIMENT

Jones, Hendrick, and Epstein (1979) have described an interesting thought experiment that touches on the major issues that we will discuss throughout this book. They title their hypothetical experiment the "Universal Parenting Machine" and describe the project as follows:

> Suppose that six infants are placed immediately after birth into a "universal parenting machine" (the UPM). To enliven the scenario, we may suppose that three infants are male and three female. The UPM is conceived as an enclosed building with advanced machinery and technology capable of taking care of all of the infants' physical needs from immediately after birth until maturity. The most critical feature of the UPM is that it is constructed so that the infants will have no human contact other than with each other during their first 18 years of life. In fact, they will not even know that other human beings exist [p. 52].

Now imagine that the creation of a UPM is within the range of our technical capabilities. Let's also assume that the UPM can be set up in such a way as to create a modern-day "Garden of Eden," complete with trees, flowers, the sounds of birds chirping, and a transparent domed roof so that our experimental children are exposed to the sights and sounds of the weather and the movements of the sun, the moon, and the stars. In other words, try to imagine that we have simulated a very pleasant acre of the real world that lacks at least one potentially important feature: we have omitted all other people and, indeed, the concept of a culture. Were we to expose six infants to this environment, there are many questions we might wish to ask about their development. Here are but a few:

- Perhaps the most basic question: Would these children interact with one another and become social creatures? If they did, several other questions could be asked.

- Would the children love one another, depend on one another, or develop stable friendships?
- Would the children ever develop a spoken language or some other efficient method of communicating complex ideas?
- Would this environment provide the kinds of stimulation that children need to develop intellectually so that they might have complex ideas to express?
- Would these children develop sex roles and/or become sexual beings at maturity?
- Would the children develop a sense of pride in their accomplishments (assuming, of course, that they were able to accomplish anything meaningful on their own)?
- Would the children's interactions be benevolent (guided by a spirit of togetherness, cooperation, and altruism) or belligerent (destructive and aggressive)?
- Would these children ever develop standards of good and evil or right and wrong to govern their day-to-day interactions?

How would the experiment turn out? That's hard to say, for this kind of project has not been conducted and, if current ethical guidelines prevail, probably never will. But this is a thought experiment, and there is nothing to prevent us from speculating about possible outcomes, with the help of what is known about social and personality development.

Recall that the product of socialization is a person who has acquired the beliefs, attitudes, and behaviors that are thought to be appropriate for members of his or her culture. How does the child become socialized? One point of view is that children are shaped by their culture. Were we to adopt this viewpoint quite literally, we might predict that our six experimental children would surely become little vegetables or semihumans in the absence of a prevailing social structure. The opposite side of the coin is that culture is shaped by people. If this point of view has any merit, we might assume that our six children would show enough initiative to interact, to develop strong affectional ties, and to create their own little society complete with a set of rules or customs to govern their

interactions. Although this suggestion may seem quite improbable, there is at least one case in which a small group of Jewish war orphans did indeed form their own "society" in the absence of adult supervision while in a German prison camp during the Second World War (Freud & Dann, 1951). This group will be discussed in detail in Chapters 6 and 14.

Of course, we can't be absolutely certain that infants raised by the UPM would create the same kind of social order the young war orphans did. Furthermore, the orphans were integrated into adult society at a very early age, so that they provide few clues about the kinds of people that our experimental children might eventually become. So where do we turn to develop some predictions about the outcome of our experiment? One possibility is to examine the existing theories of social and personality development to see what hints they can provide.

There are several theories of socialization, each of which makes assumptions about children and the ways they develop. In the following sections of this chapter, we will compare and contrast a number of these theories on the basis of the assumptions they make. Our theoretical overview will carry over into Chapters 2, 3, and 4, where we will take a closer look at several major perspectives on social and personality development.

Once we have had an opportunity to examine the major theories, our focus will shift to a most important aspect of social development: the child's earliest interpersonal relationships. You may have observed that young infants become attached to "mama" and often voice their displeasure if separated from this intimate companion. How does this attachment originate? How does it affect the infant's reactions to strangers? Why and under what circumstances will an infant become distressed when separated from its mother or from another close companion? These issues are explored in some detail in Chapter 5. Chapter 6 addresses another important question: What happens to children who do not become attached to an adult or do not develop a sense of social responsiveness during the first two to three years of life? The answers to all these questions, particularly the last, would almost certainly provide some basis for speculation about the development of children raised by a universal parenting machine.

People clearly differ in their willingness to engage others in social interaction and to seek their attention or approval. Some individuals can be described as loners, while others are outgoing and gregarious. These two types differ in what is called *sociability*, or the value they place on the presence, attention, and approval of other people. Achievement is another way in which people clearly differ. Some people take great pride in their accomplishments and seem highly motivated to achieve. Others do not appear to be terribly concerned about what they have accomplished or what they are likely to accomplish in the future. Would our six experimental children come to value the presence, attention, or approval of one another? Would they develop a motive to achieve? Perhaps a review of the factors that influence children's sociability, achievement motivation, and achievement behavior will help us to decide. These topics are discussed in Chapters 7 and 8.

Earlier, we wondered whether interactions among our six experimental children would turn out to be benevolent or belligerent. Children raised in a typical home setting display both kinds of behavior, but we should keep in mind that the socializing experiences provided by a UPM could hardly be described as typical. Nevertheless, it might be possible to make some educated guesses about the positive or negative character of these children's interactions if we had some information about the development of aggression and altruism in normally reared children. The factors that affect children's aggressive inclinations are discussed in Chapter 9. The development of altruism and prosocial behavior (generosity, helpfulness, and cooperation) is the focus of Chapter 10.

One of the reasons that human beings are able to live together in ordered societies is that they have devised laws and moral norms that distinguish right from wrong and govern their day-to-day interactions. How do children acquire a knowledge of these moral principles? What role do parents, teachers, peers, and other agents of socialization play in the moral development of the child? The answers to these questions may well provide some hints about the likelihood that children raised by a universal parenting machine would develop their own moral norms. Moral development becomes the topic of discussion in Chapter 11.

Recall that the children selected for our experiment were balanced with respect to biological sex (three males and three females). Would they eventually differentiate among themselves on the basis of gender? Would they develop a sense of masculinity and femininity and pursue different activities? Would they become sexual beings at maturity? There are reasons for predicting that the answers to all these questions would be yes, for gender is, after all, a biological characteristic. But we should keep in mind that sex roles and standards of sexual conduct are almost certainly affected by social values and customs. Thus, the sex typing and the sexual behavior of our six experimental children might well depend on the kind of social order they created, as well as on their biological heritage. The determinants of sex typing and sex-role behaviors are explored in some detail in Chapter 12.

Since our experimental children are to be raised by a machine, they will not be exposed to a nuclear family as we know it, consisting of a mother, a father, and any number of brothers and sisters. How would the lack of family ties and familial influence affect their development? Perhaps we can gain some insight on this issue after focusing on the family as an agent of socialization in Chapter 13.

Although families may have an enormous impact on their young throughout childhood and adolescence, it is only a matter of time before other societal agents begin to exert their influence. For example, infants and toddlers are frequently exposed to alternative caregivers and a host of new playmates when their working parents place them in some kind of day care. Even those toddlers who remain at home will soon begin to learn more about the outside world once they develop an interest in television. And by age 6 to 7, virtually all youngsters in Western societies are venturing outside the home to school, a setting that requires them to adjust to the demands of a new authority figure—the classroom teacher—and to interact effectively with other little people who are similar to themselves. Does exposure to television or to formal schooling contribute in any meaningful way to the shaping of one's character? Do playmates and the peer group have a significant effect on a child's social and personality development? The answers to these questions are of obvious importance to the development of our six experimental children, who are to be raised with no exposure to the electronic media and no companions other than peers. Thus, our overview of social and personality development will conclude in Chapter 14 with a discussion of three major "extrafamilial" agents of socialization—television, schools, and children's peer groups.

In sum, we cannot specify *exactly* how children raised by a universal parenting machine would turn out. After all, we have no empirical precedents from which to work. Although we will not dwell further on our hypothetical children in the text, you may want to keep them in mind and to make some educated guesses about their future as we examine the major theories of social and personality development and review a portion of the data on children's socialization that have been collected over the past 60 to 70 years. Let's begin by looking at some of the assumptions that social-developmental theorists have made about children and the socialization process.

THEORIES OF SOCIAL AND PERSONALITY DEVELOPMENT

You may never have considered yourself a theorist, but you probably are. If I were to ask you why males and females are so very different as adults when they seem so very similar as infants, you would undoubtedly give me some explanation. In so doing, you would be stating or at least reflecting your own underlying theory of sex-role development.

A theory is really nothing more than a set of concepts and propositions created by the theorist to represent or explain some aspect of his or her experience. Psychological theories help us to understand certain behavioral phenomena and allow us to derive predictions, or *hypotheses*, about future events. Par-

ents who support the adage "Spare the rod and spoil the child" are telling us something about their theory of child rearing. Specifically, they seem to be saying that a swat across the seat of the pants is an effective method of behavior control that should also have the effect of making the child feel responsible for his or her actions.

Theories of socialization are many in number and varied in focus. Several qualify as "mini-theories" that apply only to certain aspects of social and personality development. Yet, there are some global theories that make a number of basic assumptions about human nature and offer explanations for virtually all facets of the socialization process. The mini-theories are important and will be discussed when we take up the topics to which they apply. However, the major portion of this book is organized around several very broad theories of social and personality development, including *psychoanalytic theory, the biological viewpoint, social-learning theory,* and *cognitive-development theory.*

Psychoanalytic theory originated from Sigmund Freud's clinical observations of emotionally disturbed adults. We will see in the next chapter that Freud considered the emotional developments of childhood to be the building blocks of the adult personality. His emphasis on the emotional, or affective, aspects of socialization has led many of his followers to conclude that parents' child-rearing practices have a profound effect on the personality development of their children.

The biological viewpoint is similar to Freud's psychoanalytic theory in that both schools of thought believe that many human social behaviors are attributable, in part, to instincts or other attributes that have a hereditary basis. One group of biological theorists, the *ethologists*, stresses that certain patterns of social behavior are products of our evolutionary history that have persisted over time because they help us to survive. Other biologically oriented theorists, such as the *behavior geneticists*, are less inclined to attribute human social behavior to instincts stemming from our evolution as a species. However, they do stress that everyone inherits a different set of genes from his or her parents and that the particular combination of genes that one inherits will influence one's temperament, personality, and mental health. We will focus on these biological theories of social and personality development, along with the psychoanalytic approach, in Chapter 2.

In Chapter 3 we will review the most important aspects of social-learning theory. The central tenet of this approach is that the vast majority of human behavior is *learned* rather than innate or genetically programmed. Parents, teachers, and other socializing agents are said to steer the child toward socially acceptable patterns of conduct by reinforcing his or her "desirable" acts while punishing those responses that they consider undesirable or socially inappropriate. Moreover, children are thought to acquire many competent or socially adaptive behaviors as they carefully observe and then imitate the actions of parents, older siblings, and a variety of other social "models."

Cognitive-developmental theory derives from the prodigious efforts of Jean Piaget, a theorist who is concerned mainly with the course of cognitive (intellectual) development rather than the whys and wherefores of socialization. According to Piaget (1969), cognitive development progresses through a series of stages, and each succeeding stage represents a totally new and more complex version of its predecessor. Lawrence Kohlberg (1966, 1969) proceeds one step further by suggesting that social and personality development also occurs in stages. Kohlberg assumes that a person's level, or stage, of cognitive development largely determines how he or she views the world and, thus, what the person is likely to learn from his or her interactions with others. The cognitive-developmental approach is the subject of Chapter 4.

Many people find it difficult not to select a "favorite" theory of social and personality development after scanning several of these approaches for the first time. The reason that we tend to "play favorites" may be quite simple: we all make assumptions about children and the ways they develop, and perhaps we tend to favor theories that make assumptions similar to our own. See whether you find this true of yourself. Take the short quiz in Box 1-1 and compare the overall pattern of your five responses against the several patterns that appear in the key. Then, after complet-ing your study of Chapters 1–4, see whether the theory you prefer is the one that most closely matches the pattern of responses you favored when completing this exercise. (Let's note, however, that the best way to evaluate these theories is on the demonstrated ability of each to predict and explain significant aspects of human social and personality development, not on the basis of our first impressions or preferences.)

Now let's take a closer look at some of the major issues and points of contention that contemporary theorists debate.

QUESTIONS AND CONTROVERSIES ABOUT HUMAN DEVELOPMENT

Developmental theorists have different points of view on at least four basic issues:

1. Are children inherently good or inherently bad?
2. Is nature (biological forces) or nurture (environmental forces) the primary influence on human development?
3. Are children actively involved in the developmental process; or, rather, are they passive recipients of social and biological influences?
4. Is development continuous or discontinuous?

EARLY PHILOSOPHICAL PERSPECTIVES ON HUMAN NATURE

What kind of animal is man? After debating this issue for centuries, social philosophers have produced viewpoints ranging from Thomas Hobbes's (1651/1904) doctrine of *original sin*, which held that children are inherently selfish egoists who must be controlled by society, to Jean Jacques Rousseau's doctrine of *innate purity*—the notion that children are born with an intuitive sense of right and wrong that is often misdirected by society. These two viewpoints clearly differ in their implications for child rearing. Proponents of original sin argued that parents must actively restrain their egoistic offspring, while the innate purists viewed children as "noble savages"

BOX 1-1   MATCH WITS WITH THE THEORISTS

All of us have made certain assumptions about children and child rearing. Developmental theorists make assumptions too, and their assumptions largely determine what they may propose in the way of a theory. You may find it interesting to match wits with these influential scholars to see with whom you most agree (initially, at least). Answer the five questions that follow. Then compare the patterning of your five responses against the patterns that appear in the "key" at the end of this exercise. The pattern that comes closest to your own will tell you with which group of theorists you are most philosophically consistent.

1. Biological factors (for example, heredity, maturation) and social forces (for example, culture, methods of parenting) are thought to contribute to human development. All things considered, which set of forces contributes more heavily in this regard?
   a. Biological factors contribute more than 70% to developmental outcomes. *[handwritten: Bio. viewpt.]*
   b. Biological factors contribute 60–70%; social forces contribute 30–40%. *[handwritten: Cognitive/Piaget Bioviewpt.]*
   c. Biological factors and social forces are equally important. *[handwritten: Psycho — Freud]*
   d. Social forces contribute 60–70%; biological factors contribute 30–40%. *[handwritten: Social Learning/Psych Erikson]*
   e. Social forces contribute more than 70% to developmental outcomes. *[handwritten: Soc. Learning]*
2. Children are—
   a. "Seething cauldrons"—creatures whose basically negative impulses must be controlled. *[handwritten: Psy — Freud, Bioview P]*
   b. Neither inherently good nor inherently bad. *[handwritten: Soc. Learn Locke Watson]*
   c. Noble savages—creatures who are born with many positive and few negative tendencies. *[handwritten: Cognitive Piaget Rousseau, Psy+Erikson Kohlberg]*
3. Development proceeds—
   a. In stages—that is, through a series of fairly abrupt changes. *[handwritten: Psy (Freud Erik) Cog-learning Piaget Biological viewpt]*
   b. Continuously—in small increments without abrupt changes. *[handwritten: Social Learning - Watson Locke]*
4. Children are basically—
   a. Active creatures who play a major role in determining their own character. *[handwritten: 1/3 Soc-Learning; Bioviewpt. Cog. Psy Erikson]*

[handwritten top right: 2/3 Soc.learn]

   b. Passive creatures whose characters are molded by parents, teachers, and other agents of society. *[handwritten: Psy]*
5. Character attributes such as aggressiveness or dependency—
   a. First appear in childhood and remain relatively stable over time. *[handwritten: Psy - Freud & Erikson]*
   b. First appear in childhood but may change rapidly at some later time. *[handwritten: Soc. learning, Cog., Biological viewpt]*

Now transcribe your answers in the space marked "Your Pattern." Then invert the page and compare your pattern with the patterns that appear in the key. On the basis of the five assumptions you have made, are you a budding psychoanalyst, learning theorist, cognitive developmentalist, or biological theorist?

Question

Your pattern: 1   2   3   4   5

Key

*Biological theorists differ on the exact weights given to biological and social factors.

Pattern of answers					
Theory and/or theorist	1	2	3	4	5
Sigmund Freud's psychoanalytic theory.	c	a	a	b	a
Erik Erikson's psychosocial theory (a revision and extension of Freud's thinking). Note the similarities here.	d	c	a	a	a
These patterns describe the assumptions made by learning theorists. Different learning theorists make slightly different assumptions, but if your pattern closely approximates one of these, you are most philosophically consistent with the learning viewpoint.	e	b	b	a	b
	e	b	b	b	b
Jean Piaget's cognitive-developmental theory.	b	c	a	a	b
The biological perspective.	a or b*	a	a	b	b

who should be given the freedom to follow their inherently positive inclinations.

   Another view on children and child rearing was suggested by John Locke, who believed that the mind of an infant is a *tabula rasa*, or "blank slate," that is written upon by experience. In other words, children were portrayed as neither inherently good nor inherently bad, and how they will turn out should depend entirely on how they are raised. Like Hobbes, Locke argued in favor of disciplined child rearing to

ORIGINAL
SIN

INNATE
PURITY

ensure that children develop good habits and acquire few if any unacceptable impulses.

As it turns out, each of these three philosophical perspectives on human nature remains with us today in one or more contemporary theories of social and personality development. Although one may search in vain for explicit statements about human nature, the theorist will typically emphasize the positive or the negative aspects of children's character or perhaps will note that positivity or negativity of character depends on the child's experiences. These assumptions about human nature are important, for they influence the content of each developmental theory—particularly what the theory has to say about child rearing.

NATURE VERSUS NURTURE

One of the oldest controversies among developmental theorists is the "nature versus nurture" issue: Are human beings a product of their heredity and other biological predispositions, or are they shaped by the environment in which they are raised? Here are two opposing viewpoints:

> Heredity and not environment is the chief maker of man. . . . Nearly all of the misery and nearly all of the happiness in the world are due not to environment. . . . The differences among men are due to differences in the germ cells with which they were born [Wiggam, 1923, p. 42].

> Give me a dozen healthy infants, well formed, and my own specified world to bring them up in and I'll guarantee to take any one at random and train him to become any type of specialist I might select—doctor, lawyer, artist, merchant, chief, and yes, even beggarman and thief, regardless of his talents, penchants, tendencies, abilities, vocations, and race of his ancestors. There is no such thing as an inheritance of capacity, talent, temperament, mental constitution, and behavioral characteristics [Watson, 1925, p. 82].

Clearly these are extreme positions that few contemporary researchers would be willing to endorse. Today, many developmentalists believe that the relative contributions of nature and nurture depend on the aspect of development in question: social forces predominate in some areas (for example, moral development), while biological factors take precedence in others (for example, physical growth and development). However, they stress that most complex human attributes, such as temperament, personality, and mental health, are probably best viewed as the end products of a long and involved interplay between biological predispositions and environmental forces. Their advice to us, then, is to think less about nature *versus* nurture and more about how these two sets of influences combine or *interact* to produce developmental change.

ACTIVITY VERSUS PASSIVITY

Another topic of theoretical debate is the *activity/ passivity* issue. Are children curious, active creatures who largely determine how agents of society treat them? Or are they passive souls on whom society fixes its stamp? Consider the implications of these

TABULA RASA

opposing viewpoints. If it could be shown that children are extremely malleable—literally at the mercy of those who raise them—then perhaps individuals who turned out to be less than productive would be justified in suing their overseers for malfeasance. Indeed, one young man in the United States recently used this logic to bring a malfeasance suit against his parents. Perhaps you can anticipate the defense that the parents' lawyer would offer. Counsel would surely argue that the parents tried many strategies in an attempt to raise their child right but that he responded favorably to none of them. The implication is that this young man played an active role in determining how his parents treated him and therefore bears a large share of the responsibility for creating the climate in which he was raised.

As we will see in the next three chapters, there is an intermediate stance on this activity/passivity issue, one that leans more in the direction of an active child than a passive one. This "middle ground" is the view that human development is best described as a continuous *reciprocal interaction* between children and their environments (*reciprocal determinism*): the environment clearly affects the child, but the child's mannerisms and behaviors will also affect the en-

vironment. The implication is that children are *actively involved* in creating the very environments that will influence their growth and development.

CONTINUITY VERSUS DISCONTINUITY

Think for a moment about the concept of developmental change. Do you think the changes we experience along the road to maturity occur very gradually? Or would you say these changes are rather abrupt?

Continuity theorists view human development as an additive process that occurs in small steps, without sudden changes. They might represent the course of developmental change with a relatively smooth growth curve like the one in Figure 1-1A. In contrast, discontinuity, or "stage," theorists believe that the developing child proceeds through a series of abrupt changes, each of which elevates the child to a new and presumably more advanced stage of development. These stages are represented by the plateaus in the discontinuous growth curve in Figure 1-1B.

A developmental stage is a period of the life cycle characterized by a particular set of abilities, motives, behaviors, or emotions that occur together and form a coherent pattern. However, it is important to note that a stage is merely a *description* of the attributes that appear at one point in the life cycle: A theorist who summarizes the course of development with a series of stages has not necessarily explained why that development occurred. To qualify as an *explanation* of development, a stage theory must tell (1) how or why components of each stage "hang together" as an organized whole and (2) how or why children progress from stage to stage.

The continuity/discontinuity controversy is not easily resolved. Consider the following example. One teenager thought he would never grow. Although his height had been increasing at about one inch per year for several years, he was only 5′2″ at the beginning of his third year of high school. His friends (and some prospective dates) called him "shrimpie." Ah, but that glorious junior year! He grew nine inches, gained 45 pounds, and suddenly found himself being "drafted" in the earlier rounds when team captains chose players for football games in gym class.

Isn't this discontinuous development—a spurt of nine inches in one year after growing but five inches

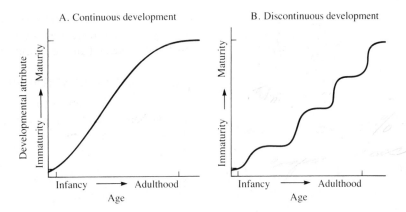

FIGURE 1-1   The course of development as described by continuity and discontinuity (stage) theorists

over the past five years? Stage theorists would certainly say it is. Continuity theorists, however, might argue that the boy's growth had been very steady during the previous five years. They would also note that he didn't grow nine inches overnight—it took a year to do so. What was happening, in their view, was that the boy was experiencing an event, puberty, that caused his rate of physical development to accelerate. But even though he was growing faster during his one-year "growth spurt," this growth remained gradual, or continuous, over that year.

One reason for the continuity/discontinuity debate is that discontinuity theorists tend to focus on the visible results of development—the obvious changes in the child with age—whereas continuity theorists are looking at the processes that give rise to these changes. Research in developmental psychology shows that different types of development are important at different periods of the life cycle. For example, the development of intimate emotional ties to close companions is particularly noteworthy during infancy and adolescence; one's gender identity and sex-role preferences are rapidly developing during the preschool period; moral reasoning undergoes dramatic changes during middle childhood and adolescence; and a strong concern about one's present and future roles in life becomes a preoccupation for many people during late adolescence and young adulthood. If we concentrate on *what it is that is developing* (for example, emotional bonds, gender

identity, moral reasoning, personal identities), social and personality development may often appear to be rather discontinuous, or "stagelike." But if we focus on the processes that underlie these developments (for example, biological maturation and learning), then development may seem much more gradual, or continuous. As we review the leading theories of child development, we will see that continuity theorists do tend to concentrate on the *processes* that underlie developmental change, whereas stage theorists are concerned mainly with the nature or *content* of these changes.

MATCHING ASSUMPTIONS WITH THEORIES

Now that we have seen the kinds of issues on which theorists differ, let's briefly consider the patterns of assumptions made by particular theories and theoretical traditions.

Psychoanalytic theory.   Sigmund Freud adopted the doctrine of original sin when he formulated his psychoanalytic theory of social and personality development. His impression was that human beings were "seething cauldrons" who must constantly seek to gratify a number of innate sexual and aggressive instincts. Like Hobbes, Freud believed that the purpose of socialization was to divert the child's socially undesirable impulses away from their natural outlets and into socially acceptable patterns of behavior. His view was that children are "molded" by the more powerful elements of society, and he depicted the young child as a relatively *passive* entity in this "socialization" process—one whose developmental outcomes (that is, personality or character) would depend largely on the emotional climate created by parents in their attempts at child rearing.

In recent years, proponents of psychoanalytic theory (Erikson, 1963, 1972; Hartmann, 1958) have reassessed Freud's views and concluded that children are not nearly so sinister or so passive as Freud had assumed. Erik Erikson argues that the child is an active, curious explorer whose lifelong attempts to master the environment are not easily explained as a displacement of primitive sexual or aggressive urges. Erikson clearly stresses the positive, adaptive aspects of our character, and, in this sense, his viewpoint resembles that of the innate purists.

The biological viewpoint.   Like Freud, biological theorists contend that children have inherited a number of attributes and behavioral predispositions that will have a profound effect on their development. But in marked contrast to Freud's passive child, the biological view is that even newborn babes are *active*, adaptive souls who are capable of influencing the character of their environments from the moment of birth. Ethologists, for example, have argued that human infants inherit several patterned behaviors (such as smiling, crying, and clinging) that serve to attract attention and/or promote contact with their caregivers—precisely the kind of experience that a baby needs to form secure emotional ties to other members of the species. Thus, the biological viewpoint is that children are neither inherently good nor inherently bad but, rather, inherently active and adaptive.

Proponents of the biological perspective tend to concentrate very heavily on the hereditary bases of behavior—the nature side of the nature/nurture issue. Nevertheless, they are well aware that human beings are largely products of their environments and that little of anything of lasting developmental significance occurs automatically. To pursue our example, infants may well be biologically predisposed to beam signals (such as smiles and cries) to their caregivers, but these innate responses will eventually wane if they fail to produce favorable reactions from unresponsive companions. (In this case, the environment might be said to have overridden a biological predisposition.) Of the four major approaches to social and personality development, the biological viewpoint is really more a "point of view" than a well-articulated theory. We will see that biological studies are often useful for pinpointing some of the causes of social *behavior*; however, they are rarely sufficient, in themselves, for explaining social and personality *development*.

Social-learning theory.   The doctrine of *tabula rasa* provides the philosophical base for several models of socialization known collectively as social-learning theory. The most influential of the early social-learning theorists was the American psychologist John B. Watson. Watson believed that children enter the world with very little in the way of ability, knowledge, or behavioral predispositions. In other words, he viewed the neonate as a blank slate who would develop very gradually according to the kinds of learning experiences provided by the environment.

Watson's strong belief in "environmental determinism" was generally accepted by other social-learning theorists until the 1960s. During that decade, Albert Bandura and his associates (Bandura, 1965; Bandura & Walters, 1963) criticized their colleagues for failing to recognize that children are active, thinking organisms who are quite capable of self-instruction, self-reinforcement, and, thus, some degree of self-determination. Bandura concedes that the newborn infant is a naive, unknowing creature who is quite receptive to environmental influence. But he suggests that the child and the environment are in a constant state of *reciprocal interaction*: the active, creative child is said to affect the environment, and the resulting environment then affects the child. Thus, the Bandurans are set apart from earlier social-learning theorists by their contention that children are active agents who have a hand in determining the character of their own socializing environment.

Cognitive-developmental theory. Cognitive-developmental theorists Jean Piaget and Lawrence Kohlberg have adopted a perspective that resembles the doctrine of innate purity. Although the cognitive theorists do not make the assumption that humans are inherently moral, they do stress the positive aspects of human development while rejecting the notion that children are passive recipients of environmental influence. Indeed, Piaget asserts that the child is an *active* explorer who is born with a need to adapt to his or her environment.

What does Piaget mean by "adaptation"? In the biological sciences, *adaptation* refers to the organism's ability to cope with its surroundings, and the function of this adaptation is survival. Piaget's adaptation serves a similar purpose: the child must understand the environment in order to function effectively within it. Piaget contends that children become increasingly adaptive as they develop intellectually, for adaptation results from the interaction between the child's evolving cognitive structures (abilities) and environmental stimuli. The environment provides the impetus for cognitive development. But Piaget stresses that the reorganization and extension of the child's cognitive abilities are undertaken *by the child when he or she is prepared for this undertaking* and are *not* "shaped" by parents, teachers, or any other external agent. In sum, active, exploring children do not simply mirror experience; they create it, and in the process they change themselves (Langer, 1969).

As the child develops intellectually and becomes capable of increasingly complex adaptations, his or her conception of self in relation to others is changing. Kohlberg (1969) emphasizes that children's reactions to parental demands, peer pressures, social models, and other interpersonal encounters depend on their cognitive construction (that is, understanding) of these events. Thus, the cognitive theorists assume that intellectual and social development occur together and represent a "fundamental unity."

The philosophical assumptions underlying each major theory of social and personality development are summarized in the "key" of the exercise in Box 1-1. You may find it helpful to use these assumptions as a framework for understanding why each theory has taken the form that it has.

In the next section of the chapter, we will focus on the "tools of the trade"—that is, the research methods that developmentalists use to test their theories and gain a better understanding of the child's world.

RESEARCH METHODS

When detectives are assigned cases to solve, they will first gather the facts, formulate hunches, and then sift through the clues or collect additional information until one of their hunches proves correct. Unraveling the mysteries of social and personality development is in many ways a similar endeavor. Investigators must carefully observe their subjects, study the information they have collected, and then use it to draw conclusions about the ways people develop.

Our focus in this section is on the methods that researchers use to gather information about developing children and adolescents. Our first task is to understand why developmentalists consider it absolutely essential to gather all these facts. We will then discuss the advantages and disadvantages of several basic fact-finding strategies and see how these techniques might be used to detect developmental change.

THE SCIENTIFIC METHOD

The study of social and personality development is appropriately labeled a scientific enterprise because modern developmentalists have adopted a value system called the scientific method that guides their attempts at understanding. The scientific method is really more of an attitude or a value than a method; the attitude dictates that, above all, investigators must be *objective* and must allow their observations (or data) to decide the merits of their thinking.

In the 17th and 18th centuries, when social philosophers were presenting their views on children and child rearing, their ideas were often interpreted as

fact. It was as if people assumed that great minds always had great insights. Very few individuals questioned the word of these well-known scholars, because the scientific method was not yet an important criterion for evaluating wisdom or knowledge.

The intent here is not to criticize the early social philosophers. In fact, today's developmentalists (and children) are indebted to these men for helping to modify the ways in which society thought about, treated, and often exploited its young (see Ariès. 1962; Despert, 1965). However, so-called great minds may produce miserable ideas on occasion, and if such poorly conceived notions have implications for the ways human beings are to be treated, it behooves us to discover these erroneous assumptions before they harm anyone. The scientific method, then, is a value that helps to protect the scientific community and society at large against flawed reasoning. The protection comes from the practice of evaluating the merits of various theoretical pronouncements against the objective record, rather than simply relying on the academic, political, or social credibility of the theorist. Of course, this means that the theorist whose ideas are being evaluated must be equally objective and, thus, willing to discard pet notions when there is evidence that they have outlived their usefulness.

BASIC FACT-FINDING STRATEGIES

Today researchers are rather fortunate in having many methods that they can use to test their hypotheses about social and personality development. This diversity of available research techniques is a strength because discoveries produced by one technique can be verified by other strategies. Such *converging evidence* is extremely important, for it demonstrates that the "discovery" one has made is truly a discovery and not merely an artifact of the method used to collect the original data.

In the pages that follow, we will first discuss the relative strengths and weaknesses of six basic research strategies: naturalistic observation, interviews, case studies, clinical methods, experiments, and natural (or quasi) experiments. We will then consider the ways developmentalists might use these strategies to detect and explain age-related changes in children's feelings, thoughts, and patterns of social behavior.

Naturalistic Observation

A research method that many developmentalists favor is naturalistic observation—observing people in their common, everyday (that is, natural) surroundings. To observe children, this would usually mean going into their homes, schools, or public playgrounds and recording what happens. Rarely will the observer try to record every event that occurs. Generally speaking, the researcher will be testing a specific hypothesis about one particular class of behavior, such as cooperation or aggression. He or she will define incidents that qualify as examples of the target behavior before beginning the study and will then focus exclusively on this type of behavior (and perhaps its antecedents and consequents if they can be determined from the observational record).

Rosalind Charlesworth and Willard Hartup (1967) used naturalistic observation to determine whether nursery school children become more pleasant to one another as they grow older. Charlesworth and Hartup first defined examples of positive social reinforcement that children might dispense to one another (for example, showing affection, cooperating, sharing, giving tangible objects such as toys). Then, over a five-week period, they carefully observed a sample of 3- and 4-year-old nursery school children, noting instances in which a child dispensed a positive social reinforcer to a classmate. The results were interesting. Not only were 4-year-olds more likely to reinforce their peers than 3-year-olds were, but they also distributed their reinforcers to a larger number of classmates. In addition, the children who gave the most social reinforcers to peers were the ones who received the most in return. So these preschoolers appeared to be partaking in a *reciprocal exchange* of positive reinforcers, a finding that suggests we could learn a great deal about the origins of social equity by observing the mutual give-and-take among young children at play in their peer groups.

The major advantage of naturalistic observation is that it allows researchers to study phenomena as they occur in the real world. However, this method has several limitations. For example, the researcher must allow subjects to become accustomed to his presence so that they are less likely to "show off" for this attentive adult or alter their behavior in other meaningful ways. Observers must also assess the *reliability* of their observations as a check on the objectivity of the procedure. Reliability is most often measured by asking a second person to witness the same events as the first observer witnesses and then comparing the two observational records. If independent observers can largely agree on what occurred, the observations are reliable. A lack of agreement indicates that the observational scheme is unreliable and in need of revision.

Perhaps the major limitation of observational research is its inability to differentiate among several possible causes for the observations made. Let's reconsider a major result of Charlesworth and Hartup's study: Do 4-year-olds reinforce peers more than 3-year-olds *because* the older children have learned that peers will return their acts of kindness? Or, rather, are 4-year-olds simply more inclined to favor group play activities that just happen to provide more opportunities to give and receive social reinforcers? The latter explanation is not at all far-fetched if the nursery school setting has few solitary (that is, one-person) toys that are sufficiently interesting to capture the attention of a typical 4-year-old. In sum, there are many variables in the natural environment that may affect children's behavior, and it is often difficult to specify which of these factors or what combination of them is responsible for a particular observation or pattern of observations. But please note that this is merely a limitation of observational research, not a devastating critique. Naturalistic observation is an excellent procedure for detecting developmental trends or changes in behavior which, once observed, may then be subjected to intensive causal analyses in later research.

Interviews, Case Studies, and the Clinical Method

Three common methods that social developmentalists use to gather information and test hypotheses are the interview, the case study, and the clinical technique. Although these approaches are similar in many respects, they differ in the extent to which research participants are treated alike by the investigator.

The interview method. A researcher who opts for the interview method will ask the child (or the parents) a series of questions about one or more aspects of the child's life. If the session is a *structured interview*, all who participate in the study are asked exactly the same questions in the same order. The purpose of this standardized, or structured, format is to treat each person alike so that the responses of different participants can be compared.

One interesting application of the interview technique is a project in which kindergarten, second-grade, and fourth-grade children responded to 24 questions designed to measure their knowledge of social stereotypes about males and females (Williams, Bennett, & Best, 1975). Each question came in response to a different short story in which the central character was described by either stereotypically masculine adjectives (for example, *tough, forceful*) or stereotypically feminine ones (for example, *emotional, excitable*). The child's task was to indicate whether the character in each story was male or female. Williams and her associates found that even kindergartners were quite knowledgeable about gender stereotypes, although children's thinking became much more stereotyped between kindergarten and the second grade. One implication of these results is that stereotyping of the sexes must begin very early if 5-year-old kindergartners are already thinking along stereotyped lines.

The interview method has some serious shortcomings. Investigators must hope that the answers they receive are honest and accurate and are not merely attempts by respondents to present themselves in a favorable or socially desirable manner. Clearly, inaccurate responses will lead to erroneous conclusions. When interviewing children of different ages, the investigator must also ensure that all questions are clearly understood by even the youngest respondents; otherwise, the age trends observed in one's study may represent differences in children's ability to comprehend and communicate rather than real underlying changes in children's feelings, thoughts, or behaviors.

In spite of these potential shortcomings, the structured interview can be an excellent research tool. Interviews are particularly useful when the interviewer *challenges* children to display what they really feel, think, or know about an issue, for the socially desirable response to such a challenge is likely to be a truthful answer.

The case study. Yet another method of studying human social and personality development is the case study approach. The researcher prepares detailed descriptions of one or more individuals and then tries to draw conclusions by analyzing these "cases." In preparing an individualized record, or "case," the investigator will typically gather many pieces of information about the individual, such as family history, socioeconomic status, educational and work history, health records, self-descriptions of significant life events, and performance on psychological tests. Much of the information in a case history comes from interviews with the individual; the questions asked are typically not standardized and may vary considerably from case to case.

In Chapter 2, we will see that Sigmund Freud was a strong proponent of the case study and used it to great advantage. Nevertheless, this method has three major shortcomings that can seriously compromise its usefulness. First, the validity of an investigator's conclusions will obviously depend on the accuracy of information received from the "cases." Unfortunately, the potential for inaccuracy is great in a method in which adult subjects try to reconstruct the causes and consequences of important events that happened years ago in childhood. Second, the data on any two (or more) individuals may not be directly comparable if the investigator has asked each participant different questions rather than posing a standard set of questions to all. Finally, the case study may lack *generalizability*—that is, conclusions drawn from the backgrounds and experiences of the particular individuals who were studied may not apply to most people. In sum, the case study approach can serve as a rich source of ideas about social and personality development. However, its limitations are many, and any conclusions drawn from case studies should be verified using other research techniques.

The clinical method. This approach is a close relative of the case study technique. The investigator will seek to test one or more hypotheses by presenting the research participant with a question, a task, or a stimulus of some sort and then inviting a response. When the participant has responded, the investigator will often ask a follow-up question or introduce a new task in the hope of clarifying the participant's original answer. This questioning then continues until the investigator has the information needed to evaluate his or her hypothesis. Although participants are often asked the same questions in the initial stages of the research, their answers to each question determine what the investigator asks next. Since participants' answers often differ, it is possible that no two participants will ever receive exactly the same treatment. In other words, the clinical method treats each subject as unique.

Jean Piaget, a famous Swiss psychologist, relied extensively on the clinical method to study children's moral reasoning and general intellectual development. The data from Piaget's research are largely protocol records of his interactions with individual children. Here is a small sample from Piaget's (1932/

1965, p. 143) work on the development of moral reasoning—a sample which shows that this young child thinks about lying in a very different way than adults do:

Piaget: Do you know what a lie is?

Clai: It's when you say what isn't true.

Piaget: Is $2 + 2 = 5$ a lie?

Clai: Yes, it's a lie.

Piaget: Why?

Clai: Because it isn't right.

Piaget: Did the boy who said $2 + 2 = 5$ know it wasn't right or did he make a mistake?

Clai: He made a mistake.

Piaget: Then if he made a mistake, did he tell a lie or not?

Clai: Yes, he told a lie.

We need only examine the richness of Piaget's thinking (as we will in Chapter 4 and throughout the text) to see that the clinical method can provide a wealth of information about developing children. However, this approach is a highly controversial technique that presents some thorny interpretive problems. We have already noted the difficulties in comparing cases or protocols generated by a procedure that treats each participant differently. Furthermore, the nonstandardized probing of each participant raises the possibility that the examiner's preexisting theoretical biases may affect the questions asked and the interpretations provided. Since conclusions drawn from the clinical method depend, in part, on the investigator's subjective assessments and interpretations, it is desirable to provide converging evidence for clinical insights by verifying them with other research techniques.

The Experimental Method

The laboratory experiment. The laboratory experiment is perhaps the most popular method of studying developing children because it permits the researcher to conduct reasonably unambiguous tests of his or her hypotheses. To introduce the essential features of this important technique, let's consider a problem that is well suited for experimental analysis.

Suppose we believe that children learn a lot from watching television and are likely to emulate the behavior of the television characters to whom they are exposed. One hypothesis we might formulate from this line of reasoning is that children who watch "helpful" television characters are likely to become more helpful themselves should they have an opportunity to assist someone in the near future.

In conducting a laboratory experiment to test this (or any) hypothesis, we would bring our participants into a controlled environment, expose them to different treatments, and record as data their responses to the treatments. The different treatments to which we expose our participants represent the *independent variable* of the experiment. To test the hypothesis we have proposed, our independent variable would be the type of television program we show to our participants: half of our children might view a program in which one or more characters were helpful to others, and the other half would view a program in which the characters were not especially helpful. Since our hypothesis centers on children's helpgiving, we would want to measure as our *dependent variable* how helpful children are after watching each type of television show. A dependent variable is called dependent because its value, or level, presumably "depends" on the value of the independent variable. In the present case, we are hypothesizing that future helpgiving will be greater for youngsters who watch programs that demonstrate helpgiving (one level of the independent variable) than for those who watch programs displaying little or no helpgiving (the second level of the independent variable). If we are careful experimenters and exercise precise control over *all* other factors that may affect children's helpgiving,[1] then the pattern of results that we have anticipated would allow us to draw a strong conclusion: watching television programs that demonstrate helpgiving causes children to become more helpful in the near future. Indeed, the most important advantage of the experimental method is that it permits a precise assessment of cause-and-effect relationships that may exist between independent and dependent variables.

Several years ago, the experiment proposed here was actually conducted (Sprafkin, Liebert, & Poulos, 1975). The 6-year-olds who participated in this study watched either an episode from the popular

Lassie series that contained a dramatic rescue scene or a *Lassie* episode that contained no outstanding acts of helpgiving. After watching one or the other show, each child began to play a game in an attempt to win a prize. While playing, he or she could hear some puppies in an adjacent area that were apparently discomforted. The dependent variable in this experiment was the amount of time children would spend away from the game giving help or comfort to the crying puppies. To help, children had to leave the game and thereby decrease their chances of winning a prize.

Was helpgiving at all influenced by the type of program the children had watched? Indeed it was, for the children who had watched the episode that emphasized helpgiving spent considerably more time comforting the distressed pups than did children who had watched the other episode. Since these youngsters were randomly assigned to watch either program and had been treated alike in every respect other than the content of the program they watched, it was reasonable to conclude that youngsters in the prosocial-programming condition were the more helpful group *because* they had watched a TV program in which helpgiving was a central theme (see also Box 1-2).

Critics of laboratory experimentation have argued that the tightly controlled laboratory "environment" is highly artificial and that children are likely to behave very differently in these surroundings than they would in a natural setting. Thus, it is quite conceivable that inferences drawn from laboratory experiments will not always apply in the real world.

The field experiment.   One way to determine whether a conclusion drawn from a laboratory experiment applies to the real world is to seek converging evidence by conducting an experiment in the natural environment—that is, a field experiment. This approach combines the advantages of naturalistic observation with the more rigorous control of an experiment. In addition, children are typically not apprehensive about participating in a strange experiment, because all the activities they undertake are everyday activities, and they may not even be aware that they are being observed.

Let's consider an example of a field experiment

that provides converging evidence for the hypothesis that children who watch prosocial television programs that display helpfulness, cooperation, and affection will themselves become more prosocially inclined. Lynette Friedrich and Aletha Stein (1973) went into a nursery school, became acquainted with the children there, and then observed how often each child was helpful, cooperative, or affectionate toward other children. This initial measure of the child's prosocial behavior provided a *baseline* against which future increases in helpfulness or cooperation could be measured. After the baseline data were collected, the children were randomly assigned to different experimental conditions. Some of the children watched prosocial television programming (*Mister Rogers' Neighborhood*) at school, three days a week for a month. Other children spent an equal amount of time at school watching neutral films featuring circuses and farm scenes. At the end of this month-long treatment phase, each child was observed daily in the nursery school setting for two additional weeks to determine whether the television programming had had any effect on his or her willingness to cooperate with others or to give help and affection.

The results of this field experiment clearly indicated that children who had watched the prosocial programming did, indeed, become more cooperative and affectionate toward their peers than they had been during the initial baseline period. Not only are these results consistent with those reported by Sprafkin et al. (1975), but they also demonstrate that conclusions drawn from that laboratory experiment are definitely applicable to the real world.

The Natural (or Quasi) Experiment

There are many issues to which the experimental method cannot or should not (for ethical reasons) be applied. Suppose, for example, that we wish to study the effects of social deprivation on infants' social and emotional development. Obviously we cannot ask one group of parents to lock their infants in an attic for two years so that we can collect the data we need. It is simply unethical to submit children to any experimental treatment that may adversely affect their physical or psychological well-being.

However, we might be able to accomplish our

BOX 1-2   *THE DIFFERENCE BETWEEN CORRELATION AND CAUSATION*

There are many strategies that one can use to study the relationship between variables such as children's exposure to prosocial television and their helpgiving. Suppose, for example, that we had *interviewed* several dozen youngsters to determine each child's favorite TV shows and then *observed* the children at play, noting that those who preferred prosocial programming were much more helpful than those who favored other kinds of televised entertainment. What these data would show is that there is a meaningful relationship, or *correlation*, between children's television preferences and their helpfulness during free play. But would this correlation imply that watching prosocial television causes children to become more helpful?

No, it would not! Although we would have detected a relationship between children's preferences for prosocial programming and their helpgiving, the direction of this relationship is not at all clear. An equally plausible interpretation for our correlational finding is that helpful children are the ones who prefer prosocial programs! Another possibility is that neither of these variables causes the other and that both are actually caused by a third variable that we have not measured. For example, if parental encourage-

ment of helpgiving causes children to become more helpful *and* to prefer prosocial TV programs, then the latter two variables may be correlated, even though their relationship is not one of cause and effect. So correlational findings point to systematic relationships between variables, but they do not establish causality.

Naturalistic observation, interviews, case studies, and the clinical method are all excellent strategies for determining whether two or more variables are correlated. But since correlations do not imply causation, these methods cannot be used to establish the underlying causes of any aspect of human development. By contrast, the experimental method allows an investigator to determine whether two variables are causally related by systematically manipulating one of these variables to observe its *effect* (if any) on the other. So when Joyce Sprafkin and her colleagues manipulated children's exposure to different kinds of television programming and found that those who had watched prosocial programs became more helpful than those who had watched other programs, they were able to conclude that exposure to prosocial programming *causes* children to become more helpful, at least in the short run.

---

research objectives through a natural (or quasi) experiment—a study in which we observe the consequences of a natural event to which subjects have been exposed. So if we were able to locate a group of children who were raised in impoverished institutions with very little contact with caregivers over the first two years, we could compare their social and emotional development with that of children raised at home in traditional family settings. This comparison would provide some information about the effects of early social deprivation on children's social and emotional development. (Indeed, precisely this kind of natural experiment is described in detail in Chapter 6.) The "independent variable" in a natural experiment is the "event" that subjects experience (in our example, the social deprivation experienced by institutionalized infants). The "dependent variable" is whatever outcome measure one chooses to study (in our example, social and emotional development).

Note, however, that researchers conducting natural experiments do not control the independent vari-

able, nor do they randomly assign participants to experimental conditions; they merely observe and record the apparent outcomes of a natural happening or event. So in the absence of tight experimental control, it is often hard to determine precisely what factor is responsible for any group differences that are found. But even though the quasi experiment is unable to make *strong* statements about cause and effect, it is nevertheless useful: it can tell us whether a natural event could possibly have influenced those who experienced it and, thus, can provide some meaningful clues about cause and effect.

DESIGNING RESEARCH TO MEASURE DEVELOPMENTAL CHANGE

We have now reviewed many of the techniques that social developmentalists use to gather information about their research participants. However, these researchers are not merely interested in looking at children's behavior at any one moment; they hope to determine how children's feelings, thoughts, and behaviors develop or change over time. How do they design their research to chart these developmental trends? Let's briefly consider three methods: cross-sectional comparisons, longitudinal comparisons, and cross-sectional/short-term longitudinal comparisons.

Cross-Sectional Comparisons

In a cross-sectional comparison groups of children who *differ in age* are studied at approximately *the same point in time*. For example, a researcher interested in determining whether children become more generous as they mature might place 6-, 8-, and 10-year-olds in a situation where they are afforded an opportunity to share a valuable commodity (say, candy or money) with needy youngsters who are less fortunate than themselves. By comparing the responses of children in the different age groups, investigators can often identify (and occasionally even explain) age-related changes in whatever aspect of development they are studying.

An important advantage of the cross-sectional method is that the investigator can collect data from children of different ages over a short time. For example, an investigator would not have to wait four years for her 6-year-olds to become 10-year-olds in order to determine whether children's generosity increases over this age range. She can merely sample children of different ages and test all samples at approximately the same time.

Notice, however, that in cross-sectional research, participants at each age level are *different* people who come from different cohorts. A *cohort* is a group of people of the same age who are exposed to similar cultural environments or historical events as they are growing up. The fact that different cohorts are always involved in cross-sectional comparisons means that any age-related effects that are found in the study may not always be due to age or development but, rather, to some other feature that distinguishes individuals in different cohorts. An example may clarify the issue. For years, cross-sectional research had consistently indicated that young adults score higher on intelligence tests than middle-aged adults, who, in turn, score higher than the elderly. But does intelligence decline with age, as these findings would seem to indicate? Not necessarily! More recent research (Baltes, 1968) reveals that individuals' intelligence test scores remain reasonably stable over the years and that the earlier studies were really measuring something quite different: cohort differences in education. The older adults in earlier cross-sectional studies had had less schooling, which could explain why they scored lower on intelligence tests than the middle-aged or young adult samples. Their test scores had not declined but, rather, had always been lower than those of the younger adults with whom they were compared.

This example points directly to a second problem with the cross-sectional method: it tells us nothing about the development of *individuals* because each person is observed *at only one point in time*. So cross-sectional comparisons cannot provide answers to questions such as "When will *my* child become more generous?" or "Will aggressive 2-year-olds become aggressive 5-year-olds?" To address issues like these, an investigator will often rely on a second kind of developmental comparison, the longitudinal method.

Longitudinal Comparisons

The longitudinal comparison is a method whereby the same children are observed repeatedly over time. For example, a researcher interested in determining whether generosity increases over middle childhood might provide 6-year-olds an opportunity to behave in a charitable fashion toward needy youngsters and then follow up with similar assessments of the generosity of these same children at ages 8 and 10.

The period spanned by a longitudinal study may be very long or reasonably short. The investigators may be looking at one particular aspect of development, such as generosity, or at many. By repeatedly testing the same subjects, investigators can assess the *stability* of various attributes and the patterns of developmental *change* for each person in the sample. In addition, they can identify *general* developmental trends by looking for commonalities in development that most or all individuals share. Finally, the tracking of several children over time will help investigators to understand the bases for *individual differences*

PHOTOS 1-1 Leisure activities of the 1930s (left) and 1980s (right). As these photos illustrate, children growing up in the 1930s had very different kinds of experiences from those of today's youth. Many believe that cross-generational changes in the environment may limit the results of a longitudinal study to the youngsters who were growing up while that research was in progress.

in development, particularly if they are able to establish that different kinds of earlier experiences lead to very different outcomes.

Although we have focused on the important advantages of the longitudinal comparison, this procedure does have several drawbacks. For example, longitudinal research can be very costly and time-consuming, particularly if the project spans a period of several years. Moreover, the focus of theory and research in social and personality development is constantly changing, so that longitudinal questions that seem very exciting at the beginning of a long-term project may seem rather trivial by the time the study ends. *Subject loss* may also become a problem: children may move away, get sick, become bored with repeated testing, or have parents who, for one reason or another, will not allow them to continue in the study. Thus, one's final conclusions may be limited to a smaller and potentially atypical (that is, non-representative) sample of healthy youngsters who do not move away and who remain cooperative over the long run.

Longitudinal research has another shortcoming that students often see right away—the *cohort*, or *cross-generational*, problem. Children in longitudinal research are usually drawn from one particular cohort, and as a result they will experience somewhat different cultural, family, and school environments than children in other cohorts. Consider, for example, that children raised in the 1940s lived in larger and typically less affluent families. What's more, they traveled less than modern children do and had no access to television or electronic computers. Clearly, these youngsters lived in a different world, and inferences drawn from longitudinal studies of such children may not apply to today's youth. Stated another way, cross-cohort (or cross-generational) changes in the environment may limit the conclusions of a longitudinal project to those children who were growing up while the study was in progress.

We have seen that the cross-sectional and the longitudinal methods each have distinct advantages and disadvantages. Might it be possible to combine the best features of both approaches? A third kind of developmental comparison—the cross-sectional/short-term longitudinal method—tries to do just that.

Cross-Sectional/Short-Term Longitudinal Comparisons

Suppose that we have developed a training program designed to increase the generosity of 6- to 10-year-old children. Before implementing the program on a large scale, we would surely want to pretest it on a smaller sample to determine whether it works. In conducting the pretest, we would also hope to answer some very practical questions such as "When can children first understand the program?" or "At what age will children respond most favorably to the training?" Finally, parents and teachers would want to know whether any immediate increases in generosity produced by our program will persist over time.

The only design that allows us to answer all these questions is the cross-sectional/short-term longitudinal comparison. This procedure combines the best features of the cross-sectional and the longitudinal approaches by selecting children of different ages (that is, different cohorts) and then studying these groups over time. For purposes of our proposed research, we might begin by administering our training program to a group of 6-year-olds, a group of 8-year-olds, and a group of 10-year-olds. Of course, we would want to randomly assign other 6-, 8-, and 10-year-olds to control groups that would not be exposed to any generosity training. The children who were "trained" would then be observed and compared with their age mates in the control group to determine (1) whether the program was immediately effective at increasing generosity, and (2) if so, at what age the program had its largest immediate impact. This is the information we would obtain had we conducted a standard cross-sectional experiment.

However, our choice of the cross-sectional/short-term longitudinal method also allows us to measure the enduring effects of our program by retesting our samples of 6- and 8-year-olds two years later. This approach has several advantages over the standard longitudinal comparison. The first is a *time saving*: in only two years, we have learned about the long-term effects of the program on children who are still between the target ages of 6 and 10. A standard longitudinal comparison would require four years to provide similar information. Second, the cross-sectional/short-term longitudinal design actually yields *more information* about long-term effects than the longitudinal approach does. If we had chosen the longitudinal method, we would have data on the long-term effects of a program administered only to 6-year-olds. However, the cross-sectional/short-term longi-

tudinal design allows us to determine whether the program has *comparable* long-term effects when administered to both 6- and 8-year-olds. Clearly, this combination of the cross-sectional and longitudinal methods provides a rather versatile alternative to either of those approaches (see Table 1-1 for a summary of the aims, implications, advantages, and disadvantages of each type of developmental comparison).

There is one additional method that we need to discuss before turning to theories of social and personality development in Chapter 2: the *cross-cultural comparison*.

CROSS-CULTURAL COMPARISONS

Developmental researchers are often hesitant to publish a new finding or conclusion until they have studied enough children to determine that their "discovery" is reliable. However, their conclusions are frequently based on children living at one point in time within one particular culture, and it is often difficult to know whether these conclusions will apply to future generations or even to children who are currently growing up in other areas around the world. Today, the generalizability of findings across samples and settings has become an important issue, for many theorists have implied that there are "universals" in human development—events and outcomes that all children share as they progress from infancy to adulthood.

Cross-cultural studies are those in which participants from different cultural backgrounds are observed, tested, and compared on some aspect of their psychological functioning. Studies of this kind serve many purposes. For example, they allow investigators to determine whether conclusions drawn about the development of children in one society apply to children growing up in other societies. So the cross-cultural comparison guards against the overgeneralization of research findings and, indeed, is the only way to determine whether there are truly "universals" in human development.

Although the cross-cultural method has led to the discovery of several developmental outcomes that most (if not all) people share, many investigators who favor and use this approach are looking for *differences* rather than similarities. They recognize that human beings develop in societies that have very different ideas about issues such as the age at which mothers should wean their infants, when and how children should be punished, what activities are most appropriate for boys and for girls, when childhood ends and adulthood begins, the treatment of the aged, and countless other aspects of social life. They have also learned that people from various cultures may differ somewhat in the ways they perceive the world, express their emotions, and solve problems. Ruth Benedict (1934) used the term *cultural relativism* to express her belief that a person's behavior can be understood only within the context of that person's cultural environment. So, social development in cross-cultural perspective is, in part, an attempt to specify how societies differ in the ways they raise their children and how these differences may then contribute to culture-specific patterns of behavior, or distinct "cultural personalities."

One classic example of cultural relativity comes from Margaret Mead's (1935) cross-cultural study of

TABLE 1-1   Three Methods of Detecting Developmental Trends

	Cross-sectional method	Longitudinal method	Cross-sectional/Short-term longitudinal method
Procedure	Observe children of different ages at one point in time	Observe children of one age on more than one occasion over time	Observe children of different ages on more than one occasion over time
Information gained	Differences in the behavior of older and younger children (children in each age group are different people)	Changes over time in the behavior of individual children	Changes over time in the behavior of children of different ages
Implications of information gained	Hints at developmental trends	Reflects developmental trends for individual children from one age group	Reflects developmental trends for individual children from several age groups
Advantages	1. Demonstrates age differences in behavior 2. Relatively inexpensive 3. Takes little time to conduct	Provides data on the development of individual children	1. Provides data on the development of individual children of different ages 2. Less time-consuming than longitudinal research 3. May be less costly and more informative than longitudinal research
Disadvantages	1. Age trends may reflect extraneous differences between older and younger children rather than true developmental change 2. Provides no data on the development of individuals because each participant is observed at only one point in time	1. Relatively expensive 2. Extremely time-consuming 3. Participants may drop out of the project 4. Cross-generational problems	1. More costly than cross-sectional research 2. More time-consuming than cross-sectional research

three primitive societies on the island of New Guinea. Despite their geographical proximity, these three groups were found to be very dissimilar in many respects. Mead described the Arapesh as a passive, nurturant people who stood in marked contrast to their neighbors, the Mundugumor, who were ruthless and aggressive. The third group, the Tchambuli, were quite different from the other two groups and from our own society. Among the Tchambuli, males were passive, nurturant, and dependent, while females were dominant, independent, and assertive. The Mead study is but one example of a large body of cross-cultural research indicating that the content of socialization, or *what* the child acquires, depends very heavily on the specific values and child-rearing practices that are endorsed by members of his or her society.

We have now reviewed a variety of research designs and techniques, each of which has definite strengths and weaknesses. When planning a research project, investigators will select a method only after carefully considering what it will take to answer the questions they are asking and then comparing these needs against available resources, such as the size of their research budget, the amount of time that they have to conduct the research, and the availability of research participants. The fact that investigators have so many methods from which to choose is advantageous in that findings obtained through one technique may then be confirmed through the use of other methodologies. So there is no "best method" for studying children and adolescents; each of the approaches that we have considered has contributed in a meaningful way to our understanding of social and personality development.

SUMMARY

Socialization is the process through which children and adolescents acquire the beliefs, values, and behaviors deemed significant and appropriate by other members of society. The study of socialization is an interdisciplinary science. Anthropologists and sociologists concentrate on the "content," or *common outcomes*, of socialization—that is, the similarities that children and adolescents display in their adjustment to society and its institutions. Psychologists focus more intently on the means by which children become socialized and on the attributes and experiences that contribute most heavily to our *individual* personalities.

The study of social and personality development is truly a theoretical discipline with four major theoretical traditions: psychoanalytic theory, the biological viewpoint, social-learning theory, and cognitive-developmental theory. The evolution of different theories is attributable, in part, to the tendency of theorists to make different assumptions about human nature and the character of human development. Sigmund Freud, the father of psychoanalytic theory, portrayed children as "seething cauldrons" who are constantly trying to gratify inborn sexual and aggressive instincts. According to Freud, the development of personality proceeds through a series of stages as parents successfully divert the child's undesirable impulses away from their natural outlets and into socially acceptable patterns of behavior. Like Freud, proponents of the biological viewpoint contend that children inherit a number of characteristics that will influence their social and personality development. But rather than characterizing children as inherently negative, self-serving creatures who are passively molded by their parents, biological theorists argue that humans are active and adaptive beings whose natural inclinations are neither inherently good nor inherently bad.

Social-learning theorists view children as blank slates who come into the world with very little in the way of ability, knowledge, or behavioral predispositions. The social-learning perspective is that socialization occurs continuously and may take either a positive or a negative path, depending on the kinds of learning experiences provided by one's environment. However, the most recent versions of social-learning theory stress that children are not merely passive pawns of environmental influence but, rather, active agents who have a hand in determining the character of their own socializing environments.

The cognitive developmentalists stress the positive

side of human nature by portraying children as active, adaptive explorers who are constantly trying to cope with the social, emotional, and intellectual demands of the environment. An important assumption made by cognitive theorists is that a child's level of cognitive development will determine her interpretations of and reactions to the social experiences and socializing environment that she encounters.

The best way to evaluate these theories is not on the basis of the assumptions they make but, rather, on their ability to predict and explain significant aspects of social and personality development. Developmentalists are fortunate to have available a variety of useful techniques for studying children and testing the predictions that theorists make. The major methods of conducting research with children and adolescents are naturalistic observation, interviews, case studies, clinical assessments, experiments, and natural (or quasi) experiments. Developmental trends are detected by adapting one or more of these techniques to provide cross-sectional or longitudinal comparisons. The cross-sectional comparison assesses developmental change by studying children of different ages at the same point in time. The longitudinal comparison detects developmental trends by repeatedly examining the same children over a period of time. A combination of the cross-sectional and the longitudinal approaches is also available to the investigator who wishes to take advantage of the best features of both strategies. Each of these research designs and techniques has advantages and disadvantages, and there is no one "best method" for studying social and personality development. When planning a research project, investigators will select a particular method and research design only after carefully considering the nature of the problem under investigation, the costs involved, the amount of time that they have to conduct the research, and the availability of research participants.

NOTES

1. There are two major aspects of experimental control. First, experimenters must ensure that they treat all participants alike in every respect other than the manipulation of the independent variable. Second, they must ensure that the participants in each condition are comparable with respect to any extraneous personal attributes (for example, level of cognitive development, prior helpfulness) that could affect their performance on the dependent variable. One way to control these extraneous personal attributes is to randomly assign participants to treatment conditions. Random assignment means that each research participant has an equal probability of being exposed to each experimental condition, with assignment of individuals to conditions typically accomplished by an unbiased procedure such as a coin flip. If the assignment is truly random, there is only a very slim chance that participants in the two (or more) experimental conditions will differ significantly on any personal characteristic that might affect their performance on the dependent variable.

REFERENCES

ARIES, P. (1962). *Centuries of childhood*. New York: Knopf.

BALTES, P. B. (1968). Longitudinal and cross-sectional sequences in the study of age and generation effects. *Human Development, 11,* 145–171.

BANDURA, A. (1965). Influence of models' reinforcement contingencies on the acquisition of imitative responses. *Journal of Personality and Social Psychology, 1,* 589–595.

BANDURA, A., & Walters, R. H. (1963). *Social learning and personality development*. New York: Holt, Rinehart and Winston.

BENEDICT, R. (1934). *Patterns of culture*. Boston: Houghton Mifflin.

CHARLESWORTH, R., & Hartup, W. W. (1967). Positive social reinforcement in the nursery school peer group. *Child Development, 38,* 993–1002.

CHILD, I. L. (1954). Socialization. In G. Lindzey (Ed.), *Handbook of social psychology*. Reading, MA: Addison-Wesley.

DESPERT, J. L. (1965). *The emotionally disturbed child: Then and now.* New York: Brunner/Mazel.

ELKIN, F. (1960). *The child and society*. New York: Random House.

ERIKSON, E. H. (1963). *Childhood and society* (2nd ed.). New York: Norton.

ERIKSON, E. H. (1972). Eight ages of man. In C. S. Lavatelli & F. Stendler (Eds.), *Readings in child behavior and child development*. San Diego, CA: Harcourt Brace Jovanovich.

FREUD, A., & Dann, S. (1951). An experiment in group upbringing. In R. Eisler, A. Freud, H. Hartmann, & E. Kris (Eds.), *The psychoanalytic study of the child* (Vol. 6). New York: International Universities Press.

FRIEDRICH, L. K., & Stein, A. H. (1973). Aggressive and prosocial television programs and the natural behavior of preschool children. *Monographs of the Society for Research in Child Development, 38*(4, Serial No. 51).

HARTMANN, H. (1958). *Ego psychology and the problem of adaptation*. New York: International Universities Press.

HOBBES, T. (1904). *Leviathan*. Cambridge: Cambridge University Press. (Original work published 1651)

JONES, R. A., Hendrick, C., & Epstein, Y. (1979). *Introduction to social psychology*. Sunderland, MA: Sinauer.

KOHLBERG, L. (1966). A cognitive-developmental analysis of children's sex-role concepts and attitudes. In E. E. Maccoby (Ed.), *The development of sex differences*. Stanford, CA: Stanford University Press.

KOHLBERG, L. (1969). Stage and sequence: The cognitive-developmental approach to socialization. In D. A. Goslin (Ed.), *Handbook of socialization theory and research*. Skokie, IL: Rand McNally.

LANGER, J. (1969). *Theories of development*. New York: Holt, Rinehart and Winston.

LOCKE, J. (1913). *Some thoughts concerning education*. Sections 38 and 40. London: Cambridge University Press. (Original work published 1690)

MEAD, M. (1935). *Sex and temperament in three primitive societies*. New York: Morrow.

PIAGET, J. (1965). *The moral judgment of the child*. New York: Free Press. (Original work published 1932)

PIAGET, J. (1969). *The psychology of the child*. New York: Basic Books.

SPRAFKIN, J. L., Liebert, R. M., & Poulos, R. W. (1975). Effects of a prosocial televised example on children's helping. *Journal of Experimental Child Psychology, 20*, 119–126.

WATSON, J. B. (1925). *Behaviorism*. New York: Norton.

WIGGAM, A. E. (1923). *The new decalogue of science*. Indianapolis: Bobbs-Merrill.

WILLIAMS, J. E., Bennett, S. M., & Best, D. L. (1975). Awareness and expression of sex-stereotypes in young children. *Developmental Psychology, 11*, 635–642.

2

PSYCHOANALYTIC THEORY AND MODERN BIOLOGICAL PERSPECTIVES

THE PSYCHOANALYTIC PERSPECTIVE

An Overview of Freud's Psychoanalytic Theory

Erik Erikson's Theory of Psychosocial Development

Psychoanalytic Theory Today

RECENT BIOLOGICAL PERSPECTIVES

Ethological Theory

The Behavior Genetics Approach

SUMMARY

REFERENCES

Our focus in this chapter is on some of the earliest and some of the newest ideas about human social and personality development. The earlier ideas stem from Sigmund Freud's psychoanalytic theory—an approach that portrays human beings as servants to inborn biological needs that play a major role in determining who we are and what we are likely to become. After briefly reviewing Freud's view of human development, we will consider what modern biological theorists have to say about innate, or inborn, determinants of personality and social behavior.

THE PSYCHOANALYTIC PERSPECTIVE

With the possible exception of Charles Darwin's theory of evolution, no scientific theory has had a greater impact on Western thought than Sigmund Freud's psychoanalytic theory. One of my former professors once claimed that Freud's name was recognized by a larger percentage of the American people than that of any other scientific personality. And he may have been correct. Many laypersons have been exposed to at least some of Freud's ideas, and it would not be surprising if friends and relatives were to ask your opinion of Freud (and his theory) when they learn that you are taking a psychology course.

Almost no one is neutral about Sigmund Freud. His followers thought him a genius even though they didn't agree with all of his ideas. Yet many of his contemporaries in the medical profession ridiculed Freud, calling him a quack, a crackpot, and other, less complimentary names. What was it about this man and his theory that made him so controversial? For one thing, he emphasized the importance of sexual urges as determinants of behavior, for children as well as for adults. In this section of the chapter, we will first consider Freud's interesting perspective on human development and then compare Freud's theory with that of his best-known follower, Erik Erikson.

AN OVERVIEW OF FREUD'S PSYCHOANALYTIC THEORY

Psychoanalytic theory is not a deductive approach that began with well-defined concepts and propositions from which hypotheses were derived and tested. Freud did not conduct laboratory experiments. He did not use objective instruments to collect his data. Nor did he ever submit his findings to statistical analysis or describe them with tables and graphs. Freud was a practicing physician (a neurologist) who formulated his psychoanalytic theory from the observations and notes that he made about the life histories of his mentally disturbed patients.

Freud observed that people are often reluctant to discuss very personal problems with a stranger, even if the stranger is a therapist. For this reason, he favored nontraditional methods of interviewing patients—methods such as hypnosis, *free association* (in which the patient discusses anything that comes to mind), and *dream analysis*. While reclining on the couch, the patient would relax and talk about anything and everything that popped into his or her head. Dreams were thought to be a particularly rich source of information, for they gave some indication of a patient's *unconscious motivations*.[1] Freud assumed that we all dream about what we really want—for example, sex and power—unhindered by social prohibitions that tend to suppress these desires when we are awake.

During the course of therapy, Freud's patients would typically begin by discussing their current problems and then work backward, describing many of the important events of their lives. Often these retrospective accounts would end with the patient's expressing extreme discomfort over one or more events that had occurred early in childhood. As Freud listened to the associations of his patients, he was struck by the fact that each event in a person's life history seemed to be related in some meaningful way to earlier events. He then realized that these "case histories" were precisely the kind of longitudinal data from which one might formulate a comprehensive theory of personality.

From his analyses of patients' dreams, slips of the tongue, unexpected free associations, and childhood

PHOTO 2-1 The psychoanalytic theory of Sigmund Freud (1856–1939) changed our thinking about developing children.

memories, Freud was able to infer that all of us experience intense conflicts that influence our behavior. As biological creatures, we have goals or motives that must be satisfied. Yet society dictates that many of these basic urges are undesirable and must be suppressed or controlled. According to Freud, these conflicts emerge at several points during childhood and play a major role in determining the course and character of one's social and personality development.

Instincts, Goals, and Motives

Freud believed that all human behavior is energized by psychodynamic forces. Presumably each individual has a fixed amount of *psychic* (mental) energy that he or she uses to think, to learn, and to perform other mental functions.

According to Freud, a child needs psychic energy in order to satisfy basic urges. And what kind of urges are children born with? Bad ones! Freud viewed the newborn as a "seething cauldron"—that is, an inherently negative creature who is relentlessly "driven" by two kinds of biological *instincts* (inborn motives), which he called *Eros* and *Thanatos*. Eros, or the life instincts, helps the child (and the species) to survive; it directs life-sustaining activities such as

respiration, eating, sex, and the fulfillment of all other bodily needs. By contrast, Thanatos—the death instincts—was viewed as a set of destructive forces present in all human beings. Freud believed that Eros is stronger than Thanatos, thus enabling us to survive rather than self-destruct. But he argued that if the psychic energy of Thanatos reached a critical point, the death instincts would be expressed in some way. For example, Freud thought that destructive phenomena such as arson, fistfights, murder, war, and even masochism (the desire to be hurt) were expressions of the death instincts.

Three Components of Personality: Id, Ego, and Superego

According to Freud (1933), the psychic energy that serves the instincts is eventually divided among three components of personality—the id, ego, and superego.

The id: Legislator of the personality. At birth, the personality is all id. The major function of the id is to serve the instincts by seeking objects that will satisfy them.

Have you ever heard a hungry baby cry until someone comes to feed him? A Freudian would say that the baby's cries and agitated limb movements are energized by the hunger instinct. Presumably the id directs these actions as a means of attracting the mother or another adult and thereby produces the object (food—or, literally, the mother's breast) that reduces hunger.

According to Freud, the id obeys the *pleasure principle* by seeking immediate gratification for instinctual needs. This impulsive thinking (also called "primary-process thinking") is rather unrealistic, however, for the id will invest psychic energy in any object that seems capable of gratifying the instincts, whether or not the object can actually do so. If we had never progressed beyond this earliest type of thinking, we might gleefully ingest wax fruit to satisfy hunger, reach for an empty pop bottle when thirsty, or direct our sexual energies at racy magazines and inflatable love dolls. Perhaps you can see the problem: we would have a difficult time satisfying our needs by relying on our irrational ids. Freud believed that these very difficulties lead to the development of the second major component of personality—the ego.

The ego: Executive of the personality. According to Freud (1933), the ego emerges when psychic energy is diverted from the id to energize important cognitive processes such as perception, learning, and logical reasoning. The goal of the rational ego is to serve the *reality principle*—that is, to find realistic ways of gratifying the instincts. At the same time, the ego must invest some of its available psychic energy to block the id's irrational thinking.

Freud stressed that the ego is both servant and master to the id. The ego's mastery is reflected by its ability to delay gratification until reality is served. But the ego continues to serve the id as an executive serves subordinates, pondering several alternative courses of action and selecting a plan that will best satisfy the id's basic needs.

The superego: Judicial branch of the personality. The superego is the person's moral arbiter. It develops from the ego, represents the ideal, and strives for *perfection* rather than for pleasure or reality (Freud, 1933).

Freud believed that 3–6-year-old children are gradually internalizing the moral standards of their parents, eventually adopting these guidelines as their own. These *internalized* "codes of conduct" form the child's superego. At this point, children do not need an adult to tell them when they have been bad; they are now aware of their transgressions and will feel guilty or ashamed of what they have done. Freud argued that the biggest task faced by parents when raising a child is to ensure that the child develops a stable superego. This internal censor is presumably the mechanism that prevents human beings from expressing undesirable sexual and aggressive instincts in ways that could threaten society and the social order.

Dynamics of the personality. We see, then, that the superego's main function is to monitor the ego—

that is, to ensure that the ego violates no moral principles. Note, however, that since the ego serves the id, the superego's major adversary is really the id. In other words, the superego attempts to persuade the ego to find socially acceptable outlets for the id's undesirable impulses—a process called *sublimation*. Sublimation might be illustrated by a person who decides to exercise vigorously or to take a cold shower in order to "drain away" unacceptable sexual urges.

Although the three components of personality may have conflicting goals or purposes, they normally do not incapacitate one another. The mature, healthy personality is best described as a dynamic set of checks and balances. The id communicates basic needs, the ego restrains the impulsive id long enough to find realistic methods of satisfying these needs, and the superego decides whether the ego's problem-solving strategies are morally acceptable. The ego is clearly "in the middle" and must serve two harsh masters by striking a balance between the opposing demands of the id and the superego.

Of course, not everyone is perfectly normal or healthy. Abnormalities or unusual quirks may arise if psychic energy is unequally distributed across the id, ego, and superego. For example, a sociopath might have a very strong id, a normal ego, and a very weak superego. In contrast, the righteous moralist may have a personality in which most of the psychic energy is controlled by a very strong superego. These are but two of the many abnormal personalities that could result from uneven distributions of psychic energy among the id, ego, and superego.

Freud's Stages of Psychosexual Development

Freud viewed the sex instinct as the most important of the life forces because he often discovered that the mental disturbances of his patients revolved around earlier sexual conflicts that they had *repressed*—that is, forced out of conscious awareness. Yet Freud's use of the term *sex* refers to much more than the need to copulate. Many simple bodily functions that most of us would consider rather asexual were viewed by

Freud as "erotic" activities, motivated by this general life force that he called the sex instinct.

Although the sex instinct is presumably inborn, Freud (1940/1964) felt that the character of this life force changes over time, as dictated by biological maturation. *Maturation* refers to changes that result from the aging process (for example, teething in infants; the growth spurt of puberty), rather than from learning, injury, or other life experiences. As the sex instinct matures, its energy, or *libido*, gradually shifts from one part of the body to another, and the child enters a new stage of *psychosexual* development. Freud called these stages "psychosexual" to underscore his view that the maturation of the sex instinct leaves distinct imprints on the developing psyche (that is, the mind, or personality).

The oral stage (birth to 1 year).   Freud was struck by the fact that infants spend much of the first year spitting, chewing, sucking, and biting on objects, and he concluded that the sex instinct must be centered on the mouth during this "oral" period. Indeed, he believed that oral activities are methods of gratifying the sex instinct, because children will suck, bite, or chew just about anything that comes into contact with their mouths—their thumbs, their lips, toys, and parts of their mother's body—even

when they are not particularly hungry or thirsty.

Freud argued that infants in the *oral stage* may adopt any of several basic methods—for example, sucking, biting, or spitting—to gratify the sex instinct. Presumably, the child will prefer one (or some combination) of these techniques over all others. This choice is thought to be important, for the child's preferred method of oral gratification may provide some indication of the kind of personality that he or she will have later in life. (To illustrate, Freud argued that biting or "oral aggression" could resurface later as a tendency toward argumentativeness. These argumentative individuals might then lean toward occupations such as law, politics, or editorial work in which the spoken or written word—for speech is an oral activity—can be used to criticize or hurt others.) Note the implication here: Freud was arguing that *early experiences may have a long-term effect on social and personality development.* In Box 2-1 we will see why he believed that earlier modes of functioning are likely to surface in the adult personality.

The anal stage (1 to 3 years).   In the second year of life, libido concentrates in the anal region as the sphincter muscles begin to mature. For the first time, the child has the ability to withhold or expel fecal material at will, and Freud believed that voluntary defecation becomes the primary method of gratifying the sex instinct.

During the anal stage, children must endure the demands of toilet training. For the first time, outside agents are interfering with instinctual impulses by insisting that the child inhibit the urge to defecate until he or she has reached the designated locale. There are, of course, many strategies that parents might adopt when seeing their child through this first "social" conflict. Freud believed that the emotional climate created by parents in their attempts to toilet-train a child is very important, for it may have a lasting effect on the child's personality.

The phallic stage (3 to 6 years).   We now come to the aspect of Freudian theory that many people find so controversial. Freud's view was that 3- to 4-year-old children have matured to the point that their

BOX 2-1 EARLY EXPERIENCES MAY AFFECT THE ADULT PERSONALITY

Freud (1940/1964) described several mechanisms that children may use to defend themselves (literally, their egos) against the anxieties or uncertainties of growing up. We have already discussed one such "defense" mechanism—sublimation, in which the child finds socially acceptable outlets for unacceptable motives. Freud believed that frequent use of these defense mechanisms may have long-term effects on the personality. For example, a teenaged girl who habitually sublimates her sexual desires by taking cold showers may become a "cleanliness nut" as an adult.

Another important ego defense mechanism is *fixation*, or arrested development. According to Freud, the child who experiences severe conflicts at any particular stage of development may be reluctant to move or incapable of moving to the next stage, where the uncertainties are even greater. The child may then fixate at the earlier stage, and further development will be arrested or at least impaired. Freud believed that some people become fixated at the level of primary-process thinking and consequently remain "dreamers" or "unrealistic optimists" throughout their lives. Others fixate on particular behaviors. An example is the chronic thumbsucker whose oral fixation is expressed later in life in substitute activities such as smoking or oral sex. In sum, Freud was convinced that childhood fixations were important determinants of many personality characteristics.

A person who experiences too much anxiety or too many conflicts at any stage of development may retreat to an earlier, less traumatic stage. Such developmental reversals are examples of an ego-defense mechanism that Freud called *regression*. Even a well-adjusted adult may regress from time to time in order to forget problems or reduce anxiety. For example, masturbation is one earlier mode of sexual functioning that a person may undertake to reduce sexual conflicts or frustrations. Dreaming is a regressive activity that enables a person to resolve conflicts and obtain pleasure through the magic of wishful thinking. Thus, regression is a third way in which earlier events, activities, and thought processes may affect the behavior of adults.

---

genitals have become an interesting and sensitive area of the body. Libido presumably flows to this area as children derive pleasure from stroking and fondling their genitals. What is so controversial? According to Freud, all children at this age develop a strong incestuous desire for the parent of the other sex. He called this period the phallic stage because he believed that the phallus (penis) assumes a critically important role in the psychosexual development of both boys and girls.

Let's examine this stage for boys. According to Freud, 4-year-old boys develop an intense sexual longing for their mothers. At the same time, they become jealous, and if they could have their way, they would destroy their chief rivals for maternal affection, their fathers. Freud called this state of affairs the *Oedipus complex* after the legendary Oedipus, king of Thebes, who unwittingly killed his father and married his mother.

Now, 3−5-year-old boys are not as powerful as King Oedipus, and they face certain defeat in their quest to win the sexual favors of their mothers. In fact, Freud suggests that a jealous young son will have many conflicts with his paternal rival and will eventually fear that his father might castrate him for this rivaling conduct. When this *castration anxiety* becomes sufficiently intense, the boy (if development is normal) will then resolve his Oedipus complex by repressing his incestuous desire for the mother and identifying with the father. This "*identification with the aggressor*" lessens the chances of castration, for the boy is no longer a rival. He will try to emulate the father, incorporating all the father's attitudes, attributes, and behaviors. In so doing, the son is likely to adopt a distinct preference for the masculine sex role and to become a "male" psychologically. Identification with the aggressor should also place the crowning touch on the boy's superego, for he will repress two of the most taboo of motives—incest and murder—and internalize the moral standards of his feared and respected rival. In short, the boy has become a well-behaved youngster—daddy's "little man."

And what about girls? Freud contends that, before

age 4, girls prefer their mothers to their fathers. But once the girl discovers that she lacks a penis, she is thought to blame her closest companion, the mother, for this "castrated" condition. This traumatic discovery results in a transfer of affection from the mother to the father. Freud believed that a girl of this age envies her father for possessing a penis and that she will choose him as a sex object in the hope of exerting some control over a person who has the valued organ that she lacks (Freud assumed that the girl's *real* underlying motive was to bear her father's child, an event that would compensate for her lack of a penis, especially if the child was male).

The female Oedipus complex (known as the *Electra complex*) bears some obvious similarities to that of the male. Children of each sex value the male phallus; girls hope to gain one, and boys hope to keep theirs. Furthermore, both boys and girls perceive the parent of the same sex as their major rival for the affection of the other parent. However, Freud was uncertain just how (or why) girls ever resolved their Electra complexes. Boys fear castration, and this intense fear forces them to renounce their Oedipus complexes by identifying with their fathers. But what do girls fear? After all, they supposedly believe that they have already been castrated, and they attribute this act of brutality to their mothers. To Freud's way of thinking, they no longer have any reason to fear the mother.

Why, then, does the Electra complex subside? Freud (1924/1961) assumed that it may simply fade away as the girl faces reality and recognizes the impossibility of possessing her father. However, he suggested that girls will develop weaker superegos than boys because their resolution of the Electra complex is not based on a fear of retaliation (castration anxiety) that would force them to internalize the ethical standards of their mothers (or their fathers).

The latency period (ages 6 to 12).
Between ages 6 and 12, the child's sex instincts are relatively quiet. The sexual traumas of the phallic stage are forgotten, and all available libido is channeled into some socially acceptable activity, such as schoolwork or vigorous play, that consumes most of the child's physical

and psychic energy. The latency period continues until puberty, when the child suddenly experiences a number of biological changes that mark the beginning of Freud's final psychosexual stage.

The genital stage (age 12 onward).
With the onset of puberty come maturation of the reproductive system, production of sex hormones, and, according to Freud, a reactivation of the genital zone as an area of sensual pleasure. The adolescent may openly express libido toward members of the other sex, but for the first time, the underlying aim of the sex instincts is reproduction. Throughout adolescence and young adulthood, libido is invested in activities—forming friendships, preparing for a career, courting, marriage—that prepare the individual to satisfy the fully mature sex instinct by having children. This genital period is the longest of Freud's psychosexual stages. It lasts from puberty to old age, when the individual may regress to an earlier stage and begin a "second childhood."

Evaluation of Freud's Theory

Few theories have generated as much interest or as much criticism as Freud's psychoanalytic model. Many critics contend that Freud's favorite interview techniques, free association and dream analysis, are unstandardized, hopelessly subjective, and thus a poor source of scientific information. Let's also recall who Freud's subjects were: a relatively small number of *clinical* patients. Were the reports of these individuals accurate, or did Freud's mentally disturbed subjects simply tell him whatever they thought he wanted to hear? Do the life histories of neurotic patients really tell us anything about the personality development of normal people? Pollsters cannot make accurate statements about public opinion by sampling a nonrepresentative population such as dock workers or old people. Why, then, should we believe that Freud's theory can be generalized beyond the abnormal population on which it is based? In sum, the theories of Freud and his closest disciples stem from unstandardized, nonobjective assessments of a population that is hardly representative of human beings in general.

Methodological criticisms notwithstanding, how plausible do you think Freud's ideas are? Do you think that we are all relentlessly driven by sexual and aggressive instincts? Could we have really experienced Oedipus or Electra complexes and simply repressed these traumatic events? And what about the role of culture in human development? In 19th- and early 20th-century Europe, there were no clinical psychologists or sex therapists, and the topic of sex was not discussed publicly in this outwardly prudish Victorian era. Could the sexual conflicts that Freud thought so important have merely been reflections of the sexually repressive culture in which his patients lived?

Few contemporary psychologists accept all of Freud's major premises and propositions. For example, there is not much evidence for the notion that the oral and anal activities of childhood predict one's later personality. Nor is there reason to believe that all children experience Oedipus and Electra complexes. To experience these conflicts, 4- to 6-year-old children would have to recognize the anatomical differences between the sexes, and there is little evidence that they do. In fact, Alan Katcher (1955) found that the majority of 4- to 5-year-olds are inept at assembling a doll so that its genitals match other parts of its body. Even 6-year-olds often made mistakes such as attaching a lower torso containing a penis to an upper body with breasts. Clearly, these "oedipal-aged" children were confused or ignorant about sex differences in genital anatomy, and it seems highly unlikely that they could be experiencing any castration anxiety or penis envy.

But we cannot reject all of Freud's ideas simply because some of them may seem a bit outlandish. Indeed, there are several reasons that Sigmund Freud will always remain an important figure in the history of the behavioral sciences. For one thing, his theory was the first systematic explanation of human behavior, and it revolutionized the study of psychology. When psychology came into being, in the middle of the 19th century, investigators were concerned with understanding isolated aspects of *conscious* experience, such as sensory processes and perceptual illusions. It was Freud who first noted that these scientists were studying the tip of the iceberg when he proclaimed that the vast majority of psychic experience lay below the level of conscious awareness. Perhaps Freud's most important contribution was his concept of unconscious motivation, the idea that much of our behavior is caused by forces or repressed conflicts of which we are not consciously aware. Freud also convinced many scientists that development occurs in stages and that the events of childhood are truly the foundation from which the adult character arises. In sum, psychoanalysis was a new look at human behavior that attempted to explain a wide range of phenomena that Freud's predecessors had not even considered. Freud was truly a great explorer who dared to navigate murky, uncharted waters. In the process, he changed our view of humankind.

ERIK ERIKSON'S THEORY OF PSYCHOSOCIAL DEVELOPMENT

As Freud became widely read, he attracted many followers. However, Freud's pupils did not always agree with the master, and eventually they began to modify some of Freud's ideas and became important theorists in their own right. Among the best known of these *neo-Freudian* scholars is Erik Erikson, who was a student of Freud's daughter, Anna.

Erikson accepts many of Freud's ideas. He agrees that people are born with a number of basic instincts and that the personality has three components: the id, ego, and superego. Erikson also assumes that development occurs in stages and that the child must successfully resolve some crisis or conflict at each stage in order to be prepared for the crises that will emerge later in life.

However, Erikson is truly a revisionist, for his theory differs from Freud's in several important respects. First, Erikson (1963, 1972) stresses that children are *active, adaptive* explorers who seek to control their environment rather than passive creatures who are molded by their parents. He has also been labeled an *ego* psychologist because he believes that an individual must first understand the *realities* of the social world (an ego function) in order to adapt successfully and show a normal pattern of personal growth. This is perhaps the major difference between Freud and Erikson. Unlike Freud, who felt that the

PHOTO 2-2 Erik Erikson (b. 1902) has emphasized the sociocultural determinants of personality in his theory of psychosocial development.

most interesting aspects of behavior stemmed from conflicts between the id and the superego, Erikson assumes that human beings are basically rational creatures whose thoughts, feelings, and actions are largely controlled by the ego.

Clearly, Erikson's thinking was shaped by his own interesting experiences. He was born in Denmark, was raised in Germany, and spent much of his adolescence wandering throughout Europe. After receiving his professional training, Erikson emigrated to the United States, where he studied college students, victims of combat fatigue during World War II, civil rights workers in the South, and American Indians. With this kind of cross-cultural background, it is hardly surprising that Erikson would emphasize social and cultural aspects of development in his own theory. Henry Maier (1969, p. 23) used these words to reflect Erikson's point of view:

> Culture adds the human aspect of living. Man lives by instinctual forces, and culture insists upon the "proper" use of these forces. [But] it is the cultural environment . . . which determines the nature of each individual's experience. The child and his parents are never alone; through the parent's conscience [many past] generations are looking upon a child's actions, helping him to integrate his relationships with their approval. . . . A culture, class, or ethnic group's basic ways of [viewing the world] are transmitted to the [child] . . . and tie the child forever to his original milieu.

In sum, Erikson believes that we are largely products of our society rather than our sex instincts. For this reason, his approach should be labeled a theory of *psychosocial* development.

Eight Life Crises

Erikson argues that all human beings face a minimum of eight major crises, or conflicts, during the course of their lives. Each crisis is primarily "social" in character and has important implications for the future. Table 2-1 compares Freud's psychosexual and Erikson's psychosocial stages. Note that Erikson's developmental stages do not end at adolescence or young adulthood. Erikson believes that the problems of adolescents and young adults are very different from those faced by parents who are raising children or by the aged who must grapple with the specter of retirement, a sense of uselessness, and death. Most contemporary psychologists would definitely agree.

As we have noted, Erikson believes that the successful resolution of each life crisis prepares the person for the next of life's conflicts. By contrast, the individual who fails to resolve one or more of the life crises is almost certain to encounter problems in the future. For example, a child who learns to mistrust other human beings in infancy may find it exceedingly difficult to trust a prospective friend or lover later in life. An adolescent who fails to establish a strong personal identity may be reluctant to commit his or her fragile sense of "self" to a "shared identity" with a prospective spouse. We see, then, that later crises may become very formidable hurdles for the individual who stumbles early.

Although Erikson believes that the crises of childhood set the stage for our adult lives, we must remember that he views human beings as rational, adaptive creatures who will struggle to the very end in their attempts to cope successfully with their social environment. Charles Dickens' Scrooge, a fictional character from *A Christmas Carol*, aptly illustrates the self-centered, "stagnated" adult—one who is failing at Erikson's seventh life crisis (and who has been unsuccessful at establishing a sense of intimacy as well). You may remember that old Scrooge was so absorbed in his own interests (making money) that he completely ignored the needs and wishes of his young storekeeper, Bob Cratchit. Scrooge's tale had a happy ending, however. By the end of the story, he had acquired a sense of intimacy and generativity that had eluded him earlier, and he was now ready to face life's final crisis in a positive frame of mind. An unlikely reversal? Not necessarily! Erikson is quite the optimist; he maintains that "there is little that cannot be remedied later, there is much [in the way of harm] that can be prevented from happening at all" (1950, p. 104).

Evaluation of Erikson's Theory

Many people prefer Erikson's theory to Freud's because they simply refuse to believe that human beings are dominated by sexual instincts. An analyst like Erikson, who stresses our rational, adaptive nature, is so much easier to accept. In addition, Erikson emphasizes many of the social conflicts and personal dilemmas that people may remember, are currently experiencing, or can easily anticipate. In the words of one student, "Erikson's theory is so relevant . . . Freud's is a figment of his *wild* imagination."

Although Erikson's ideas evolved from his many

TABLE 2-1   Erikson's and Freud's Stages of Development

Approximate age	Erikson's stage or "psychosocial crisis"	Erikson's viewpoint: Significant events and social influences	Corresponding Freudian stage
Birth to 1 year	Basic trust versus mistrust	Infants must learn to trust others to care for their basic needs. If caregivers are rejecting or inconsistent in their care, the infant may view the world as a dangerous place filled with untrustworthy or unreliable people. The mother or primary caregiver is the key social agent.	Oral
1 to 3 years	Autonomy versus shame and doubt	Children must learn to be "autonomous—to feed and dress themselves, to look after their own hygiene, and so on. Failure to achieve this independence may force the child to doubt his or her own abilities and feel shameful. Parents are the key social agents.	Anal
3 to 6 years	Initiative versus guilt	Children attempt to act grown up and will try to accept responsibilities that are beyond their capacity to handle. They sometimes undertake goals or activities that conflict with those of parents and other family members, and these conflicts may make them feel guilty. Successful resolution of this crisis requires a balance: the child must retain a sense of initiative and yet learn not to impinge on the rights, privileges, or goals of others. The family is the key social agent.	Phallic
6 to 12 years	Industry versus inferiority	Children must master important social and academic skills. This is a period when the child compares the self with peers. If sufficiently industrious, children will acquire the social and academic skills to feel self-assured. Failure to acquire these important attributes leads to feelings of inferiority. Significant social agents are teachers and peers.	Latency

and varied experiences and his observations of both normal and clinical populations, his research methods (basically consisting of unstructured interviews and nonsystematic observations) were every bit as subjective as those of Freud. Another major shortcoming of Erikson's theory is that it does not clearly specify the kinds of experiences that people must have in order to cope with and resolve various psychosocial crises. For example, what kinds of caregiving might lead an infant to trust (or mistrust) other people? Why is trust important for the child's developing sense of autonomy, initiative, or industry? Exactly how do adolescents formulate stable identities with which to face the tasks of young adulthood? Erikson is simply not very explicit about any of these important issues. His theory is a *descriptive* overview of human social and emotional development that does not do a very good job of explaining how or why this development takes place.

Researchers who study such topics as the emotional development of infants or the growth of the adolescent self-concept are beginning to pay more attention to Erikson, for they often find that their results are consistent with his descriptive framework. Many of these investigators are now using Erikson's description of psychosocial development as a general

TABLE 2-1 *continued*

Approximate age	Erikson's stage or "psychosocial crisis"	Erikson's viewpoint: Significant events and social influences	Corresponding Freudian stage
12 to 20 years	Identity versus role confusion	This is the crossroad between childhood and maturity. The adolescent grapples with the question "Who am I?" Adolescents must establish basic social and occupational identities, or they will remain confused about the roles they should play as adults. The key social agent is the society of peers.	Early genital (adolescence)
20 to 40 years (young adulthood)	Intimacy versus isolation	The primary task at this stage is to form strong friendships and to achieve a sense of love and companionship (or a shared identity) with another person. Feelings of loneliness or isolation are likely to result from an inability to form friendships or an intimate relationship. Key social agents are lovers, spouses, and close friends (of both sexes).	Genital
40 to 65 years (middle adulthood)	Generativity versus stagnation	At this stage, adults face the tasks of becoming productive in their work and raising their families or otherwise looking after the needs of young people. These standards of "generativity" are defined by one's culture. Those who are unable or unwilling to assume these responsibilities will become stagnant and/or self-centered. Significant social agents are the spouse, children, and cultural norms.	Genital
Old age	Ego integrity versus despair	The older adult will look back at life, viewing it as either a meaningful, productive, and happy experience or as a major disappointment full of unfulfilled promises and unrealized goals. One's life experiences, particularly social experiences, will determine the outcome of this final life crisis.	Genital

starting point and then trying to *explain* how children are able to develop a sense of trust, autonomy, initiative, industry, or a personal identity. So Erikson's theory is having an impact, and we will look at some of the more encouraging of the early returns as we proceed through the text.

PSYCHOANALYTIC THEORY TODAY

Today psychoanalysts represent a small minority within the community of child developmentalists. Many researchers have abandoned the psychoanalytic approach (particularly Freud's theory) because it is difficult to verify or disconfirm. Suppose, for example, that we wanted to test the basic Freudian proposition that the healthy personality is one in which psychic energy is evenly distributed among the id, ego, and superego. How could we do it? There are objective tests that we could use to select "mentally healthy" subjects, but we have no instrument that measures psychic energy or the relative strengths of the id, ego, and superego. The point is that many psychoanalytic assertions are untestable by any method other than the interview or a clinical approach, and unfortunately, these techniques are time-consuming, expensive, and among the least objective of all methods used to study developing children.

Of course, the main reason that developmental researchers have abandoned the psychoanalytic perspective is that other theories seem more compelling to them. One theoretical approach that is currently attracting a good deal of attention is the modern biological viewpoint, to which we will now turn.

RECENT BIOLOGICAL PERSPECTIVES

Freud's psychoanalytic theory obviously has strong biological overtones. Not only are inborn instincts the motivational components of his theory, but the maturation of the sex instinct was said to determine the course (or at least the stages) of social and personality development.

In this section of the chapter, we will become acquainted with two additional streams of thought that emphasize biological contributions to human social and personality development. One of these approaches, the *ethological* tradition, focuses most intently on inherited attributes that characterize all members of a species and conspire to make us *alike* (that is, contribute to common developmental outcomes). By contrast, the second approach, *behavior genetics*, is concerned mainly with determining how the unique combination of genes that each of us inherits might be implicated in making individuals *different* from one another.

ETHOLOGICAL THEORY

Ethology is the study of the biological bases of behavior, including its evolution, causation, and development (Cairns, 1979). This theoretical approach arose from the work of several European zoologists who argued that other theorists, particularly social scientists, had overlooked or simply chosen to ignore important biological contributions to human and animal behavior.

According to the ethologists, the newborn of each species come equipped with a number of inborn attributes and responses that are products of evolution. These "biologically programmed" characteristics are thought to have evolved as a result of the Darwinian process of *natural selection*. Presumably, environmental stresses or demands impinge on members of all species, ensuring that only those individuals with the most adaptive characteristics will survive to pass these attributes along to their offspring. Thus, each "species-specific" behavior is *preselected*—meaning that it has persisted over generations because it serves some function that increases the chances of survival for the individual and the species (Blurton-Jones, 1972). Examples of such preselected characteristics are the nest-building behavior of lovebirds, nut cracking by red squirrels, and crying to communicate discomfort by human infants.

When conducting research, ethologists prefer the method of naturalistic observation because they believe that "biologically programmed" behaviors that

PHOTO 2-3 The cry is a distress signal that attracts the attention of caregivers.

affect human (or animal) development are best identified and understood if they are observed in settings where they have adaptive significance (Charlesworth, 1980). Stated another way, it makes little sense to look for innate responses to the natural environment in the highly artificial context of the laboratory. (Ethologists do occasionally conduct laboratory experiments, but only to confirm or clarify observations made in the natural environment.)

When testing a hypothesis in the field, a human ethologist makes detailed records of children's interactions, noting when the critical (or target) behavior occurred and what happened immediately before and after this critical event. Of particular interest are any possible innate responses (for example, facial features or postural cues) that may have elicited or terminated the behavior in question. Ethologists believe that most of our inherited attributes have the function of promoting particular kinds of experiences that will affect our development. For example, we will see in Chapter 5 that the cry of a human infant is thought to be a biologically programmed "distress signal" that brings caregivers running. Not only are infants said to be biologically programmed to convey their distress with loud, lusty cries, but ethologists

also believe that caregivers are biologically predisposed to respond to such signals. So the adaptive significance of an infant's crying is to ensure (1) that the infant's basic needs (hunger, thirst, safety) will be met and (2) that the infant will have sufficient contact with other human beings to form primary social and emotional relationships (Bowlby, 1973).

Although ethologists are especially critical of learning theorists for largely ignoring the biological bases of behavior, they are well aware that social development would not progress very far without learning. For example, the cry of a human infant may well be an innate signal that promotes the human contact from which emotional attachments emerge. However, these emotional attachments do not simply "happen" automatically. The infant must first *learn* to discriminate familiar faces from those of strangers before he or she will show any evidence of becoming emotionally attached to a regular companion. Presumably, the adaptive significance of this kind of discriminatory learning stems from that period of evolutionary history when humans lived in the great outdoors, traveling in nomadic tribes. In those days, it was essential that youngsters become attached to familiar companions and fearful of strangers, for failure to cry in response to a strange face might make a toddler "easy pickings" for a predatory animal.

Now consider the opposite side of the coin. Some caregivers are habitually inattentive or even neglectful, so that the infant's cries rarely promote any contact with them. Such an infant will probably not form strong emotional attachments to her primary caregivers and may remain shy or emotionally unresponsive to others for years to come (Ainsworth, 1979; Sroufe, Fox, & Pancake, 1983). What this infant has learned from her early experiences is that close companions are unreliable and not to be trusted. Consequently, the child becomes ambivalent or wary around her caregivers and may later assume that other people (for example, teachers and peers) are equally untrustworthy individuals who should be avoided whenever possible.

One interesting ethological notion is the idea that there are critical periods in development. A *critical period* is a part of the life cycle during which the developing organism is particularly sensitive or responsive to certain environmental influences; outside this period, the same influences are thought to have little, if any, lasting effect. For example, some ethologists believe that the first three years of life are a critical period for the development of social and emotional responsivity in human beings. Presumably, we are most uniquely susceptible to forming close emotional ties during the first three years, and should we have little or no opportunity to do so during this period, we would find it difficult (if not impossible) to make close friends or to enter into intimate emotional relationships with other people later in life. In Chapter 6, we will see whether there is any empirical basis for this interesting and provocative claim about human social and emotional development.

In sum, ethologists clearly acknowledge that we humans are largely products of our experiences. Yet they are quick to remind us that we are also inherently biological creatures who have a number of inborn characteristics and capabilities that affect the kinds of learning experiences we are likely to have.

Contributions of the Ethological Viewpoint

If this chapter had been written in 1970, it would not have included a section on ethological theory. Although ethology came into being more than 30 years ago, the early ethologists studied animal behavior; only within the past 10 to 15 years have proponents of ethology made a serious attempt to specify the biological bases of human development. Clearly, they have not yet succeeded in providing us with a comprehensive overview of all aspects of social and personality development. However, they have made developmental researchers increasingly aware that every child has a bioevolutionary heritage that affects his or her own behavior and the reactions of others to the child.

Perhaps the most intriguing ethological notion—one that we will discuss in detail in Chapter 5—is that infants are inherently sociable creatures who are quite capable of promoting and maintaining social encounters from the day they are born. This viewpoint contrasts sharply with that of learning theorists,

who portray the infant as a *tabula rasa*, or with the cognitive view of the infant as an "asocial" creature who comes into the world equipped with only a few primitive reflexes. Ethologists also believe that our evolutionary history provides us with inborn *motivational* inclinations that affect our behavior in important ways (shades of Freud and the concept of instincts). For example, the motive of *altruism*—a concern about the welfare of others—has presumably evolved because it promotes survival of the species (an idea we will explore in more detail in Chapter 10). Box 2-2 describes some recent observations to suggest that there may be a biological basis for certain aspects of altruism.

In the late 1980s, the ethological viewpoint is itself a thriving infant—one that should continue to develop and perhaps have an even stronger impact on the field of social and personality development in the years ahead.

Criticisms of Ethology

Recall that psychoanalytic theory is often criticized as being *untestable*: How, for example, does one measure various instincts or the strength of personality components such as the id, ego, and superego? The same criticism can be aimed at the ethologists: How does one prove that certain motives or behaviors are (1) inborn or (2) products of our evolutionary history? These claims are often difficult or impossible to confirm. In addition, ethological theory is often criticized as being a retrospective, or "post hoc," *description* of development. One can easily apply evolutionary concepts to account for something that has already happened, but can the theory *predict* what is likely to happen in the future? Many developmentalists believe that it cannot.

Finally, proponents of learning theory have an interesting viewpoint on ethology. They argue that, even if the bases for certain motives or behaviors are biologically programmed, these innate responses will soon become so modified by learning that it may not be helpful to spend much time wondering about their prior evolutionary significance. Albert Bandura (1973), for example, makes the following observation when comparing the aggressive behavior of humans and animals:

BOX 2-2   IS ALTRUISM PART OF HUMAN NATURE?

Darwin's notion of "survival of the fittest" seems to argue against altruism as an inborn motive. Many have interpreted Darwin's idea to mean that powerful, self-serving individuals who place their own needs ahead of others' are the ones who are most likely to survive. If this were so, evolution would favor the development of selfish, egoistic motives—not altruism—as basic components of human nature.

Martin Hoffman (1981) has recently challenged this point of view, listing several reasons that the concept of "survival of the fittest" actually implies altruism. His arguments hinge on the assumption that human beings are more likely to receive protection from natural enemies, satisfy all their basic needs, and successfully reproduce if they live together in cooperative social units. If this assumption is correct, then cooperative, altruistic individuals would be the ones who are most likely to survive long enough to pass along their "altruistic genes" to their offspring; individualists who "go it alone" would probably succumb to famine, predators, or some other natural disaster that they could not cope with by themselves. So over thousands of generations, natural selection would favor the development of innate social motives such as altruism. Presumably, the tremendous survival value of being "social" makes altruism, cooperation, and other social motives much more plausible as components of human nature than competition, selfishness, and the like.

It is obviously absurd to argue that infants routinely help other people. However, Hoffman believes that even newborn babies are capable of recognizing and experiencing the emotions of others. This ability, known as *empathy*, is thought to be an important contributor to altruism, for a person must recognize that others are distressed in some way before he or she is likely to help. So Hoffman is suggesting that at least one aspect of altruism—empathy—is present at birth.

Hoffman's claim is based on an experiment (Sagi & Hoffman, 1976) in which infants less than 36 hours old listened to (1) another infant's cries, (2) an equally loud computer simulation of a crying infant, or (3) no sounds at all (silence). The infants who heard a real infant crying soon began to cry themselves, to display physical signs of agitation such as kicking, and to grimace. Infants exposed to the simulated cry or to silence cried much less and seemed not to be very discomforted. (A recent study by Martin & Clark, 1982, has confirmed these observations.)

Hoffman argues that there is something quite distinctive about the human cry. His contention is that infants listen to and experience the distress of (that is, empathize with) another crying infant and become distressed themselves. Of course, this finding does not conclusively demonstrate that humans are altruistic by nature. But it does imply that the capacity for empathy may be present at birth and thus serve as a biological basis for the eventual development of altruistic behavior.

[Unlike animals], man does not rely heavily on auditory, postural, or olfactory signals for conveying aggressive intent or appeasement. He has [developed] a much more intricate system of communication—namely language—for controlling aggression. National leaders can . . . better safeguard against catastrophic violence by verbal communiques than by snapping their teeth or erecting their hair, especially in view of the prevalence of baldness among the higher echelons [p. 16].

In spite of these criticisms, the ethological perspective remains a valuable addition to the field of social and personality development. It has made us aware of important biological contributors to human social behavior and has led to several discoveries that were neither anticipated nor easily explained by other theoretical approaches.

THE BEHAVIOR GENETICS APPROACH

In recent years, investigators from the fields of genetics, embryology, population biology, and psychology have asked the question "Are there specific abilities, traits, and patterns of behavior that depend very heavily on the particular combination of genes that an individual inherits, and if so, are these attributes likely to be modified by one's experiences?" Those who focus on these issues in their research are known as *behavior geneticists*.

Before we take a closer look at the field of behavior genetics, it is necessary to dispel a common myth. Although behavior geneticists view development as the process through which one's *genotype* (the set of genes one inherits) comes to be expressed as a *phenotype* (one's observable characteristics and behaviors), they are *not* strict hereditarians. Instead, they believe that most behavioral attributes are the end product of a long and involved interplay between hereditary predispositions and environmental influences. Consider the following example. A child who inherits genes for tall stature will almost certainly grow taller than one who inherits genes for short stature if these children are raised in the same environment. But if the first child receives poor nutrition early in life and the second is well nourished, they may well be about the same height as adults. Thus, the behavior geneticist is well aware that even attributes such as physical stature that seem to have a very strong hereditary component are often modified in important ways by environmental influences. This is a point to keep in mind as we discuss the implications of behavior genetics research in the pages that follow.

Methods of Assessing Hereditary Influences

Behavior geneticists use two major strategies to assess hereditary contributions to behavior: *selective breeding* and *family studies*. Each of these approaches attempts to specify the *heritability* of various attributes—that is, the amount of variation in a trait or a class of behavior that is attributable to hereditary factors.

Selective breeding studies. Members of any species, particularly humans, differ considerably in their abilities, peculiarities, and patterns of behavior. Do such differences reflect the fact that no two individuals (except identical twins) inherit the same pattern of genes?

Many investigators have tried to answer this question by seeing whether they could selectively breed particular attributes in animals. A famous example of a selective breeding experiment is R. C. Tryon's (1940) attempt to show that maze-learning ability is a heritable attribute in rats. Tryon first tested a large sample of rats for maze-learning ability, labeling those who made few errors "maze-bright" and those who made many errors "maze-dull." Then, across many successive generations, Tryon mated the brightest of the maze-bright rats with one another while also inbreeding the dullest of the maze-dull

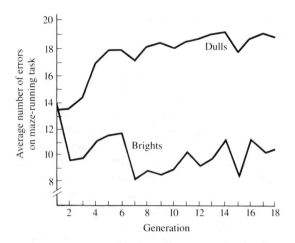

FIGURE 2-1 Maze-running performance by inbred maze-bright and maze-dull rats over 18 generations

groups.[2] The results of this selective breeding experiment appear in Figure 2-1. Note that, across generations, differences in maze-running performance between the maze-bright and the maze-dull groups became increasingly apparent. By the 18th generation, the worst performer in the maze-bright group was better at running mazes than the best performer from the maze-dull group. Thus, Tryon's data suggest that maze-learning ability in rats is influenced by hereditary factors. Other investigators have used the selective breeding technique to demonstrate clear genetic contributions to such attributes as activity level, emotionality, aggressiveness, and sex drive in rats, mice, and chickens (Plomin, DeFries, & McClearn, 1980).

Family studies. Since it is obviously unethical to conduct selective breeding studies with humans, the field of human behavior genetics relies on an alternative methodology known as the family study. In a typical family study, persons who live in the same household are compared to see how similar they are on one or more behavioral attributes. If the attribute in question is heritable, then the similarity between any two individuals who live in the same household should increase as a function of their *kinship*—that is, the extent to which they have the same genes. For example, identical twins, who developed from the same fertilized egg and have the same genotype (kinship = 1.00), should be more similar on a heritable attribute than fraternal twins or ordinary siblings, who have only half their genes in common (kinship = .50). And fraternal twins and siblings should be more similar on heritable attributes than either half-siblings (kinship = .25) or genetically unrelated children living in same home (kinship = .00).

A family study can also help us determine the extent to which various traits and behavioral attributes are affected by the environment. Consider genetically unrelated adopted children raised in the same household. Their degree of kinship with one another and with their adoptive parents is .00. Consequently, there is no reason to suspect that these youngsters will resemble one another or their adoptive parents unless their common environment plays some part in determining their standing on the trait or behavior in question. Another way that the effects of the environment can be inferred is to compare identical twins raised in the same environment with identical twins raised in different environments. The kinship of any pair of identical twins, reared together or apart, is 1.00. So if identical twins reared together are more alike on an attribute than identical twins reared apart, we can infer that the environment plays some role in determining that attribute.

We are now about ready to examine the results of a small sample of family studies to illustrate why behavior geneticists believe that our temperaments and personalities are influenced by the genes we have inherited. To evaluate this research, however, one needs to know what correlation coefficients are and how these statistics might help us to determine whether various attributes are influenced by heredity. Before proceeding, you may find it helpful to turn to Box 2-3, which discusses the concept of correlation and the role that correlations play in behavior genetics research.

Hereditary Contributions to Temperament, Personality, and Mental Health

When psychologists speak of "personality," they are referring to a broad collection of attributes—including temperament, attitudes, traits, values, and distinctive behavioral patterns (or habits)—that seem to

PHOTO 2-4 Because identical twins have identical genotypes, they are a rich source of information about possible hereditary contributions to personality and social behavior.

characterize an individual. Unfortunately, the personality consists of so many characteristics that it is virtually impossible to measure them all with any single test. However, it is possible to focus on specific aspects of personality to see whether there is any hereditary basis for the ways we behave.

Heritability of temperament. Selective breeding experiments conducted with various animal species reveal that temperamental attributes such as activity level, fearfulness, and sociability have a strong hereditary component (see McClearn, 1970). Could the same be true of humans? Behavior geneticists have tried to answer this question by comparing the temperamental similarities of pairs of identical and pairs of fraternal twins. Several such studies reveal that identical twin infants (who have inherited identical genotypes) are much more alike on temperamental dimensions such as activity level, demands for attention, and irritability than pairs of fraternal twins (Goldsmith & Gottesman, 1981; Matheny, 1980). These data imply that at least some components of human temperament are heritable. Moreover, Jerome Kagan and his associates (Kagan, Reznick, Clarke, Snidman, & Garcia-Coll, 1984) found that children who were either socially inhibited or uninhibited at age 21 months remained relatively

BOX 2-3   CORRELATIONS, CORRELATION COEFFICIENTS, AND ESTIMATES OF HERITABILITY

Simply stated, a correlation indicates whether two variables are related. In other words, if one asks whether two attributes are correlated, one wants to know whether those attributes "go together" in some meaningful way. An agricultural scientist might wish to know whether crop yield is related to rainfall. A medical researcher may seek to determine whether physical exercise is related to the incidence of heart disease. A behavior geneticist conducting a family study may wish to determine whether the IQ scores of twins are related to the IQ scores of their cotwins.

Any two variables may be *positively correlated, negatively correlated*, or *uncorrelated*. A positive correlation means that high scores on variable X are associated with high scores on variable Y and that low scores on X are associated with low scores on Y. For example, height and weight are positively correlated: children who are *taller* also tend to be *heavier*. A negative correlation means that high scores on variable X are associated with low scores on variable Y and vice versa. For example, exercise is negatively correlated with the incidence of heart disease: people who exercise *more* are *less* likely to have heart attacks. Finally, if scores on variable X are not at all associated with scores on variable Y, the two factors are said to be uncorrelated, or unrelated.

The strength, or magnitude, of a correlation can be determined statistically and is represented as a *correlation coefficient* (symbolized r) with a value between -1.00 and $+1.00$. Positive correlations range from .01 to 1.00; negative correlations range from $-.01$ to -1.00. The absolute size of a correlation coefficient (disregarding its sign) provides information about the strength of the relationship between the variables. For example, the correlation coefficients $-.70$ and $+.70$ are equal in magnitude but opposite in direction. Both are stronger relationships than a correlation of .50. A correlation coefficient of .00 indicates that the variables under consideration are unrelated.

There are two common misconceptions about correlation coefficients. First, the fact that two variables are correlated does not necessarily mean that one causes the other. For example, the positive correlation between the number of crimes reported in cities and the number of churches in those cities does not mean that churches cause crime. In this case, a third variable, population, determines both the number of crimes in a city and the number of churches built there. Although the latter two variables are correlated, the relationship between them is not one of cause and effect.

Second, people often assume that a correlation (r) of .70 is twice as large as a correlation of .35, for example, or that

inhibited or uninhibited when retested at 4 years of age. So it appears that early temperamental patterns are often reasonably stable over time.

Alexander Thomas and his colleagues (Thomas, Chess, & Birch, 1970; Thomas & Chess, 1977) have noted that certain temperamental attributes tend to cluster together. For example, highly active infants are often irritable and irregular in their feeding, sleeping, and bowel habits, whereas passive babies tend to be good-natured and regular in their habits. Thomas and Chess (1977) contend that most infants can be placed into one of three categories on the basis of their overall pattern of temperamental characteristics:

1. *The easy child.* Easygoing children are even-tempered, are typically in a positive mood, and are quite adaptable to new experiences. Their habits are regular and predictable.

2. *The difficult child.* Difficult children are active, irritable, and irregular in their habits. They often react vigorously and very negatively to changes in routine and are slow to adapt to new persons or situations.

3. *The slow-to-warm-up child.* These children are quite inactive and moody. They, too, are slow to adapt to new persons and situations, but unlike the difficult child, they typically respond to novelty or to changes in routine with mild forms of passive resistance. For example, they might resist cuddling by directing their attention elsewhere rather than by crying or kicking.

Apparently these broad temperamental patterns may also persist over time and influence the child's adjustment to a variety of settings and situations later in life. For example, children with difficult temperaments are more likely than other children to have

BOX 2-3   *continued*

a correlation of .50 is twice as large as a correlation of .25. This is incorrect. To determine the relative magnitude of any two correlations, we must compare the squared correlation coefficients. Thus, an *r* of .70 is roughly 4 times as strong as an *r* of .35 (because $.70^2 = .49$ and $.35^2 = .12$).

How can the heritability of an attribute be estimated from correlations? Suppose that we had just conducted a study of 50 families, 25 that have a pair of identical twins and 25 that have a pair of fraternal twins. While conducting the study, we measured some aspect of personality in each twin and found that the correlation between identical twins on this trait was + .50 and the correlation between fraternal twins was + .30. Since members of each twin pair live in the same household, we might assume that they have had highly similar environments. Thus, the fact that identical twins are more alike on this personality dimension than fraternal twins suggests that the trait in question is affected by heredity. Now we may wonder, just how strong is the hereditary contribution?

In recent years, behavior geneticists have proposed a statistical technique to estimate the amount of variation in a characteristic that is attributable to hereditary factors. This index, called a *heritability quotient*, is calculated as follows:

$$H = (r \text{ identical twins} - r \text{ fraternal twins}) \times 2$$

In words, the equation reads: Heritability of an attribute equals the correlation between identical twins minus the correlation between fraternal twins, all multiplied by a factor of 2 (Plomin, DeFries, & McClearn, 1980).

Now we can estimate the contribution that heredity makes to the aspect of personality that we measured in our hypothetical study. Recall that the correlation between identical twins on the attribute was + .50 and the correlation between fraternal twins was + .30. Plugging these values into the formula yields the following heritability quotient (*H*):

$$H = (.50 - .30) \times 2 = .20 \times 2 = .40$$

The heritability quotient is about .40, which, on a scale ranging from 0 (not at all heritable) to 1.00 (totally heritable), is moderate at best. We might conclude that, within the population from which our subjects were selected, this aspect of personality is influenced to some extent by hereditary factors. However, it appears that much of the variability among people on this trait is attributable to nonhereditary factors—that is, to environmental influences and to errors we may have made in measuring the trait (no measure is perfect).

---

problems adjusting to school activities, and they are often irritable and aggressive in their interactions with peers (Rutter, 1978; Thomas, Chess, & Korn, 1982). Yet Thomas and Chess (1977) find that early temperamental profiles can be modified by environmental factors—particularly the patterns of child rearing used by parents. For example, a difficult infant who has trouble adapting to new routines may become much more adaptable if parents remain calm, exercise restraint, and allow the child to respond to novelty at a leisurely pace.

In sum, the temperamental characteristics we display are clearly influenced by the genes we have inherited. However, we should keep in mind that early temperamental patterns can be altered and that the changes in temperament that are commonly observed over the course of childhood suggest that this aspect of personality is highly susceptible to environmental influence.

Heritability of adult characteristics. Psychologists have often assumed that the relatively stable traits and habits that make up our adult personalities are determined by the environment. Presumably, our feelings, attitudes, values, and characteristic patterns of behavior have been shaped by the culture in which we live and the company we keep. Behavior geneticists would not necessarily disagree with this conclusion. However, they do believe that psychologists overestimate the impact of the environment on the developing personality while underestimating the importance of hereditary factors (Goldsmith, 1983).

Family studies of personality suggest that many attributes have a hereditary component. One example of a heritable trait is *empathic concern*. A person high in empathy is a compassionate soul who recognizes the needs of others and is concerned about their welfare. In Box 2-2 we saw that newborn infants will react to the distress of other infants by becoming distressed themselves—a finding that implies that empathy may be innate. If it is, identical twins should be more similar in empathic concern than fraternal twins.

Karen Matthews and her associates (Matthews, Batson, Horn, & Rosenman, 1981) administered a test of empathic concern to 114 pairs of identical twins and 116 pairs of fraternal twins aged 42 to 57 years. These twin pairs, all males, had been raised in the same household, but most had not lived together for many years. Even though the vast majority of the twins had lived apart in different environments for long periods, the identical twins were still more alike in empathic concern ($r = .41$) than the fraternal twins ($r = .05$), suggesting that empathy is a reasonably heritable attribute. The implications of these findings are interesting. In the words of the authors, "If empathic concern for others leads to altruistic motivation, the present study provides evidence for a genetic basis for individual differences in altruistic behavior" (p. 246).

Just how heritable is the adult personality? Perhaps we can get some idea by looking at the personality resemblances among family members, as shown in Table 2-2. Note that identical twin pairs are more similar on this composite measure of personality than are either fraternal twin pairs or nontwin siblings. Were we to use the twin data to estimate the genetic contribution to personality, we might conclude that many personality traits are moderately heritable. That is, using H to stand for heritability, $H = (.52 - .25) \times 2 = .54$. Of course, one implication of a

moderate heritability coefficient is that personality is strongly influenced by environmental factors.

What features of the environment contribute most heavily to the development of our personalities? Developmentalists have traditionally assumed that the home environment is especially important in this regard. Yet, Table 2-2 reveals that genetically unrelated individuals who live in the same homes barely resemble one another on the composite personality measure. Thus, aspects of the home environment that all family members *share* must not contribute much to the development of personality.

Behavior geneticists David Rowe and Robert Plomin (1981) argue that the environmental influences that contribute most heavily to personality are those that make individuals *different* from one another—that is, events, situations, and experiences that children within any family do *not* share. An example of a "*nonshared environmental influence*" within the home is a tendency of one or both parents to respond differently to sons and daughters, to first-born and later-born children, and so on. To the extent that two siblings are treated differently by parents, they will experience different environments, which will increase the likelihood that their personalities will differ in important ways. Interactions among siblings provide another source of "nonshared" environmental influence on the developing personality. For example, an older sibling who habitually dominates a younger one may become generally assertive and dominant as a result of these home experiences. But for the younger child, this home environment is a

TABLE 2-2   Correlation Coefficients for a Composite Personality Measure for Family Members at Three Levels of Kinship

	Kinship			
	1.00	.50		.00
	Identical twins	*Fraternal twins*	*Nontwin siblings*	*Genetically unrelated children living in the same home*
Personality attributes (average correlations across several personality traits)	.52	.25	.20	.07

dominating environment that may foster the development of such personality traits as passivity, tolerance, and cooperation.

Rowe and Plomin suggest the following formula as an estimate of the effects of nonshared environmental influences on the developing personality:

$$\text{Nonshared environmental effects} = 1 - r \text{ (correlation for identical twins)}$$

They justify the use of this estimate in these words:

> Because [identical] twins are perfectly matched from a genetic standpoint, any *differences* for pair members must arise . . . from [nonshared] environmental influences. . . . One minus the correlation for identical twins is therefore an estimate of all [nonshared] environmental causes that make identical twins *different* from one another [p. 521; italics added].

Table 2-2 shows that the average correlation for identical twins across several personality attributes is + .52. Thus, it appears that nonshared environmental influences (that is, $1 - .52 = .48$) are, indeed, important contributors to personality development.

Hereditary contributions to mental health.   Is there a hereditary basis for mental illness? Might some among us be predisposed to commit deviant or antisocial acts? Although these ideas seemed absurd 20 years ago when I was a college student, it now appears that the answer to both questions is a qualified yes.

The evidence for hereditary contributions to abnormal behavior comes from family studies in which investigators calculate *concordance rates* for various disorders. In a twin study, for example, the concordance rate for a disorder is a measure of the likelihood that the second twin will exhibit the problem, given that the first one does. If concordance rates are higher for identical twins than for fraternal twins, one can conclude that the disorder is influenced by heredity.

Schizophrenia is a serious form of mental illness characterized by profound disturbances in thinking, emotional expression, and everyday behavior. One survey of 11 twin studies of schizophrenia suggested an average concordance rate of .57 for identical twins

but only .13 for fraternal twins (Gottesman & Shields, 1973). This is a strong indication that schizophrenia is a heritable disorder. In recent years, it has become increasingly apparent that heredity also contributes to abnormal behaviors and conditions such as alcoholism, criminality, depression, hyperactivity, manic-depressive psychosis, and a number of neurotic disorders (Fuller & Thompson, 1978; Mednick, 1985; Schwarz, 1979). Now, it is possible that one of your close relatives has been diagnosed as alcoholic, neurotic, manic-depressive, or schizophrenic. Rest assured that this does *not* mean that you or your children will develop these problems. Only 10–14% of children who have had one schizophrenic parent ever develop any symptoms that might be labeled "schizophrenic" (Kessler, 1975). Even if you are an identical twin whose cotwin has a serious psychiatric disorder, the odds are only between 1 in 2 and 1 in 10 (depending on the disorder) that you will ever experience anything that even approaches the problem that affects your twin.

Since identical twins are typically *discordant* (that is, not alike) with respect to various disorders, it is obvious that the environment must be a very important contributor to behavioral abnormalities and mental illnesses. In other words, people do not inherit particular disorders—they inherit genetic predispositions to develop certain illnesses or deviant patterns of behavior. But even when such a genetic predisposition has been inherited, it may take one or more very stressful experiences (for example, rejecting parents, flunking out of school, or a crumbling marriage) to trigger the illness in question.

The Character of Genotype/Environment Interactions

After reviewing a tiny portion of the literature and seeing how behavior geneticists estimate the contribution of heredity to various attributes, it should be clear that both heredity and environment contribute in important ways to our temperaments, personalities, and mental health. But how do they do so? Today, most behavior geneticists have rejected the notion that heredity contributes a set percentage to each attribute and environment contributes the rest. Even the once-popular "rubber band" hypothesis, which stated that heredity sets a range of developmental potentials for each attribute and environment determines the extent of development, is probably too simple. So how do environments act on our genotypes to influence development? In at least three ways.

Passive genotype/environment interactions. Parents contribute to a child's development in two important respects: (1) they have provided genes—the child's biological blueprint for development—and (2) they structure a social, emotional, and intellectual environment in which the child will grow. Scarr and McCartney (1983) propose that the environments parents provide for their children depend, in part, on the parents' own genotypes. And because children share genes with their parents, the rearing environments to which they are exposed are correlated (and, therefore, likely to be compatible) with their own genotypes.

The following example illustrates some developmental implications of these passive genotype/environment correlations. Parents who exercise regularly and who encourage this kind of animation tend to raise children who enjoy vigorous physical activities (Shaffer, 1985). Surely, it could be argued that the parents' own displays of physical activity and their inducements to exercise are potent environmental influences that contribute to their children's activity preferences. However, parents such as these may have a genetic predisposition to enjoy physical exercise which (1) may be passed along to their children and (2) may affect the activities that they, as parents, will try to promote. Thus, not only are their children exposed to a rearing environment that encourages vigorous physical exercise, they may also have inherited genes that predispose them to be responsive to that environment. In other words, these youngsters may come to enjoy physical exercise for both hereditary and environmental reasons—and the influences of heredity and environment are inextricably intertwined.

Evocative genotype/environment interactions. Earlier, we noted that the environmental influences that may contribute most heavily to personality are "nonshared" experiences that make individuals *different* from one another. Could it be that any two children (even siblings) are likely to be treated differently by others because they have inherited differing genotypes and thus elicit different reactions from their companions?

Scarr and McCartney (1983) think so. Their notion of evocative genotype/environment correlations assumes that a child's heritable attributes will affect the behavior of others toward the child. For example, smily, active babies may receive more attention and social stimulation than moody and passive ones. Teachers may respond more favorably to physically attractive students than to their less attractive classmates. Clearly, these reactions of other people to the child (and the child's attributes) are environmental influences that will play an important role in shaping that child's personality. So once again we see an intermingling of hereditary and environmental influences, in which heredity affects the character of the social environment in which the personality develops.

Active (niche-picking) genotype/environment interactions. Finally, Scarr and McCartney (1983) propose that the environments children prefer and seek out will depend in part on the children's genetic characteristics. For example, grade-school students who have inherited muscular physiques may be genetically predisposed to prefer rough-and-tumble sporting activities, whereas their classmates with other physiques may be more inclined to choose other methods of passing their leisure time, such as reading or playing board games. The implication, then, is that people with different genotypes will *actively* select different "environmental niches" for themselves—niches that will then have a powerful effect on their future social, emotional, and intellectual development.

Developmental implications. The relative importance of these three kinds of genotype/environment interactions is thought to change over the course of development. During the first two years, infants and toddlers are not free to roam the neighborhood, choosing friends and environmental niches. Most of their time is spent at home in an environment that parents structure for them, so that passive genotype/environment interactions are particularly important early in life. But once children reach school age and venture away from home every day, they suddenly become much freer to pick their own interests, activities, friends, and hangouts. Thus, active, niche-building interactions should exert more and more influence on the developing personality as the child matures. Finally, evocative genotype/environment interactions are always important; that is, a person's heritable attributes and patterns of behavior may influence the ways others react to him or her throughout life.

If this theory has any merit, then virtually all siblings other than identical twins should come to resemble each other less and less over time as they emerge from the relatively similar rearing environments that parents impose during the early years and begin to actively select different environmental niches for themselves. Indeed, there is some support for this assertion. Pairs of genetically unrelated adoptees who live in the same home do show some definite similarities in conduct and in intellectual performance during early and middle childhood (Scarr & Weinberg, 1978). Since these adoptees share no genes with each other or with their adoptive parents, their resemblances must be attributable to their common rearing environments. Yet by late adolescence, genetically unrelated siblings no longer resemble each other in intelligence, personality, or any other aspect of behavior, presumably because they have selected very different environmental niches, which, in turn, have steered them along differing developmental paths (Scarr & McCartney, 1983; Scarr, Webber, Weinberg, & Wittig, 1981). By contrast, pairs of identical twins bear a close behavioral resemblance to each other throughout childhood and adolescence. Why should this be? Scarr and McCartney suggest two reasons: (1) not only do identical twins elicit similar reactions from other people, but (2) their identical genotypes predispose them to prefer and to select very similar environments (that is, friends, interests, and activities), which will exert comparable influences on these twin pairs and virtually guarantee that they will continue to resemble each other over time.

Contributions and Criticisms of the Behavior Genetics Approach

Human behavior genetics is a relatively new discipline that is beginning to have a strong influence on the ways behavioral scientists look at social and personality development. Only 30 years ago, it was generally assumed that our personalities are shaped by the familial and cultural contexts in which we live. Presumably, everyone had a different personality because no two persons were exposed to precisely the same set of experiences as they were growing up. Today, we have a plausible alternative explanation for individual differences in social and personal behavior: with the exception of identical twins, no two persons inherit precisely the same set of genes from their parents. Of course, the implication of this point of view is that our temperaments, personalities, and characteristic patterns of social conduct depend in part on the hereditary blueprints that our parents passed along to us when we were conceived.

Yet, the finding that many components of personality appear to be heritable (that is, influenced by genetic factors) in no way implies that genotype determines behavior or that environmental influences are unimportant. In fact, two of the major contributions of the behavior genetics approach are the notions that (1) our genotypes influence the kinds of environments that we are likely to experience and (2) virtually all behavioral attributes of lasting developmental significance represent a long and involved interplay between the forces of nature and nurture. Perhaps Donald Hebb (1980) was not too far off in stating that behavior is determined 100 percent by heredity and 100 percent by the environment, for it appears that these two sets of influences are inextricably intertwined.

Interesting as these ideas may seem, there are those who argue that the behavior genetics approach is more accurately characterized as a descriptive overview of development than as a well-articulated theory. One reason for this sentiment is that behavior geneticists use the term *environment* in a very global way, making little or no attempt to measure environmental influences or to specify how the environment acts on the individual to influence behavior. Perhaps you can see the problem: the critics contend that one has not *explained* development by merely postulating that unspecified environmental forces act in unknown ways on a person's genotype to produce behavioral phenotypes.

How does the environment impinge upon the individual to influence his conduct and character? What environmental influences, given when, are particularly noteworthy in this regard? As we will see in our next chapter, social-learning theorists have explored these very issues in some detail.

SUMMARY

This chapter focuses on some of the oldest and some of the newest ideas about human social and personality development. The older ideas stem from Sigmund Freud's *psychoanalytic theory*. Freud was a practicing neurologist who developed his theory from his observations of neurotic patients—observations that led him to conclude that human beings are born with two kinds of urges, or instincts: *Eros*, the life instincts, and *Thanatos*, the death, or destructive, instincts. Freud believed that these instincts were the source of all *psychic* (or mental) energy—the energy that one uses to think, to learn, and to perform other mental functions that are necessary to gratify one's inborn goals or motives.

According to Freud, a newborn infant has a primitive, undifferentiated personality consisting of the instincts (Eros and Thanatos) and a few basic reflexes. This is the *id*, the component of personality that represents all of one's basic needs, wishes, and motives. The *ego* is formed as psychic energy is diverted from the id to activate important cognitive processes, such as perception, learning, and logical reasoning, which help the child to find realistic methods of gratifying the instincts. The *superego* is the ethical component of the personality. It develops from the ego, and its function is to determine whether the ego's methods of satisfying the instincts are moral or immoral.

Freud believed that social and personality development progresses through a series of five *psychosexual stages*—oral, anal, phallic, latency, and genital—that parallel the maturation of the sex instinct. Freud assumed that the activities and conflicts that emerge at each psychosexual stage would have lasting effects on the developing personality.

Erik Erikson has extended Freud's theory by concentrating less on the sex instinct and more on important sociocultural determinants of human development. According to Erikson, people progress through a series of eight *psychosocial* stages. Each stage is characterized by a particular social conflict or "crisis" that the individual must successfully resolve in order to develop in a healthy direction. Erikson's first five stages occur at the same ages as Freud's psychosexual stages, but they differ from Freud's stages in several respects. Erikson's last three stages, which occur during young adulthood, middle age, and old age, are important extensions of Freud's developmental scheme.

Although psychoanalytic theory has strong biological overtones, there are two recent approaches—*ethology* and *behavior genetics*—that focus even more intently on biological contributions to social and personality development. The ethologists concentrate on inherited attributes that conspire to make human beings similar to one another (that is, contribute to common developmental outcomes). Ethologists believe that children are born with a number of adaptive responses that have evolved over the course of human history and serve to channel development along particular paths. Although ethologists recognize that we are largely products of our experiences, they remind us that we are biological creatures whose innate characteristics affect the kinds of learning experiences that we are likely to have.

Behavior geneticists concentrate on those biological attributes that conspire to make individuals different from one another. Their major research method is to look for behavioral similarities and differences among family members to determine whether heredity contributes to important psychological attributes. These family studies indicate that our unique genotypes play important roles in the development of temperament, personality, and abnormal patterns of behavior. Yet, these findings do not imply that our genes determine our social conduct and personalities or that environmental influences are unimportant. Indeed, two of the major contributions of the behavior genetics approach are the notions that (1) our genotypes influence the kinds of environments that we are likely to experience and (2) all behavioral attributes of lasting developmental significance are products of a long and involved interplay between the forces of nature and nurture.

NOTES

1. *Unconscious motivation* was Freud's term for urges, wishes, and fears that influence one's thinking and behavior even though one is unaware of them.

2. This was a well-controlled experiment in that Tryon occasionally took offspring from each of the two groups and placed them with foster mothers from the other group. This cross-fostering procedure helps to ensure that any differences in maze-learning ability between the offspring of the two strains are due to selective breeding (heredity) rather than to the type of early stimulation that the young animals received from their mother figure (environment).

REFERENCES

AINSWORTH, M. D. S. (1979). Attachment as related to mother-infant interaction. In J. S. Rosenblatt, R. A. Hinde, C. Beer, & M. Busnel (Eds.), *Advances in the study of behavior* (Vol. 9). Orlando, FL: Academic Press.

BANDURA, A. (1973). *Aggression: A social learning analysis.* Englewood Cliffs, NJ: Prentice-Hall.

BLURTON-JONES, N. (1972). Characteristics of ethological studies of human behavior. In N. Blurton-Jones (Ed.), *Ethological studies of child behavior.* London: Cambridge University Press.

BOWLBY, J. (1973). *Attachment and loss.* Vol. 2: *Separation.* London: Hogarth Press.

CAIRNS, R. B. (1979). *Social development: The origins and plasticity of interchanges.* New York: W. H. Freeman.

CHARLESWORTH, W. R. (1980). Teaching ethology of human behavior. *Human Ethology Newsletter, 28,* 7–9.

ERIKSON, E. H. (1950). In M. J. E. Senn (Ed.), *Symposium on the healthy personality.* New York: Josiah Macy Jr. Foundation.

ERIKSON, E. H. (1963). *Childhood and society* (2nd ed.). New York: Norton.

ERIKSON, E. H. (1972). Eight ages of man. In C. S. Lavatelli & F. Stendler (Eds.), *Readings in child behavior and child development.* San Diego, CA: Harcourt Brace Jovanovich.

FREUD, S. (1933). *New introductory lectures in psychoanalysis.* New York: Norton.

FREUD, S. (1961). The dissolution of the Oedipus complex. In J. Strachey (Ed. and trans.), *The standard edition of the complete psychological works of Sigmund Freud* (Vol. 19). London: Hogarth Press. (Original work published 1924)

FREUD, S. (1964). An outline of psychoanalysis. In J. Strachey (Ed. and trans.), *The standard edition of the complete psychological works of Sigmund Freud* (Vol. 22). London: Hogarth Press. (Original work published 1940)

FULLER, J. L., & Thompson, W. R. (1978). *Genetic basis of behavior.* St. Louis: Mosby.

GOLDSMITH, H. H. (1983). Genetic influences on personality from infancy to adulthood. *Child Development, 54,* 331–355.

GOLDSMITH, H. H., & Gottesman, I. I. (1981). Origins of variation in behavioral style: A longitudinal study of temperament in young twins. *Child Development, 52,* 91–103.

GOTTESMAN, I. I., & Shields, J. (1973). Genetic theorizing and schizophrenia. *British Journal of Psychiatry, 122,* 17–18.

HEBB, D. O. (1980). *Essay on mind.* Hillsdale, NJ: Erlbaum.

HOFFMAN, M. L. (1981). Is altruism a part of human nature? *Journal of Personality and Social Psychology, 40,* 121–137.

KAGAN, J., Reznick, R. J., Clarke, C., Snidman, N., & Garcia-Coll, C. (1984). Behavioral inhibition to the unfamiliar. *Child Development, 55,* 2212–2225.

KATCHER, A. (1955). The discrimination of sex differences by young children. *Journal of Genetic Psychology, 87,* 131–143.

KESSLER, S. (1975). Psychiatric genetics. In D. A. Hamburg & K. Brodie (Eds.), *American handbook of psychiatry.* Vol. 6: *New psychiatric frontiers.* New York: Basic Books.

MAIER, H. W. (1969). *Three theories of child development.* New York: Harper & Row.

MARTIN, G. B., & Clark, R. D., III. (1982). Distress crying in neonates: Species and peer specificity. *Developmental Psychology, 18,* 3–9.

MATHENY, A. P. (1980). Bayley's Infant Behavior Record: Behavioral components and twin analysis. *Child Development, 51,* 1157–1167.

MATTHEWS, K. A., Batson, C. D., Horn, J., & Rosenman, R. H. (1981). "Principles in his nature which interest him in the fortune of others . . .": The heritability of empathic concern for others. *Journal of Personality, 49,* 237–247.

McCLEARN, G. E. (1970). Genetic influences on behavior and development. In P. H. Mussen (Ed.), *Carmichael's manual of child psychology* (Vol. 1). New York: Wiley.

MEDNICK, S. (1985, March). Crime in the family tree. *Psychology Today,* pp. 58–61.

PLOMIN, R., DeFries, J. C., & McClearn, G. E. (1980). *Behavioral genetics: A primer.* New York: W. H. Freeman.

ROWE, D. C., & Plomin, R. (1981). The importance of nonshared (E_1) environmental influences in behavioral development. *Developmental Psychology, 17,* 517–531.

RUTTER, M. (1978). Family, area, and school influences in the genesis of conduct disorders. In L. Hersov, M. Berber, & D. R. Shaffer (Eds.), *Aggression and antisocial behavior in childhood and adolescence.* Oxford: Pergamon Press.

SAGI, A., & Hoffman, M. L. (1976). Empathic distress in newborns. *Developmental Psychology, 12,* 175–176.

SCARR, S., & McCartney, K. (1983). How people make their own environments: A theory of genotype/environment effects. *Child Development, 54,* 424–435.

SCARR, S., Webber, P. L., Weinberg, R. A., & Wittig, M. A. (1981). Personality resemblance among adolescents and their parents in biologically-related and adoptive families. *Journal of Personality and Social Psychology, 40,* 885–898.

SCARR, S., & Weinberg, R. A. (1978). The influence of "family background" on intellectual attainment. *American Sociological Review, 43,* 674–692.

SCHWARZ, J. C. (1979). Childhood origins of psychopathology. *American Psychologist, 34,* 879–885.

SHAFFER, D. R. (1985). *Familial patterns of physical activities and exercise.* Unpublished manuscript, University of Georgia.

SROUFE, L. A., Fox, N. E., & Pancake, V. R. (1983). Attachment and dependency in developmental perspective. *Child Development, 54,* 1615–1627.

THOMAS, A., & Chess, S. (1977). *Temperament and development.* New York: Brunner/Mazel.

THOMAS, A., Chess, S., & Birch, H. G. (1970). The origin of personality. *Scientific American, 223,* 102–109.

THOMAS, A., Chess, S., & Korn, S. (1982). The reality of difficult temperament. *Merrill-Palmer Quarterly, 28,* 1–20.

TRYON, R. C. (1940). Genetic differences in maze learning in rats. *Yearbook of the National Society for Studies in Education, 39,* 111–119.

3

SOCIAL-LEARNING THEORY

(continues)

EVALUATION OF SOCIAL-LEARNING THEORY

Contributions of Social-Learning Theory

Criticisms of the Social-Learning Approach

SUMMARY

REFERENCES

Let's suppose that we have been transported back to the year 1910. We have just registered for a new semester, and here we are awaiting the first lecture of the first psychology course that our college has ever offered. At precisely one minute before the hour, the professor enters the hall through a side door, takes his place at the lectern, and announces to the hushed gathering: "Students, we have been given the opportunity this term to survey a new science called psychology, or the study of the mind." We listen eagerly as the professor informs us that the first half of the term will deal with the theories of a Viennese neurologist by the name of Sigmund Freud. As the professor describes Freud's view of the mind, it all comes back to us, for we, as visitors from the future, have already heard of Freud and probably know something about his ideas. The professor then begins to describe the work of several experimental psychologists who may be somewhat less familiar to us, including William James, Hermann Ebbinghaus, and Edward Titchener. We are told that these men share an interest in phenomena such as emotions, volition, consciousness, and the *subjective* experience of everyday sensory events—color, sound, motion, and pain. We can already anticipate an interesting semester in the new course, which should help us solve many mysteries of the mind.

Had we taken this course three years later, we would surely have learned of another psychologist, John B. Watson, who vehemently objected to the discipline's mentalistic overtones. In 1913 Watson proclaimed:

> The time seems to have come when psychology must disregard all references to consciousness, when it need no longer delude itself into thinking that it is making mental states the object of observation. We have become so enmeshed in speculative questions concerning the elements of the mind, the nature of conscious content . . . that I, as an experimental student, feel that something is wrong with our premises and the types of problems which develop from them. There is no longer any guarantee that we all mean the same thing when we use the terms now current in psychology. . . .
> Psychology, as the behaviorist views it, is a purely objective, experimental branch of natural science. Its theoretical goal is the prediction and control of *behavior*. Introspection [thinking about one's own inter-

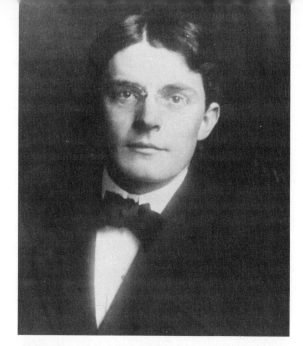

PHOTO 3-1 John B. Watson (1878–1958) was the founder of behaviorism and the first social-learning theorist.

nal states] forms no essential part of its methods, nor is the scientific value of its data dependent upon the readiness with which they lend themselves to interpretation in terms of consciousness. The behaviorist . . . recognizes no dividing line between man and brute. The behavior of man, for all its refinement and complexity, forms only a part of the behaviorist's total scheme of investigation [pp. 158–163; italics added].

Although Watson was first and foremost a learning theorist, he had some very pointed things to say about developmental processes. For example, a basic premise of his doctrine of *behaviorism* was that the "mind" of an infant is a *tabula rasa* and that *learned* associations between stimuli and responses are the building blocks of human development. According to Watson, development does not proceed through a series of stages; it is a continuous process marked by the gradual acquisition of new and more sophisticated *behavioral* patterns, or habits. Watson believed that only the simplest of human reflexes (for example, sucking, grasping) are inborn and that all of the significant aspects of one's personality are learned.

Before we take a closer look at Watson's early contributions to the field of social and personality development, it is necessary to understand what behaviorists mean by the term *learning* and to get some idea of the methods by which learning can occur.

WHAT IS LEARNING?

Learning is one of those deceptively simple terms that are actually quite complex and difficult to define. Most psychologists think of learning as a change in behavior (or behavioral potential) that satisfies the following three criteria (Domjan & Burkhard, 1986):

1. The individual now thinks, perceives, or reacts to the environment in a *new way*.
2. This change is clearly the result of one's *experiences*—that is, attributable to repetition, study, practice, or the observations one has made, rather than to heredity or maturational processes or to physiological damage resulting from injury.
3. The change is *relatively permanent*. Facts, thoughts, and behaviors that are acquired and immediately forgotten have not really been learned; and temporary changes attributable to fatigue, illness, or drugs do not qualify as learned responses.

HOW DOES LEARNING OCCUR?

Learned responses or habits may be acquired in at least four ways: by *repetition* (or mere exposure), by *classical conditioning*, by *operant conditioning*, and by *observation*. Let's briefly consider each of these processes.

Mere Exposure

Odds are that you can recall an occasion when you gradually became more positive toward a song, a new food, an idea, or an acquaintance the more often you encountered that stimulus. It turns out that these "mere exposure" effects are quite real: over the past several years, social psychologists have discovered that we tend to develop favorable attitudes toward objects, activities, and persons that we encounter on a regular basis—even though we may never touch the objects, partake in the activities, or interact with the persons (Harrison, 1977; Moreland & Zajonc, 1980). Although people may say they know what they like, it seems that they often *learn* to like what they know (Domjan & Burkhard, 1986).

Classical Conditioning

A second way that one may learn is through classical conditioning. In classical conditioning, a neutral stimulus that initially has no effect on the subject comes to elicit a response of some sort by virtue of its association with a second, nonneutral stimulus that always evokes the response.

To illustrate classical conditioning, consider that young children are unlikely to lick their lips (or to do much else other than listen) the first two or three times they hear the jingling of an approaching ice-cream truck. In other words, this jingling is an initially neutral stimulus in that it does *not* elicit lip licking. Ice cream, however, will normally elicit lip licking. In the language of classical conditioning, ice cream is an *unconditioned stimulus* (*UCS*), and lip licking is an unlearned or *unconditioned response* (*UCR*) to ice cream. If a child hears the jingling of an ice-cream truck *and* then receives an ice-cream cone on several days in succession, she should come to associate this jingling with the presentation of ice cream and may begin to lick her lips at the sound of the approaching vehicle. Clearly, the child's behavior has changed as a result of her experiences. In the terminology of classical conditioning, she is now emitting a *conditioned response* (*CR*), lip licking, to an initially neutral or *conditioned stimulus* (*CS*)—the jingling of the ice-cream truck (see Figure 3-1).

Although the lip-licking response described in this example may seem rather mundane, it is quite conceivable that every one of us has learned many things through classical conditioning—things that continue to affect us today. In fact, we will soon see why John B. Watson believed that many fears, phobias, and other conditioned emotional responses may be acquired through a form of classical conditioning.

Operant (or Instrumental) Conditioning

In classical conditioning, learned responses are elicited by a conditioned stimulus. Operant (or instrumental) conditioning is quite different: it requires the learner to first emit a response of some sort (that is, to actively operate on the environment) and then associate this action with the particular outcomes, or consequences, it produces.

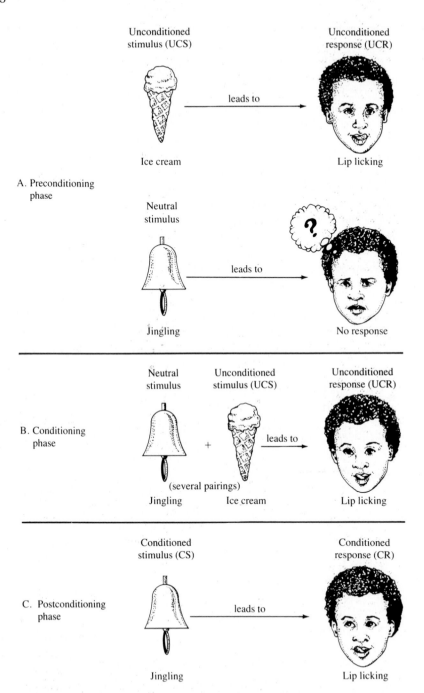

FIGURE 3-1   The three phases of classical conditioning. In the preconditioning phase, the unconditioned stimulus (UCS) always elicits an unconditioned response (UCR), while the conditioned stimulus (CS) never does. During the conditioning phase, the CS and UCS are paired repeatedly and eventually associated. At this point, the learner passes into the postconditioning phase, in which the CS alone will elicit the original response (now called a conditioned response, or CR).

Two kinds of consequences are important in operant conditioning—*reinforcers* and *punishments*. Reinforcers are consequences that promote operant learning by increasing the likelihood that the response will occur in the future. For example, a mother who praises her son for sharing a cookie with a playmate is using praise as a reinforcer. And if the boy values his mother's praise and recognizes that sharing is what produced this pleasant outcome, he is likely to share again with his friend when the opportunity presents itself. By contrast, punishments are consequences that suppress a response and may decrease the likelihood that it will occur again in the future. For example, an infant whose hands are slapped every time she reaches for her mother's glasses may soon refrain from doing so. An adolescent who is grounded for sassing his father will probably think twice before repeating this "mistake." In sum, operant conditioning is a very common form of learning in which freely emitted responses become either more or less probable, depending on the consequences (reinforcers and punishments) they produce.

Observational Learning

Observational learning is a fourth process by which we acquire new feelings, attitudes, and behaviors. If a child watches someone do something or listens attentively to that person's reasoning, then the child may learn to do, think, or feel as that other person did. Even toddlers can learn by observation. A 2-year-old boy may discover how to approach and pet the family dog simply by noting how his older sister does it. A 6-year-old girl may acquire a negative attitude toward members of a minority group after hearing her parents talk about these people in a disparaging way. In the language of observational learning, the individual who is observed and imitated is called a social *model*. Over the years, children are exposed to hundreds of social models and will have the opportunity to learn literally thousands of responses (some good, some bad) simply by observing others displaying them.

WATSON'S LEGACIES

John B. Watson surely qualifies as the first *social-learning* theorist. His view that children are shaped by their environments carried a stern message for parents—that it was they who were largely (if not wholly) responsible for what their child would become. Watson (1928) stressed that parents must begin to train their child at birth if they wished him or her to develop good habits, and he was particularly concerned that coddling, kissing, and other displays of affection would make parents' attempts at proper socialization all the more difficult. He favored an approach in which youngsters were treated

> as though they were young adults. Dress them, bathe them with care and circumspection. Let your behavior always be objective and kindly firm. Never hug and kiss them, never let them sit on your lap . . . shake hands with them in the morning. Give them a pat on the head if they have made an extraordinarily good job of a difficult task. . . . In a week's time, you will find how easy it is to be perfectly objective with your child and at the same time kindly. You will be utterly ashamed at the mawkish, sentimental way you have been handling [your child] [1928, pp. 81–82].

Watson's ideas contrasted sharply with those of Freud and with those of contemporary maturational theorists such as Arnold Gesell. Indeed, Gesell (1928) portrayed young children as biological creatures whose development would unfold according to nature's grand (maturational) plan. His message to parents was to provide good care but, basically, to sit back and relax.

Why was Watson so convinced that young children are remarkably malleable organisms, subject to any and all kinds of environmental influence? It seems that his views stemmed in large part from his own earlier research suggesting that infantile fears and other emotional reactions are easily acquired through classical conditioning. In 1920, for example, Watson and Rosalie Raynor presented a gentle white rat to an 11-month-old named Albert. Albert's initial reactions were positive ones: he crawled toward the rat and played with it as he had previously with a dog and a rabbit. Then came the conditioning phase. Every time little Albert reached for the white rat, Watson would sneak up behind him and bang a steel rod loudly with a hammer. Little Albert would then cry and shy away from the rat. In this case, the loud noise is the unconditioned stimulus (UCS) because it elicits fearful behavior (the UCR) without any learning having taken place. Did little Albert eventually associate the white rat with the loud noise and come to fear his furry playmate? Indeed he did, and he also learned to shy away from other furry things, such as cats, balls of cotton, and a fur coat. This extension, or *generalization*, of fear to objects other than the rat illustrates that emotional responses acquired through classical conditioning can be very powerful indeed. And since Watson's day, other researchers have repeatedly demonstrated that many of our attitudes and prejudices may also be acquired through a classical conditioning process (see Staats & Staats, 1958).

But perhaps the most important contribution of Watson's early research was the message it conveyed to other behaviorists, virtually all of whom worked with animals. The message was clear: apparently human behavior obeyed many of the most basic laws of learning theory. This was an immensely important demonstration, for it helped to convince a number of influential learning theorists that *human* social and personality development was a topic worthy of their scientific scrutiny.

Since Watson's day, three major theories have been proposed to explain how social learning occurs and how it contributes to the process of human development. Two of these theories, the *neo-Hullian* approach and Skinner's *operant-learning* model, are not nearly as influential as they once were and therefore will be mentioned only briefly. We will then carefully examine the model that most contemporary social-learning theorists favor—the *cognitive social-learning* approach of Albert Bandura and his associates.

NEO-HULLIAN THEORY

The origins of the first comprehensive social-learning theory can be traced to 1936, the year a group of anthropologists, psychologists, and sociologists began an interdisciplinary seminar at Yale University. The goal of the Yale group was rather ambitious: these scientists hoped to construct a theory of human development based on principles of learning outlined earlier by Clark Hull, a famous experimental psychologist who worked with animals. Their task

would prove to be a formidable one, for at that time Freud's psychoanalytic viewpoint was the dominant theory of human development. Several of the Yale theorists were well versed in psychoanalytic principles, and they believed that any theory they might construct would never gain widespread acceptance unless it was able to explain all the developmental phenomena that Freud had described.

The theory that evolved from the Yale seminar differed from Freud's psychoanalytic approach in four important respects. First, instincts played virtually no role in this neo-Hullian theory. Second, the personality was no longer described as a system composed of an id, ego, and superego. Instead, the neo-Hullians used the term *habit* to describe the relatively stable aspects of one's character, where a habit was defined as a well-learned association between a stimulus and a response. Presumably, our interactions with other people will lead to the development of many well-ingrained habits, which collectively make up our personalities. Third, members of the Yale group assumed that development occurs continuously and is not at all stagelike. Neo-Hullians John Dollard and Neal Miller (1950) described the personality as a system-in-transition: people will interact with one another until the day they die, and these new social encounters are continually modifying their existing habits. Finally, each individual was said to develop a unique habit structure (or personality) because no two persons are ever exposed to precisely the same set of social-learning experiences.

THE MOTIVATIONAL COMPONENTS OF PERSONALITY

According to the neo-Hullians, human behavior is motivated not by instincts, but by *primary* and *secondary drives*. Primary drives are unlearned motives, such as hunger, thirst, pain, or the need for sexual gratification, that impel the organism into action (note the similarity here to Freud's instincts). Dollard and Miller (1950) propose that these primary drives are all that is present at birth and are the principal motivators of human behavior throughout the first year of life. Presumably, the goal of a drive-ridden organism is to reduce whatever drive the organism is

PHOTOS 3-2 Neal Miller (b. 1909), left, and John Dollard (1900–1980), right, proposed an explanation of social and personality development that was based on Clark Hull's theory of learning.

experiencing. In fact, neo-Hullians define learning as the development of a response (habit) that proves to be a reliable method of reducing a drive.

Many human goals and motives would appear to be unrelated to the primary drives. But are they really? One of the major assumptions of neo-Hullian theory is that a large proportion of human behavior eventually comes under the control of secondary drives. Secondary drives are all motives that are not present at birth and must be acquired as a result of experience. And how are they acquired? Dollard and Miller (1950) propose that secondary drives are elaborations or extensions of a primary motive that are likely to develop whenever a stimulus or class of stimuli is repeatedly associated with one or more of the primary drives. Consider the following example.

Fear is said to be a secondary drive that motivates escape or avoidance behavior. As a first-grader, I became afraid of dogs. Every day on my quarter-mile trek to school, I had to pass a number of households guarded by four-legged protectors that would bark and often charge after me, nipping at my heels. Now, I mean to say that I was terrified. A neo-Hullian would argue that I had associated dogs with a primary drive stimulus—pain—and as a result had acquired a fear of dogs. Incidentally, I soon learned that running from my canine tormentors only made matters worse.

A better strategy was to sneak down the road, concealing myself behind bushes and trees, but unfortunately it often took what seemed like hours to reach my destination. Generating excuses for my mother to chauffeur me to and from school was the most effective "habit" that I developed to deal with my fear of dogs.

THE NEO-HULLIAN EXPLANATION OF SOCIAL LEARNING

Recall that the most basic goal of a drive-ridden organism is to reduce whatever drive it is experiencing. According to Dollard and Miller (1950), responses that are effective at reducing a drive are *reinforcing*. When a child is reinforced for responding in a particular way to a stimulus—that is, when his response reduces a drive—the act that the child has performed will become conditioned to that stimulus. Stated another way, the child will associate the reinforced response with a particular cue, and at that point learning has occurred. Dollard and Miller assumed that responses must be reinforced before they will be learned. Moreover, they believed that learned responses that are often reinforced will become stronger, whereas previously acquired habits that are no longer reinforced are likely to decline in strength and eventually drop out of the subject's behavioral repertoire (this latter process is known as *extinction*).

Neo-Hullians argue that there are two kinds of reinforcers that promote social learning: *primary reinforcers* and *secondary reinforcers*. Primary reinforcers are substances or activities, such as food, water, and sex, that reduce primary drives. Secondary reinforcers are initially neutral objects or activities that acquire some value by virtue of their association with one or more primary reinforcers. Take money, for example. Children do not value money until they discover that coins and currency can be used to purchase goods, such as candy and soda, that reduce primary drives. But once money becomes a valuable commodity (that is, a secondary reinforcer), the child acquires a motive (or secondary drive) to obtain money, and any response that "earns" him money will be reinforced.

Dollard and Miller (1950) contend that most of our everyday behaviors are motivated by secondary (or acquired) drives and sustained by secondary reinforcers. For example, human beings are said to develop a "need for social approval" which motivates any behavior that is likely to be reinforced by a smile, a pat on the back, or some other form of social acceptance or approval. Other complex human motives that were said to evolve originally from primary drives include the needs for affiliation, love, competence, achievement, power, status, and security. Each of these "acquired drives" was thought to motivate a variety of social behaviors that could be "strengthened" by one or more secondary reinforcers.

When parents attempt to train or "socialize" a child, they are trying to induce their youngster to make "socially appropriate" responses to a variety of cues. Neo-Hullians assume that often the child's most probable responses to a stimulus or situation may be quite effective at reducing drives but are not the kinds of acts that parents are likely to condone. For example, masturbation may reduce the sex drive but is likely to elicit negative reactions from others if displayed openly. But do young boys stop fondling their genitals because they struggle through an Oedipus complex and fear that they might be castrated (as Freud had assumed)? Dollard and Miller (1950) considered this scenario highly improbable. Instead,

they argue that masturbation will eventually wane (extinguish) as parents discourage this activity while encouraging socially desirable alternative responses (for example, vigorous play) that will satisfy one or more acquired drives, such as the need for approval, competence, or exploration.

In sum, neo-Hullian theorists portray development as the changes that occur in a child's behavior as a result of his or her experiences. The ideal outcome of these learning experiences is a collection of habits (that is, a personality) that is structured so that the most probable responses to any given stimulus are both socially desirable and effective at reducing a primary or secondary drive.

The role of culture in social learning. At first glance, neo-Hullian theory may seem a rather bland approach to the study of human social and personality development. Dollard and Miller were not particularly interested in describing the course of normal development or in listing the habits that characterize the healthy or the abnormal personality. Instead they emphasized the *process* of habit formation by trying to explain *how* social learning (and hence social and personality development) takes place. However, Dollard and Miller were well versed in social anthropology, and they stressed that each individual is largely a product of his or her cultural, subcultural, and familial backgrounds. In their view, the experimental psychologist can contribute to a theory of socialization by helping us to understand important learning *processes* and principles that transcend cultural influence. But they believed that sociologists and social anthropologists can play an equally important role by calling our attention to various cultural forces that determine the *content* of social learning. In sum, Miller and Dollard (1941) viewed their own work as but one piece of the developmental puzzle, noting:

> No psychologist would venture to predict the behavior of a rat without knowing on what arm of a T-maze the [reward] is placed. It is no easier to predict the behavior of a human being without knowing the conditions of his "maze." . . . Culture . . . is a statement of the design of the human maze, of the type of reward involved, and of what responses are to be rewarded. [Culture] is in this sense a recipe for

learning. . . . Even within the same society, the mazes which are run by two individuals may seem the same but actually be quite different. . . . No personality analysis of two people can be accurate [if it] does not take into account these . . . differences in the types of responses which have been rewarded [pp. 5–6].

SKINNER'S OPERANT-LEARNING THEORY

While the neo-Hullians were formulating their theory of social and personality development, psychologist B. F. Skinner was conducting research with animals and discovering important principles that would lead to a second social-learning theory—one that served as an important link between the neo-Hullian approach and the viewpoint that many behaviorists favor today. Perhaps Skinner's most radical departure from the earlier neo-Hullian theory was his assertion that internal drives play little or no role in human social learning. Instead, he argued that most of the social responses that we acquire are freely emitted operants that become either more or less probable as a function of their consequences. Stated another way, Skinner (1953) proposes that the vast majority of behavior (both animal and human) is motivated by *external* stimuli—reinforcers and punitive events—rather than by internal forces, or drives.

How are these operants acquired? As noted earlier, operant learning occurs when a person emits a response and is reinforced for that action. In Skinner's theoretical framework, a reinforcer is not something that reduces a drive but, rather, any event that increases the probability that a response will be repeated. Thus, if a 3-year-old girl were to comfort her doll while playing, receive a hug from her proud mother, and then resume her comforting with renewed vigor, a Skinnerian would say that the mother's hug had reinforced the girl's nurturant behavior.

Reinforcers may be either *positive* or *negative* in character. The girl in the preceding example received positive reinforcement, because a pleasant or positive stimulus (a hug) was *added* to the situation after the behavior (comforting) had occurred, and the re-

sponse was subsequently repeated. Thus, positive reinforcers can be thought of as rewards that are consequences of a particular behavior. Negative reinforcement, in contrast, is any unpleasant stimulus that is *removed from the situation* once a particular response has occurred. Suppose that a mother tickles her child until the child utters "I love you, mommy." Prolonged tickling is an aversive stimulus, and its removal should increase the probability that the child will say "I love you, mommy" whenever this mother acts as if she might tickle her child in the future. In sum, both positive and negative reinforcers serve to increase the probability that a response will be repeated. However, Skinner proposed that many parents do not fully appreciate the power of negative reinforcement and hence will not often use it to shape the behavior of their children.

You may be thinking "Wait a minute—virtually all parents use aversive stimuli to control their children's behavior!" And indeed they do. But Skinnerians are careful to distinguish between negative reinforcement and punishment. Recall that a negative reinforcer is an aversive stimulus that is *withdrawn* when the child performs a desirable act (that is, one that the reinforcing agent hopes to instill). By contrast, the most familiar form of punishment involves the *presentation* of an aversive stimulus when the child emits an undesirable response. In other words, the purpose of punishment is roughly opposite to that of reinforcement—to *suppress* unacceptable acts rather than to strengthen acceptable ones. A boy who is banished to his room for refusing to share toys with his sister will probably not repeat his stingy antics, at least not while in the presence of the punitive agent. A Skinnerian would argue that the punitive agent has attempted to suppress the boy's stingy behavior by presenting aversive stimuli as a consequence of that particular course of action.

So it is true that parents often use punishment as a means of controlling their children's behavior; and there is a case to be made for its use, particularly when the punished behavior is something dangerous like playing with matches or probing electrical sockets with metallic objects. Yet operant-learning theorists contend that punishment is generally less effective than reinforcement at producing desirable changes in behavior, because punishment merely suppresses ongoing or established responses without teaching anything new. For example, a toddler who is punished for grabbing food with his hands is likely to stop eating altogether rather than to learn to use his spoon. A much simpler way to promote this desirable alternative response is to reinforce it (Skinner, 1953). Operant theorists also note that punishment may have some undesirable side effects, such as making the child angry or resentful toward the punitive agent. There is even some evidence that punishment can backfire and have effects opposite to those intended, for parents who use harsh forms of punishment in an attempt to suppress their children's aggressive acts often end up raising extremely aggressive children. We will explore the reasons for this paradoxical effect when we take up the topic of aggression in Chapter 9.

Skinner has taught animals to perform a wide variety of behaviors, including incredible feats such as inducing pigeons to play table tennis, by carefully reinforcing the component responses of these complex behavioral systems. Is it possible that children learn socially desirable operants as their parents, teachers, and other agents of socialization carefully shape these responses through the administration of reinforcement? Indeed it is. Even infants are susceptible to operant conditioning, as we see in the following example.

Paul Weisberg (1963) exposed 3-month-old infants to four experimental treatments to see whether he could increase the frequency with which they babbled. The infants in one experimental group received social stimulation in the form of smiles and gentle pats on the tummy whenever they happened to babble (*contingent* social stimulation). A second group was given the same kinds of social stimulation, but these gestures were *noncontingent*; that is, they were presented at random and did not depend on the infants' babbling behavior. Two other groups received nonsocial stimulation (the sound of chimes) that was either contingent or noncontingent on their babbling responses. Weisberg found that neither noncontingent social stimulation nor the sound of chimes was sufficient to reinforce babbling behavior. Babbling (a social operant) became more frequent only when it was accompanied by *contingent* social stimulation.

PHOTO 3-3   B. F. Skinner (b. 1904) formulated a social-learning theory that emphasizes the role of external stimuli in controlling human behavior.

In analyzing these results, Skinner would argue that it makes little sense to attribute the babbling of the latter infants to a "babbling" drive or to any other internal motive. Instead, the infants appeared to have become more "vocal" because babbling produced *external* stimuli (smiles and pats) that stimulated its repetition.

Weisberg's study is only one of many showing that freely emitted social operants can be conditioned. In fact, it has been argued (see Gewirtz, 1969; Skinner, 1953) that virtually all significant human behaviors are "conditioned" responses established through principles of operant learning.

Recently, a number of learning theorists have noted some serious deficiencies in Skinner's operant analysis of human development. Perhaps Skinner's most vociferous critic is Stanford University psychologist Albert Bandura. Bandura (1977) has argued that, even though human social behaviors are subject to the laws of operant conditioning, we do not know that these responses are actually acquired through that process. Furthermore, Bandura has criticized the Skinnerians for their assumption that external stimuli—the reinforcers that shape responses and the cues that direct these responses—control most human behavior. Indeed, Bandura calls this the *radical behaviorist* position, radical because it ignores people's cognitive capabilities and thus their ability to produce their own cues and to construct their own reinforcement contingencies. Finally, Bandura notes that reinforcement may play a very different role in the learning process than that suggested by either the neo-Hullians or the Skinnerians. Read on and you will see what he means.

BANDURA'S COGNITIVE SOCIAL-LEARNING THEORY

When contemporary developmentalists use the term *social-learning theory*, they are probably referring to the theory of Albert Bandura and his associates (Bandura, 1971, 1977; Bandura & Walters, 1963; Mischel, 1979). This "Banduran" approach shares some important features with its neo-Hullian and Skinnerian predecessors. For example, all three theories contend that a person's social-learning experiences determine his or her personality. Moreover, the three approaches use roughly the same terminology and consider the concepts of "cue," "response," "reinforcement," "punishment," "acquisition" (learning), and "extinction" to be important theoretical constructs. But despite these basic commonalities, Bandura's theory of social learning is very different from the neo-Hullian and the Skinnerian approaches.

HOW DOES BANDURA DIFFER FROM OTHER SOCIAL-LEARNING THEORISTS?

Notice that "drive" is not included in the list of important theoretical elements presented above. The Skinnerians were first to criticize the neo-Hullian assertion that human behavior is motivated by primary and secondary drives, and Bandura echoes their criticism. He views the term *drive* as a circular motivational label that does little more than *describe* the behavior to which it refers. For example, a drive theorist who observes a person trying to amass a fortune ascribes that behavior to an "acquired drive" for money that can be inferred from the person's "money-seeking" behavior. Bandura (1977) notes:

It is not the existence of motivated behavior that is being questioned, but whether such behavior is at all explained by ascribing it to the action of [drives]. The limitations of this type of analysis can be illustrated by considering a common activity, such as reading. . . . People spend large sums . . . purchasing reading material; . . . they engage in reading for hours on end; and they can become emotionally upset when deprived of reading material [such as a missed newspaper]. . . .

One could ascribe [reading behavior] to the force of a "reading drive." . . . However, if one wanted to *predict* what people read, when, how long, and the order in which they choose to read different material, one would look not for drives, but for preceding inducements and expected benefits derived from reading [p. 3; italics added].

In other words, Bandura maintains that the social-learning theorist must identify the antecedent stimuli (cues) that trigger a response and the consequences (rewards or punishments) that maintain, alter, or suppress that response before he or she can *explain* why the response occurred. So why do people read? For any number of reasons. One person may be reading because she finds the activity pleasurable; another reader may be studying for an exam; a third may be trying to understand his income tax form; a fourth may be planning a vacation. To attribute the behavior of these four persons to a "reading drive" is, in Bandura's opinion, a grossly oversimplified analysis of their activities.

To this point, the Skinnerians and the Bandurans are in perfect agreement. But as we have previously noted, Skinnerian theorists assume that external stimuli—environmental cues and extrinsic reinforcers—are the primary determinants of human behavior. Bandura rejects this assertion because it ignores the individual's cognitive capabilities. Indeed, we will soon see that a response to any particular stimulus or situation depends not so much on the reinforcers or punishments that are actually forthcoming as on the person's impressions, or *cognitive representations*, of the consequences that his actions are likely to have.

Finally, recall that both the neo-Hullians and the Skinnerians assume that a child must first perform a response and then be reinforced for his or her actions before that response will be learned. Bandura disagrees. In 1965, he made what was then considered a radical statement: children can learn by merely obser-ving the behavior of a social model, *even though they have never attempted the responses they have witnessed or received any reinforcement for performing them.* Note the implications here: Bandura is propos-ing a type of "no trial" learning in which the learned response is neither motivated by a drive state, elicited by a conditioned stimulus, nor strengthened by a rein-forcer. Impossible, said many learning theorists, for Bandura's proposition seems to ignore important principles of both classical and operant conditioning.

An Example of "No Trial" Learning without Reinforcement

But Bandura was right, although he first had to con-duct what is now considered a classic experiment to prove his point (Bandura, 1965). At the beginning of this experiment, nursery school children were taken one at a time to a semidarkened room to watch a short film. As they watched, they saw an adult model direct an unusual sequence of aggressive responses toward an inflatable Bobo doll, hitting the doll with a mallet while shouting "Sockeroo!," throwing rubber balls at the doll while shouting "Bang, bang, bang!," and so on (see Photo 3-5). There were three experimental conditions. Children in the *model rewarded* condi-tion saw the film end as a second adult appeared and gave the aggressive model some candy and a soft drink for her "championship performance." Children assigned to the *model punished* condition saw an ending in which a second adult scolded and spanked the model for beating up on Bobo. Finally, children in the *no consequences* condition simply watched the model beat up on Bobo without receiving any reward or punishment.

When the film ended, each child was left alone in a playroom that contained a Bobo doll and many of the props that the model had used to work Bobo over. Hidden observers then watched the child, recording all instances in which he or she imitated one or more of the model's aggressive acts. These observations would reveal how willing the children were to *per-form* the responses they had seen the model display. The results of this "performance" test appear on the left-hand side of Figure 3-2. Here we see that chil-dren in the model-rewarded and the no-consequences

PHOTO 3-4 Albert Bandura (b. 1925) has emphasized the cognitive aspects of social learning in his theory of social and personality development.

conditions imitated more of the model's aggressive acts than children who had seen the model punished for aggressive behavior. At the very least, these re-sults indicate that subjects in the first two conditions had learned some rather novel aggressive responses without being reinforced themselves and without having had a previous opportunity to perform them. This looks very much like the kind of "no trial" obser-vational learning that Bandura had proposed.

The Learning/Performance Distinction

But one question remained: Had the children in the model-rewarded and the no-consequences conditions actually *learned more* from observing the model than children who had seen the model punished? To find out, Bandura devised a second test in which he per-suaded children to show just how much they had learned. Each child was offered some juice and trin-kets for reproducing all of the model's behaviors that he or she could remember. The results of this "learning" test, which appear in the right-hand por-tion of Figure 3-2, clearly show that children in each of the three conditions learned about the same amount by observing the model. Apparently children in the model-punished condition had imitated fewer of the model's responses on the initial "performance" test

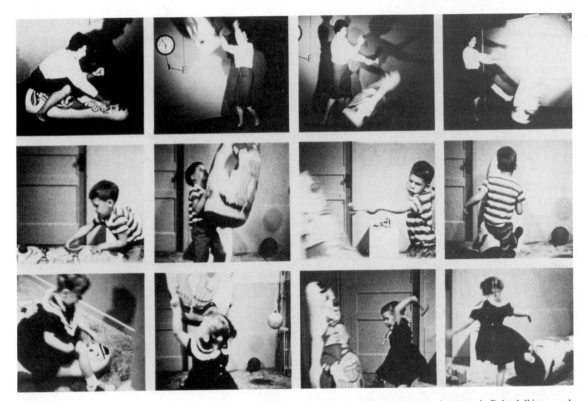

PHOTO 3-5 In Bandura's classic experiment, children who had watched an adult model show aggression toward a Bobo doll in several distinctive ways (top row) performed similar acts themselves (middle and bottom rows), even though they hadn't been reinforced for committing such acts.

because they felt that they too might be punished for striking Bobo. But offer them a reward, and they show that they have learned much more than their initial performances might have implied.

In sum, it is important to distinguish what children *learn* by observation and their willingness to *perform* these responses. Bandura's (1965) experiment shows that reinforcement is not necessary for observational learning. What reinforcement does is to increase the likelihood that the child will perform that which he or she has already learned by observing the model's behavior.

Observational Learning and Social/Personality Development

Bandura (1977) believes that the vast majority of the habits we acquire during our lifetimes are learned by observing and imitating other people. According to

Bandura, there are several reasons that observational learning plays such a prominent role in social and personality development. First, learning by observation is much more efficient than the trial-and-error method. When observers can learn by watching a model perform flawlessly, they are spared the needless errors that might result from attempts to perfect the same skills and abilities on their own. For this reason, parents soon discover that it is much easier to instill socially acceptable behaviors by displaying or describing these responses for the child than by differentially reinforcing the child's unguided actions. Second, many complex behaviors could probably never be learned unless children were exposed to people who modeled them. Take language, for example. It seems rather implausible that parents could ever shape babbling into words, not to mention grammatical speech, merely by rewarding and punishing

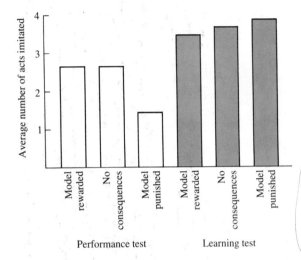

FIGURE 3-2 Average number of aggressive responses imitated during the performance test and the learning test for children who had seen a model rewarded, punished, or receiving no consequences for her actions

these random vocalizations. Yet children who lack some bit of grammatical knowledge will soon alter their sentence constructions after hearing this rule of grammar reflected in the speech of a companion (Bandura & Harris, 1966; Zimmerman, 1977). Finally, observational learning permits the young child to acquire many new responses in a large number of settings where her "models" are simply pursuing their own interests and are not trying to teach her anything in particular. Of course, some of the behaviors that young children observe and may try to imitate are actions that adults display but would like to discourage—practices such as swearing, eating between meals, and smoking. Bandura's point is that children are continually learning both desirable and undesirable responses by "keeping their eyes (and ears) open," and he is not at all surprised that social and personality development proceeds so very rapidly along so many different paths.

HOW DO WE LEARN BY OBSERVATION?

It would be highly inappropriate to conclude that Bandura and his associates are the only social-learning theorists who recognize the importance of observational learning. Both Miller and Dollard

(1941) and Skinner (1953) believe that many behaviors are acquired through the influence of example; but their theories of imitative learning require that a modeled response be performed by the observer and then reinforced before the response will be learned.

Perhaps you can see the problem with these theories. They certainly cannot explain the results of Bandura's (1965) experiment or any example of *delayed imitation* where (1) the observer does not imitate the modeled response in the setting where it occurred, (2) reinforcement is not forthcoming to either the model or the observer, and (3) the observer does not display the acquired response until days, weeks, or even months later. Instances of delayed imitation are common among children. Almost every young boy watches his father shave and then tries to shave himself at a later date when daddy is no longer present to serve as a "shaving" model. In this case, the model was not reinforced for shaving and is not likely to reinforce his son for undertaking what is clearly a dangerous activity for little boys.

How, then, does the child acquire the component responses involved in the act of shaving? Bandura suggests that this and all other successful instances of imitative learning occur *while the observer attends to the model and before the observer's imitative responses have been performed or reinforced.* What the observer acquires is *symbolic representations* of the model's behavior that are stored in memory and retrieved at a later date to guide his own attempts to imitate. Bandura contends that the acquisition of modeled behavior is governed by four interrelated processes: *attention, retention, motoric reproduction*, and *motivation*.

Attentional processes. Virtually all children are exposed to a large number of social models, including parents, teachers, siblings, peers, Scout leaders, and media heroes. However, Bandura (1977) notes that (1) a child must first attend carefully to any model to learn by observation and (2) some models are more worthy of attention than others.

Whom are young children likely to select as social models? According to Bandura (1977), the most likely candidates are people who are warm and nurturant (socially responsive) and/or appear competent and powerful. Indeed, Joan Grusec and Rona Abramovitch (1982) found that nursery school children will often attend to and imitate their teachers (powerful, competent models) and those classmates who are typically warm and responsive to them. Moreover, 5–8-year-olds prefer to imitate age mates or older models rather than a younger child because they believe that younger children are less competent than they are (Brody & Stoneman, 1981; Graziano, Brody, & Bernstein, 1980).

Attainment of certain developmental milestones will also affect the child's choice of models. For example, once children are fully aware of their gender and know that it will never change (a milestone reached by most between 5 and 7 years of age), they will pay much more attention to models of their own sex (Grusec & Brinker, 1972). And as people mature, they develop certain interests, attitudes, and values and will normally prefer models who are in some way similar to themselves—friends or people in the same occupation, ethnic group, political party, and so on. But even though our choice of models may become somewhat more restricted over time, we continue to learn by observing others for the rest of our lives.

Retention processes. An observer must also commit the model's behavior to memory if he or she is to reproduce these responses later when the model is no longer present to serve as a guide. According to Bandura (1977), observers use two methods to retain the important elements of a modeled sequence. The first is the *imaginal representational system*; observers simply form retrievable sensory images of what they have seen. For example, a boy may attend to the acrobatics of a basketball star such as "Dr. J." (Julius Erving), form images of what he has seen, and then use these images to guide his own play on the basketball court. Observers may also make use of the *verbal representational system* by translating what they have observed into summary verbal labels. Verbal coding enables the observer to store a great deal of information in a label that is easily retrieved. Moreover, it permits the observer to retain complex responses that would be difficult or impossible to remember by any other method. Imagine how hard it

would be to open a combination lock if the model's dial-turning responses were not summarized by a verbal label such as L49, R37, L18.

A large amount of evidence suggests that symbolic coding of modeled activities does enhance the observational learning of both children and adults. For example, children who are told to describe a model's actions as they observe them are later able to reproduce more of these responses than children who do not describe the model's behavior (Coates & Hartup, 1969). By contrast, children who are prevented from verbally encoding a model's behavior (by counting to themselves as they watch the model) are *less* capable of reproducing the model's actions than those who did not perform distracting mental activities (Bandura, Grusec, & Menlove, 1966).

Motoric reproduction processes. Symbolic representations of a modeled sequence must be translated into action before the observer can be said to have imitated the model's behavior. The rate at which this motoric reproduction unfolds depends, in part, on the observer's ability to execute all the component responses. Learners who possess the requisite skills may be able to achieve errorless imitation with little or no practice. But if one or more constituent responses are lacking, the observer will fail to emulate the model. The point is that we often learn things from models that we cannot reproduce ourselves. For example, a 4-foot 2-inch boy may have acquired and retained symbolic representations of "Dr. J.'s" moves to the basket, but, lacking the height and agility of this amazing basketball star, he may never be able to execute a whirlybird dunk.

The adage "Practice makes perfect" certainly applies to much of our observational learning. As a novice golfer, I studied many books and "pro shop" films in an attempt to learn all facets of the Jack Nicklaus swing. I knew all the "rules"—left arm straight, head down, eyes on the ball—but I had real problems reproducing Jack's swing, or at least its results. One of my problems was that I was unable to observe my own swing to determine whether it matched my symbolic representation of the Nicklaus swing. By consulting with other golfers and by making self-corrective adjustments based on the results I was achieving, I finally developed a golf swing that satisfied me (although it would hardly have satisfied Jack Nicklaus). Bandura would describe my experience as fairly typical, for he argues that "in most everyday learning, people usually achieve only rough approximations of new patterns of behavior by modeling and [then] refine them through self-corrective adjustments on the basis of informative feedback from performance" (1971, p. 8).

Motivational processes (reinforcement). Bandura distinguishes acquisition (learning) from performance because people do not enact everything they learn. Recall that children in the model-punished condition of Bandura's (1965) experiment were initially quite reluctant to imitate the model's aggressive responses. They had seen the model spanked for her actions and might well have assumed that they would be punished for imitating her behavior. But when the children were offered incentives to imitate, learned responses that had previously been inhibited were promptly translated into action. These data led Bandura to conclude that the main function of both direct and vicarious reinforcement is to regulate the *performance* of learned behavior.[1]

However, Bandura (1969) concedes that reinforcement may play a small part in the *acquisition* of modeled responses. If an observer knows *in advance* that he will be reinforced for correctly imitating a model, this promise of reward should motivate him to attend carefully to the model's actions and to expend some effort in retaining what he has witnessed. Thus, incentives that are anticipated before observing the model's behavior may indeed promote observational *learning*.

In summarizing his theory of observational learning, Bandura (1969) stresses:

> It is evident . . . that observers do not function as passive video-tape recorders which indiscriminately register and store all modeling stimuli encountered in everyday life. . . . Observational learning constitutes a complex multiprocess phenomenon in which absence of appropriate matching responses following exposure to modeling stimuli may result from failures [to pay attention], inadequate transformation of modeled events to symbolic modes of representation, retention decrements, motor deficiencies, or unfavorable conditions of reinforcement [pp. 142–143].

Clearly, what is new about Bandura's theory is the proposition that social learning is primarily a *cognitive* activity that requires neither the enactment nor the reinforcement of the responses that we acquire. Yet it can also be argued that our willingness to *perform* learned responses is also under cognitive control. In the Bandura (1965) experiment, for example, children who had seen the model rewarded for aggressive behavior were initially much more willing to imitate the model's actions than those who had seen the model punished. While observing the consequences of the model's behavior, these youngsters had formed very different impressions (that is, cognitions) about the likely outcomes of their own imitative responses—impressions that then affected their willingness to display what they had learned by observation. According to Bandura, what determines whether we will enact the responses we have learned is not the actual consequences we receive for performing such acts but, rather, the consequences that we expect. And Bandura's (1965) experiment proves his point: when children in the model-punished condition were later led to expect positive outcomes for imitating the model, they became every bit as willing to do so as their counterparts in the model-rewarded condition.

THE ACTIVE INDIVIDUAL: SELF-CONTROL THROUGH SELF-REINFORCEMENT

An adequate theory of social and personality development must explain not only how habits and behavioral tendencies are acquired but also how they are regulated and maintained. Bandura (1977) concedes that many of our habits and mannerisms are profoundly affected by the approving or disapproving responses they elicit from other people. But he also notes that people often misinterpret the idea that "human behavior is controlled by its consequences" to mean that our actions are "at the mercy" of environmental influences. Bandura's counterargument is that much of human behavior is *self-regulated* by *self-produced consequences* (self-reinforcement).

An artist who sculpts a bust from clay does not require someone at her side to differentially reinforce her every move until an acceptable product emerges.

Rather, the artist has her own idea of what constitutes acceptable work and will perform self-corrective adjustments until her project meets these standards. The result of this self-scrutinizing may often be a product that far exceeds the standards of acceptable art for the layperson or, indeed, for other artists. I once knew an artist who, in his own words, had never created a "finished" product, because he was never satisfied with any of his paintings. Although this person made a substantial sum of money from the sale of his work, his failure to match his own standards of artistic merit was the major impetus for his eventual selection of another occupation.

This example of self-monitoring is not at all unusual. Bandura contends that people set performance standards for themselves in many areas and respond to their accomplishments either positively or negatively in accordance with these self-imposed demands.

Origins of self-reinforcement. According to Bandura (1977), children acquire their standards of self-reinforcement through direct instruction and observational learning. Parents often try to teach certain performance standards by offering their child incentives for behavior that meets or exceeds these criteria. For example, a mother may praise her son or provide him with some material reinforcer, such as money or toys, for every grade of "B" or above on his report card. As a result of this reinforcement, the child may come to consider the grade "B" an indicator of a job well done and respond to his subsequent academic accomplishments in a self-approving or self-critical fashion depending on their departure from this acquired performance standard.

Several experiments (reviewed in Bandura, 1971) show that children also learn standards of self-reinforcement displayed by social models and use these performance criteria to evaluate their own social behavior. Of course, some models are more effective in this regard than others. Generally speaking, children attempt to compare themselves with models who are similar to themselves in competence or ability. For example, a 4-year-old who is learning to swim will most likely compare her accomplishments with those of another novice swimmer.

Bandura suggests that our standards of self-reinforcement play a major role in the shaping of our self-concepts. He defines *self-esteem* in terms of the discrepancies between a person's behavior and the accomplishments that he or she has selected as indications of personal merit. A man who consistently fails to satisfy his self-imposed behavioral demands will evaluate himself negatively and be low in self-esteem. But if his accomplishments frequently match or exceed his performance standards, he will think well of himself and enjoy high self-esteem. Thus, a person's feelings about the self depend on more than his or her absolute accomplishments and the reactions of others to these accomplishments. Rather, the self-concept depends on the "goodness of fit" between one's behavior and one's *own* performance expectancies. Bandura (1971) notes that many very competent people who clearly "have it made" in the eyes of others may hold negative opinions of themselves for failing to reach their own lofty aspirations. He concludes that

> a harsh system of self-reinforcement gives rise to depressive reactions, chronic discouragement, feelings of worthlessness, and a lack of purposefulness. Excessive self-disparagement, in fact, is one of the defining characteristics of psychotic depression. [Researchers] have shown [that] depressed adults evaluate their performances as significantly poorer than do nondepressed subjects, even though their actual achievements are the same [p. 31].

Maintenance of self-reinforcement contingencies. Many of the performance standards that we set for ourselves apply to activities that originally were of little intrinsic interest to us. For example, few children enter grammar school with a strong desire to excel at particular subjects such as language or arithmetic. Yet once they set performance standards to shoot for (such as doing all of their homework every day), many students will forgo interesting TV programs and other enticements until they have achieved their objectives. They may even feel so good about their perseverance that they actively reward themselves in some way for their accomplishments (for example, treating themselves to an ice-cream cone or a movie). And should someone fail to meet an exacting standard, her self-imposed punishment might take many forms, not the least of which may be feeling very bad about herself.

Bandura is not at all impressed by the fact that people monitor their performances and will often reward themselves. From his perspective, the challenging questions that must be answered are "Why do people *deny* themselves available rewards over which they have full control, why do they adhere to exacting standards that require difficult performances, and why do they *punish* themselves?" (1971, p. 33; italics added).

Bandura concedes that external incentives such as praise, social recognition, and awards surely contribute to the maintenance of high performance standards, whereas few accolades are bestowed on people who reward themselves for mediocre accomplishments. Modeling influences may also contribute to the maintenance of high standards. A person who often sees others refuse to reward themselves for substandard performances is less likely to reinforce his own trivial accomplishments. But in recent years, Bandura (1982) has argued that the primary motivation for adhering to exacting performance standards comes not from the external environment but from within the individual. Once we set goals for which to strive, *self*-satisfaction becomes conditional on achieving these objectives. Accordingly, we feel extremely proud, competent, or "efficacious" when we succeed, and we may feel anxious, guilty, shameful, or downright incompetent should our performances fall short of our self-imposed demands. So *cognitively based* perceptions of competence, or *self-efficacy*, stemming from successes contribute in a major way to the maintenance of high performance standards.

Self-efficacy as a contributor to personality development. Just how important are these feelings of self-efficacy for social and personality development? Bandura suggests that they may be crucial. In a recent set of experiments, Bandura (1982) has shown that children are most likely to undertake, persist at, and ultimately succeed at novel or ambiguous tasks that they *think* they are capable of performing well, whereas they tend to avoid or give up on activities at which they feel less capable or efficacious. Consider one possible implication of such an observation. If parents were to repeatedly stress to their daughter that math is something "boys do better at," these statements might persuade the girl to devote less time to math than to her other classes, resulting, perhaps, in lower math grades and ultimately in "math anxiety," or the perception that she is not very good at this subject. Not feeling particularly efficacious at math, the girl may subsequently choose to avoid taking electives in math, statistics, and computer science, thereby barring the doors to many occupations that depend heavily on well-developed quantitative skills. Bandura (1982) suggests that each of us is constantly processing, evaluating, and reevaluating information about his or her strengths and weaknesses, thereby forming a unique pattern of self-perceived competencies. These perceptions of self-efficacy then affect the activities we choose to pursue (or to avoid) and, thus, largely determine who we are and what we are likely to become.

SOCIAL LEARNING AS RECIPROCAL DETERMINISM

Early versions of social-learning theory were largely tributes to John Watson's *doctrine of environmental determinism*: young, unknowing children were viewed as passive recipients of environmental influence who would become whatever parents, teachers, and other agents of society groomed them to be. In fact, B. F. Skinner, the famous "radical behaviorist" of recent times, has taken a position that many students find hard to accept: not only are we products of our experiences, but we have little to say in determining the character of those experiences. In other words, Skinner (1971) is arguing that "free will," or the concept of conscious choice, is merely an illusion.

Now contrast Skinner's position with that of Bandura (1977), who has repeatedly emphasized that children are active, thinking beings who contribute in many ways to their own development. Observational learning, for example, requires the observer to actively attend to, encode, and retain the behaviors displayed by social models. Moreover, children are often free to choose the models to whom they will attend and hence have some say about what they will learn from others.

Let's also recall that children are active in another

important respect—they are often responsible for creating the very reinforcers that maintain old habits and strengthen new ones. Suppose that a little boy discovers that he can gain control over desirable toys by assaulting his playmates. In this case, control over a desired toy is a satisfying outcome that reinforces the child's aggressive behavior. But note that the reinforcer here is produced by the child himself—through his aggressive actions. Not only has bullying behavior been reinforced (by obtaining the toy), but the character of the play environment has changed. Our bully becomes more inclined to victimize his playmates in the future, whereas those playmates who are victimized may become even more inclined to "give in" to the bully (see Figure 3-3).

In sum, cognitive-learning theorists such as Bandura (1977) and Richard Bell (1979) characterize social and personality development as a continuous *reciprocal interaction* between children and their environments. The situation or "environment" that a child experiences will surely affect the child, but the child's behavior is thought to affect the environment as well. The implication is that children are actively involved in shaping the very environments that will influence their growth and development.

ATTRIBUTION (OR SOCIAL INFORMATION-PROCESSING) THEORY

Bandura's characterization of children as active information processors, who organize experience by making mental notes about their strengths, their weaknesses, and the likely consequences of their behavior, is certainly shared by proponents of attribution (or social information-processing) theory. The major assumption of this promising new approach is that all of us (children and adults alike) are constantly seeking explanations, or *causal attributions*, for both our own and other people's behaviors. Theorizing about attributional processes can be traced to Fritz Heider (1958), a social psychologist who believed that all human beings are characterized by two strong motives: (1) the need to form a coherent understanding of the world and (2) the need to exert some control over the environment and, thus, become the "captain of one's own ship." To satisfy these motives, a person must be able to predict how people are likely to behave in a variety of situations and to understand why they behave in these ways. Without such knowledge, the world might seem a random, incoherent place that we would find impossible to adapt to or control.

Heider presumed that all human beings are intrinsically motivated to attend to and encode social experiences and to construct naive theories of human behavior in an attempt to make sense of all this information. Thus, whenever we see someone perform an act that catches our eye, we analyze the situation in which the behavior occurs, compare it with similar situations from the past (and/or the actor's prior behaviors), and formulate hypotheses about the underlying *cause* of the actions we have witnessed.

According to Heider, a person who is seeking to explain some noteworthy behavior will tend to attribute it either to *internal* causes (for example, some characteristic or disposition of the actor) or to *external* causes (for example, something about the situation that elicited the actor's behavior or is otherwise responsible for it). This is an important distinction, for the kinds of causal attributions we make about our own or other people's behavior can influence our reactions to that behavior and, hence, the kinds of social-learning experiences that we are likely to have. Consider the following example.

Suppose a 10-year-old boy is walking across the playground when he is suddenly smacked in the back of the head by a Frisbee. He turns around and sees no one but a single classmate, who is laughing at this turn of events. What kind of "theory" does the child formulate to explain his classmate's conduct? It is likely that the boy will interpret his classmate's laughter as a sign that the classmate *intended* to hit him, and he will probably attribute the classmate's behavior to some internal (or dispositional) cause, such as the classmate's aggressiveness. Consequently, the boy is likely to be angry and may respond with some form of counteraggression. But had the classmate expressed concern about having hit the boy with the Frisbee, and had there been another classmate

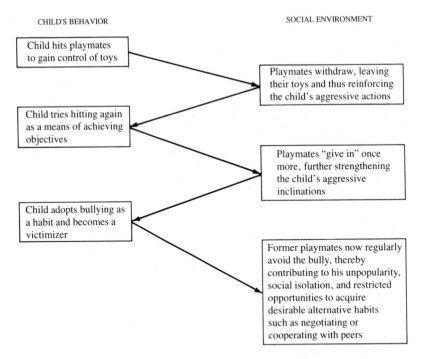

CHILD'S BEHAVIOR

SOCIAL ENVIRONMENT

Child hits playmates to gain control of toys

Playmates withdraw, leaving their toys and thus reinforcing the child's aggressive actions

Child tries hitting again as a means of achieving objectives

Playmates "give in" once more, further strengthening the child's aggressive inclinations

Child adopts bullying as a habit and becomes a victimizer

Former playmates now regularly avoid the bully, thereby contributing to his unpopularity, social isolation, and restricted opportunities to acquire desirable alternative habits such as negotiating or cooperating with peers

FIGURE 3-3   Reciprocal determinism: a hypothetical example showing how a child both influences and is influenced by the social environment

present to whom the Frisbee was apparently being thrown, it is likely that the boy would view the act of hitting him as *unintentional* and perhaps attribute it to some external (or situational) cause, such as the wind deflecting the Frisbee's path. Thus, the child is not as likely to be angry, and his behavioral response should be very different than if he had held the classmate personally responsible for the hurt that he had experienced.

According to attribution theory, we also attribute our *own* behavior to internal or external causes, and the kinds of self-attributions we make have important implications for the future. If you score 100% on a test that all your classmates say was particularly difficult, you are likely to attribute your success to internal factors, such as ability or hard work. But if other students say the test was easy, you are more likely to attribute your success to the unchallenging nature of the exam—an external cause. In both cases, the outcome is the same—you scored 100%—but the

implications for the future differ depending on the attribution you make. In the first instance, you are more likely to reward yourself for your achievement, which, in itself, should contribute to perceptions of self-efficacy for this particular subject. But if the test is perceived as easy, your accomplishment is not particularly noteworthy and may contribute little if anything to your perceived self-worth.

Attribution theory and cognitive social-learning theory are similar in at least two important respects. Both approaches maintain that we are largely products of our experiences. Moreover, proponents of each theory stress that our *cognitive interpretations* of social-learning experiences will have a much stronger influence on our subsequent behavior than the tangible outcomes, or consequences, of these events. Yet the two theories also differ in important ways. For example, social-learning theorists have generally assumed that children's interpretations of experience will change over time because the older child will have different kinds of experiences to interpret than younger children do. By contrast, attribution theorists argue that developmental trends in children's interpretations of experience reflect underlying changes that are occurring in the ways children process information to form causal attributions. So proponents of attribution theory ascribe much more importance to the impact of cognitive development on social and personality development than their counterparts from the social-learning tradition.

On a practical note, learning theorists and attribution theorists often disagree about how children are likely to interpret various aspects of experience. Suppose, for example, that the father of an extremely selfish child were to ask you "How can I convince Jimmy that he should share his toys with his playmates?" If you were a social-learning theorist, you might tell him to carefully monitor Jimmy's behavior and then provide some sort of tangible reinforcer (such as a cookie or the promise of a new toy) whenever Jimmy shares with a companion. Of course, your hope would be that Jimmy would come to associate such pleasantries with sharing, eventually concluding that acts of generosity are inherently satisfying activities that he wants to perform—activities of which he can feel proud (or which are worthy of some other kind of *self*-reinforcement).

Attribution theorists (for example, Lepper, 1981) would respectfully disagree with such a strategy. In their view, if Jimmy isn't inclined to share his toys but finds himself doing so for a cookie or a new toy, then he is apt to attribute his sharing behavior to the incentives he receives (a situational cause). Thus, he may never come to perceive himself as a generous person (a dispositional cause for sharing) or to view sharing as an intrinsically satisfying act. Oh, Jimmy will learn that sharing "pays off," all right, but only in the presence of someone who will *reward* personal sacrifices. Consequently, he is unlikely to share (and may become even more selfish) if an adult is not around to monitor and encourage this behavior.

How, then, would an attribution theorist approach this problem? Perhaps by relying on more subtle forms of social reinforcement that communicate to Jimmy that he has behaved in a competent and responsible manner when he shares his toys with a playmate. Not only is the child less likely to view his sharing as a ploy to win a tangible reward, but the reasoning that accompanies the praise should make Jimmy feel proud of himself (or self-efficacious) and allow him to make a dispositional attribution for his praiseworthy conduct (for example, "I share because *I* am a good boy who knows how to treat his friends"). Consequently, Jimmy may be more inclined to share toys with playmates in the future because he wants to live up to his new self-image as a mature and responsible playmate.

Which of these opposing viewpoints is correct? As we will see in later chapters, there is some support for both. Clearly, tangible reinforcers can be used to promote socially desirable acts such as sharing that children might not choose to perform on their own. But once they begin to undertake such behavior, it seems that more subtle forms of reinforcement that foster dispositional attributions may be more effective at sustaining the activity than the continued administration of tangible rewards. In fact, we will see that there are many occasions when the offer of tangible reinforcers can actually undermine children's intrinsic interest in desirable activities by convincing them that they are performing these behaviors merely to obtain a reward.

EVALUATION OF SOCIAL-LEARNING THEORY

"The more things change, the more they remain the same." It might be argued that this epigram describes the evolution of social-learning theory. Recall that John Watson, the first social-learning theorist, objected to the study of subjective, mentalistic phenomena. He argued that overt behavior was the appropriate subject matter for psychologists and that virtually all such behavior was determined by forces external to the organism. The neo-Hullians largely agreed with Watson except for their assertion that certain organismic characteristics such as primary and secondary drives are important determinants of behavior. Next came the Skinnerians, who took Watson quite literally. Skinner and his disciples argued that drives and cognitive activities are unnecessary to explain behavior. From their perspective, human behavior is controlled by external stimuli that evoke various responses and by reinforcing (or punishing) stimuli that maintain, alter, or suppress these responses. But the circle is beginning to close. Bandura and his associates emphasize that children do have "minds," which they use to affect the course and outcome of their development (a sentiment that is clearly echoed by causal attribution theorists). Thus, it is fair to say that most contemporary social-learning theorists are once again interested in the "mentalistic" determinants of behavior.

CONTRIBUTIONS OF SOCIAL-LEARNING THEORY

Developmentalists have benefited from the social-learning viewpoint in many ways. One very positive feature of this approach is that behaviorists stress *objectivity* in all phases of their work. Their units of analysis are typically objective behavioral responses rather than subjective phenomena that are hard to observe or measure. Behaviorists carefully define their concepts, make clear-cut predictions, and conduct tightly controlled experiments to provide objective evidence for the suspected causes of developmental change. The demonstrated success of their approach has encouraged researchers from all theoretical backgrounds to become more objective when studying developing children.

The learning theorist's emphasis on overt behavior and its immediate causes has also produced a number of important clinical insights and practical applications. For example, many problem behaviors can now be treated rapidly by various behavior modification techniques in which the therapist (1) identifies the reinforcers that sustain undesirable habits and eliminates them while (2) reinforcing alternative behaviors that are more socially desirable. Thus, childhood phobias such as a fear of school can often be eliminated in a matter of days or weeks, rather than the months (or years) that a psychoanalyst might take, probing the child's unconscious, trying to find the underlying conflict that is producing the phobic reaction.

But surely the major contribution of the social-learning approach is the wealth of information it has provided about developing children. After studying how children interpret and react to various environmental influences, learning theorists have helped us to understand how and why children form emotional attachments to others, adopt sex roles, come to abide by moral rules, form friendships, and so on. Throughout this text, we will see that much of what is known about social and personality development stems from the research of "behavioral," or learning, theorists.

CRITICISMS OF THE SOCIAL-LEARNING APPROACH

In spite of its strengths, many view the learning approach as an oversimplified account of social and personality development. Consider its explanation of individual differences: presumably, individuals follow different developmental paths because no two persons grow up in exactly the same environment. Yet critics are quick to note that each person comes into the world with something else that is an equally plausible explanation for his or her "individuality"— a unique genetic inheritance. Children also mature at different rates, a factor that affects how other people will respond to them (for an interesting example, see the material in Chapter 14 on rate of maturation and popularity) and how they will react to the behavior of other people. The point to be made is that our genetic characteristics and maturational timetables may have direct effects on development, or they may have indirect effects by determining what we are capable of learning (or would find reinforcing) at any given point in the life cycle. And when we recall the "behavior genetics" argument that our genotypes may affect the kinds of environments that we prefer and seek out, it does appear that social-learning theorists may have oversimplified the issue of individual differences in development by downplaying the contribution of important biological factors.

Is the social-learning approach truly a developmental theory? Many critics would say it is not, and there is some justification for their viewpoint. Nowhere in any social-learning theory do we find references to ages and stages of development. Social-learning theorists have been much more concerned with outlining a general set of principles to explain how people of *all* ages form new habits and discard old ones. So the social-learning approach is a "process" approach that has little to say about specific age-related changes in behavior.

Despite the popularity of recent cognitively oriented learning theories that stress the child's active role in the developmental process, there are those who say that *no* social-learning theorist pays enough attention to the *cognitive* determinants of development. Indeed, these latter critics suggest that a child's cognitive abilities progress through a series of qualitative changes (or stages) that social-learning theorists completely ignore. Furthermore, they argue that a child's impressions of and reactions to the social environment depend largely on his or her level of cognitive development. Recently, this "cognitive developmental" perspective has attracted many followers, and for reasons that should become quite apparent in the next chapter as we review the basic premises and implications of this interesting approach.

SUMMARY

The father of social-learning theory was John B. Watson, a psychologist who claimed that newborn infants are *tabulae rasae* who are gradually conditioned by their environments to feel, think, and act in certain characteristic ways. Watson believed that learned associations between stimuli and responses (habits) are the building blocks of human development. Presumably, social and personality development is a continuous process marked by the gradual acquisition of new and more sophisticated habits. These habits may be acquired by repeated exposure to a stimulus, classical conditioning, operant conditioning, or observational learning.

Since Watson's day, researchers have offered several explanations of social and personality development based on the principles of various learning theories. *Neo-Hullian* theorists assume that one's personality consists of a set of habits, each of which represents a learned association between a stimulus and a response. According to the neo-Hullians, human behavior is motivated by *primary* and *secondary* *drives*. Responses that prove to be reliable sources of drive reduction are learned and become habits. Presumably, the goal of socialization is to help children to acquire habits that are both socially acceptable and effective at reducing a drive.

By contrast, *Skinnerian* (or operant-learning) theorists believe that drives play little or no role in human social learning. Instead they argue that most of our actions are freely emitted operants that become either more or less probable as a function of their consequences. In other words, human behavior is said to be controlled by *external* stimuli—reinforcers and punitive events—rather than by internal forces, or drives.

According to Bandura's *cognitive social-learning* theory, many habits and personality attributes are responses acquired by observing the behavior of social models. Bandura makes an important distinction between learning and performance. He has shown that a response need not be reinforced or even performed in order to be learned. Learning is viewed as a *cognitive* activity that occurs as the observer attends to, codes, and mentally rehearses the model's behavior and before that behavior is reinforced. From Bandura's perspective, reinforcers and punitive events are performance variables that motivate the learner to display—or suppress—what he or she has already learned.

Bandurans suggest that children play an active role in their own socialization. The process of observational learning requires the observer to actively attend to, code, rehearse, and enact the behavior displayed by social models. Furthermore, children are said to regulate their own behavior by rewarding acts that are consistent with learned standards of acceptable conduct and punishing acts that are inconsistent with those standards. Finally, Bandura emphasizes that all psychological functioning can be described as a continuous reciprocal interaction between personal, behavioral, and environmental factors: the environment is said to affect the child, but the child's behavior also affects the environment. The implication of Bandura's reciprocal influence model is that children are actively involved in shaping the very environments that influence their development.

Causal attribution theorists also portray children as active, thinking beings who are constantly seeking explanations, or causal attributions, for their own behavior and that of other people. The kinds of attributions that children make about their own and others' behaviors are assumed to influence their future behavior, which, in turn, will affect the kinds of social-learning experiences that they are likely to have.

Among the strengths of the social-learning approach are its objectivity, its practical applications, and the wealth of information it has helped to generate about developing children and adolescents. Nevertheless, the learning approach is often criticized as a nondevelopmental model that discounts or ignores important biological and cognitive contributions to social and personality development.

NOTES

1. Vicarious consequences are the rewards and punishments experienced by social models. Bandura's (1965) experiment showed that the consequences of the model's behavior affected the willingness of observers to display what they had learned through observation. Thus, vicarious rewards and punishments are thought to regulate the performance of learned responses in much the same way as rewards and punishments that are administered directly to the learner.

REFERENCES

BANDURA, A. (1965). Influence of models' reinforcement contingencies on the acquisition of imitative responses. *Journal of Personality and Social Psychology, 1*, 589–595.

BANDURA, A. (1969). *Principles of behavior modification.* New York: Holt, Rinehart and Winston.

BANDURA, A. (1971). *Social learning theory.* Morristown, NJ: General Learning Press.

BANDURA, A. (1977). *Social learning theory.* Englewood Cliffs, NJ: Prentice-Hall.

BANDURA, A. (1982). Self-efficacy mechanism in human agency. *American Psychologist, 37*, 122–147.

BANDURA, A., Grusec, J. E., & Menlove, F. L. (1966). Observational learning as a function of symbolization and incentive set. *Child Development, 37*, 499–506.

BANDURA, A., & Harris, M. (1966). Modification of syntactic style. *Journal of Experimental Child Psychology, 4*, 341–352.

BANDURA, A., & Walters, R. H. (1963). *Social learning and personality development.* New York: Holt, Rinehart and Winston.

BELL, R. Q. (1979). Parents, child, and reciprocal influences. *American Psychologist, 34*, 821–826.

BRODY, G. H., & Stoneman, Z. (1981). Selective imitation of same-age, older, and younger peer models. *Child Development, 52*, 717–720.

COATES, B., & Hartup, W. W. (1969). Age and verbalization in observational learning. *Developmental Psychology, 1*, 556–562.

DOLLARD, J., & Miller, N. E. (1950). *Personality and psychotherapy: An analysis in terms of learning, thinking, and culture.* New York: McGraw-Hill.

DOMJAN, M., & Burkhard, B. (1986). *The principles of learning and behavior* (2nd ed.). Monterey, CA: Brooks/Cole.

GESELL, A. (1928). *Infancy and human growth.* New York: Macmillan.

GEWIRTZ, J. L. (1969). Mechanisms of social learning: Some roles of stimulation and behavior in early human development. In D. A. Goslin (Ed.), *Handbook of socialization theory and research.* Skokie, IL: Rand McNally.

GRAZIANO, W. G., Brody, G. H., & Bernstein, S. (1980). Effects of information about future allocation and peer's motivation on peer reward allocations. *Developmental Psychology, 16*, 475–482.

GRUSEC, J. E., & Abramovitch, R. (1982). Imitation of peers and adults in a natural setting: A functional analysis. *Child Development, 53*, 636–642.

GRUSEC, J. E., & Brinker, D. B. (1972). Reinforcement for imitation as a social learning determinant with implications for sex-role development. *Journal of Personality and Social Psychology, 21*, 149–158.

HARRISON, A. A. (1977). Mere exposure. In L. Berkowitz (Ed.), *Advances in experimental social psychology* (Vol. 10). Orlando, FL: Academic Press.

HEIDER, F. (1958). *The psychology of interpersonal relations.* New York: Wiley.

LEPPER, M. R. (1981). Intrinsic and extrinsic motivation in children: Detrimental effects of superfluous social controls. In W. A. Collins (Ed.), *Minnesota Symposia on Child Psychology* (Vol. 14). Minneapolis: University of Minnesota Press.

MILLER, N. E., & Dollard, J. (1941). *Social learning and imitation.* New Haven, CT: Yale University Press.

MISCHEL, W. (1979). On the interface of cognition and personality: Beyond the person-situation debate. *American Psychologist, 34*, 740–754.

MORELAND, R. L., & Zajonc, R. B. (1980). Is stimulus recognition a necessary condition for the occurrence of exposure effects? *Science, 207*, 557–558.

SKINNER, B. F. (1953). *Science and human behavior.* New York: Macmillan.

SKINNER, B. F. (1971). *Beyond freedom and dignity.* New York: Knopf.

STAATS, A. W., & Staats, C. K. (1958). Attitudes established by classical conditioning. *Journal of Abnormal and Social Psychology, 57*, 37–40.

WATSON, J. B. (1913). Psychology as the behaviorist views it. *Psychological Review, 20*, 158–177.

WATSON, J. B. (1928). *Psychological care of the infant and child.* New York: Norton.

WATSON, J. B., & Raynor, R. (1920). Conditioned emotional reactions. *Journal of Experimental Psychology, 3*, 1–14.

WEISBERG, P. (1963). Social and nonsocial conditioning of infant vocalization. *Child Development, 34*, 377–388.

ZIMMERMAN, B. J. (1977). Modeling. In H. Hom & P. Robinson (Eds.), *Psychological processes in early education.* Orlando, FL: Academic Press.

4

COGNITIVE-DEVELOPMENTAL THEORY

ORIGINS OF PIAGET'S THEORY

PIAGET'S VIEW OF INTELLIGENCE

The Child as a Constructor of Reality

Cognitive Schemata: The Structural Aspects of Intelligence

How Is Knowledge Gained? The Functional Basis of Intelligence

PIAGET'S STAGES OF COGNITIVE DEVELOPMENT

The Sensorimotor Stage (Birth to 2 Years)

The Preoperational Stage (Approximately 2 to 7 Years)

The Concrete-Operational Stage (Approximately 7 to 11 Years)

The Formal-Operational Stage (Age 11–12 and Beyond)

(continues)

If I had written this book 25 years ago, it would not have included a chapter on cognitive-developmental theory. Although the theory itself has been around for more than 60 years, its widespread application to social-developmental issues and problems is relatively recent. This "new look" at social and personality development stems from the work of several cognitive theorists (Baldwin, 1906; Bruner, Olver, & Greenfield, 1966; Kohlberg, 1966; Werner, 1957), but the major contributor is unquestionably Jean Piaget, a Swiss scholar who has been studying the processes and products of intellectual development since 1920.

We will soon discover that Piaget's theory is not a well-articulated theory of socialization. It is more accurately characterized as a theory of psychological functioning that has important implications for social and personality development. According to Piaget, the child is neither driven by undesirable instincts nor "molded" by environmental influences. Piaget and his followers view children as curious, active explorers who respond to the environment according to their *understanding* of its essential features. Presumably, any two children might react very differently to some aspect of the environment if they interpret it differently. To predict how a child will respond to a praising mother, a scolding teacher, or a bossy playmate, one has to know how the child perceives, or construes, that event.

The term *cognitive development* refers to the changes that occur in our mental abilities over the course of our lives. According to Piaget, children pass through four major stages of cognitive growth between birth and early adulthood. Each successive stage is thought to represent a new and more complex method of intellectual functioning that will play a major role in determining (1) how the child encodes, interprets, and responds to environmental events and, thus, (2) what effects these events are likely to have on the child's social and personality development.

ORIGINS OF PIAGET'S THEORY

Piaget was a man of many interests. At the age of 10 he published his first scientific article, about a rare albino sparrow, and he was already a regular con-

tributor to the scientific literature long before earning a Ph.D. in zoology at the age of 21. Piaget's secondary interest was *epistemology* (the branch of philosophy concerned with the origins of knowledge), and he hoped desperately to be able to integrate his two academic concerns. At that point, he felt psychology was the answer. He then journeyed to Paris, spending two years at the Sorbonne studying clinical psychology, logic, and philosophy of science. During his stay in Paris, Piaget was offered a position standardizing intelligence tests at the Alfred Binet laboratories. His decision to accept this position had a profound influence on the direction of his career.

Many of us would find the task of standardizing an intelligence test rather tedious. It requires that one administer a large number of precisely worded questions to children of different ages in order to determine the age at which the majority of test takers can correctly answer each individual item. However, Piaget soon became more interested in children's *incorrect* answers when he discovered that youngsters of roughly the same age were making similar kinds of mistakes—errors that were typically quite different from the incorrect responses of younger or older children. Could these age-related differences in children's error patterns reflect developmental steps or stages in the process of intellectual growth? Piaget thought so, and he began to suspect that *how* children think is a much better indicator of their cognitive abilities than *what* they may happen to know.

When his own three children were born, Piaget made detailed notes on their intellectual abilities, carefully observing how they reacted to various objects, events, and problems that he presented to them. Many of Piaget's ideas about intelligence and about intellectual development during infancy are based on these naturalistic observations of his own children.

Piaget's theory gradually took shape over a number of years as he broadened his horizons and began to study a larger sample of developing children. Many of Piaget's theoretical insights came from his use of the *clinical method*, a question-and-answer technique that he devised to measure the ways children attacked various problems and thought about everyday issues. By carefully questioning a large number of children in several age groups, Piaget was able to identify four methods (or patterns) of reasoning that are age-related and, in his opinion, represent different stages of intellectual growth.

PIAGET'S VIEW OF INTELLIGENCE

Many psychologists define intelligence as a person's mental capacity or ability to profit from experience. They measure intelligence by asking the child a series of questions and totaling the number of correct answers, which is then compared against the norms for children of that age to yield an *intelligence quotient*, or *IQ*. Piaget became dissatisfied with this "psychometric" approach because he felt that IQ tests overemphasize intellectual content, or *what* the child thinks, while ignoring the question how or why the child thinks these things. As a result, he turned away from the study of intellectual content and began to investigate the *process* of thinking.

Piaget's definition of intelligence reflects his background in biology. He viewed intelligence as a basic life function that helps the organism adapt to its environment. He added that intelligence "is a form of *equilibrium* toward which all [cognitive structures] tend" (1950, p. 6). So according to Piaget, intellectual activity is undertaken with one goal in mind: to produce a balanced, or harmonious, relationship between one's thought processes and the environment (such a balanced state of affairs is called *cognitive equilibrium*). Piaget stressed that the environment is constantly challenging the child, for many novel stimuli and events are not immediately understood. He believed that these imbalances (or *cognitive disequilibriums*) between the child's modes of thinking and environmental events would prompt the child to make mental adjustments that would enable her to cope with puzzling new experiences and thereby restore cognitive equilibrium. In sum, Piaget's view of intelligence is an "interactionist" model which implies that mismatches between one's internal mental schemes and the external environment stimulate cognitive activity and intellectual growth.

PHOTO 4-1   The theory of cognitive development of Swiss scholar Jean Piaget (1886–1980) has several important implications for our understanding of social and personality development.

THE CHILD AS A CONSTRUCTOR OF REALITY

According to Piaget, the child is a *constructivist*—an organism that acts on novel objects and events and thereby gains some understanding of their essential features. He notes:

> Knowledge is not a copy of reality. To know an object, to know an event is not simply to look at it and make a mental copy or image of it. To know is to [mentally] modify, to transform the object, and to understand the way the object is constructed. A . . . [cognitive] operation is thus the essence of knowledge . . . which [defines] the object of knowledge [as cited in Jennings, 1967].

Piaget stresses that the child's constructions of reality (that is, interpretations of objects and events) will depend on the knowledge base available to him at that point in time: the more immature the child's cognitive system, the more limited his interpretation of an environmental event. Consider the following example:

> A four-year-old child and his father are watching the setting sun. "Look Daddy. It's hiding behind the mountain. Why is it going away? Is it angry?" The

father grasps the opportunity to explain to his son how the world works. "Well, Mark, the sun doesn't really feel things. And it doesn't really move. It's the earth that's moving. It turns on its axis so that the mountain moves in front of the sun. . . ." The father goes on to other explanations of relative motion, interplanetary bodies and such. The boy . . . firmly and definitely responds, "But *we're* not moving. *It* is. Look, it's going down" [Cowan, 1978, p. 11].

This child is making an important assumption here that dominates his attempt at understanding— namely, that the way he sees things must correspond to the way they are. Obviously, it is the sun that is moving, ducking behind the mountain as if it were a live being who was expressing some feeling or serving a definite purpose by hiding. However, the father knows the characteristics that distinguish animate from inanimate objects (and a little about astronomy as well), so that he is able to construct a very different interpretation of the "reality" that he and his son have witnessed.

COGNITIVE SCHEMATA: THE STRUCTURAL ASPECTS OF INTELLIGENCE

Piaget uses the term *schemata* to refer to the models, or mental structures, that we create to represent, organize, and interpret our experiences. A *schema* is a pattern of thought or action that is similar in some respects to what the layperson calls a strategy or a concept. Piaget (1952, 1977) has described three kinds of intellectual structures: behavioral (or sensorimotor) schemata, symbolic schemata, and operational schemata.

Behavioral (or sensorimotor) schemata. A

behavioral schema is an organized pattern of behavior that a child uses to represent and respond to an object or an experience. These are the first psychological structures to emerge, and for much of the first two years of life, an infant's knowledge of objects and events is limited to that which she can represent through overt actions. Stated another way, infants younger than 18 months are not yet capable of organizing experience or solving problems on a purely "mental" level.

An example of a behavioral schema, one that most of us use on a regular basis, is tying our shoelaces. We don't have to think consciously about the component responses involved in tying our shoes; this knowledge is acquired by experience and becomes represented in our muscles (Bruner, 1964).

Symbolic schemata. During the second year,

children reach a point at which they can solve problems and think about objects and events without having acted on them. In other words, they are now capable of representing actions mentally and using these mental symbols, or symbolic schemata, to satisfy their objectives. Consider the following observation of the antics of Jacqueline, Piaget's 16-month-old daughter:

> Jacqueline had a visit from a little boy [18 months of age] . . . who, in the course of the afternoon got into a terrible temper. He screamed as he tried to get out of a playpen and pushed it backward, stamping his feet. Jacqueline stood watching him in amazement, never having witnessed such a scene before. The next day, she herself screamed in her playpen and tried to move, stamping her foot . . . several times in succession [Piaget, 1951, p. 63].

Clearly, Jacqueline was imitating the responses of her absent playmate, even though she had not performed those actions at the time they were modeled. It appears that she must have represented the model's behavior in some internal, symbolic form that preserved the original scene and guided her later imitation.

Operational schemata. The thinking of children aged 7 and older is characterized by a third type of schema, the operational structure. A *cognitive operation* is an internal mental activity that a person performs on his or her objects of thought. Common cognitive operations include mental activities such as *reversibility* (reversing an action in one's head; see Figure 4-1) and all the actions implied in mathematical symbols such as $+$, $-$, $\times$, $\div$, $=$, $<$, and $>$. As we will see later in the chapter, these cognitive operations permit children to construct rather complex intellectual schemata that will enable them to think

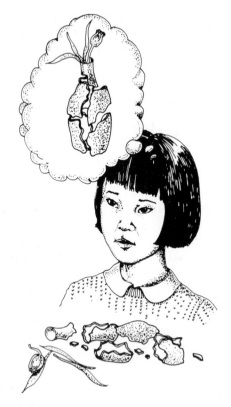

FIGURE 4-1 Reversibility is a cognitive operation that develops during middle childhood

logically and systematically—first about their actual experiences and eventually about abstract or hypothetical events.

HOW IS KNOWLEDGE GAINED? THE FUNCTIONAL BASIS OF INTELLIGENCE

How do children construct and modify their intellectual schemata? Piaget believes that all cognitive structures are created through the operation of two inborn intellectual functions, which he calls organization and adaptation. *Organization* is the process by which children combine existing schemata into new and more complex intellectual structures. For example, a toddler may initially believe that anything that flies is a "birdie." As he gradually discovers that many things that are not birds can also fly, he may

organize this knowledge into a new and more complex mental structure such as this one:

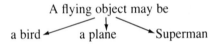

According to Piaget, organization is inborn and automatic: children are constantly organizing their available schemata into higher-order systems or structures.

The goal of organization is to further the process of adaptation. As its name implies, *adaptation* is the process of adjusting to the demands of the environment. According to Piaget, adaptation occurs through two complementary activities: assimilation and accommodation.

Assimilation is the process by which the child tries to interpret new experience in terms of her existing models of the world—the schemata that she already possesses. Imagine the reaction of an infant who is exposed for the first time to a beach ball. She may first try to grasp it with one hand and thus assimilate it into her "grasping" schema in much the same way that rattles, rubber animals, and other crib toys have been assimilated in the past. In other words, the infant is trying to adapt to a novel stimulus by construing it as something familiar—namely, something to be grasped.

However, truly novel objects, events, and experiences may be difficult or impossible to incorporate into existing schemata. Piaget (1952) believed that people who assimilate novel stimuli will often have to *accommodate* to these stimuli—that is, modify their existing schemata to make them compatible with the novel input. For example, the infant may have to alter her grasping structure (accommodate) by using two hands instead of one in order to assimilate a beach ball into that particular schema. So assimilation and accommodation are viewed as complementary aspects of most adaptive acts.

What motivates the child to assimilate environmental stimuli and to accommodate to these objects and events? Piaget is clear on this point: "His position is simply that there is an intrinsic need for cognitive . . . structures, once generated by functioning, to perpetuate themselves by more functioning. Schemas

AN INFANT ACCOMMODATING HIS MOUTH TO THE SHAPE OF AN OBJECT

are [active] and one of their important, built-in properties is repeated assimilation of anything assimilable in the environment" (Flavell, 1963, p. 78).

We can compare the adaptive activities of cognitive schemata to the behavior of an ameba. This one-celled animal is a perpetual "eating machine" that engulfs food particles, changes shape, and grows. *Cognitive growth* occurs in a somewhat similar fashion. Children extend their schemata to novel aspects of the environment, and, in the process of ingesting (assimilating) this environmental "nutriment," their schemata are accommodated, or changed. The product of this intellectual functioning is adaptation, a state of equilibrium between the child's cognitive structures and the environment.

But equilibrium is short-lived, according to Piaget. Just as an ameba repeatedly changes shape by ingesting more food, one's cognitive structures are repeatedly changing (accommodating) as newer experiences are assimilated. And even during periods when children are not experiencing anything new, they are actively reorganizing their existing knowledge into higher-order schemata. So two kinds of activity—organization and adaptation—make possible a progressively greater understanding of the world. Piaget stressed that these intellectual functions operate in a reciprocal fashion: assimilations bring about new accommodations, which stimulate reorganizations, which, in turn, allow further assimilations, and so on. Over the long run, cognitive abilities will eventually mature to an extent

that the child is capable of thinking about old issues in a completely new way and will pass from one stage of intellectual development to the next higher stage.

PIAGET'S STAGES OF COGNITIVE DEVELOPMENT

Piaget has identified four major periods of cognitive development: the sensorimotor stage (birth to 2 years), the preoperational stage (2 to 7 years), the stage of concrete operations (7 to 11 years), and the stage of formal operations (11 years and beyond). These stages of intellectual growth represent completely different levels of cognitive functioning and form what Piaget calls an *invariant developmental sequence*. The invariant-sequence notion means that all children progress through the stages in precisely the same order. According to Piaget, there can be no skipping of stages, because each successive stage builds on its immediate predecessor.

Piaget's model of cognitive development has important implications for social and personality development. For example, if cognition develops in stages, the child's methods of organizing social experiences will differ from those of adults and thus *cannot* be the direct result of adult teaching. Unlike social-learning theorists, who view development as a product of learning, cognitive theorists argue that *learning is a product of one's level of development*. That is, the modes of thinking (cognitive structures) that characterize a particular stage of development largely determine how the child will interpret his interactions with other people and hence what he may learn from these social encounters (Kohlberg, 1969). With this assumption in mind, let's now consider how children's thinking changes from birth through adolescence.

THE SENSORIMOTOR STAGE (BIRTH TO 2 YEARS)

The sensorimotor stage spans the first two years, or the period that psychologists refer to as infancy. The dominant cognitive structures are behavioral schemata, which evolve as infants begin to coordinate their *sensory* input and *motor* responses in order to "act on" and get to "know" the environment.

During the first two years of life, infants evolve from reflexive creatures with very limited knowledge into planful problem solvers who have already learned a great deal about themselves, their close companions, and the objects and events in their everyday worlds. So dramatic are the infant's cognitive advances that Piaget divides the sensorimotor period into six substages (see Table 4-1, p. 88), which describe the child's gradual transition from a reflexive to a reflective organism. Our review will focus on three important aspects of the infant's sensorimotor development: problem-solving skills, imitative abilities, and the object concept.

Growth of Problem Solving

Over the first eight months, infants begin to act on objects and to discover that they can make interesting things happen. However, these discoveries emerge very gradually. Piaget believes that neonates[1] are born with only a few basic reflexes (for example, sucking, grasping) that assist them in satisfying biological needs such as hunger. During the first month, their activities are pretty much confined to exercising their innate reflexes, assimilating new objects into these reflexive schemes (for example, sucking on objects other than nipples), and accommodating their reflexes to these novel objects. The first coordinated habits emerge at 1–4 months of age as infants discover by chance that various responses that they can produce (for example, sucking their thumbs, making sounds by cooing) are satisfying and, thus, worthy of repetition. These responses, called *primary circular reactions*, are centered on the infant's own body. They are called "primary" because they are the first habits to appear and "circular" because the pleasure they bring stimulates their repetition.

Between 4 and 8 months of age, infants discover (again by chance) that they can make interesting things happen to *external* objects (such as making a rubber duck quack by squeezing it). These responses, called *secondary circular reactions*, also tend to be repeated for the pleasure they bring. Of what possible significance are these simple habits for social and personality development? According to Piaget, infants are discovering the limits and capabilities of their own bodies during the first four months and then recognizing that external objects are separate from their "physical selves" by the middle of the first year. Thus, making a distinction between "self" and "nonself" is viewed as the first step in the development of a personal identity, or self-concept.

Between 8 and 12 months of age, infants are suddenly able to coordinate two or more actions to achieve their objectives. For example, were you to place a toy that the child wanted under a cushion, the child might lift the cushion with one hand while using the other to grab the toy. In this case, the act of lifting the cushion is not a pleasurable response in itself; nor is it emitted by chance. Rather, it represents part of a larger *intentional* schema in which two initially unrelated responses—lifting and grasping—are coordinated as a means to an end.

At 12 to 18 months of age, infants begin to experiment with objects and will try to invent totally new methods of solving problems or reproducing interesting results. For example, a child who originally squeezed a rubber duck to make it quack may now decide to drop it, step on it, or crush it with a pillow to see whether these actions will have the same or different effects on the toy. These trial-and-error exploratory schemata, called *tertiary circular reactions*, signal the emergence of true curiosity.

A dramatic development takes place between 18 and 24 months of age: children begin to internalize their behavioral schemata to construct mental symbols, or images. Suddenly, 18–24-month-olds are capable of solving problems mentally, without resorting to trial-and-error experimentation. This ability, called *inner experimentation*, is illustrated in Piaget's interaction with his son, Laurent:

> Laurent is seated before a table and I place a bread crust in front of him, out of reach. Also, to the right of the child I place a stick, about 25cm. long. At first, Laurent tries to grasp the bread . . . and then he gives up . . . Laurent again looks at the bread, and without moving, looks very briefly at the stick, then suddenly grasps it and directs it toward the bread. . . . [He then] draws the bread to him [Piaget, 1952, p. 335].

Clearly, Laurent has an important insight: the stick can be used as an extension of his arm to obtain a distant object. Trial-and-error experimentation is not apparent in this case, for Laurent's "problem solving" occurred at an internal, symbolic level.

Development of Imitation

Piaget recognized the important adaptive significance of imitation, and he was very interested in its development. His own observations led him to believe that infants are incapable of imitating novel responses displayed by a model until 8 to 12 months of age. Moreover, the imitative schemes of these young infants are rather imprecise. Were you to bend and straighten your finger, the infant might mimic you by opening and closing her entire hand! For 8–12-month-olds, precise imitation of even the simplest responses may come very slowly, only after days (or even weeks) of practice (Kaye & Marcus, 1981).

Voluntary imitation becomes much more precise at age 12 to 18 months, as we see in the following example:

> At [1 year and 16 days of age, Jacqueline] discovered her forehead. When I touched the middle of mine, she first rubbed her eye, then felt above it and touched her hair, after which she brought her hand down a little and finally put her finger on her forehead [Piaget, 1951, p. 56].

Between 18 and 24 months of age, infants reach a point where they are capable of *deferred imitation*—the ability to reproduce the behavior of an *absent* model. When we discussed symbolic schemata, we noted an example of deferred imitation— Jacqueline's reproduction of her playmate's temper tantrum 24 hours later. According to Piaget, older infants are capable of deferred imitation because they can now internalize their behavioral schemata, thereby forming mental symbols or images of a model's behavior that will serve as a guide for its later reproduction.

Recently a number of investigators have concluded that Piaget may have badly underestimated the imitative abilities of infants. For example, at least two experiments have shown that infants only 12 to 14 months of age may be capable of deferred imitation

(Abravanel & Gingold, 1985; Meltzoff, 1985), although they are not as proficient at such imitative displays as 18- to 24-month-olds. And in Box 4-1 we will see that some investigators now believe infants are capable of a very special form of imitation as early as the first few days and weeks of life.

The Object Concept: Out of Sight Is Not Necessarily Out of Mind

Even though infants are not yet operating on a symbolic level, they are nevertheless forming simple concepts as they begin to recognize similarities and differences among objects and events and to treat perceptually similar phenomena alike (Younger, 1985). One of the more notable achievements of the sensorimotor period is the development of the object concept—the idea that people, places, and things continue to exist when they are no longer visible or otherwise detectable through the senses.

If you were to remove your watch and cover it with a coffee mug, you would be well aware that the watch continues to exist even though it is not visible. Objects have a permanence for us; out of sight is not necessarily out of mind. Yet babies are not initially aware of this basic fact of life. Throughout the first four months, infants will not search for attractive objects that vanish; were they interested in a watch that was then covered by a mug, they would soon lose interest, almost as if they believed that the watch had lost its identity by being transformed into a mug (Bower, 1982). At age 4 to 8 months, infants will retrieve attractive objects that are partly concealed or hidden under a transparent cover; but their continuing failure to search for objects that are completely concealed suggests that, from their perspective, disappearing objects may no longer exist.

The first signs of an emerging object concept appear at 8 to 12 months of age. However, object permanence is far from complete, as we see in Piaget's demonstration with 10-month-old Jacqueline:

> Jacqueline is seated on a mattress without anything to disturb or distract her. . . . I take her [toy] parrot from her hands and hide it twice in succession under the mattress, on her left [point A]. Both times Jacqueline looks for the object immediately and grabs it. Then I take it from her hands and move it

BOX 4-1   CAN NEONATES IMITATE FACIAL EXPRESSIONS?

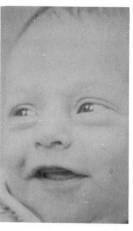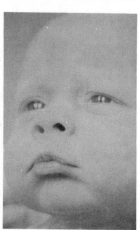

Can newborns imitate? As shown in these photos, neonates can apparently reproduce certain facial expressions and gestures displayed by an adult model.

Several years ago, Andrew Meltzoff and Keith Moore (1977) reported a startling set of results. Apparently, 12- to 21-day-old infants were able to imitate an adult model's simple facial expressions—actions such as mouth openings, tongue protrusions, and a puckering of the lips. However, these initial findings were greeted with much

very slowly before her eyes to the corresponding place on her right, under the mattress [point B]. Jacqueline watches this movement . . . but at the moment when the parrot disappears [at point B] she turns to her left and looks where it was before [at point A] [1954, p. 51].

Jacqueline's response is typical of children at this age. When searching for a disappearing object, the 8- to 12-month-old will often look in the place where it was previously *found* rather than the place where it was last seen. In other words, the child acts as if her *behavior* determined where the object was to appear, and consequently she does not treat the object as if it existed independent of her own activity.

Between 12 and 18 months of age, the object concept improves. Infants will now track the visible movements of objects and search for them where they were last seen. Yet the object concept is not complete, for the child cannot make the mental inferences necessary to represent and understand *invisible* displacements. Thus, if you conceal an attractive toy in

your hand, place your hand behind a barrier and deposit the toy there, remove and open your empty hand, and ask the child to find the toy, 12- to 18-month-olds will search where the toy was last seen—in your hand—rather than looking behind the barrier.

By 18 to 24 months of age, children are capable of mentally representing invisible displacements and using these mental inferences to guide their search for objects that disappear. The object concept is now complete.

In Chapter 5 we will see that the object concept may play an important role in the development of the child's first true emotional attachments. Cognitive theorists have proposed that infants cannot form close emotional ties to regular companions unless these individuals have a "permanence" about them. After all, it would seem rather difficult to establish a meaningful and lasting relationship with a person who "ceases to exist" whenever he or she passes from view.

BOX 4-1   *continued*

skepticism. After all, this particular imitative scheme involves matching a facial gesture that babies can see with their own expressions, which they cannot see—a sophisticated skill that Piaget claimed was not available until 8 to 12 months of age. Some critics dismissed the infant's responses as pseudo imitation: perhaps very young infants will pucker, open their mouths, or stick out their tongues because face-to-face interaction with the adult has excited them (see Olson & Sherman, 1983). Others wondered whether the adult model might not be subconsciously mimicking the facial expressions of the infants. Although both these possibilities could conceivably account for Meltzoff and Moore's original results, they are less plausible explanations for recent demonstrations that *calm* infants only 36–72 hours old can reproduce the facial gestures of adult models under conditions where *the model gestured first* and the infant's imitative *reactions* were recorded on videotape (Field, Woodson, Greenberg, & Cohen, 1982; Meltzoff & Moore, 1983). Since the babies in these latter studies were so very young, we might seriously entertain the possibility that neonates are biologically prepared to imitate the facial gestures of their companions.

To date, there is little evidence that very young infants are capable of imitating anything other than facial gestures, and additional demonstrations of facial imitation will be necessary before all the skeptics are likely to conclude that neonates possess this ability. So the controversy continues, although many developmentalists now concede that neonates probably can imitate a limited number of facial expressions.

Of what possible significance is this very special form of imitation? An ethologist might answer by arguing that facial imitation is an inborn ability that enables infants to respond contingently to caregivers, thereby eliciting their attention and affection. Indeed, we will see in Chapter 5 that very young infants have a number of other inborn characteristics that help them to elicit the kinds of affectionate social contact from caregivers that are necessary for normal social and emotional development. So if neonates really are capable of imitating the facial gestures of close companions, it is quite conceivable that facial imitation serves this same important function.

An Overview of Sensorimotor Development

The child's achievements during the sensorimotor period are truly remarkable. In two short years, infants have evolved from reflexive and largely immobile creatures into planful thinkers who can move about on their own, solve some problems in their heads, form simple concepts, and even communicate many of their thoughts to their companions. Table 4-1 presents a brief summary of the major intellectual accomplishments of the first two years.

THE PREOPERATIONAL STAGE (APPROXIMATELY 2 TO 7 YEARS)

During the preoperational stage, children are becoming increasingly proficient at constructing and using mental symbols to think about the objects, situations, and events they encounter. But despite these advances in symbolic reasoning, Piaget's descriptions of preoperational intelligence focus mainly on the limitations or deficiencies in children's thinking. Indeed, he calls this period "preoperational" because he believes that preschool children have not yet acquired the cognitive operations (and operational schemata) that would enable them to think logically.

Piaget divides the preoperational stage into two phases: the *preconceptual* period (2–4 years of age) and the *intuitive* period (4–7 years).

The Preconceptual Period

Emergence of symbolic thought. The *preconceptual period* is marked by the sudden appearance of the symbolic function: the ability to make one thing—a word or an object—stand for, or represent, something else. For example, words soon come to represent objects, persons, and events, so that the child can now easily reconstruct and make reference to the past and talk about items that are no longer present. Pretend play also emerges at this time. Toddlers often pretend to be people they are not (mommies, superheroes), and they may play these roles with props such as a shoebox or a stick that symbolize other objects such as a baby's crib or a ray gun. These kinds of symbolic play activities enable the 2–4-year-old to construct what adults often call a make-believe or a fantasy world. Although some parents are concerned when their preschool children immerse themselves in a world of make-believe and begin to invent imaginary playmates, Piaget feels that these are basically healthy activities. In Box 4-2 we take a closer look at children's play and see how these "pretend" activities may contribute to the child's social, emotional, and intellectual development.

Deficits in preconceptual reasoning. Piaget calls this period "preconceptual" because he believes that the ideas, concepts, and cognitive processes of 2–4-year-olds are very primitive by adult standards. For example, it appeared to Piaget that preschool children know little about cause-and-effect relationships because they rely on *transductive reasoning*. The transductive thinker reasons from the particular to the particular: when any two events occur together (covary), the child is likely to assume that one has caused the other. One day when Piaget's daughter had missed her usual afternoon nap, she remarked "I haven't had a nap, so it isn't afternoon." In this case, Lucienne reasoned from one particular (the nap) to another (the afternoon) and erroneously concluded that her nap determined when it was afternoon.

According to Piaget, the most striking deficiency in children's preoperational reasoning is a characteristic that he calls *egocentrism*—a tendency to view the world from one's own perspective and to

TABLE 4-1   Summary of the Substages and Intellectual Accomplishments of the Sensorimotor Period

Piagetian Substage	Methods of solving problems or producing interesting outcomes	Imitation skills	Object concept
1. Reflex activity (0–1 month)	Exercise and accommodation of inborn reflexes	Some imitation of facial expressions[a]	Tracks moving object but ignores its disappearance
2. Primary circular reactions (1–4 months)	Repeating interesting acts that are centered on one's own body	Repetition of own behavior that is mimicked by a companion	Looks intently at the spot where an object disappeared
3. Secondary circular reactions (4–8 months)	Repeating interesting acts that are directed toward external objects	Same as in Substage 2	Searches for partly concealed object
4. Coordination of secondary schemata (8–12 months)	Combining actions to solve simple problems (first evidence of intentionality)	Ability to eventually imitate novel responses after gradually accommodating a crude first attempt at imitation	First glimmering of object permanence; searches for and finds concealed object that has not been visibly displaced
5. Tertiary circular reactions (12–18 months)	Experimenting to find new ways to solve problems or reproduce interesting outcomes	Systematic imitation of novel responses	Searches for and finds object that has been visibly displaced
6. Invention of new means through mental combinations (18–24 months)	First evidence of insight as the child solves problems at an internal, symbolic level	Deferred imitation of the actions of absent models	Object concept is complete; searches for and finds objects that have been hidden through invisible displacements

[a]Imitation of facial expressions is apparently an inborn ability that may bear little relation to the voluntary imitation that appears later in the first year (Field, Woodson, Greenberg, & Cohen 1982; Meltzoff & Moore, 1983).

have difficulty recognizing another person's point of view. Examples of this self-centeredness can be found in children's speech as well as their thinking. Here is a sample conversation in which the egocentrism of a 4-year-old named Sandy comes through as she describes an event she has witnessed:

Sandy: Uncle David, it got on your car and scratched it.

Adult: What did?

Sandy: Come, I'll show you. (*She takes her uncle outside and shows him a scratch on the top of his new car.*)

Adult: Sandy, what made the scratch?

Sandy: Not me!

Adult (*laughing*): I know, Sandy, but how did the scratch get there?

Sandy: It got on the car and scratched it with its claws.

Adult: What did?

Sandy (*looking around*): There! (*She points to a cat that is walking across the street.*)

Adult: Oh, a cat! Why didn't you tell me that in the first place?

Sandy: I did!

Note that Sandy has made little or no attempt to adapt her speech to the needs of her listener, because she assumes that her uncle shares her perspective and must already know what caused the scratch on his car. On another occasion, Sandy was asked how many sisters she had, and she said "Two." Next she was asked whether Shelley (her older sister) had two sisters, and she replied "No, Shelley has one sister—Shannon!" Can you see the egocentrism in Sandy's reasoning? Her problem is that she does not assume Shelley's perspective and realize that she too is Shelley's sister. Instead she operates strictly from her own point of view.

In recent years, cognitive theorists have proposed that the egocentrism of younger children helps to explain why they are often rather cruel, selfish, inconsiderate, or unwilling to help one another. If these "insensitive" youngsters do not yet realize how their own actions make others feel, they may not readily experience the remorse and sympathy that might inhibit antisocial behavior or elicit acts of kindness. This hypothesized link between one's cognitive abilities and social behaviors will be explored in some detail when we consider the topics of social cognition, aggression, altruism, and moral development in Chapters 7, 9, 10, and 11.

The Intuitive Period

The intuitive thinking that characterizes 4–7-year-olds is little more than an extension of preconceptual thought, although children are now slightly less egocentric and somewhat more proficient at using images and symbols in their reasoning. The child's thinking is called "intuitive" because his understanding of objects and events is centered on their single most salient perceptual feature—the way things appear to be.

Classification and whole/part relations. The limitations of a perceptually based, intuitive logic are apparent when 4–7-year-olds work on *class inclusion* problems that require them to think about whole/part relations. One such problem presents children with a set of wooden beads, most of which are brown, with a few white ones thrown in. If the preoperational child is asked whether these are all wooden beads, he answers yes. If asked whether there are more brown beads than white beads, he will once again answer correctly. However, if he is then asked "Are there more brown beads or more wooden beads?," he will usually say "More brown beads." Notice that the child can conceive of a whole class (wooden beads) when responding to the first question and of two distinct classes (brown and white beads) when responding to the second. Yet the third question, which requires him to *simultaneously* relate a whole class to its component parts, is too difficult. The child's thinking about class inclusion is now *centered* on the one most salient perceptual feature—the color of the beads—so that he fails to consider that brown beads and white beads can be combined to form a larger class of wooden beads.[2]

BOX 4-2 *PLAY IS SERIOUS BUSINESS*

Play is an intrinsically satisfying activity—something that young children do for the fun of it (Rubin, Fein, & Vandenberg, 1983). Since toddlers and preschool children spend a large percentage of their waking hours at one form of play or another, we might wonder what effects these pleasurable activities will have on their social, emotional, and intellectual development.

Play begins very early in life as babies begin to repeat acts that they find satisfying or pleasurable. Piaget (1951) suggests that play is an *adaptive* activity that permits infants to practice their competencies in a relaxed and carefree way. Presumably the opportunity to manipulate novel objects and to play social games such as peek-a-boo will help to nurture curiosity, object permanence, inner experimentation, and other cognitive advances.

At 11–13 months of age, *pretend play* begins (Rubin et al., 1983). The earliest forms of pretend play are simple acts in which infants pretend to engage in familiar activities such as eating, sleeping, or drinking from a cup. As children enter the preoperational stage, their play becomes further removed from everyday activities and much more complex. They can now substitute one object (for example, a block) for another (a car) and use language in inventive ways to construct rich fantasy worlds for themselves. One notable example is that many preoperational children create "imaginary playmates" who are

given names and personality traits and who will remain near and dear to their creators during this period (Singer, 1973). Once again, Piaget views these symbolic play activities as a means for energetic young children to practice and perfect their emerging conceptual skills, thereby setting the stage for further social and intellectual growth.

Recently investigators have begun to confirm some of Piaget's ideas about play. Jeffrey Dansky (1980) observed a group of preschool children and divided them into players (those who often engage in pretend play) and nonplayers (those who rarely do). One week later, these children were observed after they had been given a number of unusual play objects such as clothespins, matchboxes,

The conservation problem. Other examples of children's intuitive reasoning come from Piaget's famous conservation studies (Flavell, 1963). One of these experiments begins with having the child adjust the volumes of liquid in two identical containers until each is said to have "the same amount to drink." Next the child sees the experimenter pour the liquid from one of these tall, thin containers into a short, broad container. He is then asked whether the remaining tall, thin container and the shorter, broader container have the same amount of liquid (see Figure 4-2 for an illustration of the procedure). Children younger than 6 or 7 will usually say that the tall, thin receptacle contains more liquid than the short, broad one. The child's thinking about liquids is apparently centered on one perceptual feature—the relative heights of the columns (tall column = more liquid). In Piaget's terminology, preoperational children are incapable of

conservation: they do not yet realize that certain properties of a substance (such as its volume or mass) remain unchanged when its appearance is altered in some superficial way.

Why do preoperational children fail to conserve? Simply because their thinking is not yet *operational*. According to Piaget, either of two cognitive operations is necessary for conservation. The first is *reversibility*—the ability to mentally undo, or reverse, an action. At the intuitive level, the child is incapable of mentally reversing the flow of action and therefore does not realize that the liquid in the short, broad container would attain its former height if it were poured back into the tall, thin container. Second, the child must be able to overcome his or her "centered" thinking in order to recognize that immediate appearances can be deceiving. Piaget suggests that children begin to "decenter" as they acquire a cognitive operation

BOX 4-2   *continued*

and paper clips. Dansky found that his "players" were more likely than "nonplayers" to use these objects in a novel, creative way. In a similar vein, Hutt and Bhavnani (1976) found that children who were judged low in exploratory play as toddlers tended five years later to be low in curiosity and to experience problems in their personal and social adjustment. By contrast, those who had been active explorers as toddlers were more likely to score high on tests of creativity and to be judged curious and independent during the grade school years. Finally, Jennifer Connolly and Anna-Beth Doyle (1984) report that preschool children who "pretend" a lot are both more socially mature and more popular with their peers than children of the same age who "pretend" less often. After reviewing the literature on children's play, Rubin et al. (1983) concluded that Piaget was right: play activities clearly foster the development of cognitive and social skills.

Play may also serve as a means of coping with emotional crises and reducing interpersonal conflicts. Piaget points out that young children are often obliged to follow rules and adapt to a social world that they do not fully understand. When children are upset by the imposition of a rule, they can cope with these conflicts and crises by retreating into a fantasy world that permits them to reflect on the incidents that have been so discomforting. Piaget argues that "it is primarily [emotional] conflicts that reappear in

symbolic play. . . . If there is a [disciplinary] scene at lunch . . . one can be sure that an hour or two afterward it will be re-created with dolls and brought to a happier solution. Either the child disciplines her doll . . . or in play she accepts what had not been accepted at lunch (such as finishing a bowl of soup she does not like, especially if it is the doll who finishes it symbolically). . . . Generally speaking, symbolic play helps in the resolution of conflicts and also in the compensation of unsatisfied needs [and] the *inversion of roles* such as obedience and authority" [Piaget & Inhelder, 1969, p. 60; italics added].

The italicized portion of Piaget and Inhelder's statement hints at another major function of symbolic play—role taking. During the preschool period, children become cowboys, firefighters, doctors, lawyers, nurses, or space travelers by simply donning the appropriate attire and pretending to be these things. They can become powerful authority figures (such as parents) by enacting that role with dolls or with younger brothers and sisters. In other words, pretend play enables preschool children to try out roles that other people play while encouraging them to think about the feelings of the individuals who actually live these roles. In the process, they will learn from their enactments and further their understanding of the social world in which they live (Rubin et al., 1983).

---

called *compensation*—the ability to focus on several aspects of a problem at the same time. Children at the intuitive stage are unable to attend simultaneously to both height and width when trying to solve the liquid conservation problem. Consequently, they fail to recognize that increases in the width of a column of liquid compensate for decreases in its height to preserve its absolute amount.

"Intuitive" impressions of social phenomena.   The child's thinking about social attributes and events is also rather "intuitive" at this time. For example, 3–5-year-olds clearly understand that they are boys or girls and that everyone can be classified according to gender. But the thinking of these young children about gender and its implications is quite egocentric and is dominated by appearances or "perceptual realities." Thus, a 4-year-old boy might well

say he could become a mommy if he wanted to or might conclude that a woman who cuts her hair short, wears men's clothing, and goes to work as a construction worker is now a man (see Tarvis & Wade, 1984). Impressions such as these suggest that preschool children have not yet conserved the concept of gender. In Chapter 12, we will see that the conservation of gender is an important contributor to sex-role development that is not attained until age 5 to 7, when most children are acquiring cognitive operations and beginning to use them in their thinking.

Has Piaget Underestimated the Preoperational Child?

Are preschool children really as illogical, intuitive, and hopelessly egocentric as Piaget claims? Apparently not. Consider, for example, that one

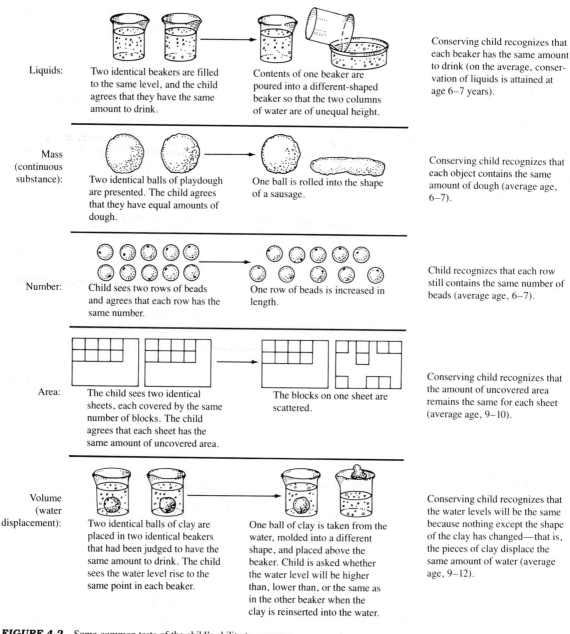

Liquids: Two identical beakers are filled to the same level, and the child agrees that they have the same amount to drink.

Contents of one beaker are poured into a different-shaped beaker so that the two columns of water are of unequal height.

Conserving child recognizes that each beaker has the same amount to drink (on the average, conservation of liquids is attained at age 6–7 years).

Mass (continuous substance): Two identical balls of playdough are presented. The child agrees that they have equal amounts of dough.

One ball is rolled into the shape of a sausage.

Conserving child recognizes that each object contains the same amount of dough (average age, 6–7).

Number: Child sees two rows of beads and agrees that each row has the same number.

One row of beads is increased in length.

Child recognizes that each row still contains the same number of beads (average age, 6–7).

Area: The child sees two identical sheets, each covered by the same number of blocks. The child agrees that each sheet has the same amount of uncovered area.

The blocks on one sheet are scattered.

Conserving child recognizes that the amount of uncovered area remains the same for each sheet (average age, 9–10).

Volume (water displacement): Two identical balls of clay are placed in two identical beakers that had been judged to have the same amount to drink. The child sees the water level rise to the same point in each beaker.

One ball of clay is taken from the water, molded into a different shape, and placed above the beaker. Child is asked whether the water level will be higher than, lower than, or the same as in the other beaker when the clay is reinserted into the water.

Conserving child recognizes that the water levels will be the same because nothing except the shape of the clay has changed—that is, the pieces of clay displace the same amount of water (average age, 9–12).

FIGURE 4-2   Some common tests of the child's ability to conserve

recent review of the literature on children's causal reasoning (Sedlak & Kurtz, 1981) suggests that even 3-year-olds recognize that (1) causes precede rather than follow effects and (2) an event that always precedes an effect (100% covariation) is more likely to be its cause than are other events that occasionally precede it. Although these are simple causal rules, they indicate that 3–4-year-olds have some understanding of causality and will not always resort to transductive reasoning.

According to Piaget (1970), children younger than 6 or 7 cannot conserve because they are too intellectually immature to understand and use the cognitive operations of reversibility and compensation that would enable them to solve conservation problems. Yet Dorothy Field (1981) has shown that 4-year-olds can learn to conserve through *identity training*—that is, by being taught that the object or substance transformed in a conservation task is still the *same* object or substance, regardless of its new appearance. In fact, 5–6-year-olds who have never been trained will often conserve things through this identity principle long before they acquire the logical operations of reversibility and compensation (Acredolo, 1982).

Finally, there is new evidence on children's egocentrism. John Flavell (Flavell, Everett, Croft, & Flavell, 1981) showed 3-year-olds a card with a dog on one side and a cat on the other. The card was then held vertically between the child (who could see the dog) and the experimenter (who could see the cat), and the child was asked which animal the experimenter could see. The 3-year-olds performed flawlessly, indicating that they could assume the experimenter's perspective and infer that he must be seeing the cat rather than the animal they could see. This and similar demonstrations reveal that preoperational children are not nearly so egocentric as Piaget had thought. However, we shouldn't assume that 2–7-year-olds are capable of seeing or appreciating another person's point of view in all situations, particularly those in which they must infer abstract, nonobservable information such as a person's motives or intentions. In Chapter 7, we will see how social perspective-taking skills gradually evolve over time, thereby enabling us to achieve a richer understanding of both our own activities and the behavior of other people.

In sum, the evidence we have reviewed clearly indicates that preoperational children are not nearly so illogical, intuitive, or self-centered as Piaget had assumed. However, Piaget is undoubtedly correct in arguing that their thinking will become much more orderly and rational once they begin to understand and use cognitive operations such as reversibility and compensation.

THE CONCRETE-OPERATIONAL STAGE (APPROXIMATELY 7 TO 11 YEARS)

During the concrete-operational period, children are rapidly acquiring cognitive operations and applying these important new skills when thinking about objects, situations, and events that they have seen, heard of, or otherwise experienced. Recall from our earlier discussion that a cognitive operation is an internal mental schema that enables the child to modify and reorganize her images and symbols and to reverse these transformations in her head. For example, the operation of reversibility allows the child to mentally reverse the flow of action and thereby recognize that a column of water that has assumed a new appearance would once again look the same if she were to pour it back into its original container. The operations of cognitive *addition* and *subtraction* permit the child to discover the logical relation between whole classes and subclasses by mentally adding the parts to form a superordinate whole and then reversing this action (subtracting) to once again think of the whole class as a collection of subclasses. Thus, the ability to operate on one's objects of thought takes the 7- to 11-year-old far beyond the static and centered thinking of the preoperational stage.

To this point, we have talked about two operational structures: class inclusion and conservation. Let's briefly consider two more.

Mental representation of actions. According to Piaget, the concrete operator is finally able to construct accurate mental representations of a complex series of actions. Suppose, for example, that we were to ask a 5-year-old preoperational child and his 10-year-old sister to sketch a map of the route to their grandmother's house across town. Even if the younger child walks there every day, he will probably fail to produce an accurate map. His problem, according to Piaget, is that he cannot conjure up a mental representation of the entire route. By contrast,

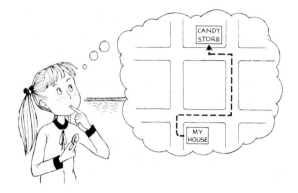

the older, operational child will find this mapmaking task rather easy, for it simply requires her to transcribe the "cognitive map" in her head (Piaget & Inhelder, 1956).

Relational logic.   A better understanding of relations and relational logic is one of the hallmarks of concrete-operational thinking. For example, concrete operators are capable of *seriation*, an operation that enables them to arrange a set of stimuli along a quantifiable dimension, such as length. A related ability is the concept of *transitivity*, which describes the relations between the elements in a serial order. If, for example, John is taller than Mark, who is taller than Sam, then John has to be taller than Sam. Although this inference seems elementary to us, children show little awareness of the transitivity principle before the stage of concrete operations.

Two additional observations are worthy of note. First, *pre*operational children can be trained to seriate and to make simple transitive inferences, so that the basic ability to understand the relations "less than" and "greater than" must precede the development of cognitive operations (Gelman & Baillargeon, 1983). Second, the transitive inferences of concrete operators are generally limited to real objects that are physically present. Indeed, 7- to 11-year-olds do not yet apply this relational logic to abstract signifiers such as the xs, ys, and zs that we use in algebra.

Summing up.   After touching on the accomplishments of the concrete-operational period, we can perhaps appreciate why many societies begin to

formally educate their young at 6 to 7 years of age. This is precisely the time when children are decentering from perceptual illusions and acquiring the cognitive operations that will enable them to comprehend arithmetic, to classify animals, people, objects, and events, to think more systematically about cause and effect, and to understand the relations between upper- and lower-case letters, between letters and the printed word, between words and sentences, and so on.

Although the acquisition and use of cognitive operations represent a significant step beyond the perceptually based "intuitive" logic of the preoperational period, the child's cognitive development is far from complete. Piaget chose the name "*concrete* operations" because he believed that children at this stage can apply their operational schemata only to objects, situations, or events that are *real* or *imaginable*. Indeed, we are about to see that 7- to 11-year-olds find it very difficult to think logically about any abstract idea or hypothetical proposition that has no basis in reality.

THE FORMAL-OPERATIONAL STAGE (AGE 11–12 AND BEYOND)

By age 11 or 12, many children are entering the last of Piaget's intellectual stages—formal operations. Perhaps the most important characteristic of formal-operational thinking is its flexibility. No longer is thinking tied to the observable or imaginable, for formal operators can reason quite logically about abstract ideas that may have no basis in reality.

Reactions to hypothetical propositions.   One way to determine whether a preadolescent has crossed over into the stage of formal operations is to present a thought problem that violates her views about the real world. The concrete operator, whose thinking is tied to objective reality, will often balk at hypothetical propositions. In fact, she may even reply that it is impossible to think about objects that don't exist or events that could never happen. In contrast, formal operators enjoy thinking about hypotheticals and are likely to generate some very unusual and creative responses. In Box 4-3 we can see the differences between concrete-operational and formal-operational thinking as children consider a hypothetical proposition that was presented in the form of an art assignment.

Hypothetical-deductive reasoning: The systematic search for answers and solutions.

The formal operator's approach to problem solving becomes increasingly systematic and abstract—much like the hypothetical-deductive reasoning of a scientist. We can easily compare the reasoning of formal operators with that of their younger counterparts by examining their responses to Piaget's famous "four beaker" problem:

> The child is given four similar flasks containing colorless, odorless liquids which are perceptually identical [but contain different chemicals]. We number them (1) . . . (2) . . . (3) . . . and (4). We add a bottle (with an eyedropper) which we call g. Mixing chemicals $1 + 3 + g$ will yield a yellow color. The experimenter presents to the subject two [unlabeled] glasses, one containing chemicals $1 + 3$, the other containing chemical 2. In front of the subject, he pours several drops of g into each of the two glasses and notes the different reactions. Then the subject is asked to simply reproduce the yellow color in a test tube, using flasks 1, 2, 3, 4, and g as he wishes [Inhelder & Piaget, 1958, pp. 108–109].

Children at the concrete-operational stage attack this problem by *doing what they saw the experimenter do*: they mix a few drops of g with chemicals from each of the four flasks and thus fail to produce the yellow color. At this point, concrete operators may say something like "I tried them all and nothing works." Usually they have to be coaxed to go beyond their visual experiences to mix three chemicals, and their higher-order combinations tend to be unsystematic. In fact, concrete operators who stumble on the correct solution by this trial-and-error approach are often unable to reproduce the yellow color when asked to repeat the process.

The formal operator begins in the same way as the concrete operator, but he subsequently proceeds to test every possible combination of three chemicals when the binary combinations (that is, $1 + g, 2 + g, 3 + g, 4 + g$) fail to solve the problem. Furthermore,

the formal operator generates the higher-order combinations according to a rational, systematic plan, often beginning with $1 + 2 + g$ and proceeding through $1 + 3 + g, 1 + 4 + g, 2 + 3 + g$, and so on until all possible combinations have been tested and the one correct solution identified. The verbalizations that accompany the formal operator's problem-solving behavior are likely to include many "if . . . then" propositional statements that characterize the logic used in hypothetical-deductive reasoning. These statements rarely appear in the protocols on concrete-operational children.

In sum, formal-operational thinking is rational, systematic, and abstract. The formal operator can now "think about thinking" and operate on *ideas* as well as tangible objects and events. Piaget believes that these new cognitive abilities are almost certain to have a dramatic impact on the adolescent's feelings, goals, and behaviors, for teenagers are suddenly able to reflect on weighty abstractions such as morality and justice, as well as more personal concerns such as their present and future roles in life, their beliefs and values, and the way things "are" as opposed to the way things "ought to be." Consequently, the adolescent approaching intellectual maturity is apt to become a bit of a philosopher, and his preoccupation with thinking and its products is the hallmark of the formal-operational period.

Does everyone achieve formal operations?

Piaget has argued that the transition from concrete to formal operations occurs very gradually. Presumably, 11–13-year-olds who are just entering the formal stage should be able to consider hypothetical propositions such as the three-eye problem, but it may be another three to four years before they are capable of the planful, systematic reasoning necessary to solve abstract puzzles such as the four-beaker problem. Piaget never identified a stage of reasoning beyond formal operations, and he thought that most people would reach this highest level of intellect by age 15–18.

Recently, investigators have been finding that adolescents are much slower to acquire formal operations than Piaget had thought. In fact, Edith

BOX 4-3   *CHILDREN'S RESPONSES TO A HYPOTHETICAL PROPOSITION*

Piaget has argued that the thinking of concrete operators is reality-bound. Presumably most 9-year-olds would have a difficult time thinking logically about objects that don't exist or events that could never happen. By contrast, children entering the stage of formal operations were said to be quite capable of considering hypothetical propositions and carrying them to a logical conclusion. Indeed, Piaget suspected that many formal operators would even enjoy this type of cognitive challenge.

Several years ago, a group of concrete operators (9-year-old fourth-graders) and a group of children who were at or rapidly approaching formal operations (11- to 12-year-old sixth-graders) completed the following assignment:

> Suppose that you were given a third eye and that you could choose to place this eye anywhere on your body. Draw me a picture to show where you would place your "extra" eye, and then tell me why you would put it there.

All the 9-year-olds placed the third eye *on the forehead between their two natural eyes.* It seems as if these children called on their concrete experiences to complete their assignment: eyes are found somewhere around the middle of the face in all people. One 9-year-old boy remarked that the third eye should go between the other two because "that's where a cyclops has his eye." The rationales for this eye placement were rather unimaginative. Consider the following examples:

Jim *(age 9½):*   I would like an eye beside my two other eyes so that if one eye went out, I could still see with two.

Vickie *(age 9):*   I want an extra eye so I can see you three times.

Tanya *(age 9½):*   I want a third eye so I could see better.

By contrast, the older, formal-operational children gave a wide variety of responses that were not at all dependent on what they had seen previously. Furthermore, these children thought out the advantages of this hypothetical situation and provided rather imaginative rationales for placing the "extra" eye in unique locations. Here are some sample responses:

Ken *(age 11½):*   *(Draws the extra eye on top of a tuft of hair.)* I could revolve the eye to look in all directions.

John *(age 11½):*   *(Draws his extra eye in the palm of his left hand.)* I could see around corners and see what kind of cookie I'll get out of the cookie jar.

Tony *(age 11):*   *(Draws a close-up of a third eye in his mouth.)* I want a third eye in my mouth because I want to see what I am eating.

When asked their opinions of the "three eye" assignment, many of the younger children considered it rather silly and uninteresting. One 9-year-old remarked "This is stupid. Nobody has three eyes." However, the 11–12-year-olds enjoyed the task and continued to pester their teacher

Neimark's (1979) review of the literature suggests that a sizable percentage of American adults do not reason at the formal level and that there are some societies where no one solves Piaget's formal-operational problems.

Why is it that some people fail to attain formal operations? One possibility is that these individuals may not have had the kinds of schooling that stress logic, mathematics, and science—experiences that Piaget believes will facilitate the transition to formal operations. Another possibility is that some individuals may not have the intellectual capacity to move from concrete to formal operations. Indeed, adolescents or adults who score even slightly below average on standardized intelligence tests rarely if ever reason at the formal level (Inhelder, 1966;

Jackson, 1965). Finally, it may be that most if not all adults are *capable* of formal reasoning but will do so only on problems that hold their interest or are of vital importance to them. For example, a competent auto mechanic might engage in genuine hypothetical-deductive reasoning when troubleshooting a car with engine problems but not in most other day-to-day activities. Indeed, Tulkin and Konner (1973) found that hunters from preliterate societies will often reason at the formal level on at least one task—tracking prey. Clearly, this is an activity of great importance to them that requires the systematic testing of inferences and hypotheses. So the failure of many adolescents and adults to *perform* at the formal-operational level on Piaget's test problems may be precisely that—a *performance* deficit rather than a

BOX 4-3 *continued*

for "fun" art assignments "like the eye problem" for the remainder of the school year.

So the results of this demonstration are generally consistent with Piaget's theory. Older children who are at or rapidly approaching formal operations are more likely than younger concrete operators to generate logical and creative responses to a hypothetical proposition and to enjoy this type of reasoning.

Tanya's, Ken's, and John's responses to the "third eye" assignment.

competence deficit. Their less than optimal performance may simply reflect either a lack of interest or a lack of experience with the test problems rather than an inability to reason at the formal level.

Let's first consider several of the more common criticisms of Piaget's approach before we take a closer look at how this theory has changed our view of social and personality development.

EVALUATION OF PIAGET'S THEORY

Jean Piaget has had a profound impact on the study of cognitive development in particular and child development in general. Like all noteworthy theories, Piaget's theory has stimulated an enormous amount of research. And as often happens when theories are scrutinized, some of this research points to some possible shortcomings in Piaget's approach.

CRITICISMS OF PIAGET'S APPROACH

The timing issue. The most frequent complaint about Piaget's theory is that children do not always display various intellectual skills or enter a particular stage of development when Piaget says they should. Yet, Piagetians do not believe that this "timing" issue is an important criticism. They argue that Piaget was interested mainly in identifying the *sequencing* of intellectual stages and that his age norms are rough approximations at best. As it turns out, later research has generally confirmed Piaget's sequential hypothesis: the sequencing of intellectual abilities that Piaget observed in his Swiss samples also describes the course and content of intellectual growth for children from hundreds of countries, cultures, and subcultures that have now been studied (Flavell, 1985). Although cultural factors do influence the *rate* of cognitive growth, the direction of development proceeds from sensorimotor intellect to preoperational thinking to concrete operations to (in many cases) formal operations.

The stage issue.   Other researchers have questioned Piaget's notion that the child's thinking develops in stages (see Flavell, 1985). If cognitive growth is stagelike, then why should it take several years before a 7-year-old who can conserve liquids and mass will be able to pass other problems, such as the conservation of volume (see Figure 4-2), that require precisely the same cognitive skills? Piaget was aware of such inconsistencies and had an explanation for them. Presumably children who can conserve liquids and mass but not volume are at a *stage* (concrete operations) where operational schemata are the dominant mental structures. Their problem is that they have not yet organized their operational structures in a way that would enable them to solve the very difficult "conservation of volume" problem.

Perhaps you can anticipate the critics' response. They argue that if cognitive growth is gradual and continuous, without sudden transformations to higher levels of functioning, then it is misleading to talk about distinct stages of intellectual growth. Although cognitive abilities do seem to emerge in a particular sequence, this intellectual progression may not be as "stagelike" as Piaget assumed.

Does Piaget's theory explain cognitive development?   Perhaps the major shortcoming of Piaget's theory is that it does not clearly indicate how children move from one stage of intellect to the next. After considering the issue, Piaget (1970) concluded that the maturation of the brain and the nervous system interacts with the child's experiences to promote cognitive growth. Presumably children are always assimilating new experiences, accommodating to those experiences, and reorganizing their schemata into increasingly complex mental structures. Maturation was thought to influence intellectual development by affecting the ways children can act on objects and events, which, in turn, will determine what they can learn from their experiences. As children continue to construct and reorganize their cognitive schemata, they will eventually come to think about old information in new ways and begin the gradual transition from one stage of intellect to the next.

Clearly, this rather vague explanation of cognitive growth raises more questions than it answers. For example, we might wonder what maturational changes are necessary before children can progress from sensorimotor to preoperational functioning or from concrete operations to formal operations. What kinds of experiences must a child have before he will construct mental symbols, understand cognitive operations, or begin to operate on ideas and think about hypotheticals? Piaget is simply not very explicit about these or any other mechanisms that might enable a child to move to a higher stage of intellect. As a result, a growing number of researchers now look on his theory as an elaborate *description* of cognitive development that has little if any explanatory value (Gelman & Baillargeon, 1983).

CONTRIBUTIONS OF PIAGET'S THEORY

Although Piagetian theory has some real shortcomings and leaves many questions unanswered, Piaget surely qualifies as the father of cognitive psychology and a leading figure in the history of the behavioral sciences. Indeed, it is almost inconceivable that our knowledge of intellectual development could have progressed to its present level had Piaget pursued his early interests in zoology and never worked with developing children.

Although his primary interest was in charting children's cognitive growth, we will see that Piaget made several important contributions to the study of social and personality development, most notably in the areas of moral reasoning (see Chapter 11) and peer relations (Chapter 14). Indeed, Piaget's notion that social development depends on cognitive development has spawned a whole new area of developmental research—the study of *social cognition*. Students of social cognition seek to determine (1) how children come to understand the thoughts, emotions, intentions, and behaviors of themselves and other people and (2) how this knowledge affects their own social behavior. The development of social cognition is the primary focus of Chapter 7, and the links between one's social-cognitive abilities and various aspects of social and personality development are discussed throughout the text.

Finally, Piaget had a profound influence on one person in particular—a young university professor named Lawrence Kohlberg who has formulated his own cognitive-developmental theory of social and personality development.

KOHLBERG'S EXTENSION OF PIAGET'S THEORY

Lawrence Kohlberg of Harvard University has used Piaget's earlier theory as a framework for understanding the growth of such social phenomena as emotional attachments, sociability, gender identities, sex typing, altruism, and moral reasoning. The basic assumptions that underlie Kohlberg's (1969) cognitive-developmental approach to socialization are as follows:

1. Cognitive development proceeds through the invariant sequence of stages that Piaget has described.

2. Emotional development parallels cognitive development. For example, true emotional attachments cannot occur until the infant develops a certain level of object permanence; sympathetic reactions that promote altruism require a lessening of egocentrism and the development of perspective-taking (role-taking) skills.

3. Social development can be described as changes that occur in the self-concept as the child compares herself with other people and acquires more and more information about her niche in the social environment.

4. The child's social cognition (or understanding of the thoughts, needs, motives, and emotions of other people) will depend on her *role-taking* abilities. The more advanced the child's role taking, the better able she will be to understand the needs of others and why they behave as they do. These changes in social cognition will then contribute to a restructuring of the *self*-concept (a step in social and personality development).

5. The direction of social and personality development is toward a state of equilibrium, or *reciprocity*, between the child's actions and the actions of others toward the child. To achieve a state of social equilibrium, the child must establish a stable, workable identity so that others will respond to her in a predictable fashion. For example, children eventually develop gender identities ("I'm a girl" or "I'm a boy") that remain constant across all situations and role relationships. The establishment of a stable gender identity is a social analogue of conservation, and it depends on the same logical operations as physical conservations.

In sum, Kohlberg's view is that social and personality development proceeds through an invariant sequence of qualitatively distinct stages. The behaviors that characterize each social stage are said to depend on the interplay between two important factors: (1) the child's level of cognitive development and (2) the kinds of social experiences the child encounters. Thus, the cognitive-developmental approach to socialization differs from other stage theories, such as the psychoanalytic approaches of Freud and Erikson, by stressing the impact of cognition and intellectual development. Kohlberg (1969) defends this emphasis by stating:

> On the logical side, our approach claims that social development is cognitively based because any description of the shape or pattern of social responses necessarily entails some cognitive dimensions. Description of the organization of the child's social responses entails a description of the way in which he perceives, or conceives, the social world and the way in which he conceives himself. . . .
>
> On the empirical side the cognitive-developmental approach derives from the fact that most marked . . . changes in the psychological development of the child are cognitive, in the mental age or IQ sense.

The influence of intelligence on children's social attitudes and behavior is such that it has a greater number of social-behavior correlates than any other aspect of personality [pp. 372–373].

Kohlberg does not deny the importance of social learning as a contributor to social and personality development. Quite the contrary: he argues that socialization could not progress very far if the child failed to assimilate social experiences and accommodate to these experiences. But Kohlberg is quick to remind us that the child's existing cognitive structures determine *how* he or she interprets social experiences and, hence, *what* is likely to be learned from interacting with others.

Kohlberg's stages of social and personality development vary considerably depending on which aspect of socialization he is considering. For example, the stage sequence involved in sex-role development is normally completed by the time the child enters concrete operations (age 7), whereas moral development may continue well into young adulthood. Clearly, Kohlberg and the many cognitive theorists whom he has influenced have had some rather interesting and provocative ideas about socialization—ideas that we will examine in some detail as we discuss the aspects of social and personality development to which their theories apply.

PHOTO 4-2   Lawrence Kohlberg (b. 1927) has formulated a cognitive-developmental theory of socialization that has influenced research on altruism, sociability, sex typing, and moral development.

SUMMARY

Jean Piaget has formulated a theory of intellectual development that has important implications for social and personality development. According to Piaget, intellectual activity is a basic life function that helps the child to adapt to the environment. He describes children as active, inventive explorers who are constantly constructing *schemata* to represent what they know and modifying these cognitive structures through the processes of *organization* and *adaptation*. Organization is the process by which children rearrange their existing knowledge into higher-order structures, or schemata. Adaptation is the process of adjusting successfully to the environment, and it occurs through two complementary activities: *assimilation* and *accommodation*. Assimilation is the process by which the child tries to interpret new experiences in terms of her existing schemata. Accommodation is the process of modifying one's existing schemata in order to interpret (or otherwise cope with) new experiences. Presumably, cognitive growth results from the interplay of these intellectual functions: assimilations stimulate accommodations, which induce the reorganization of schemata, which allows further assimilations, and so on.

Piaget believes that intellectual growth proceeds through an invariant sequence of stages that can be summarized as follows:

Sensorimotor period (0–2 years).   Over the first two years, infants come to "know" and understand objects and events by acting on them. The behavioral (or sensorimotor) schemata that a child creates to adapt to his surroundings are eventually internalized to form mental symbols that enable the child to understand the permanence of objects (including people), to imitate the behavior of absent models, and to solve simple problems on a mental level without resorting to trial and error.

Preoperational period (roughly 2–7 years).

Symbolic reasoning becomes increasingly apparent during the preoperational period as children begin to use words and images in inventive ways in their play activities. Although 2- to 7-year-olds are becoming more and more knowledgeable about the world in which they live, their thinking is quite deficient by adult standards. Piaget describes preschool children as highly *egocentric*: they view events from their own perspective and have difficulty assuming another person's point of view. And their thinking is characterized by *centration*: when they encounter something new, they tend to focus only on one aspect of it—its most obvious, or perceptually salient, feature. Consequently, they often fail to solve problems that require them to evaluate several pieces of information simultaneously.

Concrete operations (roughly 7–11 years).

During the period of concrete operations, children can think logically and systematically about concrete objects, events, and experiences. They can now perform arithmetical operations in their heads and mentally reverse the effects of physical actions and behavioral sequences. The acquisition of these and other *cognitive operations* permits the child to conserve, seriate, make transitive inferences, and construct mental representations of a complex series of events.

Formal operations (age 11 or 12 and beyond).

Formal-operational thinking is rational, abstract, and much like the hypothetical-deductive reasoning of a scientist. At this stage, adolescents can "think about thinking" and operate on ideas as well as tangible objects and events. However, many adolescents and adults may fail to reason at the formal level, particularly if they score below average on intelligence tests or have not had the kinds of educational experiences that promote the development of this highest form of intellect.

Although Piaget has accurately described the normal *sequence* of intellectual development, he often underestimates and occasionally overestimates the child's cognitive capabilities. Some investigators have challenged Piaget's assumption that development occurs in stages, while others have criticized his theory for failing to specify how children progress from one stage of intellect to the next. But despite its shortcomings, Piaget's theory has contributed enormously to our understanding of cognitive development and has spawned a new area of study—*social cognition*. Students of social cognition seek to determine how children interpret the thoughts, motives, emotions, and behaviors of themselves and other people and how this knowledge affects their social behavior and personality development.

Lawrence Kohlberg has used Piaget's theory as a framework for understanding many social-developmental phenomena. Kohlberg's most basic assumption is that social and personality development parallels cognitive development and therefore occurs in stages. Kohlberg's stages of social and personality development vary considerably for different social attributes. We will review these stages in some detail when we discuss the aspects of development to which they apply.

NOTES

1. *Neonate* is the term developmentalists use to refer to an infant who is less than 1 month of age.

2. *Centered thinking* (or *centration*) is Piaget's term for the child's tendency to focus on only one aspect of a problem when two or more aspects are relevant.

REFERENCES

ABRAVANEL, E., & Gingold, H. (1985). Learning via observation during the second year of life. *Developmental Psychology, 21,* 614–623.

ACREDOLO, C. (1982). Conservation/nonconservation: Alternative explanations. In C. J. Brainerd (Ed.), *Processes in cognitive development* (Vol. 1). New York: Springer-Verlag.

BALDWIN, J. M. (1906). *Social and ethical interpretations in mental development.* New York: Macmillan.

BOWER, T. G. R. (1982). *Development in infancy.* New York: W. H. Freeman.

BRUNER, J. S. (1964). The course of cognitive growth. *American Psychologist, 19,* 1–15.

BRUNER, J. S., Olver, R. R., & Greenfield, P. M. (1966). *Studies in cognitive growth.* New York: Wiley.

CONNOLLY, J. A., & Doyle, A. (1984). Relation of social fantasy play to social competence in preschoolers. *Developmental Psychology, 20,* 797–806.

COWAN, P. A. (1978). *Piaget: With feeling.* New York: Holt, Rinehart and Winston.

DANSKY, J. (1980). Make-believe: A mediator of the relationship between play and associative fluency. *Child Development, 51,* 576–579.

FIELD, D. (1981). Can preschool children really learn to conserve? *Child Development, 52,* 326–334.

FIELD, T. M., Woodson, R., Greenberg, R., & Cohen, D. (1982). Discrimination and imitation of facial expressions by neonates. *Science, 218,* 179–181.

FLAVELL, J. H. (1963). *The developmental psychology of Jean Piaget.* New York: Van Nostrand Reinhold.

FLAVELL, J. H. (1985). *Cognitive development.* Englewood Cliffs, NJ: Prentice-Hall.

FLAVELL, J. H., Everett, B. H., Croft, K., & Flavell, E. R. (1981). Young children's knowledge about visual perception: Further evidence for the level 1–level 2 distinction. *Developmental Psychology, 17,* 99–103.

GELMAN, R., & Baillargeon, R. (1983). A review of Piagetian concepts. In J. H. Flavell & E. M. Markman (Eds.), *Handbook of child psychology.* Vol. 3: *Cognitive development.* New York: Wiley.

HUTT, C., & Bhavnani, R. (1976). Predictions from play. In J. S. Bruner, A. Jolly, & K. Sylva (Eds.), *Play.* New York: Penguin Books.

INHELDER, B. (1966). Cognitive development and its contribution to the diagnosis of some phenomena of mental deficiency. *Merrill-Palmer Quarterly, 12,* 299–319.

INHELDER, B., & Piaget, J. (1958). *The growth of logical thinking from childhood to adolescence.* New York: Basic Books.

JACKSON, S. (1965). The growth of logical thinking in normal and subnormal children. *British Journal of Educational Psychology, 35,* 255–258.

JENNINGS, F. G. (1967, May 20). Jean Piaget: Notes on learning. *Saturday Review,* pp. 81–83.

KAYE, K., & Marcus, J. (1981). Infant imitation: The sensorimotor agenda. *Developmental Psychology, 17,* 258–265.

KOHLBERG, L. (1966). A cognitive-developmental analysis of children's sex-role concepts and attitudes. In E. E. Maccoby (Ed.), *The development of sex differences.* Stanford, CA: Stanford University Press.

KOHLBERG, L. (1969). Stage and sequence: The cognitive-developmental approach to socialization. In D. A. Goslin (Ed.), *Handbook of socialization theory and research.* Skokie, IL: Rand McNally.

MELTZOFF, A. N. (1985). Immediate and deferred imitation in fourteen- and twenty-four-month-old infants. *Child Development, 56,* 62–72.

MELTZOFF, A. N., & Moore, M. K. (1977). Imitation of facial and manual gestures by human neonates. *Science, 198,* 75–78.

MELTZOFF, A. N., & Moore, M. K. (1983). Newborn infants imitate adult facial gestures. *Child Development, 54,* 702–709.

NEIMARK, E. D. (1979). Current status of formal operations research. *Human Development, 22,* 60–67.

OLSON, G. M., & Sherman, T. (1983). A conceptual framework for the study of infant mental processes. In L. P. Lippitt (Ed.), *Advances in infancy research* (Vol. 3). Norwood, NJ: Ablex.

PIAGET, J. (1950). *The psychology of intelligence.* San Diego, CA: Harcourt Brace Jovanovich.

PIAGET, J. (1951). *Play, dreams, and imitation in childhood.* New York: Norton.

PIAGET, J. (1952). *The origins of intelligence in children.* New York: International Universities Press.

PIAGET, J. (1954). *The construction of reality in the child.* New York: Basic Books.

PIAGET, J. (1970). Piaget's theory. In P. H. Mussen (Ed.), *Carmichael's manual of child psychology* (Vol. 1). New York: Wiley.

PIAGET, J. (1977). The role of action in the development of thinking. In W. F. Overton & J. M. Gallagher (Eds.), *Knowledge and development* (Vol. 1). New York: Plenum Press.

PIAGET, J., & Inhelder, B. (1956). *The child's conception of space.* New York: Norton.

PIAGET, J., & Inhelder, B. (1969). *The psychology of the child.* New York: Basic Books.

RUBIN, K. H., Fein, G., & Vandenberg, B. (1983). Play. In E. M. Hetherington (Ed.), *Handbook of child psychology.* Vol. 4: *Socialization, personality, and social development.* New York: Wiley.

SEDLAK, A. J., & Kurtz, S. T. (1981). A review of children's use of causal inference principles. *Child Development, 52,* 759–784.

SINGER, J. (1973). *The child's world of make believe.* Orlando, FL: Academic Press.

TARVIS, C., & Wade, C. (1984). *The longest war: Sex differences in perspective* (2nd ed.). San Diego, CA: Harcourt Brace Jovanovich.

TULKIN, S. R., & Konner, M. J. (1973). Alternative conceptions of intellectual functioning. *Human Development, 16,* 33–52.

WERNER, H. (1957). The concept of development from a comparative and organismic point of view. In D. B. Harris (Ed.), *The concept of development.* Minneapolis: University of Minnesota Press.

YOUNGER, B. (1985). The segregation of items into categories by ten-month-old infants. *Child Development, 56,* 1574–1583.

5

EARLY SOCIAL AND EMOTIONAL DEVELOPMENT I:
EMOTIONAL GROWTH AND ESTABLISHMENT OF AFFECTIONAL TIES

ARE BABIES EMOTIONAL CREATURES?

Facial and Vocal Expressions of Emotion

Recognizing Emotions: Can Babies Read Faces and Voices?

Emotions and Early Social Development

A DEFINITION OF ATTACHMENT

THE CAREGIVER'S ATTACHMENT TO THE INFANT

Early Emotional Bonding

Infant Characteristics That Promote Caregiver-to-Infant Attachments

Problems in Establishing Caregiver-to-Infant Attachments

(continues)

In 1891 G. Stanley Hall stated that adolescence is the most crucial stage of life for the development of personality. Hall characterized the teenage years as a time when interests are solidified, long-lasting friendships emerge, and important decisions are made about one's education, career, and (in those days) choice of a mate. In other words, he viewed adolescence as the period when individuals assume personal and interpersonal identities that will carry them through their adult lives.

This viewpoint was soon challenged by Sigmund Freud (1905/1930), who believed that many of the decisions an adolescent makes about the future are predetermined by his or her reactions to earlier life experiences. In fact, Freud proclaimed that the foundations of the adult personality are laid during the first five to six years of life and that the process of personality development begins the moment that a baby is first handed to his or her parents.

Today we know that Freud was right in at least one respect: social and emotional development does begin very early in life. Although few contemporary theorists believe that our personalities are "set in stone" during the first five or six years, it is now apparent that the kinds of emotional relationships that infants develop with their close companions may well affect the ways they relate to other people later in life. Early social experiences are important—and infancy is truly a sensitive period for social and personality development.

Our primary focus over the next two chapters will be a major social and emotional milestone of infancy—the development of affectional ties between children and their closest companions. We will briefly review what is known about infants' ability to recognize and display emotions and then see how developmentalists define a true emotional attachment. At this point, we will concentrate on the *process* of becoming attached and will try to determine how infants and their companions establish these close emotional ties. Next, we will consider two common fears that attached infants often display and see why these fearful reactions often emerge during the latter part of the first year. And in Chapter 6, we will continue our discussion of early social development by reviewing the rapidly expanding base of evidence that suggests that the kinds of emotional attachments that infants are able to establish (or the lack thereof) may have very important implications for their later social, emotional, and intellectual well-being.

ARE BABIES EMOTIONAL CREATURES?

Do babies have feelings? Do they experience and display specific emotions such as happiness, sadness, fear, and anger the way that older children and adults do? Most new parents think they do. In one recent study, more than half the mothers of 1-month-old infants said their babies displayed distinct affective (that is, emotional) responses to indicate interest, surprise, joy, anger, and fear (Johnson, Emde, Pannabecker, Stenberg, & Davis, 1982). Although one might argue that this is simply a case of proud mothers reading much too much into the behavior of their babies, there is now reliable evidence that infants—even very young ones—are indeed emotional creatures.

FACIAL AND VOCAL EXPRESSIONS OF EMOTION

Over the past several years, Carroll Izard and his colleagues at the University of Delaware have studied emotional expression in infants by videotaping babies' responses to such events as grasping an ice cube, having a toy taken away, or seeing their mothers return after a separation (Izard, 1982; Trotter, 1983). Izard's procedure is straightforward: he asks raters, who are unaware of the events that an infant has experienced, to tell him what emotion the child is feeling from the facial expression that the child displays. These studies reveal that different adult raters observing the same expression reliably see the same emotion in a baby's face. Apparently, infants are quite capable of communicating their feelings.

Izard's experiments have led him to conclude that various emotions appear at different times over the first two years. At birth, babies show interest, distress (in response to pain), disgust, and the suggestion of a smile. Angry expressions appear at 3–4 months—about the same time that infants acquire sufficient control of their limbs to push unpleasant stimuli away. Sadness also emerges at about this time, and fear makes its appearance at age 5–7 months, followed by shame and shyness. Finally, complex emotions such as guilt and contempt are first observed during the second year of life.

Babies can also express emotions vocally. Apparently, healthy neonates are capable of producing at least three distinct cries: a rhythmic "hunger" cry that starts with a whimper and becomes louder and more sustained; a "mad" cry that is also rhythmic but much more intense; and a "pain" cry that begins with a loud shriek, followed by a brief silence and then more vigorous crying. Peter Wolff (1969) devised an interesting experiment to see whether young, relatively inexperienced mothers could distinguish these three cries. While supposedly observing the neonates in their own rooms, Wolff played a tape recording of the infant crying and waited for the mothers to respond. And respond they did: at the sound of a pain cry, mothers immediately came running to see what was wrong. However, mothers responded much more slowly (if at all) to either "hungry" or "mad" cries. So it appears that different cries convey very different messages, even to new mothers who have had little experience with babies.

Critics of such demonstrations argue that the so-called "emotional" expressions of infancy are really nothing more than global displays of positive and negative affect. However, these critics have not adequately explained how adults are able to show such remarkable agreement about the specific feeling an infant is experiencing (for example, distress versus disgust) when they have nothing more to go on than a tape recording of the infant's facial or vocal expression. Moreover, babies react in predictable ways to particular kinds of experiences. During the first few weeks, soft sounds or novel visual displays are likely to elicit signs of interest and the suggestion of a smile. When given an inoculation, 2-month-old infants show the facial expression that Izard (and

Interest: brows raised; mouth may be rounded; lips may be pursed.

Fear: mouth retracted; brows level and drawn up and in; eyelids lifted.

Disgust: tongue protruding; upper lip raised; nose wrinkled.

Joy: bright eyes; cheeks lifted; mouth forms a smile.

Sadness: corners of mouth turned down; inner portion of brows raised.

Anger: mouth squared at corners; brows drawn together and pointing down; eyes fixed straight ahead.

PHOTOS 5-1   Young infants display a variety of emotional expressions.

others) call distress, whereas older infants react with anger (Izard, Hembree, Dougherty, & Coss, 1983). And there is even some consistency to children's affective displays, for the infants who react more vigorously to a distressing event on one occasion are likely to remain the most vigorous responders when retested several months later (Hyson & Izard, 1985). So it appears that early patterns of affective expression are tied to specific kinds of eliciting events and are relatively stable over time. Regardless of whether one calls them "emotions" (and most contemporary researchers do), it is obvious that infants are able to communicate a variety of feelings to their close companions.

RECOGNIZING EMOTIONS: CAN BABIES READ FACES AND VOICES?

When do infants first notice and respond to the emotional expressions of other people? Surprising as it may seem, they are prepared to react to certain vocal signals at birth or shortly thereafter. In Box 2-2, for example, we learned that neonates who hear another infant cry will soon begin to cry themselves, thus showing their responsiveness to the distress of another baby.[1] Over the first year, parents (particularly mothers) speak to infants in high-pitched tones that are acoustic concomitants of positive emotions such as happiness (Fernald & Simon, 1984). By the end of the neonatal period (age 4–6 weeks), infants can discriminate their mothers' voices from those of female strangers when the mother speaks in her normal high-pitched "happy" tone but not when she speaks in a monotone (Mehler, Bertoncini, Barriere, & Jassik-Gerschenfeld, 1978). Of course, this does not mean that infants recognize that their mothers are "happy"; but it does imply that they are closely attending to the parameters of speech by which we convey emotions.

There is considerable debate about when infants are first capable of detecting emotions in the *facial* expressions of other people. In an early study (La Barbera, Izard, Vietze, & Parisi, 1976), 4- to 6-month-old infants were shown slides of adult faces expressing joy or anger or a neutral emotion. These youngsters looked longer at the joyful expression than at the other two, thus suggesting that they could discriminate happy emotions from neutral or negative ones. However, other investigators (for example, Oster, 1981) have argued that what may have captured the infants' attention was not the model's "happy" emotion at all but, rather, the physical contrast between the smiling model's teeth and the rest of the face—a contrast not apparent in the angry or neutral emotive display. Subsequent research suggests that the critics may be right: infants younger than 4 to 6 months are relatively insensitive to emotional configurations shown in photographs, although their performance improves dramatically (at least for distinguishing the emotions of happiness,

fear, and anger) between 7 and 9 months of age (see Caron, Caron, & Myers, 1985; Nelson & Dolgin, 1985).

At about the same time that infants are beginning to recognize emotional expressions in photographs, they are becoming quite proficient at reading their mothers' emotional reactions to uncertain situations and using this information to regulate their own behavior. This *social referencing* function is nicely illustrated in two recent studies in which 8–10-month-old infants were approached by strangers (normally a fear-provoking event at this age). In both studies, infants responded much more favorably to the stranger's approach if their mothers had either spoken positively to the stranger or issued a warm greeting than if the mothers had reacted neutrally or negatively toward this person (Boccia & Campos, 1983; Feinman & Lewis, 1983). Although mothers and other close companions will remain the primary source of information about uncertain situations throughout infancy, 15-month-old infants have at least begun to rely on the emotional reactions of less familiar acquaintances as cues for how they should be feeling or responding to strange settings or circumstances (Feiring, Lewis, & Starr, 1984).

EMOTIONS AND EARLY SOCIAL DEVELOPMENT

What role do infants' emotions play in early social development? Clearly, they serve a communicative function that is likely to affect the behavior of caregivers. For example, cries of distress summon close companions. Early suggestions of a smile or expressions of interest may convince caregivers that their baby enjoys their company and is willing to strike up a social relationship with them. Later expressions of fear or sadness serve as feedback that the infant is insecure or feeling blue and is in need of attention or comforting. Anger may imply that the infant wishes her companions to cease whatever they are doing that is upsetting her, whereas joy serves as a prompt for caregivers to prolong an ongoing interaction or perhaps signals the baby's willingness to accept new challenges. Thus, infants' emotions are adaptive in that they promote social contact and help caregivers to adjust their behavior to the infant's needs and goals. Stated another way, the emotional expressions of infancy help infants and their close companions to "get to know each other."

At the same time, the infant's emerging ability to recognize and interpret the emotions of others is a tremendously important achievement that enables the child to infer how he should be feeling or behaving in a variety of situations. The beauty of this social referencing is that children can *quickly* acquire knowledge in this way. For example, a sibling's joyful reaction to the family pooch should indicate that this "ball of fur" is a friend rather than an unspeakable monster. A mother's look of distress and overt expression of concern might immediately suggest that the knife in one's hand is an implement to be avoided. And given the frequency with which expressive caregivers direct an infant's attention to important aspects of the environment, it is likely that the information inherent in their emotional displays will contribute in a major way to the child's understanding of the world in which he lives.

A DEFINITION OF ATTACHMENT

Social developmentalists have discovered that the young of most higher species form close emotional ties to their mothers or a "mother figure" during infancy. To the layperson, this "attachment" appears to be a bond of love that is often attributed to maternal tendencies such as "mother instinct" or "mother love." Developmentalists are willing to concede that mothers and other close companions are likely to become attached to an infant long before the infant is attached to them. However, it now appears that mother love must be nurtured and that most infants are capable of promoting such a caregiver-to-infant bond from the moment of birth.

Just what is a social *attachment*? John Bowlby (1958, 1973) uses the term to refer to the *strong and enduring affectional ties* that bind a person to his or her most intimate companions. According to Bowlby, people who are attached will *interact often* and will try to *maintain proximity* to each other.

Thus, an 8-month-old boy who is attached to his mother may show his attachment by doing whatever it takes—crying, clinging, approaching, or following—to establish or maintain contact with her. Leslie Cohen (1974) adds that attachments are *selective* in character and imply that the company of some people (*attachment objects*) is more pleasant or reassuring than that of others. For example, a 2-year-old girl who is attached to her mother should prefer the mother's company to that of a stranger whenever she is upset, discomforted, or afraid.

Although our focus in this chapter is on the attachments that develop between infants and their close companions, there are many other kinds of attachments that individuals may form. For example, children may become attached to playmates and form solid friendships. Adults are typically attached to their mates. In fact, people often develop intense attachments to those cuddly kittens, puppies, or other house pets that respond to them and seem to enjoy their company. All these relationships are similar in that the attachment object is someone (or something) special with whom we are motivated to maintain contact.

How do infants and caregivers become attached to each other? Let's address this important issue by looking first at caregivers' reactions to infants.

THE CAREGIVER'S ATTACHMENT TO THE INFANT

People sometimes find it hard to understand how a parent might become attached to a neonate. After all, newborn infants can be demanding little creatures who drool, spit up, fuss, cry, dirty their diapers on a regular basis, and often require a lot of attention at all hours of the day and night. Since babies are associated with so many distasteful consequences, why don't their parents learn to dislike them?

One reason that parents may overlook or discount the negative aspects of child care is that they have often begun to form emotional attachments to their infant *before* they experience many of the unpleasantries of parenthood. Marshall Klaus and John Kennell

(1976) believe that caregivers can become emotionally bonded to an infant during the first few hours after birth—provided that they are given an opportunity to get to know their baby. And just what kinds of contact are necessary to promote this early emotional bonding? Let's see what Klaus and Kennell have to say.

EARLY EMOTIONAL BONDING

Several years ago, Klaus and Kennell (1976) proposed that a mother's attitude toward her infant may depend, in part, on her experiences with that child shortly after giving birth. Specifically, they hypothesized that early skin-to-skin contact between mothers and their babies would make mothers more responsive to their infants and thereby promote the development of strong mother-to-infant emotional bonds.

To test this hypothesis, Klaus and Kennell studied 28 young mothers who had just delivered full-term, healthy infants. During their three-day stay in the hospital, half the mothers followed the traditional routine: they saw their babies briefly after delivering, visited with them 6–12 hours later, and then had half-hour feeding sessions with their infants every four hours. The mothers in the second, or "extended contact," group were permitted five "extra" hours a day to cuddle their babies, including an hour of skin-to-skin contact that took place within three hours of birth. At the end of these three-day routines, the two groups of mothers went home and began to care for their infants full-time.

One month later, Klaus and Kennell interviewed the 28 mothers, examined their babies, and filmed each mother feeding her infant. The results of this follow-up were striking: mothers who had had extensive early contact with their infants seemed much more involved with them and held them much closer during their feeding sessions than mothers who had experienced the normal hospital routine. Perhaps even more remarkable were the results of a second follow-up conducted when the babies were a year old: mothers from the extended-contact group were still more soothing, cuddling, and nurturing, and they were also more likely than mothers from the "normal routine" group to report that they missed

their babies while away from home at work. As for the infants, those who had had extended early contact with their mothers outperformed those who had not on tests of physical and mental development.

Klaus and Kennell believe that the amount of early contact a mother has with her infant is less important than the *timing* of that contact. In the hospital setting, mothers who have had some close contact with their babies in the first 10–12 hours of life tend to caress their infants more and hold them closer while feeding than do mothers whose initial contacts with their infants were delayed or abbreviated (Gaulin-Kremer, Shaw, & Thoman, 1977; Grossmann, Thane, & Grossmann, 1981). Kennell, Voos, and Klaus (1979) suggest that the first 6–12 hours is a *sensitive period* for the emotional bonding of a mother to her infant: presumably mothers are most likely to develop the strongest possible affection for their babies if they have had skin-to-skin contact with them during this particular time.

Why Might Early Contact Be Important?

Why do mothers build these emotional bridges to their infants just after giving birth? Kennell et al. (1979) have suggested that hormones present at the time of delivery may help to focus the mother's attention on her baby and make her more susceptible to forming an early attachment. If these hormones should dissipate before a mother has any extended contact with her infant, she will presumably become less responsive to her baby, much as animals do if separated from their offspring in the first few hours after giving birth.

Although the "hormonal mediation" hypothesis may seem to account for the findings we have reviewed, there are reasons to question this interpretation of early emotional bonding. For one thing, mothers who have had close contact with their infants soon after giving birth are not always more nurturant or more involved with their babies (Svejda, Campos, & Emde, 1980), particularly if their pregnancies were unplanned (Grossmann et al., 1981). Moreover, the hormonal hypothesis cannot explain why fathers who are present at the birth (or soon thereafter) often become so fascinated with their neonate, wishing to touch, hold, or caress the baby. Indeed, some investigators (for example, Greenberg & Morris, 1974) have interpreted fathers' "engrossment" with their babies as a form of emotional bonding that is similar to that experienced by mothers and is obviously not attributable to the presence of pregnancy hormones.

If the hormonal mediation hypothesis does not explain the early affection or engrossment that parents often display toward their newborn infants, then what does? One idea offered by ethologists is the notion that caregivers are genetically predisposed to react favorably and with affection to a neonate's pleasing social overtures (see Bowlby, 1973). Of course, there may be other plausible explanations for these early "engrossment" effects—explanations that make no reference to any innate predispositions of the parent. Consider a possibility suggested by social-psychological research on the interpretation of emotions. Perhaps the intense emotional arousal (fear or apprehension) that parents experience during childbirth is *reinterpreted* in a positive light when they are handed an infant who gazes attentively at them, grasps their fingers, and seems to snuggle in response to their caresses. If parents should then attribute these positive feelings *to the baby and her behavior*, it is easy to see how they might feel rather affectionate toward their neonate and become emotionally involved with her. However, parents who have little or no early contact with their neonates are unable to attribute their existing emotional arousal to a beautiful, responsive baby. In fact, they often end up labeling their emotions as exhaustion or a sense of relief that the ordeal of pregnancy and childbirth is finally over (Grossman, Eichler, Winickoff, & Associates, 1980). Perhaps you can see that these latter attributions are unlikely to make parents feel especially affectionate toward the child they have just borne.

Is Early Contact Necessary for Optimal Development?

Klaus and Kennell's sensitive-period hypothesis implies that new parents show a basic "readiness" to become emotionally involved with their infant during the first few hours after the baby is born. As we have seen, there is some evidence to support this proposition. However, Klaus and Kennell also claim that parents who have had little or no contact with their neonates during the sensitive period may never become as attached to these infants as they might had they had skin-to-skin contact with them during the first few hours. This second theoretical proposition is much more controversial.

In her recent review of the emotional-bonding literature, Susan Goldberg (1983) reports that mothers who have had early contact with their infants do seem to be somewhat more responsive and affectionate toward their babies for the first three days of life. But in contrast to Klaus and Kennell's research, Goldberg finds that these "early contact" effects are not large and may not last very long. In the one study in which mothers and infants were carefully observed over a nine-day period, the advantages of early contact steadily declined over time. By the ninth day after birth, early-contact mothers were no more affectionate or responsive toward their infants than mothers who had had no skin-to-skin contact with their babies for several hours after delivery. Indeed, the delayed-contact mothers showed a dramatic increase in responsiveness over the nine-day observation period—suggesting that the hours immediately after birth are not nearly so critical as Klaus and Kennell assumed (Goldberg, 1983).

Michael Rutter (1979) is another theorist who believes that the events of the first few hours are unlikely to have a permanent effect on mother/infant relationships. To support his claim, Rutter notes that adoptive parents often develop close emotional ties to their children even though they have rarely had *any* contact with their adoptees during the neonatal period. In fact, the likelihood that a mother and her infant will become securely attached is just as high in adoptive families as in nonadoptive ones (Singer, Brodzinsky, Ramsay, Steir, & Waters, 1985).

Sara Rode and her associates (Rode, Chang, Fisch, & Sroufe, 1981) have recently followed up on a number of 12–19-month-old infants who had been born prematurely (or seriously ill) and had spent the first several weeks of their lives in intensive care. Although many of the parents occasionally visited their children in the hospital, they did not have the close early contact with their babies that Klaus and Kennell believe to be necessary for optimal parent-to-infant emotional bonding. Nevertheless, Rode et al. found that the vast majority of these infants were closely attached to their parents during the second year of life. In fact, the percentage of securely attached infants in Rode's sample (71%) compares favorably with the 66–70% typically observed among 12-month-old, full-term infants who have had a fair amount of early contact with their caregivers (Ainsworth, Blehar, Waters, & Wall, 1978). Rode and her associates concluded that

> although prematurity and physical separation place stress on the family system, of greater importance to the infant-caregiver attachment relationship may be the length of time that the infant has been at home with the caregiver and the quality of care experienced. The quality of the infant-caregiver attachment relationship is a product of the entire history of infant-caregiver interaction. While the earliest days and hours are important . . . attachment is a process that evolves during the first year of life [p. 190].

In sum, research on early emotional bonding suggests that parents can become highly involved with their infants during the first few hours if they are permitted to touch, hold, cuddle, and play with their babies. As a result, many hospitals have altered their routines to allow and encourage these kinds of experiences. However, it appears that this early contact is neither crucial nor sufficient for the development of strong parent-to-infant or infant-to-parent attachments. Stable attachments between infants and caregivers are not formed in a matter of minutes, hours, or days: they build rather slowly from social interactions that take place over many weeks and months. So there is absolutely no reason for parents who do not have early skin-to-skin contact with their infant to assume that they will have problems establishing a warm and loving relationship with the child.

INFANT CHARACTERISTICS THAT PROMOTE CAREGIVER-TO-INFANT ATTACHMENTS

John Bowlby (1958, 1969) believes that human infants are born with a repertoire of reflexes and other physical characteristics that are likely to elicit highly favorable reactions from their caregivers. For example, the rooting,[2] sucking, and grasping reflexes may lead parents to believe that their infant enjoys being close to them. Other reactions such as the reflexive smile (see Box 5-1), laughter, or spontaneous bab-

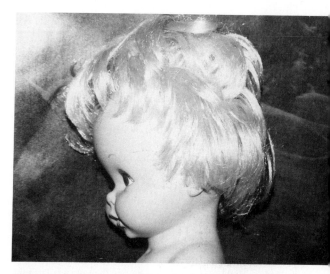

PHOTO 5-2   The kewpie-doll syndrome. A short face, round protruding cheeks, and an elongated forehead are characteristics that make an infant appear "cute" and thereby elicit people's attention.

bling are also likely to have a positive effect on close companions. In fact, parents may interpret their infant's smiles, laughs, and babbles as indications that the child is contented and that they are effective caregivers. Thus, a smiling or babbling infant can reinforce caregiving activities and thereby increase the likelihood that parents or other nearby companions will want to attend to this happy little person in the future.

Even the reflexive cry, which parents frequently describe as aversive, can promote caregiver-to-infant attachments. Bowlby views the cry as a "distress signal" that elicits the approach of those who are responsible for the infant's care and safety. Presumably, responsive caregivers who are successful at quieting their babies will then become the beneficiaries of positive responses, such as smiling and babbling, that should reinforce their caregiving behavior and make them feel even closer to their contented infants.

Oh, Baby Face: The Kewpie-Doll Syndrome

Konrad Lorenz (1943) has argued that a baby's "kewpie doll" appearance (large forehead; chubby, protruding cheeks; soft, rounded features) makes the

BOX 5-1   *THE ASOCIAL SMILE BECOMES A SOCIAL SIGNAL*

John Bowlby (1958, 1969) believes that smiling is a bio-logically programmed response that plays an important role in the development of affectional ties between caretakers and their infants. Smiling does begin very early, although the neonate's first smiles are not necessarily "social": soft sounds, changes in brightness, and the appearance of new visual patterns are examples of nonsocial stimuli that may elicit smiles from very young infants (Ambrose, 1963; Bower, 1982). Some neonates will even smile in their sleep (Emde, Gaensbauer, & Harmon, 1976). So these early smiles appear to be *reflexive* responses to a variety of internal or external events. In fact, this smile often strikes observers as more of a grimace than a true smile.

True *social smiling* begins as early as 3 weeks of age, when the sound of a female voice may produce a grin. In the fifth or sixth week of life, the human face (particularly the eyes) replaces the female voice as the most potent elicitor of smiling (Wolff, 1963). By 3–4 months of age, infants are apt to crack broad smiles in response to either a familiar or a strange face, although they may be quicker to smile at familiar company (Bowlby, 1969; Dunkeld, 1978). Apparently the onset of social smiling is influenced by both genetic and maturational factors. For example, identical twins are more similar than fraternal twins in the age at which they begin to smile at faces (Freedman, 1965). Moreover, infants who are born six weeks premature do not begin to smile at social stimuli until 12 weeks of age—about six weeks behind full-term infants (Dittrichova, 1969). However, premature and full-term infants start to

smile at approximately the same *conceptional* age—46 weeks—indicating that maturation plays an important role in the emergence of social smiling.

Once infants begin to smile at caregivers, their tendency to keep smiling at them may depend, in part, on caregivers' reactions to these signals. Parents often interpret the in-fant's smile as a wonderful thing; in fact, one study found that an adult's most typical response to a baby's smile was to smile back at the baby (Gewirtz & Gewirtz, 1968). And how do infants react to smiles and other social ges-tures? They smile all the more at their playful companions (Brackbill, 1958; Wahler, 1967). At about 6 months of age, most infants who have been raised in a home setting with their parents become quite selective, generally saving their smiles for familiar company. This *discriminated smiling response* is one sign that an infant is becoming attached to his close companions.

Learning theorists explain the increasingly social charac-ter of an infant's smile by analyzing the interactions be-tween infants and caregivers. Presumably an infant will smile more and more at faces because her parents, siblings, and other caregivers will reinforce these greetings by smil-ing at, speaking to, or otherwise entertaining her. Moreov-er, a baby's smile can reinforce caregiving activities and increase the amount of time that parents and other caregiv-ers will *want* to spend with their happy, responsive infant. So continued interactions between a smiling infant and a responsive caregiver should lead to an increase in recipro-cal smiling and to the development of a "special" rela-

infant appear cute or lovable to caregivers. Recently, Thomas Alley (1981) found that adults aged 18–47 judged line drawings of "babyish" faces to be much "cuter" than those of 4-year-old children. When com-menting on the babyish figures, Alley's subjects often described them as "adorable" or "pleasant to look at" or noted that "you receive pleasure from a cute person" (p. 653). Younger boys and girls also react positively to babyish facial features, although girls begin to show an even stronger interest in infants after reaching menarche (Goldberg, Blumberg, & Kriger, 1982). Finally, infants clearly differ in physical attractiveness (Hildebrandt, 1983), and adults often respond more favorably to attractive babies than to unattractive ones (Hildebrandt & Fitz-gerald, 1981; Stephan & Langlois, 1984). So it

seems that infantlike facial features (or the "kewpie doll" look) may help to elicit the kinds of attention from caregivers that will promote social attachments. However, more research is needed to tell us whether adults actually find it easier to become attached to highly attractive infants than to babies whose facial features are somewhat less than attractive.

Interactional Synchrony

One thing that many new parents find absolutely fascinating about infants is that their babies often seem so responsive to them. Full-term, healthy babies are particularly responsive to the sound of the human voice. When spoken to, neonates will often open their eyes, look at their caregivers, synchronize their bodily movements with the breaks and pauses in

BOX 5-1 *continued*

tionship that both parties enjoy. Here, then, is what seems a very plausible explanation for the origin of a discriminated smiling response in young infants.

Cognitive theorists stress that the development of the social smile may also depend on the child's cognitive and perceptual growth. According to Jerome Kagan (1971), infants are active information processors who try to understand what they are experiencing by matching these events to their existing schemata. Presumably, when infants can assimilate events into their cognitive schemata, they will indicate their pleasure at this accomplishment by cracking a broad smile.

Cognitive-perceptual theorists would point out that infants are developing schemata for familiar patterns during the second month of life—precisely the time that they begin to smile regularly at faces. Perhaps the first social smiles simply indicate that the infant recognizes the human face as a familiar pattern. At 3 to 4 months of age, when infants are first capable of discriminating faces, they suddenly become quicker to smile at a familiar face. However, the fact that the infant still smiles at unfamiliar faces suggests that his schema for faces is very general. As the child's facial schema becomes more differentiated, only familiar faces will be recognized and will elicit smiles. Thus, the discriminated smiling response may arise because strange faces are now simply too discrepant with the child's existing schemata to be assimilated and "understood."

In sum, the smile is initially an asocial, reflexive re-

Few signals will attract as much attention as a baby's social smile.

sponse that becomes increasingly "social" in character over the first six months of life. Although biological factors may determine the onset of social smiling, the further development of the smile from an indiscriminate social signal to a greeting reserved for close companions depends on the child's cognitive development and experiences with caregivers.

---

a companion's speech, and occasionally even vocalize themselves (Condon & Sander, 1974; Rosenthal, 1982). Moreover, Craig Peery (1980) reports that 1-day-old infants are already synchronizing their head movements with those of adults: frame-by-frame photographic analyses of the interactions between infants and an admiring female adult revealed that each infant reliably (1) withdrew his or her head at the approach of the adult and (2) approached the adult as she withdrew her head. Clearly, infants are capable of engaging in synchronized interactions with caregivers from the first day of life.

Over the next several weeks and months, caregivers and infants will ordinarily have many opportunities to interact and to develop and perfect *synchronized routines* that both parties will probably enjoy.

Psychologists who have observed these exquisite interactions have likened them to "dances" in which the partners take turns responding to each other's lead. Daniel Stern (1977) has provided a written account of one such "dance" that occurred as a mother was feeding her 3-month-old infant:

A normal feeding, not a social interaction, was underway. Then a change began. While talking and looking at me, the mother turned her head and gazed at the infant's face. He was gazing at the ceiling, but out of the corner of his eye he saw her head turn toward him and he turned to gaze back at her . . . now he broke rhythm and stopped sucking. He let go of the nipple . . . as he eased into the faintest suggestion of a smile. The mother abruptly stopped talking and, as she watched his face begin to transform, her eyes opened a little wider and her eyebrows raised a bit.

His eyes locked on to hers, and together they held motionless for an instant. . . . This silent and almost motionless instant continued to hang until the mother suddenly shattered it by saying "Hey!" and simultaneously opened her eyes wider, raising her eyebrows further, and throwing her head up toward the infant. Almost simultaneously, the baby's eyes widened. His head tilted up and, as his smile broadened, the nipple fell out of his mouth. Now she said, "Well, hello! . . . Heello . . . Heeelloo," so that her pitch rose and the "hellos" became longer and more emphatic on each successive repetition. With each phrase, the baby expressed more pleasure, and his body resonated almost like a balloon . . . filling a little more with each breath. The mother then paused and her face relaxed. They watched each other expectantly for a moment . . . then the baby suddenly took an initiative. . . . His head lurched forward, his hands jerked up, and a fuller smile blossomed. His mother was jolted into motion. She moved forward, mouth open and eyes alight, and said "Oooooh . . . ya wanna play do ya . . . yeah? . . ." And off they went [p. 3].

In this example, it was the mother who started the episode by gazing at the baby's face and capturing his attention. However, young infants are quite capable of initiating, maintaining, and even terminating these synchronized exchanges if they become overly excited or discomforted in some way. In the interaction that Stern describes, the mother soon became much more boisterous in her play and raised her voice to a level where her baby appeared apprehensive. At this point, the baby tried to withdraw from the game by looking away. Once he had composed himself, he gazed again at his mother and "exploded into a big grin." The mother then became even more playful than before, and the baby immediately frowned and looked away. Clearly, he had had enough excitement for the moment. The mother picked up on this signal and gave the baby his nipple, and he began to feed once again. Their synchronized social exchange was suddenly over.

In sum, infants seem naturally responsive to other people—almost as if they had an innate capacity for engaging in synchronized interaction. Stern (1977) has suggested that these synchronized routines may occur several times a day and are important contributors to social attachments. As an infant continues to interact with a particular caregiver, he will learn what this person is like and how he can regulate her attention. Of course, the caregiver will probably become more proficient at interpreting the baby's social and emotional signals and will learn how to adjust her behavior to successfully capture and maintain his attention. As the caregiver and the infant practice their routines and become better "dance partners," their relationship should become more satisfying for both parties and may eventually blossom into a strong reciprocal attachment.

PROBLEMS IN ESTABLISHING CAREGIVER-TO-INFANT ATTACHMENTS

Although we have talked as if caregivers invariably became attached to their infants, this does not always happen. As we will see, some babies are hard to love, some caregivers are hard to reach, and some environments are not very conducive to the establishment of secure emotional relationships.

Some Babies May Be Hard to Love

Although we have emphasized that neonates are remarkably proficient at attracting attention and sustaining social interactions, many babies lack certain qualities that would endear them to their caregivers. For example, premature infants (that is, babies born at least three weeks before their due dates) are not only inalert and unresponsive to others' bids for attention, but they also tend to be physically unattractive and slow to smile and frequently emit high-pitched, nonrhythmic cries that are perceived as much more aversive than those of healthy, full-term infants (Frodi et al., 1978; Zeskind, 1980). Moreover, some full-term and otherwise healthy infants have difficult temperaments: they are at risk of alienating close companions because they are extremely active and irritable, are irregular in their habits, and will resist or ignore caregivers' social overtures (Crockenberg, 1981).

Recent research shows that adults may have a hard time establishing stable and synchronized routines with very irritable and/or unresponsive infants (Greene, Fox, & Lewis, 1983; Thoman, Acebo, & Becker, 1983). Indeed, Greene et al. (1983) report that infants who often cry during social interactions seem to disrupt the development of a positive reciprocal relationship with their caregivers. Although the mothers of these fretful infants are quite willing to provide comfort and attend to basic needs, they spend less time in playful and affectionate social exchanges than mothers whose babies are less fretful and more responsive to social play.

Learned helplessness theory (Seligman, 1975) helps to explain why socially aloof infants might alienate their caregivers. In its most basic form, the theory states that people will become apathetic and will stop trying to control their environments should they perceive little or no connection between their actions and the rewards or punishments they receive. Thus, caregivers who are repeatedly unsuccessful at soothing an irritable infant or at bidding for the attention of an unresponsive one may simply stop trying to achieve these objectives, choosing instead to provide their child with only the most basic and routine care (see Donovan & Leavitt, 1985).

Fortunately, most parents will eventually establish satisfying routines and become quite attached to their difficult or unresponsive infants. One way to help the process along is to identify neonates who may be difficult to love and then teach their caregivers how to elicit favorable reactions from these sluggish or irritable companions. In Box 5-2, we will take a closer look at one such training program that appears to be quite effective at achieving these aims.

Some Caregivers Are Hard to Reach

Caregivers sometimes have personal quirks or characteristics that seriously hinder or even prevent them from establishing close emotional ties to their infants. A caregiver who is chronically depressed, for example, may not be sufficiently responsive to an infant's social signals to establish a synchronous and satisfying relationship. In fact, Marian Radke-Yarrow and her associates (Radke-Yarrow, Cummings, Kuczynski, & Chapman, 1985) report that insecure attachments are the *rule* rather than the exception if the child's primary caregiver has been diagnosed as clinically depressed.

A caregiver's own family history is also an important consideration. Parents who were themselves unloved, neglected, or abused as children may expect their babies to be "perfect" and to love them right away. When the infant is irritable, fussy, and inattentive (as all infants will be at times), these emotionally insecure adults are apt to feel as if the baby had rejected them. They may then withdraw their affection—sometimes to the point of neglecting the child—or become physically abusive (Rutter, 1979; Steele & Pollack, 1974).

Problems may also arise if caregivers try to follow preconceived notions about how infants should be raised rather than adjusting their parenting to the infant's state or temperamental characteristics. For example, a father who believes that his baby requires a large amount of stimulation may end up overexciting an "excitable" infant; a mother who is afraid of spoiling her baby may be reluctant to soothe a child who has become overly excited (Korner, 1974). Unfortunately, caregivers who often misread their baby's signals and end up trying to fit a square peg into a round hole may be less likely to establish the kind of interactional synchrony with their infant that would help them to become attached to her (Sprunger, Boyce, & Gaines, 1985).

Finally, some caregivers may be disinclined to love their babies because their pregnancies were unplanned and their infants are unwanted. In one study conducted in Czechoslovakia (Matejcek, Dytrych, & Schuller, 1979), mothers who had been denied permission to abort an unwanted pregnancy were judged to be less closely attached to their children than a group of same-aged mothers of similar marital and socioeconomic status who had not requested an abortion. Although both the "wanted" and the "unwanted" children were physically healthy at birth, over the next nine years the unwanted children were more frequently hospitalized, made lower grades in school, had less stable family lives and poorer relations with peers, and were generally more irritable than the children whose parents had wanted them. Here, then, are data suggesting that a caregiver's failure to become emotionally attached to an infant could have long-term effects on the child's physical, social, emotional, and intellectual well-being.

Of course, these findings do not imply that all wanted children will be loved or that all unwanted children will remain unloved. Nevertheless, it would appear that mothers who give birth to an unplanned and unwanted child are less likely than mothers who plan their pregnancies to become closely attached to their infants.

BOX 5-2   *BRAZELTON TRAINING: EFFECTS ON PARENTS AND INFANTS*

Irritable, unresponsive, and apathetic infants who are at risk of alienating their close companions can often be identified very soon after birth by virtue of their low scores on the *Brazelton Neonatal Behavioral Assessment Scale*. This simple test, which is usually administered on the third day of life and repeated several days later, is a measure of the infant's neurological health and responsiveness to stimulation. It assesses the strength of 20 infant reflexes as well as the infant's reactions to 26 situations, many of which are "social" in character (for example, responses to cuddling, the infant's orientation to the examiner's face and voice, general alertness, and irritability). High-risk infants who may fail to establish synchronized routines with caregivers are fairly easy to spot: their performance on the test is characterized by mild irritability, inalertness, lack of attention to social stimuli, and poor motor control (Brazelton, 1979; Waters, Vaughn, & Egeland, 1980). Dr. T. Berry Brazelton (1979) believes that many of the emotional difficulties forecasted by low scores on the Brazelton test can be prevented if parents of these unresponsive babies learn how to properly stimulate and comfort their infants.

One method of teaching parents how to interact with their babies is to have them either watch or take part as the Brazelton Neonatal Behavioral Assessment Scale is administered to their child. The Brazelton test is well suited as a teaching device because it is designed to elicit many of the infant's most pleasing characteristics, such as smiling, cooing, and gazing. As the test proceeds, parents will see that their neonate can respond positively to other people, and they will also learn how to elicit these pleasant interactions.

"Brazelton training" has proved to be an effective strategy indeed. Mothers of high-risk children who have had the Brazelton procedure demonstrated to them become more responsive in their face-to-face interactions with their babies. In addition, the infants of these mothers score higher on the Brazelton test one month later than high-risk infants whose mothers were not trained (Widmayer & Field, 1980).

Other investigators (Myers, 1982; Worobey & Belsky, 1982) have found that Brazelton training also has positive effects on the parents of healthy, responsive infants. In Barbara Myers's (1982) study, either mothers or fathers in a treatment group were taught to give the Brazelton test to their neonates, while parents in a control group received no such training. When tested four weeks later, parents who had received the Brazelton training were more knowledgeable about infant behavior, more confident in their caretaking abilities, and more satisfied with their infants than control parents. In addition, fathers who had been trained reported that they were much more involved in caring for their infants at home than fathers who had received no training.

Although many hospitals provide brief instructions on how to diaper and bathe a baby, parents are seldom told anything about the neonate's basic abilities, such as whether newborns can see, hear, or respond to people. Brazelton training clearly illustrates what a new baby is capable of doing, and it appears to have a number of positive effects on both parents and their infants. Clearly this technique may prove to be somewhat less effective in the long run than extensive interventions in which a child care professional visits the family regularly over the first year, observing parent/child interactions and providing guidance when necessary (Barrera, Rosenbaum, & Cunningham, 1986). However, Barbara Myers (1982), a strong proponent of the Brazelton technique, argues that "the treatment is relatively inexpensive, it only takes about an hour, and the parents reported enjoying it. This type of intervention needs to be tested [further] on other populations . . . for possible consideration as a routine portion of a hospital's postpartum care" (p. 470).

Some Environments Are Hazardous to the Formation of Healthy Attachments

To this point, we have noted that the character of an adult's attachment to his or her infant is influenced by the adult's characteristics as well as the infant's. However, we should also recognize that interactions between infants and caregivers take place within a broader social and emotional context that may affect how a particular caregiver and infant will react to each other. For example, mothers who must care for several small children with little or no assistance may find themselves unwilling or unable to devote much attention to their newest baby, particularly if the infant is at all irritable or unresponsive (Belsky, 1980; Crockenberg, 1981). Indeed, researchers have consistently reported that the more children a woman has had, the more negative her attitudes toward children become, and the more difficult she thinks her children are to raise (Garbarino & Sherman, 1980; Hurley & Hohn, 1971).

In recent years, family sociologists have argued that the quality of a caregiver's relationship with his or her spouse can have a dramatic effect on parent/infant interactions. For example, parents who are depressed about an unhappy marriage sometimes look to their babies for love and attention when their spouses fail to satisfy these emotional needs (Steele & Pollack, 1974). However, they will probably fail to find the support they are seeking, for Jeffrey Cohn and Edward Tronick (1982) report that 3-month-old infants soon become wary and begin to protest should their mothers behave as if they were depressed. Cohn and Tronick suggest that the infant's negative reaction to depression may further depress the adult and make it difficult for him or her to establish a satisfying routine with the child. This problem may be particularly apparent if the baby has already shown a tendency to be irritable and unresponsive. Indeed, Jay Belsky (1981) reported that neonates who are "at risk" for later emotional difficulties (as indicated by their poor performance on the Brazelton scale) are likely to have nonsynchronous interactions with their parents *only when the parents are unhappily married.* Taken together, these findings indicate that a stormy marriage is a major environmental hazard that can hinder or even prevent the establishment of close emotional ties between parents and their infants.

THE INFANT'S ATTACHMENT TO CAREGIVERS

Although adults may become emotionally attached to an infant very soon after the baby is born, the infant will require a little more time to form a genuine attachment to caregivers. Many theories have been proposed to explain how and why infants become emotionally involved with the people around them. But before we consider these theories, we should briefly discuss the stages that babies go through in becoming attached to a close companion.

DEVELOPMENT OF PRIMARY SOCIAL ATTACHMENTS

Several years ago, Rudolph Schaffer and Peggy Emerson (1964) studied the development of social attachments by following a group of Scottish infants from early infancy to 18 months of age. Once a month, mothers were interviewed to determine (1) how the infant responded when separated from close companions in seven situations (for example, being left in a crib; being left in the presence of strangers) and (2) the persons to whom the infant's separation responses were directed. A child was judged to be attached to someone if separation from that person reliably elicited a protest.

Schaffer and Emerson found that infants pass through the following steps, or stages, as they develop close ties with their caregivers:

• *The asocial stage (0–6 weeks).* The very young infant is largely an asocial creature: many kinds of social and nonsocial stimuli will elicit favorable reactions, and few produce any kind of protest. By the end of this period, infants are beginning to show a distinct preference for social stimuli, such as a smiling face.

• *The stage of indiscriminate attachment (6 weeks to 6–7 months).* During this period, infants prefer human company, and they are apt to protest when an adult puts them down or leaves them alone. However, the children's protests are truly indiscriminate: they dislike being separated from anyone, whether strangers or regular companions.

It now appears that the social preferences of 3–6-month-old infants are not nearly so "indiscriminate" as Schaffer and Emerson had thought. Three-month-old infants can easily discriminate their mothers' faces from those of strangers (Barrera & Maurer, 1981), and babies apparently recognize their mothers' voices (and odors, if breast-fed) during the first two weeks of life (Cernoch & Porter, 1985; DeCasper & Fifer, 1980). Between 3 and 6 months of age, infants are more likely to smile at their mothers than at unfamiliar companions (Watson, Hayes, Vietze, & Becker, 1979) and are often more quickly soothed by a regular caregiver (Bower, 1982). But despite this emerging preference for familiar company, 3- to 6-month-old infants are no more likely to protest the departure of a regular companion than that of a stranger.

• *The stage of specific attachments (about age 7 months).* At about 7 months of age, infants begin to protest only when separated from one particular individual, usually the mother (see Figure 5-1). In addition, many infants begin to fear strangers at about this time. Schaffer and Emerson interpret these data as an indication that the infants have formed their first genuine attachments.

• *The stage of multiple attachments.* Within weeks after forming their initial attachments, about half the infants in Schaffer and Emerson's study were becoming attached to other people (fathers, siblings, grandparents, or perhaps even a regular babysitter). By 18 months of age, very few infants were attached to only one person, and some were attached to five or more.

Schaffer and Emerson originally believed that infants who are multiply attached have a "hierarchy" of attachment objects and that the person at the top of the list is their most preferred companion. However, later research indicates that each of the infant's attachment objects may serve a slightly different function, so that the person whom an infant prefers most may depend on the situation. For example, most infants prefer the mother's company if they are upset or frightened (Lamb & Stevenson, 1978). However, fathers seem to be preferred as playmates, possibly because much of the time they spend with their infants is "play time," and fathers are more likely than mothers to play unusual, rough-and-tumble games that infants seem to enjoy (Clarke-Stewart, 1978; Lamb, 1981).[3] Schaffer (1977) is now convinced that "being attached to several people does not necessarily imply a shallower feeling toward each one, for an infant's capacity for attachment is not like a cake that has to be [divided]. Love, even in babies, has no limits" (p. 100).

THEORIES OF ATTACHMENT

If you have ever cared for a kitten or a puppy, you may have noticed that pets seem most responsive to the person who feeds them. Is this true of human

FIGURE 5-1 The developmental course of attachment during infancy

infants? Some theorists think so, but many others disagree. We will now look at several theories that attempt to explain how (or why) infants become attached to their regular companions.

For years, theorists have argued about the reasons that babies come to "love" their caregivers. The history of this theoretical controversy is interesting because each theory makes different assumptions about the part that infants play in their social relationships and the roles that caregivers must enact in order to win the baby's affection. The four theories that have been most influential are those reviewed in Chapters 2 through 4—psychoanalytic theory, learning theory, cognitive-developmental theory, and ethological theory.

Psychoanalytic Theory: Attachments Develop from Oral Activities

According to Freud, infants are "oral" creatures who derive pleasure from such activities as sucking, biting, and mouthing objects. Presumably the infant will invest psychic energy in and become attached to any person or object that provides oral pleasure. Thus, infants were thought to become emotionally involved with their mothers because it is usually the mother who gives pleasure to the oral child by feeding her. Freud believed that infants will become securely attached to their mothers if the mother is relaxed and generous in her feeding practices, thereby allowing the child a lot of oral pleasure.

Erik Erikson also believes that the feeding situation is a major contributor to social attachments. According to Erikson, a mother who lets her infant go hungry at times or who weans her baby too early is likely to have an anxious child who fails to develop a sense of trust in other people. Erikson contends that an untrusting child may become overdependent—one who will "lean on" others, not necessarily out of love or a desire to be near but solely to ensure that his or her needs are met. Presumably children who have not learned to trust others during infancy are likely to avoid close mutual-trust relationships throughout their lives.

Before we examine the research on feeding practices and their contribution to social attachments, we need to consider another viewpoint that assumes that feeding is important—learning theory.

Learning Theory: Rewardingness Leads to Love

Learning theorists consider the mother a logical attachment object for her baby. Not only do mothers feed their infants, they also change them when they are wet or soiled, provide warmth, tender touches, and soft, reassuring vocalizations when they are upset or afraid, and promote changes in the "scenery" in what otherwise could be a rather monotonous environment for babies who cannot get up and move about on their own. What will a baby make of all this? According to learning theorists, an infant will eventually associate the mother with pleasant feelings and pleasurable sensations, so that she becomes a conditioned stimulus for positive outcomes (in the language of learning theory, a *secondary reinforcer*). Once the mother (or any other caregiver) has attained the status of a conditioned, or secondary, reinforcer, the infant is attached—he will now do whatever is necessary (smile, coo, babble, or follow) to attract the caregiver's attention or to remain near this valuable and rewarding person.

Like psychoanalytic theorists, many learning theorists believe that feeding is important in determining the quality of an infant's attachment to the primary caregiver. Robert Sears (1963) suggests two reasons that feeding may be a special kind of caregiving activity. First, the mother is often able to sit down with her infant and provide *many comforts*—including warmth and tactile, visual, and vocal stimulation, as well as satisfying the baby's hunger and thirst—*all at once*. Second, feeding is an activity that should elicit positive responses from the infant (smiling, cooing) that are likely to increase a caregiver's affection for the child. So feeding is thought to be important because it provides positive reinforcers to both the caregiver and her infant—reinforcers that will strengthen their feelings of affection for each other.

Just how important is feeding?   In 1959 Harry Harlow and Robert Zimmerman reported the results of a study designed to compare the importance of feeding and tactile stimulation for the development of social attachments in infant monkeys. The monkeys were separated from their mothers in the first day of life and reared for the next 165 days by two surrogate mothers. As you can see in Photo 5-3, each surrogate mother had a face and a well-proportioned body constructed of wire. However, the body of one surrogate (the "cloth mother") was wrapped in foam rubber and covered with terrycloth. Half the infants were always fed by this warm, comfortable cloth mother, the remaining half by the rather uncomfortable "wire mother." At several points during the experiment, the attachment of each infant to its surrogate mothers was measured by noting how much time the infant spent in close contact with each mother as well as which mother the infant would run to when frightened.

If feeding is especially important to the development of primary social attachments, we would expect the monkeys to spend more time in contact with the mother who had fed them, regardless of the amount of tactile comfort she provided. We would also expect the monkeys to run to the feeding mother whenever they were upset or afraid. However, Harlow and Zimmerman found that all the infants spent more time on the cloth mother, *regardless of which mother had fed them* (see Figure 5-2). In addition, all infants showed a clear preference for the cloth mother when they were frightened by novel stimuli (marching toy bears, wooden spiders) that were placed in their cages. Apparently the cloth mothers provided the reassurance the infants were seeking, for Harlow and Zimmerman (1959) noted that

> in spite of their abject terror, the infant monkeys, after reaching the cloth mother and rubbing their bodies about hers, rapidly come to lose their fear of the frightening stimuli. Indeed, within a minute or two most of the babies were visually exploring the thing which so shortly before had seemed an object of evil. The bravest of the babies would actually leave the mother and approach the fearful monsters, under, of course, the protective gaze of their mothers [p. 423].

Clearly, the implication of Harlow and Zimmerman's classic study is that feeding is *not* the most important determinant of an infant's attachment to caregivers.

Although Harlow's subjects were monkeys, research with human infants paints a similar picture. In their study of Scottish infants, Schaffer and Emerson (1964) asked each mother the age at which her child had been weaned, the amount of time it had taken to wean the child, and the feeding schedule (regular interval or demand feeding) that she had used with her baby. None of these feeding practices predicted the character of an infant's attachment to his or her mother. In fact, Schaffer and Emerson found that, in 39% of the cases, the person who usually fed, bathed, and changed the child (typically the mother) was not even the child's primary attachment object! These findings are clearly damaging to any theory that states that feeding and feeding practices are the primary determinants of the child's first social attachment.

Current viewpoints. How, then, do attachments develop? Contemporary learning theorists would argue that feeding plays a role in the process but that satisfying the child's hunger is only one of the many nice things that caregivers do for their infants. Presumably the visual, tactile, and vocal stimulation that adults provide when they interact with their infants will also make these regular companions seem rather attractive or rewarding (Gewirtz, 1969). Although "contact comfort" may be a powerful contributor to attachments in infant monkeys, Harriet Rheingold

PHOTO 5-3 The wire and cloth surrogate mothers used in Harlow's research. Infant monkeys remain with the cloth mother even though they must stretch to the wire mother in order to feed. This was one of the observations that led Harlow to conclude that feeding is not the most important contributor to primary social attachments.

(1961) has argued that visual and auditory contact between a mother and her infant is more important than either feeding or physical contact for promoting attachments in human beings. Rheingold's hypothesis receives some support from an experiment by Roedell and Slaby (1977), who found that over a three-week period 5-month-old infants developed a preference for an adult who provided visual and auditory stimulation *from a distance*, as opposed to a second adult who regularly stroked, rocked, and patted them.

In sum, learning theorists now believe that infants are attracted to people who are quick to respond to their signals and who provide them with a variety of pleasant or rewarding experiences. Indeed, Schaffer and Emerson (1964) found that the two aspects of a mother's behavior that predicted the character of her infant's attachment to her were (1) her responsiveness to the infant's behavior and (2) the total amount of stimulation she provided. Mothers who responded quickly to their infants' social signals and who often played with their babies had infants who were closely attached to them.

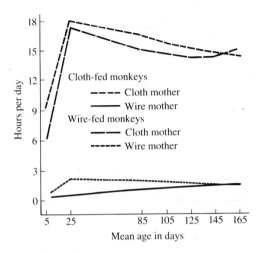

FIGURE 5-2 Average amount of time infant monkeys spent in contact with their cloth and wire mother surrogates. The monkeys spent much more of their time clinging to the cloth mother, regardless of which mother had fed them.

Cognitive-Developmental Theory: Attachments Depend on Cognitive Development

Proponents of Jean Piaget's cognitive-developmental theory believe that an infant's ability to form social attachments depends, in part, on his level of intellectual development. Before an attachment can occur, the infant must be able to discriminate familiar persons (that is, potential attachment objects) from strangers. He must also recognize that close companions continue to exist even when they are absent (Kohlberg, 1969; Schaffer, 1971). This latter ability is an example of the object concept (or *object permanence*), discussed in Chapter 4. Presumably infants who recognize that objects (or persons) have a permanent existence will develop stable schemata for people with whom they regularly interact. They should then prefer these people to all others and may even protest when they cannot locate their close companion(s).

Is the timing of social attachments related to cognitive development? Apparently so. In their classic study of Scottish infants, Schaffer and Emerson (1964) noted that attachments normally appear during the third quarter of the first year (age 7–9

months)—precisely the time that infants begin to show some evidence of acquiring the object concept. Drawing from these observations and the work of Piaget, Schaffer (1971) then proposed that attachments will not occur until the fourth sensorimotor substage, when infants first begin to search for and find objects hidden behind a screen.

An experiment by Barry Lester and his associates (Lester, Kotelchuck, Spelke, Sellers, & Klein, 1974) was designed to evaluate Schaffer's hypothesis. In this study, 9-month-old and 12-month-old infants were given a test that measured their level of object permanence. Then each infant was exposed to a number of brief separations from the mother, the father, and a stranger. The results lend some support to the cognitive-developmental viewpoint. The 9-month-old infants who scored high (Stage 4 or above) in object permanence showed stronger protests when separated from their mothers than infants who scored lower (Stage 3 or below). Among the 12-month-old infants, those who scored high in object permanence showed more separation protest at the departure of *either the mother or the father* than infants whose object permanence was less well developed. Neither age group protested separations from a stranger. Using separation protest as evidence of attachment, it would appear that the cognitively advanced 9-month-olds were attached to their mothers, while the cognitively advanced yearlings were attached to both parents. Thus, Lester's findings not only are consistent with the developmental stages of attachment reported by Schaffer and Emerson (1964) but also indicate that the timing of the primary attachment is related to the child's level of object permanence.

Ethological Theory: Attachments May Be Biologically Programmed

Ethologists have proposed an interesting explanation for social attachments that is sometimes called "evolutionary" theory because of its distinct evolutionary overtones. The major assumption of the ethological approach is that all animals, including human beings, are born with a number of species-specific "signals," or behavioral tendencies, that promote certain social behaviors (Ainsworth, Bell, & Stayton, 1974;

Bowlby, 1969, 1973). Presumably these innate signals are products of a species' evolutionary history, and each of these attributes serves some purpose that increases the chances of survival for the individual and the species.

What is the purpose of a social attachment? According to John Bowlby (1969, 1973), infant/caregiver attachments serve the same function for all species—namely, to protect the young from prolonged discomfort, from predators, and perhaps from fear itself. Of course, ethologists would argue that the long-range purpose of the primary social attachment is to ensure that the young of each successive generation live long enough to reproduce, thereby enabling the species to survive.

Let's briefly consider some of the evidence that led Bowlby to propose his evolutionary theory of attachment.

Attachment in precocial birds. More than 100 years ago, investigators first noted that chicks would follow almost any moving object—another chicken, a duck, or a human being—as soon as they were able to walk (Spaulding, 1873). Konrad Lorenz (1937) observed the same "following response" in young goslings, a behavior he labeled *imprinting* (or stamping in). Lorenz also noted that (1) imprinting is automatic (that is, the young fowl does not have to be taught to follow), (2) imprinting occurs only within a narrowly delimited *critical period* after the bird has hatched,[4] and (3) imprinting is irreversible—once the bird begins to follow a particular object, it will remain attached to it. Although later research has challenged some of Lorenz's original conclusions (see Rajecki, 1977), contemporary ethologists remain firm in their belief that imprinting is an innate response that attaches an infant to its mother, thereby increasing the infant's chances of survival.

Attachment in mammals. The tendency to cling to or to maintain physical contact with the mother is commonly observed among infants of many mammalian species. We have previously touched on Harry Harlow's work showing the importance of tactile stimulation and contact comfort for the development of primary attachments in infant monkeys. Although the attachment of a young monkey to its primary caregiver is certainly not an example of imprinting, Harlow's research convinced John Bowlby that the tendency of young animals to cling to their mothers is an inborn, *preadapted* response that promotes the development of social attachments.

Attachment in human infants. According to Bowlby (1969, 1973), human infants have inherited a number of responses that help them to maintain contact with a caregiver. Three of these response systems—sucking, grasping, and following (first by keeping the caregiver in sight and later by crawling or walking)—are said to serve an *executive function*: they are initiated by the infant and require only a minimal response from the caregiver. Two other responses, smiling and vocalizing (crying or babbling), serve a *signaling function* by encouraging caregivers to approach the infant and to provide some kind of attention or comfort. A baby's "kewpie doll" appearance is yet another inborn characteristic that may make an infant seem desirable to others (Alley, 1981). Thus, infants are said to be *active* participants in the attachment process: their role (initially, at least) is to emit a number of preprogrammed signals that are likely to attract attention or influence the behavior of caregivers.

Bowlby contends that adults are biologically programmed to respond to an infant's signals in much the same way that infants are programmed to react to the sight, sound, warmth, and touch of their caregivers. As a mother (or other primary caregiver) becomes more proficient at reading and reacting to her baby's signals, the infant should become ever more responsive to her. The end result of these increasingly personal interactions is the development of a *mutual* bond, or attachment, between the infant and his or her most intimate companion(s).

A common misunderstanding. A hasty reading of ethological theory might lead one to conclude that human attachments are "automatic"—that all the child requires to form one is a caregiver with whom to interact. This view is incorrect. Although infants may be preprogrammed to beam various signals to other people, these innate responses may eventually wane if they fail to produce favorable reactions from an unresponsive caregiver (Ainsworth et al., 1978). So infants are not biologically programmed to attach themselves to the closest available human; attachments are a product of a *history* of interaction in which each participant has learned to respond in a meaningful way to the social signals of his or her partner. In Chapter 6, we will consider some of the consequences that infants may experience when their primary caregivers are habitually unresponsive to their bids for attention.

Comparing the Four Theoretical Approaches

Although the four theories we have reviewed are different in many respects, each theory has had something to offer. Even though feeding practices are not as important as psychoanalytic theorists had originally thought, it was Sigmund Freud who stressed that we will need to know more about mother/infant interactions if we are to understand how babies form emotional attachments. Learning theorists followed up on Freud's ideas and concluded that caregivers play an important role in the infant's emotional development. Presumably the infant is likely to view a responsive companion who provides many comforts as a rewarding individual who is worthy of affection. Ethologists can agree with this point of view, but they would add that the infant is an active participant in the attachment process. That is, infants emit preprogrammed signals to which caregivers are biologically predisposed to respond. Thus, ethologists view infants as socially adept creatures who are capable of promoting the very interactions from which attachments are likely to develop. Finally, cognitive theorists have contributed to our understanding of early emotional development by showing that the timing of social attachments is related to the child's level of intellectual development. In sum, it makes no sense to tag one of these theories as "correct" and to ignore the other three, for each theory has helped us to understand how and why infants become attached to their most intimate companions.

DEVELOPMENT OF FEARFUL REACTIONS

At about the same time that infants are establishing close affectional ties to a caregiver, they often begin to display negative emotional outbursts that may puzzle or even annoy their close companions. In this section we will look at two of the common fears of infancy—stranger anxiety and separation anxiety—and try to determine why these negative reactions are likely to emerge during the second half of the first year.

STRANGER ANXIETY

Nine-month-old Billy is sitting on the floor in the den when his mother leads a strange person into the room. The stranger suddenly walks toward the child, bends over, and says "Hi, Billy! How are you?" If Billy is like many 9-month-olds, he may stare at the stranger for a moment and then turn away, whimper, and crawl toward his mother.

This wary reaction to a stranger, or stranger anxiety, stands in marked contrast to the smiling, babbling, and other positive greetings that infants often emit when approached by a familiar companion. Schaffer and Emerson (1964) noted that most of the infants in their sample reacted positively to strangers up until the time they had formed an attachment (usually at about 7 months of age) but then became fearful of strangers shortly thereafter. Studies of North American children tend to confirm this finding: wary reactions to strangers often emerge at 6–7 months of age, peak at 8–10 months, and gradually decline in intensity over the second year (Sroufe, 1977). However, stranger anxiety may never completely subside, for 2-, 3-, and even 4-year-olds are apt to show at least some signs of wariness when approached by a stranger in an unfamiliar setting (Greenberg & Marvin, 1982).

At one time, stranger anxiety was thought to be a true developmental milestone—that is, an inevitable response to unfamiliar company that supposedly characterized all infants who had become attached to

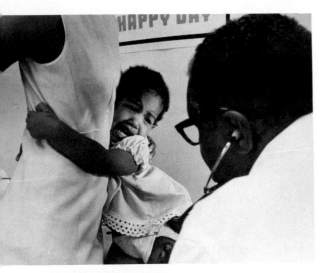

PHOTO 5-4   Although infants become more tolerant of strangers during the second year, stranger anxiety is a reaction that may never completely subside. Unavoidable contact with an intrusive stranger is likely to upset many 2-, 3-, and even 4-year-olds.

a caregiver. However, recent research indicates that infants are not always afraid of strangers and, in fact, may sometimes react rather positively to an unfamiliar companion (Bretherton, Stolberg, & Kreye, 1981; Rheingold & Eckerman, 1973). Before we try to understand why 6–12-month-old infants are sometimes wary of strangers, it may be helpful to note the circumstances under which stranger anxiety is most likely to occur.

When Will Infants Fear a Stranger?

Among the many factors that affect an infant's reactions to a stranger are the availability of a familiar companion, the setting in which the stranger appears, the ways the stranger responds to the infant, and the stranger's physical characteristics.

Availability of familiar companions.   Infants react much more negatively to the approach of a stranger when they are separated from their mothers or other close companions. In one study, strangers approached 6–12-month-old infants who were sitting either on their mothers' laps or in infant seats a few feet away. Although fewer than one third of the

infants showed a wary reaction when seated with their mothers, about two thirds of them frowned, turned away, whimpered, or cried if they were seated only four feet from their mothers (Morgan & Ricciuti, 1969). Apparently contact with a loved one provides a sense of security that enables infants to respond more constructively to the approach of a stranger. This is particularly true if caregivers treat the stranger like a friend or use a positive tone of voice when talking to their infants about the stranger (Feinman & Lewis, 1983; Feiring et al., 1984).

The setting.   A number of years ago, a student noted that her baby reacted much more negatively to strangers while visiting the supermarket than at home. Her hypothesis was that babies are apprehensive in unfamiliar settings and that this wariness is then magnified by the approach of an unfamiliar person.

Later research suggests that this young woman was a rather astute observer. Alan Sroufe and his associates (Sroufe, Waters, & Matas, 1974) found that few 10-month-old infants were wary of strangers when tested within the familiar confines of the home but that most of them reacted negatively to strange companions when tested in an unfamiliar laboratory. Sroufe et al. also found that an infant's familiarity with a strange setting made a difference: whereas only 50% of the infants were apprehensive when they had had ten minutes to get used to a strange room, over 90% became upset if a stranger approached within a minute after they had been placed there. Clearly, the setting in which a stranger appears is an important determinant of an infant's reactions to that person.

The stranger's behavior.   After reviewing the literature, Alan Sroufe (1977) concluded that an infant's response to a stranger often depends on the stranger's behavior. Strangers who initially keep their distance and then approach slowly while smiling, talking, or offering a familiar toy are likely to elicit a positive reaction from a 10–12-month-old. Presumably some of the apprehension surrounding the approach of an unfamiliar person can be offset if the stranger behaves in a friendly manner (like a caregiver) and offers a familiar object (such as a toy) with which the child will feel comfortable. By contrast, intrusive strangers who approach rapidly and force themselves on the child (for example, by trying to pick her up) are likely to elicit a fearful reaction.

Some investigators have argued that an infant will react quite favorably to any stranger who allows the child to regulate their initial interactions. Mary Levitt (1980) tested this hypothesis by exposing 10-month-old infants to a stranger who wanted to play peek-a-boo. In the *contingent response* condition, the infant could control the stranger's peek-a-boo behavior: every time the child touched a cylinder in front of him or her, the stranger opened a curtain and said "Hi, [baby's name]." In the *noncontingent response* condition, the stranger simply opened the curtain and vocalized a total of 14 times according to a schedule that the infant could not control. After playing peek-a-boo for seven minutes, the stranger reappeared, approached the child, and lifted him or her. Figure 5-3 shows the results in simplified form. Note that infants who had been able to control the stranger's peek-a-boo behavior reacted much more positively to the stranger's later intrusions than infants who had had no prior control over the stranger. Apparently, strange adults can become "friends" if they allow the infant to regulate their earliest interactions.

Do Levitt's findings imply that strangers should never initiate games or activities with a potentially wary infant? *No, they do not.* Recently, Inge Bretherton and her associates (Bretherton et al., 1981) have found that 12–24-month-old children are quite willing to play with a friendly stranger who actively bids for their attention as long as the stranger (1) is not overly intrusive and (2) offers a toy (or suggests an activity) with which the infant is familiar. In fact, friendly strangers are apt to be more successful at establishing rapport with an infant if they cautiously take the initiative and allow the infant to control the pace of their activities rather than sitting back and waiting for the child to initiate an interaction with them (Bretherton et al., 1981).

The strange child: Friend or fiend. A number of years ago, Michael Lewis and Jeanne Brooks (1974) exposed 7–19-month-old infants to strange

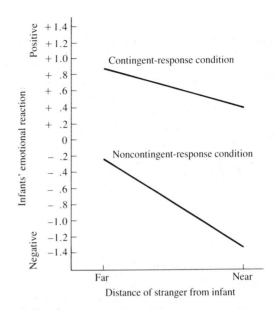

FIGURE 5-3 Emotional reactions of 10-month-old infants to the approach of a stranger. Infants in the contingent condition, who had had some control over the stranger's peek-a-boo behavior, reacted favorably to the stranger's approach. In contrast, infants in the noncontingent condition were quite wary of a stranger they could not control, and their wariness increased as the stranger became more intrusive.

adults and a strange child (a 4-year-old girl). As the adults approached, the infants became quite wary. However, the approach of the strange child typically elicited a mildly *positive* reaction. Could the infants have been responding favorably to the child because she was relatively small, as they were? To find out, Brooks and Lewis (1976) exposed 7–24-month-old infants to a strange adult, a strange child, and an adult midget who was the same size as the strange child. The infant reacted much more negatively to both the normal-sized adult and the midget than to the child. Surely these subjects did not prefer the strange child solely on the basis of size; otherwise they would have reacted positively to the "child-sized" midget. Apparently, adultlike facial features were the cues that elicited a wary response.

Although infants may initially react to other children as if they were friends rather than fiends, it is not at all unusual for a youngster to become wary of peers at some point during the second year (Jacobson,

1980; Kagan, Kearsley, & Zelazo, 1975). In the following section, we will take a closer look at this "delayed reaction" to unfamiliar peers as we consider how various developmental theorists would explain stranger anxiety.

Why Are Infants Wary of Strangers?

We have seen that stranger anxiety follows a regular developmental course, normally emerging at about the same time as the primary social attachment. But why do children who are attached to someone suddenly become wary of strangers? Let's consider three points of view.

The "fear of separation" hypothesis.

Psychoanalytic and social-learning theorists (Sears, 1963; Spitz, 1950) have proposed that a child's stranger anxiety actually represents a fear of becoming separated from or losing the person(s) to whom he or she is attached. Consistent with this point of view are the observations that wary reactions first appear *after* the infant has become attached to someone and that attached infants will often cling to their mothers or other close companions when a stranger approaches (Morgan & Ricciuti, 1969; Schaffer & Emerson, 1964). However, the "fear of separation" hypothesis does not explain why infants sometimes react very positively to strangers and may continue to do so even after they have seen their mothers leave the room (Ainsworth et al., 1978). How can we explain these findings?

The ethological perspective.

John Bowlby (1973) suggests that there are a number of events that qualify as natural clues to danger. In other words, some situations have been so frequently associated with danger through a species' evolutionary history that a fear or avoidance response has become innate, or "biologically programmed." Avoidance or wariness of strangers is presumably one example of a class of preprogrammed fears that are elicited by stimuli that are unfamiliar to the child.

Critics had a field day with this explanation when it was first proposed. After all, couldn't one reasonably argue that many stimuli, including the child's eventual attachment objects, should be sufficiently unfamiliar to elicit a protest almost from birth if Bowlby's notion of "stranger anxiety as an innate fear response" were correct? Bowlby's reply to this criticism is straightforward: An infant's cognitive and perceptual abilities are very immature at birth. Consequently, it will take some time for the child to learn what is familiar and to discriminate these persons, objects, and events from those that are unfamiliar. But once such discriminations are possible, the infant's biologically programmed "fear of the unfamiliar" should be readily apparent.

Indeed, some support for a biological mediation of stranger anxiety can be found in the behavior genetics literature. Specifically, identical twins (who share identical genes) are much more similar than fraternal twins in the age at which they begin to fear strangers (Freedman, 1965; Plomin & DeFries, 1985).

Why does stranger anxiety become less intense during the second year? Mary Ainsworth (Ainsworth et al., 1974) believes that infants become less wary of strangers as they begin to use their attachment objects as *secure bases* who encourage a second preprogrammed behavior—exploring the environment. According to Ainsworth and her associates (1974),

> The dynamic balance between exploratory and attachment behavior has significance from an evolutionary point of view. Whereas attachment behaviors . . . serve a protective function during the long, helpless infancy of a species such as the human . . . exploratory behaviors reflect a genetic basis for an infant to be interested in novel features of the environment, to approach them, manipulate them, . . . to play, and to learn more about the nature of his environment and the properties of the objects in it. It is an advantageous arrangement for an infant . . . to explore without straying too far from an adult who can protect him [p. 104].

In sum, stranger anxiety is thought to wane as the child explores the environment and finds that many novel stimuli (including friendly strangers) can be interesting and enjoyable in their own right.

Two questions remain. If 7–10-month-old infants are programmed to fear unfamiliar people, then (1) why don't they fear strange children, and (2) why do they then become wary of peers in the second year of life? Cognitive theorists have proposed an explanation for stranger anxiety that addresses both these issues.

The cognitive-developmental viewpoint.

Jerome Kagan (1972) believes that stranger anxiety is a natural outgrowth of the infant's perceptual and cognitive development. Kagan suggests that 6–8-month-olds have developed stable schemata for the faces of familiar companions and that a strange face is now a discrepant and potentially fear-producing stimulus. He notes that children of this age will typically stare at a stranger before they begin to protest. Presumably this short visual fixation is not a fear-induced "freezing" but, rather, a period of *hypothesizing*: the infant is examining the discrepant stimulus and trying to explain what it is or what has become of the familiar faces that match his or her schema for human beings. Failing to answer these questions, the child becomes wary of the stranger and may cry in an attempt to summon familiar company. As infants mature, they are gradually exposed to many strangers, and their schema for faces will become more generalized. Therefore, a 2-year-old is unlikely to be upset at the sight of a strange face, because strangers are now easily assimilated into the infant's very broad facial schema.

According to the cognitive viewpoint, infants who see only a small number of people should soon develop stable schemata for these regular companions and perhaps come to fear strangers at an early age. By contrast, infants who are often exposed to strangers (for example, relatives, babysitters, and family friends) should be slow to develop a stable schema for "caregivers" and therefore may be relatively unperturbed by a stranger. Support for this proposition comes from a study by Rudolph Schaffer (1966), who found that infants who are wary of strangers at an early age are likely to come from small families and to have had very little contact with people from outside the immediate household.

Why are 7–10-month-old infants *not* afraid of strange children? Perhaps because babies of this age are cared for mainly by adults and do not have well-developed schemata for children. As a result, an unfamiliar child may simply represent an *interesting*

stimulus that is far too discrepant from the infant's schema for "caregivers" to generate much anxiety. However, Jerome Kagan and his associates (Kagan et al., 1975) believe that an unfamiliar child will become an object of apprehension once the infant has developed a schema for children (based on siblings or playmates) and then discovers that the small stranger does not match this "child schema."

In a longitudinal study, Joseph Jacobson (1980) found that infants do become wary of unfamiliar peers at some point between the ages of 10 and 14½ months. Moreover, Jacobson's infants had been given a test of cognitive development at 10 months of age. Jacobson discovered that the infants who had scored highest on this cognitive test were most wary of strange peers at 12 months of age, while those who had scored lower showed their greatest anxiety at age 14½ months. So the time at which infants are most apprehensive around other children will depend, in part, on their rate of cognitive development.

Summing up.

We have seen that stranger anxiety is a rather complex emotional response that varies with the availability of familiar companions, the setting, and the identity and behavior of the stranger, as well as the infant's developmental level and genetic predisposition to be wary. Clearly, there is no one correct explanation for this interesting phenomenon: each of the above explanations has received some support and has helped us to understand why infants are sometimes apprehensive when they come face to face with a stranger.

SEPARATION ANXIETY

At 7–12 months of age, many infants begin to show signs of discomfort when separated from their mothers or other familiar companions. For example, 10-month-old Tony, restrained in his playpen, is likely to cry if he sees his mother put on a coat and pick up a purse as she prepares to go shopping. If unrestrained and exposed to the same scene, 15-month-old Ben might run and cling to his mother or at least follow her to the door. As she leaves and closes the door behind her, Ben will probably cry. These reactions reflect the infants' separation anxiety. Separation anxiety normally appears during the latter half of the first year (at about the time infants are forming primary social attachments), peaks at 14–20 months, and gradually becomes less frequent and less intense throughout infancy and the preschool period (Kagan, 1983; Weinraub & Lewis, 1977).

Children raised in some cultural settings protest separations from their mothers at an earlier age than North American or European infants. For example, Mary Ainsworth (1967) found that Ugandan infants begin to fear separations from their mothers as early as 5–6 months of age. Why? One reason may be that Ugandan babies have much more close contact with their mothers than is typical in Western cultures—these infants sleep with their mothers, nurse for at least two years, and go wherever their mothers go, riding on the mother's hips or across her back in a cotton sling. So Ugandan infants may be quick to protest separations from their mothers because these separations are very unusual events.

Explanations for Separation Anxiety

There are several reasons that an infant might protest a separation from loved ones. Let's consider three points of view.

The "conditioned anxiety" hypothesis.

Psychoanalytic theorists and some learning theorists have proposed that infants may learn to fear separations from their caregivers if prior discomforts (for example, hunger, wet diapers, and pain) have been especially frequent or intense during periods when caregivers were not present to relieve them. In other words, infants may associate prolonged or intense discomfort with the caregiver's absence and then express their "conditioned anxiety" by protesting whenever the caregiver is about to depart.

One problem with the "conditioned anxiety" hypothesis is that it cannot explain why infants are *less* likely to protest separations from their mothers at home (where they have previously suffered many discomforts) than in a laboratory environment where they have never been before (Rinkoff & Corter, 1980). In addition, "conditioned anxiety" cannot explain the *early* separation protests seen among Ugandan infants, who have rarely been separated from their mothers and therefore have had little or no opportunity to associate pain and discomfort with the mother's absence. Let's now consider a second point of view that offers an explanation for both these findings.

The ethological viewpoint.   Ethologists have argued that children are biologically programmed to fear many strange or uncertain situations, including strange people, strange settings, and the "strange circumstance" in which they are separated from their familiar companions (Bowlby, 1973; Stayton, Ainsworth, & Main, 1973). According to the ethological viewpoint, infants should show stronger separation protests in a strange laboratory environment because this unfamiliar setting magnifies the apprehension they will ordinarily experience when separated from a caregiver. Moreover, ethologists would argue that Ugandan infants are quick to protest separations from their mothers because these separations occur so very infrequently that they qualify as highly unusual (that is, fear-provoking) events (Ainsworth, 1967).

Why does separation anxiety become less intense toward the end of the second year? According to ethologists, a fear of separation will gradually wane as the child's innate exploratory activities become increasingly apparent and he or she begins to initiate brief separations by using the mother (or another close companion) as a secure base from which to explore.

Apparently infants are much less likely to fear separations *that they initiate themselves*. Harriet Rheingold and Carol Eckerman (1970) found that 10-month-olds were perfectly willing to leave their mothers and venture alone into a strange room in order to play there. However, a second group of 10-month-olds typically cried when they were placed in this same strange room and then were left alone as their mothers departed. It appears that the first group of infants were not discomforted in the strange setting because they knew where their mothers were and were using them as a secure base from which to explore the environment.

Of course, the infant's willingness to explore will depend on the setting, the accessibility of caregivers, and the presence of other people. Alan Sroufe (1977) reports that infants are much more likely to explore an unfamiliar setting if a caregiver is present.

Moreover, Helen Samuels (1980) found that infants will venture much farther from their mothers and stay away longer when a brother or sister is present to pull them away from their "secure bases." However, an exploring infant will typically retreat toward a caregiver if confronted by a stranger (Bretherton & Ainsworth, 1974) or if the caregiver should become less accessible by moving away from the child or pursuing an interest of her own, such as reading or sewing (Rinkoff & Corter, 1980; Jones, 1985; Sorce & Emde, 1981).

In sum, ethologists view separation anxiety as an innate reaction that helps to protect the young of a species from harm or discomfort by ensuring that they will remain near their caregivers. Yet the caregivers who serve this protective function are also instrumental in alleviating separation anxiety. By serving as a secure base for exploratory activities, the caregiver encourages the infant to venture into the unknown and to become increasingly familiar with the environment. As a result, the child should eventually become more tolerant of separations and much less wary of stimuli (strangers and unfamiliar settings) that have previously been a source of concern.

The cognitive viewpoint. Cognitive-developmental theorists propose another explanation of separation anxiety that complements the ethological viewpoint. Jerome Kagan (1972, 1976) believes that infants develop not only schemata for familiar faces (those of caregivers) but also schemata for a familiar person's probable whereabouts. In other words, the infant may schematize "familiar faces in familiar places." Kagan notes that infants are often separated from their mothers in the course of day-to-day living and generally do not protest these brief separations. For example, if a mother proceeds into the kitchen, leaving her 10-month-old son on the living-room floor, the infant is likely to stop playing and watch her depart and then resume his previous activity without protesting her absence. This separation is not protested, because the child is able to explain where his mother has gone; that is, he has previously developed a schema for mother-in-the-kitchen. But should the mother pick up her coat and purse and walk out the front door, the child will find it difficult to account for her whereabouts and will

probably cry. In sum, cognitive theorists believe that infants are most likely to protest separations when they cannot understand where their absent companions may have gone or when they are likely to return.

The results of a home-based observational study (Littenberg, Tulkin, & Kagan, 1971) are quite consistent with Kagan's cognitive hypothesis. In this study, 15-month-old infants showed little separation protest when mother departed through a doorway she used often but considerable protest when she left through a door that she used infrequently, such as the entry to a closet or the cellar. The children were separated from their mothers in both cases, but they protested only when they could not account for the mother's whereabouts.

Kagan's theory also explains the results of an interesting study by Carl Corter and his associates (Corter, Zucker, & Galligan, 1980). Nine-month-old infants first accompanied their mothers to a strange room (room A) and shortly thereafter watched the mothers exit into a second room (room B). Few of the infants protested this separation; most of them continued to play for a while with the toys that were present before crawling into the adjoining room and finding their mothers. In cognitive terms, it is reasonable to assume that the infants had formed a schema for the absent mother's whereabouts once they had found her in room B. At this point, the infants and their mothers reentered room A and spent a short time together before the mother departed once again. But on this second trial, she proceeded into another adjoining room (room C) and thus violated the infant's schema for her probable whereabouts. This time the majority of the infants fussed or cried! And where did these distressed youngsters go to search for their mothers? Generally, they crawled to the doorway that *matched their schemata* (room B) rather than to the portal through which they had most recently seen the mother depart (room C). Here, then, is another demonstration that infants are most likely to protest separations from a caregiver when they are uncertain of her whereabouts.

Notice that these 9-month-olds were looking for "mama" *where they had previously found her* rather than where she was last seen. This is precisely the type of error made by Piaget's 8–12-month-old infants as they first began to realize that objects have a permanence about them. Must infants have reached this initial phase in the development of the object concept before they will begin forming hypotheses about the probable location of an absent caregiver? Probably so. If an infant did not recognize that a departing caregiver continued to exist, he or she would not try to determine her location and might not even protest her absence. As it turns out, we have already discussed a study that supports this line of reasoning. Recall that Barry Lester and his associates (1974) found that infants who had not yet reached the very first phase in the development of object permanence generally failed to protest when separated from their mothers and fathers.

On Easing the Pain of Separations

At some point, virtually all parents will find it necessary to leave their infants and toddlers in an unfamiliar setting (such as a nursery or a day-care center) or in the company of a stranger (for example, a babysitter) for hours at a time. Are there ways to make these separations easier or more tolerable for a young child?

Indeed there are. Marsha Weinraub and Michael Lewis (1977) found that toddlers who were separated from their mothers in an unfamiliar setting cried less and played more constructively if the mother took the time to explain that she was leaving and would soon return. Apparently, brief explanations that inform the child that he or she should "play until mommy returns" are more effective at reducing separation distress than lengthy explanations (Adams & Passman, 1981). The problem with a lengthy discourse is that it is probably quite discrepant with the caregiver's usual practices. In other words, if the child has no schema for lengthy explanations, he or she may perceive the upcoming separation as something "out of the ordinary" and become very concerned.

Some parents try to prepare their toddlers for an upcoming separation by explaining the situation to the child anywhere from a few hours to a few days in advance. This approach may work with preschool children who have the language skills and cognitive abilities to ask pertinent questions and to rehearse the situation in their own minds, but it may backfire with younger children who lack these problem-solving capabilities. Indeed, Roderick Adams and Richard

Passman (1980) found that 2-year-olds who had been prepared at home for an upcoming separation later played less constructively and were more likely to try to follow their departing mothers than were toddlers who had not been told of the separation in advance.

Separations are also less painful for older infants and toddlers if they have some reminder of the home setting with them, such as a favorite stuffed animal or a security blanket (Passman & Weisberg, 1975). Recently, Richard Passman and Kathleen Longeway (1982) found that toddlers who were given sharply focused photographs of their mothers were reasonably tolerant of separations: they played more and stayed longer in an unfamiliar playroom than toddlers who were given unrecognizable (blurred) photographs of their mothers. Apparently a clear physical representation of the mother reduces separation distress, and it may help a child to remember whatever explanation a mother has given for her departure (although this latter assumption remains to be tested). Although all the children in Passman and Longeway's study were at least 20 months of age, we know that infants are capable of recognizing photographs of their mothers early in the first year (Barrera & Maurer, 1981) and that they have already begun to carefully examine and to smile at photographs of their parents by age 9–12 months (Brooks-Gunn & Lewis, 1981). So it is possible that even a 9–12-month-old infant, who is unlikely to understand a verbal explanation, can be made less discomforted during necessary separations if a substitute caregiver is able to produce a photograph of the infant's absent companion(s).

Reactions to the Loss of an Attachment Object

To this point, the research we have reviewed has focused on children's rather immediate responses to *short-term* separations from attachment objects. How do young children react to permanent or prolonged separations from their loved ones? Do they eventually stop protesting or perhaps even forget these special companions?

Seeking to answer these questions, John Bowlby (1960) studied the behavior of children aged 15 to 30 months who were hospitalized for chronic illnesses and, thus, separated from their mothers for a long period. According to Bowlby, most of these children progressed through three behavioral phases during their separations. In the initial, *protest* phase, the child tried to regain his or her mother by crying, demanding her return, and resisting the attention of caretakers. This phase lasted from a few hours to more than a week. Next came the phase of *despair*. It seemed to Bowlby as if the child had given up hope of ever being reunited with his or her mother. The child became apathetic and unresponsive to toys and to other people and appeared to be in "a deep state of mourning." Finally, the child entered what Bowlby calls the stage of *detachment*. At this point the child appeared to have recovered, for he or she showed a renewed interest in play activities, caretakers, and other features of the environment. But the child's relationship with the mother had changed. When the mother visited, the child was cool and largely indifferent, showing hardly any protest when she left once again. It was almost as if the children were in the process of undoing their attachments to their mothers. Bowlby's observations have now been replicated by Heinicke and Westheimer (1965), who studied the behavior of 2- to 3-year-old children left by their parents in a residential nursery for periods ranging from two weeks to three months.

Bowlby notes that a fourth separation phase, *permanent withdrawal from human relationships*, may occur if the child's separation from the mother is extremely prolonged or if the child loses a series of temporary attachment objects, such as nurses or babysitters, while separated from the mother. In either case, the child often becomes uninterested in contacting others. He or she is still able to communicate with other people on their initiative but becomes more egocentric as attention shifts from human beings to fuzzy toys or other inanimate objects.

Michael Rutter (1979) has carefully reviewed these and other pertinent data and concluded that children's reactions to long-term separations are nowhere near as uniform as Bowlby suggests. According to Rutter, most children who are securely attached to their caregivers may protest and show some "despair" over a long-term separation, but they are unlikely to "detach" themselves either from their close companions (that is, parents) or from human beings in general. However, Rutter claims that those infants and toddlers who have shaky, insecure relationships with companions at home may well put some psychological distance between themselves and these persons, almost as if they were becoming detached. And should the child's attachments be sufficiently insecure, he or she may indeed choose to withdraw from human contact, sinking into a state of "affectionless psychopathology" in which it becomes exceedingly difficult to be emotionally involved with anyone.

Clearly Rutter is proposing that there are not one but perhaps several kinds of attachments that children may form with caregivers and that different kinds of attachments may have different implications for the child's future social and emotional well-being. In Chapter 6, we will see that he is right on both counts. And would you care to hazard a guess about whether an insecure attachment with a close companion is better than no attachment at all? This is another issue we will consider in the next chapter as we review what is known about the social, emotional, and intellectual development of children who are denied opportunities to form social attachments during the early years of their lives.

SUMMARY

It appears that even very young infants are emotional creatures. At birth, babies are capable of expressing interest, distress, disgust, and pleasure (as indexed by their primitive smiles). Sadness and anger first appear at 3–4 months of age, followed a few months later by clear expressions of fear, shame, and shyness; complex emotions such as guilt and contempt emerge during the second year. There is some debate about when infants first recognize the emotional expressions of other people. A neonate will respond differently to vocal indications of pleasure than to those signifying distress. However, infants seem relatively insensitive to visual configurations of emotion until the latter half of the first year.

Emotions play at least two important roles in an infant's social development. The child's own emotional expressions are adaptive in that they promote social contact with others and assist caregivers in adjusting their behaviors to the infant's needs and goals. At the same time, the infant's ability to recognize and interpret the emotions of other people serves an important *social referencing* function by helping the child to infer how he or she should be feeling or behaving in a wide variety of situations.

Infants begin to form affectional ties to their close companions during the first year of life. These "bonds of love," or *attachments*, serve many purposes and are important contributors to social and emotional development. Attachments are usually reciprocal relationships, for parents and other intimate companions will often become attached to the infant.

Parents may become emotionally involved with an infant during the first few hours if they have close contact with their baby during this period. An initial bond may then be strengthened as the infant begins to emit social signals (smiles, vocalizations) that attract the attention of caregivers and make them feel that the baby enjoys their company. Eventually the infant and a close companion will establish highly synchronized interactive routines that are satisfying to both parties and are likely to blossom into a reciprocal attachment. However, some parents may have a difficult time becoming attached to their infant if the child is irritable, unresponsive, or unwanted, if they are unhappily married or have other problems that prevent them from devoting much attention to the baby, or if they follow preconceived notions about child rearing rather than adjusting their parenting to the infant's state and temperament.

Most infants have formed a primary social attachment to a close companion by 6–8 months of age, and within weeks they are establishing these affectional ties with other regular companions. Many theories have been proposed to explain how and why infants form attachments. Among the most influential theories of attachment are the psychoanalytic, the learning-theory, the cognitive-developmental, and the ethological viewpoints. Although these theories make different assumptions about the roles that infants and caregivers play in the formation of attachments, each viewpoint has contributed to our understanding of early social and emotional development.

At about the time infants are becoming attached to a close companion, they often begin to display two negative emotions, or "fears." *Stranger anxiety* is the child's wariness of unfamiliar people. It is by no means a universal reaction and is most likely to occur in response to an intrusive stranger who appears in an unfamiliar setting where loved ones are unavailable. *Separation anxiety* is the discomfort infants may feel when separated from the person or persons to whom they are attached. As infants develop intellectually and begin to move away from attachment objects to explore the environment, they will become increasingly familiar with strangers and better able to account for the absences of familiar companions. As a result, both stranger anxiety and separation anxiety will decline in intensity toward the end of the second year.

The effects of prolonged or permanent separations from a loved one depend on the quality of the child's emotional relationship with the departed person. Children who have stable ties with caregivers often protest and may show some short-term depression, or despair, over the loss of an attachment object. However, those who are insecure in their emotional relationships may become "detached" from loved ones and, in extreme cases, may withdraw from human contact and experience difficulties becoming involved with anyone.

NOTES

1. Although ethologists have suggested that such crying may be a precursor of empathy, another interpretation is that infants find the sound of crying to be aversive and will chime in to convey their own distress.

2. The rooting reflex is an innate response: when an object brushes the cheek, an infant will turn its head in the direction of the touch, searching for something to suck.

3. Fathers' contributions to their infants' social and emotional development will be discussed at length in Chapter 6.

4. A *critical period* is a relatively brief period in the life cycle during which an organism is particularly sensitive to certain environmental influences. Presumably, the same experiences provided before or after this period will have little if any effect. In the case of imprinting, the argument is that young fowl must be exposed to an "imprinting" stimulus during their critical period for imprinting or they will not become attached to a caregiver.

REFERENCES

ADAMS, R. E., & Passman, R. H. (1980, March). *The effects of advance preparation upon children's behavior during brief separation from their mother.* Paper presented at annual meeting of the Southeastern Psychological Association, Washington, D.C.

ADAMS, R. E., & Passman, R. H. (1981). The effects of preparing two-year-olds for brief separations from their mothers. *Child Development, 52,* 1068–1070.

AINSWORTH, M. D. S. (1967). *Infancy in Uganda: Infant care and the growth of love.* Baltimore: Johns Hopkins University Press.

AINSWORTH, M. D. S., Bell, S. M., & Stayton, D. J. (1974). Infant-mother attachment and social development: Socialization as a product of reciprocal responsiveness to signals. In M. P. M. Richards (Ed.), *The integration of the child into a social world.* London: Cambridge University Press.

AINSWORTH, M. D. S., Blehar, M. C., Waters, E., & Wall, S. (1978). *Patterns of attachment: A psychological study of the strange situation.* Hillsdale, NJ: Erlbaum.

ALLEY, T. R. (1981). Head shape and the perception of cuteness. *Developmental Psychology, 17,* 650–654.

AMBROSE, J. A. (1963). The concept of a critical period in the development of social responsiveness in early infancy. In B. M. Foss (Ed.), *Determinants of infant behavior* (Vol. 2). London: Methuen.

BARRERA, M. E., & Maurer, D. (1981). Recognition of mother's photographed face by the three-month-old infant. *Child Development, 52,* 714–716.

BARRERA, M. E., Rosenbaum, P. L., & Cunningham, C. E. (1986). Early home intervention with low-birth-weight infants and their parents. *Child Development, 57,* 20–23.

BELSKY, J. (1980). Child maltreatment: An ecological integration. *American Psychologist, 35,* 320–335.

BELSKY, J. (1981). Early human experience: A family perspective. *Developmental Psychology, 17,* 3–23.

BOCCIA, M., & Campos, J. (1983, April). *Maternal emotional signalling: Its effects on infants' reactions to strangers.* Paper presented at the biennial meeting of the Society for Research in Child Development, Detroit, MI.

BOWER, T. G. R. (1982). *Development in infancy.* New York: W. H. Freeman.

BOWLBY, J. (1958). The nature of the child's tie to his mother. *International Journal of Psychoanalysis, 39,* 350–373.

BOWLBY, J. (1960). Separation anxiety. *International Journal of Psychoanalysis, 41,* 89–113.

BOWLBY, J. (1969). *Attachment and loss.* Vol. 1: *Attachment.* London: Hogarth Press.

BOWLBY, J. (1973). *Attachment and loss.* Vol. 2: *Separation.* London: Hogarth Press.

BRACKBILL, Y. (1958). Extinction of the smiling response in infants as a function of reinforcement schedule. *Child Development, 29,* 114–124.

BRAZELTON, T. B. (1979). Behavioral competence of the newborn infant. *Seminars in Perinatology, 3,* 35–44.

BRETHERTON, I., & Ainsworth, M. D. S. (1974). Responses of one-year-olds to a stranger in a strange situation. In M. Lewis & L. Rosenblum (Eds.), *The origins of fear.* New York: Wiley.

BRETHERTON, I., Stolberg, U., & Kreye, M. (1981). Engaging strangers in proximal interaction: Infants' social initiative. *Developmental Psychology, 17,* 746–755.

BROOKS, J., & Lewis, M. (1976). Infants' responses to strangers: Midget, adult, and child. *Child Development, 47,* 323–332.

BROOKS-GUNN, J., & Lewis, M. (1981). Infant social perception: Responses to pictures of parents and strangers. *Developmental Psychology, 17,* 647–649.

CARON, R. F., Caron, A. J., & Myers, R. S. (1985). Do infants see emotional expressions in static faces? *Child Development, 56,* 1552–1560.

CERNOCH, J. M., & Porter, R. H. (1985). Recognition of maternal axillary odors by infants. *Child Development, 56,* 1593–1598.

CLARKE-STEWART, K. (1978). And daddy makes three: The father's impact on the mother and the young child. *Child Development, 49,* 466–478.

COHEN, L. J. (1974). The operational definition of human attachment. *Psychological Bulletin, 4,* 207–217.

COHN, J. F., & Tronick, E. Z. (1982). Three-month-old infants' reactions to simulated maternal depression. *Child Development, 53,* 185–193.

CONDON, W. S., & Sander, L. W. (1974). Neonate movement is synchronized with adult speech: Interactional participation and language acquisition. *Science, 183,* 99–101.

CORTER, C. M., Zucker, K. J., & Galligan, R. F. (1980). Patterns in the infant's search for mother during brief separation. *Developmental Psychology, 16,* 62–69.

CROCKENBERG, S. B. (1981). Infant irritability, mother responsiveness, and social support influences on the security of infant-mother attachment. *Child Development, 52,* 857–865.

DeCASPER, A. J., & Fifer, W. P. (1980). Of human bonding: Newborns prefer their mothers' voices. *Science, 208,* 1174–1176.

DITTRICHOVA, J. (1969). The development of premature infants. In R. J. Robinson (Ed.), *Brain and early development.* London: Academic Press.

DONOVAN, W. L., & Leavitt, L. A. (1985). Simulating conditions of learned helplessness: The effects of interventions and attributions. *Child Development, 56,* 594–603.

DUNKELD, J. (1978). *The function of imitation in infancy.* Unpublished doctoral dissertation, University of Edinburgh.

EMDE, R. N., Gaensbauer, T. J., & Harmon, R. J. (1976). *Emotional expression in infancy: A biobehavioral study.* New York: International Universities Press.

FEINMAN, S., & Lewis, M. (1983). Social referencing at 10 months: A second-order effect on infants' responses to strangers. *Child Development, 54,* 878–887.

FEIRING, C., Lewis, M., & Starr, M. D. (1984). Indirect effects and infants' reactions to strangers. *Developmental Psychology, 20,* 485–491.

FERNALD, A., & Simon, T. (1984). Expanded intonational contours in mothers' speech to newborns. *Developmental Psychology, 20,* 104–113.

FREEDMAN, D. G. (1965). Hereditary control of early social behaviors. In B. M. Foss (Ed.), *Determinants of infant behavior* (Vol. 3). London: Methuen.

FREUD, S. (1930). *Three contributions to the theory of sex.* New York: Nervous and Mental Disease Publishing Co. (Original work published 1905)

FRODI, A. M., Lamb, M. E., Leavitt, L. A., Donovan, W. L., Neff, C., & Sherry, D. (1978). Fathers' and mothers' responses to the faces and cries of normal and premature infants. *Developmental Psychology, 14,* 490–498.

GARBARINO, J., & Sherman, D. (1980). High-risk neighborhoods and high-risk families: The human ecology of child maltreatment. *Child Development, 51,* 188–198.

GAULIN-KREMER, E., Shaw, J. L., & Thoman, E. B. (1977, March). *Mother-infant interaction at first encounter: Effects of variation in delay after delivery.* Paper presented at the biennial meeting of the Society for Research in Child Development, New Orleans.

GEWIRTZ, H. B., & Gewirtz, J. L. (1968). Caretaking settings, background events, and behavior differences in four Israeli child-rearing environments: Some preliminary trends. In B. M. Foss (Ed.), *Determinants of infant behavior* (Vol. 4). London: Methuen.

GEWIRTZ, J. L. (1969). Mechanisms of social learning: Some roles of stimulation and behavior in early human development. In D. A. Goslin (Ed.), *Handbook of socialization theory and research.* Skokie, IL: Rand McNally.

GOLDBERG, S. (1983). Parent-infant bonding: Another look. *Child Development, 54,* 1355–1382.

GOLDBERG, S., Blumberg, S. L., & Kriger, A. (1982). Menarche and interest in infants: Biological and social influences. *Child Development, 53*, 1544–1550.

GREENBERG, M. T., & Marvin, R. S. (1982). Reactions of preschool children to an adult stranger: A behavioral systems approach. *Child Development, 53*, 481–490.

GREENBERG, M. T., & Morris, N. (1974). Engrossment: The newborn's impact upon the father. *American Journal of Orthopsychiatry, 44*, 520–531.

GREENE, J. G., Fox, N. A., & Lewis, M. (1983). The relationship between neonatal characteristics and three-month mother-infant interaction in high-risk infants. *Child Development, 54*, 1286–1296.

GROSSMAN, F. K., Eichler, L. S., Winickoff, S. A., & Associates. (1980). *Pregnancy, birth, and parenthood: Adaptations of mothers, fathers, and infants.* San Francisco: Jossey-Bass.

GROSSMANN, K., Thane, K., & Grossmann, K. E. (1981). Maternal tactile contact of the newborn after various post-partum conditions of mother-infant contact. *Developmental Psychology, 17*, 158–169.

HALL, G. S. (1891). The contents of children's minds on entering school. *Pedagogical Seminary, 1*, 139–173.

HARLOW, H. F., & Zimmerman, R. R. (1959). Affectional responses in the infant monkey. *Science, 130*, 421–432.

HEINICKE, C. M., & Westheimer, I. (1965). *Brief separations.* New York: International Universities Press.

HILDEBRANDT, K. A. (1983). Effect of facial expression variations on ratings of infants' physical attractiveness. *Developmental Psychology, 19*, 414–417.

HILDEBRANDT, K. A., & Fitzgerald, H. E. (1981). Mothers' responses to infant physical appearance. *Infant Mental Health Journal, 2*, 56–61.

HURLEY, J. R., & Hohn, R. L. (1971). Shifts in child-rearing attitudes linked with parenthood and occupation. *Developmental Psychology, 4*, 324–328.

HYSON, M. C., & Izard, C. E. (1985). Continuities and changes in emotional expressions during brief separation at 13 and 18 months. *Developmental Psychology, 21*, 1165–1170.

IZARD, C. E. (1982). *Measuring emotions in infants and children.* New York: Cambridge University Press.

IZARD, C. E., Hembree, E. A., Dougherty, L. M., & Coss, C. L. (1983). Changes in two- to nineteen-month-old infants' facial expressions following acute pain. *Developmental Psychology, 19*, 418–426.

JACOBSON, J. L. (1980). Cognitive determinants of wariness toward unfamiliar peers. *Developmental Psychology, 16*, 347–354.

JOHNSON, W., Emde, R. N., Pannabecker, B., Stenberg, C., & Davis, M. (1982). Maternal perception of infant emotion from birth through 18 months. *Infant Behavior and Development, 5*, 313–322.

JONES, S. S. (1985). On the motivational bases for attachment behavior. *Developmental Psychology, 21*, 848–857.

KAGAN, J. (1971). *Change and continuity in infancy.* New York: Wiley.

KAGAN, J. (1972). Do infants think? *Scientific American, 226*, 74–82.

KAGAN, J. (1976). Emergent themes in human development. *American Scientist, 64*, 186–196.

KAGAN, J. (1983). Stress and coping in early development. In N. Garmezy & M. Rutter (Eds.), *Stress, coping and development in children.* New York: McGraw-Hill.

KAGAN, J., Kearsley, R. B., & Zelazo, P. R. (1975). The emergence of initial apprehension to unfamiliar peers. In M. Lewis & L. Rosenblum (Eds.), *Friendship and peer relations.* New York: Wiley.

KENNELL, J. H., Voos, D. K., & Klaus, M. H. (1979). Parent-infant bonding. In J. D. Osofsky (Ed.), *Handbook of infant development.* New York: Wiley.

KLAUS, H. M., & Kennell, J. H. (1976). *Maternal-infant bonding.* St. Louis: Mosby.

KOHLBERG, L. (1969). Stage and sequence: The cognitive-developmental approach to socialization. In D. A. Goslin (Ed.), *Handbook of socialization theory and research.* Skokie, IL: Rand McNally.

KORNER, A. F. (1974). The effect of the infant's state, level of arousal, sex, and ontogenetic stage on the caregiver. In M. Lewis & L. A.

Rosenblum (Eds.), *The effect of the infant on its caregiver.* New York: Wiley.

LA BARBERA, J. D., Izard, C. E., Vietze, P., & Parisi, S. A. (1976). Four- and six-month-old infants' visual responses to joy, anger, and neutral expressions. *Child Development, 47*, 535–538.

LAMB, M. E. (1981). The development of father-infant relationships. In M. E. Lamb (Ed.), *The role of the father in child development.* New York: Wiley.

LAMB, M. E., & Stevenson, M. (1978). Father-infant relationships: Their nature and importance. *Youth and Society, 9*, 277–298.

LESTER, B. M., Kotelchuck, M., Spelke, E., Sellers, M. J., & Klein, R. E. (1974). Separation protest in Guatemalan infants: Cross-cultural and cognitive findings. *Developmental Psychology, 10*, 79–85.

LEVITT, M. J. (1980). Contingent feedback, familiarization, and infant affect: How a stranger becomes a friend. *Developmental Psychology, 16*, 425–432.

LEWIS, M., & Brooks, J. (1974). Self, others, and fear: Infants' reactions to people. In M. Lewis & L. A. Rosenblum (Eds.), *The origins of fear.* New York: Wiley.

LITTENBERG, R., Tulkin, S., & Kagan, J. (1971). Cognitive components of separation anxiety. *Developmental Psychology, 4*, 387–388.

LORENZ, K. Z. (1937). The companion in the bird's world. *Auk, 54*, 254–273.

LORENZ, K. Z. (1943). Die angeboren Formen möglicher Erfahrung [The innate forms of possible experience]. *Zeitschrift für Tierpsychologie, 5*, 233–409.

MATEJCEK, Z., Dytrych, Z., & Schuller, V. (1979). The Prague study of children born from unwanted pregnancies. *International Journal of Mental Health, 7*, 63–74.

MEHLER, J., Bertoncini, J., Barriere, M., & Jassik-Gerschenfeld, D. (1978). Infant recognition of mother's voice. *Perception, 7*, 491–497.

MORGAN, G. A., & Ricciuti, H. N. (1969). Infants' responses to strangers during the first year. In B. M. Foss (Ed.), *Determinants of infant behavior* (Vol. 4). London: Methuen.

MYERS, B. J. (1982). Early intervention using Brazelton training with middle-class mothers and fathers of newborns. *Child Development, 53*, 462–471.

NELSON, C. A., & Dolgin, K. G. (1985). The generalized discrimination of facial expressions by seven-month-old infants. *Child Development, 56*, 58–61.

OSTER, H. (1981). "Recognition" of emotional expression in infancy? In M. E. Lamb & L. R. Sherrod (Eds.), *Infant social cognition: Empirical and theoretical considerations.* Hillsdale, NJ: Erlbaum.

PASSMAN, R. H., & Longeway, K. P. (1982). The role of vision in maternal attachment: Giving 2-year-olds a photograph of their mother during separation. *Developmental Psychology, 18*, 530–533.

PASSMAN, R. H., & Weisberg, P. (1975). Mothers and blankets as agents for promoting play and exploration by young children in a novel environment: The effects of social and nonsocial attachment objects. *Developmental Psychology, 11*, 170–177.

PEERY, J. C. (1980). Neonate and adult head movement: No and yes revisited. *Developmental Psychology, 16*, 245–250.

PLOMIN, R., & DeFries, J. C. (1985). *Origins of individual differences in infancy.* Orlando, FL: Academic Press.

RADKE-YARROW, M., Cummings, E. M., Kuczynski, L., & Chapman, M. (1985). Patterns of attachment in two- and three-year-olds in normal families and families with parental depression. *Child Development, 56*, 884–893.

RAJECKI, D. W. (1977). Social psychology from an ethological perspective. In C. Hendrick (Ed.), *Perspectives on social psychology.* Hillsdale, NJ: Erlbaum.

RHEINGOLD, H. L. (1961). The effect of environmental stimulation upon social and exploratory behavior in the human infant. In B. M. Foss (Ed.), *Determinants of infant behavior* (Vol. 1). London: Methuen.

RHEINGOLD, H. L., & Eckerman, C. D. (1970). The infant separates himself from his mother. *Science, 168*, 78–83.

RHEINGOLD, H. L., & Eckerman, C. D. (1973). Fear of the

stranger: A critical examination. In H. W. Reese (Ed.), *Advances in child development and behavior* (Vol. 8). Orlando, FL: Academic Press.

RINKOFF, R. F., & Corter, C. M. (1980). Effects of setting and maternal accessibility on the infant's response to brief separation. *Child Development, 51,* 603–606.

RODE, S. S., Chang, P., Fisch, R. O., & Sroufe, L. A. (1981). Attachment patterns of infants separated at birth. *Developmental Psychology, 17,* 188–191.

ROEDELL, W. C., & Slaby, R. G. (1977). The role of distal and proximal interaction in infant social preference formation. *Developmental Psychology, 13,* 266–273.

ROSENTHAL, M. K. (1982). Vocal dialogues in the neonatal period. *Developmental Psychology, 18,* 17–21.

RUTTER, M. (1979). Maternal deprivation, 1972–1978: New findings, new concepts, new approaches. *Child Development, 50,* 282–305.

SAMUELS, H. R. (1980). The effect of an older sibling on infant locomotor exploration of a new environment. *Child Development, 51,* 607–609.

SCHAFFER, H. R. (1966). The onset of fear of strangers and the incongruity hypothesis. *Journal of Child Psychology and Psychiatry, 7,* 95–106.

SCHAFFER, H. R. (1971). *The growth of sociability.* Baltimore: Penguin Books.

SCHAFFER, H. R. (1977). *Mothering.* Cambridge, MA: Harvard University Press.

SCHAFFER, H. R., & Emerson, P. E. (1964). The development of social attachments in infancy. *Monographs of the Society for Research in Child Development, 29*(3, Serial No. 94).

SEARS, R. R. (1963). Dependency motivation. In M. Jones (Ed.), *Nebraska Symposium on Motivation* (Vol. 11). Lincoln: University of Nebraska Press.

SELIGMAN, M. E. P. (1975). *Helplessness: On depression, development, and death.* New York: W. H. Freeman.

SINGER, L. M., Brodzinsky, D. M., Ramsay, D., Steir, M., & Waters, E. (1985). Mother-infant attachments in adoptive families. *Child Development, 56,* 1543–1551.

SORCE, J. F., & Emde, R. N. (1981). Mother's presence is not enough: Effect of emotional availability on infant exploration. *Developmental Psychology, 17,* 737–745.

SPAULDING, D. A. (1873). Instinct with original observation in young animals. *MacMillans Magazine, 27,* 282–283.

SPITZ, R. A. (1950). Anxiety in infancy. *International Journal of Psychoanalysis, 31,* 139–143.

SPRUNGER, L. W., Boyce, W. T., & Gaines, J. A. (1985). Family-infant congruence: Routines and rhythmicity in family adaptations to a young infant. *Child Development, 56,* 564–572.

SROUFE, L. A. (1977). Wariness of strangers and the study of infant development. *Child Development, 48,* 1184–1199.

SROUFE, L. A., Waters, E., & Matas, L. (1974). Contextual determinants of infant affectional response. In M. Lewis & L. A. Rosenblum (Eds.), *The origins of fear.* New York: Wiley.

STAYTON, D. J., Ainsworth, M. D. S., & Main, M. B. (1973). Development of separation behavior in the first year of life: Protest, following, and greeting. *Developmental Psychology, 9,* 213–225.

STEELE, B. F., & Pollack, C. B. (1974). A psychiatric study of parents who abuse infants and small children. In R. E. Helfer & C. H. Kempe (Eds.), *The battered child.* Chicago: University of Chicago Press.

STEPHAN, C. W., & Langlois, J. H. (1984). Baby beautiful: Adult attributions of infant competence as a function of infant attractiveness. *Child Development, 55,* 576–585.

STERN, D. (1977). *The first relationship: Infant and mother.* Cambridge, MA: Harvard University Press.

SVEJDA, M. J., Campos, J. J., & Emde, R. N. (1980). Mother-infant "bonding": Failure to generalize. *Child Development, 51,* 775–779.

THOMAN, E. B., Acebo, C., & Becker, P. T. (1983). Infant crying and stability in the mother-infant relationship: A systems analysis. *Child Development, 54,* 653–659.

TROTTER, R. J. (1983, August). Baby face. *Psychology Today,* pp. 14–20.

WAHLER, R. G. (1967). Infant social attachments: A reinforcement theory interpretation and investigation. *Child Development, 38,* 1079–1088.

WATERS, E., Vaughn, B. E., & Egeland, B. R. (1980). Individual differences in infant-mother attachment relationships at age one: Antecedents in neonatal behavior in an urban, economically disadvantaged sample. *Child Development, 51,* 208–216.

WATSON, J. S., Hayes, L. A., Vietze, P., & Becker, J. (1979). Discriminative infant smiling to orientations of talking faces of mother and stranger. *Journal of Experimental Child Psychology, 28,* 92–99.

WEINRAUB, M., & Lewis, M. (1977). The determinants of children's responses to separation. *Monographs of the Society for Research in Child Development, 42*(4, Serial No. 172).

WIDMAYER, S., & Field, T. (1980). Effects of Brazelton demonstrations on early interactions of preterm infants and their teen-age mothers. *Infant Behavior and Development, 3,* 79–89.

WOLFF, P. H. (1963). Observations on the early development of smiling. In B. M. Foss (Ed.), *Determinants of infant behavior* (Vol. 2). London: Methuen.

WOLFF, P. H. (1969). The natural history of crying and other vocalizations in early infancy. In B. M. Foss (Ed.), *Determinants of infant behavior* (Vol. 4). London: Methuen.

WOROBEY, J., & Belsky, J. (1982). Employing the Brazelton scale to influence mothering: An experimental comparison of three strategies. *Developmental Psychology, 18,* 736–743.

ZESKIND, P. S. (1980). Adult responses to the cries of low and high risk infants. *Infant Behavior and Development, 3,* 167–177.

6

EARLY SOCIAL AND EMOTIONAL DEVELOPMENT II:
IMPLICATIONS FOR
FUTURE DEVELOPMENT

INDIVIDUAL DIFFERENCES IN THE QUALITY OF ATTACHMENTS

How Do Infants Become Securely or Insecurely Attached?

Long-Term Correlates of Secure and Insecure Attachments

Maternal Employment and Alternative Caregiving: Do They Hinder Children's Emotional Development?

THE UNATTACHED INFANT: EFFECTS OF RESTRICTED SOCIAL CONTACTS DURING INFANCY

Effects of Social Isolation in Dogs

Social Deprivation in Monkeys

Social Deprivation in Humans

Three Theoretical Perspectives on Social Deprivation Effects

Can Children Recover from Early Developmental Impairments?

SUMMARY

REFERENCES

My sister once asked whether it was normal for a 10-month-old to be a "mama's boy." She then proceeded to tell me that her son Jacob almost always cried when she left him alone and often tried to crawl to wherever she had gone. Actually, she was overstating the case. Jacob did cry when his mother disappeared from view at grandma's house or left him alone for more than five to ten minutes at home. But in most cases Jacob reacted rather normally to a separation from his mother: he watched intently as she left and then continued whatever he was doing. My sister and I talked for a while about the nature of relationships between mothers and infants, and we eventually decided that Jacob's attachment to her was one indication that he was well on his way to becoming a socially responsive little boy.

Had he been there, Sigmund Freud would surely have endorsed our conclusion. Freud (1905/1930) repeatedly argued that the emotional events and experiences of infancy can have any number of long-term effects on developing children. In fact, he stressed that the formation of a stable mother/infant emotional bond is *absolutely necessary* for normal social and personality development, a sentiment shared by ethologist John Bowlby and the best-known psychoanalytic theorist of recent times, Erik Erikson. Erikson's view is that secure emotional attachments to caregivers provide the infant with a basic sense of *trust* that will permit him or her to form close affectional ties to other people later in life. Learning theorists such as Harry Harlow (who studied monkeys) and Robert Sears (who studied humans) believe that close contact with a mother figure allows the infant to acquire a repertoire of social skills that will enable him or her to interact effectively and appropriately with other members of the species. In sum, almost everyone agrees that the emotional events of infancy are very influential in shaping one's future development.

There are at least two ways to evaluate this "early experience" hypothesis. First, one could try to determine whether infants who do not become securely attached to their parents turn out any different from those who do. Second, one could look at what happens to infants who have had little or no contact with a mother figure during the first two years and do not

become attached to anyone. In the pages that follow, we will consider the findings and implications of both these lines of inquiry.

INDIVIDUAL DIFFERENCES IN THE QUALITY OF ATTACHMENTS

Mary Ainsworth and her associates (Ainsworth, Blehar, Waters, & Walls, 1978) have found that infants differ in the type (or quality) of attachments that they have with their caregivers. Ainsworth measures the quality of an infant's attachment by exposing the child to a *"strange situations" test* consisting of a series of eight episodes designed to gradually escalate the amount of stress that the baby will experience (see Table 6-1). By recording and analyzing the child's responses to these episodes—that is, exploratory activities, reactions to strangers and to separations, and, in particular, the child's behaviors when reunited with the close companion—we can usually place his or her attachment into one of the following three categories:

1. *Secure attachment.* About 70% of 1-year-old infants fall into this category. The securely attached infant actively explores while alone with the mother and is visibly upset by separation. The infant *greets the mother warmly when she returns and will welcome physical contact with her.* The child is outgoing with strangers while the mother is present.

2. *Insecure attachment (anxious and resistant).* About 10% of 1-year-olds fall into this category. These infants appear quite anxious and are unlikely to explore while the mother is present, and they become very distressed as the mother departs. But when the mother returns, the infants are ambivalent: they will *try to remain near her,* although they seem to resent her for having left them, and they are *likely to resist physical contact initiated by the mother.* Anxious/resistant infants are quite wary of strangers, even when their mothers are present.

3. *Insecure attachment (anxious and avoidant).* These infants (about 20% of 1-year-olds) seem uninterested in exploring when alone with their mothers. Moreover, they show little distress when separated

from the mother but will generally *turn away so as to ignore or to avoid contact with her when she returns*. Anxious/avoidant infants are not particularly wary of strangers but may sometimes avoid or ignore them in much the same way that they avoid or ignore their mothers.

From these descriptions, it would appear that securely attached infants are reasonably happy individuals who have established an affectionate relationship with their primary caregivers. By contrast, infants in the anxious/resistant category are drawn to their mothers but seem not to trust them, while infants who are anxious and avoidant appear to derive little if any comfort from their mothers, almost as if they were somewhat "detached" from them.

HOW DO INFANTS BECOME SECURELY OR INSECURELY ATTACHED?

Ainsworth (1979) has suggested that the quality of an infant's attachment to his or her mother depends largely on the kinds of interactions that the mother

and the infant have had. For example, it appears that mothers of *securely attached* infants are responsive caregivers from the very beginning: they are highly sensitive to their infants' signals, emotionally expressive, and likely to encourage their infants to explore; moreover, they seem to enjoy close contact with their babies (Ainsworth, 1979; Ainsworth et al., 1978). Ainsworth believes that infants learn what to expect from other people from their early experiences with primary caregivers. When a caregiver is sensitive to the infant's needs and easily accessible, the infant should derive comfort and pleasure from their interactions and become securely attached.

Mothers of *anxious and resistant* infants seem interested in their babies and willing to provide close physical contact. However, they frequently misinterpret their infants' signals and have generally failed to establish synchronized routines with them. In some cases, part of the problem may be attributable to a "difficult" infant, for Everett Waters and his associates found that infants classified as anxious/resistant

TABLE 6-1   The Eight Episodes That Make Up the Strange-Situations Test

Episode number	Persons present	Duration	Brief description of actions
1	Mother, baby, and observer	30 seconds	Observer introduces mother and baby to experimental room, then leaves. (Room contains many appealing toys scattered about.)
2	Mother and baby	3 minutes	Mother is nonparticipant while baby explores; if necessary, play is stimulated after 2 minutes.
3	Stranger, mother, and baby	3 minutes	Stranger enters. First minute: stranger silent. Second minute: stranger converses with mother. Third minute: stranger approaches baby. After 3 minutes mother leaves unobtrusively.
4	Stranger and baby	3 minutes or less	First separation episode. Stranger's behavior is geared to that of baby.
5	Mother and baby	3 minutes or more	First reunion episode. Mother greets and/or comforts baby, then tries to settle him again in play. Mother then leaves, saying "bye-bye."
6	Baby alone	3 minutes or less	Second separation episode.
7	Stranger and baby	3 minutes or less	Continuation of second separation. Stranger enters and gears her behavior to that of baby.
8	Mother and baby	3 minutes	Second reunion episode. Mother enters, greets baby, then picks him up. Meanwhile stranger leaves unobtrusively.

at 1 year of age had often been rather irritable and unresponsive as neonates (Waters, Vaughn, & Egeland, 1980). Yet the infant's behavior cannot be the only contributor to an anxious/resistant attachment, since many difficult babies will eventually become securely attached to their caregivers. Ainsworth (1979) has noted that mothers of anxious/resistant infants tend to be *inconsistent* in their caregiving—at times they react very enthusiastically to their babies, although their responses to the infant often depend more on their own moods than on the infant's behavior. As a result, the infant becomes both anxious and resentful when he learns that he cannot count on the mother for the emotional support and comfort that he needs (see also Belsky, Rovine, & Taylor, 1984).

The mothers of *anxious and avoidant* infants differ from other mothers in several respects. For example, they are very impatient with their babies, angry or resentful when the infant interferes with their own plans and activities, and quite unresponsive to the infant's signals (Ainsworth, 1979; Egeland & Farber, 1984). Moreover, they often express negative feelings about their infants, and on those occasions when they do respond positively to their children, they tend to limit their expressions of affection to brief kisses rather than hugging or cuddling (Tracy & Ainsworth, 1981). Ainsworth (1979) believes that these mothers are rigid, self-centered people who are likely to reject their babies. Indeed, Byron Egeland and Alan Sroufe (1981) found that rejecting mothers (particularly those who express their rejection by abusing their infants) are the ones who are likely to have infants classified as anxious and avoidant.

Yet caregivers need not be extremely unresponsive or actively reject their child to promote an anxious/avoidant relationship. Jay Belsky and his associates (Belsky, Rovine, & Taylor, 1984) have discovered that some infants classified as anxious and avoidant have overzealous mothers who are constantly providing them with high levels of stimulation, even during periods when the child doesn't care to be stimulated. Perhaps these infants have learned to cope with intrusive maternal involvement by simply turning away from or avoiding their rather insensitive caregivers so as not to become overaroused (Belsky et al., 1984).

Caregivers or Infants as Architects of Attachment Quality?

To this point we have talked as if mothers were primarily responsible for the kinds of attachments their infants form. Not everyone agrees with this view. Jerome Kagan (1984), for example, has argued that the strange-situations test may really measure individual differences in infants' temperaments rather than the quality of their attachments. Accordingly, a temperamentally "difficult" infant who resists changes in routine and is upset by novelty may become so distressed by the strange-situations procedure that he is unable to respond constructively to his mother's comforting. He is thus classified by Ainsworth as "anxious and *resistant*." By contrast, an easygoing infant who is a bit shy or "slow to warm up" may appear calm and detached in the strange-situations paradigm and, thus, is apt to be classified as "anxious and *avoidant*." So Kagan's *temperament hypothesis* implies that infants, not caregivers, are the primary architects of their "attachment classifications." Presumably, the attachment behaviors that a child shows are overt reflections of his or her own temperament.

However, critics of the temperament hypothesis (for example, Sroufe, 1985) cite several observations that are damaging to that view. For example, many infants are securely attached to one parent and insecurely attached to the other—a pattern that we should not expect if attachment classifications were merely reflections of a child's relatively stable temperamental characteristics. Moreover, the quality of an infant's attachment to a particular caregiver can change relatively quickly if the caregiver experiences life changes (for example, divorce, a return to work) that significantly alter the way he or she interacts with the child (Thompson, Lamb, & Estes, 1982; Vaughn, Egeland, Waters, & Sroufe, 1979). Relatively stable aspects of temperament should not be so readily modifiable. Finally, several recent longitudinal studies have measured infant temperament, infant social behavior, and maternal caregiving over the first year to see which of these factors (or what combination of them) best predicts the quality of infant attachment at age 12 months. I shall concentrate on one of these studies in particular (Goldberg, Perrotta, Minde, & Corter, 1986) because the infants in this project were all premature and, thus, likely to display the sluggish, unresponsive temperamental characteristics that might place them at risk of developing insecure attachments. At three-month intervals over the first year, ratings were made of (1) the infants' social behaviors, (2) the mothers' caregiving styles (for example, acceptance of the child, sensitivity to social signals, accessibility), and (3) the infants' temperamental characteristics. At the end of the year, infants were tested in the strange-situations paradigm to determine the type of attachment they had to their mothers. The results were clear: the best predictor of infants' later attachment classifications was *the style of caregiving their mothers had used*, and neither infant social behaviors nor infant temperamental characteristics reliably forecasted the quality of these attachments (see also Belsky, Rovine, & Taylor, 1984, and Crittenden, 1985, for similar patterns of results). And it is important to add that the majority of Goldberg's temperamentally sluggish, "at risk" infants ended up establishing *secure* attachments with their mothers rather than the anxious, insecure relationships that might have been anticipated by Kagan's temperament hypothesis.

In sum, the research we have reviewed suggests that caregivers, not infants, are the primary architects of the quality of infants' attachments. Indeed, one recent study (Weber, Levitt, & Clark, 1986) suggests that, if temperamental variables are at all related to the security (or insecurity) of attachments, it is the mother's temperament that makes the difference, not the child's.[1] Of course, this observation is quite consistent with Ainsworth's views on the origins of secure and insecure attachments if it is reasonable to assume that a mother's temperamental characteristics will influence the type of caregiving she provides.

To this point we have focused only on the quality of the infant's attachment to his or her mother. Do you think that the kind of attachment an infant has to the mother will have any effect on the infant's relationship with the father? We will explore this issue in the next section as we take a closer look at some of the ways fathers contribute to their infants' social and emotional development.

Fathers as Attachment Objects

In 1975, Michael Lamb described fathers as the "forgotten contributors to child development." And he was right. Until the mid-1970s, fathers were largely ignored or treated as "biological necessities" who played only a minor role in the social and emotional development of their infants and toddlers. Indeed, the literature on fatherhood at that time focused mainly on the effects of father *absence* (due to death or divorce), and even then, it was felt that the absence of the father would have little if any impact on the child until the preschool period (that is, ages 2–5) and beyond.

One reason that fathers were ignored may have been that they spend much less time interacting with infants and toddlers than mothers do (Belsky, Gilstrap, & Rovine, 1984; Parke, 1981). However, fathers often appear to be just as interested in and emotionally involved with their newborn infants as mothers are (Greenberg & Morris, 1974; Parke, 1981), and they become increasingly responsive to their infants' social and emotional signals over the first year of the child's life (Belsky, Gilstrap, & Rovine, 1984). How do infants react to dad's increasing involvement?

Michael Lamb (1981) reports that many infants form attachments to their fathers during the third quarter of the first year, particularly if the fathers spend a lot of time with them. Lamb also notes that fathers and mothers respond in different ways to their babies. Mothers are more likely than fathers to hold their infants, to soothe them, to play traditional games, and to care for their needs; fathers are more likely than mothers to provide playful physical stimulation and to initiate unusual or unpredictable games that infants often enjoy (Lamb, 1981). Although many infants prefer their mothers' company when upset or afraid, fathers are generally preferred as playmates. However, the playmate role is only one of many that fathers assume. Most fathers are quite skillful at soothing and comforting their distressed infants, and they may also serve as a "secure base" from which their babies will venture to explore the environment (Lamb, 1981). In other words, fathers are rather versatile companions who can assume any and all of the functions normally served by the other parent (of course, the same is true of mothers).

Now, if parents are so versatile, why do you suppose fathers and mothers often behave so very differently toward their infants? Many investigators believe that the answer is simple—the mother quickly assumes the role of primary caregiver, thereby pushing the father in another direction if he hopes to play a special role in the infant's life. Although this "social roles" hypothesis seems reasonable, it cannot easily account for the results of a recent study by Michael Lamb and his associates (Lamb, Frodi, Hwang, Frodi, & Steinberg, 1982). Lamb et al. found that, even in nontraditional families where the father has served as the child's primary caregiver, mothers continue to be the most nurturant or comforting parent. The implication of these findings is that a parent's biological gender or early sex typing may have a greater influence on his or her reactions to an infant than the parent's actual involvement in caregiving activities.

Although research on fatherhood is still a new endeavor, we have already learned that the father is a very important contributor to his infant's social, emotional, and intellectual development. Let's take a closer look at these findings.

Fathers' impact on intellectual activities. In one of the earliest intensive studies of fatherhood, Alison Clarke-Stewart (1978, 1980) found that infants whose fathers were highly involved with them scored higher on intelligence tests than those whose fathers were less involved. Easterbrooks and Goldberg (1984) have essentially corroborated these findings with a sample of young toddlers. Children whose fathers were highly involved with them and sensitive to their needs expressed more positive affect while working at a cognitive challenge (a jigsaw puzzle) and persisted longer at the task than those whose fathers were less sensitive and involved. Moreover, Easterbrooks and Goldberg report that the fathers' *sensitivity* to their toddlers' needs was a better predictor of the children's cognitive performance than fathers' overall involvement in caregiving activities. So even with fathers, the type or *quali-*

ty of interaction is a more important determinant of the child's developmental outcomes than the sheer amount of contact the father provides.

Fathers as contributors to social and emotional development. Does the kind of attachment that an infant establishes with his or her mother affect the infant's relationship with the father? Not necessarily. Mary Main and Donna Weston (1981) used the strange-situations test to measure the quality of infants' attachments to both their mothers and their fathers. They found that the quality of the child's attachment to one parent did not predict the type of attachment relationship that the infant had with the second parent. Of the 43 infants tested, 12 were securely attached to both parents, 11 were secure with the mother but insecure with the father, 10 were insecure with the mother but secure with the father, and 11 were insecurely attached to both parents.

What does the father add to a child's social and emotional development? One way to find out is to compare the social behavior of infants who are securely attached to their fathers and infants whose relationships with their fathers are insecure. Main and Weston adopted this strategy by exposing their four groups of infants to a friendly stranger in a clown costume who first spent several minutes trying to play with the child and then turned around and cried when a person at the door told the clown he would have to leave. As the clown went through his routine, the infants were observed and rated for (1) the extent to which they were willing to establish a positive relationship with the clown (low ratings indicated that the infant was wary or distressed) and (2) signs of emotional conflict (that is, indications of psychological disturbance such as curling up in the fetal position on the floor or vocalizing in a "social" manner to a wall). Table 6-2 shows the results of this stranger test. Note that infants who were securely attached to both parents were the most socially responsive group. Equally important is the finding that infants who were securely attached to *at least one parent* were more friendly toward the clown and less emotionally conflicted than infants who had insecure relationships with both parents. In sum, this study illustrates the important role that fathers play in their infants' social and emotional development. Not only are infants more socially responsive when they are securely attached to *both* parents, but it also appears that a secure attachment to the father can help to prevent harmful consequences (emotional disturbances; an exaggerated fear of other people) that may otherwise result when infants are insecurely attached to their mothers.

LONG-TERM CORRELATES OF SECURE AND INSECURE ATTACHMENTS

Does the quality of an infant's attachment relationships predict his or her later behavior? Apparently so. And even though the existing data are somewhat limited in that they focus almost exclusively on infants' attachments to their mothers, the long-term correlates of these secure and insecure attachments are very interesting indeed. For example, Susan Londerville and Mary Main (1981) found that infants who were securely attached at 12 months of age are more likely than those who were insecurely attached to obey their mothers and to cooperate with female strangers at 21 months of age. Moreover, infants who were securely attached at 12–18 months are more curious at age 2 and more sociable with peers, and by age 3 they are even more comfortable *competing* with a strange adult at a game than children with a history of insecure attachment (Lutkenhaus, Grossmann, & Grossmann, 1985; Matas, Arend, & Sroufe, 1978; Pastor, 1981). And it is interesting to note that, from a peer's point of view, securely attached 2–3-year-olds are much more attractive as playmates than are children who are insecurely attached. In fact, peers often respond in an overtly negative or aggressive

way to playmates classified as "anxious and resistant" (Jacobson & Wille, 1986).

The relationship of early attachment to social and intellectual behavior during the *preschool* period is nicely illustrated in a study by Everett Waters and his associates. Waters, Wippman, and Sroufe (1979) first measured the quality of children's attachments at 15 months of age and then observed these children in a nursery school setting at age 3½. Children who had been securely attached to their mothers at age 15 months were now social leaders in nursery school: they often initiated play activities, were generally sensitive to the needs and feelings of other children, and were very popular with their peers. Observers described these children as curious, self-directed, and eager to learn. By contrast, children who had been insecurely attached at age 15 months were socially and emotionally withdrawn, were hesitant to engage other children in play activities, and were described by observers as less curious, less interested in learning, and much less forceful in pursuing their goals. By age 4 to 5, children who had been securely attached as infants were still more curious, more responsive to peers, and much less dependent on adults than their classmates who had been insecurely attached (Arend, Gove, & Sroufe, 1979; Sroufe, Fox, & Pancake, 1983).

Clearly, these findings are consistent with Erik Erikson's ideas about the importance of developing an early sense of "trust" in other people. Perhaps securely attached infants who have learned to trust an easily accessible and responsive caregiver become curious problem solvers later in life because they feel comfortable at venturing away from an attentive parent to explore and, as a result, they learn how to

TABLE 6-2 Average Levels of Social Responsiveness and Emotional Conflict Shown by Infants Who Were Either Securely or Insecurely Attached to Their Mothers and Fathers

Measure	Pattern of attachment			
	Securely attached to both parents	*Secure with mother, insecure with father*	*Insecure with mother, secure with father*	*Insecurely attached to both parents*
Social responsiveness	6.94	4.87	3.30	2.45
Emotional conflict	1.17	1.00	1.80	2.50

Note: Social responsiveness ratings could vary from 1 (wary, distressed) to 9 (happy, responsive). Conflict ratings could vary from 1 (no conflict) to 5 (very conflicted).

answer questions and how to solve problems on their own. Moreover, securely attached infants may be quite sociable and rather popular with their peers because they have already established pleasant relationships with responsive caregivers and have learned from these experiences that human beings are likely to react positively to their social gestures. By contrast, an anxious, insecure infant who has not learned to trust her caregivers may find it exceedingly difficult to trust other people. In fact, the insecurities surrounding her interpersonal relationships may make the child less interested in the novel aspects of her environment, thereby hindering her exploratory activities and preventing her from developing the individual initiative that would help her to answer questions and to solve problems.

Fortunately, the future is not always so bleak for infants who are insecurely attached. As we noted earlier, a secure relationship with another person, such as the father (or perhaps a grandparent or an older sibling), may help to prevent the harmful consequences of an insecure attachment to the mother. In addition, it is quite possible for an initially insecure attachment to become more secure over time. One reason infants become insecurely attached in the first place is often that their mothers have withdrawn from caregiving activities because of life stresses of their own, such as health or marital problems, financial woes, and lack of emotional support from friends and family members. Recently, researchers have been finding that initially insecure infants are likely to become securely attached if the lives of their close companions become less stressful (Vaughn et al., 1979). Often these positive developments take place as highly stressed and emotionally unresponsive mothers begin to receive emotional support and assistance from a close friend, a spouse, or a grandparent (Crockenberg, 1981; Egeland & Sroufe, 1981).

However, it is also possible for securely attached infants to become insecurely attached if their caregivers experience life changes that make them less accessible and less responsive to their children. Ross Thompson and his colleagues (Thompson, Lamb, & Estes, 1982) have found that secure attachments sometimes change for the worse if the mother returns

to work or if the child begins to receive regular caregiving from someone else (for example, a babysitter or a day-care agency). Unlike diamonds, attachments are not forever: any event that drastically alters the ways an infant and caregiver respond to each other is likely to have a significant effect on the quality of their emotional relationship.

But it would be wrong to create the impression that all mothers will undermine the security of their infants' attachments by returning to work or enrolling their children in a day-care center. At it turns out, the effects of maternal employment and alternative caregiving are bidirectional: although some securely attached infants will become insecure, at least as many insecure infants will develop secure attachments to their mothers after the mother has returned to work or enrolled them in a day-care facility (Thompson et al., 1982). In the next section we will take a closer look at the effects of maternal employment and alternative caregiving and try to determine why these events and experiences do not affect all children in the same way.

MATERNAL EMPLOYMENT AND ALTERNATIVE CAREGIVING: DO THEY HINDER CHILDREN'S EMOTIONAL DEVELOPMENT?

Working mothers are no longer exceptions to the rule. In the United States, over half of all mothers who live with their husbands are now employed outside the home, and the percentage of working mothers in single-parent households is even higher (Hoffman, 1984). Not only does work take a mother away from her child for several hours a day, but her infants or preschool children will also have to adjust to some kind of alternative caregiving—either in-home or out-of-the-home care by a babysitter or relative or care provided by a group day-care center (Etaugh, 1980). Are these daily separations and contacts with alternative caregivers likely to undermine an infant's attachment to the mother? Will they have a harmful effect on a child's social and emotional development? Let's first consider the effects of maternal employment.

Maternal Employment and the Infant's Relations with Caregivers

Mothers who work outside the home are obviously less accessible to their children (at least during working hours) than mothers who remain at home full-time. One recent study found that working mothers spent much less time alone with their children than nonemployed mothers did; and the more hours these mothers worked, the less time they spent playing with their infants and toddlers (Easterbrooks & Goldberg, 1985). Nevertheless, a recent review of the literature suggests that maternal employment, in itself, is unlikely to have adverse effects on the vast majority of young children (Hoffman, 1984). According to Lois Hoffman (1984), working mothers can be quite successful at establishing secure relationships with their infants and toddlers if they compensate for their lack of available time for their children by being particularly sensitive and responsive when they do interact with them. Moreover, Easterbrooks and Goldberg (1985) find that families spend just as many hours together in "family" activities in households where mothers work as in those where only the father is employed. So it is quite conceivable that intensive *family* interactions provide all the experience an infant needs to become (or remain) securely attached to a working mother.

Yet there is another side to this story—one that we must consider before drawing any firm conclusions of our own. Most of the studies that show no differences in the emotional development of children of working mothers and those whose mothers are not employed have focused on *two-parent, middle-class* families. Thus, the working mothers in this research may have been relatively advantaged in that other adults (the fathers) were available to assume some of the child care responsibilities and to encourage them as they tried to maintain warm, loving relationships with their infants and toddlers. Can we assume that the results of these studies would also apply to economically disadvantaged families, particularly those in which the working mothers are single parents and have no spousal support?

Probably not. In a recent study of economically disadvantaged mothers and their infants, Vaughn, Gove, and Egeland (1980) found that infants whose mothers had returned to work before the infants' first birthday were much more likely to develop anxious/avoidant attachments than infants from similar backgrounds whose mothers cared for them at home. Moreover, the likelihood that these infants' attachments would become (or remain) insecure over time was greater if the working mother was a single parent. Although some of the difficulties these infants experienced may be attributable to the unstable day care they received (80% of them had experienced at least one change in alternative caregivers), the data imply that an early return to work by mothers who must raise their children without support from a spouse can impede the development of secure emotional attachments.

What are the effects of a mother's return to work during the second year, after the infant has already formed an attachment to her? In their study of economically disadvantaged families, Vaughn et al. (1980) found that half the infants whose mothers returned to work after the infants' first birthday changed attachment classifications. Yet the direction of these changes was very interesting in that insecure infants were about as likely to become securely attached after their mothers' return to work as secure infants were to become insecurely attached. Moreover, a recent short-term longitudinal study of *two-parent, middle-class* families (Owen, Easterbrooks, Chase-Lansdale, & Goldberg, 1984) found that not one infant classified as securely attached at age 12 months became insecurely attached after the mother had returned to work. Of course, it is possible that an infant from virtually any background could become insecurely attached if his mother's return to work significantly alters the ways she reacts to his social overtures and emotional needs (see Thompson, Lamb, & Estes, 1982). But the bulk of the evidence suggests that emotionally responsive mothers, particularly those who have the support of their husbands, need not worry about undermining an already secure relationship with an infant should they decide to return to work.

Finally, an unexpected outcome of the longitudinal study by Owen et al. (1984) is worth noting here. Infants whose mothers returned to work in the second year occasionally became more insecure in their relationships with their *fathers*! The authors explain this finding by speculating that fathers often spend more time on routine household chores after their wives return to work and, as a result, may become less physically and emotionally responsive to their infants. Will these emerging insecurities eventually subside as fathers become more proficient at striking a balance between housework and caregiving activities? At this point we can't say, for the research that could tell us remains to be conducted. And in view of the important roles that fathers play in their children's social and emotional development, perhaps such research should become a priority.

Effects of Infant Day Care

The dramatic rise in maternal employment over the past 25 years means that increasing numbers of infants and toddlers have had to adjust to some kind of alternative caregiving, or "day care." Who looks after these youngsters while their parents are away at work? Perhaps the best data on this question come from a nationally representative sample of 55,000 employed women in the United States, each of whom had a child under 1 year of age in day care (Klein, 1985). As shown in Table 6-3, the percentages of children in various kinds of day care differ somewhat depending on the mothers' employment status. When the mother works part-time, infants are frequently cared for in their own homes by their fathers or other relatives. By contrast, infants whose mothers work full-time are more likely to be placed in someone else's home, and more often than not the alternative caregiver is not related to the child. Finally, it is

worthy of note that fewer than 10% of the infants in this sample were placed in day-care centers (that is, caregiving environments designed to handle large numbers of children and organized somewhat like a nursery school) and that the vast majority of preschool children whose mothers work will never experience any center-based alternative care (Roupp & Travers, 1982). This is an interesting observation because most of our knowledge about the effects of day care is based on studies of children in day-care centers! Therefore, we must be very cautious about generalizing the findings we will discuss to the larger population of children receiving alternative care.

Day care and the mother/infant relationship. Although some developmentalists have voiced an opinion that young children deserve good mothering and that a mother's place is in the home (for example, Fraiberg, 1977; Packard, 1983), it was Bowlby's work on children's reactions to separation (Bowlby, 1960, 1973) that made day care a controversial subject. Bowlby has argued that any of several caregiving arrangements that deny an infant access to his or her one special companion (usually the mother) could have rather severe emotional consequences for the child. Those familiar with Bowlby's research soon begin to speculate. Would regular and prolonged exposure to alternative caregivers undermine an infant's emotional security? Is there a danger that infants in day care will form close attachments to their alternative caregivers and become less responsive to or even "detached" from their biological parents?

TABLE 6-3 Percentages of Infants in Various Day-Care Arrangements as a Function of Mother's Employment Status

| | Caregiving arrangements | | | | | | |
| | Home care | | | Care in another home | | | |
Mother's employment status	Fathers	Grandparent or other relative	Non-relative	Grandparent or other relative	Non-relative	Day-care center	Other
Part-time (less than 35 hours/week)	22.8	14.1	6.5	17.8	14.1	3.3	21.3
Full-time (more than 35 hours/week)	8.9	13.9	6.3	20.8	28.0	6.3	15.8

Although infants and toddlers are often visibly distressed when they first enter day care, most children in day-care centers soon adjust to the daily routine and will often become attached to their substitute caregivers (Belsky, 1985; Etaugh, 1980). However, there is little evidence that these attachments undermine a child's emotional relationships with parents: given a choice, most children who receive group day care continue to prefer their mothers to their substitute caregivers (Cummings, 1980; Ragozin, 1980). Finally, there are even some data to indicate that *excellent* day care provided by sensitive and responsive companions improves the social skills and may even promote the intellectual development of children from economically disadvantaged homes (O'Connell & Farran, 1982; Zeskind & Ramey, 1981). In sum, these findings paint a very rosy picture, suggesting that mothers need not worry about harming their children or subverting their own emotional relationships with them should they leave their youngsters with a substitute caregiver.

However, we must be extremely cautious in interpreting these outcomes. Most of the studies that show no differences between day-care children and children raised at home have looked at *middle-class samples* in which the alternative care was of *unusually high quality* (Anderson, Nagle, Roberts, & Smith, 1981). Unfortunately, we cannot be sure that the results of these studies would apply to economically disadvantaged children, who may often receive much less stimulating kinds of day care. In addition, we have already seen that some securely attached infants from middle-class homes become insecurely attached when their mothers return to work and/or arrange for them to receive alternative care (Thompson et al., 1982). So although many youngsters are not adversely affected by alternative caregiving, the fact remains that these arrangements can disrupt the emotional development of some children.

Why do children differ in their reactions to day care? Let's consider two possibilities.

Age at entry. One factor that may affect a child's responses to alternative care is the child's age at the time day care begins. Recently, researchers have been finding that infants from both lower-class and middle-class backgrounds are much more likely to develop insecure attachments to their mothers if the mother returns to work before the child's first birthday and the child receives full-time (all day) alternative care (Schwartz, 1983; Vaughn et al., 1980; see also Box 6-1). Moreover, older preschool and school-age children who began day care early in infancy are sometimes found to be more aggressive toward their peers and less cooperative with adults than children who entered day care as toddlers (Belsky & Steinberg, 1978; Etaugh, 1980; Haskins, 1985).

However, Jerome Kagan and his associates reported that one group of infants who began to participate in a very high-quality day-care program at age 3½ to 5½ months were not adversely affected. When later given the strange-situations test, these infants were securely attached to their mothers. Moreover, their performance on other assessments of social, emotional, and intellectual growth was quite comparable to that of a second group of children from similar social backgrounds who had been cared for at home by their mothers (Kagan, Kearsley, & Zelazo, 1978). So it seems that early exposure to alternative caregiving need not be harmful, provided the care is excellent.[2]

Quality of alternative care. According to experts on alternative care, an excellent day-care facility is one that has (1) a reasonable child-to-caregiver ratio (4–12 children per adult), (2) caregivers who are warm, emotionally expressive, and responsive to children's bids for attention, (3) little staff turnover so that children can become familiar and feel comfortable with their new adult companions, (4) a "curriculum" made up of games and activities that are age-appropriate, and (5) an "administration" that is willing (or, better yet, eager) to confer with parents about the child's progress (Anderson et al., 1981; Kagan et al., 1978). Given adequate training and resources, and some effort on the substitute caregiver's part, all these criteria can be achieved by a relative or regular sitter providing in-home care, a nonrelative operating a day-care home,[3] or a formal day-care center.

Unfortunately, we know very little about the quality of care that children *typically* receive in different caregiving arrangements. Rubenstein and Howes (1979) found that alternative caregiving in high-quality day-care centers tends to be more affectionate and play-oriented than the care that children receive at home from nonworking mothers, whereas other investigators have reported that nonworking mothers provide more sensitive and responsive caregiving than substitute caregivers in unregulated day-care homes (Rubenstein, Pedersen, & Yarrow, 1977; Stith & Davis, 1984). Yet these observations are based on very small samples, and there is considerable variation in the quality of care provided in each of these kinds of arrangements. Some day-care centers provide poor care, whereas some day-care homes may be excellent. Additional research that focuses on the quality of all kinds of day care is sorely needed.

But regardless of the setting in which care is given, it is now apparent that the quality of day care that children receive can make a difference. For example, we have seen that even very young infants who experience alternative caregiving are likely to become securely attached to their parents if the care they receive is outstanding (Kagan et al., 1978). In addition, children are more likely to become attached to their substitute caregivers and to profit from the day-care curriculum when they interact with the same caregiver over a long period and when the caregiver is knowledgeable about children and responsive to their needs (Anderson et al., 1981; Belsky, 1985; Cummings, 1980). The size of the day-care group is also important: children who are cared for in smaller groups (15 or fewer) are more outgoing with their peers and score higher on standardized tests than children who are part of larger aggregations (Roupp, Travers, Glantz, & Coelen, 1979).

Perhaps we can summarize by concluding that most children who receive good alternative care are unlikely to suffer any adverse effects as a result of their day-to-day separations from working parents. However, the outcome may not be so favorable for a very young infant who receives substandard day care from an unresponsive caregiver (or a series of caregivers), particularly if the working mother hasn't the support of a spouse and/or lacks the time, patience, or energy to respond sensitively to her baby's signals when she does come home (Vaughn et al., 1980).

THE UNATTACHED INFANT: EFFECTS OF RESTRICTED SOCIAL CONTACTS DURING INFANCY

Some infants have very limited contacts with adults during the first year or two of life and do not appear to become attached to anyone. Occasionally these socially deprived youngsters are reared at home by very abusive or neglectful caregivers, but most of them are found in understaffed institutions where they may see a caregiver only when it is time to be fed, changed, or bathed. Will these unattached infants suffer as a result of their early experiences? If so, how are they likely to differ from children raised at home by a responsive caregiver, and what, if anything, can be done to "normalize" their developmental progress? These are the issues we will consider in the pages that follow.

We will begin by looking at the immediate and long-range effects of social deprivation on puppies and infant monkeys. Although this may seem a strange way to approach questions about socially deprived humans, there are several good reasons for reviewing the animal literature. For one thing, socially deprived humans are rather hard to come by: very few babies are raised without a primary caregiver, and it is clearly unethical to subject human infants to conditions of prolonged social deprivation when we have reason to suspect that these experiences will prove harmful to their development. But animals can be subjected to varying degrees of deprivation in controlled experiments that permit the investigator to infer cause-and-effect relationships. This is hardly the ideal solution, for one can never be absolutely certain that findings obtained for animals will hold for humans. However, animals do develop, and the development of monkeys, like that of human infants, takes place over a period of years. Infant monkeys also form emotional attachments to their mothers—attachments that closely resemble the human infant's emotional ties to close companions. So it would seem that tightly controlled experimental studies of socially deprived monkeys may help us to understand the behavior of human beings who have not had an opportunity to become attached to a primary caregiver.

BOX 6-1   *EARLY EMOTIONAL DEVELOPMENT IN THE KIBBUTZ*

Early in the 20th century when Zionist pioneers founded their first collective settlements, or kibbutzim, a system of communal child care was employed to enable a greater number of adults to perform economically productive work. Over the years, this system of child rearing has become something of an institution, and it is quite common today in Israel. In the modern kibbutz, women are granted brief maternity leaves to deliver and care for their neonates but will generally return to work within 6 to 12 weeks after the child is born. During the hours that mothers are working, their children are cared for by specially designated caretakers (called *metaplot*; singular, *metapelet*), each of whom looks after three to four children of the same age. Children typically stay with the same metapelet for 12 to 15 months, when they are reassigned to another metapelet. All children remain with peers and the metapelet throughout the day, except for the period between 4:00 and 7:00 P.M., when they are with their parents. At night, children of the kibbutz are assigned to *biet tinokot* and *biet yeladim* ("children's homes"), where they are looked after by "watchwomen" who periodically walk from residence to residence. Because many women in the kibbutz take turns as watchwomen, these caregivers are often quite unfamiliar to the children.

Abraham Sagi and his colleagues (Sagi et al., 1985) point out that child-rearing practices in the kibbutz differ substantially from those considered optimal by Ainsworth and her associates. Not only do children receive alternative

care from a very early age, but they have less contact with parents than home-reared infants do and are monitored at night by unfamiliar watchwomen, who have many children to look after and may be slow to respond to a child's distress or other bids for attention. Moreover, women serving as primary caregivers, or metaplot, are *assigned* to this work, and they may or may not be enthusiastic about serving in that capacity. For all these reasons, Sagi et al. presumed that the incidence of insecure attachments would be greater among kibbutz-reared infants than among children from the United States or Israeli children raised in home settings.

To test this hypothesis, Sagi et al. administered the strange-situations test to 86 kibbutz-reared infants aged 11 to 14 months. Each child was tested three times to assess the quality of his or her attachment to the mother, the father, and the metapelet. The resulting data were then compared with the patterns of attachment observed among U.S. children and among a second sample of 36 home-reared Israeli infants.

As we see in examining the table, Sagi et al. found that insecure attachments were more common among kibbutz-reared infants than among their U.S. counterparts or Israeli children raised at home. The latter comparison is particularly interesting in that the home-reared Israeli infants were recruited from day-care centers and, thus, were themselves receiving alternative care (although not from the early age that kibbutz-reared infants had).

Although it is tempting to conclude that *early* entry into

EFFECTS OF SOCIAL ISOLATION IN DOGS

Thompson and Melzack (1956) describe an interesting series of experiments designed to measure the effects of social isolation on the development of Scottish-terrier puppies. Each puppy assigned to the experimental group was separated from its mother immediately after weaning and housed in a cage with opaque sides. These pups were then isolated from other puppies and humans for several months. By contrast, puppies assigned to the control group were reared (1) with other dogs in the laboratory or (2) in a home setting with human caretakers.

After seven to ten months both groups were tested for their fear of strange stimuli, their relative dominance, and their social responsiveness. Thompson

and Melzack found that the isolated puppies were much more agitated when exposed to novel stimuli, such as an umbrella opening, than the control puppies. They were also less dominant than control puppies when placed in a situation where they had to compete with the control puppies for a bone. The results of the social responsiveness test were particularly interesting. Social responsiveness was measured by releasing the puppy into a large pen that contained two other dogs confined to opposite corners of the pen by chicken-wire partitions. The isolates were observed to pay very little attention to other dogs, spending most of their time sniffing around and exploring the pen itself. Control pups, in contrast, spent a considerable amount of time barking at, wagging their tails at, and examining the other

BOX 6-1 continued

alternative care is the factor responsible for the higher incidence of insecure attachments among kibbutz-reared infants, such an explanation, by itself, is much too simplistic. Apparently the quality of caregiving that infants had received from the metaplot is also of critical importance. Not only did an infant's attachment to his or her metapelet predict the quality of the infant's attachment to his or her father, but most infants under the care of a particular metapelet established exactly the same kind of attachment to her. Thus, some metaplot have characteristics that promote secure attachments, whereas other metaplot seem to promote insecure attachments. Although these latter findings are intriguing in their own right, they also lend support to the results of U.S. studies (see text) that find that early entry into day care presents few if any adjustment problems when alternative caregivers are enthusiastic about their responsibilities, warm and emotionally expressive, and sensitive to children's needs.

Finally, it is important to note that kibbutz-reared infants who do establish insecure relationships with their metapelet or their parents are hardly doomed to a life of emotional insecurity. Recall that kibbutzniks are routinely reassigned to new metaplot in the second year, a practice that provides them another opportunity to become secure emotionally with a very close companion. Indeed, studies of kibbutz-reared preschoolers (for example, Levy-Shiff, 1983; Maccoby & Feldman, 1972) find that most 2- to 3-year-old kibbutzniks eventually establish close ties to their parents

and are as well adjusted, both emotionally and to formal nursery school routines, as U.S. or Israeli children who have been raised at home. However, it is important to emphasize that the long-term outcomes may be nowhere near as positive for children (kibbutz-raised or otherwise) who continue to receive alternative care from someone who is unresponsive to them and insensitive to their needs.

Attachment Patterns Observed among Three Groups of Infants

	Type of attachment	
Sample	Insecure	Secure
U.S. sample		
with mother	33%	66%
Kibbutz sample		
with mother	49	48
with father	44	54
with metapelet	52	45
Home-reared Israeli sample		
with mother	25	75

Note: Percentages in some rows do not add to 100% because some infants were judged to be unattached or their attachments were not easily classifiable.

dogs. Follow-up observations revealed that the isolates' relative lack of social responsiveness persisted for several years.

The latter finding comes as no surprise to John Scott. Scott and his colleagues (Elliot & Scott, 1961; Scott, 1962, 1968; Scott & Marston, 1950) have studied the development of social attachments in dogs and concluded that the period between 3 and 12 weeks of age is critical for the development of social responsiveness. Isolation during this period (as was the case in Thompson and Melzack's study) should prevent puppies from ever becoming highly receptive to the presence of other dogs or human beings. Indeed, Freedman, King, and Elliot (1961) reported that cocker-spaniel pups that had been isolated for 14 weeks were not susceptible to training because

they fled whenever a human approached.

Other investigators have found that isolated puppies develop rather strange behaviors during their period of confinement. For example, Fuller and Clark (1966a, 1966b) report that a puppy isolated during the period of primary social attachments often adopts bizarre postures, such as cringing in a corner of a test room with one paw raised above its head and its body forced into the angle formed by the walls. Scott (1968) suggests that the isolate may simply be trying to retreat from the strange stimuli afforded by the new environment or may perhaps derive comfort from contact similar to that provided by the walls of its isolation chamber.

These few studies reveal that isolate pups differ from normally reared pups in many ways. Perhaps

PHOTO 6-1 Isolate monkeys often display unusual postures.

the most notable difference is the relative lack of social responsiveness characterizing puppies that have not had an opportunity to become attached to a caretaker or some other companion during their period of primary socialization.

SOCIAL DEPRIVATION IN MONKEYS

Many investigators have studied the effects of early social deprivation on rhesus monkeys, and their findings are remarkably consistent: monkeys isolated for the first six months of life or longer show extremely abnormal patterns of behavior that persist into adulthood. One of the best known of these research programs is that of Harry and Margaret Harlow (1977). The Harlows isolated rhesus monkeys at birth by placing them in individual wire cages where they could see and hear but could not touch other monkeys (partial social deprivation) or in stainless-steel cubicles in which all light was diffused, sounds were filtered, temperature and air flow were controlled, and even feeding and cleaning of the chambers were automated (total social deprivation). These two kinds of isolation produced similar effects.

Three months of social deprivation left infants in a state of emotional shock. When removed from isolation, the infant avoided other monkeys and generally gave the appearance of being terrified by clutching at

itself, crouching, or burying its head in its arms as if trying to shut out this strange new world (see Photo 6-1). So here we see a commonality in the effects of social isolation on puppies and monkeys: abnormal postural adjustments. The isolate monkeys also showed abnormal behaviors such as self-biting, rocking, and pulling out tufts of their hair. However, these three-month isolates eventually recovered. Daily 30-minute play periods with a normal age mate soon led to the development of effective social relationships that persisted into adolescence and adulthood.

The prognosis was not nearly so optimistic for infants isolated six months or longer. The six-month isolates clearly avoided normal age mates during free-play sessions, preferring instead to play by themselves with toys. What little social responsiveness they did show was directed toward other isolates, leading the Harlows to conclude that "misery prefers miserable company." Normally reared infant monkeys usually go through a phase of aggressive play as they near their first birthday. Yet when the six-month isolates were attacked by other infants, they accepted the abuse without offering much of a defense. Bad as this behavioral pattern may sound, the effects of 12 months of social isolation were even worse. The Harlows describe the plight of their 12-month isolates as follows:

> Monkeys that have been isolated for twelve months are very seriously affected. . . . Even primitive and simple play activity is almost nonexistent. With these isolated animals no social play is observed [either with controls or with other isolates] and aggressive behavior is never demonstrated. Their behavior is a pitiful combination of apathy and terror as they crouch at the sides of the room, meekly accepting the attacks of the more [emotionally] healthy control monkeys. We have been unable to test them in the playroom beyond a ten-week period because they are in danger of being seriously injured or even killed by the others [1977, p. 95].

Follow-up studies of monkeys isolated six months or longer have found that the isolates develop bizarre patterns of social and sexual behavior during adolescence and adulthood. Harlow describes the adult sexual behavior of these monkeys as follows:

> When the [isolate] females were smaller than the sophisticated [normally reared, breeding] males, the

PHOTO 6-2 Typical abusive behavior of "motherless" mother monkeys toward their own infants.

girls would back away and sit down facing the males [an inadequate attempt at sexual posturing], looking appealingly at these would-be consorts. Their hearts were in the right place, but nothing else was. When the females were larger than the males, we can only hope that they misunderstood the males' intentions, for after a brief period of courtship, they would attack and maul the ill-fated male. Females show no respect for a male they can dominate. [Isolate] males were equally unsatisfactory. They approached the [normal] females with a blind . . . misdirected enthusiasm. Frequently, the males would grasp the females by the side of the body and thrust laterally, . . . working at cross purposes with reality. Even the most persistent attempts by these females to set the boys straight came to naught. Finally, these females either stared at the males with complete contempt or attacked them in utter frustration [Harlow, 1962, p. 5].

Isolates as mothers. What kind of mothers do isolate females make?[4] Harlow and his associates (Harlow, Harlow, Dodsworth, & Arling, 1966) found that these "motherless mothers" frequently pushed their infants away, refusing to let them nurse, and sometimes even subjected them to severe physical abuse. Several infants were actually killed. Others had to be separated from their mothers almost immediately in order to ensure their survival. For example:

In one instance the infant was separated within an hour of birth after the mother had bitten off or mangled six fingers. Two weeks later after the infant had recovered, it was replaced with the mother, but she immediately started to bite the infant's toes and the infant was then permanently removed [Harlow et al., 1966, p. 90].

Two other remarkable findings emerged from Harlow's study of "motherless mothers." First, the surviving offspring of these brutal or indifferent mothers showed a relatively normal pattern of social development. Thus, unloving mothers are better than no mothers at all, a finding that undoubtedly surprised many social-developmental theorists. Second, the "motherless mothers" who were blessed with second and even third babies suddenly became adequate mothers. Harlow et al. (1966) proposed that the first infants may have served a socializing function by partially compensating for the previous social deprivation of the isolates, thereby allowing these "motherless mothers" to develop enough social responsiveness to accept subsequent babies. The notion that infants may serve as socializing agents for their mothers is supported by the observation that "motherless mothers" played (in a fashion characteristic of preadolescents) with their second and third babies, whereas normal rhesus mothers have ordinarily ceased to play with any monkey once they reach maturity. But despite the vast improvement in their maternal behaviors, the "motherless mothers" continued to display incompetent social and sexual responsiveness toward other adult monkeys.

Can isolate monkeys recover? Harlow and his associates initially believed that the first six months of life was a *critical period* for the social development of rhesus monkeys. Presumably rhesus infants who were denied social stimulation and who remained unattached to another monkey for six months or longer would become forever incapable of establishing normal social and emotional relationships. However, a later experiment by Steven Suomi and Harry Harlow (1972) challenged this point of view by showing that the isolation syndrome can be reversed.

Suomi and Harlow isolated four male rhesus infants for a six-month period and then exposed the isolates to 26 weeks of "therapy." The therapists in this case were younger rhesus females who were 3 months of age at the beginning of the therapy sessions. Why younger therapists? For two reasons. First, normally reared age mates are likely to attack the passive isolates and will accept these strangers only if they defend themselves. Unfortunately, the isolates do not defend themselves; instead, they withdraw and their condition worsens. By contrast, a 3-month-old infant has not yet become active and aggressive in its play; the initial response of the younger infant is to approach and cling tenaciously to the passive isolate rather than working him over. Suomi and Harlow reasoned that an emotionally disturbed isolate might be able to tolerate the presence of a relatively passive, nonaggressive infant and perhaps would even learn to respond to the younger therapist's playful antics. Once the isolate had been "drawn out of his shell," both he and his younger companion might then progress together toward the development of normal social behaviors.

For the first four weeks of the project, each isolate saw his therapist for two-hour periods, three days a week. Contact time was gradually increased so that by the 12th week of therapy each isolate and his younger therapist had contact with each other and with a second isolate/therapist pair several times a week. All the isolates were severely disturbed when they emerged from isolation, and their abnormal behaviors persisted for the first 60 days of the program. But by the end of the 26 weeks of therapy, the isolates had recovered. Their behavioral abnormalities had largely disappeared, and their play antics were virtually indistinguishable from those of their socially competent therapists. In no way did these isolates resemble the rather pitiful, socially inept creatures described in earlier reports. Follow-up studies of these "rehabilitated" monkeys found their behavior to be perfectly normal and age-appropriate two years later (Cummins & Suomi, 1976).

Melinda Novak (1979) has now used this *younger-peer therapy* to treat rhesus monkeys who were isolated for their entire first year. Novak reports that even these profoundly disturbed 12-month isolates will eventually become socially and sexually competent as adults if they are eased into a rehabilitative program with a younger therapist.

Clearly, these dramatic reversals contradict the

PHOTO 6-3 Younger "therapist" monkey clinging to the back of her older isolate playmate.

critical-period hypothesis—a viewpoint that implied that the devastating social and emotional consequences of prolonged isolation were permanent and irreversible. Perhaps it is more accurate to say that the first six months of life is a "sensitive" period when normally reared monkeys are rapidly developing important social skills and becoming attached to their mothers. Although social deprivation interferes with these activities and produces a rather disturbed young monkey, recovery is possible if the patient is given the proper therapy.

SOCIAL DEPRIVATION IN HUMANS

Fortunately, there are both legal and ethical constraints to prevent researchers from isolating human infants for scientific purposes. Yet in the recent past, physicians and psychologists began to discover that infants in some orphanages and foundling homes were being raised under conditions that resembled those experienced by Harlow's socially deprived monkeys. For example, it was not uncommon for an impoverished institution to have but one caregiver for every 12 to 20 infants. Moreover, the caregivers in these understaffed institutions rarely saw the infants except to bathe and change them or to prop a bottle against the infant's pillow at feeding times. Infants were often housed in separate cribs with sheets hung over the railings so that, in effect, they were isolated from the world around them. To make matters worse, babies in the more impoverished of these institutions had no crib toys to manipulate and few if any opportunities to get out of their cribs and practice motor skills. Compared with infants raised in a typical home setting, these institutionalized children received very little in the way of social or sensory stimulation.

Early Studies of Institutionalized Infants

Since the early 1940s, several investigators have reported the same reliable and quite alarming outcome: children raised for the first year of life in impoverished and understaffed institutions are likely to show signs of severe developmental retardation (Goldfarb, 1943, 1945, 1947; Provence & Lipton, 1962; Ribble, 1943; Spitz, 1945). Typically these infants appear quite normal for the first three to six months of life: they cry for attention, smile and babble at caregivers, and make all the proper postural adjustments when they are about to be picked up. But in the second half of the first year their behavior begins to change. Compared with home-reared infants, institutional children seldom cry, coo, or babble; they adopt rigid body postures and often fail to accommodate to the handling of caregivers when such contact is forthcoming; their language is grossly retarded; and they often appear either forlorn and uninterested in their caregivers or emotionally starved, with an insatiable need for affection. Here are two descriptions of these children:

> While the children in 'Nursery' [who were cared for by their mothers] developed into normal, healthy toddlers, a two-year observation of 'Foundling-home' showed that the emotionally starved children never learned to speak, to walk, to feed themselves. With one or two exceptions . . . those who survived were human wrecks who behaved in a manner of agitated or of apathetic idiots [Spitz, 1949, p. 149].

> Outstanding were his soberness, his forlorn appearance, and lack of animation. . . . He did not turn to adults to relieve his distress. . . . He made no demands. . . . As one made active and persistent efforts at a social exchange he became somewhat

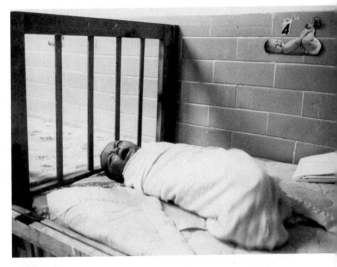

PHOTO 6-4 Children raised in barren, understaffed institutions show many signs of developmental retardation.

more responsive, animated and . . . active, but lapsed into his depressed . . . appearance when the adult became less active . . . if you crank his motor you can get him to go a little; but he can't start on his own [Provence & Lipton, 1962, pp. 134–135].

What are these institutionalized infants like as schoolchildren, adolescents, and adults? The answer seems to depend on just how depriving the institution is as well as how much time the children spend there. William Goldfarb (1943, 1947) compared the developmental progress of two groups of children: a group who left an understaffed orphanage for foster homes during the first year of life ("foster children") and a second group who spent their first three years at the orphanage before departing for foster homes ("institution children"). The children in these two groups were comparable in age, sex, and the socioeconomic backgrounds of their biological parents. The developmental progress of each group was periodically assessed by interviewing and observing the children and by giving them a battery of tests. The children were studied at four ages: 3½, 6½, 8½, and 12.

Goldfarb found that the institution children performed less well than the foster children on almost all the tests he administered. They scored lower on all tests of intelligence, particularly those emphasizing conceptual skills and abstract reasoning. Compared with foster children, the institution children were socially immature and remarkably dependent on adults, even when adult assistance appeared unnecessary. Language and speech problems often plagued these children, and they were much more prone than the foster children to displays of temper, hyperactivity, aggression, deception, and acts of destruction. Goldfarb reported that the institution children seemed almost incapable of forming close interpersonal attachments. By adolescence, they were often loners who had a difficult time relating to peers or family members.

Barbara Tizard (1977; Tizard & Hodges, 1978) has recently compared similar groups of institutionalized and early-adopted children and found that some of the developmental impairments described by Goldfarb also characterized her institutional samples. The institutions in which Tizard's children lived had high ratios of staff to children, so that children were not socially deprived. However, they were cared for by 50 to 80 different caregivers over the first few years of life and rarely became attached to a particular individual. By age 8 Tizard's institutional children and late adoptees were intellectually normal and socially outgoing, and several of them had even formed close emotional ties to a housemother or an adoptive parent. But despite these encouraging signs, children who had spent at least four years in the institution had few close friends and were much more unpopular, restless, and disobedient at school than children raised from late infancy in a family setting. So it seems that prolonged institutionalization can have adverse effects that are very difficult to overcome.

Emotional Deprivation and the Failure to Thrive

Otherwise healthy children living in homes where there is lots of emotional turmoil and very little affection often appear rather apathetic or depressed and are likely to lag far behind their age mates in physical growth and motor development. This "failure to thrive" syndrome may characterize as many as 3% of preschool children in the United States and up to 5% of all patients admitted to pediatric hospitals (Lipsitt, 1979).

Perhaps the most intriguing research on the failure-to-thrive syndrome was reported by Lytt Gardner (1972). Gardner studied the development of physically healthy, nonabused infants and toddlers who had received adequate physical care but very little affection from emotionally unresponsive parents. These home-reared but emotionally deprived youngsters showed many of the same abnormalities as children raised in understaffed institutions: apathy and apparent depression, a forlorn appearance, rigid body postures, retarded physical and motor development, depressed vocalization, and so on. One case involved twins—a boy and a girl—who developed quite normally for the first four months. Soon thereafter, the twins' father lost his job, their mother became pregnant with an unwanted baby, and the parents blamed each other for the hardships they were experiencing. The father then moved out of the house, and the mother focused her resentment on her infant son, becoming increasingly detached and unresponsive to his bids for attention (she did, however, provide him with adequate nutrition and physical care). Although his sister remained socially responsive and continued to grow normally, the boy at 13 months of age often failed to react to social stimulation and *was only about the size of an average 7-month-old infant*. In other words, his growth was severely retarded, a condition Gardner called *deprivation dwarfism* (see Figure 6-1).

It is important to emphasize that the "deprivation dwarfs" Gardner studied were free of organic abnormalities and had received adequate nutrition and physical care. But all these children came from disordered family environments where they had been rejected by one parent and often by both. Gardner states emphatically that deprivation dwarfism is directly related to the infant's early social/emotional deprivation, and his conclusions are based on the behavior of many deprivation dwarfs hospitalized for observation and treatment. The following passage describes a typical case:

> The 15-month-old child quickly responded to the attention she received from the hospital staff. She gained weight and made up for lost growth; her emotional state improved strikingly. Moreover, these changes were demonstrably unrelated to any change

FIGURE 6-1 Three-year-old, treated for deprivation dwarfism 18 months earlier, actually lost weight on return to the care of a mother who appeared detached and unemotional in her relationship with the boy. His skeletal maturity on return to the hospital was at the level of a 15-month-old's; he was listless and lay on his back most of the time, his legs spraddled in a characteristic "frog" position.

in food intake. During her stay in the hospital she received the same standard nutrient dosage she had received at home. It appears to have been the enrichment of her social environment, not of her diet, that was responsible for the normalization of her growth [Gardner, 1972, p. 78].

It is relatively easy to explain the depressed social responsiveness observed among Gardner's deprivation dwarfs: these youngsters haven't had enough face-to-face contact with playful, responsive caregivers to acquire many socially responsive behaviors (such as social smiling) or even to learn that other human beings can be interesting. But why do you suppose emotional deprivation might inhibit a child's physical growth and development?

Apparently the answer is not related to diet, for when Gardner's deprivation dwarfs received ample doses of responsive social stimulation in the hospital, they soon began to grow rapidly on the same diet on which they had "failed to thrive" at home. Current thinking on the subject is that lack of social and emotional stimulation may inhibit secretion of the pituitary *growth hormone*, a substance known to be essential for the normal growth and development of body cells (Tanner, 1978). Indeed, Gardner (1972) noted that deprivation dwarfs have abnormally low levels of growth hormone in their bloodstreams during periods of subnormal growth. And when these youngsters entered the hospital and began to receive responsive caregiving, the secretion of growth hormone resumed, apparently enabling them to grow rapidly and make up the ground lost while they were socially and emotionally deprived.

THREE THEORETICAL PERSPECTIVES ON SOCIAL DEPRIVATION EFFECTS

Studies of institutionalized children (and, indeed, of those who fail to thrive) are "experiments of nature" that were not designed in a laboratory and are subject to a variety of methodological criticisms (see Longstreth, 1981; Pinneau, 1955). However, many of the results we have reviewed are so consistent across studies that most researchers have stopped arguing about whether deprivation effects are real. Today the issue is "Why do they occur?"

The Maternal Deprivation Hypothesis

Psychologists such as John Bowlby (1973) and René Spitz (1965) believe that infants will not develop normally unless they receive the warm, loving attention of a stable mother figure to whom they can become attached. Presumably children raised in understaffed institutions and animals reared in isolation will show developmental impairments because they have not had an opportunity to become emotionally involved with that special someone—typically their mother—who is constantly looking after them and attending to their needs.

Popular as this explanation was when it first appeared, there is no evidence that infants need to be "mothered" by a single caregiver in order to develop normally. Studies of adequately staffed institutions in the Soviet Union, the People's Republic of China, and Israel reveal that infants who are cared for by many responsive caregivers appear quite normal and are as well adjusted at 2–3 years of age as noninstitutionalized infants and toddlers who are reared at home (Bronfenbrenner, 1970; Kessen, 1975; Levy-Shiff, 1983). Moreover, we have seen that Harlow's infant monkeys who were isolated for three months eventually recovered from their early developmental abnormalities without ever being exposed to a mother figure. All they needed was stimulation provided through daily contacts with other monkeys of the same age. In a similar vein, Freud and Dann (1951) reported that a group of six war orphans raised together from early infancy in a German concentration camp were neither mentally retarded nor socially unresponsive at 3 years of age, despite their very limited contact with their parents (who had been executed in Hitler's gas chambers) or other adult prisoners.[5] Apparently the stimulation that these orphans provided one another was sufficient to prevent serious developmental abnormalities. So infants need not become attached to a single mother figure in order to develop normally.

The Stimulus Deprivation Hypothesis

Other psychologists have proposed a stimulus deprivation hypothesis to explain the behavioral abnormalities of children raised in understaffed institutions. The central theme of this explanation is that infants require a variety of sensory inputs, or "stimulus feedings," in order to become responsive to the environment and to show a normal pattern of development. Proponents of the stimulus deprivation hypothesis argue that impoverished, understaffed institutional settings are breeding grounds for developmental abnormalities because they provide the infant with a monotonous sensory environment where *there is little if any stimulation to encourage any sort of responsiveness*, be it social responsiveness, exploratory behavior, cognitive functioning, or emotional expression. And what kind of stimulation is most important? Lawrence Casler (1965) suggests that "perhaps any source—an impersonal caretaker, or even a machine—would be satisfactory, so long as the dosage of stimulation were approximately correct" (p. 141).

Would infants in understaffed institutions develop normally if they received periodic doses of sensory stimulation? Probably not. C. L. Pratt (1967, 1969) tried to reverse the effects of social isolation on infant monkeys by providing enriched visual stimulation in the form of "slide shows" (pictures of inanimate objects and other monkeys). This treatment had no real therapeutic effect—the infants remained socially inept. By contrast, three-month isolates who received *social* stimulation through contacts with age mates did eventually overcome their deficiencies and develop age-appropriate patterns of social behavior.

The Social Stimulation Hypothesis

Many investigators now believe that infants in poorly run institutions develop abnormally because they have very little exposure to anyone who responds contingently to their social signals. Sally Provence and Rose Lipton (1962) studied a sample of healthy institutionalized infants who had toys to play with, some visual and auditory exposure to other infants, but limited contact with adult caregivers. In other words, these infants were "socially deprived" although they were certainly not "stimulus deprived." In spite of the variety of stimulation that the infants received, they showed roughly the same early patterns of social, emotional, and intellectual impairment that characterized the institutional children from earlier studies. If we contrast this finding with the normal development of Chinese, Russian, and Israeli infants who are raised by a multitude of caregivers in communal settings, we can draw an interesting conclusion: *infants apparently need sustained interactions with responsive companions in order to develop normally*. Recall that we came to the same conclusion when we looked at the origins of the primary social attachment: infants who have regular interactions with *sensitive* and *responsive* caregivers are the ones who are likely to become securely attached to their close companions.

Why are interactions with responsive people so important? Probably because the social stimulation an infant receives is likely to depend on the infant's own behavior: people often attend to the child *when* he or she cries, smiles, babbles, or gazes at them. This kind of association between one's own behavior and the behavior of caregivers may lead infants to believe that they have some *control* over their social environment. Thus, the infant may become more sociable as she learns that she can use her social signals to attract the attention and affection of her responsive companions (see Finkelstein & Ramey, 1977).

Now consider the plight of institutionalized infants who may emit many signals and rarely receive a response from their overburdened or inattentive caregivers. What are these children likely to learn from their early experiences? Probably that attempts to attract the attention of others are useless, for nothing they do seems to matter to anyone. Consequently, they may develop a sense of "*learned helplessness*" and simply stop trying to exercise any control over the environment. Here, then, is a very plausible explanation for the finding that socially deprived infants are often rather passive, withdrawn, and apathetic.

CAN CHILDREN RECOVER FROM EARLY DEVELOPMENTAL IMPAIRMENTS?

Earlier we noted that severely disturbed young monkeys can overcome the effects of prolonged social isolation if they receive the proper kinds of therapy. Is the same true of human beings? Can children who start out in an understaffed institutional setting recover from their initial handicaps, and if so, what will they require in the way of corrective therapy?

There is now a wealth of evidence that socially deprived infants can recover from their handicaps if they are placed in homes where they receive ample doses of individualized attention from affectionate and responsive caregivers (Clarke & Clarke, 1976; Rutter, 1981). One notable example is a study by Wayne Dennis (1973), who compared the development of two groups of children who had lived in an understaffed Lebanese institution. Children in one group were adopted into good homes before their second birthday. Although they had developmental quotients in the mentally retarded range at the time of their adoptions, these children eventually attained IQ scores that were only slightly below average after spending several years in a stimulating home environment. By contrast, children who remained in the institution continued to score in the mentally retarded range on all intelligence tests.

The *quality* of the home environment in which children live affects their chances of recovering from early developmental impairments. Lee Willerman and his associates found that 1-year-olds with social, motor, and mental handicaps are unlikely to recover if they live in economically disadvantaged homes where they receive little social or intellectual stimulation from their caregivers (Willerman, Broman, & Fiedler, 1970). However, children who are placed in "enriched" home environments may show dramatic recoveries. Audrey Clark and Jeanette Hanisee (1982) studied a group of Asian children who were adopted by highly educated and relatively affluent American parents, many of whom were teachers, ministers, or social workers. The adoptees had all been separated from their biological parents and had lived in institutions, foster homes, or hospitals before coming to the United States. Many were war orphans who had early histories of malnutrition or serious illness. But in spite of the severe environmental insults they had endured, these children made remarkable progress. After only two to three years in their highly stimulating adoptive homes, the Asian adoptees scored significantly *above* average on both a standardized intelligence test and an assessment of social maturity.

The prognosis for recovery may also depend on the *amount of time* the child has spent in a severely depriving environment. It appears that prolonged social and sensory deprivation that begins early in the first year and lasts as long as three years is likely to produce serious social, emotional, and intellectual handicaps that are difficult to overcome (Dennis, 1973; Goldfarb, 1943, 1947; Rutter, 1981). For example, we have noted that Goldfarb's institution children, who had spent their first three years in an understaffed orphanage, remained somewhat socially, emotionally, and intellectually deficient as adolescents despite having lived in foster homes during the preceding eight to nine years. Do such findings imply that the first three years is a critical period for the social, emotional, and intellectual development of human beings, as Bowlby (1973) and others have proposed?

At this point, no one can be certain that *all* the effects of prolonged social and emotional deprivation are *completely* reversible. However, many theorists believe that those who favor a critical-period hypothesis are being overly pessimistic. It stands to reason that children who develop severe problems when deprived for long periods might take longer to overcome their handicaps than children whose early deprivation was relatively brief. Moreover, we have to wonder how Goldfarb's institution children would have fared had they been adopted into enriched home environments such as those of the Asian adoptees in Clark and Hanisee's (1982) study. Clearly, the fact that Goldfarb's institution children showed some deficiencies as adolescents in no way implies that they were *incapable* of recovery, as proponents of the critical-period hypothesis might have us believe.

It was only a short time ago that six months of isolation was thought to have irreversible effects on the social and emotional development of rhesus monkeys. Yet Harry Harlow and his associates were able to perfect a therapy to treat the harmful consequences of early social deprivation and bring even their most profoundly disturbed 12-month isolates back to a state of normality. This younger-peer therapy has now been used by Wyndol Furman, Don Rahe, and Willard Hartup (1979) to modify the behavior of socially withdrawn preschool children. Children who had been identified as social isolates in a day-care setting were exposed to a series of play sessions with a partner who was either their age or 18 months younger. The results were clear: withdrawn children who had played with a partner became much more socially outgoing in their day-care classrooms than social isolates who had not taken part in any play sessions. In addition, the improvements in sociability were greatest for those withdrawn children who had played with a *younger* partner (see Figure 6-2). So Furman et al. (1979) obtained results with humans that are similar to those reported earlier for emotionally disturbed monkeys. Although Furman's withdrawn children could hardly be classified as emotionally ill, the results of this study are sufficiently encouraging to suggest the younger-peer treatment as one possible therapy for children who are more severely disturbed.

In sum, infants who have experienced social and sensory deprivation over the first two years show a strong capacity for recovery when placed in a stimulating home environment where they receive individual attention from responsive caregivers. Even severely disturbed children who are adopted after spending several years in understaffed institutions will show dramatic improvements, compared with their counterparts who remain in a barren institutional setting (Dennis, 1973; Rutter, 1981). And rather than being discouraged by handicaps that continue to plague many late adoptees, we could just as easily treat their partial recoveries as an encouraging sign— one that may lead to the discovery of environmental interventions and therapeutic techniques that will enable these victims of prolonged social and emotional deprivation to put their lingering deficiencies behind them.

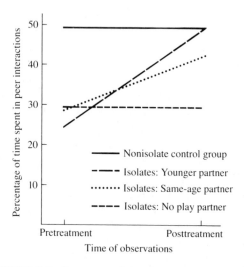

FIGURE 6-2   Percentages of time that children spent interacting with peers before and after engaging in play sessions with a younger or a same-age partner

SUMMARY

Psychologists from many theoretical backgrounds believe that the social and emotional events of infancy are very influential in shaping one's future development. Two ways of evaluating this *early experience* hypothesis are (1) to look for variations in the development of children who form different kinds of attachments to close companions and (2) to see what happens to socially deprived infants who have had few if any opportunities to become emotionally involved with anyone.

Children differ in the security of their attachments to caregivers. A securely attached infant is one who derives comfort from close companions and can use them as safe bases for exploration. Insecurely attached infants do not venture far from their attachment objects even though they derive very little comfort or security from their contacts with them. A secure attachment is fostered by caregivers who are very responsive and affectionate toward their babies. The quality of the infant's attachments may affect his or her later behavior, and for this reason it is advantageous for the child to be attached to the father and other close companions as well as the mother. Children who are securely attached are generally more curious than insecurely attached infants and are more interested in learning, more cooperative, and friendlier toward adults and peers. Moreover, these differences persist throughout the preschool period and possibly much longer. It was once feared that regular separations from attachment objects would undermine a child's emotional security. However, there is little evidence that a mother's employment outside the home or alternative caregiving by day-care workers will have such an effect, provided that the day care is of high quality and the mother is responsive to her child when she is at home.

Some infants have had very limited contacts with caregivers during the first year or two of life, and as a result they do not become attached to anyone. Both monkeys and children who experience little social contact during infancy are likely to be withdrawn, apathetic, and (in humans) intellectually deficient. The longer infants suffer from social and sensory deprivation, the more disturbed they become. However, both monkeys and humans have a strong capacity for recovery and may overcome many of their initial handicaps if placed in settings where they will receive ample amounts of individual attention from responsive companions.

NOTES

1. Although a child's temperamental characteristics may predict his or her reactions to certain aspects of the strange-situations test (for example, responses to strangers), they do not reliably forecast the *total pattern* of the child's responses across all eight episodes of the strange situations. Recall that it is the total pattern of the child's responses that determines his or her attachment classification, not discrete reactions to particular episodes or events.

2. Unfortunately, the kind of high-quality, center-based day care that Kagan et al. (1978) describe is not always available, particularly to mothers from economically disadvantaged backgrounds who often have very little money and must return to work soon after giving birth in order to get by. Perhaps you can see the irony here: the families that may have the greatest need for excellent day care are those that are least able to afford it.

3. Day-care homes are households in which an adult caregiver (often a mother with children of her own) is paid for looking after the children of one or more working mothers.

4. You may be wondering how the motherless mothers ever became pregnant if their sexual behavior was truly inadequate. In some cases, breeding males overpowered them or helped the more cooperative ones to attain a satisfactory coital posture. In other cases, isolate females were placed in a specially constructed "breeding rack" that restrains, positions, and supports the female during copulation.

5. All six of these children arrived at the concentration camp during the first few months of life and were together for the remainder of their confinement. They received about the same amount of attention from adults that is normally received by children in severely depriving institutional settings. We will take a closer look at these remarkable orphans in Chapter 14 when we consider the important functions that the peer group fulfills in a child's social and personality development.

REFERENCES

AINSWORTH, M. D. S. (1979). Attachment as related to mother-infant interaction. In J. S. Rosenblatt, R. A. Hinde, C. Beer, & M. Busnel (Eds.), *Advances in the study of behavior* (Vol. 9). Orlando, FL: Academic Press.

AINSWORTH, M. D. S., Blehar, M. C., Waters, E., & Wall, S. (1978). *Patterns of attachment: A psychological study of the strange situation.* Hillsdale, NJ: Erlbaum.

ANDERSON, C. W., Nagle, R. J., Roberts, W. A., & Smith, J. W. (1981). Attachment to substitute caregivers as a function of center quality and caregiver involvement. *Child Development, 52,* 53–61.

AREND, R., Gove, F. L., & Sroufe, L. A. (1979). Continuity of individual adaptation from infancy to kindergarten: A predictive study of ego-resiliency and curiosity in preschoolers. *Child Development, 50,* 950–959.

BELSKY, J. (1985). Two waves of day-care research: Developmental effects and conditions of quality. In R. Ainslie (Ed.), *The child and the day care setting.* New York: Praeger.

BELSKY, J., Gilstrap, B., & Rovine, M. (1984). The Pennsylvania infant and family development project I: Stability and change in mother-infant and father-infant interaction in a family setting at one, three, and nine months. *Child Development, 55,* 692–705.

BELSKY, J., Rovine, M., & Taylor, D. G. (1984). The Pennsylvania infant and family development project, III: The origins of individual differences in infant-mother attachment: Maternal and infant contributions. *Child Development, 55,* 718–728.

BELSKY, J., & Steinberg, L. D. (1978). The effects of day care: A critical review. *Child Development, 49,* 929–949.

BOWLBY, J. (1960). Separation anxiety. *International Journal of Psychoanalysis, 41,* 89–113.

BOWLBY, J. (1973). *Attachment and loss.* Vol. 2: *Separation.* London: Hogarth Press.

BRONFENBRENNER, U. (1970). *Two worlds of childhood: U.S. and U.S.S.R.* New York: Russell Sage Foundation.

CASLER, L. (1965). The effects of extra tactile stimulation on a group of institutionalized infants. *Genetic Psychology Monographs, 71,* 137–175.

CLARK, E. A., & Hanisee, J. (1982). Intellectual and adaptive performance of Asian children in adoptive American settings. *Developmental Psychology, 18,* 595–599.

CLARKE, A. M., & Clarke, A. D. B. (1976). *Early experience: Myth and evidence.* New York: Free Press.

CLARKE-STEWART, K. A. (1978). And daddy makes three: The father's impact on the mother and young child. *Child Development, 49*, 466–478.

CLARKE-STEWART, K. A. (1980). The father's contribution to children's cognitive and social development in early childhood. In F. A. Pedersen (Ed.), *The father-infant relationship: Observational studies in the family setting.* New York: Praeger.

CRITTENDEN, P. M. (1985). Maltreated infants: Vulnerability and resilience. *Journal of Child Psychology and Psychiatry, 26*, 85–96.

CROCKENBERG, S. B. (1981). Infant irritability, maternal responsiveness, and social support influences on the security of mother-infant attachment. *Child Development, 52*, 857–865.

CUMMINGS, E. M. (1980). Caregiver stability and day care. *Developmental Psychology, 16*, 31–37.

CUMMINS, M. S., & Suomi, S. J. (1976). Long-term effects of social rehabilitation in rhesus monkeys. *Primates, 17*, 43–51.

DENNIS, W. (1973). *Children of the crèche.* New York: Appleton-Century-Crofts.

EASTERBROOKS, M. A., & Goldberg, W. A. (1984). Toddler development in the family: Impact of father involvement and parenting characteristics. *Child Development, 55*, 740–752.

EASTERBROOKS, M. A., & Goldberg, W. A. (1985). Effects of early maternal employment on toddlers, mothers, and fathers. *Developmental Psychology, 21*, 774–783.

EGELAND, B., & Farber, E. A. (1984). Mother-infant attachment: Factors related to its development and changes over time. *Child Development, 55*, 753–771.

EGELAND, B., & Sroufe, L. A. (1981). Attachment and early maltreatment. *Child Development, 52*, 44–52.

ELLIOT, O., & Scott, J. P. (1961). The development of emotional stress reactions to separation in puppies. *Journal of Genetic Psychology, 99*, 3–22.

ETAUGH, C. (1980). Effects of nonmaternal care on children: Research evidence and popular views. *American Psychologist, 35*, 309–319.

FINKELSTEIN, N. W., & Ramey, C. T. (1977). Learning to control the environment in infancy. *Child Development, 48*, 806–819.

FRAIBERG, S. (1977). *Every child's birthright: In defense of mothering.* New York: Basic Books.

FREEDMAN, D. G., King, J. A., & Elliot, O. (1961). Critical period in the social development of dogs. *Science, 133*, 1016–1017.

FREUD, A., & Dann, S. (1951). An experiment in group upbringing. In R. S. Eisler, A. Freud, H. Hartmann, & E. Kris (Eds.), *The psychoanalytic study of the child* (Vol. 6). New York: International Universities Press.

FREUD, S. (1930). *Three contributions to the theory of sex.* New York: Nervous and Mental Disease Publishing Company. (Original work published 1905)

FULLER, J. L., & Clark, L. D. (1966a). Genetic and treatment factors modifying the post-isolation syndrome in dogs. *Journal of Comparative and Physiological Psychology, 61*, 251–257.

FULLER, J. L., & Clark, L. D. (1966b). Effects of rearing with specific stimuli upon post-isolation syndrome in dogs. *Journal of Comparative and Physiological Psychology, 61*, 258–263.

FURMAN, W., Rahe, D. F., & Hartup, W. W. (1979). Rehabilitation of socially withdrawn preschool children through mixed-age and same-age socialization. *Child Development, 50*, 915–922.

GARDNER, L. J. (1972). Deprivation dwarfism. *Scientific American, 277*, 76–82.

GOLDBERG, S., Perrotta, M., Minde, K., & Corter, C. (1986). Maternal behavior and attachment in low-birth-weight twins and singletons. *Child Development, 57*, 34–46.

GOLDFARB, W. (1943). The effects of early institutional care on adolescent personality. *Journal of Experimental Education, 12*, 107–129.

GOLDFARB, W. (1945). Effects of psychological deprivation in infancy and subsequent stimulation. *American Journal of Psychiatry, 102*, 18–33.

GOLDFARB, W. (1947). Variations in adolescent adjustment in institutionally reared children. *Journal of Orthopsychiatry, 17*, 449–457.

GREENBERG, M., & Morris, N. (1974). Engrossment: The newborn's impact upon the father. *American Journal of Orthopsychiatry, 44*, 520–531.

HARLOW, H. F. (1962). The heterosexual affectional system in monkeys. *American Psychologist, 17*, 1–9.

HARLOW, H. F., & Harlow, M. K. (1977). The young monkeys. In *Readings in developmental psychology today* (2nd ed.). Del Mar, CA: CRM Books.

HARLOW, H. F., Harlow, M. K., Dodsworth, R. O., & Arling, G. L. (1966). Maternal behavior of rhesus monkeys deprived of mothering and peer associations as infants. *Proceedings of the American Philosophical Society, 110*, 88–98.

HASKINS, R. (1985). Public school aggression among children with varying day-care experience. *Child Development, 56*, 689–703.

HOFFMAN, L. W. (1984). Maternal employment and the young child. In M. Perlmutter (Ed.), *Minnesota Symposia on Child Psychology* (Vol. 17). Hillsdale, NJ: Erlbaum.

JACOBSON, J. L., & Wille, D. E. (1986). The influence of attachment pattern on developmental changes in peer interaction from the toddler to the preschool period. *Child Development, 57*, 338–347.

KAGAN, J. (1984). *The nature of the child.* New York: Basic Books.

KAGAN, J., Kearsley, R. B., & Zelazo, P. R. (1978). *Infancy: Its place in human development.* Cambridge, MA: Harvard University Press.

KESSEN, W. (1975). *Childhood in China.* New Haven, CT: Yale University Press.

KLEIN, R. P. (1985). Caregiving arrangements by employed women with children under 1 year of age. *Developmental Psychology, 21*, 403–406.

LAMB, M. E. (1975). Fathers: Forgotten contributors to child development. *Human Development, 18*, 245–266.

LAMB, M. E. (1981). The development of father-infant relationships. In M. E. Lamb (Ed.), *The role of the father in child development.* New York: Wiley.

LAMB, M. E., Frodi, A. M., Hwang, C., Frodi, M., & Steinberg, J. (1982). Mother- and father-infant interaction involving play and holding in traditional and nontraditional Swedish families. *Developmental Psychology, 18*, 215–221.

LEVY-SHIFF, R. (1983). Adaptation and competence in early childhood: Communally-raised kibbutz children versus family raised children in the city. *Child Development, 54*, 1606–1614.

LIPSITT, L. P. (1979). Critical conditions in infancy: A psychological perspective. *American Psychologist, 34*, 973–980.

LONDERVILLE, S., & Main, M. (1981). Security of attachment, compliance, and maternal training methods in the second year of life. *Developmental Psychology, 17*, 289–299.

LONGSTRETH, L. E. (1981). Revisiting Skeels' final study: A critique. *Developmental Psychology, 17*, 620–625.

LUTKENHAUS, P., Grossmann, K. E., & Grossmann, K. (1985). Infant-mother attachment and style of interaction with a stranger at the age of three years. *Child Development, 56*, 1538–1542.

MACCOBY, E. E., & Feldman, S. (1972). Mother-attachment and stranger-reactions in the third year of life. *Monographs of the Society for Research in Child Development, 37*(1, Serial No. 146).

MAIN, M., & Weston, D. R. (1981). The quality of the toddler's relationship to mother and to father: Related to conflict and the readiness to establish new relationships. *Child Development, 52*, 932–940.

MATAS, L., Arend, R. A., & Sroufe, L. A. (1978). Continuity of adaptation in the second year: The relationship between quality of attachment and later competence. *Child Development, 49*, 547–556.

NOVAK, M. A. (1979). Social recovery of monkeys isolated for the first year of life: II. Long-term assessment. *Developmental Psychology, 15*, 50–61.

O'CONNELL, J. C., & Farran, D. C. (1982). Effects of day-care experience on the use of intentional communicative behaviors in a sample of socioeconomically depressed infants. *Developmental Psychology, 18*, 22–29.

OWEN, M. T., Easterbrooks, M. A., Chase-Lansdale, L., & Goldberg, W. A. (1984). The relation between maternal employment status and stability of attachments to mother and to father. *Child Development, 55*, 1894–1901.

PACKARD, V. (1983). *Our endangered children: Growing up in a changing world*. Boston: Little, Brown.

PARKE, R. D. (1981). *Fathers*. Cambridge, MA: Harvard University Press.

PASTOR, D. L. (1981). The quality of mother-infant attachment and its relationship to toddlers' initial sociability with peers. *Developmental Psychology, 17*, 326–335.

PINNEAU, S. R. (1955). The infantile disorders of hospitalism and anaclitic depression. *Psychological Bulletin, 52*, 429–452.

PRATT, C. L. (1967). *Social behavior of rhesus monkeys reared with varying degrees of peer experience*. Unpublished master's thesis, University of Wisconsin.

PRATT, C. L. (1969). *Effect of different degrees of early stimulation on social development*. Unpublished doctoral dissertation, University of Wisconsin.

PROVENCE, S., & Lipton, R. C. (1962). *Infants in institutions*. New York: International Universities Press.

RAGOZIN, A. S. (1980). Attachment behavior of day-care children: Naturalistic and laboratory observations. *Child Development, 51*, 409–415.

RIBBLE, M. (1943). *The rights of infants*. New York: Columbia University Press.

ROUPP, R., & Travers, J. (1982). Janus faces day care: Perspectives on quality and cost. In E. Zigler & E. W. Gordon (Eds.), *Day care: Scientific and social issues*. Boston: Auburn House.

ROUPP, R., Travers, J., Glantz, F., & Coelen, C. (1979). *Children at the center: Final report of the National Day Care Study*. Cambridge, MA: Abt Associates.

RUBENSTEIN, J. L., & Howes, C. (1979). Caregiving and infant behavior in day care and in homes. *Developmental Psychology, 15*, 1–24.

RUBENSTEIN, J. L., Pedersen, F., & Yarrow, L. (1977). What happens when mother is away: A comparison of mothers and substitute caregivers. *Developmental Psychology, 13*, 529–530.

RUTTER, M. (1981). *Maternal deprivation revisited* (2nd ed.). New York: Penguin Books.

SAGI, A., Lamb, M. E., Lewkowicz, K. S., Shoham, R., Dvir, R., & Estes, D. (1985). Security of infant-mother, -father, and -metapelet attachments among kibbutz-reared Israeli children. In I. Bretherton & E. Waters (Eds.), Growing points of attachment theory and research. *Monographs of the Society for Research in Child Development, 50*(1–2, Serial No. 209).

SCHWARTZ, P. (1983). Length of day-care attendance and attachment behavior in eighteen-month-old infants. *Child Development, 54*, 1073–1078.

SCOTT, J. P. (1962). Critical periods in behavior development. *Science, 138*, 949–957.

SCOTT, J. P. (1968). *Early experience and the organization of behavior*. Monterey, CA: Brooks/Cole.

SCOTT, J. P., & Marston, V. P. (1950). Critical periods affecting the development of normal and maladjustive social behavior in puppies. *Journal of Genetic Psychology, 77*, 25–60.

SPITZ, R. A. (1945). Hospitalism: An inquiry into the genesis of psychiatric conditions in early childhood. In A. Freud (Ed.), *The Psychoanalytic Study of the Child* (Vol. 1). New York: International Universities Press.

SPITZ, R. A. (1949). The role of ecological factors in emotional development in infancy. *Child Development, 20*, 145–155.

SPITZ, R. A. (1965). *The first year of life: A psychoanalytic study of normal and deviant object relations*. New York: International Universities Press.

SROUFE, L. A. (1985). Attachment classification from the perspective of infant-caregiver relationships and infant temperament. *Child Development, 56*, 1–14.

SROUFE, L. A., Fox, N. E., & Pancake, V. R. (1983). Attachment and dependency in developmental perspective. *Child Development, 54*, 1615–1627.

STITH, S. M., & Davis, A. J. (1984). Employed mothers and family day care substitute caregivers: A comparative analysis of infant care. *Child Development, 55*, 1340–1348.

SUOMI, S. J., & Harlow, H. F. (1972). Social rehabilitation of isolate reared monkeys. *Developmental Psychology, 6*, 487–496.

TANNER, J. M. (1978). *Fetus into man: Physical growth from conception to maturity*. Cambridge, MA: Harvard University Press.

THOMPSON, R. A., Lamb, M. E., & Estes, D. (1982). Stability of infant-mother attachment and its relationship to changing life circumstances in an unselected middle-class sample. *Child Development, 53*, 144–148.

THOMPSON, W. R., & Melzack, R. (1956). Early environment. *Scientific American, 114*, 38–42.

TIZARD, B. (1977). *Adoption: A second chance*. London: Open Books.

TIZARD, B., & Hodges, J. (1978). The effect of early institutional rearing on the development of eight-year-old children. *Journal of Child Psychology and Psychiatry, 19*, 99–118.

TRACY, R. L., & Ainsworth, M. D. S. (1981). Maternal affectionate behavior and infant-mother attachment patterns. *Child Development, 52*, 1341–1343.

VAUGHN, B. E., Egeland, B. R., Waters, E., & Sroufe, L. A. (1979). Individual differences in infant-mother attachment at twelve and eighteen months: Stability and change in families under stress. *Child Development, 50*, 971–975.

VAUGHN, B. E., Gove, F. L., & Egeland, B. R. (1980). The relationship between out-of-home care and the quality of infant-mother attachment in an economically disadvantaged population. *Child Development, 51*, 1203–1214.

WATERS, E., Vaughn, B. E., & Egeland, B. R. (1980). Individual differences in mother-infant attachment relationships at age one: Antecedents in neonatal behavior in an urban, economically disadvantaged sample. *Child Development, 51*, 208–216.

WATERS, E., Wippman, J., & Sroufe, L. A. (1979). Attachment, positive affect, and competence in the peer group: Two studies in construct validation. *Child Development, 50*, 821–829.

WEBER, R. A., Levitt, M. J., & Clark, M. C. (1986). Individual variation in attachment security and strange situation behavior: The role of maternal and infant temperament. *Child Development, 57*, 56–65.

WILLERMAN, L., Broman, S. H., & Fiedler, M. (1970). Infant development, pre-school IQ, and social class. *Child Development, 41*, 69–77.

ZESKIND, P. S., & Ramey, C. T. (1981). Preventing intellectual and interactional sequelae of fetal malnutrition: A longitudinal, transactional, and synergistic approach to development. *Child Development, 52*, 213–218.

7

THE SELF,
SOCIAL COGNITION,
AND SOCIABILITY

DEVELOPMENT OF THE SELF

One Self or Two?

The Self as Separate from Others

When Do Children Recognize Themselves?

The Preschooler's Conceptions of Self

Conceptions of Self in Middle Childhood and Adolescence

Self-Esteem: The Affective Component of Self

KNOWING ABOUT OTHERS

Age Trends in Impression Formation

Theories of Social-Cognitive Development

SOCIABILITY: DEVELOPMENT OF THE "SOCIAL" SELF

Sociability during the First Three Years

Individual Differences in Sociability

Sociability during the Preschool Period

Is Sociability a Stable Attribute?

SUMMARY

REFERENCES

Who am I?

> I'm a person who says what I think . . . not [one]
> who's going to say one thing and do the other. I'm
> really lucky. I've never [drunk or] done drugs, but
> I'm always high. I love life. I'm about five years
> ahead of my age. I've got a lot of different business
> interests . . . a construction company, oil wells, land
> . . . I'm trying everything. I travel a lot . . . it's
> difficult to be traveling and in school at the same time.
> [People] perceive me as being unusual . . . very
> mysterious, and I hope they see me as being a com-
> petitor, because I do all my talking on the field.
>
> HERSCHEL WALKER, college student and
> running back of the Dallas Cowboys
> (as quoted by Blount, 1986)

How would you answer the "Who am I" question?
If you are like most adults, you would probably
respond by mentioning attributes such as your gender, those of your personal characteristics that you
consider particularly noteworthy (for example, honesty, sincerity, friendliness, kindness), perhaps your
political leanings, religious preferences (if any), and
occupational aspirations or attainments, and your
strongest interests and values. In so doing, you would
be describing that elusive concept that psychologists
call the *self*.

Although no one knows you as well as you do, it is
a safe bet that much of what you know about yourself
stems from your contacts and experiences with other
people. When a college sophomore tells us that he is a
friendly, likable guy who is active in his fraternity,
the Black Student Union, and the Campus Crusade
for Christ, he is saying that his past experiences with
others and the groups to which he belongs are important determinants of his personal identity. Several
decades ago, sociologists Charles Cooley (1902) and
George Herbert Mead (1934) proposed that the self-
concept evolves from social interactions and will
undergo many changes over the course of a lifetime.
Indeed, Cooley used the term *looking-glass self* to
emphasize that a person's understanding of his identity is a reflection of how other people react to him:
one's self-concept is the image cast by a social
mirror.

Cooley and Mead believed that the self and social
development are completely intertwined—that they
emerge together and that neither can progress very far

without the other. Presumably neonates experience
people and events as "streams of impressions" and
will have absolutely no concept of "self" until they
realize that they exist independent of the objects and
individuals that they encounter regularly. Once infants make this important distinction between self
and nonself, they will establish interactive routines
with their close companions (that is, develop socially) and will learn that their behavior elicits predictable reactions from others. In other words, they are
acquiring information about the "social self" based
on the ways people respond to their overtures. As
they acquire some language and begin to interact with
a larger number of other people, children's self-
concepts will change. Soon toddlers are describing
themselves in categorical terms such as age ("I this
many"), size and gender ("I big boy, not a baby"),
and activities ("I run—zoom!") that are reflections of
how others respond to or label them. Mead (1934)
concluded that

> the self has a character that is different than that of the
> physiological organism proper. The self is something
> which . . . is not initially there at birth but arises in the
> process of social development. That is, it develops in
> a given individual as a result of his relations to that
> process as a whole and to other individuals within the
> process.

Do babies really have no sense of self at birth? This
issue is explored in the first section of the chapter,
where we will trace the growth of the self-concept
from infancy to young adulthood. We will then consider what developing children know about other
people and see that this aspect of social cognition
parallels the development of the self-concept. Finally, we will begin to look at some of the important
outcomes of social development that help children to
define a sense of self. In this chapter, we will focus on
sociability, or the child's willingness to engage others
in social interaction. In Chapter 8, we will see how
active and curious infants begin to take pride in their
ability to make things happen—a pride that often
blossoms into a strong motive to achieve. Chapters 9
and 10 focus on the development of aggressive tendencies and altruistic inclinations (that is, the willingness to cooperate, to share, and to help others).
Our concern in Chapter 11 shifts to moral and ethical

issues as we follow the child's transformation from an egocentric and reputedly self-indulgent organism to a moral philosopher of sorts who has internalized certain ethical principles to evaluate his or her own conduct and the behavior of other people. And in Chapter 12, we will examine the sex-typing process and note that the child's emerging conception of self as a male or a female may exert a powerful influence on his or her thoughts, feelings, and patterns of conduct.

Let's now return to the starting point and see how children come to know and understand this entity that we call the "self."

DEVELOPMENT OF THE SELF

Just what do psychologists mean by the term *self*? If we go by what they study in their research, we might define the self as *a person's impressions of the traits, motives, values, and behaviors that combine to make him or her a unique individual.* So self by this definition is roughly equivalent to a *self-concept*—the person as seen from his or her own point of view. Others have argued that such an "operational" definition is too restrictive and that we would be more accurate in simply describing the self as the "individual" (that is, the human entity) who is being studied (Mischel, 1977). And as we will see in the next several paragraphs, there are those who believe that neither of these definitions adequately depicts the richness, complexity, and sense of personalism implied by the term *self*.

ONE SELF OR TWO?

The 19th-century psychologist William James (1890) was the first to propose that there is not one self but two: the *I* (or self-as-knower) and the *Me* (or self-as-known). In other words, he viewed the self as both a *subject* who has experiences, thinks, and constructs knowledge and an *object* who can be reflected on or thought about. James put it this way:

> Whatever I may be thinking of, I am always at the same time more or less aware of *myself*, of my *personal* existence. At the same time, it is I who am aware. . . . [as if] the total self . . . were duplex, partly

known and knower, partly object and partly subject . . . which for shortness we may call one the *Me* and the other the *I* [p. 53].

James believed that the "I" was the central aspect of self, which, from one's own point of view, doesn't change very much over time. What changes, according to James, is the "Me," the objective manifestations of self that the "I" (and, indeed, other people) perceive and react to. Thus, when giving the interview quoted at the beginning of this chapter, football star Herschel Walker recognizes that despite his new-found wealth and fame (changes in "Me") he is still only Herschel, an entity ("I") that has always been the same and is inherently no better or worse than anybody else. When asked about the adulation he receives from his fellow students, Walker replies: "It's something I've tried to discourage. I'm honored by it; but sort of ashamed of it. The way I make the best of it is to show people I'm still Herschel Walker from Wrightsville, GA. I'm just like an average person" (Blount, 1986, p. 20c).

Contemporary social psychologists make a similar distinction between the self as an active, thinking organism (subjective self) and the self as an object of thought (objective self) that influences and is influenced by others (see Duvall & Wicklund, 1972). Moreover, it appears that adults reliably differ in the extent to which they are aware of and will consciously monitor their inner, or private, selves, which other people can't see, and the outer, or "public," components of self, which are normally available for public scrutiny (Scheier & Carver, 1981).

Which of these aspects of self develops first? Most contemporary researchers believe that the "I," or private self-as-knower, must surely be the first to appear; presumably an infant must first know *that she is* (or that she exists independent of other entities) before she can understand *who* or *what* she is (Harter, 1983). When do infants first differentiate themselves from other people, objects, and environmental events? At what point do they sense their uniqueness and form *stable* self-images? What kinds of information do young children use to define the self? And how do their self-images and feelings of self-worth change over time? These are some of the issues we will explore as we trace the development of self from infancy through adolescence.

THE SELF AS SEPARATE FROM OTHERS

Like Cooley and Mead, many developmentalists believe that infants are born without a sense of self. Psychoanalytic theorist Margaret Mahler (Mahler, Pine, & Bergman, 1975) likens the newborn to a "chick in an egg" who has no reason to differentiate the self from the surrounding environment. After all, every need the child has is soon satisfied by his or her ever-present companions, who are simply "there" and have no identities of their own. Only as the ego begins to form, at 4–6 months of age, will infants recognize that they are separate from their caregivers. In Mahler's words, the child is now in the process of "hatching" from the mother's protective shell and spreading his wings to establish an identity of his own.

Piaget agrees that neonates are born without any knowledge of self. But as they apply their reflexive schemata to the world around them, things begin to change. During the period of primary circular reactions (1–4 months), infants are repeating pleasurable acts that are centered on their own bodies (for example, sucking their thumbs and waving their arms). At 4–8 months (or the period of secondary circular reactions), infants have begun to repeat actions centered on some aspect of the *external* environment (for example, shaking a rattle or squeezing a noise-making toy). Thus, children may learn the limits of their own bodies during the first four months and may recognize that they can operate on objects external to this physical self by the middle of the first year. If 8-month-old infants could talk, they might answer the question "Who am I?" by saying "I am a looker, a chewer, a reacher, and a grabber who acts on objects and makes things happen."

But not everyone agrees that it takes infants 4 to 6 months to become self-aware. Recall from Chapter 5 that even 1-day-old infants can synchronize their movements with those of an adult, as shown by their tendency to withdraw their heads at the approach of an adult's head and to move their heads forward when the adult withdrew hers (Peery, 1980). We have also noted that breast-fed infants less than 2 weeks old can already discriminate their mothers' axillary odors from those of other lactating females (Cernoch & Porter, 1985) and that they already recognize their

mothers' voices and prefer them to those of female strangers (DeCasper & Fifer, 1980). Very young infants are also aware of contingencies and seem to understand that they can make things happen. At age 3 weeks, they are often emitting "fake cries" (crying sounds of low pitch and intensity that differ substantially from distress cries) that are either designed to attract the attention of caregivers or repeated because the child has discovered that she can make interesting noises and continues to do so for the sheer pleasure of experimenting with sounds (Wolff, 1969). By age 8 weeks, infants delight at the discovery that they can make a brightly colored mobile rotate (by turning their heads on a pressure-sensitive pillow that activates the mobile), and they will soon become apathetic about the same mobile if they are unable to control its movement (Watson & Ramey, 1972). Observations such as these have convinced some developmentalists that infants have both the powers of discrimination and the sense of agency to recognize that they exist, independent of other people, during the first month or two of life, and possibly even sooner (Samuels, 1986; Stern, 1983).

At this point, no one can be absolutely certain about the age at which infants become self-aware. We now know that neonates are hardly the "autistic" creatures that Mahler has described, and given the remarkable perceptual and discriminative feats of which they are capable, we might well entertain the possibility that babies are never totally unable to distinguish themselves from the environment. Yet Piaget, Mahler, and others are undoubtedly correct in one sense, for any primitive self-awareness that may be present very early will surely become much more refined (and much more apparent to scientists who study it) over the first 4–8 months of the child's life.

WHEN DO CHILDREN RECOGNIZE THEMSELVES?

Recognizing that one is separate from objects and close companions is only the first step in the development of a personal identity. Although a 5–6-month-old infant may have a subjective sense of self (I) and nonself (they, it), we might wonder whether she perceives herself as a physical object that continues to exist in space and over time. In other words, does the child have a firm self-image? Can she recognize herself?

One way to find out might be to place infants in front of a mirror and see how they respond to their reflections. Researchers who have adopted this strategy find that 5–8-month-olds enjoy looking in a mirror and will often reach out and touch their reflected images (Bertenthal & Fischer, 1978; Lewis & Brooks-Gunn, 1979). By 9–12 months of age, infants recognize the correspondence, or contingency, between their own actions and those of a mirror image, and they often delight in making the image do whatever they do. Does this gleeful reaction to the reflected image mean that the infant recognizes *himself* in the mirror? Not necessarily, for it might be argued that he enjoys looking at and playing with his mirror image because this interesting "companion" is the most responsive playmate he has ever seen (Damon & Hart, 1982).

Michael Lewis and Jeanne Brooks-Gunn (1979) have studied the development of self-recognition by applying a spot of rouge to infants' noses and then placing them before a mirror.[1] If infants have schemata for their own faces and recognize their mirror images as themselves, they should soon notice the discrepant red dot and reach for or wipe their *own* noses. When Lewis and Brooks-Gunn subjected 9–24-month-olds to this rouge test, they found that a few of the 15–17-month-olds and the vast majority of the 18–24-month-olds touched their own noses rather than those of their mirror images. In other words, they recognized the images as reflections of themselves and inferred that they must have a strange dot on their faces—something that warranted further investigation.

By 18 months of age, many infants recognize static representations of themselves, such as a photograph taken earlier (Lewis & Brooks-Gunn, 1979). Recall that this is precisely the age when the object concept is maturing and infants are internalizing their sensorimotor schemata to form mental images. So it seems that the ability to recognize the self is closely related to the child's level of cognitive development. Even children with Down's syndrome and a variety of other mental deficiencies can recognize themselves in a mirror if they have attained a mental age of at least 18–20 months (Hill & Tomlin, 1981).

PHOTO 7-1 Recognizing one's own mirror image is an important milestone in the development of "self."

Although a certain level of cognitive development seems necessary for self-recognition, social experiences are probably of equal importance. Gordon Gallup (1979) finds that adolescent chimpanzees can easily recognize themselves in a mirror (as shown by the rouge test) unless they have been reared in complete social isolation. In contrast to normal chimps, social isolates react to their mirror images as if they were looking at another animal! So the term *looking-glass self* applies to chimpanzees as well as to humans: reflections cast by a "social mirror" enable normal chimps to develop a knowledge of self, whereas a chimpanzee that is denied these experiences will fail to acquire a personal identity.

How does social interaction help children and chimpanzees to form stable schemata for their own faces? What kinds of social experiences might be important in this regard? Karen Schneider-Rosen and Dante Cicchetti (1984) hypothesized that the exploratory competencies and sense of self-efficacy associated with a secure mother/infant attachment may be the skills that contribute most directly to self-recognition. Calling on the attachment literature, they then proposed that interactions with *responsive* caregivers are the kinds of social experience that promote secure attachments *and* the early onset of self-awareness. Schneider-Rosen and Cicchetti tested their hypotheses with a sample of 19-month-old infants and found that 73% of the children who recognized themselves in a mirror were securely attached to their mothers and only 27% were insecurely attached. However, Michael Lewis and his associates (Lewis, Brooks-Gunn, & Jaskir, 1985) have recently contradicted these findings by reporting that self-recognition occurs earlier among infants who are *insecurely* attached to their mothers. So what these contradictory outcomes show is that just how the social "looking glass" contributes to one's earliest images of "me"—the physical self—is a topic that is not well understood and one that is certainly worthy of additional research.

THE PRESCHOOLER'S CONCEPTIONS OF SELF

Once children acquire language, they begin to tell us what they know about their emerging self-concepts. By the end of the second year, some toddlers are already using the personal pronouns *I, me, my*, and *mine* when referring to the self and *you* when addressing a companion (Lewis & Brooks-Gunn, 1979). This linguistic distinction between *I* and *you* suggests that 2-year-olds now have a firm concept of "self" and "others" (who are also recognized as selves) and have inferred from their conversations that *I* means the person (or self) who is speaking whereas *you* refers to whomever is spoken to. By contrast, autistic children (whose conceptions of self are often very disordered or even lacking on the rouge test) frequently misuse these personal pronouns and may fail to use them at all (Fraiberg & Adelson, 1976; Spiker & Ricks, 1984).

Emergence of the Categorical Self

Once children realize that they are separate and distinct from their companions, they begin to notice some of the ways that people differ and to categorize themselves on these dimensions, a classification called the *categorical self*. Age is one of the first social categories that children recognize and incorporate into their self-concepts. By the end of the first year, children can easily discriminate a strange baby from a strange adult, and given a choice, they much

prefer to play with the infant (Lewis & Brooks-Gunn, 1979). Apparently infants classify others as "children" or "adults" on the basis of perceptual cues such as size, tone of voice, and facial configuration. The importance of facial features was illustrated by Brooks and Lewis (1976), who found that infants react much more enthusiastically when approached by a 4-year-old (with childlike features) than by an adult midget of the same height.

The child's use of age as a social category becomes much more refined during the preschool period (Edwards, 1984). Children aged 3 to 5 who examine photographs of people aged 1 to 70 can easily classify them as "little boys and girls" (photographs of 2- to 6-year-olds), "big boys and girls" (7- to 13-year-olds), "mothers and fathers" (14- to 49-year-olds), and "grandmothers and grandfathers" (age 50 and older).

Gender is another social category that children recognize and react to very early in life. Brooks-Gunn and Lewis (1981) found that 9- to 12-month-old infants can easily discriminate photographs of strange women from those of strange men, and they are more likely to smile at the women. Those 2- to 3-year-olds who have acquired gender labels such as *mommy* and *daddy* or *boy* and *girl* can correctly identify people in photographs as males and females, even though they are not always certain about their own gender identities (Brooks-Gunn & Lewis, 1982; Thompson, 1975). Further, 3- to 4-year-olds are quite aware that they are "boys" or "girls," although many of them believe that they could change sex if they really wanted to (Kohlberg, 1969). And by the time they enter school, children know that they will always be males or females and have already learned many cultural stereotypes about men and women (Williams, Bennett, & Best, 1975). Clearly, one's gender identity is an extremely important aspect of the "categorical self"—one that we will discuss at length in Chapter 12.

Who Am I? Responses of Preschool Children

When asked to describe themselves, preschoolers dwell on their physical characteristics, their possessions and interpersonal relationships, and the actions they can perform (Damon & Hart, 1982). In one

PHOTO 7-2   Preschool children's sense of self is based largely on the activities they are able to perform.

study (Keller, Ford, & Meachum, 1978), 3- to 5-year-olds were asked to say ten things about themselves and to complete the sentences "I am a ———" and "I am a boy/girl who ———." Approximately 50% of the children's responses to these probes and questions were *action* statements such as "I play baseball" or "I walk to school." By contrast, psychological descriptions such as "I'm happy" or "I like people" were rare among these 3- to 5-year-olds. So it seems that preschool children have a somewhat "physicalistic" conception of self that is based mainly on their ability to perform various acts and make things happen.

These findings would hardly surprise Erik Erikson. In his theory of psychosocial development, Erikson (1963) proposes that 2- to 3-year-olds are struggling to become independent, or autonomous, while 4- to 5-year-olds who have achieved a sense of *autonomy* are now acquiring new skills, achieving important objectives, and taking great pride in their accomplishments. According to Erikson, it is a healthy sign when preschool children define themselves in terms of their activities, for an activity-based self-concept reflects the sense of *initiative* they will need in order to cope with the difficult lessons they must learn at school.

Awareness of One's "Public" and "Private" Selves

When adults think about the self, they know that they have a "public" self (or selves) that others see and a "private," *thinking* self that is not available for public scrutiny. Do young children make this distinction between public self (or "self as known") and private self ("self as knower")?

One way to find out is to ask young children "how" or "where" they think and whether other people can observe them thinking. Flavell, Shipstead, and Croft (1978) tried this approach and found that children older than 3½ generally know (1) that dolls can't think, even though they have heads, (2) that their own thinking goes on inside their heads, and (3) that another person cannot observe their thought processes. In addition, most 4- to 5-year-olds know that private mental activities are controlled by their brains (or their minds), whereas they mistakenly assume that this unseen organ is not involved in overt acts that others can see, such as making a face or telling a story (Johnson & Wellman, 1982). Finally, Lev Vygotsky (1934) noted that 4- to 5-year-olds are beginning to make a clear distinction between "speech for self" and "speech for others." Speech for self, which often accompanies problem-solving activities, is now abbreviated, may be nearly inaudible, and contains many indefinite referents such as "this" or "get it" that are not likely to be understood by anyone other than the child. By contrast, communicative speech, which is intended for others, is boldly articulated and usually consists of complete sentences.

In sum, it appears that children begin to acquire the concept of a private, thinking self that others can't see between the ages of 3½ and 5. However, we still don't know the point at which a child will first recognize that the *products* of thinking are private, so that other people are often unable to determine exactly what he or she is thinking about.

CONCEPTIONS OF SELF IN MIDDLE CHILDHOOD AND ADOLESCENCE

In Chapter 4 we learned that children's thinking gradually becomes less concrete and more abstract as they progress from middle childhood through adolescence. Is the same true of one's personal identity, or self-concept? To find out, Raymond Montemayor and Marvin Eisen (1977) asked 4th-, 6th-, 8th-, 10th-, and 12th-graders to write 20 different answers to the question "Who am I?" They found that younger children (9- to 10-year-olds) do describe themselves in much more concrete terms than preadolescents (11- to 12-year-olds), who, in turn, are more concrete and less abstract than adolescents. Generally speaking, the younger children mentioned categorical information such as name, age, gender, and address, as well as their physical attributes and favorite activities. However, adolescents defined themselves in terms of their traits, beliefs, motivations, and interpersonal affiliations. This developmental shift toward a more abstract or "psychological" view of self can be seen in the responses of three participants:

9-year-old: My name is Bruce C. I have brown eyes. I have brown hair. I love! sports. I have seven people in my family. I have great! eye site. I have lots! of friends. I live at . . . . I have an uncle who is almost 7 feet tall. My teacher is Mrs. V. I play hockey! I'm almost the smartest boy in the class. I love! food. . . . I love! school.

11½-year-old: My name is A. I'm a human being . . . a girl . . . a truthful person. I'm not pretty. I do so-so in my studies. I'm a very good cellist. I'm a little tall for my age. I like several boys . . . I'm old fashioned. I am a very good swimmer . . . I try to be helpful. . . . Mostly I'm good, but I lose my temper. I'm not well liked by some girls and boys. I don't know if boys like me. . . .

17-year-old: I am a human being . . . a girl . . . an individual . . . I am a Pisces. I am a moody person . . . an indecisive person . . . an ambitious person. I am a big curious person . . . I am lonely. I am an American (God help me). I am a Democrat. I am a liberal person. I am a radical. I am conservative. I am a pseudoliberal. I am an Atheist. I am not a classifiable person (i.e., I don't want to be) [pp. 317–318].

When grade school children do use psychological labels to describe the self, they apply them in a concrete fashion, viewing these attributes as absolute and unchanging. For example, an 8- to 11-year-old who says that she is "kind" is likely to believe that kindness is a stable and enduring aspect of her personality that will always characterize her interactions with others (Mohr, 1978; Rotenberg, 1982). But adolescents who describe themselves with a trait such as "kindness" may recognize that any number of extenuating circumstances can cause them to act in a way that is inconsistent with their self-descriptions. For example, a "kindly" 20-year-old might say "I help my brother with his homework, but I don't help my sister with hers because my brother really needs help, while my sister is lazy. I mean it's fair to help him and not her" (Damon & Hart, 1982, p. 858). What the adolescent has done is to integrate a stable attribute (kindness) with a belief (help only those who need help) to produce an abstract conception of self that provides a logical explanation for two actions that appear inconsistent.

Robert Selman (1980) has studied children's growing awareness of their private selves by asking them to consider the following dilemma:

> Eight-year-old Tom is trying to decide what to buy his friend Mike for a birthday present. By chance, he meets Mike on the street and learns that Mike is extremely upset because his dog Pepper has been lost for two weeks. In fact, Mike is so upset that he tells Tom "I miss Pepper so much that I never want to look at another dog . . ." Tom goes off only to pass by a store with a sale on puppies. Only two are left and these will soon be gone.

Children were first asked whether Tom should buy Mike one of the puppies. To probe their understanding of the distinction between the private self and one's public image, they were then asked questions such as "Can you ever fool yourself into thinking that you feel one way when you really feel another?" and "Is there an inside and an outside to a person?"

Selman found that children younger than 6 did not distinguish between private feelings and public behavior, responding to the questions with statements such as "If I say that I don't want to see a puppy again, then I really won't ever want to." By contrast, most 8-year-olds recognize the difference between inner states and outward appearances, and they are likely to say that Mike would really be happy to have another puppy. So somewhere between the ages of 6 and 8, children become much more aware of their subjective, "inner" selves and will think of this private self as the true self.

In early adolescence, thinking about the private self becomes much more complex. Selman (1980) proposes that young adolescents are "aware of their own self-awareness" and believe that they can *control* their inner feelings. For example, a 14-year-old might react to the loss of a pet by noting "I can fool myself into not wanting another puppy if I keep saying to myself, I don't want a puppy; I don't ever want to see another puppy." However, older adolescents eventually realize that they cannot control all their subjective experiences because their feelings and behaviors may be influenced by factors of which they are *not consciously aware.* Consider the response of one older adolescent when asked "Why did Mike say he didn't want to ever see another puppy?"

> [Mike] might not want to admit that another dog could take Pepper's place. He might feel at one level that it would be unloyal to Pepper to just go out and replace the dog. He may feel guilty about it. He doesn't want to face these feelings, so he says no dog. (Experimenter: Is he aware of this?) Probably not [Selman, 1980, p. 106].

In sum, children's understanding of their public and private selves becomes increasingly abstract from middle childhood through adolescence. The concrete 6-year-old who feels that her public image is an accurate portrayal of self will gradually become a reflective adolescent who not only distinguishes between the public and private selves but also recognizes that the private "self as knower" may not always understand why the public self behaves as it does.

SELF-ESTEEM: THE AFFECTIVE COMPONENT OF SELF

There is another side to the self-concept that we have not considered: children's feelings about (or evaluations of) the qualities that they perceive themselves as having. This aspect of self is called self-esteem. Children with high self-esteem generally feel quite positive about their perceived characteristics, whereas those with low self-esteem view the self in a less favorable light.

Susan Harter (1982) has developed a 28-item self-concept scale that asks children to evaluate their competencies in four areas:

1. *Cognitive competence.* Doing well in school,

feeling smart, remembering things easily, understanding what they read.
2. *Social competence.* Having a lot of friends, being popular, being important to one's classmates, feeling liked.
3. *Physical competence.* Doing well at sports, being chosen early for games, being good at new games, would rather play than watch.
4. *General self-worth.* Sure of myself, am a good person, happy the way I am, want to stay the same.

Each of the 28 items requires the child to select one of two statements that is "most like me" and then to indicate whether that statement is "sort of true for me" or "really true for me." Figure 7-1 shows a sample item from the cognitive competencies subscale. Each item is scored from 1 to 4; a score of 1 (far left-hand box) indicates low perceived competence on that item and a score of 4 (far right-hand box) indicates high perceived competence. Responses to items on each of the four subscales are then summed and averaged to determine how positively the child evaluates his or her cognitive competencies, social competencies, physical competencies, and general self-worth.

Harter (1982) administered her self-concept scale to 2097 third- through ninth-graders and also asked teachers to rate each child on a similar 28-item scale. Several interesting findings emerged from this study. First, even third-graders (8-year-olds) perceive themselves in either favorable or unfavorable terms on each of the four subscales—indicating that children's feelings about the self (or self-esteem) are well established by middle childhood. Second, children make important distinctions about their competencies in different areas, so that their "self-esteem" depends on the situation in which they find themselves. For example, a star student who considers himself bad at sports and other physical activities may enjoy high self-esteem in the classroom while feeling inadequate on the playground. Finally, Harter found that children's evaluations of self seem to be accurate reflections of how others perceive them. For example, subjects' ratings of their cognitive competencies were positively correlated with their own

Really true for me	Sort of true for me					Sort or true for me	Really true for me
☐	☐	Some kids often forget what they learn	but	Other kids can remember things easily		☐	☐

FIGURE 7-1   A Sample Item for Harter's Cognitive Competencies Subscale

achievement scores and their teachers' ratings of their cognitive competencies. Their ratings of interpersonal skills and competencies in the social area were confirmed by peers who had been asked to rate each classmate in terms of how good a friend that person was. Moreover, children who had rated themselves high in physical competencies were more frequently chosen for sporting activities and were rated higher on physical competence by gym teachers than their classmates who had rated themselves low in physical competencies. Taken together, these results suggest that both self-knowledge and self-esteem may depend to a large extent on the way others perceive and react to our behavior. This is precisely the point that Charles Cooley (1902) was making when he coined the term *looking-glass self* to explain how we construct a self-image.[2]

Which Competencies Are Most Important?

Although children evaluate their competencies in many areas, it appears that some attributes are more important than others. For example, fourth-, fifth-, and sixth-graders typically define their self-worth in terms of their cognitive and social competencies, so that children who enjoy the highest self-esteem are those who do well in school and have lots of friends (Coopersmith, 1967; Kokenes, 1974). Once again, these findings would not surprise Erik Erikson, who believes that the major psychosocial crisis that grade school children face is *industry versus inferiority*. According to Erikson, 6- to 12-year-olds are now measuring themselves against their peers to determine who they are and what they are capable of. The major goal of the grade school child is to achieve a sense of personal and interpersonal competence by acquiring important technological and social skills—

reading, writing, an ability to cooperate, and a sense of fair play—that are necessary to win the approval of both adults and peers. Children who acquire these skills should feel good about themselves because they are developing the sense of "industriousness" that will prepare them for their next developmental hurdle—the identity crisis of adolescence. Those who fail to acquire important academic and social skills will feel inferior (that is, have low self-esteem) and may have a difficult time establishing a stable identity later in life (Erikson, 1963).

Erikson believed that the determinants of self-esteem will change as children enter adolescence and begin the long process of establishing stable social, sexual, and occupational identities. Recent research suggests that he may have been right: eighth- to tenth-graders who feel good about themselves and who have made a preliminary commitment to a social or occupational identity are those who have warm and supportive relationships with their parents, a teacher who cares about them, and/or a close circle of friends (Berndt, 1982; Kokenes, 1974; Waterman, 1982). In other words, the social looking glass by which young adolescents define and evaluate the self now consists of a smaller group of "significant others" rather than most or all others.

Changes in Self-Esteem from Middle Childhood through Adolescence

Although the finding is by no means universal (see Savin-Williams & Demo, 1984), a number of investigators have reported that self-esteem often declines at age 12 to 13 (Rosenberg, 1979; Simmons, Blyth, Van Cleave, & Bush, 1979) and then gradually increases over the next several years (McCarthy & Hoge, 1982; O'Malley & Bachman, 1983). One explanation for young adolescents' declining self-esteem is that many of them are experiencing the physical upheaval of puberty and are becoming overly critical and self-conscious about their changing body images. Indeed, overweight youngsters are very likely to show a precipitous decline in self-esteem at some point during adolescence (Mendelson & White, 1985), and those 12–16-year-olds who are least satisfied about their physical appearance tend to have negative self-images (Lerner, Iwawaki, Chihara, & Sorell, 1980; Simmons et al., 1979). Other possible explanations for a decline in perceived worth are (1) that young adolescents are moving from elementary school, where they are the oldest and most revered pupils, to junior high, where they are the youngest and least competent (Harter, 1983), and (2) that these young "formal operators" are beginning to think about the concept of an "ideal self" (the person they ought to be), so that any major discrepancies between who they are and "what they should be" will lower their self-esteem.

According to Erikson (1963), adolescents experience a decline in self-worth because they are now reevaluating themselves and their goals as they search for a stable identity. Erikson proposed that the many physical, cognitive, and social changes that occur at puberty force the young adolescent to conclude "I ain't what I ought to be, I ain't what I'm gonna be, but I ain't what I was" (1950, p. 139). In other words, 12- to 15-year-olds face an *identity crisis* in that they are no longer sure who they are and yet must also grapple with the question "Who will I become?" A failure to answer these questions leaves them confused and uncertain about their self-worth. However, Erikson proposed that adolescents would eventually view themselves in more positive terms if they achieved a stable identity with which to approach the tasks of young adulthood.

In recent years, investigators have taken a closer look at the adolescent identity crisis and found that many people go through several phases, or "identity statuses," before establishing anything approaching a stable identity (or identities). In Box 7-1, we will consider some of these findings and see that the development of a firm, future-oriented self-image is a gradual and uneven process that may take much longer than Erikson had assumed.

KNOWING ABOUT OTHERS

There are some interesting parallels between the child's knowledge of self and knowledge of others. For example, infants begin to form attachments to their caregivers and to become wary of strangers after they discover that other people are separate entities and not merely extensions of the self (Mahler et al., 1975). Yet they recognize their regular companions and know that these people continue to exist long before they recognize themselves in a mirror or a photograph. As we learned earlier, many 2–3-year-olds can correctly label pictures of males and females, even though they are not always certain of their own gender identities. And although 3-year-olds can easily place photographs into age categories such as "little children" and "big children," they are not always sure about the category to which they belong (Edwards & Lewis, 1979). In sum, it appears that infants are aware of their own existence as active, independent entities (the "I" component of self) before they know much about their standing in relation to other people (Harter, 1983). And once this sense of "I" as an independent entity is firmly established, it seems that they begin to pay particular attention to other people, noticing how they differ and using this information to formulate a self-concept (the "me" component of self). Perhaps Gordon Gallup (1979) was right in arguing that a person must have some knowledge of others before he or she can understand the self.

What kinds of information do children use when forming impressions of other people? How do their impressions of others change over time? And what skills might children be acquiring that would explain these changes in social cognition? These are the issues we will consider in the pages that follow.

AGE TRENDS IN IMPRESSION FORMATION

Children younger than 6 or 7 are likely to characterize their friends and acquaintances in the same concrete, observable terms that they use to describe themselves. For example, preschool children often say that they like their "best friend" because (1) the friend lives nearby, so that they can play together (availability and shared activities), (2) the friend is good-looking (physical appearance), and/or (3) the friend has interesting toys (possessions). When these youngsters do use a psychological term to describe a liked or disliked other, it is typically a very general attribute such as "He is *nice*" or "She is *naughty*"—the same kind of diffuse psychological label that they occasionally use to describe the self (Hayes, Gershman, & Bolin, 1980; Livesley & Bromley, 1973).

Between the ages of 7 and 10, children begin to rely less on concrete attributes (for example, possessions and physical characteristics) and more on psychological terms when describing the self and others (Livesley & Bromley, 1973; Peevers & Secord, 1973). Carl Barenboim (1981) has recently proposed a three-step developmental sequence to describe the changes in children's impressions during the grade school years:

1. *Behavioral comparisons phase.* If asked to talk about people they know, 6- to 8-year-olds will compare and contrast their acquaintances in concrete *behavioral* terms, such as "Billy *runs* faster than Jason" or "She *draws* best in our whole class." Before this phase, children usually describe the behavior of their companions in absolute terms (for example, "Billy's fast") without making explicit comparisons.

2. *Psychological constructs phase.* As they continue to observe definite regularities in a companion's behavior, 8- to 10-year-olds should begin to base their impressions on the stable *psychological* attributes, or traits, that the person is now presumed to have. For example, an 8- to 10-year-old might describe well-known classmates with statements such as "He's a stubborn idiot" or "She's generous." However, children at this phase are not yet comparing their acquaintances on these psychological dimensions.

3. *Psychological comparisons phase.* By preadolescence (age 11 or 12), children should begin to *compare* and *contrast* others on important psychological dimensions. The statement "Bill is much more shy than Ted" is an example of a psychological comparison.

Barenboim evaluated his proposed developmental sequence by asking 6-, 8-, and 10-year-olds to describe three persons whom they knew well. Each of the child's

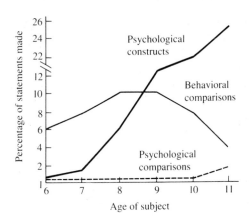

FIGURE 7-2 Percentages of descriptive statements classified as behavioral comparisons, psychological (traitlike) constructs, and psychological comparisons for children between the ages of 6 and 11

descriptive statements was classified as a behavioral comparison, a psychological construct (or traitlike statement), or a psychological comparison. The children were then retested one year later, so that data were available for subjects of all ages between 6 and 11.

Several interesting findings emerged. As we see in Figure 7-2, the impressions of younger children were usually stated in behavioral terms. Use of behavioral comparisons increased between the ages of 6 and 8 and began to decline at age 9. However, 9- to 11-year-olds were relying much more heavily on psychological constructs during the same period when the use of behavioral comparisons was becoming less common. The longitudinal data were also consistent with Barenboim's proposed developmental sequence: over the year between the original test and the retest, virtually all the subjects had either stayed at the same phase of impression formation or moved forward (for example, from behavioral comparisons to the psychological constructs phase). Note, however, that even the 11-year-olds rarely used psychological comparisons when stating their impressions of other people.

When do children begin to compare others on important psychological dimensions? To find out, Barenboim repeated his study with 10-, 12-, 14-, and 16-year-olds and found that the vast majority of 12–16-year-olds had progressed to this third level of

BOX 7-1   *WHAT AM I TO BE? A CLOSER LOOK AT THE ADOLESCENT IDENTITY CRISIS*

Perhaps you can recall a time during the teenage years when you were confused about who you were, what you should be, and what you were likely to become. Do you remember how you resolved your adolescent identity crisis? Is it possible that you have not resolved it yet? And what role do you think an experience like college might play in the process of identity formation?

James Marcia (1966) has carefully analyzed what Erik Erikson had to say about the adolescent identity crisis and has concluded that, at any given point in time, adolescents and young adults can be classified into one of four "identity statuses":

1. *Identity diffusion.* Individuals classified as diffuse have not made firm commitments to particular value systems, ideologies, or plans for the future and are not actively trying to form such commitments. They may not yet have experienced an identity crisis or, having experienced one, were unable to resolve it.

2. *Identity foreclosure.* A person is classified as a foreclosure if he or she has never experienced an identity crisis but has made preliminary commitments to particular goals, values, and beliefs. This may occur when parents or other authority figures suggest an identity to the adolescent (for example, "You'll go to med school, Johnny") and he or she accepts their wishes without really evaluating them.

3. *Moratorium.* This status describes the person who is currently experiencing a strong identity crisis and is actively exploring a number of values, interests, ideologies, and prospective careers in an attempt to find a stable identity in which to grow and embrace the challenges of young adulthood.

4. *Identity achievement.* The identity achiever has resolved his or her crisis by making relatively strong commitments to an occupation, a sexual orientation, and/or a political or religious ideology. Marcia's interpretation of Erikson's theory led him to believe that adolescents must experience an identity crisis (hence, the moratorium status) before achieving a stable identity. However, it is possible to progress from identity diffusion to the moratorium phase, skipping the foreclosure status.

Age Trends in Identity Formation

Although Erikson is not terribly precise about the age at which he expected adolescents to establish stable identities,

he assumed that identity crises were a hallmark of early adolescence and that they would eventually be resolved over a period of several years. Yet even these rather vague predictions about timing may be overly optimistic. Philip Meilman (1979) used a structured interview to access the identity statuses of college-bound boys between 12 and 18, 21-year-old college males, and 24-year-old adult males. As shown in the graph, only 20% of the 18-year-olds, 40% of the college students, and slightly over half of the 24-year-olds had established a mature identity status. Note, however, that there was evidence of a clear developmental progression: identity diffusion and the foreclosure status became less common among older subjects, whereas nearly 25% of the 18-year-olds, 52% of the 21-year-olds, and 68% of the 24-year-olds had either reached the moratorium status or achieved stable identities.

One problem with Meilman's study is that subjects came from a very restricted sample; all were college-bound or college-educated males. Archer (1982) has recently studied a broader cross-section of male and female 6th-, 8th-, 10th-, and 12th-graders and reported a similar set of findings. The vast majority of Archer's subjects were classified as identity diffuse or foreclosures, the largest increase in identity achievement coming between the 10th and 12th grades. However, Archer reports that only 19% of the 12th-graders' responses could be classified as moratoriums or identity achievement—a figure that is remarkably similar to the 24% of all 18-year-olds who had achieved these statuses in Meilman's study. Taken together, these studies indicate that American youth do not experience a strong identity crisis until late adolescence. It also appears that a substantial percentage of young adults are still searching for and trying to establish a personal identity.

One Identity or Many?

Not only might the formation of a stable identity take longer than Erikson assumed, it is apparently an uneven process. Archer's structured interview assessed subjects' identity statuses in four areas: occupational choice, sex-role attitudes, religious beliefs, and political ideologies. Only 5% of her adolescents were found to have the same identity status in each area, and more than 90% had two or three identity statuses across the four areas. Vocational choice

BOX 7-1   *continued*

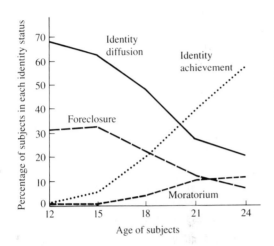

Percentage of subjects in each of Marcia's four identity statuses as a function of age. Note that resolution of the identity crisis occurs much later than Erikson assumed: only 4% of the 15-year-olds and 20% of the 18-year-olds had achieved a stable identity.

was the area in which subjects were most likely to have achieved a stable identity; the largest number of identity diffusions came in the area of political ideology.

Effects of College Attendance on Identity Formation

Gordon Munro and Gerald Adams (1977) compared college students with their working peers in order to assess the effects of college attendance on the process of identity formation. Although the two groups were comparable in the area of occupational identity, the working youth were further along in the process of establishing stable religious and political identities. Munro and Adams concluded that full-time employment "might stimulate rapid movement toward identity formation, while college attendance might be seen as an extended moratorium period" (p. 523). Indeed, one recent longitudinal study found that college students often regress from identity achievement to the moratorium status at some point in their academic careers (Adams & Fitch, 1982).

In sum, the establishment of a stable adult identity (or identities) is a very gradual process that often extends into young adulthood, particularly if the individual is exposed to a college community in which old viewpoints are likely to be challenged and new alternatives presented. However, let's not be too critical of the college environment, for the vast majority of college students emerge from their four years of higher education with "identity statuses" that are much less diffuse than those they had as entering freshmen (Waterman, 1982).

Identity Status and Establishment of Intimacy

Erikson (1963) proposed that successful resolution of the identity crisis is necessary before one can enter into a truly intimate relationship with another adult. To Erikson, true intimacy is a reciprocal commitment in which each partner must give of himself or herself to achieve a *shared* identity. True intimacy need not imply sexuality, but it does imply a mutual trust and a genuine sensitivity to the needs, wishes, and aspirations of one's partner. Presumably, the major psychosocial crisis of young adulthood is the struggle to establish an intimate relationship with someone, a goal that Erikson believed is next to impossible for the person who is confused about his or her own identity.

Recent research is generally consistent with Erikson's point of view. Fitch and Adams (1983), for example, report that the majority of college students showing mature identity statuses (that is, moratorium or achievement) as freshmen or sophomores had established intimate relationships one year later, whereas those with diffuse identities had rarely achieved intimacy with anyone over the next 12 months. Moreover, identity status is a much better predictor of one's entry into intimate relationships for college alumni, who have had several years to live within their identities, than for college students, whose identity crises may be less firmly resolved (Whitbourne & Tesch, 1985). Although these findings are early returns, they do suggest that the establishment of a stable personal identity is a significant developmental milestone—one that helps pave the way for the growth of strong and enduring emotional commitments later in life.

impression formation. By contrast, fewer than 15% of the 10-year-olds *ever* used a psychological comparison when talking about their companions.

Why do children progress from behavioral comparisons to psychological constructs to psychological comparisons? Why do their own self-concepts become increasingly abstract during this same period of time? In the following section we will consider three contrasting but not altogether inconsistent points of view.

THEORIES OF SOCIAL-COGNITIVE DEVELOPMENT

The three theories that are most often used to explain developmental trends in social cognition are Piaget's cognitive-developmental approach, attribution theory, and Robert Selman's role-taking analysis.

Cognitive-Developmental Theory

According to cognitive-developmental theorists, the ways children think about the self and other people depend to a large extent on their levels of cognitive development. Recall from Chapter 4 that children younger than 6 or 7 are usually functioning at Piaget's preoperational stage—their thinking tends to be static and to center on the most salient perceptual aspects of stimuli and events. Thus it would hardly surprise a Piagetian to find that 4–7-year-olds describe both themselves and other people in concrete, observable terms (that is, appearance, possessions, and actions that the person can perform).

The thinking of 7–10-year-olds will change in many ways as these youngsters enter Piaget's concrete-operational stage. For example, egocentrism is becoming less pronounced, so that children may begin to appreciate that other people may have points of view that differ from their own. Concrete operators are also decentering from perceptual illusions, becoming more proficient at classifying objects and events, and beginning to recognize that certain properties of an object remain invariant despite changes in its appearance (conservation). These emerging abilities to look beyond overt appearances and to infer underlying invariances might seem to explain why 8–10-year-olds are suddenly noting definite regularities in their own and others' behavior and using

psychological constructs, or traits, to describe these patterns.

At age 11 to 12, children are entering formal operations and are now able to think more logically and systematically about abstractions. Although the concept of a psychological trait is indeed an abstraction, it is one based on regularities in concrete, observable behaviors, perhaps explaining why *concrete* operators can think in these terms. However, a trait *dimension* is even more of a mental inference or abstraction that has few if any concrete referents. Thus, the ability to think in these terms and to reliably order individuals along such dimensions (as is necessary in making psychological comparisons) implies that a person is able to operate on abstract concepts—a formal-operational ability.

Barenboim (1981) favored a cognitive-developmental interpretation when seeking to explain why children progress from behavioral comparisons to psychological constructs to psychological comparisons. And his conclusions seem quite reasonable when we recall that the shift from behavioral comparisons to psychological constructs occurs at age 8–9, soon after children have entered Piaget's concrete-operational stage and are becoming increasingly proficient at detecting regularities or invariances and classifying such events. Moreover, the shift from psychological constructs to psychological comparisons occurs at about age 12, precisely the time when many children are entering formal operations and acquiring the ability to operate on abstractions. So the points at which we see major transitions in children's impressions of the self and others are generally consistent with the Piagetian interpretation of these events.

The Attributional (or Social Information-Processing) Perspective

Causal attribution theorists such as Fritz Heider (1958) and Harold Kelley (1973) have argued that the attributions we make about the causes of social behavior will largely determine how we perceive and react to ourselves and other people. Presumably, children's self-perceptions and impressions of others will change as they become more proficient at inferring the reasons that people behave as they do.

According to Secord and Peevers (1974), there are three major milestones in the development of children's understanding of the self and others. First, children must recognize that individuals can be the *cause* of various actions. They must then realize that such actions are often guided by *intentions*. Finally, they must understand that people may behave in predictable and consistent ways (that is, people have *stable* traits and dispositions). Let's briefly consider the points at which each of these milestones might be achieved.

People as causal agents. When do children first understand that people can "cause" various events? Probably very early in life. Indeed, we've previously touched on Watson and Ramey's (1972) demonstration that 8-week-old infants are already aware of contingencies between their actions and outcomes: babies who had learned to control the rotation of a mobile (by turning their heads and tripping an electrical switch) gleefully continued to do so, whereas other infants soon became apathetic about the same rotating mobile if they could not control its movement. Surely what the first group of infants found so intriguing about the mobile was not that it moved, but that they could *cause* it to move.

Although young children rarely use causal terminology if asked to explain why an event occurred, studies that rely on *nonverbal* measures reveal that even 3-year-olds know that (1) people must ordinarily be present before they might be considered the cause of an event and (2) an actor's behaviors must *precede* the event to be its cause. To illustrate the latter (*temporal priority*) principle, Kun (1978) showed 3-year-olds sets of pictures such as

A. Scott pulled the dog's tail
B. The dog bit Scott
C. Scott cried

and then asked them whether A or C had caused B. The children reliably chose picture A, evidently recognizing that something Scott had done previously had caused the dog to bite him. So for simple situations where there appear to be a small number of possible causes for an event, preschool children are quite aware that people can be (and often are) the causal agents.

Inferring intentionality. Knowing that a person has caused an event does not necessarily imply that the child understands the actor's intentions. If someone were to throw a baseball, hitting a 4-year-old in the head, the child would know that the pain he was experiencing was caused by the person who had thrown the ball. But in order to interpret this situation as an adult might, the child must now decide whether the pain he is experiencing was deliberate (intentional) or accidental.

When do children first understand that an actor might perform an act fully intending to produce a given effect? Surprising as it may seem, there is now evidence that even 3-year-olds recognize that actors intend to produce their "successes" when striving to achieve a goal (see Shultz & Wells, 1985). In fact, the attributional error shown by many preschool children is to assume that *most social behaviors are intentional*. As a result, they often fail to distinguish deliberate acts from accidents until they are 5 to 6 years of age (see Shantz, 1983, for a review of the literature). When deciding whether an act or its consequences were intended or not, 5–7-year-olds often rely on a *foreseeability heuristic*: if the actor's behavior was voluntary and its effects could have been predicted, then the behavior was intentional. Moreover, 5–7-year-olds tend to rely on a *valence heuristic*: actions producing desirable outcomes for the actor are more likely to be viewed as intentional than those producing aversive outcomes. In sum, children are becoming much more proficient at distinguishing deliberate acts from accidental ones during the early grade school years (Shantz, 1983).

Understanding of dispositional characteristics. Even knowing that an actor has caused a foreseeable and intended event is not sufficient information, in itself, to perceive the actor as having stable traits or dispositions. In order to view someone as exhibiting a trait, the perceiver must first view the actor's behavior as *internally caused*, rather than attributable to situational constraints, and then infer that this "personal" cause is reasonably stable over time and across situations.

An example may help to illustrate some of the challenges children face when deciding between internal and external attributions. Suppose Johnny stays in from recess to help the birthday boy, Jimmy, with his schoolwork. Jimmy is anxious to finish his schoolwork because he wants to ride his shiny new birthday bicycle. Can Jimmy assume that Johnny really wants to help him (a personal or dispositional cause), or, rather, should he simply conclude that "Johnny has helped me so that I might let him ride my new bike" (an external cause)? According to causal attribution theory (Kelley, 1973), there are several schemata that Jimmy might use to infer the meaning of Johnny's behavior:

1. *The consistency schema.* Is Johnny often helpful, or does he rarely behave this way? If he consistently assists other people, then his willingness to help Jimmy is apt to be viewed as internally caused.

2. *The distinctiveness schema.* Does Johnny often help me and not other kids (high distinctiveness), or, rather, does he tend to help whoever seems to need assistance (low distinctiveness)? If Johnny is helpful to lots of other kids (that is, his behavior is low in distinctiveness), then Jimmy is more likely to assume that the helpgiving was internally caused.

3. *The consensus schema.* Do other kids often help me (high consensus), or is Johnny one of the few who do (low consensus)? Presumably, Jimmy is more likely to attribute Johnny's behavior to internal causes if Johnny is one of the few who will help. Acts that everyone will perform are high in consensus and likely to be perceived as externally (that is, situationally) caused.

4. *Multiple sufficient causes and the discounting schema.* Of course, there may often be several plausible causes for an actor's behavior. In our example, Johnny may be helping Jimmy because he wants to (internal cause); because Jimmy has a new bike that Johnny might get to ride (a situational cause); or for *both* reasons. According to the *discounting principle* (Kelley, 1973), the role of a given cause in producing an event will be discounted to some extent if other plausible causes are also present. Thus, Jimmy is somewhat less likely to conclude that Johnny's helpfulness is internally motivated if Jimmy has just received a shiny new bike for his birthday (alternative "external" cause) than if Jimmy has no attractive possessions that Johnny might be hoping to use (no apparent external motivation).

By the time children enter grade school, they are using information about the consistency, the distinctiveness, and (occasionally) the consensus of an actor's behavior to determine whether personal qualities of the actor or situational constraints are responsible for an action (Sedlak & Kurtz, 1981; Shantz, 1983). There is some disagreement, though, about when children first use the discounting principle. Many investigators find no evidence for its use among 5–7-year-olds (see Shantz, 1983), whereas others report that even 5-year-olds will discount internal causes for an actor's behavior when plausible external causes are also present (Dalenberg, Bierman, & Furman, 1984).[3] These age trends in the use of causal schemata suggest a very interesting question: If 5- and 6-year-olds often make dispositional attributions, deciding that an actor's behavior reflects his or her personal motives and characteristics, then why do they not use psychological constructs (traits) when describing the self and others? A recent study by William Rholes and Diane Ruble (1984) suggests an answer.

In Rholes and Ruble's study, children aged 5 to 10 first heard stories in which an actor's behavior varied in either consistency or distinctiveness—information that they might have used to make personal or situational attributions. The following is an example of a "high consistency" story that would be expected to yield a dispositional attribution about the actor's high ability:

> Yesterday Sam threw the basketball through the hoop almost every time he tried. In the past, Sam has almost always thrown the ball through the hoop when he tried to.

After hearing the stories, children were asked to make either dispositional or situational attributions for the actor's most recent behavior and to answer a series of questions to determine whether they viewed an actor's dispositions as *stable* causes of his or her conduct. In the basketball story, for example, children might be asked "How many times do you think Sam could throw the ball through the hoop in the future?" (stability over time) or "How many other kinds of throwing games would Sam do well at?" (stability over situations).

As expected, Rholes and Ruble found that even 5-

and 6-year-olds made dispositional attributions about the actor's current behavior if that action was either high in consistency or low in distinctiveness. But when it came to the *prediction* questions, children younger than 9 did not seem to recognize that dispositions are stable across situations. Thus, 5–8-year-olds who viewed Sam as having high ability in basketball did not realize that Sam probably has the perceptual-motor skills to do well at other, similar games.

So it appears that children younger than 8 or 9 may fail to describe the self and others in "traitlike" terms not because they fail to make internal attributions (as attribution theorists had originally thought) but because they are uncertain about the *stability* of internal causes and personal characteristics. Stated another way, traitlike terms are not very meaningful for younger children. Should a 6-year-old use a trait such as "kind" to describe someone, she is apt to be describing an apparent internal cause for that person's recent "kindly" behavior rather than referring to a stable attribute that has definite implications for the person's future conduct. By contrast, traitlike terms are much more salient to a 9-year-old, who can use a label like "kind" as a brief and convenient way of expressing his knowledge that a person who shows kindness in one situation is apt to display the same inclination in a variety of other situations.

Why do children fail to recognize the stability of personal attributes until age 8 or 9? Social information-processing theorists might argue that 5–8-year-olds have simply not had enough experience at applying causal schemata and comparing actors' behaviors over time and across situations to have developed the *concept* of stable and abiding personal characteristics (Rholes & Ruble, 1984). However, cognitive-developmental theorists attribute the younger child's shortcomings to a cognitive deficit: specifically, younger children's *static and centered thinking*, which focuses on the "here and now" (that is, the way things are at present), prevents them from recognizing the regularities or invariances in conduct that would lead to the inference of stable traits and dispositions. Robert Selman (1980) tends to side with the cognitive theorists on this issue, but he proceeds one step further, arguing that a mature understanding of the self and others depends to a large extent on one particular aspect of cognitive growth—the development of role-taking skills. Let's take a closer look.

Selman's Role-Taking Analysis of Interpersonal Understanding

According to Selman (1980), children will become much more proficient at understanding themselves and other people as they acquire the ability to discriminate their own perspectives from those of their companions and to see the relations between these potentially discrepant points of view. The underlying assumption of Selman's theory is straightforward: in order to "know" a person, one must be able to assume his perspective and understand his thoughts, feelings, motives, and intentions—in short, the *internal* factors that account for his behavior. If a child has not yet acquired these important role-taking skills, she may have little choice but to describe her acquaintances in terms of their external attributes—that is, their appearance, their activities, and the things they possess.

Selman has studied the development of role-taking skills by asking children to comment on a number of interpersonal dilemmas. Here is one example (from Selman, 1976, p. 302):

> Holly is an 8-year-old girl who likes to climb trees. She is the best tree climber in the neighborhood. One day while climbing down from a tall tree, she falls . . . but does not hurt herself. Her father sees her fall. He is upset and asks her to promise not to climb trees any more. Holly promises.
> Later that day, Holly and her friends meet Shawn. Shawn's kitten is caught in a tree and can't get down. Something has to be done right away or the kitten may fall. Holly is the only one who climbs trees well enough to reach the kitten and get it down but she remembers her promise to her father.

After listening to the dilemma, the children were asked:

1. Does Holly know how Shawn feels about the kitten?
2. How will Holly's father feel if he finds out she climbed the tree?
3. What does Holly think her father will do if he finds out she climbed the tree?
4. What would you do in this situation?

After analyzing children's responses to these questions, Selman concluded that role-taking abilities progress through a series of stages, which appear in Table 7-1.

Apparently these role-taking stages represent a true developmental sequence, for 40 of 41 boys who were repeatedly tested over a five-year period showed a steady forward progression from stage to

TABLE 7-1   Selman's Stages of Social Perspective Taking

Stage	Typical responses to the "Holly" dilemma
0. *Egocentric or undifferentiated perspective* roughly 3 to 6 years) Children are unaware of any perspective other than their own. They assume that whatever they feel is right for Holly to do will be agreed on by others.	Children often assume that Holly will save the kitten. When asked how Holly's father will react to her transgression, these children think he will be "happy becaue he likes kittens." In other words, these children like kittens themselves, and they assume that Holly and her father also like kittens. They do not recognize that another person's viewpoint may differ from their own.
1. *Social-informational role taking* (roughly 6 to 8 years) Children now recognize that people can have perspectives that differ from their own but believe that this happens *only* because these individuals have received different information. The child is still unable to think about the thinking of others and know in advance how others will react to an event.	When asked whether Holly's father will be angry because she climbed the tree, the child may say "If he didn't know why she climbed the tree, he would be angry. But if he knew why she did it, he would realize that she had a good reason." Thus, the child is saying that if both parties have exactly the same information, they will reach the same conclusion.
2. *Self-reflective role taking* (roughly 8 to 10 years) Children now know that their own and others' points of view may conflict even if they have received the same information. They are now able to consider the other person's viewpoint. They also recognize that the other person can put himself in their shoes, so that they are now able to anticipate the person's reactions to their behavior. However, the child cannot consider his own perspective and that of another person at the same time.	If asked whether Holly will climb the tree, the child might say "Yes. She knows that her father will understand why she did it." In so doing, the child is focusing on the father's consideration of Holly's perspective. But if asked whether the father would want Holly to climb the tree, the child usually says no, thereby indicating that he is now assuming the father's perspective and considering the father's concern for Holly's safety.
3. *Mutual role taking* (roughly 10 to 12 years) The child can now simultaneously consider her own and another person's points of view and recognize that the other person can do the same. At this point, each party can put the self in the other's place and view the self from that vantage point before deciding how to react. The child can also assume the perspective of a disinterested third party and anticipate how each participant (self and other) will react to the viewpoint of his or her partner.	At this stage, a child might describe the outcome of the "Holly" dilemma by taking the perspective of a disinterested third party and indicating that she knows that both Holly and her father are thinking about what each other is thinking. For example, one child remarked: "Holly wanted to get the kitten because she likes kittens, but she knew that she wasn't supposed to climb trees. Holly's father knew that Holly had been told not to climb trees, but he couldn't have known about [the kitten]. He'd probably punish her anyway just to enforce his rule."
4. *Social and conventional system role taking* (roughly 12 to 15 and older) The young adolescent now attempts to understand another person's perspective by comparing it with that of the social system in which he operates (that is, the view of the "generalized other"). In other words, the adolescent expects others to consider and typically assume perspectives on events that most people in their social group would take.	A Stage 4 adolescent might think that Holly's father would become angry and punish her for climbing the tree because fathers generally punish children who disobey. However, adolescents sometimes recognize that other people are nontraditional or may have a personal viewpoint quite discrepant from that of the "generalized other." If so, the subject might say the reaction of Holly's father will depend on the extent to which he is unlike other fathers and does not value absolute obedience.

stage with no skipping of stages (Gurucharri & Selman, 1982). Perhaps the reason these role-taking skills develop in one particular order is that they are closely related to Piaget's invariant sequence of cognitive stages (Keating & Clark, 1980). As we see in Table 7-2, most concrete operators are at Selman's second or third level of role taking, whereas many formal operators have reached the fourth and final role-taking stage.

It is important to understand the relationship between egocentrism and role taking. Shantz (1983) points out that these two constructs are often confused; writers have tended to view egocentrism as the opposite of role taking while equating nonegocentric functioning with skillful role taking. Yet the relationship is not that simple. It is true that the ability to recognize and appreciate another person's divergent point of view would seem to require a decline in egocentrism. However, one may become less egocentric without becoming a skillful role taker. So despite the meaningful links between children's role-taking stages and their performance on Piagetian cognitive measures and IQ tests (see Pellegrini, 1985), there is reason to believe that other, *noncognitive* influences contribute in important ways to one's role-taking abilities. Could social experiences play such a role? Yes, indeed, for we are about to see that a child's proficiency as a role taker both influences and is influenced by the kinds of social interactions he or she has had.

Role taking and social behavior. As children acquire important role-taking skills, their relationships with other people will begin to change. For example, we've seen that preschool children (at Selman's egocentric stage) think of "friends" as people who live nearby and play together. But once children recognize that playmates may have different motives and intentions (Selman's Stage 1), they begin to think of a friend as anyone who tries to do nice things for another person. Later, at Stage 2, children understand that the term *friend* implies a *reciprocal* relationship in which the parties involved act with mutual respect, kindness, and affection (Furman & Bierman, 1983, 1984; Selman, 1980). Finally, young adolescents who are becoming more knowledgeable about the preferences and personalities of their acquaintances begin to view a "friend" as a person with similar interests and values who is willing to share intimate information with them (Berndt, 1982). In sum, children become much more selective about whom they call a friend as they begin to understand the viewpoints of their peers and are better able to determine who among these companions has an outlook on life that is reasonably well coordinated with their own.

A child's role-taking skills may also affect his or her status in the peer group. Lawrence Kurdek and Donna Krile (1982) recently found that the most popular children among groups of third- to eighth-graders are those who have well-developed role-taking skills. Moreover, children who have established intimate friendships score higher on tests of role-taking abilities than their classmates without close friends (McGuire & Weisz, 1982).

TABLE 7-2 Percentages of Children and Adolescents at Each of Selman's Role-Taking Stages as a Function of their Level of Cognitive Development

Piaget's stage	Role-taking stage				
	0 Egocentric	*1* Social- informational	*2* Self- reflective	*3* Mutual	*4* Social systems
Concrete operations	0	14	32	50	4
Transitional (late concrete)	1	3	42	43	10
Early formal operations	0	6	6	65	24
Consolidated formal operations	0	12[a]	0	38	50

[a]Since only 8 consolidated formal operators were found in the sample, this figure of 12% represents only one subject.

Why are mature role takers likely to enjoy such a favorable status in the peer group? A recent study by Lynne Hudson and her associates (Hudson, Forman, & Brion-Meisels, 1982) provides one clue. Second-graders who had tested either high or low in role-taking ability were asked to teach two kindergarten children how to make caterpillars out of construction paper. As each tutor worked with the kindergartners, his or her behavior was videotaped for later analysis. Hudson et al. found that all the older tutors were willing to assist their younger pupils if the kindergartners *explicitly asked for help*. However, good role takers were much more likely than poor role takers to respond to a kindergartner's subtle or *indirect* requests for help. For example, exaggerated straining with scissors and frequent glances at the tutor usually elicited a helpful response from a good role taker but nothing more than a smile from a poor role taker. Apparently, good role takers are better able to infer the needs of their companions so that they can respond accordingly—an ability that may help to explain why they are so popular with their peers and quite successful at establishing close friendships.

Effects of social interaction on role taking. Although our understanding of the self and others will influence our social behavior, it appears that the reverse is also true: our social experiences can affect the ways we think about the self and other people. For example, Jean Piaget (1965) has argued that playful interactions among grade school children promote the development of important role-taking skills. By assuming different roles while playing together, young children should become more aware of discrepancies between their own perspectives and those of their playmates. And when conflicts arise in play, children must learn to integrate their points of view with those of their companions (that is, compromise) in order for play to continue. So Piaget assumes that equal-status contacts among peers are an important contributor to social perspective taking and the growth of interpersonal understanding.

Diane Bridgeman (1981) tested this hypothesis in an interesting study with fifth-graders. Students in a *cooperative interdependence* condition were divided into six-person study groups. Each person in each

group was assigned various lessons that he or she was required to learn and then teach to the other group members. Since each student had access only to his or her own materials, the members of each group were clearly dependent on one another. Indeed, the tutors had to be good listeners and recognize what their pupils didn't understand and would need to know (a form of perspective taking) in order for the group members to learn all the material for which they were responsible. Students assigned to the *control* condition were required to learn exactly the same material, which was taught in the classroom by their teachers.

When tested before the experiment, students in the two conditions were found to be comparable in role-taking abilities. But by the end of the eight-week experiment, children in the cooperative learning groups had typically become better role takers, while those in the control condition had not. Apparently Piaget was right in arguing that a person's role-taking skills will depend, in part, on the kinds of social experiences that he or she has had.

Are some forms of peer contact better than others at promoting the development of interpersonal awareness? Janice Nelson and Francis Aboud (1985) think so. Nelson and Aboud proposed that disagreements among friends are particularly important because children tend to be more open and honest with their friends than with nonfriend acquaintances. As a result, disagreeing friends should be more likely than disagreeing acquaintances to provide each other with the information needed to recognize and appreciate their conflicting points of view.

Nelson and Aboud tested this line of reasoning in an experiment with 8–10-year-olds. Each child in the sample first took a test of "social knowledge" to measure his or her level of reasoning about interpersonal issues such as "What is the thing to do if you lose a ball that belongs to one of your friends?" After taking the test, pairs of friends and pairs of nonfriend acquaintances[4] discussed one of the interpersonal issues on which they had initially disagreed, and their discussions were tape-recorded. When the discussion was over, each member of the pair was taken aside by the experimenter and asked to offer a solution for the problem that the pair had discussed.

The results clearly showed that friends responded to interpersonal conflict in a different way than nonfriends. While discussing the issue on which they disagreed, friends were more critical of their partners than nonfriends were, but they were also more likely to fully explain the rationales for their own points of view—precisely the kind of information that might be expected to promote an awareness of each other's perspectives. When tested before the discussion, pairs of friends and pairs of nonfriend acquaintances made comparable scores on the social knowledge test. But after the discussion, friends' final answers to the issue they had discussed were at a higher level of social understanding than their original answers, whereas the final answers of nonfriend acquaintances hadn't changed appreciably from pretest to posttest. These results are "early returns"—too new to have yet been replicated—but they do suggest that equal-status contacts *among friends* may be particularly important to the development of role-taking skills and interpersonal understanding.

Postscript

Although many questions remain to be answered about the development of self and interpersonal awareness, this much is certain: Cooley and Mead were quite correct in suggesting that social cognition and social development are completely intertwined—that they occur together and that neither can progress very far without the other. Lawrence Kohlberg (1969) reached the same conclusion, arguing that social development produces changes in both the child's self-concept and his or her impressions of other people. These latter developments then influence the child's future social interactions, which, in turn, will affect his or her impressions of the self and the social environment.

Now that we have touched briefly on the topic of social cognition, it is time to consider many of the important social events, experiences, and outcomes that seem to influence the self-concepts of developing children. We will begin, in the last section of this chapter, by looking at an aspect of social development that is receiving ever-increasing attention—the growth of sociability.

SOCIABILITY: DEVELOPMENT OF THE "SOCIAL" SELF

Sociability is a term that researchers use to describe the child's willingness to engage others in social interaction and to seek their attention or approval. Although sociable interactions and emotional attachments are sometimes confused, they are easily distinguished. Recall that an attachment is a relatively *strong* and *enduring* affectional tie between the child and a particular person (for example, the mother or father). By contrast, *sociability* refers to the friendly gestures that the child makes to a much wider variety of targets (peers, strange adults, teachers), and the resulting social relationships are often temporary and emotionally uninvolving (Ainsworth, 1972; Clarke-Stewart, Umeh, Snow, & Pederson, 1980). Some of the confusion surrounding these two constructs stems from the fact that both originate from the child's earliest interactions with caregivers, who usually become both attachment objects and targets for sociable gestures. But even though children may eventually become sociable with any number of other people, they will form attachments to very few.

SOCIABILITY DURING THE FIRST THREE YEARS

Months before infants form their first attachments, they are already smiling, cooing, and trying to attract the attention of their companions. By 6 weeks of age, many infants prefer human company to nonsocial forms of stimulation, and they are apt to protest whenever *any* adult puts them down or walks off and leaves them alone (Schaffer & Emerson, 1964). Even another baby may elicit a response from an infant. Touching first occurs at 3 to 4 months of age (Vincze, 1971), and by the middle of the first year, infants will often smile at their tiny companions, vocalize, offer toys, and gesture to one another (Hay, Nash, & Pedersen, 1983; Vandell, Wilson, & Buchanan, 1980). Perhaps children seem so sociable at such an early age because other people—even little people— are likely to notice and respond to their bids for attention.

Although infants do respond to each other's gestures and bids for attention, investigators have wondered just how "sociable" these interactions really are. Edward Mueller and his associates (Mueller & Lucas, 1975; Mueller & Vandell, 1979) have proposed that children pass through three distinct stages of sociability in their interactions with other children. In the first, or *object-centered*, stage, children may cluster around a single toy but will pay much more attention to the object than to one another. But during the second, or *simple interactive*, stage, children frequently respond to the behavior of peers. In fact, one child will often try to regulate the behavior of another, as we see in the following example:

> Larry sits on the floor and Bernie turns and looks toward him. Bernie waves his hand and says "da," still looking at Larry. He repeats the vocalization three more times before Larry laughs. Bernie vocalizes again and Larry laughs again. This same sequence . . . is repeated twelve more times before Bernie . . . walks off [Mueller & Lucas, 1975, p. 241].

Are these brief "action-reaction" episodes examples of true social discourse? Perhaps, but it is also possible that infants at this stage are so egocentric that they simply think of a peer as a particularly interesting and responsive "toy" over which they have some control (Brownell, 1986).

Finally, older infants and toddlers progress to a third, or *complementary interactive*, stage in which their interactions are clearly "social" in character. Children now emit signals (smiles, vocalizations) fully intending to influence their playmates and expecting the playmates to respond (Kavanaugh & McCall, 1983). Play during this stage is characterized by role reversals and a primitive kind of reciprocity. For example, a Stage 3 toddler who has received a toy from a playmate might immediately return the favor by offering the playmate another toy. Children are also beginning to take turns playing complementary roles, such as chaser and chasee in a game of tag. Although the first evidence of such complementary interaction may appear as early as 16–18 months, children will become much more proficient at turn taking and other forms of cooperative exchange by the end of the second year (Brownell, 1986).

Are children becoming more responsive to strange adults in the same way they are with peers? Alison Clarke-Stewart tried to answer this question by observing 60 infants as they interacted with their mothers and an adult stranger at 12, 18, 24, and 30 months of age (Clarke-Stewart et al., 1980). The results of her longitudinal study were clear: children became much more friendly and outgoing toward both their mothers and the adult stranger over the period between 12 and 30 months of age. These findings parallel the results of an earlier study (Maccoby & Feldman, 1972) in which children became much less anxious around strangers between the ages of 2 and 3. In fact, Maccoby and Feldman (1972) reported that many distressed 3-year-olds could be comforted by a strange adult and did not require that their mothers be present in order to sustain a friendly interaction with a stranger (see also Lutkenhaus, Grossmann, & Grossmann, 1985).

INDIVIDUAL DIFFERENCES IN SOCIABILITY

Researchers who study infants and toddlers have found that some youngsters are simply more sociable than others. At least three hypotheses have been proposed to account for these individual differences in sociability: the genetic hypothesis, the "security of attachment" hypothesis, and the "ordinal position" hypothesis.

The Genetic Hypothesis—Sociability as a Heritable Attribute

There is now evidence to suggest that one's genotype influences one's responsiveness to other people (Goldsmith, 1983). Over the first year, identical twins are much more similar than fraternal twins in their frequency of social smiling and their fear of strangers (Freedman, 1974), and these differences in sociability are still apparent when pairs of identical and fraternal twins are retested at 18 and 24 months of age (Matheny, 1983). In fact, Sandra Scarr's (1968) study of 6–10-year-old twin pairs suggests that genetic influences on sociability are often detectable well into middle childhood. Scarr found that identical twins were more similar than fraternal twins on measures of their desire to affiliate with others (as rated by their mothers) as well as their "friendliness" and "shyness" (as rated by an adult observer). Moreover, some of the mothers in Scarr's study were mistaken about whether their twins were monozygotic (identical) or dizygotic (fraternal). Yet in each case of mistaken identity, the degree of similarity between members of a twin pair was more in line with their actual zygosity than with their mother's belief about their zygosity. That is, identical twins raised mistakenly as fraternals were as much alike as identical twins raised as identicals. Fraternal twins raised mistakenly as identicals were as dissimilar as fraternals raised as fraternals. The results for these older, misclassified twin pairs are very important, for they indicate that genetic influences on sociability are long-lasting and may never be completely overridden by social influences.

Although sociability appears to be a heritable attribute, environmental influences can play a major role in its expression. In a recent adoption study, Daniels and Plomin (1985) found a significant correlation between the shyness of adopted toddlers and the sociability of their *biological* mothers: shy toddlers tended to have mothers who were low in sociability, whereas nonshy toddlers had mothers who were more outgoing. This finding argues for a genetic influence on sociability in view of the fact that biological mothers and their adopted-away toddlers have genes in common. However, Daniels and Plomin also reported a significant correlation between the shyness of adopted toddlers and the sociability of their *adoptive* mothers, and the magnitude of this relationship was nominally greater than that between the toddlers and their biological mothers! Since adoptive mothers and their adopted children have *no* genes in common, environmental factors must have been responsible for their resemblance on these sociability measures.

What early environmental events are likely to influence a child's social responsiveness? One likely candidate is the quality of the child's emotional attachments.

The "Security of Attachment" Hypothesis

Although attachment and sociability represent different social systems, Mary Ainsworth (1979) believes that the quality of a child's attachments will affect his or her reactions to other people. Ainsworth's position is that children who are insecurely attached to one or more unresponsive companions will be rather anxious and inhibited in the presence of others and much less sociable than children who are securely attached.

Most of the available evidence is consistent with Ainsworth's hypothesis. Infants who are securely attached to their mothers at 12 to 19 months of age are more likely than those who are insecurely attached to (1) obey their mothers, (2) cooperate with and make positive social gestures toward a strange adult, (3) act sociably around other infants, and (4) be friendly, outgoing, and popular with their peers some three to four years later in nursery school (LaFreniere & Sroufe, 1985; Londerville & Main, 1981; Pastor, 1981; Thompson & Lamb, 1983). Moreover, two secure attachments are apparently better than one: toddlers who are secure with their mothers *and* their fathers are more socially responsive and less conflicted about interacting with a strange adult than are children who are insecure with one or both parents (Main & Weston, 1981). Perhaps Ainsworth is right in arguing that securely attached children are sociable children because they have learned to trust their responsive caregivers and assume that other people will also welcome their bids for attention.

The "Ordinal Position" Hypothesis

Years ago, Stanley Schachter (1959) reported an interesting finding: in times of stress or uncertainty, first-borns prefer to affiliate with other people, while later-borns would rather face their problems alone. Although his subjects were adults, Schachter suspected that first-born children, who have enjoyed an exclusive relationship with their parents, are generally more sociable than later-borns.

Deborah Vandell (Vandell, Wilson, & Whalen, 1981) evaluated this "ordinal position" hypothesis by placing pairs of 6-month-old infants together and watching them play. Vandell found that first-borns were more likely than later-borns to approach and take turns gesturing to each other. In a similar study of 3-year-olds, Margaret Snow, Carol Jacklin, and Eleanor Maccoby (1981) found that first-borns (particularly "only" children) were both more socially outgoing and more aggressive than later-borns. The later-borns in this study often stood around watching others play, and they were somewhat more likely than first-borns to withdraw from social contacts.

There are at least two reasons that a child's ordinal position in the family may influence his or her responsiveness to peers. For one, only children and other first-borns tend to receive more attention from parents than later-borns do (Lewis & Kreitzberg, 1979). Thus, first-borns may be particularly sociable because they have had many positive social experiences at home—experiences that encourage them to be more outgoing with their peers. In addition, it is possible that later-borns have learned to be wary and somewhat inhibited around other people—particularly little people—because they are often dominated, bullied, or ridiculed by their older and more powerful siblings (Abramovitch, Corter, & Lando, 1979). Vandell et al. (1981) reported a finding that is consistent with this "social power" hypothesis: first-borns who had often interacted with an *older* child from outside the family were less sociable than first-borns who had had little contact with an older child. Apparently, frequent exposure to older, more powerful companions (siblings or little friends of the family) can make a child a bit hesitant to approach and interact with a new playmate.

Perhaps parents could help their later-borns to become more friendly and outgoing by reserving special play periods for these youngsters—times when the younger child can be at the center of their attention. In this way, they may help these newer members of the family to feel important and loved and to learn that other people can be pleasant, responsive companions. Another strategy that parents might follow is to find other children about the same age for their later-borns to play with. This suggestion is based on the finding that infants and toddlers who often play with children *their own age* are friendlier and more outgoing than those who are rarely exposed to age mates (Mueller & Vandell, 1979; Vandell et al., 1981).

SOCIABILITY DURING THE PRESCHOOL PERIOD

Between the ages of 2 and 5, not only do children become more outgoing, but the ways in which they express their sociability will also change as they make social overtures to a much wider audience. Observational studies suggest that 2- to 3-year-olds are more likely than older children to remain near an adult and to seek physical affection, whereas the sociable behaviors of 4- to 5-year-olds normally consist of playful bids for attention or approval that are directed at peers rather than adults (Hartup, 1983; Sullivan, 1953).

As preschool children spend more and more time socializing with their peers, they become much less inclined to play alone or to seek the attention of adult companions (Harper & Huie, 1985). Are there consequences for youngsters who "buck this trend" by continuing to show a distinct preference for adult companionship?

Indeed there are. Moore and Updegraff (1964) explored the relationship between a child's social status (popularity) in the nursery school group and his or her sociability toward adults and toward peers. The results were clear. Preference for adult companionship clearly hindered the child's acceptance into the peer group, whereas children who were highly sociable with their peers tended to be quite popular. Since most youngsters are becoming increasingly peer-oriented during the preschool years, it is hardly surprising that a child who habitually shuns peer contact in favor of adults might face serious difficulties in his or her relations with peers. Other children may perceive this child as a "mama's boy" or the "teacher's pet." By contrast, children who frequently seek the attention or approval of peers are taking an important first step toward establishing good peer relations and eventually being accepted as a "regular guy" or "one of the gang"—an important milestone, indeed, as we will see in the final section of the chapter.

Effects of Nursery School on Children's Sociability

Does the nursery school experience have any noticeable effect on children's sociability? John Shea (1981) addressed this issue by observing 3- and 4-year-olds as they entered nursery school and began to attend classes two, three, or five days a week. As children mingled on the playground, their behavior was videotaped, and individual acts were classified on five dimensions: aggression, rough-and-tumble play, distance from the nearest child, distance from the teacher, and frequency of peer interaction. Over a ten-week observation period, children gradually ventured farther from the teacher as they became much more playful and outgoing with one another and much less forceful and aggressive. Moreover, these changes in sociability were most noticeable for the children who attended school five days a week and least apparent (but detectable nevertheless) for those who attended twice a week. Shea concluded that nursery school attendance has a very positive effect on children's reactions to other children.

However, there are exceptions to the rule. James Pennebaker and his associates (Pennebaker, Hendler, Durrett, & Richards, 1981) found that children rated *low* in sociability by their parents and teachers miss more days of nursery school because of illness than children who are rated highly sociable. This was a particularly interesting finding, for the health records of the less sociable (and presumably sickly) children indicated that they had been no less healthy than their more sociable classmates before entering nursery school. Pennebaker et al. suggest that shy and otherwise unsociable children often find the nursery school setting threatening and aversive. As a result, they may feign illnesses in order to stay home, or they may actually suffer from stress-induced disorders such as gastric problems and tension headaches. Unfortunately, these socially inhibited "absentees" may be the ones who would profit most from the social curriculum of nursery school—if only they could acquire a few basic skills that would enable them to interact more effectively with their classmates. In Box 7-2 we will consider some of the strategies that researchers have used to improve the social skills of extremely unsociable children.

Who Raises Sociable Children?

Although the data are somewhat limited, it appears that parents who are warm and supportive and who *require* their children to follow certain rules of social etiquette (for example, "Be nice"; "Play quietly"; "Don't hit") are likely to raise well-adjusted sons and daughters who relate well to both adults and peers (Baumrind, 1971). By contrast, permissive parents who set few standards and exert little control over their children often raise youngsters who are aggres-

PHOTO 7-3   Children who prefer the company of adults tend to be unpopular with their peers.

sive and unpopular with their peers and who may resist or rebel against rules set by other adults (for example, teachers). There is also evidence that children of overprotective mothers (particularly boys) are quite sociable when interacting with adults but are often anxious and inhibited around their peers (Kagan & Moss, 1962; Martin, 1975). This finding might be explained by the fact that a highly protective mother frequently encourages her children to remain near her side. As a result, an overprotected son may be rejected as a "sissy" by other children, an experience that may prompt him to seek the company of friendly adults and to avoid peers.

The finding that securely attached children are generally outgoing and popular suggests that sensitive, responsive caregiving contributes to the development of sociability. MacDonald and Parke (1984) hypothesized that the character of *playful* interactions between parents and their children is especially significant in this regard, for in the context of play, parents are social partners whose style of interacting with the child will undoubtedly influence the ways in which the child reacts to other playmates.

MacDonald and Parke then observed 3–5-year-olds as they played with peers and with each of their parents at home. The results of this study were indeed interesting and differed somewhat depending on the

BOX 7-2   *IMPROVING THE SOCIAL SKILLS OF UNSOCIABLE CHILDREN*

Unsociable children are usually deficient at a number of very basic social skills, such as successfully initiating play activities, cooperating, communicating their needs, giving help, affection, and approval to their peers, and resolving interpersonal conflicts (Asher, 1986). During the past few years, investigators have devised a number of "therapies" aimed at improving the social skills of withdrawn or otherwise unpopular children who can't seem to get along with others. Among the more common of these approaches are the following:

Reinforcing Socially Appropriate Behaviors

In their excellent review of the literature on social skills training, Melinda Combs and Diana Slaby (1977) point out that adults can shape socially appropriate responses such as cooperation and sharing by reinforcing these actions and ignoring examples of "inappropriate" behavior, such as aggression and solitary play. Another method of encouraging children to make social contacts is to place them in charge of valuable resources that they must dispense to the peer group. Frank Kerby and Curt Tolar (1970) tried this approach with a withdrawn 5-year-old. Each day for several days, the boy was given a large bag of candies. He was then told to ask his classmates what kind of candy they wanted and to give them the candy of their choice. After distributing all the candies, the boy was praised by his teacher and given some candy (and a nickel) for his efforts. Observations during later free-play periods revealed that this child became much more outgoing and cooperative with his peers. It seems that the candy gave him a reason to initiate social interactions. And in the process he acquired some basic social skills and enhanced his status as he dispensed valuable commodities to his classmates.

One problem with relying exclusively on contingent reinforcement to improve children's social skills is that any gains achieved may fade away once the "therapy" ends. According to Combs and Slaby (1977), contingent reinforcement will be most effective if administered on a regular basis to the *entire peer group* rather than given occasionally to the unsociable children. The group reinforcement procedure not only reinforces unsociable peers

for interacting appropriately with their classmates but also allows them to see others reinforced for this kind of behavior. There are several ways for adults to structure the environment so that it becomes possible to reinforce a group of children for appropriate social conduct. For example, they might persuade children to work at tasks or to strive for goals that require cooperation among all present. And even simple strategies such as giving children "social" toys to play with (cards, checkers, and the like) should provide ample opportunities for adults to reinforce examples of appropriate social behavior.

Modeling Social Skills

Albert Bandura finds that modeling therapies can be a very effective means of reducing childhood fears and phobias. For example, children who are highly fearful of dogs will soon begin to approach and even pet these furry monsters after seeing a number of fearless peer models apparently enjoying themselves as they play with dogs (Bandura & Menlove, 1968). Would a similar form of therapy help shy or solitary children overcome any concerns they might have about approaching and interacting with peers?

Apparently so. In one study (Cooke & Apolloni, 1976), live models demonstrated certain social skills—for example, smiling at others, sharing, initiating positive physical contacts, and giving verbal compliments—to withdrawn grade school children. This procedure proved effective at increasing each type of behavior that the model had enacted. The training also had two desirable side effects. First, the withdrawn children began to show increases in other positive social behaviors that had not been modeled. Second, the frequency of positive social responses among *untrained* children also increased, apparently in direct response to the friendly gestures made by their classmates who had received the social skills training. Thus, modeling strategies can produce marked changes in a child's social skills—changes that benefit both the child and the peers with whom he or she interacts. It seems that the modeling approach works best when the model is similar to the child, when he initially acts shy and withdrawn, and when his socially skillful actions are accompanied by some form of

sex of the child. Boys who were comfortable and relaxed with peers had fathers who engaged in a lot of physical play and mothers who were highly verbal and involved with them, whereas boys who displayed

negative and abrasive interactions with peers had directive fathers who often issued commands to the child and provided him few opportunities to control the pace of their interactions. Girls who were com-

BOX 7-2 continued

commentary that directs the observer's attention to the purposes and benefits of behaving appropriately toward others (Asher, Renshaw, & Hymel, 1982).

Cognitive Approaches to Social Skills Training

The cognitive approach to social skills training differs from a reinforcement or a modeling approach in that children are more *actively involved* in thinking about, talking about, practicing, and imagining the consequences of certain social overtures (Combs & Slaby, 1977). One argument advanced in favor of this approach is that the child's active and explicit involvement in the social skills training may lead to a greater understanding, internalization, and generalization of the skills that are learned.

Coaching is a technique in which the therapist models or displays one or more social skills, explains the rationales for using them, allows children to practice such behavior, and then suggests how the children might improve on their performance. Sherrie Oden and Steven Asher (1977) coached third- and fourth-grade social isolates on four important social skills—how to participate in play activities, how to take turns and share, how to communicate effectively, and how to give attention and help to peers. Not only did the children who were coached become more outgoing and positive, but follow-up measures a year later revealed that these former isolates had achieved even further gains in social status (see also Bierman, 1986; Ladd, 1981). Apparently the benefits of a coaching strategy are even greater if this approach is combined with other forms of social skills training, such as encouraging children to work together toward the attainment of cooperative goals (Bierman & Furman, 1984).

Role-playing techniques are another type of cognitive therapy that seems to improve children's social skills. Myrna Shure and George Spivack (1978) devised a ten-week program to help preschool children generate and then evaluate solutions to a number of interpersonal problems. Children role-played these situations with puppets and were encouraged to discuss the impact of their solutions on the feelings of all parties involved in a conflict. Shure and Spivack found that fewer aggressive solutions were offered

Coaching can be effective at improving the social skills of withdrawn children.

the longer the children had participated in the program. Moreover, the children's classroom adjustment (as rated by teachers) improved as they became better able to think through the social consequences of their own actions.

Summing Up

Clearly, there are several methods that might be used to improve the social skills of unsociable children and head off the potentially harmful effects of poor peer relations. Perhaps the way to treat extremely shy and withdrawn children is to begin with a technique that produces fairly immediate results—for example, contingent reinforcement or modeling. Once these isolates have been drawn out of their shells and have seen that peer contacts can be rewarding, they may then be ready for coaching or the kinds of role-playing and problem-solving experiences that are apparently quite effective at producing long-term gains in sociability and peer acceptance.

fortable, relaxed, and outgoing with peers had fathers who were verbally expressive and involved with them, whereas girls who displayed negative or abrasive peer interactions had fathers whose play was

highly physical in character and mothers who were directive and commanding. If there is a common theme here that applies to both boys and girls, it would seem to be that a directive, controlling parental style fosters the development of poor social skills and nonharmonious peer interactions. Indeed, Bhavnagri and Parke (1985) recently found that the mothers who were least successful at facilitating playful, sociable exchanges between pairs of unacquainted 2-year-olds were those who were the most directive and controlling while trying to encourage the toddlers to play together.

IS SOCIABILITY A STABLE ATTRIBUTE?

Several longitudinal studies suggest that sociability is a reasonably stable attribute from about age 2 onward. Wanda Bronson (1985) found that, between the ages of 12 and 24 months, indicators of sociability such as a child's initial reactions to play sessions, willingness to initiate social interactions, and time spent interacting with other children become much more consistent and predictable over time. Thus, a 12-month-old who is highly sociable today may not be tomorrow, whereas this kind of inconsistency is not often seen among 2-year-olds. Bronson also found that measures of children's sociability at 2 years of age predicted their sociability at age 3½ in nursery school, whereas sociability measured when these children were only 12–14 months of age did not. Other investigators working with older children have also found that sociability remains fairly stable over time. In other words, if a child is quite friendly and outgoing during nursery school or the early grade school years, chances are that he or she will become a highly sociable adolescent or young adult (Kagan & Moss, 1962; Schaefer & Bayley, 1963).

Merrill Roff and his associates (Roff, 1974; Roff, Sells, & Golden, 1972) have collected longitudinal data on the interpersonal behavior of thousands of developing children. One of the most reliable findings in this research is that unsociable children who are *rejected by their peers* run the risk of experiencing serious emotional disturbances later in life—problems such as delinquency, neurotic and psychotic disorders, and sexual deviations, to name a few. We will be returning to this intriguing relationship between poor peer relations and later emotional difficulties in Chapter 14, where we will discuss the many important roles that peers play in a child's social and personality development. But even without considering the issue further at this point, it should be apparent that the task of becoming appropriately sociable is an important developmental hurdle—one that may call for therapeutic intervention if children are extremely shy, uncomfortable, or aggressive around their peers.

SUMMARY

In recent years there has been a revival of interest in the psychology of the self. *Self* is a term that researchers use to refer to a person's impressions of the combination of attributes that makes him or her a unique individual. The self seems to have two distinct components: the "*I*" (or subjective self-as-knower) and the "*Me*" (or the self-as-an-observable-object that one can think about).

Although there is some disagreement among contemporary theorists, the prevailing point of view is that infants cannot distinguish between the self and nonself (objects, other people) until 4–6 months of age. The "I" (or self-as-knower) develops first. But by 18–24 months of age, the "Me" (or self-as-object) emerges as children form stable self-images (as indicated by their ability to recognize themselves in a mirror) and soon begin to categorize themselves along socially significant dimensions such as age and sex. The self-concepts of preschool children are very concrete, centering on their physical attributes, their possessions, and the activities they can perform. Older grade school children typically describe the self in terms of psychological attributes, whereas adolescents have a more abstract conception of self that includes not only their stable attributes but also their beliefs, attitudes, and values.

Grade school children differ in their perceived self-worth, or *self-esteem*. Children who feel good about their cognitive and social competencies tend to do better at school and have more friends than their classmates who feel socially and intellectually inadequate. Self-esteem often declines in early adolescence and then gradually increases over the next several years. Among the factors that may be responsible for young adolescents' declining self-esteem are (1) dissatisfactions about their changing body images, (2) the loss of status they experience upon entering junior high and becoming the youngest and least competent pupils, and (3) the sense of confusion that results as they perceive the need to establish a stable identity and begin to reevaluate themselves and their goals.

There are some interesting parallels between children's knowledge of self and their knowledge of others. Children younger than 6 or 7 are likely to describe friends and acquaintances in the same concrete, observable terms (physical attributes and activities) that they use to describe the self. By age 8 to 10, children begin to see regularities in the behavior of both themselves and others and will often base their impressions of an acquaintance on the stable psychological constructs, or "traits," that this person is presumed to have. As they approach adolescence, their impressions become much more abstract as they begin to compare and contrast their friends and acquaintances on a number of psychological attributes. The growth of self-knowledge and interpersonal understanding is related to changes that are occurring in children's intellectual and social information-processing abilities and their role-taking skills. To truly know a person, one must be able to assume his perspective and understand his thoughts, feelings, motives, and intentions—in short, the internal factors that account for his behavior. Both cognitive development and social experiences are important contributors to one's proficiency as a role taker.

Sociability is a term that refers to the child's tendency to approach and interact with other people and to seek their attention or approval. Although children become much more sociable over the first three years, some infants are more outgoing than others. Three factors that may contribute to these individual differences in sociability are the child's genotype, the security of his or her interpersonal attachments, and the child's ordinal position in the family.

During the preschool period, children become much more playful and outgoing with one another and much less inclined to seek the companionship of adults. Nursery school attendance often accelerates this trend, although children who are initially low in sociability sometimes become even more withdrawn

and inhibited if they lack the social skills to interact effectively with their nursery school classmates. Warm, supportive parents who require their children to follow certain rules of social etiquette and are not overly directive or controlling tend to raise sons and daughters who establish good relations with both adults and peers. By contrast, permissive parents who exert little or no control are likely to have children who resist adult authority and are aggressive and unpopular with their peers.

Sociability is a stable attribute from about age 2 onward. A child who is quite friendly and outgoing during nursery school and the grade school years is likely to become a highly sociable adolescent or young adult. Unsociable children who are rejected by their classmates run an above-average risk of experiencing serious emotional difficulties later in life. Thus, the task of becoming appropriately sociable is an important developmental hurdle—one that may require therapeutic intervention if children are extremely shy, uncomfortable, or aggressive around their peers.

NOTES

1. Rather than simply dabbing a spot of rouge on the child's nose, Lewis and Brooks-Gunn had mothers wipe their children's ostensibly "dirty" faces and apply the rouge without mentioning it or calling attention to what they were doing.

2. Harter and Pike (1984) have recently developed a perceived competence scale for preschool and early grade school children (4–7-year-olds) and found that youngsters in this age range do tend to perceive themselves in relatively favorable or unfavorable terms on a couple of dimensions: general competence and social acceptance. However, the authors were hesitant to label these self-perceptions as a firm sense of self-esteem because 4–7-year-olds' impressions of their general competencies and social acceptance are not terribly accurate and, hence, may partly reflect a *desire* to be liked or to be "good" at a variety of activities rather than a firm set of beliefs about their actual competencies.

3. A point worth noting here is that use of an attributional principle such as discounting is *not* an ability or a "trait" that children suddenly acquire and display from that day forward, for their tendency to rely on such schemata will depend very heavily on the quality of the information they are processing and the type of judgment they are asked to

make. For example, if information about two or more plausible causes for an outcome is very clear and unambiguous to them, then young children may well make use of the discounting principle. By contrast, Colleen Surber (1984) finds that even adults may fail to employ the discounting schema when the information they must consider to do so is of dubious reliability and/or when their own theorizing about a phenomenon suggests that its causes are positively rather than inversely related.

4. A nonfriend acquaintance, in this study, was a classmate who was rated "OK" but not a close friend.

REFERENCES

ABRAMOVITCH, R., Corter, C., & Lando, B. (1979). Sibling interaction in the home. *Child Development, 50,* 997–1003.

ADAMS, G. R., & Fitch, S. A. (1982). Ego stage and identity status development: A cross-sequential analysis. *Journal of Personality and Social Psychology, 43,* 574–583.

AINSWORTH, M. D. S. (1972). Attachment and dependency: A comparison. In J. L. Gewirtz (Ed.), *Attachment and dependency.* Washington, DC: Winston.

AINSWORTH, M. D. S. (1979). Attachment as related to mother-infant interaction. In J. G. Rosenblatt, R. A. Hinde, C. Beer, & M. Busnel (Eds.), *Advances in the study of behavior* (Vol. 9). Orlando, FL: Academic Press.

ARCHER, S. L. (1982). The lower age boundaries of identity development. *Child Development, 53,* 1551–1556.

ASHER, S. R. (1986). An overview of intervention research with unpopular children. In S. R. Asher & J. Coie (Eds.), *Assessment of children's social status.* New York: Cambridge University Press.

ASHER, S. R., Renshaw, P. D., & Hymel, S. (1982). Peer relations and the development of social skills. In S. G. Moore (Ed.), *The young child: Reviews of research* (Vol. 3). Washington, DC: National Association for the Education of Young Children.

BANDURA, A., & Menlove, F. L. (1968). Factors determining vicarious extinction of avoidance behavior through symbolic modeling. *Journal of Personality and Social Psychology, 8,* 99–108.

BARENBOIM, C. (1981). The development of person perception in childhood and adolescence: From behavioral comparisons to psychological constructs to psychological comparisons. *Child Development, 52,* 129–144.

BAUMRIND, D. (1971). Current patterns of parental authority. *Developmental Psychology Monographs, 4*(No. 1, Pt. 2).

BERNDT, T. J. (1982). The features and effects of friendship in early adolescence. *Child Development, 53,* 1447–1460.

BERTENTHAL, B. I., & Fischer, K. W. (1978). Development of self-recognition in the infant. *Developmental Psychology, 14,* 44–50.

BHAVNAGRI, N., & Parke, R. D. (1985, April). *Parents as facilitators of preschool peer-peer interaction.* Paper presented at the biennial meeting of the Society for Research in Child Development, Toronto.

BIERMAN, K. L. (1986). Process of change during social skills training with preadolescents and its relation to treatment outcome. *Child Development, 57,* 230–240.

BIERMAN, K. L., & Furman, W. (1984). The effects of social skills training and peer involvement on the social adjustment of preadolescents. *Child Development, 55,* 151–162.

BLOUNT, R. (1986, May 4). "I'm about five years ahead of my age." *Atlanta Journal and Constitution,* pp. 17c–20c.

BRIDGEMAN, D. L. (1981). Enhanced role-taking through cooperative interdependence: A field study. *Child Development, 51,* 1231–1238.

BRONSON, W. C. (1985). Growth in the organization of behavior over the second year of life. *Developmental Psychology, 21,* 108–117.

BROOKS, J., & Lewis, M. (1976). Infants' response to strangers: Midget, adult, and child. *Child Development, 47,* 323–332.

BROOKS-GUNN, J., & Lewis, M. (1981). Infant social perception: Responses to pictures of parents and strangers. *Developmental Psychology, 17,* 647–649.

BROOKS-GUNN, J., & Lewis, M. (1982). The development of self-knowledge. In C. B. Kopp & J. B. Krakow (Eds.), *The child: Development in a social context.* Reading, MA: Addison-Wesley.

BROWNELL, C. A. (1986). Convergent developments: Cognitive-developmental correlates of growth in infant/toddler peer skills. *Child Development, 57,* 275–286.

CERNOCH, J. M., & Porter, R. H. (1985). Recognition of maternal axillary odors by infants. *Child Development, 56,* 1593–1598.

CLARKE-STEWART, K. A., Umeh, B. J., Snow, M. E., & Pederson, J. A. (1980). Development and prediction of children's sociability from 1 to 2½ years. *Developmental Psychology, 16,* 290–302.

COMBS, M. L., & Slaby, D. A. (1977). Social skills training with children. In B. B. Lahey & A. E. Kazdin (Eds.), *Advances in clinical child psychology.* New York: Plenum.

COOKE, T., & Apolloni, T. (1976). Developing positive social-emotional behaviors: A study of training and generalization effects. *Journal of Applied Behavior Analysis, 9,* 65–78.

COOLEY, C. H. (1902). *Human nature and the social order.* New York: Scribner's.

COOPERSMITH, S. (1967). *The antecedents of self-esteem.* New York: W. H. Freeman.

DALENBERG, C. J., Bierman, K. L., & Furman, W. (1984). A reexamination of developmental changes in causal attributions. *Developmental Psychology, 20,* 575–583.

DAMON, W., & Hart, D. (1982). The development of self-understanding from infancy through adolescence. *Child Development, 53,* 841–864.

DANIELS, D., & Plomin, R. (1985). Origins of individual differences in infant shyness. *Developmental Psychology, 21,* 118–121.

DeCASPER, A. J., & Fifer, W. P. (1980). Of human bonding: Newborns prefer their mothers' voices. *Science, 208,* 1174–1176.

DUVALL, S., & Wicklund, R. A. (1972). *A theory of objective self-awareness.* Orlando, FL: Academic Press.

EDWARDS, C. P. (1984). The age group labels and categories of preschool children. *Child Development, 55,* 440–452.

EDWARDS, C. P., & Lewis, M. (1979). Young children's concepts of social relations: Social functions and social objects. In M. Lewis & L. Rosenblum (Eds.), *The child and its family: The genesis of behavior* (Vol. 2). New York: Plenum.

ERIKSON, E. H. (1950). In M. J. E. Senn (Ed.), *Symposium on the healthy personality.* New York: Josiah Macy Jr. Foundation.

ERIKSON, E. H. (1963). *Childhood and society* (2nd ed.). New York: Norton.

FITCH, S. A., & Adams, G. R. (1983). Ego identity and intimacy status: Replication and extension. *Developmental Psychology, 19,* 839–845.

FLAVELL, J. H., Shipstead, S. G., & Croft, K. (1978). *What young children think you see when their eyes are closed.* Unpublished data, Stanford University.

FRAIBERG, S., & Adelson, E. (1976). Self-representation in young blind children. In Z. Jastrzembska (Ed.), *The effects of blindness and other impairments on early development.* New York: American Foundation for the Blind.

FREEDMAN, D. G. (1974). *Human infancy: An evolutionary perspective.* Hillsdale, NJ: Erlbaum.

FURMAN, W., & Bierman, K. L. (1983). Developmental changes in young children's conceptions of friendship. *Child Development, 54,* 549–556.

FURMAN, W., & Bierman, K. L. (1984). Children's conceptions of friendship: A multimethod study of developmental changes. *Developmental Psychology, 20,* 925–931.

GALLUP, G. G., Jr. (1979). Self-recognition in chimpanzees and man: A developmental and comparative perspective. In M. Lewis & L. A. Rosenblum (Eds.), *Genesis of behavior*. Vol. 2: *The child and its family*. New York: Plenum.

GOLDSMITH, H. H. (1983). Genetic influences on personality from infancy to adulthood. *Child Development, 54*, 331–355.

GURUCHARRI, C., & Selman, R. L. (1982). The development of interpersonal understanding during childhood, preadolescence, and adolescence: A longitudinal follow-up study. *Child Development, 53*, 924–927.

HARPER, L. V., & Huie, K. S. (1985). The effects of prior group experience, age, and familiarity on the quality and organization of preschoolers' social relationships. *Child Development, 56*, 704–717.

HARTER, S. (1982). The perceived competence scale for children. *Child Development, 53*, 87–97.

HARTER, S. (1983). Developmental perspectives on the self-system. In P. H. Mussen (Ed.), *Handbook of child psychology*. Vol. 4: *Socialization, personality and social development*. New York: Wiley.

HARTER, S., & Pike, R. (1984). The pictorial scale of perceived competence and social acceptance for young children. *Child Development, 55*, 1969–1982.

HARTUP, W. W. (1983). Peer relations. In P. H. Mussen (Ed.), *Handbook of child psychology*. Vol. 4: *Socialization, personality and social development*. New York: Wiley.

HAY, D. F., Nash, A., & Pedersen, J. (1983). Interaction between six-month-old peers. *Child Development, 54*, 557–562.

HAYES, D. S., Gershman, E., & Bolin, L. J. (1980). Friends and enemies: Cognitive bases for preschool children's unilateral and reciprocal relationships. *Child Development, 51*, 1276–1279.

HEIDER, F. (1958). *The psychology of interpersonal relations*. New York: Wiley.

HILL, S. D., & Tomlin, C. (1981). Self-recognition in retarded children. *Child Development, 52*, 145–150.

HUDSON, L. M., Forman, E. R., & Brion-Meisels, S. (1982). Role-taking as a predictor of prosocial behavior in cross-age tutors. *Child Development, 53*, 1320–1329.

JAMES, W. (1890). *Principles of psychology* (Vol. 1). New York: Henry Holt.

JOHNSON, C. N., & Wellman, H. M. (1982). Children's developing conceptions of the mind and brain. *Child Development, 53*, 222–234.

KAGAN, J., & Moss, H. A. (1962). *Birth to maturity*. New York: Wiley.

KAVANAUGH, R., & McCall, R. (1983). Social influencing among 2-year-olds: The role of affiliative and antagonistic behaviors. *Infant Behavior and Development, 6*, 39–52.

KEATING, D., & Clark, L. V. (1980). Development of physical and social reasoning in adolescence. *Developmental Psychology, 16*, 23–30.

KELLER, A., Ford, L. H., Jr., & Meachum, J.A. (1978). Dimensions of self-concept in preschool children. *Developmental Psychology, 14*, 483–489.

KELLEY, H. H. (1973). The process of causal attribution. *American Psychologist, 28*, 107–128.

KERBY, F. D., & Tolar, H. C. (1970). Modification of preschool isolate behavior: A case study. *Journal of Applied Behavior Analysis, 3*, 309–314.

KOHLBERG, L. (1969). Stage and sequence: The cognitive-developmental approach to socialization. In D. A. Goslin (Ed.), *Handbook of socialization theory and research*. Skokie, IL: Rand McNally.

KOKENES, B. (1974). Grade level differences in factors of self-esteem. *Developmental Psychology, 10*, 954–958.

KUN, A. (1978). Evidence for preschoolers' understanding of causal direction in extended causal sequences. *Child Development, 49*, 218–222.

KURDEK, L. A., & Krile, D. (1982). A developmental analysis of the relation between peer acceptance and both interpersonal understanding and perceived social self-competence. *Child Development, 53*, 1485–1491.

LADD, G. W. (1981). Effectiveness of a social learning method for enhancing children's social interaction and peer acceptance. *Child Development, 52*, 171–178.

LaFRENIERE, P. J., & Sroufe, L. A. (1985). Profiles of peer competence in the preschool: Interrelations between measures, influence of social ecology, and relation to attachment history. *Developmental Psychology, 21*, 56–69.

LERNER, R. M., Iwawaki, S., Chihara, T., & Sorell, G. T. (1980). Self-concept, self-esteem, and body attitudes among Japanese male and female adolescents. *Child Development, 51*, 847–855.

LEWIS, M., & Brooks-Gunn, J. (1979). *Social cognition and the acquisition of self*. New York: Plenum.

LEWIS, M., Brooks-Gunn, J., & Jaskir, J. (1985). Individual differences in visual self-recognition as a function of mother-infant attachment relationship. *Developmental Psychology, 21*, 1181–1187.

LEWIS, M., & Kreitzberg, V. S. (1979). Effects of birth-order and spacing on mother-infant interactions. *Developmental Psychology, 15*, 617–625.

LIVESLEY, W. J., & Bromley, D. B. (1973). *Person perception in childhood and adolescence*. London: Wiley.

LONDERVILLE, S., & Main, M. (1981). Security of attachment, compliance, and maternal training methods in the second year of life. *Developmental Psychology, 17*, 289–299.

LUTKENHAUS, P., Grossmann, K. E., & Grossmann, K. (1985). Infant-mother attachment at twelve months and style of interaction with a stranger at the age of three years. *Child Development, 56*, 1538–1542.

MACCOBY, E. E., & Feldman, S. (1972). Mother-attachment and stranger-reactions in the third year of life. *Monographs of the Society for Research in Child Development, 37*(1, Serial No. 146).

MacDONALD, K., & Parke, R. D. (1984). Bridging the gap: Parent-child play interaction and peer interactive competence. *Child Development, 55*, 1265–1277.

MAHLER, M. S., Pine, F., & Bergman, A. (1975). *The psychological birth of the human infant*. New York: Basic Books.

MAIN, M., & Weston, D. R. (1981). The quality of the toddler's relationship to mother and father: Related to conflict and the readiness to establish new relationships. *Child Development, 52*, 932–940.

MARCIA, J. E. (1966). Development and validation of ego identity status. *Journal of Personality and Social Psychology, 3*, 551–558.

MARTIN, B. (1975). Parent-child relations. In F. D. Horowitz (Ed.), *Review of child development research* (Vol. 4). Chicago: University of Chicago Press.

MATHENY, A. P. (1983). A longitudinal twin study of the stability of components from Bayley's Infant Behavior Record. *Child Development, 54*, 356–360.

McCARTHY, J. D., & Hoge, D. R. (1982). Analysis of age effects in longitudinal studies of adolescent self-esteem. *Developmental Psychology, 18*, 372–379.

McGUIRE, K. D., & Weisz, J. R. (1982). Social cognition and behavioral correlates of preadolescent chumship. *Child Development, 53*, 1478–1484.

MEAD, G. H. (1934). *Mind, self, and society*. Chicago: University of Chicago Press.

MEILMAN, P. W. (1979). Cross-sectional age changes in ego identity status during adolescence. *Developmental Psychology, 15*, 230–231.

MENDELSON, B. D., & White, D. R. (1985). Development of self-body-esteem in overweight youngsters. *Developmental Psychology, 21*, 90–96.

MISCHEL, T. (1977). *The self: Psychological and philosophical issues*. Oxford: Basil Blackwell.

MOHR, D. M. (1978). Development of attributes of personal identity. *Developmental Psychology, 14*, 427–428.

MONTEMAYOR, R., & Eisen, M. (1977). The development of self-conceptions from childhood to adolescence. *Developmental Psychology, 13*, 314–319.

MOORE, S., & Updegraff, R. (1964). Sociometric status of preschool children related to age, sex, nurturance-giving, and dependency. *Child Development, 35*, 519–524.

MUELLER, E., & Lucas, T. (1975). A developmental analysis of peer interactions among toddlers. In M. Lewis & L. Rosenblum (Eds.), *Friendship and peer relations*. New York: Wiley.

MUELLER, E., & Vandell, D. L. (1979). Infant-infant interaction. In J. Osofsky (Ed.), *Handbook of infant development*. New York: Wiley.

MUNRO, G., & Adams, G. R. (1977). Ego-identity formation in college students and working youth. *Developmental Psychology, 13*, 523–524.

NELSON, J., & Aboud, F. E. (1985). The resolution of social conflict among friends. *Child Development, 56*, 1009–1017.

ODEN, S., & Asher, S. R. (1977). Coaching children in social skills for friendship making. *Child Development, 48*, 495–506.

O'MALLEY, P. M., & Bachman, J. G. (1983). Self-esteem: Change and stability between ages 13 and 23. *Developmental Psychology, 19*, 257–268.

PASTOR, D. L. (1981). The quality of mother-infant attachment and its relationship to toddlers' initial sociability with peers. *Developmental Psychology, 17*, 326–335.

PEERY, J. C. (1980). Neonate and adult head movement: No and yes revisited. *Developmental Psychology, 16*, 245–250.

PEEVERS, B. H., & Secord, P. F. (1973). Developmental changes in attribution of descriptive concepts to persons. *Journal of Personality and Social Psychology, 27*, 120–128.

PELLEGRINI, D. S. (1985). Social cognition and competence in middle childhood. *Child Development, 56*, 253–264.

PENNEBAKER, J. W., Hendler, C. S., Durrett, M. E., & Richards, P. (1981). Social factors influencing absenteeism due to illness in nursery school children. *Child Development, 52*, 692–700.

PIAGET, J. (1965). *The moral judgment of the child*. New York: Free Press.

RHOLES, W. S., & Ruble, D. N. (1984). Children's understanding of dispositional characteristics of others. *Child Development, 55*, 550–560.

ROFF, M. F. (1974). Childhood antecedents of adult neurosis, severe bad conduct, and psychological health. In D. F. Ricks, A. Thomas, & M. Roff (Eds.), *Life history research in psychopathology* (Vol. 3). Minneapolis: University of Minnesota Press.

ROFF, M. F., Sells, S. B., & Golden, M. M. (1972). *Social adjustment and personality development in children*. Minneapolis: University of Minnesota Press.

ROSENBERG, M. (1979). *Conceiving the self*. New York: Basic Books.

ROTENBERG, K. J. (1982). Development of character constancy of self and other. *Child Development, 53*, 505–515.

SAMUELS, C. (1986). Bases for the infant's development of self-awareness. *Human Development, 29*, 36–48.

SAVIN-WILLIAMS, R. C., & Demo, D. H. (1984). Developmental change and stability in adolescent self-concept. *Developmental Psychology, 20*, 1100–1110.

SCARR, S. (1968). Environmental bias in twin studies. *Eugenics Quarterly, 15*, 34–40.

SCHACHTER, S. (1959). *The psychology of affiliation*. Stanford, CA: Stanford University Press.

SCHAEFER, E. S., & Bayley, N. (1963). Maternal behavior, child behavior, and their intercorrelations from infancy through adolescence. *Monographs of the Society for Research in Child Development, 28* (Serial No. 87).

SCHAFFER, H. R., & Emerson, P. E. (1964). The development of social attachments in infancy. *Monographs of the Society for Research in Child Development, 29* (3, Serial No. 94).

SCHEIER, M. F., & Carver, C. S. (1981). Private and public aspects of self. In L. Wheeler (Ed.), *Review of personality and social psychology* (Vol. 2). Beverly Hills, CA: Sage.

SCHNEIDER-ROSEN, K., & Cicchetti, D. (1984). The relationship between affect and cognition in maltreated infants: Quality of attachment and the development of visual self-recognition. *Child Development, 55*, 648–658.

SECORD, P. F., & Peevers, B. H. (1974). The development and attribution of person concepts. In T. Mischel (Ed.), *Understanding other persons*. Totowa, NJ: Rowman & Littlefield.

SEDLAK, A. J., & Kurtz, S. T. (1981). A review of children's use causal inference principles. *Child Development, 52*, 759–784.

SELMAN, R. L. (1976). Social-cognitive understanding: A guide to educational and clinical practice. In T. Lickona (Ed.), *Moral development and behavior: Theory, research and social issues*. New York: Holt, Rinehart and Winston.

SELMAN, R. L. (1980). *The growth of interpersonal understanding*. Orlando, FL: Academic Press.

SHANTZ, C. U. (1983). Social cognition. In P. H. Mussen (Ed.), *Handbook of child psychology*, Vol. 3: *Cognitive development*. New York: Wiley.

SHEA, J. D. C. (1981). Changes in interpersonal distances and categories of play behavior in the early weeks of preschool. *Developmental Psychology, 17*, 417–425.

SHULTZ, T. R., & Wells, D. (1985). Judging the intentionality of action-outcomes. *Developmental Psychology, 21*, 83–89.

SHURE, M. B., & Spivack, G. (1978). *Problem-solving techniques in childrearing*. San Francisco: Jossey-Bass.

SIMMONS, R. G., Blyth, D. A., Van Cleave, E. F., & Bush, D. M. (1979). Entry into early adolescence: The impact of school structure, puberty, and early dating on self-esteem. *American Sociological Review, 44*, 948–967.

SNOW, M. E., Jacklin, C. N., & Maccoby, E. E. (1981). Birth-order differences in peer sociability at thirty-three months. *Child Development, 52*, 589–595.

SPIKER, D., & Ricks, M. (1984). Visual self-recognition in autistic children: Developmental relationships. *Child Development, 55*, 214–225.

STERN, D. N. (1983). The early development of schemas of self, other, and "self with other." In J. D. Lictenberg & S. Kaplan (Eds.), *Reflections on self psychology*. Hillsdale, NJ: Erlbaum.

SULLIVAN, H. S. (1953). *The interpersonal theory of psychiatry*. New York: Norton.

SURBER, C. F. (1984). Inferences of ability and effort: Evidence for two different processes. *Journal of Personality and Social Psychology, 46*, 249–268.

THOMPSON, R. A., & Lamb, M. E. (1983). Security of attachment and stranger sociability in infancy. *Developmental Psychology, 19*, 184–191.

THOMPSON, S. K. (1975). Gender labels and early sex-role development. *Child Development, 46*, 339–347.

VANDELL, D. L., Wilson, K. S., & Buchanan, N. R. (1980). Peer interaction in the first year of life: An examination of its structure, content, and sensitivity to toys. *Child Development, 51*, 481–488.

VANDELL, D. L., Wilson, K. S., & Whalen, W. T. (1981). Birth-order and social experiences differences in infant-peer interaction. *Developmental Psychology, 17*, 438–445.

VINCZE, M. (1971). The social contacts of infants and young children reared together. *Early Child Development and Care, 1*, 99–109.

VYGOTSKY, L. S. (1934). *Thought and language*. Cambridge, MA: M.I.T. Press.

WATERMAN, A. S. (1982). Identity development from adolescence to adulthood: An extension of theory and a review of research. *Developmental Psychology, 18*, 341–358.

WATSON, J. S., & Ramey, C. T. (1972). Reactions to response contingent stimulation in early infancy. *Merrill-Palmer Quarterly, 18*, 219–228.

WHITBOURNE, S. K., & Tesch, S. A. (1985). A comparison of identity and intimacy statuses in college students and alumni. *Developmental Psychology, 21*, 1039–1044.

WILLIAMS, J. E., Bennett, S. M., & Best, D. L. (1975). Awareness and expression of sex stereotypes in young children. *Developmental Psychology, 11*, 635–642.

WOLFF, P. H. (1969). The natural history of crying and other vocalizations in early infancy. In B. M. Foss (Ed.), *Determinants of infant behavior* (Vol. 4). London: Methuen.

8

ACHIEVEMENT

Two basic aims of socialization are to encourage children to pursue important goals and to convince them to take pride in their accomplishments. During my elementary and high school days, I had several heart-to-heart talks with my parents (of the kind you may remember) about the value of writing essays and memorizing the countless passages that were required of me in English and history classes. Both my parents took the position that I should strive to do my best, whatever the assignment, because successful completion of these scholastic activities would promote the self-confidence I would need to become a success in life. My parents' outlook was very typical of adults in many Western societies where children are often encouraged to be independent and competitive and to do well in whatever activities they may undertake—in short, to become "achievers." Although the meaning of achievement varies somewhat from society to society, a recent survey of 30 cultures reveals that people all over the world value personal attributes such as self-reliance, responsibility, and a willingness to work hard to attain important objectives (Fyans, Salili, Maehr, & Desai, 1983).

Must these valued attributes be taught? Social-learning theorists think so, although others disagree. Psychoanalytic theorist Robert White (1959) proposes that children are intrinsically motivated to "master" the environment. He calls this striving for mastery *effectance motivation* after the young child's tendency to "effect" various acts, with little or no parental prompting, that will enable her to cope with the demands of the environment and the people within it. Note the similarity of White's position to that of Piaget, who believes that children are intrinsically motivated to assimilate and accommodate to new experiences, thereby *adapting* to the environment.

Throughout this text, we have stressed that human infants are curious, active explorers who are constantly striving to understand, and to exert some control over, the world around them. But even though this basic propensity for competence and achievement may be innate, it is obvious that some children try harder than others to master their school assignments, their music lessons, or the positions they play on the neighborhood softball team. How can we explain these individual differences? Is there a "motive to achieve" that children must acquire? What kinds of home, family, and scholastic experiences are likely to promote achievement behavior? And how do children's self-images and their expectations about succeeding or failing affect their aspirations and accomplishments? These are the issues we will consider in the pages that follow.

DEFINITIONS OF INDEPENDENCE AND ACHIEVEMENT

When developmentalists talk about an "independent" person, they mean someone who is able to accomplish many goals without assistance. The concept of achievement extends far beyond a sense of independence. Children who are high achievers are not only self-reliant; they are also likely to evaluate the *quality* of their performance against some standard of merit or excellence.

The motivational view of achievement. Achievement has been looked at in two very different ways. David McClelland and his associates (McClelland, Atkinson, Clark, & Lowell, 1953) talk of the child's *need for achievement* (n Ach), which they define as a "learned motive to compete and to strive for success whenever one's behavior can be evaluated against a standard of excellence" (p. 78). In other words, high "need-achievers" have learned to take *pride* in their ability to meet or exceed high standards, and it is this sense of *self*-fulfillment that motivates them to work hard, to be successful, and to try to outperform others when faced with new challenges.

McClelland measures achievement motivation by asking subjects to examine a set of four pictures and then write a story about each as part of a test of "creative imagination." These four pictures show people working or studying, although each is sufficiently ambiguous to suggest any number of themes (see Photo 8-1). The subject's need for achievement (n Ach) is determined by counting the achievement-related statements that he or she includes in the four stories (the assumption being that subjects are projecting themselves and their motives into their themes). For example, a high need-achiever might respond to Photo 8-1 by saying that these men have been working for months on a new scientific breakthrough that will revolutionize the field of medicine, whereas a low need-achiever might say that the workers are glad the day is over so that they can go home and relax.

A behavioral view of achievement. In contrast to McClelland's viewpoint, Vaughn Crandall and his associates depict achievement as a behavioral, rather than a motivational, construct. According to Crandall, Katkovsky, and Preston (1960), "Achievement is any *behavior* directed toward the *attainment of approval* or the *avoidance of disapproval* for competence in performance in situations where standards of excellence are operable" (p. 789; italics added). Crandall and his associates argue that there is no single, overriding motive to achieve that applies to all achievement tasks. Instead, they propose that children will show different strivings in different skill areas (for example, art, schoolwork, sports) depending on the extent to which they value doing well in each area and their expectations that they can succeed.

Notice that McClelland and Crandall clearly differ on the issue of what reinforces achievement behavior. McClelland and his associates have adopted a neo-Hullian point of view, arguing that the sense of *pride* stemming from one's high accomplishments is reinforcing (and will sustain achievement behavior in the future) because it satisfies an *intrinsic* need for competence or achievement. However, Crandall and his associates counterargue that one need not talk about internal needs or drives that must be satisfied in order to explain why people strive to meet exacting standards. Instead, they propose that achievement behaviors are simply a class of *instrumental* responses designed to win the approval (or to avoid the disapproval) of significant others, such as parents, teachers, and peers.

Which of these viewpoints is correct? Perhaps both are, although any two persons may differ in the extent to which their accomplishments are motivated by intrinsic or extrinsic concerns. Susan Harter (1981)

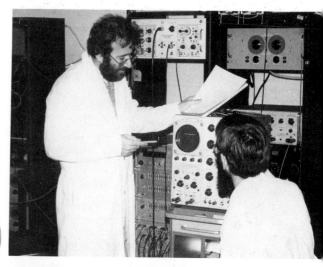

PHOTO 8-1 Scenes like this one were used by David McClelland and his associates to measure achievement motivation.

finds that some children do view achievement tasks as a means of satisfying personal needs for competence or mastery (an *intrinsic orientation* very similar to McClelland's view of *n* Ach), whereas others strive to do well in order to earn external incentives such as grades, prizes, or social approval (an *extrinsic orientation* that other theorists have called "social achievement"). Harter measures children's orientations to achievement with a 30-item questionnaire that asks whether the reasons they perform various activities are intrinsic justifications (I like challenging tasks; I like to solve problems myself) or extrinsic ones (I do things to get good grades, to win the teacher's approval, and so on). Preliminary research with this new measure shows that children who are intrinsically oriented to achieve are more likely than those who are extrinsically oriented (1) to prefer challenging problems over simpler ones and (2) to view themselves as highly competent at schoolwork and other cognitive activities.

We will now turn to the major theories of achievement to see why children might adopt different achievement orientations and how this choice of an orientation might influence their future accomplishments.

THEORIES OF ACHIEVEMENT MOTIVATION AND ACHIEVEMENT BEHAVIOR

The theories that have contributed most to our understanding of achievement motivation and achievement behavior are (1) the McClelland/Atkinson need achievement theory, (2) Crandall's social-learning theory, and (3) the attributional (or social information-processing) approach. In this section of the chapter we will compare and contrast these influential points of view.

NEED ACHIEVEMENT THEORY

The first major theory of achievement was the "need achievement" approach, a motivational model that stemmed from the pioneering efforts of David McClelland and his associates at Wesleyan University and was later revised by John Atkinson of the University of Michigan.

McClelland's Theory of Achievement Motivation

In 1938 Henry Murray published *Explorations in Personality*, a text that had a profound influence on students of human behavior. Murray outlined a personality theory that included a taxonomy of human needs. He discussed 28 basic human needs—for example, the need for sex, the need for affiliation, the need for nurturance—including the need for achievement (*n* Ach), which he defined as "the desire or tendency to do things as rapidly and/or as well as possible" (p. 164).

David McClelland and his associates at Wesleyan University read Murray's work and became interested in the development of achievement motivation. McClelland et al. (1953) viewed *n* Ach as a learned motive that, like all other complex social motives, is acquired on the basis of rewards and punishments that accompany certain kinds of behavior. If children are frequently reinforced for independence, competitiveness, and success and if they meet with disapproval when they fail, their achievement motivation should be rather strong. But a child can hardly be expected to develop a strong need for achievement if he or she is not often encouraged to be independent, competitive, and highly competent in day-to-day activities and endeavors. In sum, the strength of an individual's achievement motive was thought to depend on the quality of his or her "achievement" training. McClelland et al. believed that the quality of achievement training received by children varied as a function of their culture, their social class, and the attitudes of their parents about the value of independence and achievement.

The first task faced by the Wesleyan group was to develop a method of measuring achievement motivation. What was needed was an instrument that measured the strength of one's desire to compete and to excel in situations where standards of excellence are operable.

McClelland and his associates settled on the story-writing technique described earlier because they believed that a person's true underlying motives might well be reflected in his fantasy life—that is, dreams, wishes, idle thoughts, and daydreams. They soon discovered that people varied a great deal in the amount of achievement imagery they displayed when writing stories about ambiguous work or study scenes. The next step, then, was to validate this measure by showing that people who scored high in the need for achievement would actually turn out to be high achievers, whereas those who scored low would display more modest accomplishments.

The relationship between achievement motivation and achievement behavior. Is achievement motivation related in some meaningful way to achievement behavior? Indeed it is. Several studies conducted during the 1950s revealed that college students who score high in *n* Ach tend to have higher grade-point averages than those who score low (Bendig, 1958; McClelland et al., 1953; Weiss, Wertheimer, & Groesbeck, 1959). Moreover, Minor and Neel (1958) found that high need-achievers select higher-status occupations than low need-achievers. So it seems that people who express a strong desire to achieve on the McClelland fantasy measure of *n* Ach often do achieve at higher levels than those who test low in achievement motivation.

The achieving society. What would happen if large numbers of high need-achievers were present in a culture at a given time? Would that culture take large strides forward, showing clear signs of technological or economic growth in the years ahead? McClelland asked these questions after reading the work of German sociologist Max Weber. In his book *The Protestant Ethic and the Spirit of Capitalism* (1904/1930), Weber noted that the Protestant countries of Europe were more productive and economically advanced than their Roman Catholic counterparts. He attributed this difference to the "Protestant ethic," a doctrine that encourages self-reliance, delay of gratification, and an evaluation of work as good in itself. In sum, Weber argued that the Protestant religious ideology was conducive to the development of a spirit of capitalism and increased economic productivity.

McClelland reanalyzed these arguments in terms of his own theory of achievement motivation. The central theme of his analysis can be summarized as follows:

Protestant $\longrightarrow$ Independence $\longrightarrow$ High need $\longrightarrow$ Economic
ideology   and   achievers   growth
                achievement
                training by
                socialization
                agents

There are data consistent with McClelland's model. First, McClelland, Rindlisbacher, and de Charms (1955) found that Protestant parents expect their children to show evidence of independence at an earlier age than Catholic parents do. This finding is consistent with the model's first link, the link between the Protestant ideology and child-rearing techniques. McClelland et al. also report that the Protestants among a group of German boys attained significantly higher *n* Ach scores than the Catholics. This finding, in conjunction with the first, is consistent with the model's second link. Finally, McClelland (1955) found that in 1950, more than four decades after Weber's observations, Protestant countries (such as Australia, Canada, Great Britain, Sweden, and the United States) were still more economically advanced than Catholic countries (such as Austria, France, Ireland, Italy, and Spain). Although a num-

ber of factors other than societal differences in *n* Ach could have contributed to this last finding, McClelland nevertheless proposed a more general hypothesis that *the economic growth and development of a society should be predictable from the average level of achievement motivation of its populace.*

A direct test of this hypothesis appears in McClelland's (1961) book *The Achieving Society.* McClelland assessed the mean *n* Ach of each of 23 countries in a most interesting fashion. He simply obtained readers used in the primary grades in each country and scored the stories in these books for achievement imagery in the same way he typically scored stories that subjects might produce themselves. Children's readers were selected for study because they represent the popular culture of the country and, as such, are probably a reasonably good indication of the amount of achievement training that grade school children are receiving at any given time. Readers from the 1920s and the year 1950 were sampled. McClelland's goal was to see whether he could predict the subsequent economic growth of a country from the amount of achievement imagery present in its readers during the 1920s.

Economic growth was indexed by increases in the amount of electricity a country consumed between 1929 and 1950. Why did McClelland use this particular measure? For two reasons. First, use of electricity is highly correlated with most other measures of economic growth. Second and more important, the electricity-consumption index does not automatically handicap countries lacking natural resources such as coal or oil, for electricity can be produced in many ways. As he predicted he would, McClelland found a substantial correlation ($r = +.53$) between the number of achievement themes in a country's readers during the 1920s and the country's increase in electrical consumption for the period 1929 to 1950. Although this relationship is consistent with his hypothesis, it does not necessarily mean that the *n* Ach of a society affects its subsequent economic growth. One rival hypothesis is that economic growth already underway during the 1920s was responsible for both a country's preoccupation with achievement during the 1920s and its later economic growth. But if prior economic growth had been the causal agent, then the country's economic growth between 1929 and 1950 should be highly correlated with the number of achievement themes in its readers in 1950. *No such relationship was observed.* Thus, McClelland's cross-cultural data suggest that achievement motivation precedes economic growth and that a nation's mean *n* Ach is a barometer of its future economic accomplishments.[1]

Problems with McClelland's approach. Although McClelland's work seems to imply that achievement motivation is a reliable predictor of achievement behavior at both the individual and the group (or cultural) level, other investigators were having some difficulty replicating his findings. Virginia Crandall (1967), for example, found that children high in *n* Ach outperformed their low-need-achieving age mates in fewer than half the studies she reviewed. Moreover, John Atkinson (1964) noticed that high and low achievers often differed in their emotional reactions to achievement contexts: high achievers welcomed new challenges, whereas low achievers seemed to dread them. Why is it that achievement motivation often fails to forecast achievement behavior? Could there be other, competing motives that make achievement contexts so threatening to some people that their performance is impeded? Atkinson and his associates thought so, as we will see in their revision of McClelland's theory.

Atkinson's Expectancy × Value Model of Achievement

In outlining his theory of achievement motivation, Atkinson (1964) proposed that

> in addition to a general disposition to achieve success [called the motive to achieve success (M_s), or the achievement motive], there is also a general disposition to avoid failure, called *motive to avoid failure* [M_{af}]. Where the motive to achieve might be characterized as a capacity for reacting with pride in accomplishment, the motive to avoid failure can be conceived as a capacity for reacting with shame and embarrassment when the outcome of performance is failure. When this disposition is aroused in a person, as it is aroused whenever it is clear . . . that his performance will be evaluated and failure is a distinct possibility, the result is anxiety and a tendency to withdraw from the situation [p. 244].

According to Atkinson, a person's tendency to approach or avoid achievement activities depends on the relative strength of these *two* competing motives. A person who willingly accepts new challenges and accomplishes a lot was presumed to have a motive to attain success that is considerably stronger than his or her motive to avoid failure (that is, $M_s > M_{af}$). By contrast, the low achiever who shies away from challenges and accomplishes little was thought to have a motive to avoid failure that is stronger than his or her motive to attain success (that is, $M_{af} > M_s$). So in Atkinson's theory, the relationship between one's achievement motivation (M_s) and achievement behavior is clearly influenced by the strength of the motive to avoid failure (M_{af}).

Atkinson proposed that our willingness to work hard and strive for success in any given context will also depend on (1) our expectancies of attaining success (P_s) and avoiding failure (P_f) on the task at hand and (2) the incentive value of achieving success (I_s) and avoiding failure (I_f) in that particular situation. So his theory includes three components: *motivation*, consisting of the conflicting motives to attain success and to avoid failure, *expectancy*, consisting of the person's subjective estimate of the likelihood of attaining success and avoiding failure, and *value*, consisting of the relative attractiveness of success and the aversiveness of failure. How do these factors combine to affect achievement behavior? Atkinson expressed his theory mathematically with the formula

Achievement striving = $(M_s \times P_s \times I_s) - (M_{af} \times P_f \times I_f)$

Although this equation appears rather formidable, its implications are relatively simple. If someone is oriented toward success and not overly concerned about failure, then her achievement behavior will depend on her expectations of mastering the challenge she faces and the perceived value of the success that she might attain. Thus, she will work hard for valuable goals that she thinks she can achieve but will not knock herself out to achieve trivial goals or those that she sees no hope of accomplishing. By contrast, if a person is more concerned about the embarrassment of failing than the thrill of success, he is apt to avoid challenging tasks where the probability of success is uncertain and to choose instead to pursue goals that are either easy to attain (thus avoiding the embarrassment of failure) or very difficult (thereby explaining away a failure by pointing to the extreme difficulty of the task). Indeed, studies of risk-taking behavior (reviewed in Atkinson, 1964) reveal that people high in the motive to attain success do choose to work at tasks or to play games of moderate difficulty, for which the probability of succeeding is uncertain, whereas those high in fear of failure shun moderately difficult tasks in favor of those that are either very easy or very difficult.

Consider another implication of Atkinson's theory that may strike closer to home. If you are a psychology major, you probably consider psychology courses more important to you than a course like geology that is outside your major. If we can assume that the grade one will attain in a course is uncertain at the beginning of an academic term, then Atkinson's theory makes some interesting predictions. Students who are more concerned about attaining success than avoiding failure (that is, $M_s > M_{af}$) should work harder and perhaps obtain better grades in courses they consider important to them (I_s is high) than in those they consider unimportant (I_s is low). By contrast, students who are more concerned about avoiding failure than achieving success (that is, $M_{af} > M_s$) may actually perform *worse* in important than in unimportant courses. Why? Because failure in an important course is especially threatening to these individuals (I_f is high). Consequently, they may become very anxious about the prospect of failing, and this anxiety may cause their performance to suffer.

These ideas were tested in a study by Joel Raynor (1970). Males from an introductory psychology class took both the McClelland fantasy measure of *n* Ach (used to define M_s) and the Test Anxiety Questionnaire, an objective paper-and-pencil test that measures one's anxiety about being evaluated (used to define M_{af}). Raynor predicted that when $M_s > M_{af}$, the student would be persistent in trying to achieve in his psychology course, particularly if that course was perceived as important to the accomplishment of career goals. However, it seemed reasonable to assume that if $M_{af} > M_s$, the student might not do any better in psychology if the course was perceived as

career-relevant than career-irrelevant, and according to Atkinson's theory, he might even do worse.

Table 8-1 presents the results. As predicted, students for whom $M_s > M_{af}$ (those in the top row) obtained significantly *higher* grades if they considered introductory psychology relevant to their future careers. However, students for whom $M_{af} > M_s$ actually obtained *lower* grades if their psychology course was considered career-relevant. We see, then, that one's performance in achievement contexts depends on far more than one's level of *n* Ach (or achievement motivation). To predict how a person is likely to perform when faced with a challenge, it also helps to know something about the person's fear of failure (M_{af}) as well as his or her *expectancies* of succeeding or failing and the perceived *value* of the goal.

CRANDALL AND CRANDALL'S SOCIAL-LEARNING THEORY OF ACHIEVEMENT

Vaughn and Virginia Crandall's social-learning theory of achievement is an important link between the McClelland/Atkinson motivational approaches that we just reviewed and the more recent attributional models that are currently in vogue. The social-learning approach differs from its predecessors in several important respects. For example, the Crandalls were dismayed that achievement theorists were largely neglecting children and the developmental aspects of achievement behavior, so that they focused on *children's* achievement in their own research. Moreover, we have already noted Vaughn

TABLE 8-1 Mean Grade-Point Averages in Introductory Psychology as a Function of Achievement-Related Motives and the Relevance of the Course to Future Careers

Achievement profiles	Relevance of course to one's future	
	Low	High
$M_s > M_{af}$	2.93	3.37
$M_{af} > M_s$	3.00	2.59

Note: Mean grade-point averages are computed on a 4.00 scale where A = 4, B = 3, C = 2, D = 1, F = 0.

Crandall's view that achievement is a *behavioral*, rather than a motivational, construct and that the reinforcement for achievement behavior is *extrinsic* to the self (that is, the approval of social agents, such as parents and teachers) rather than an intrinsic need to feel proud or to satisfy an acquired achievement motive. Finally, the Crandalls do not think of achievement as a global, or unitary, attribute. Instead, they argue that there are many areas in which children may achieve, including schoolwork, sporting activities, hobbies, domestic skills, and making friends, to name a few. Presumably, a child's willingness to set high standards and work to attain them may differ from area to area depending on (1) his or her *expectancies* of succeeding and winning recognition for these efforts and (2) the perceived *value* of such recognition. So the Crandalls' theory does share one important feature with Atkinson's approach—it too is an expectancy/value theory of achievement.

But despite the inclusion of cognitive constructs such as achievement expectancy and achievement value in their model, the Crandalls' approach is appropriately labeled social-learning theory. Not only do the Crandalls view achievement as a behavioral, rather than a motivational, construct, but they also stress that achievement training begins at home and that the ways parents respond to their child's accomplishments will play a major role in shaping the child's achievement expectancies, achievement values, and achievement behaviors. Later in the chapter we will focus on the roles that parents play in encouraging (and sometimes discouraging) children's propensities for achievement. For now, however, let's see what the Crandalls have to say about the relationship between achievement expectancies and achievement behavior.

Achievement Expectancies and Children's Achievement Behavior

In her review of the literature on children's achievement, Virginia Crandall (1967) noted that children's levels of achievement motivation often failed to forecast their actual accomplishments. This result was not terribly surprising to her, because she believed that a global measure such as *n* Ach is much too broad to capture a child's feelings about striving to achieve in a particular domain such as schoolwork or physical activities.

Crandall discovered that children differ not only in their *general* motivation to achieve but also in their expectations of achieving in *different skill areas*. Do these expectations of doing well (or poorly) have any meaningful effect on children's achievement behavior? Indeed they do! Were we to review the literature, we would find that intelligence (IQ) is an important determinant of academic achievement (Shaffer & Shaffer, 1985). Yet it is not at all uncommon for children with high IQs and low academic expectancies to earn *poorer* grades than their classmates who have lower IQs and high academic expectancies (Battle, 1966; Crandall, 1967). So regardless of whether we are talking about adults, as Atkinson did, or Battle's and Crandall's child subjects, expectations of success and failure are powerful determinants of achievement behavior: people who expect to achieve usually do, whereas those who expect to fail may spend little time and effort pursuing goals that they believe to be out of reach.

Why Do I Succeed (or Fail)? Locus of Control and Children's Achievement Behavior

Drawing on the work of social-learning theorist Julian Rotter (1966), Virginia Crandall and her associates proposed that children's expectations of succeeding or failing will depend very critically on another aspect of their personalities—locus of control. *Locus of control* is a term that Rotter used to describe the extent to which people believe that their behavior determines their outcomes. Some people, called *internalizers*, assume that they are usually responsible for what happens to them. If an internalizer were to receive an A on an essay, she would probably attribute the high mark to her ability to write or to the effort she had expended in preparing the paper (personal, or internal, causes). Other people, known as *externalizers*, believe that their outcomes depend more on luck, fate, or the actions of others than on their own abilities or efforts. Thus, an externalizer is likely to attribute an A grade on an essay to luck ("The teacher just happened to like this one"), indiscriminate grading, or some other external cause.

Crandall believes that an internal locus of control (internality) is conducive to achievement: children must necessarily assume that their efforts will lead to positive outcomes if they are to strive for success and become high achievers. Externalizers are not expected to strive for success or to become high achievers, because they assume that their efforts do not necessarily determine their outcomes.

Children's locus of control is usually measured by administering the *Intellectual Achievement Responsibility Questionnaire*, a 34-item scale that taps one's perceptions of responsibility for pleasant and unpleasant outcomes. Each item describes an achievement-related experience and asks the child to select either an internal or an external cause for that experience (see Figure 8-1 for sample items). The more "internal" responses the child selects, the higher his internality score. Children who choose few internal responses are classified as externalizers.

In their recent review of more than 100 studies, Maureen Findley and Harris Cooper (1983) found that internalizers do earn higher grades and will typically outperform externalizers on standardized tests of academic achievement. In fact, one rather extensive study of minority students in the United States revealed that children's beliefs in internal control were a better predictor of their academic achievements than were their *n* Ach scores, their parents' child-rearing practices, or the type of classroom and teaching styles to which these students had been exposed (Coleman et al., 1966). So Crandall was right in assuming that a willingness to take personal responsibility for one's successes is conducive to achievement behavior.

Although these data appear to support Crandall's theory, it turns out that children's beliefs about the causes of their successes and failures are nowhere near as consistent as Crandall assumed them to be. Some children (typically high achievers) are inclined to attribute their successes to internal factors such as high ability while attributing their failures either to external factors such as task difficulty or to internal causes that they can easily overcome (such as insufficient effort). Other children are equally inconsistent, but in a different way. These youngsters (who tend to be low achievers) often attribute their suc-

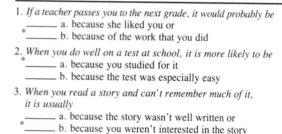

1. *If a teacher passes you to the next grade, it would probably be*
   _____ a. because she liked you or
   * _____ b. because of the work that you did

2. *When you do well on a test at school, it is more likely to be*
   * _____ a. because you studied for it
   _____ b. because the test was especially easy

3. *When you read a story and can't remember much of it, it is usually*
   _____ a. because the story wasn't well written or
   * _____ b. because you weren't interested in the story

*Denotes the "internal" response for each sample item.

FIGURE 8-1   Sample items from the Intellectual Achievement Responsibility Questionnaire

cesses to either hard work or external causes such as the ease of the task, while attributing their failures to internal causes such as lack of ability (Dweck & Elliott, 1983; Weiner et al., 1974). Clearly, these contrasting patterns are difficult to interpret according to Crandall's model, which assumes that (1) the child adopts a relatively *stable* locus of control and (2) an *internal locus* (or internality) is conducive to achievement. Not only does the perceived locus of causality often differ for successes and failures, but children who adopt internal explanations for their failures tend to be low, rather than high, achievers! Although these observations are problematic for Crandall's theory, they begin to make some sense within the framework of attribution (or social information-processing) theory, to which we will now turn.

ATTRIBUTIONAL MODELS OF ACHIEVEMENT

Attributional theories of achievement are based on the premise that human beings are active information processors who will sift through the data available to them, seeking to explain why they succeed or fail in various achievement contexts. Presumably the causal attributions that we make about our outcomes in one particular context, or situation, will influence our *expectancies* about future successes or failures in similar situations. And given the strong link between achievement expectancies and achievement behavior, it seems reasonable to assume that our beliefs

PHOTO 8-2   If youngsters believe that they are personally responsible for their successes, they are more likely to become high achievers.

about the underlying causes of our successes and failures can have a powerful effect on our motivation to persist at various achievement tasks in the future.

Weiner's Attribution Theory

Bernard Weiner (1974; Weiner et al., 1974) has developed an attributional model of achievement that focuses most directly on the cognitive concomitants of achievement outcomes and was clearly influenced by Crandall's and Rotter's previous work on locus of control. According to Weiner, a person who is trying to explain a success or a failure might attribute that outcome to any of four causes: (1) his own *ability* (or lack thereof), (2) the amount of *effort* he expended in performing the task, (3) the *difficulty* of the task, and (4) the influence of *luck* (either good or bad). Notice that two of these four causes, ability and effort, describe qualities or characteristics of the person undertaking the activity (*internal* causes), whereas the other two, task difficulty and luck, are more accurately characterized as *external*, or environmental, factors. So far, the model sounds very similar to Crandall's theorizing about locus of control. However, Weiner goes on to argue that the four causes also differ along a *stability* dimension: ability and task difficulty are reasonably stable factors, whereas

the amount of effort one expends on a task and the influence of luck are highly variable (unstable) from situation to situation. Weiner assumes that the "locus of control" and the "stability" dimensions are independent of each other, so that there are four possible causes for an achievement-related outcome, as summarized in Table 8-2.

The following example illustrates some of the principles of Weiner's theory. Imagine that you have just watched a 9-year-old achieve something that he considers significant indeed—hitting a grand-slam home run in a Little League game. As he tears around the bases, you begin to wonder how he accomplished this feat. Weiner suggests that your search for a cause is a two-step process. First, you would try to determine whether the locus of causality is internal or external. Since you know that this boy has a dismal batting average (low ability) and doesn't practice much (low effort), you conclude that there must be an *external* explanation for his smashing success. Your next step, then, would be to decide whether his success is attributable to a stable or an unstable cause. Since the pitcher was a burly 12-year-old who throws pitches at 80 miles per hour, you are reluctant to attribute the home run to the ease of the task (low task difficulty would be a stable cause). Then you remember that the batter had *closed his eyes* and swung the bat as hard as he could while up at the plate, thus leading you to conclude that his success is unlikely to be repeated soon (unstable cause) because this boy was *lucky*!

Contributions of "stability" and "locus of control" to achievement behavior.   Weiner believes that it is important to distinguish the locus of an achievement-related outcome (internal versus external) from the perceived stability of that outcome because each of these judgments has different con-

TABLE 8-2   Weiner's Classification Scheme for the Perceived Determinants of Achievement Outcomes

	Locus of control	
Stability	Internal cause	External cause
Stable cause	Ability	Task difficulty
Unstable cause	Effort	Luck

sequences. The stability dimension is thought to be important for forming *expectancies*, or predictions, about how someone will perform given similar circumstances in the future. If we should succeed at a task and attribute this outcome to a stable cause such as our high ability or the ease of this task for us, then it seems reasonable to assume that we should succeed at similar activities in the future. But if our success is attributed to an unstable cause that can vary considerably from situation to situation (our hard work or good luck), then we should not be quite so confident of attaining future successes. Conversely, if we should fail at a task and attribute this negative outcome to stable causes that we can do little about (low ability or high task difficulty), we are likely to expect to fail at similar tasks in the future, whereas attribution of failure to unstable causes such as bad luck or not trying very hard allows for the possibility of improvement and a more positive achievement expectancy. Note the distinction here between Weiner's theory and Crandall's: whereas Crandall believed that it was the locus of control for an achievement outcome that determined one's expectancies about future accomplishments, Weiner argues that it is the perceived *stability* of that outcome that contributes most to achievement expectancies. Indeed, the data we have reviewed are quite consistent with Weiner's theory. High achievers expect to succeed because they attribute their successes to high ability (a stable, internal cause). Failures don't affect their achievement expectancies, because they are most often attributed to insufficient effort (an unstable, internal cause). By contrast, low achievers expect to fail because they often attribute failures to their lack of ability (a stable, internal cause). Successes don't affect their achievement expectancies, because they are most often attributed to high effort (an unstable, internal cause). So it is only when the cause for an outcome is perceived to be stable that the outcome is likely to influence one's achievement expectancies.

Now, if the perceived stability of achievement-related outcomes determines achievement expectancies, what role does locus of control play? According to Weiner, judgments about the internality or externality of an achievement-related experience will affect the *value* of that outcome for the perceiver, which, in turn, influences his or her achievement

motivation. Weiner proposes that we are more likely to value, and to reward ourselves for, successes that we attribute to internal causes. Thus, obtaining an A on a class exam should make you feel better and more inclined to work to repeat your success if you attribute the grade to your high ability or to effort (internal factors) rather than to good luck, indiscriminate grading, or the fact that the test was easy (external causes). Furthermore, failures that we attribute to internal causes are more likely to reflect *negatively* on our self-esteem, and perhaps make us less inclined to strive for future successes, than are failures that we attribute to external causes. Clearly, it seems fruitless to work hard to reverse a poor grade if we feel that we have no ability in the subject matter; in fact, this course may suddenly seem less important or valuable, and we might be inclined to drop it. But if we can attribute our poor mark to an *external* cause such as a difficult and ambiguous exam, the failure should not make us feel especially critical of ourselves or undermine our feelings about either the value of the course or the advisability of studying for future exams.

We see, then, that Weiner's attribution model is yet another example of an expectancy/value theory of achievement. Our beliefs about the locus of causality for achievement outcomes affect our valuation of these successes and failures, whereas our attributions about the stability of those causes affect our achievement expectancies. Together these two factors (expectancy and value) determine our willingness to undertake and persist at future achievement-related activities (see Figure 8-2 for a schematic overview of Weiner's model).

Social-cognitive determinants of children's achievement attributions.

Weiner worked with adults when developing his theory, and there is now a large amount of evidence that adults clearly distinguish among ability, effort, task difficulty, and luck when seeking to explain their successes and failures (Weiner, 1982; Weiner et al., 1974). Moreover, adults often draw some rather sophisticated conclusions about these four causal factors, such as assuming that ability and effort are inversely related. For example, if a person succeeds at a challenging task while expending little effort, we assume that she

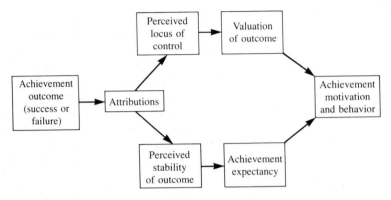

FIGURE 8.2 A schematic representation of Weiner's attribution theory of achievement

has high ability—much higher ability than a second person who achieves the same success but has to work very hard to do so. Are children capable of distinguishing among the four causal components of Weiner's model? Do they make the same kinds of causal attributions about successes and failures that adults do?

Apparently not. Before age 7 or so, children almost invariably believe that they have high abilities and that they will do well on achievement tasks, even after repeated failures (Dweck & Elliott, 1983; Stipek, 1984). Why do these youngsters so often overestimate their future accomplishments? Part of the problem may be wishful thinking—young children might confuse their *desire* to do well with their ability to do well and conclude that they can always succeed if they really want to. Deborah Stipek and her associates (Stipek, Roberts, & Sanborn, 1984) recently found some support for this "wishful thinking" hypothesis. In Stipek's research, some 4-year-olds were offered an attractive incentive (marbles—thought to stimulate wishful thinking about success) for performing a complex task, and their many errors while performing were *not* made obvious to them. Other children were offered no incentive and their errors were made obvious. Finally, children in a control group simply indicated how they thought they would do without any mention being made of incentives or the quality of their previous performance. Stipek et al. found that children in the wishful-thinking group, who had been offered an attractive incentive, felt that their chances of future success

were greater than the control subjects did, even though both these groups had been failing at the task. Thus, when children really want to succeed, they expect to, regardless of their previous failures. However, we should not conclude that young children are always oblivious to their poor performance, for the results also indicated that children who had been offered no incentives and whose failures were made obvious to them had lower achievement expectancies than their counterparts in either the wishful-thinking or the control group.

Another reason that youngsters may often overestimate their likelihood of future success is that they fail to distinguish between ability and effort. In Chapter 7, we learned that children begin to view the self and other people in stable, dispositional terms at some point between 7 and 9 years of age. So if young children do not yet recognize that ability is a stable or relatively enduring attribute, they may confuse ability with effort and assume that they can always succeed if they *try* hard enough.

John Nicholls and Arden Miller (1984) have reviewed the available literature and concluded that children's thinking about ability and effort may pass through as many as four levels, or stages:

Level 1: Effort or outcome is ability. This level characterizes many 5-year-olds. Children focus mainly on effort and occasionally on outcomes when making ability judgments. People who try harder are seen as smarter even if they get a lower score. If the child focuses on outcomes, then people who score higher are said to have worked harder (even if they have not) and thus are perceived as smarter.

Level 2: Effort is the cause of outcomes. Now children think that the amount of effort one expends is the primary determinant of success and failure. Equal effort will lead to equal outcomes. And if two persons achieve the same goal after working different amounts of time, the child will assume that the person who worked longer made mistakes or that the one who spent less time at the task must have tried harder while she was working.

Level 3: Effort and ability are partially differentiated. Effort is still the primary, but no longer the only, cause of achievement outcomes. If two persons experience equal outcomes after unequal efforts, the child may say that one is brighter than the other. However, some confounding of effort and ability is still apparent, because these same two persons would be expected to achieve exactly the same outcomes if they applied equal effort.

Level 4: Ability is capacity. Ability and effort are now clearly differentiated. The child now realizes that if two persons have equal attainments, the one who worked harder has less ability than the person who breezed through the task.

In their recent study of children's thinking about ability and effort, Nicholls and Miller (1984) asked second-, fifth-, and eighth-graders to compare the ability of either themselves or a peer with that of another person who had achieved *exactly the same score* after expending either *more* or *less* effort on a set of experimental tasks. When asked which person was smarter, 7-year-old second-graders reliably chose the person who had expended more effort, whereas the 13-year-old eighth-graders picked the lazier child who had expended little effort. All four levels of reasoning about ability and effort were observed in this study, and as we see in Table 8-3, there was evidence of a clear age progression: second-graders tended to be at levels 1 and 2, whereas many eighth-graders recognized the inverse relation between ability and effort, thereby falling into level 4.

Recently, Nicholls and Miller (1985) have shown that there are four similar levels of reasoning about the concepts of luck and skill. Five-year-olds believe that children who try harder will perform better on both "luck" tasks, where outcomes are determined by chance, and "skill" tasks, where outcomes really do depend on effort. By contrast, most 12- to 13-year-olds know that only luck influences outcomes in games of chance, whereas effort will affect one's likelihood of success on tasks requiring skill.

Notice that many children are treating ability, effort, luck, and task difficulty as separate and distinct by age 12 to 13—about the time that they are approaching formal operations and might be capable of the kinds of rapid mental reversals that should enable them to see how these four causes can vary along *two* abstract dimensions—locus of control and stability—*at the same time.* Do these observations imply that Weiner's theory is not relevant to children younger than 12 or 13? No, they do not. Even though younger children may not always think about Weiner's four causes for achievement-related

TABLE 8-3 Numbers of Children at Each Grade Falling into Each of the Four Levels of Reasoning about Ability and Effort

	Level of reasoning			
Grade	*1* *Effort or outcome* *is ability*	*2* *Effort causes* *outcomes*	*3* *Incomplete* *differentiation*	*4* *Ability is* *capacity*
2nd (7-year-olds)	10	44	6	0
5th (10-year-olds)	4	22	12	22
8th (13-year-olds)	3	5	9	43

outcomes in precisely the same ways that many adults do, we will see in the next section that 8–12-year-olds develop general attributional patterns or styles that (1) are clearly based on information about the locus of control and perceived stability of their achievement outcomes and (2) can have a profound effect on their future achievement behavior.

Dweck's Learned-Helplessness Theory

Recently, Carol Dweck and her associates have taken a closer look at the *patterns* of attributions that children display when explaining their achievement outcomes and the effects of these attributional styles on subsequent achievement behavior. In this research, children are asked to undertake a series of achievement tasks, in which their "successes" and "failures" are often determined by the experimenter. Of interest are the kinds of attributions children offer to account for such outcomes and their willingness to persist at and expend effort on similar achievement tasks in the future.

Dweck and her colleagues (see Dweck, 1978, for a review) find that there are reliable individual differences in the ways children react to failure experiences. Some children appear to be "*mastery oriented*"; they tend to attribute failures to unstable causes, particularly lack of effort, and will often show increased persistence and improved performance on subsequent achievement tasks. By contrast, children who view their failures as stemming from stable, internal causes, such as a lack of ability, often show little effort expenditure and marked deterioration of performance on future achievement tasks. In fact, many who fell into the latter category appeared to give up in the face of failure and were now incapable of solving problems of the kind they had easily mastered only a short time earlier. It appeared to Dweck that these youngsters were demonstrating a form of *learned helplessness*: if failures are attributed to a lack of ability that the child can do little about, then there is little if any reason to work hard trying to solve these or similar problems. Consequently, the child simply stops trying and acts helpless.

It is important to note that children who display this learned-helplessness syndrome are *not* merely the least competent members of a typical classroom.

In fact, Dweck (1978) reports that the previous academic attainments of helpless subjects often equal or exceed those of their mastery-oriented classmates! In a similar vein, Deborah Phillips (1984) has recently studied the achievement orientations of a large number of *high-ability* fifth-graders, about 20% of whom had academic self-concepts that seriously underestimated their abilities. The high-ability students who held inaccurate self-perceptions displayed several aspects of the learned-helplessness syndrome: compared with children who had accurate perceptions of their own abilities, members of this self-denigrating group (1) set less demanding achievement standards for themselves and held lower expectancies for success, (2) were portrayed by their teachers as showing poor persistence in academic activities, and (3) tended to attribute their successes to unstable causes, such as effort, rather than to stable ones, such as high ability. So it appears that almost anyone, even highly competent children who have often succeeded at achievement tasks, could eventually learn to stop trying and act helpless in the face of failure.

How does learned helplessness develop? Dweck and her colleagues (Dweck, Davidson, Nelson, & Enna, 1978) believe that the ways teachers evaluate their students can play a very important role in promoting either a "mastery" or a "helpless" orientation. If a teacher should praise children's intellectual competencies when they succeed but stress the nonintellectual aspects of their work (sloppiness, lack of effort) when criticizing poor performances, students are likely to assume that they are certainly smart enough and would do better if they tried harder. In other words, this pattern of evaluation should encourage them to attribute successes to stable causes (ability) and failures to unstable ones (low effort), thereby promoting the development of a mastery orientation. Now contrast this evaluative style with one in which the teacher praises nonintellectual aspects of good performances, such as neatness or effort expenditure, while focusing more exclusively on students' poor problem-solving strategies when they fail. This pattern of evaluation seems likely to encourage youngsters to attribute successes to unstable causes (high effort) and failures to stable ones (lack of ability)—

precisely the attributional style often observed among children displaying the helplessness syndrome. Dweck et al. have observed fifth-grade teachers as they gave their students evaluative feedback and found that teachers did indeed use different patterns with different students. Some students received the evaluative pattern thought to contribute to a mastery orientation, whereas others received the pattern thought to contribute to learned helplessness. But do these patterns really have such effects on children's achievement orientations?

Dweck et al. (1978) tried to answer this question in an interesting experiment. Fifth-graders worked on a series of 20 word puzzles (anagrams), half of which were easy and half of which were insoluble. The experimenter's evaluation of the child's performance on failure trials was then manipulated. Children assigned to the *mastery pattern* condition heard the experimenter respond to their failures by focusing on nonintellectual aspects of their performance about half the time (for example, "You didn't do very well that time—it wasn't neat enough") and on their incorrect solutions on the other half of the failure trials (for example, "You didn't get the word right"). Children assigned to the *helpless pattern* condition heard the experimenter focus *only* on the incorrectness of their solutions on *all* failure trials (for example, "You didn't get the word right"). After completing the word puzzles and working on another puzzle at which they were told that they were not doing very well, the children were asked to respond anonymously to the following attribution question: "If the man told you that you did not do very well . . . why do you think that was?: (a) I did not try hard enough [effort], (b) the man was too fussy [agent], (c) I am not very good at it [ability]."

The answers children gave to this question were quite consistent with Dweck's hypothesis. Table 8-4 reveals that 75% of the children who had received the helpless pattern of evaluation attributed their failure on the second puzzle to their own lack of ability. By contrast, 75% of the children who had received the mastery pattern of evaluation either attributed their failures to a lack of effort or externalized the blame altogether by saying that the evaluator was too fussy. These strikingly different attributional styles are all

the more remarkable when we note that they took less than an hour to establish in this experiment. So it seems reasonable to conclude that similar patterns of evaluative feedback from teachers, given consistently over a period of months or years, might well contribute to the development of the contrasting "helpless" and "mastery" orientations so often observed among grade school children.

Obviously, giving up in the face of a challenge is not the kind of achievement orientation that teachers would hope to encourage. What can be done to help these "helpless" children become more persistent at achievement tasks, particularly tasks that are difficult to master quickly and require concentrated and prolonged effort? One solution might be to make teachers more aware of how their reactions to their students' performance affect children's achievement orientations. Another might be to develop specific techniques or therapies aimed at teaching children how to break complex tasks into more manageable bites and to recognize that failures can and often should be attributed to causes such as a lack of effort that they can eventually overcome. In Box 8-1 we will take a closer look at some of the strategies that researchers have used to alleviate learned helplessness in grade school children.

A FINAL COMMENT ON THEORIES OF ACHIEVEMENT

Although the five theories that we have reviewed differ in many respects, each has something important to offer. McClelland was the first to demonstrate convincingly that people differ in their *motivation* to achieve, although his notion that achievement motivation was a global attribute that predicted one's reactions to virtually all achievement tasks now

TABLE 8-4 Percentage of Children in Each Condition Attributing Failure Feedback to a Lack of Ability, a Lack of Effort, or an Overly Fussy Evaluator

	Type of attribution		
Evaluative pattern	*Lack of ability*	*Lack of effort*	*Fussy evaluator*
Helpless pattern	75	25	0
Mastery pattern	25	65	10

BOX 8-1 ON HELPING THE HELPLESS TO ACHIEVE

How might we encourage helpless children to persist at tasks at which they have repeatedly failed? One method favored by behavior therapists (for example, Skinner, 1968) is a programmed learning approach in which children are taught that they can succeed by receiving many success experiences on the very problems that they have previously failed. However, advocates of this procedure stress the importance of structuring the therapy so that the child is *unlikely to fail*, for errors are assumed to undermine one's motivation to persist at achievement tasks.

By contrast, Carol Dweck believes that such a success-only therapy is likely to prove ineffective. The reason for her skepticism is that helpless children tend to attribute successes to unstable causes such as high effort or luck that (1) do not necessarily imply that one will perform well in the future and (2) do not allow children to deal constructively with failure. Moreover, it is children's beliefs about the causes of their *failures* that trigger the learned-helplessness syndrome in the first place! Dweck believes that learned helplessness is likely to be overcome only if helpless children begin to attribute their failures to unstable causes—such as insufficient effort—that they can do something about, rather than viewing them as reflecting on their lack of ability, which is not so easily modifiable. Presumably, treatments designed to accomplish this aim would persuade helpless children to try harder after experiencing failures and, thus, enable them to deal more constructively with the less than optimal performances that they (like all children) are likely to experience in the years ahead.

Dweck (1975) tested her hypotheses by identifying a group of 12 helpless children and exposing them to a series of math problems at which they repeatedly failed, so that they began to act helpless. At this point therapy was begun.

Half the children experienced 25 sessions of *success only* therapy: they worked at math problems, invariably succeeding, and were rewarded with tokens for their accomplishments. The remaining children were exposed to 25 sessions of *attribution retraining* that were identical to the success-only sessions, with one major exception: during each training session, the child experienced three prearranged "failures." On these failure trials, the experimenter noted that the child had not worked fast enough and said "That means you should have tried harder." Thus, a rather explicit attempt was made to convince these youngsters that failures can stem from a lack of effort rather than a lack of ability. Following the 25 training sessions, subjects in both therapy groups worked the series of math problems that they had repeatedly failed at the beginning of the experiment. Their performance was recorded, as were their responses to several prearranged failures and the attributions they made to account for these failures.

The results of this experiment were quite clear. After the therapy was completed, helpless children in the attribution-retraining condition now performed much better on the math problems that they had initially failed. They no longer gave up in the face of failure, and they were now much more inclined to attribute their failures to a lack of effort rather than to low ability. By contrast, helpless children assigned to the success-only condition showed no such improvement in performance. They continued to attribute their failures to low ability rather than to a lack of effort, and if anything, they were now even less willing to persist in the face of failure than before the therapeutic intervention. So we see that merely showing helpless children that they are capable of succeeding is not enough! To alleviate learned helplessness, one must teach children to respond more constructively to their *failures* by viewing these

seems badly overstated. Atkinson's revision of need achievement theory pointed to the existence of a competing "motive to avoid failure" that can make people shy away from challenging tasks to avoid the embarrassment of failing. Moreover, Atkinson's model and the Crandalls' subsequent social-learning approach broke important new ground by emphasizing that achievement-related cognitions such as one's *expectancies* of succeeding and the incentive *value* of

success are important determinants of achievement behavior. Weiner's later attribution theory grew out of the Crandalls' approach and focused much more intently on how specific cognitions about the *causes* of achievement outcomes contribute to one's achievement expectancies and the perceived value of success and failure experiences. Finally, Dweck's learned-helplessness model begins to take us back to the starting point by demonstrating that well-

BOX 8-1 *continued*

experiences as something that they can overcome if they try harder.

On a practical note, Licht and Dweck (1984) have proposed that certain academic subjects such as math and science may be particularly difficult for helpless children. The problem with these particular subjects is that they often contain unfamiliar and seemingly confusing terms and concepts at the beginning of new units—precisely the kinds of material that may pique the curiosity of mastery-oriented youngsters while convincing helpless ones that these subjects are much too complex for them to understand. To test this hypothesis, Licht and Dweck presented groups of helpless and mastery-oriented fifth-graders with two versions of new academic material, provided time for the children to master this material, and then tested them to see what they had learned. One version of the material was written in clearly understandable language in which all new concepts were carefully defined; the second version presented the same material in a somewhat confusing (but grammatically correct) style that would require persistent effort from the child to achieve the same level of understanding. The results of this experiment, which appear in the graph, were quite consistent with Licht and Dweck's hypothesis. Notice that a sizable majority of both the helpless and the mastery-oriented children did well on the exam if they had read the clear version of the new material. By contrast, only about one third of the helpless children (compared with 72% of their mastery-oriented classmates) mastered the material presented in the complex version. It appeared that many helpless youngsters simply gave up and stopped trying to learn if they had faced early difficulties in understanding the subject matter.

Perhaps teachers could assist their more "helpless" pupils to assimilate difficult new concepts by restructuring

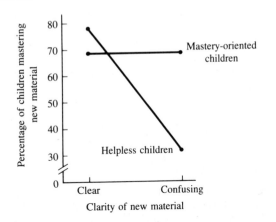

Percentages of children who mastered new academic material as a function of the clarity of that material and the children's achievement orientations

lesson plans to show how new material builds on information that students already know. For example, one might introduce the concept of multiplication by going slow and showing the child how this operation is really an extension of addition, rather than simply presenting the multiplication tables and requiring children to memorize them. The beauty of this "cumulative" approach is that it links new concepts to familiar ones and, thus, should be less likely to make the helpless child dwell on perceived inadequacies or the prospect of failing. And if Licht and Dweck's findings are any guide, it would seem that this cumulative, incremental approach to instruction will benefit the more helpless members of a class without undermining the performance of their mastery-oriented classmates.

ingrained attributional styles or patterns affect children's *motivation* (or lack thereof) to persist at challenging tasks that they have initially failed to master. So as we concluded when reviewing the various theories of attachment, it makes no sense to brand any single achievement theory as "correct" and to ignore the others. Each of these theories has helped us to understand why children often differ so dramatically in response to the challenges they face.

SOCIAL AND SITUATIONAL INFLUENCES ON CHILDREN'S ACHIEVEMENT

Now that we have reviewed the major achievement theories, it is time to ask some very practical questions about the development of children's propensities for achievement. For example, is a child's achievement orientation at all influenced by the culture or subculture in which he is raised? Anthropologists and sociologists think so, as we will see in the following section. Developmentalists have been concerned with another important issue: Are some home environments or patterns of child rearing more conducive to achievement than others? Social and educational psychologists have focused on particular social and situational determinants of achievement. How, for example, do peers and other social models influence children's achievement behavior? Might a teacher's impressions of a child's abilities have any meaningful effect on the child's future accomplishments? When should adults try to encourage achievement by rewarding it, and under what circumstances might such a strategy backfire? And how can we explain the finding that girls and young women reliably underestimate their propensities for achievement, whereas boys and young men tend to overestimate theirs? These are some of the issues we will consider as we review the many social and situational contributors to children's achievement orientations.

CULTURAL AND SUBCULTURAL INFLUENCES ON ACHIEVEMENT

There is now evidence that a child's cultural heritage does affect his or her achievement orientation. In one study, Barry, Child, and Bacon (1959) hypothesized that societies dependent on an agricultural or pastoral economy (those that accumulate food) would stress obedience, responsibility, and cooperation when raising their children. Groups that do not accumulate food (hunting and fishing societies) were expected to train their children to be independent, assertive, and venturesome. In other words, both types of society were expected to stress the kinds of values that are necessary to maintain their way of life. Barry et al. used existing anthropological data to review the economic characteristics and child-rearing techniques of 104 mostly underdeveloped, preliterate societies from all over the world. As predicted, they found that agricultural and pastoral societies placed strong pressures on their children to be responsible, cooperative, and obedient, whereas hunting and fishing societies stressed assertiveness, self-reliance, and the pursuit of individual goals.

Berry (1967) extended these findings by comparing members of high- and low-food-accumulative cultures on a measure of independence and conformity. Arctic Eskimos, a people who are forced by their geography to hunt and fish for a living, served as the low-food-accumulative group. The Temne of Sierra Leone, a group whose livelihood depends on the successful planting, harvesting, and rationing of a single crop (rice), were selected as the high-food-accumulative group. Individuals from these two societies were asked to make comparisons among lines that differed in length. For each comparison, the subject was shown a standard line and eight test lines. The subject's task was to select the test line that was the same length as the standard. Before each judgment, the experimenter presented fictitious group norms by telling the subject "Most Temne (Eskimo) people say this line [an incorrect choice] is equal in length to the standard." The incorrect line that was five lines away from the correct one served as the contrived group norm for each trial (see Figure 8-3). The distance of the subject's choice away from the correct line and in the direction of the contrived norm served as a measure of conformity for that trial. A total conformity score was determined by simply adding across trials the number of lines a subject's choices were away from the correct lines.

As expected, Berry found that the Temne largely conformed to the contrived group norms, whereas the Eskimos disregarded normative information and displayed their independence by selecting the correct lines (or lines very close to the correct ones). One Temne illustrated the cultural roots of his conformity by stating "When Temne people choose a thing, we must all agree with the decision—that is what we call cooperation" (Berry, 1967, p. 417). Eskimo subjects spoke infrequently while making their judgments, although they sometimes flashed confident smiles as they rejected the group norm in favor of a line much nearer to the correct one.

We see, then, that people from different societies think of achievement in very different ways. To a person from a food-accumulative society, achievement implies that one must suppress individualism and work for the greater good of the group. By contrast, people from other societies are much more likely to stress individual accomplishments and evi-

The top line on the stimulus card is the standard. On each trial, the subject is informed that one of the other lines (designated here by the asterisk) was most often perceived to be the same length as the standard by members of a reference group. The correct choice for this card is the second line from the bottom.

FIGURE 8-3 A common method of measuring conformity to group norms

dence of personal merit as indications that one has achieved.

Of course, the members of any given culture will vary considerably in their levels of achievement motivation, their expectations of achieving should they try, and their actual achievement behavior. Large multiethnic countries such as the United States or the Soviet Union are particularly interesting in this regard, for such a society is more accurately characterized as a collection of subcultures that show certain similarities but differ in many respects. One of the ways that subcultures differ is in their attitudes toward achievement.

Ethnic Variations in Achievement

Many years ago, Bernard Rosen (1959) compared the achievement orientations of mothers and sons from six ethnic groups living in the northeastern United States: Blacks, French Canadians, Italians, Jews, Greeks, and White Protestants. Mothers were interviewed to assess their attitudes about achievement, their emphasis on independence training, and the educational and vocational aspirations that they held for their sons. The sons' achievement motivation (n Ach) was also measured. Rosen found significant differences among the six ethnic groups on these measures—differences that persisted when variations in social class among the six groups were controlled. Generally speaking, Jewish, White Protestant, and Greek mothers held higher achievement aspirations for their sons than Italian, French Canadian, and Black mothers. The sons' n Ach scores were highly correlated with these aspirations. Look-

ing at child-rearing practices, Rosen discovered that Jewish and White Protestant mothers expected earlier evidence of self-reliance from their children than mothers in the other four ethnic groups. Moreover, Jewish, White Protestant, and Greek mothers were more likely than Italian, French Canadian, and Black mothers to encourage their sons to accomplish individual rather than group goals. So Rosen's study suggests that ethnic variations in achievement motivation do exist and are at least partly attributable to differences in (1) parental attitudes about achievement and (2) the kinds of achievement training that parents provide for their children (see also Hess, 1970, and Laosa, 1981, for similar findings).

Social-Class Differences in Achievement

Members of a culture also differ in their social-class standing, or socioeconomic status—that is, their positions within a society that is stratified according to status and power. In Western societies, the most common measures of a family's social class—family income, prestige of parents' occupations, and parents' educational levels—are based on the family's current or prior accomplishments. So in these cultures, social class is clearly an achievement-related construct, and it is perhaps not surprising to find that children from middle- and upper-class backgrounds score higher in n Ach and are more likely to do well in school than children from the lower socioeconomic strata. (See Hess, 1970, for an extensive review of the literature.)

One possible contributor to social-class differences in achievement is general intelligence: middle- and upper-class children tend to score higher on intelligence tests than lower- and working-class children (Minton & Schneider, 1980). Although the correlations between children's socioeconomic standing and their performance on intelligence tests are not very high (averaging about .25 to .30 across studies), there are those who believe that children from the upper socioeconomic strata have an "intellectual advantage" that partly accounts for their greater achievements.

But a word of caution is in order. Intelligence (or IQ) tests are merely assessments of intellectual *performance* and may seriously underestimate the test taker's intellectual *competencies*. And unfortunately, it appears that many standardized intelligence tests are heavily loaded with test items that are likely to be more familiar to children from the middle and upper socioeconomic strata (Anastasi, 1976). Clearly, such a class-linked bias in the content of the test itself would imply that IQ tests may often underestimate the intellectual abilities of children from lower- and working-class backgrounds. So we simply cannot be certain that social-class differences in intellectual *abilities* explain class-linked variations in achievement, because our best estimates of intelligence (IQ scores) are influenced by other class-linked characteristics that are unrelated to ability.

The fact that intelligence is *not* the sole contributor to class differences in achievement-related activities is illustrated by Sewell, Haller, and Straus's (1957) survey of 4167 high school seniors. This sample was large enough to allow Sewell et al. to control for the effects of intelligence while looking for class-linked variations in occupational aspirations. Even though they controlled for intellectual differences, Sewell et al. found that middle- and upper-class students expected to enter higher-status occupations than students from the lower socioeconomic strata did. This is an interesting outcome in view of the fact that there are no reliable class differences in occupational interests or values during the elementary school years (Hess, 1970). It appears that, somewhere along the line, the "American dream" of being able to rise above one's origins is subverted as children are encouraged to pursue occupations congruent with their socioeconomic status. Why do you suppose this happens?

One reason that youngsters from the lower socioeconomic strata may forgo lofty aspirations is directly related to their economic status. Many lower- and working-class students simply haven't the monetary resources to further their education or to attend the "better" schools. As a result, they are at a disadvantage when trying to compete for the prestigious jobs that society looks upon as indicators of personal achievement.

Let's consider a second possibility. Several studies (reviewed in Crandall, 1963, and Hess, 1970) suggest that parents and teachers expect middle- and upper-class children to get good grades in elementary school, to attend college, and ultimately to enter professional or other high-status vocations. By contrast, lower- and working-class parents are less likely to emphasize the importance of grades, attending college, or striving toward a high-status career. These parents encourage their children to choose a steady job, regardless of its prestige value. So it appears that middle- and upper-class children are expected to "get ahead," while lower- and working-class children are expected to "get by." As Crandall has aptly noted, "Such class-linked attitudes, values, and expectations are bound to influence children's achievement motivations, [aspirations], and performances" (p. 425).

Although they would not quibble with the findings we have reviewed, there are some theorists who believe that socioeconomic status is not even the most important contributor to class-linked variations in achievement. One such theorist is Jonathan Turner, whose interesting ideas are presented in Box 8-2.

HOME AND FAMILY INFLUENCES ON ACHIEVEMENT

As early as 6 months of age, infants already differ in their willingness to explore the environment and their attempts to control objects, situations, and the actions of other people (Yarrow et al., 1983). Moreover, these early differences in mastery behavior are better predictors of children's intellectual performance at age 2½ than are the children's own first-year scores on infant intelligence tests (Messer et al., 1986). Although the amount of mastery behavior that young infants display is related to their level of maturity (as indexed by standardized tests of infant development), social experiences will soon begin to affect the child's curiosity and problem-solving behavior. For example, infants who are securely attached to their mothers at age 12–18 months are more likely than those who are insecurely attached (1) to venture away from the mother to successfully negotiate and explore a strange environment (Cassidy, 1986; Matas, Arend, & Sroufe, 1978) and (2) to display a strong sense of curiosity, self-reliance, and an eagerness to solve problems some four years later in kindergarten (Arend, Gove, & Sroufe, 1979). It is

BOX 8-2 *AN ALTERNATIVE INTERPRETATION OF SOCIAL-CLASS DIFFERENCES IN ACHIEVEMENT*

Jonathan Turner (1970) has suggested that a child's socioeconomic status may be less important as a determinant of his or her achievement orientation than the role played by the head of the household in attaining that status. Turner reasoned that fathers in entrepreneurial occupations—those who run their own businesses or have supervisory responsibility—are more likely than fathers in nonentrepreneurial occupations to stress independence and achievement when raising their sons. If his reasoning is correct, one could hypothesize that, regardless of their socioeconomic status, boys from entrepreneurial households would exhibit a higher level of achievement motivation than boys whose fathers worked at nonentrepreneurial occupations.

Turner tested his hypothesis by first administering the McClelland test of achievement motivation to 639 seventh- and eighth-grade boys. Each boy also provided information about his father's work, and Turner classified these occupations as *entrepreneurial* or *nonentrepreneurial* and as *white collar* (nonmanual office or organizational work that is usually considered a middle-class occupation) or *blue collar* (manual labor such as farming or carpentry that is usually considered a working-class occupation). The results of Turner's study were consistent with his hypotheses. As we can see in the table, sons of both white-collar and blue-collar entrepreneurs displayed a higher level of

achievement motivation than sons of nonentrepreneurs. Clearly, the role assumed by fathers in their work (entrepreneurial versus nonentrepreneurial) was a better predictor of their sons' achievement motivation than the socioeconomic status of the fathers' occupations. Turner also found that 50% of the white-collar workers in his sample qualified as entrepreneurs, compared with only 16% of the blue-collar workers. This finding suggests that class differences in achievement may occur because a higher percentage of middle-class children are raised in entrepreneurial households, where independence and achievement are likely to be stressed.

Turner's study would seem to indicate that children from *any* social class can be high in achievement motivation if the family environment encourages achievement-related activities. Unfortunately, Turner collected no data on the child-rearing practices of the parents in his sample, and so we cannot be sure that parents in entrepreneurial households really do stress independence and achievement more than parents in nonentrepreneurial households. And even if entrepreneurs were found to be more encouraging of achievement, we would still want to know which of their child-rearing practices are most effective in this regard. There is now a rather extensive literature on parental contributions to children's achievement. These findings are discussed in the pages that follow.

Average Achievement Motivation Scores of Sons as a Function of the Socioeconomic and Entrepreneurial Status of Their Fathers

Social status of father	Entrepreneurial status of father	
	Entrepreneurs	Nonentrepreneurs
White collar (middle class)	9.7 ($N = 136$)	4.7 ($N = 138$)
Blue collar (working class)	8.8 ($N = 57$)	3.6 ($N = 308$)

not that securely attached children are any more intellectually competent; instead, they seem to be more *willing* than insecurely attached children to *apply* their competencies to the new challenges they encounter (Belsky, Garduque, Hrncir, 1984). So it would seem that a secure emotional bond with a close companion may be an important contributor to achievement *motivation*.

The Home Environment as a Contributor to Achievement

A young child's tendency to explore, to acquire new skills, and to solve problems will also depend on the character of the home environment and the challenges it provides. Bettye Caldwell and Robert Bradley have developed an instrument called the *HOME*

Inventory (Home Observation for Measurement of the Environment) that allows a researcher to visit an infant or a preschool child at home and gain a good idea of just how challenging that home environment is (Caldwell & Bradley, 1978). The HOME inventory consists of 45 statements, each of which is scored *yes* (the statement is true of this home) or *no* (the statement is not true of this home). In order to gather the information to complete the inventory, the researcher will (1) ask the child's mother to describe her daily routine and child-rearing practices, (2) carefully observe the mother as she interacts with her child, and (3) note the kinds of play materials that the parent makes available to the child. The 45 bits of information collected are then grouped into the six categories, or subscales, in Table 8-5. The home then receives a score on each subscale. The higher the scores across all six subscales, the more challenging the home environment.

Does the quality of the home environment predict children's achievement behavior? To find out, William van Doorninck and his associates (van Doorninck, Caldwell, Wright, & Frankenberg, 1981) visited the homes of 50 12-month-old infants from lower-class backgrounds and used the HOME inventory to classify these settings as stimulating (high HOME scores) or unstimulating (low HOME scores). Five to nine years later, the research team followed up on these children by looking at their standardized achievement test scores and the grades they had earned at school. As we see in Table 8-6, the quality of the home environment at 12 months of age predicted children's academic achievement several years later. Two out of three children from stimulating homes were now performing quite well at school, whereas 70% of those from unstimulating homes were doing very poorly. Although the seeds of mastery motivation may well be innate, it seems that the joy of discovery and problem solving is unlikely to blossom in a barren home environment where the child has few problems to solve and limited opportunities for learning.

Which aspects of the home environment contribute most to children's propensities for achievement?

TABLE 8-5 Subscales and Sample Items from the HOME Inventory

Subscale 1: Emotional and verbal responsivity of the mother (11 items)
  Sample items: Mother responds to child's vocalizations with a verbal response
                Mother's speech is clear, distinct, and audible
                Mother caresses or kisses child at least once during visit

Subscale 2: Avoidance of restriction and punishment (8 items)
  Sample items: Mother neither slaps nor spanks child during visit
                Mother does not scold or derogate child during visit
                Mother does not interfere with the child's actions or restrict child's movements more than three
                times during visit

Subscale 3: Organization of physical and temporal environment (6 items)
  Sample items: Child gets out of house at least four times a week
                Child's play environment appears safe and free of hazards

Subscale 4: Provision of appropriate play materials (9 items)
  Sample items: Child has push or pull toy
                Parents provide learning equipment appropriate to age—mobile, table and chairs, highchair,
                playpen, and so on
                Mother provides toys or interesting activities for child during interview

Subscale 5: Maternal involvement with child (6 items)
  Sample items: Mother "talks" to child while doing her work
                Mother structures the child's play periods

Subscale 6: Opportunities for variety in daily stimulation (5 items)
  Sample items: Father provides some caretaking every day
                Mother reads stories at least three times weekly
                Child has three or more books of his own

Bradley and Caldwell (1984b) find that the HOME subscales measuring the "variety of stimulation" the child receives and the "appropriateness of play materials" are stronger predictors of children's later first-grade achievement scores than the subscale measuring maternal responsivity. Moreover, later research shows that the maternal responsivity scale and the "variety of stimulation"/"play materials" scales are truly independent dimensions—that is, separable aspects of one's home environment (Stevens & Bakeman, 1985). So what these findings seem to imply is that the amount and variety of age-appropriate stimulation that the child receives at home has an effect on achievement above and beyond that predicted by factors related to maternal responsivity, such as the quality of the child's attachments. Stated another way, the security of one's attachments and the challenges provided by the home environment are both important contributors to children's achievement orientations.

The demands that parents make of their child and the ways they respond to his or her accomplishments can also influence the child's will to achieve. In our next section we will take a closer look at some of the child-rearing practices that seem to encourage (or discourage) the development of achievement motivation.

Child-Rearing Practices and Children's Achievement Orientations

What kinds of child-rearing practices encourage achievement motivation? In their book *The Achievement Motive*, McClelland et al. (1953) propose that parents of high need-achievers (1) stress independence training and (2) expect their children to be self-reliant at an earlier age than parents of low need-achievers do.

Marian Winterbottom (1958) tested these predictions by measuring the achievement motivation of 29 boys aged 8 to 10 and then comparing their scores against the child-rearing strategies their mothers had used. The results supported McClelland's hypotheses: mothers of high need-achievers expected their sons to be independent at an earlier age than mothers of low need-achievers. In addition, mothers of high need-achievers were more likely than mothers of low need-achievers to reinforce self-reliance with a hug and a kiss. Winterbottom concluded that *early* independence training given with lots of warmth and affection is an important contributor to children's achievement motivation.

Bernard Rosen and Roy D'Andrade (1959) suggest that direct *achievement training* (encouraging children to do things well) is at least as important to the development of achievement motivation as independence training (encouraging children to do things on their own). To evaluate their hypothesis, Rosen and D'Andrade visited the homes of boys who had tested either high or low in achievement motivation and asked these 9- to 11-year-olds to work at difficult and potentially frustrating tasks—for example, building a tower out of irregularly shaped blocks while blindfolded and using only one hand. To assess the kind of independence and achievement training the boys received at home, the investigators asked parents to watch their son work and to give any encouragement or suggestions that they cared to. The results were clear. Both mothers and fathers of high need-achievers set lofty standards for their boys to accomplish and were noticeably concerned about the quality of their sons' performance. They gave many helpful hints and were quick to praise their sons for meeting one of their performance standards. By contrast, parents of low need-achievers (particularly

TABLE 8-6   Quality of Home Environment at 12 Months of Age and Children's Academic Achievement Five to Nine Years Later

Quality of home environment at age 12 months	Academic achievement	
	Average or high (top 70% of students)	*Low (bottom 30% of students)*
Stimulating	20 children	10 children
Unstimulating	6 children	14 children

fathers) stressed neither independence nor achievement training. They often told their sons how to perform the tasks and became rather irritated whenever the boys experienced any difficulty. Finally, the high need-achievers tended to outperform the low need-achievers, and they seemed to enjoy the tasks more as well. So it appears that independence, achievement motivation, and achievement behavior are more likely to develop when parents encourage children to do things on their own *and to do them well.*

However, a caution is in order. *Early* independence and achievement training can backfire and cause a child to shy away from challenging tasks if parents accentuate the negative by *punishing failures* and *responding neutrally to successes* (for example, taking the child's achievements for granted). Indeed, children whose parents react to their accomplishments in these ways often develop a strong motive to avoid failure [M_{af}] (Teeven & McGhee, 1972). The children who show the highest levels of achievement motivation are those who are encouraged to "do their best" by parents who *reward successes* and *are not overly critical of an occasional failure.*

Parental reactions to a child's successes and failures may also influence the child's locus of control. Children who score high in *internality* tend to have parents who frequently *reward successes* and *respond neutrally to failures* (Katkovsky, Crandall, & Good, 1967). Indeed, this is precisely the pattern of parental response that should facilitate a mastery orientation to achievement by (1) encouraging children to take personal credit for successes while (2) motivating them to *try harder* to overcome their deficiencies (because success will ultimately be rewarded). By contrast, youngsters who deny personal responsibility for their outcomes and score high in *externality* tend to have parents who are *neutral toward successes* and who *punish failures.* Attributing failures to external causes may seem adaptive to these children, for such a strategy serves as a defense against the threat of punishment (Katkovsky et al., 1967). And perhaps you can see how this early "external" orientation could evolve into a sense of learned helplessness if teachers often cite poor problem-solving skills as a cause for substandard performance, thus eventually convincing the child that his or her failures really reflect a lack of ability.

Parental Control and Achievement: The Baumrind Study

Diana Baumrind (1971) has taken a slightly different approach by considering how global patterns of parental control might affect children's achievement orientations. Baumrind's subjects were 134 preschool children and their parents. Each child was observed on several occasions in nursery school and at home, and the resulting data were used to rate the child on dimensions of instrumental competence, such as self-reliance and achievement motivation. Parents were also interviewed to determine their child-rearing practices and observed while interacting with their children at home. When Baumrind analyzed the parental data, she found that individual parents generally used one of three patterns of parental control, which she describes as follows:

The *authoritarian* parent attempts: to shape, control, and evaluate the behavior of the child in accordance with a set standard of conduct, usually an absolute standard, theologically motivated and formulated by a higher authority. She values obedience as a virtue and favors punitive, forceful measures to curb self-will at points where the child's actions or beliefs conflict with what she thinks is right conduct. . . . She does not encourage verbal give and take, believing that the child should accept her word for what is right. . . .

The *authoritative* parent, by contrast with the authoritarian parent, attempts: to direct the child's activities but in a rational . . . manner. She encourages verbal give and take, and shares with the child the reasoning behind her policy. She values . . . *both autonomous self-will and disciplined conformity.* Therefore, she exerts firm control at points of parent-child divergence, but does not hem the child in with restrictions. She [balances] her own special rights as an adult [against] the child's individual interests. . . . The authoritative parent . . . sets standards for future conduct [and] uses reason as well as power to achieve her objectives. She . . . does not regard herself as infallible or divinely inspired. . . .

The *permissive* parent attempts: to behave in a nonpunitive, acceptant, and affirmative manner toward the child's impulses, desires, and actions. She consults with him about policy decisions and gives

explanations for family rules. She makes few demands . . . [and] presents herself as a resource for him
to use as he wishes, not as an active agent responsible
for shaping or altering his . . . behavior. She allows
the child to regulate his own activities, . . . avoids the
exercise of control, and does not encourage him to
obey externally-defined standards. She uses reason
but not overt power to accomplish her ends [1971,
pp. 22–23].

Baumrind found that authoritative parents are
more likely than either authoritarian or permissive
parents to have children who are highly independent
and achievement-oriented. Both authoritative and
authoritarian parents set standards for their children
and are quite controlling. But the authoritarian parent
dominates the child, allowing little if any freedom of
expression, whereas the authoritative parent is careful to permit the child enough autonomy so that he or
she can develop a sense of self-reliance and a feeling
of pride in personal accomplishments. Baumrind's
results indicate that maintaining a firm sense of control over a child can be a very beneficial child-rearing
practice. It is only when the controlling parent severely restricts the child's autonomy and uses arbitrary
or irrational methods of control that the child is likely
to rebel or fall far short of satisfying parental demands and expectations.

Permissive parents do not demand much of their
children, do not discourage immature responses, and
do not actively encourage self-reliant behavior. Children of permissive parents (especially boys) tend to
be selfish, aggressive, rather aimless, and quite low
in independence and achievement. Perhaps we are
not too far off if we describe their behavioral profile
as the "spoiled brat" syndrome.

Ninety-eight of Baumrind's subjects (and their
parents) were observed once again when the children
were 8 to 9 years old (Baumrind, 1977). Children of
authoritative parents were still relatively high in
achievement motivation and seemed to enjoy intellectual challenges, whereas children of permissive
parents were relatively unskilled (and uninterested)
in achievement-related activities. So not only do
early patterns of parental control influence children's
achievement orientations, but their effects seem to
persist over time.

PHOTO 8-3 Parents who encourage achievement are likely to
raise children who are motivated to achieve.

Modeling Influences on Children's Achievement Behavior

We have seen that all but the most permissive of
parents set standards of achievement for their children and expect them to live up to these standards.
But a child might also acquire achievement standards
by observing the behavior of social models and
adopting the criteria that these people use to evaluate
their own accomplishments. In fact, several studies
indicate that children are quick to adopt a model's
achievement standards in situations where they have
no preexisting standards of their own (Bandura,
1977; Liebert & Ora, 1968).

It so happens that children are exposed to many
models and may often observe discrepant or contradictory standards of achievement. Consider a case
where parents impose a very stringent standard on
their child while adopting a very lenient standard for
themselves. Such a discrepancy makes one wonder
how a child would then behave when not under the
watchful eyes of parents. Will the child do as they say
or, rather, do as they do? An experiment by McMains
and Liebert (1968) suggests an answer.

McMains and Liebert had fourth-graders play a
bowling game with an adult model. Although the
game appeared to be a game of skill, it was actually

"rigged" to produce a fixed pattern of scores. In the training phase of the experiment, the model always imposed a stringent achievement standard on the child: the child had to obtain a score of 20 before receiving a reward. Half the children were assigned to a *consistent-training condition* in which the model used the same stringent standard to evaluate his own performance. The remaining children were assigned to a *discrepant-training condition* in which the model used a more lenient achievement standard (a score of 15) than the one he had imposed on the child. At the end of the training phase, each child was left alone to play the bowling game and to reinforce his or her own performance. Children who reinforced themselves only when they attained a score of 20 were said to have adopted the stringent standard that the model had imposed during the training phase.

The children's average self-leniency scores—that is, the average number of times they rewarded themselves for scores lower than the stringent standard—appear in Table 8-7. Note that children were very likely to do *exactly what the model had done*. When the model used a stringent standard that was *consistent* with the one he had imposed on the child, that standard was adopted by the child: children in the consistent-training condition did not often reward their substandard performances. But when the model was lenient in evaluating his own behavior, the children often abandoned the stringent standard that they

had been taught and adopted the lenient standard that the model had actually used. Thus, the achievement standards a child adopts are strongly influenced by the *behavior* of others. Parents who set stringent standards for their children are well advised to reinforce these performance criteria by imposing the same (or even stricter) standards on themselves.

When do children start to evaluate their accomplishments by comparing them with the performance of others? Apparently this kind of social comparison begins rather early. Harriet Mosatche and Penelope Bragonier (1981) observed 3- to 4-year-olds at play and noted that the vast majority of them compared themselves with a peer at least once during the 15-minute period that each child was observed (for example, "My spaceship is higher than yours"; "I can run faster than you"). And by the time children reach the first grade, they are very interested in using social comparison to evaluate their performance if the other person is in some way *similar* to themselves (France-Kaatrude & Smith, 1985). Yet it is important to note that 6- to 7-year-olds use comparative information only to evaluate the *merits* (or lack thereof) of their performance, not to infer their own or others' *abilities* (Aboud, 1985; Ruble, Boggiano, Feldman, & Loebl, 1980). Use of comparative performances to infer ability (a stable disposition) does not appear until age 8 or 9, precisely the time that children begin to pay particularly close attention to underlying regularities in behavior and to think of these patterns as reflecting stable traits (Barenboim, 1981; Rholes & Ruble, 1984). So it seems that the process of social comparison allows younger children to decide whether their achievement *outcomes* are good or bad, while helping older children to infer whether their *ability*, or capacity for achievement, is high, average, or low.

Birth Order, Family Size, and Children's Achievement Behavior

There are now several studies to suggest that first-born children show a greater propensity for achievement than later-borns. First-borns are overrepresented among populations of eminent people and college students (Bradley, 1968; Schachter, 1963), and they score higher than later-borns on tests of

TABLE 8-7 Average Self-Leniency Scores as a Function of the Consistency of the Model's and the Child's Achievement Criteria during the Training Phase of the Experiment

Conditions	Average self-leniency score (5.00 = maximum score possible)	
	Boys	Girls
Consistent training (model used stringent standard)	1.83	.25
Discrepant training (model used lenient standard)	4.91	4.04

Note: The model always imposed a stringent standard on the child.

English and mathematics achievement (Eysenck & Cookson, 1969; Paulhus & Shaffer, 1981), verbal achievement (Breland, 1974), and verbal reasoning (Kellaghan & MacNamara, 1972). In addition, first-borns are somewhat higher in *n* Ach and hold higher educational aspirations than later-borns (Glass, Neulinger, & Brim, 1974; Sampson & Hancock, 1967).

Carmi Schooler (1972) proposed that the greater attainments of first-borns stem not from their ordinal position within the family but from social-class differences in family size: since lower- and working-class parents tend to have larger families than middle- and upper-class parents, a greater percentage of the later-borns in these studies may come from the lower socioeconomic strata, where achievement is less likely to be stressed. Although Schooler's argument is a plausible explanation for many of the older (pre-1970) studies, *recent work continues to demonstrate birth-order differences in achievement even when the effects of family size and social class are controlled.* One interesting aspect of this recent research is the finding that family size also has an effect: the more children in the family, the lower the child's attainments (see Breland, 1974; Kellaghan & MacNamara, 1972).

There are two explanations of birth-order (and family-size) variations in achievement that seem plausible to me. The first explanation, which I will call the *"parental socialization"* hypothesis, contends that first-borns (and children from small families) receive more direct achievement training from their parents than later-borns (and children from large families). The parents of later-borns (and those who have a large number of children) simply haven't as much time to spend with each successive child. The second explanation, which I will call the *"mental mediation"* hypothesis, suggests that birth order and family size are variables that affect the child's intellectual development, which will influence his or her capacity to achieve.

The parental socialization hypothesis. One finding consistent with the parental socialization hypothesis is that parents hold higher achievement expectancies for first-borns than for later-borns (Bas-

kett, 1985). But do these expectancies influence the achievement training that parents provide for their children? Apparently so. Mary Rothbart (1971) tested the parental socialization hypothesis by asking 56 mothers to supervise the performance of their 5-year-olds on a series of achievement tasks. Half the children were first-borns and half later-borns. To control for family size, Rothbart selected her participants from two-child families in which both children were the same sex. Experimental sessions were tape-recorded to determine whether mothers were behaving differently toward first-borns and later-borns while supervising their performance.

Rothbart discovered that mothers spent an equal amount of time interacting with first-born and later-born children. However, the quality of the interaction differed: mothers gave more complex technical explanations to the first-borns. In addition, mothers put more pressure on first-borns to achieve and were more anxious about the quality of their performance. When Rothbart then looked at the children's performance, she found that first-borns attained higher scores than later-borns on all but one of the experimental tasks. Clearly, these findings are consistent with the notion that first-borns receive more direct achievement training from their parents than later-borns (see also Hilton, 1967; Lewis & Kreitzberg, 1979).

The mental mediation (or confluence) hypothesis. The mental mediation hypothesis was proposed by Zajonc (1975; Zajonc, Markus, & Markus, 1979) to explain the remarkable findings of Belmont and Marolla (1973). Belmont and Marolla had analyzed the military records of almost 400,000 males, representing nearly the entire population of young men who had been born in Holland between 1944 and 1947. Data available for each man included an IQ score and other biographical information that was used to determine his social class, birth order, and family size. Controlling for both social class and birth order, Belmont and Marolla found that family size had a significant effect on IQ. As we see in Figure 8-4, *the brightest children tended to come from the smaller families.* When the researchers then looked at the effects of birth order within any given

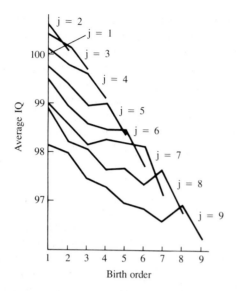

FIGURE 8-4   Average scores on a nonverbal measure of intelligence as a function of the examinee's birth order and the size of his family. Note that subjects from smaller families score higher on this test than subjects from large families. We also see that, within a given family size, children born early tend to obtain higher IQs than those born late.

family size, there was a clear birth-order effect: *first-borns outperformed second-borns, who outperformed third-borns*, and so on down the line. These findings are not unique to Dutch males, having now been replicated in samples of males and females from several countries (Zajonc et al., 1979).

Zajonc offers a very simple explanation for these birth-order and family-size effects that rests on one important assumption: a child's intellectual development depends on *the average intellectual level of all family members*—that is, the intellectual climate of the household. Clearly, first-borns should have an advantage because they are initially exposed *only* to adults, whose intellectual levels are relatively high. By contrast, a second child experiences a less stimulating intellectual environment because she is exposed to a cognitively immature older sibling as well as to her parents. A third child is further disadvantaged by the presence of *two* relatively immature older siblings. Zajonc (1975) concludes:

> With each additional child, the family's intellectual environment depreciates. . . . Children who grow

up surrounded by people with higher intellectual levels [first-borns and children from small families] have a better chance to achieve their maximum intellectual powers than children . . . from large families who spend more time in a world of child-sized minds, . . . develop more slowly and therefore attain lower IQs [p. 39].

According to this "confluence" model, older children have another advantage in that they can further their intellectual competencies (as well as their achievements) by teaching younger siblings. Moreover, longer intervals between births should be advantageous to both older and younger siblings. When children are widely spaced, the older child has more time alone with parents, and the younger child is exposed to a much older child companion who is now reasonably mature.

Although Zajonc's confluence theory is appealing for its simplicity, its predictions do not always ring true. On the positive side, older female siblings do seem to benefit intellectually from teaching younger brothers and sisters (Paulhus & Shaffer, 1981), and it appears that the intellectual climate of the household (as indexed by the HOME inventory) does depreciate as family size increases (Bradley & Caldwell, 1984a). Yet Zajonc's model would predict that children growing up in homes with *three* mature adults (say, two parents and a grandparent) should score higher on IQ tests than those exposed only to their two parents; but they don't (Brackbill & Nichols, 1982). Moreover, longer intervals between births do not always facilitate children's intellectual development as Zajonc's "sibling spacing" hypothesis would imply (Brackbill & Nichols, 1982; Galbraith, 1982). Finally, birth-order and family-size effects (on intelligence, at least) tend to be quite small and are more likely to be observed when large numbers of families are compared. Thus, the trends that emerge for the population as a whole may or may not apply to the members of any *particular* family. Clearly, not all first-borns are brighter than average; nor do all later-borns score lower in IQ (or achieve less) than their older brothers and sisters.

Summing up.   After reviewing the literature, it seems reasonable to conclude that the greater attainments of first-borns and children from small families stem, in part, from the fact that these youngsters often receive more direct achievement training than later-borns or children from large families. And although first-borns and children from smaller families do tend to score higher in IQ than later-borns and children from large families, it remains for future research to determine whether these small variations in intellectual performance help to explain birth-order and family-size differences in achievement.

SOME PERSONAL AND SITUATIONAL INFLUENCES ON ACHIEVEMENT

In this final section of the chapter, we will briefly consider three potentially important contributors to children's achievement orientations: (1) the beliefs that teachers hold about a child's propensity for achievement, (2) the effects of tangible reinforcers on children's evaluation of achievement-related activities, and (3) the impact of gender (and sex-linked expectancies).

Teacher Expectancies and Children's Achievements: The Pygmalion Effect

Earlier we noted that children's interpretations of their achievement outcomes may depend largely on the patterns of praise and criticism their teachers use when responding to their successes and failures. We also saw that the same teacher might react in different ways to roughly the same accomplishments displayed by different pupils. Do teachers' beliefs about a student's *capacity* for achievement affect the way they treat that child? Do these expectancies affect children's achievement behavior?

Several years ago, Robert Rosenthal and Lenore Jacobson (1968) conducted an interesting experiment to measure the effects of teacher expectancies on children's intellectual and academic progress. Students in grades 1 through 6 took a nonverbal IQ test. Their teachers were then led to believe that this test predicted which students would show sudden spurts of intellectual growth during the academic year. Each teacher was given the names of five students in the class who might very well prove to be "rapid bloomers." In fact, the so-called rapid bloomers were randomly selected from the class rosters. The only way they differed from the other children was that their teachers now expected more of them. Yet when the students were retested at the end of the academic year, Rosenthal and Jacobson found that, among the first- and second-graders, *the so-called rapid bloomers showed significantly greater gains in IQ and reading achievement than the other students in the class*. In other words, children who were expected to do well did, in fact, do better than other students of comparable ability.

Since the publication of this study, several other investigators have reported similar findings (Beez, 1968; Seaver, 1973), so that the "teacher expectancy" effect appears to be real. Somehow teachers must be communicating their expectancies to students, thereby improving the self-concepts (and the will to achieve) of the "rapid bloomers" while making other students feel that they are not especially bright or expected to do well. The implication is that students are becoming the objects of their teachers' self-fulfilling prophecies in what Rosenthal and Jacobson call the *Pygmalion effect.*

How do teachers derive these impressions of their students? Probably from the students' prior academic backgrounds, achievement test scores, and performance during the first few weeks of a school year. In addition, many teachers get some idea of what they can expect of a student from their experiences with the student's older brothers and sisters. When a teacher has taught a child's older siblings, the child's performance in the classroom depends, in part, on how the older siblings performed (Seaver, 1973). If the older sibs were good students, the younger sib ends up achieving more than students of comparable ability whose older siblings were taught by a different instructor. And if the older sibs were poor students, then the younger sib achieves less than students of comparable ability whose older siblings were taught by a different instructor. So the Pygmalion effect works both ways: teachers' expectancies may either facilitate or inhibit a child's academic achievement, depending on the direction of these expectancies.

Jere Brophy and Thomas Good (1970) observed student/teacher interactions in four first-grade classrooms in an attempt to identify the processes that underlie teacher expectancy effects. They found that students expected to do well were treated very differently than those expected to do poorly. For example, teachers demanded better performance from the "high expectancy" students and were more likely to praise these children for answering questions correctly (perhaps leading the high-expectancy students to suspect that they had high abilities). By contrast, "low expectancy" students were more likely to receive criticism from the teacher when they answered questions incorrectly (for example, "That's a stupid answer"), a response that might lead them to believe that their failures reflected a *lack* of ability. On those occasions when high-expectancy students did answer incorrectly, the teacher often responded by rephrasing the question until the child got it right (thus implying that the child's failures could be overcome by trying harder). Clearly, these findings are reminiscent of Dweck's results: high-expectancy students received a pattern of evaluation that is associated with a mastery orientation, whereas low-expectancy students were being treated in ways that can lead to learned helplessness. So there is nothing magical about the Pygmalion effect: "Teachers do, in fact, communicate differential performance expectations to different children through their classroom behavior, and the nature of this differential treatment is such as to encourage the children to begin to respond in ways which would confirm teacher expectancies" (Brophy & Good, 1970, p. 373).

But let's not be too critical of teachers for forming opinions of their students. All of us form impressions of the people in our lives, and these impressions often affect their behavior for better or worse. However, teachers probably should be made aware of the impact their expectancies may have on their students. Perhaps the clever instructor can even use this knowledge to "get the most" out of nearly every child in the class by setting educational objectives that the child can realistically achieve, communicating these *positive* expectancies to the child, and then praising the *ability* the child has shown whenever he or she reaches one of these academic milestones.

Effects of Material Rewards on Achievement Behavior

Children often take part in achievement-related activities, such as reading storybooks or working numerical puzzles, for the sheer fun of it. An activity that is valued for its own sake and does not require external prompts or rewards in order to continue is said to be *intrinsically* motivated.

Yet schoolwork and other forms of "achievement" behavior are not intrinsically motivating for some young children. Parents and teachers often try to promote an interest in these activities (or at least persuade children to work at them) by offering inducements such as money, praise, and gold stars for achievement at home and in the classroom. Rewards such as these that are not inherent in the activities they reinforce are called *extrinsic* reinforcers.

Learning theorists have clearly demonstrated that the offering and presentation of extrinsic reinforcement can promote new learning and motivate young children to undertake and complete activities that are not intrinsically satisfying to them (Loveland & Olley, 1979; McLoyd, 1979). For example, a teacher who offers her "nonreaders" a gold star for every ten minutes that they spend reading may well increase the reading activities of these children, who would not ordinarily read on their own. But what effect would this incentive have on the class "bookworms" who read avidly because reading is intrinsically satisfying?

Attribution theorists (for example, Lepper, 1982) suggest that children who perform intrinsically satisfying activities as a means of obtaining extrinsic reinforcement may come to like these activities less. The rationale for this prediction is straightforward: intrinsic interest in an activity may be discounted as a cause of one's behavior and even undermined if the child decides he or she is performing the activity to earn a tangible reward.

An experiment by Lepper, Greene, and Nisbett (1973) provides clear support for the attribution hypothesis. Children aged 3 to 5 who showed considerable intrinsic interest in drawing with colored felt pens were promised a special certificate if they would draw a picture for a visiting adult (expected-reward condition). Other preschool children who were equally interested in drawing with felt pens engaged in the same drawing activities and either received an unexpected certificate for their work (unexpected-reward condition) or did not receive a certificate (no-reward condition). Then, 7 to 14 days later, the children were observed during free-play periods to determine whether they still wanted to draw with the felt pens. Lepper et al. found that children who had contracted to draw a picture for an extrinsic reinforcer now spent less of their free time drawing with the pens (8.6%) than children who had received no reward (16.7%) or those who had received the reward as a surprise (18.1%). Note that the reward itself did not undermine intrinsic motivation, for children in the unexpected-reward condition continued to show as much intrinsic interest in drawing as those who were not rewarded. It was only when children had previously drawn *in order to obtain a reward* that extrinsic reinforcement undermined intrinsic interest.

Reducing one's interest in intrinsically satisfying activities is not the only undesirable effect that introduction of external incentives may have. Children who are offered such incentives for undertaking activities they already enjoy may subsequently lower their achievement aspirations, choosing to perform easy rather than difficult problems so as not to miss out on the rewards (Condry & Chambers, 1982; Harter, 1978). And unfortunately, this sudden tendency to forgo significant challenges is most apparent among those children who initially displayed the strongest intrinsic interest in the rewarded activities (Pearlman, 1984).

Do these observations mean that parents and teachers should never reward children's noteworthy accomplishments at activities that the children enjoy? No, they do not! Extrinsic rewards can sustain and even increase intrinsic interest in an activity, provided that the reinforcer is given only for *successful* task performance rather than for merely working at the task (Pallak, Costomiris, Sroka, & Pittman, 1982). Why? Because rewards given for successes serve an important *informational* function: namely, they allow children to attribute the positive outcomes of their behavior to their *competence* in that activity (a stable, internal cause) rather than to a desire to obtain the extrinsic reinforcer (an unstable, external cause). Consequently, children are likely to perform the rewarded acts in the future because rewards given for noteworthy successes have increased their perceptions of self-efficacy.

In sum, the implications of this line of research are reasonably clear. Extrinsic reinforcers can be used both at home and in the classroom to strengthen or sustain those activities that children will *not* ordinarily perform on their own. However, parents, teachers, and other social agents must guard against creating unnecessary and uninformative reward systems that are likely to decrease children's interest in activities that they already like and will perform for the fun of it.

Sex Differences in Achievement

How often have you heard the maxims "That's a man's job," "Women are just not suited for this kind of work (activity) (study)," "A woman's place is in the home"? In the vast majority of the world's societies, men are expected to pursue a career of some sort, while women, if not actively discouraged from harboring these aspirations, are at least trained for the tasks of child care and managing a household. Indeed, many who have read the Judeo-Christian scriptures have come away with the impression that such sex-linked divisions of labor are God's will. No less a religious authority than Pope Pius XII once stated: "A woman's function, a woman's way, a woman's natural bent is motherhood. Every woman is called to be a mother."

Do I repeat these sexist proverbs to enrage my female students and colleagues? Of course not! I do so simply to remind you of the well-ingrained cultural teachings that foster the impression that women ought to serve men, who are, after all, the "achieving" sex. Over the past two decades, a number of women's organizations have challenged the assertion that females are less *capable* of achievement or inherently inferior to males. *And they are correct!* Women are no less intelligent than men (Maccoby & Jacklin, 1974) and, in many Western societies, have achieved noteworthy successes at virtually all occupations heretofore labeled "masculine" (Tarvis & Wade, 1984). Yet all too often, these arguments fall on deaf ears. In this regard it is interesting to note that many women (even college students) believe that they are less capable than men and that the successes they do achieve are attributable to factors other than their own abilities (see Chapter 12 for a discussion of these findings).

Let's now set common impressions aside and see what social-developmentalists have to say about sex differences in achievement.

Sex differences in achievement expectancies. Although there are tremendous individual differences among members of each sex, girls generally outperform boys during elementary school, and boys eventually close the gap and may even outperform girls in certain subjects (for example, mathematics) during high school and college. But despite their early accomplishments, grade school girls often *underestimate* their capacity for academic achievement, whereas boys consistently *overestimate* theirs (Crandall, 1969). In fact, kindergarten and first-grade girls already think they are not as good as boys at concept formation tasks and arithmetic, even though they are earning higher grades in arithmetic and have outperformed their male classmates on tests of concept learning (Entwisle & Baker, 1983; Ruble, Parsons, & Ross, 1976). And it is disturbing to note that the *brightest* females are the ones who underestimate their competencies the most; high-achieving girls occasionally display lower expectancies of future success than their average- or low-achieving female classmates (Dweck & Elliott, 1983; Stipek & Hoffman, 1980). How can we account for these puzzling outcomes?

Home influences. Many theorists believe that sex differences in achievement expectancies originate at home. The idea here is not that parents fail to encourage their daughters to achieve but that parental actions and expectancies can lead males and females to look at achievement in very different ways. For example, parents "model" different roles for their children in families where the father pursues a career while the mother stays home to manage the household. Even if both parents work, children can form different impressions of the academic competencies of males and females if it is the father who usually helps them with their "tough" math and science homework. Finally, it seems that parents often expect more in the way of academic achievement from sons than from daughters (Parsons, Ruble, Hodges, & Small, 1976). In one recent study, Jacquelynne Parsons and her associates (Parsons, Adler, & Kaczala, 1982) found that parents of 5th- through 11th-graders believe that mathematics courses are easier, more important, and somewhat more enjoyable for their

boys than for their girls. Do these parental attitudes affect children's own impressions of their mathematical aptitude and their prospects for future success in math? Yes, indeed! Even though the males and females in Parsons's sample *did not differ* in their previous performance in math, the children's beliefs about their own mathematical *abilities* were more in line with their parents' beliefs about their math aptitude and potential than with their own past experiences in math! So it appears that parents' sex-stereotyped beliefs about their children's academic potential may be an important determinant of the sex differences we find in children's academic self-concepts. "By attributing their daughters' performances to hard work and their sons' to high ability, parents may be teaching their sons and daughters to draw different inferences regarding their abilities from equivalent achievement experiences" (Parsons et al., 1982, p. 320).

Scholastic influences. Teachers may also contribute to sex differences in achievement expectancies by responding differently to the accomplishments of male and female students. In their observational study of evaluative feedback in the classroom, Dweck et al. (1978) found that teachers' responses to boys' successes and failures were of the kind that promote a mastery orientation—that is, teachers praised the intellectual aspects of the boy's work when a boy succeeded while focusing more on nonintellectual factors (sloppiness of work; lack of effort) to account for his failures. Girls received a different evaluative pattern—teachers often stressed the nonintellectual aspects of a girl's work (that is, neatness; high effort) when she succeeded while focusing on her intellectual shortcomings when she failed. So instructors may unwittingly provide their female students with patterns of verbal evaluation that leave girls little choice but to attribute failures to their own lack of ability. Of course, this is precisely the belief that should lead female students to underestimate the likelihood of future academic success and could even result in learned helplessness.

Why are the brightest female students often the ones who underestimate their future academic accomplishments the most? A study by Jacquelynne

Parsons and her associates (Parsons, Kaczala, & Meece, 1982) provides one clue. Parsons et al. looked at teachers' use of praise in five classrooms where male and female students clearly differed in their achievement expectancies. The results were indeed interesting. Teachers were more likely to praise the work of girls they expected to do *poorly* than that of girls they expected to do well. But just the opposite was true of boys, who received more praise if the teacher expected them to do well rather than poorly. Notice that the pattern of praise received by female students in these classrooms does *not* reflect the teachers' true expectations about their future academic accomplishments. Perhaps you can see how a star female student who is rarely praised for her achievements might eventually conclude that she must lack ability or that academic success is not very important for girls, particularly when the star male students and her less competent female classmates receive far more praise from the teacher than she does.

What can we conclude about sex differences in achievement? As we have noted previously, women have often been discouraged (and sometimes even prevented) from practicing traditionally masculine occupations. And given that many contemporary females underestimate their scholastic capabilities and may even conclude that academic success is somehow less important for them than it is for males, it should come as no surprise to learn that women continue to be seriously underrepresented in the so-called achieving roles of most societies (that is, politics and the professions). Indeed, these are precisely the kind of statistics that people often cite when arguing that males achieve more than females or that males are the "achieving" sex.

Yet I feel very uncomfortable in leaving you with such an impression, particularly in view of the fact that you probably know several women who have exceeded the educational and occupational attainments of most men. Perhaps the most accurate statement we can make about sex differences in achievement is that men and women have historically differed in their *areas* of achievement rather than in their needs or capacities for achieving. As recently as

the early 1970s in the United States, fewer than 5% of doctors, 10% of lawyers, and 17% of managers and administrators were women, and fewer than 7% of college females aspired to a traditionally "masculine" profession (U.S. Bureau of the Census, 1972). However, the times have clearly changed. When America's college class of 1985 began college, in the fall of 1980, 27% of the women said they intended to pursue careers in business, engineering, law, or medicine—a fourfold increase since 1966 (American Council on Education, 1981). So it is likely that many of the negative stereotypes about the ability of women to succeed in so-called masculine pursuits will crumble over the next 20 years as females achieve, in ever-increasing numbers, in politics, professional occupations, skilled trades, and virtually all other walks of life. To oppose such a trend is to waste a most valuable resource—the efforts and abilities of more than half the world's population.

SUMMARY

Two important aims of socialization are to encourage children to become self-reliant and to take pride in their accomplishments. An *independent* child is one who is able to accomplish many objectives without the assistance of others. The concept of *achievement* extends beyond a sense of independence: the achieving child not only relies on his or her own efforts to attain many goals but also evaluates personal accomplishments against certain standards of excellence. The *need for achievement* (*n* Ach) is a learned motive to compete and to strive for success. Achievement behavior is any behavior directed toward attaining personal satisfaction or social approval in situations where standards of excellence are applicable.

Five major theories of achievement were discussed: McClelland's need achievement theory, Atkinson's revision and extension of McClelland's approach, the Crandalls' social-learning theory, Weiner's attribution theory, and Dweck's learned-helplessness theory. McClelland was the first to demonstrate that people differ in their *motivation* to achieve (*n* Ach), although his notion that *n* Ach was a global attribute that predicted one's reactions to all achievement tasks now seems badly overstated. Atkinson's revision of McClelland's theory pointed to the existence of a competing "motive to avoid failure" (M_{af}) that can make people shy away from achievement tasks in order to avoid the embarrassment of failing. Moreover, Atkinson's model and the Crandalls' subsequent social-learning theory broke new ground by demonstrating that achievement-related cognitions, such as one's *expectancies* of success and failure and the *incentive value* of succeeding (or avoiding failure), are important determinants of achievement behavior. Weiner's later attribution theory grew out of the Crandalls' approach and focused much more intently on how specific beliefs about the *causes* of one's successes and failures contribute to achievement expectancies and the incentive value of various achievement outcomes. Finally, Dweck's learned-helplessness model begins to touch bases with the earlier theories of achievement motivation by showing that the *patterns* of attributions that children display when explaining their achievement outcomes will affect their willingness to persist at challenging tasks that they have initially failed to master. Although these five achievement theories differ in many respects, each viewpoint has made important contributions to our understanding of children's achievement orientations.

There is considerable variation among different cultural and subcultural groups in the character of achievement-related goals and activities. Cross-cultural data suggest that the economy of a society influences the personalities of its members. Societies that depend on an agricultural or pastoral economy train their children to be cooperative and conforming. As a result, children from these societies are less independent, assertive, and achievement-oriented than children raised in societies that depend on hunting and fishing for their subsistence, where assertiveness and individual accomplishment are necessary for survival.

A person's ethnic and social-class background may affect his or her propensity for achievement. Some ethnic groups in North America hold higher achievement aspirations for their children, expect earlier evidence of self-reliance, and have children who are higher in *n* Ach than other ethnic groups. Children from the lower socioeconomic strata are generally lower in both achievement motivation and academic performance than children from middle- or upper-class backgrounds. There are several plausible explanations for the greater achievements of middle- and upper-class children. These children tend to score higher on intelligence tests, they have loftier aspirations, and they have the resources and the support of parents and teachers in pursuing these aspirations. In addition, they are more likely than lower- and working-class children to be raised in an entrepreneurial household, where independence and achievement are very important values.

There are many ways in which the home and family context might influence a child's propensity for achievement. Infants who are securely attached to responsive caregivers and whose home environments offer many age-appropriate problems and challenges are likely to become curious nursery school children who will later do well at school. Parents may either promote or inhibit their child's interest in achievement-related activities by virtue of their child-rearing practices. Early independence and achievement training facilitate the development of achievement motivation if the parent rewards the child's accomplishments and is not overly critical of failure. Parents who rarely reward achievement and who frequently criticize failures have children who develop a strong motive to avoid failure. *Authoritative* parents, who control the child's activities without imposing severe restrictions on his or her autonomy, have children who are self-reliant and achievement-oriented. *Authoritarian* parents, who are restrictive and domineering, and *permissive* parents, who set few if any achievement standards, tend to have children who are somewhat immature, aimless, and relatively uninterested in achievement.

First-borns and children from small families are likely to display higher levels of academic achievement than later-borns and children from large families. One explanation for these findings that has received some support is the *parental socialization hypothesis*: first-borns and children from smaller families receive more direct achievement training from their parents than later-borns and children from large families. In addition, the *mental mediation hypothesis* suggests that birth order and family size are variables that affect the child's intellectual development, which, in turn, influences his or her capacity for achievement. Although first-borns and children from smaller families do tend to score higher on IQ tests, it is not yet clear that these minor variations in intellectual performance contribute in any meaningful way to birth-order and family-size differences in achievement.

Teachers' expectancies often influence the achievements of their pupils. If a teacher expects a student to do well, the student is likely to exhibit higher levels of achievement than if the teacher has no expectations about his or her performance. The reverse is also true: when teachers expect pupils to perform poorly, the performance of those pupils is likely to suffer. Teachers contribute to this "expectancy effect," or *Pygmalion effect*, by demanding better performance of high-expectancy students and praising their successes while criticizing the failures of low-expectancy students and giving these pupils fewer opportunities to correct their mistakes.

Offering tangible rewards can be a very effective method of inducing children to work at achievement-related activities, particularly if these activities are not intrinsically satisfying to them. But one must take care not to set up unnecessary and uninformative reward systems that are likely to undermine children's intrinsic interest in activities that they already like and will perform for the fun of it.

Although girls generally outperform boys throughout elementary school, they tend to underestimate their academic capabilities and future accomplishments, whereas boys tend to overestimate their own abilities and likelihood of future success. Parents contribute to these sex differences in achievement expectancies by (1) modeling different roles for their children, (2) expecting more of their sons than their daughters, and (3) attributing sons' achievements to high ability and daughters' achievements to hard work. Teachers may also encourage these latter attributions by reacting differently to the academic accomplishments of males and females. Given that girls often underestimate their scholastic abilities and may even conclude that academic success is less

important for them than for boys, it should not be surprising to find that females are underrepresented in the professions and other so-called achieving roles of most societies. However, females are no less capable of achievement than males, and their ever-increasing contributions to virtually all the heretofore "masculine" professions are rapidly exploding the myth that males are the achieving sex.

NOTES

1. This conclusion is strengthened by the results of a second study in which the *n* Ach scores for readers used in 39 countries in the year 1950 predicted the economic growth of those countries between 1952 and 1958 (McClelland, 1961).

REFERENCES

ABOUD, F. E. (1985). Children's application of attribution principles to social comparisons. *Child Development, 56*, 682–688.

AMERICAN COUNCIL ON EDUCATION. (1981, February). More college women pursue traditionally male careers. *Higher Education and National Affairs*, p. 4.

ANASTASI, A. (1976). *Psychological testing*. New York: Macmillan.

AREND, A., Gove, F. L., & Sroufe, L. A. (1979). Continuity of individual adaptation from infancy to kindergarten: A predictive study of ego-resiliency and curiosity in preschoolers. *Child Development, 50*, 950–959.

ATKINSON, J. W. (1964). *An introduction to motivation*. Princeton, NJ: Van Nostrand.

BANDURA, A. (1977). *Social learning theory*. Englewood Cliffs, NJ: Prentice-Hall.

BARENBOIM, C. (1981). The development of person perception from childhood to adolescence: From behavioral comparisons, to psychological constructs, to psychological comparisons. *Child Development, 52*, 129–144.

BARRY, H., Child, I. L., & Bacon, M. K. (1959). The relation of child training to subsistence economy. *American Anthropologist, 61*, 51–63.

BASKETT, L. M. (1985). Sibling status effects: Adult expectations. *Developmental Psychology, 21*, 441–445.

BATTLE, E. S. (1966). Motivational determinants of academic competence. *Journal of Personality and Social Psychology, 4*, 634–642.

BAUMRIND, D. (1971). Current patterns of parental authority. *Developmental Psychology Monographs*, No. 1, pp. 1–103.

BAUMRIND, D. (1977, March). *Socialization determinants of personal agency*. Paper presented at the biennial meeting of the Society for Research in Child Development, New Orleans.

BEEZ, W. V. (1968). Influences of biased psychological reports on teacher behavior and pupil performance. *Proceedings of the 76th Annual Convention of the American Psychological Association, 3*, 365–366.

BELMONT, L., & Marolla, F. A. (1973). Birth order, family size and intelligence. *Science, 182*, 1096–1101.

BELSKY, J., Garduque, L., & Hrncir, E. (1984). Assessing performance, competence, and executive capacity in infant play: Relations to home environment and security of attachment. *Developmental Psychology, 20,* 406–417.

BENDIG, A. W. (1958). Predictive and postdictive validity of need achievement measures. *Journal of Educational Research, 52,* 119–120.

BERRY, J. W. (1967). Independence and conformity in subsistence-level societies. *Journal of Personality and Social Psychology, 7,* 415–418.

BRACKBILL, Y., & Nichols, P. L. (1982). A test of the confluence model of intellectual development. *Developmental Psychology, 18,* 192–198.

BRADLEY, R. H. (1968). Birth order and school-related behavior: A heuristic review. *Psychological Bulletin, 70,* 45–51.

BRADLEY, R. H., & Caldwell, B. M. (1984a). The HOME inventory and family demographics. *Developmental Psychology, 20,* 315–320.

BRADLEY, R. H., & Caldwell, B. M. (1984b). The relation of infants' home environments to achievement test performance in the first grade: A follow-up study. *Child Development, 55,* 803–809.

BRELAND, H. M. (1974). Birth order, family configuration, and verbal achievement. *Child Development, 45,* 1011–1019.

BROPHY, J. E., & Good, T. L. (1970). Teachers' communication of differential expectations for children's classroom performance: Some behavioral data. *Journal of Educational Psychology, 61,* 365–374.

CALDWELL, B. M., & Bradley, R. H. (1978). *Manual for the Home Observation for Measurement of the Environment.* Little Rock: University of Arkansas at Little Rock.

CASSIDY, J. (1986). The ability to negotiate the environment: An aspect of infant competence as related to quality of attachment. *Child Development, 57,* 331–337.

COLEMAN, J. S., Campbell, E. Q., Hobson, C. J., McPartland, J., Mood, A. M., Weinfeld, F. D., & York, R. L. (1966). *Equality of educational opportunity.* Report from U.S. Office of Education. Washington, DC: U.S. Government Printing Office.

CONDRY, J., & Chambers, J. (1982). Intrinsic motivation and the process of learning. In D. Grune & M. R. Lepper (Eds.), *The hidden costs of rewards.* Hillsdale, NJ: Erlbaum.

CRANDALL, V. C. (1967). Achievement behavior in young children. In *The young child: Reviews of research.* Washington, DC: National Association for the Education of Young Children.

CRANDALL, V. C. (1969). Sex differences in expectancy of intellectual and academic reinforcement. In C. P. Smith (Ed.), *Achievement-related motives in children.* New York: Russell Sage Foundation.

CRANDALL, V. J. (1963). Achievement. In H. W. Stevenson (Ed.), *Child psychology* (Vol. 1). Chicago: University of Chicago Press.

CRANDALL, V. J., Katkovsky, W., & Preston, A. A. (1960). A conceptual formulation of some research on children's achievement development. *Child Development, 31,* 787–797.

DWECK, C. S. (1975). The role of expectations and attributions in the alleviation of learned helplessness. *Journal of Personality and Social Psychology, 31,* 674–685.

DWECK, C. S. (1978). Achievement. In M. E. Lamb (Ed.), *Social and personality development.* New York: Holt, Rinehart and Winston.

DWECK, C. S., Davidson, W., Nelson, S., & Enna, B. (1978). Sex differences in learned helplessness: II. The contingencies of evaluative feedback in the classroom; III. An experimental analysis. *Developmental Psychology, 14,* 268–276.

DWECK, C. S., & Elliott, E. S. (1983). Achievement motivation. In E. M. Hetherington (Ed.), *Handbook of child psychology* (Vol. 4). New York: Wiley.

ENTWISLE, D. R., & Baker, D. P. (1983). Gender and young children's expectations for performance in arithmetic. *Developmental Psychology, 19,* 200–209.

EYSENCK, H. J., & Cookson, D. (1969). Personality in primary school children: 3. Family background. *British Journal of Educational Psychology, 40,* 117–131.

FINDLEY, M. J., & Cooper, H. M. (1983). Locus of control and academic achievement: A literature review. *Journal of Personality and Social Psychology, 44,* 419–427.

FRANCE-KAATRUDE, A., & Smith, W. P. (1985). Social comparison, task motivation, and the development of self-evaluative standards in children. *Developmental Psychology, 21,* 1080–1089.

FYANS, L. J., Jr., Salili, F., Maehr, M. L., & Desai, K. A. (1983). A cross-cultural exploration into the meaning of achievement. *Journal of Personality and Social Psychology, 44,* 1000–1013.

GALBRAITH, R. C. (1982). Sibling spacing and intellectual development: A closer look at the confluence model. *Developmental Psychology, 18,* 151–173.

GLASS, D. C., Neulinger, J., & Brim, O. G. (1974). Birth order, verbal intelligence, and educational aspiration. *Child Development, 45,* 807–811.

HARTER, S. (1978). Pleasure derived from challenge and the effects of receiving grades on children's difficulty level choices. *Child Development, 49,* 788–799.

HARTER, S. (1981). A new self-report scale of intrinsic versus extrinsic orientation in the classroom: Motivational and informational components. *Developmental Psychology, 17,* 300–312.

HESS, R. D. (1970). Social class and ethnic influences upon socialization. In P. H. Mussen (Ed.), *Carmichael's manual of child psychology* (Vol. 2). New York: Wiley.

HILTON, I. (1967). Differences in the behavior of mothers toward first- and later-born children. *Journal of Personality and Social Psychology, 7,* 282–290.

KATKOVSKY, W., Crandall, V. C., & Good, S. (1967). Parental antecedents of children's beliefs in internal-external control of reinforcements in intellectual achievement situations. *Child Development, 38,* 765–776.

KELLAGHAN, T., & MacNamara, J. (1972). Family correlates of verbal reasoning ability. *Developmental Psychology, 7,* 49–53.

LAOSA, L. M. (1981). Maternal behavior: Sociocultural diversity in modes of family interaction. In R. W. Henderson (Ed.), *Parent-child interaction: Theory, research, and prospects.* Orlando, FL: Academic Press.

LEPPER, M. R. (1982). Social cognition processes, attributions of motivation, and the internalization of social values. In E. T. Higgins, D. W. Ruble, & W. W. Hartup (Eds.), *Social cognition and social behavior: Developmental perspectives.* Cambridge: Cambridge University Press.

LEPPER, M. R., Greene, D., & Nisbett, R. E. (1973). Undermining children's intrinsic interest with extrinsic reward: A test of the overjustification hypothesis. *Journal of Personality and Social Psychology, 28,* 129–137.

LEWIS, M., & Kreitzberg, V. S. (1979). Effects of birth order and spacing on mother-infant interactions. *Developmental Psychology, 15,* 617–625.

LICHT, B. G., & Dweck, C. S. (1984). Determinants of academic achievement: The interaction of children's achievement orientations with skill area. *Developmental Psychology, 20,* 628–636.

LIEBERT, R. M., & Ora, J. P. (1968). Children's adoption of self-reward patterns: Incentive level and method of transmission. *Child Development, 39,* 537–544.

LOVELAND, K. K., & Olley, J. G. (1979). The effect of external reward on interest and quality of task performance in children of high or low intrinsic motivation. *Child Development, 50,* 1207–1210.

MACCOBY, E. E., & Jacklin, C. N. (1974). *The psychology of sex differences.* Stanford, CA: Stanford University Press.

MATAS, L., Arend, R. A., & Sroufe, L. A. (1978). Continuity of adaptation in the second year: The relationship between quality of attachment and later competence. *Child Development, 49,* 547–556.

McCLELLAND, D. C. (1955). *Studies in motivation.* New York: Appleton-Century-Crofts.

McCLELLAND, D. C. (1961). *The achieving society.* New York: Free Press.

McCLELLAND, D. C., Atkinson, J. W., Clark, R. A., & Lowell, E. L. (1953). *The achievement motive.* New York: Appleton-Century-Crofts.

McCLELLAND, D. C., Rindlisbacher, A.. & de Charms, R. C.

(1955). Religious and other sources of parental attitudes toward independence training. In D. C. McClelland (Ed.), *Studies in motivation.* New York: Appleton-Century-Crofts.

McLOYD, V. C. (1979). The effects of extrinsic rewards of differential value on high and low intrinsic interest. *Child Development, 50,* 1010–1019.

McMAINS, M. J., & Liebert, R. M. (1968). The influence of discrepancies between successively modeled self-reward criteria on the adoption of a self-imposed standard. *Journal of Personality and Social Psychology, 8,* 166–171.

MESSER, D. J., McCarthy, M. E., McQuiston, S., MacTurk, R. H., Yarrow, L. W., & Vietze, P. M. (1986). Relation between mastery behavior in infancy and competence in early childhood. *Developmental Psychology, 22,* 366–372.

MINOR, C. A., & Neel, R. G. (1958). The relationship between achievement motive and occupational preference. *Journal of Counseling Psychology, 5,* 39–43.

MINTON, H. L., & Schneider, F. W. (1980). *Differential psychology.* Monterey, CA: Brooks/Cole.

MOSATCHE, H. S., & Bragonier, P. (1981). An observational study of social comparison in preschoolers. *Child Development, 52,* 376–378.

MURRAY, H. (1938). *Explorations in personality.* New York: Oxford University Press.

NICHOLLS, J. G., & Miller, A. T. (1984). Reasoning about the ability of self and others: A developmental study. *Child Development, 55,* 1990–1999.

NICHOLLS, J. G., & Miller, A. T. (1985). Differentiation of the concepts of luck and skill. *Developmental Psychology, 21,* 76–82.

PALLAK, S. R., Costomiris, S., Sroka, S., & Pittman, T. S. (1982). School experience, reward characteristics, and intrinsic motivation. *Child Development, 53,* 1382–1391.

PARSONS, J. E., Adler, T. F., & Kaczala, C. M. (1982). Socialization of achievement attitudes and beliefs: Parental influences. *Child Development, 53,* 310–321.

PARSONS, J. E., Kaczala, C. M., & Meece, J. L. (1982). Socialization of achievement attitudes and beliefs: Classroom influences. *Child Development, 53,* 322–339.

PARSONS, J. E., Ruble, D. N., Hodges, K. L., & Small, A. W. (1976). Cognitive-developmental factors in emerging sex differences in achievement-related expectancies. *Journal of Social Issues, 32,* 47–61.

PAULHUS, D., & Shaffer, D. R. (1981). Sex differences in the impact of number of younger and number of older siblings on scholastic aptitude. *Social Psychology Quarterly, 44,* 363–368.

PEARLMAN, C. (1984). The effects of level of effectance motivation, IQ, and a penalty/reward contingency on the choice of problem difficulty. *Child Development, 55,* 537–542.

PHILLIPS, D. (1984). The illusion of incompetence among academically competent children. *Child Development, 55,* 2000–2016.

RAYNOR, J. O. (1970). Relationships between achievement-related motives, future orientation, and academic performance. *Journal of Personality and Social Psychology, 15,* 28–33.

RHOLES, W. S., & Ruble, D. N. (1984). Children's understanding of dispositional characteristics of others. *Child Development, 55,* 550–560.

ROSEN, B. C. (1959). Race, ethnicity, and the achievement syndrome. *American Sociological Review, 24,* 47–60.

ROSEN, B. C., & D'Andrade, R. (1959). The psychosocial origins of achievement motivation. *Sociometry, 22,* 185–218.

ROSENTHAL, R., & Jacobson, L. (1968). *Pygmalion in the classroom: Teacher expectation and pupils' intellectual development.* New York: Holt, Rinehart and Winston.

ROTHBART, M. K. (1971). Birth order and mother-child interaction in an achievement situation. *Journal of Personality and Social Psychology, 17,* 113–120.

ROTTER, J. (1966). Generalized expectancies for internal versus external control of reinforcement. *Psychological Monographs: General and Applied, 80* (1, Whole No. 609), 1–28.

RUBLE, D. N., Boggiano, A. K., Feldman, N. S., & Loebl, J. H.

(1980). Developmental analysis of the role of social comparison in self-evaluation. *Developmental Psychology, 16,* 105–115.

RUBLE, D. N., Parsons, J. E., & Ross, J. (1976). *Self-evaluative responses in an achievement setting.* Unpublished manuscript, Princeton University.

SAMPSON, E. E., & Hancock, F. T. (1967). An examination of the relationship between ordinal position, personality, and conformity: An extension, replication, and partial verification. *Journal of Personality and Social Psychology, 5,* 398–407.

SCHACHTER, S. (1963). Birth order, eminence, and higher education. *American Sociological Review, 28,* 757–767.

SCHOOLER, C. (1972). Birth order effects: Not here, not now! *Psychological Bulletin, 78,* 161–175.

SEAVER, W. B. (1973). Effects of naturally induced teacher expectancies. *Journal of Personality and Social Psychology, 28,* 333–342.

SEWELL, W. H., Haller, A. O., & Straus, M. A. (1957). Social status and educational and occupational aspiration. *American Sociological Review, 22,* 67–73.

SHAFFER, D. R., & Shaffer, G. S. (1985). Intelligence: Measuring mental performance. In D. R. Shaffer, *Developmental psychology: Theory, research, and applications.* Monterey, CA: Brooks/Cole.

SKINNER, B. F. (1968). *The psychology of teaching.* New York: Appleton-Century-Crofts.

STEVENS, J. H., Jr., & Bakeman, R. (1985). A factor analytic study of the HOME scale for infants. *Developmental Psychology, 21,* 1196–1203.

STIPEK, D. J. (1984). Young children's performance expectancies: Logical analysis or wishful thinking? In J. Nicholls (Ed.), *The development of achievement motivation.* Greenwich, CT: JAI Press.

STIPEK, D. J., & Hoffman, J. M. (1980). Children's achievement related expectancies as a function of academic performance histories and sex. *Journal of Educational Psychology, 72,* 861–865.

STIPEK, D. J., Roberts, T. A., & Sanborn, M. E. (1984). Preschool-age children's performance expectations for themselves and another child as a function of the incentive value of success and the salience of past performance. *Child Development, 55,* 1983–1989.

TARVIS, C., & Wade, C. (1984). *The longest war: Sex differences in perspective* (2nd ed.). San Diego, CA: Harcourt Brace Jovanovich.

TEEVEN, R. C., & McGhee, P. E. (1972). Childhood development of fear of failure motivation. *Journal of Personality and Social Psychology, 21,* 345–348.

TURNER, J. H. (1970). Entrepreneurial environments and the emergence of achievement motivation in adolescent males. *Sociometry, 33,* 147–165.

U.S. BUREAU OF THE CENSUS. (1972). *Money income in 1971 of families and persons in the United States* (Current Population Reports, Series P-60, No. 85). Washington, DC: U.S. Government Printing Office.

VAN DOORNINCK, W. J., Caldwell, B. M., Wright, C., & Frankenberg, W. K. (1981). The relationship between twelve-month home stimulation and school achievement. *Child Development, 52,* 1080–1083.

WEBER, M. (1930). *The Protestant ethic and the spirit of capitalism* (T. Parsons, Trans.). New York: Scribner's. (Original work published 1904)

WEINER, B. (1974). *Achievement and attribution theory.* Morristown, NJ: General Learning Press.

WEINER, B. (1982). An attribution theory of motivation and emotion. In H. Krohne & L. Laux (Eds.), *Achievement, stress, and anxiety.* Washington, DC: Hemisphere.

WEINER, B., Frieze, I., Kukla, A., Reed, L., Rest, S., & Rosenbaum, R. M. (1974). Perceiving the causes of success and failure. In E. E. Jones, D. E. Kanouse, H. H. Kelley, R. E. Nisbett, S. Valins, & B. Weiner (Eds.), *Attribution: Perceiving the causes of behavior.* Morristown, NJ: General Learning Press.

WEISS, P. M., Wertheimer, M., & Groesbeck, B. (1959). Achievement motivation, academic aptitude, and college grades. *Educational and Psychological Measurement, 19,* 663–666.

WHITE, R. W. (1959). Motivation reconsidered: The concept of competence. *Psychological Review, 66*, 297–333.

WINTERBOTTOM, M. (1958). The relation of need for achievement to learning experiences in independence and mastery. In J. Atkinson (Ed.), *Motives in fantasy, action, and society*. Princeton, NJ: Van Nostrand.

YARROW, L. J., McQuiston, S., MacTurk, R. H., McCarthy, M. E., Klein, R. P., & Vietze, P. M. (1983). Assessment of mastery motivation during the first year of life: Contemporaneous and cross-age relationships. *Developmental Psychology, 19*, 159–171.

ZAJONC, R. B. (1975, August). Birth order and intelligence: Dumber by the dozen. *Psychology Today*, pp. 39–43.

ZAJONC, R. B., Markus, H., & Markus, G. B. (1979). The birth order puzzle. *Journal of Personality and Social Psychology, 37*, 1325–1341.

9

AGGRESSION

(continues)

SOCIAL INFLUENCES ON AGGRESSION

Cultural and Subcultural Influences

Familial Influences

Effects of the Mass Media on Children's Aggression

METHODS OF CONTROLLING AGGRESSION

Catharsis: A Dubious Strategy

Eliminating the Payoffs for Aggression

Modeling and Coaching Strategies

Creating Nonaggressive Environments

Empathy as a Deterrent to Aggression

SUMMARY

REFERENCES

On a clear afternoon in early May 1970 I found myself lying on the ground, coughing from tear gas and hoping that I would survive the ordeal of the moment. The scene: Kent State University. Just seconds before, a column of Ohio National Guardsmen had turned and fired on a group of bystanders, killing four and wounding several others. Surprisingly, the mood of many people around me was not one of terror but one of retribution. Within minutes there was talk of locating weapons and extracting revenge from the guardsmen. The potential for an even stronger confrontation was apparent, and it is fortunate, I think, that school administrators decided to close the university before additional blood could be spilled.

Human aggression is a pervasive phenomenon. We need not look beyond the evening news to observe instances of brutality, for rapes, kidnappings, shoot-outs, and murders are everyday items for Dan Rather and his colleagues in the network and local news bureaus. Elliot Aronson (1976) has described a book that surely qualifies as the shortest capsule history of the world, a 10- to 15-page chronological listing of the most important events in human history. Perhaps you can guess how it reads. That's right: one war after another, with a few other happenings such as the birth of Christ sandwiched in between. If an extraterrestrial being somehow obtained a copy and deciphered it, he or she would be forced to conclude that we are extremely hostile and aggressive creatures who should probably be avoided.

What makes humans aggressive? Most vertebrates do not try to kill members of their own species, as we sometimes do. Is aggression a part of human nature or, rather, something that children must learn? Is there any hope for peaceful coexistence among people with conflicting interests? If so, how is our aggressiveness to be modified or controlled? These are but a few of the issues that will be considered in the pages that follow.

COMMON DEFINITIONS OF AGGRESSION

Most of us have an implicit definition of aggression. Rape is an act that almost everyone would consider violent and aggressive. But the passionate lovemaking of consenting partners is generally considered nonaggressive behavior. Whenever I introduce the topic of aggression in my classes, I ask students to define the term in their own words. As I write these definitions on the board, classmates invariably begin to argue about the meaning of aggression and the kinds of behavior that should be considered aggressive. These debates are hardly surprising in view of the fact that social scientists have argued the very same issues for 40 to 50 years. At this point it may be useful to look at some of the most common definitions of aggression.

AGGRESSION AS AN INSTINCT

Could aggression be an instinct—a basic component of human nature? Freud thought so, describing the *Thanatos* (or death instinct) as the factor responsible for the generation of aggressive energy in all human beings. Freud held a "hydraulic" view of aggression: hostile, aggressive energy would build up to a critical level and then be discharged through some form of violent, destructive behavior.

Psychoanalytic theorists are not the only ones who have adopted this viewpoint. The famous ethologist Konrad Lorenz described aggression as a fighting instinct triggered by certain "eliciting" cues in the environment. In his book *African Genesis*, Robert Ardrey (1967) has gone so far as to imply that the human being "is a predator whose natural instinct is to kill with a weapon" (p. 322). Although there are several important differences between psychoanalytic and ethological perspectives on aggression, both schools of thought maintain that aggressive behavior results from an innate propensity for violence.

BEHAVIORAL DEFINITIONS OF AGGRESSION

Most behavioral theorists think of aggression not as an instinct or a drive but, rather, as a special class of social behavior that is acquired and maintained through precisely the same processes—reinforcement and observational learning—as any other type of social behavior. Among the more frequently cited behavioral definitions of aggression is that of Arnold Buss (1961), who characterized an aggressive act as "a response that delivers noxious stimuli to another organism" (p. 3).

Notice that Buss's definition emphasizes the *consequences of action* rather than the intentions of the actor. According to Buss, any act that delivers pain or discomfort to another creature has to be considered aggressive. Yet how many of us consider our dentists aggressive when they drill on our teeth, producing some pain in the process? Is a klutzy dance partner being aggressive when he or she steps on our toes? And is a sniper who misses his target any less aggressive just because no physical harm has been done?

Although you are certainly free to disagree, most people would consider the sniper's behavior aggressive while viewing the dentist's and the dance partner's actions as careless or accidental. In making this pattern of attributions, people are relying on an *intentional definition* of aggression, which implies that an aggressive act is *any form of behavior designed to harm or injure another living being who is motivated to avoid such treatment* (Baron & Byrne, 1984). Note that this intentional definition would classify as aggressive all acts in which harm is intended but not done (for example, a violent kick that misses its target) while excluding accidental injuries or activities such as rough-and-tumble play in which participants are enjoying themselves with no harmful intent.

However, an intentional definition of aggression is not without its problems, for it is often exceedingly difficult to infer a person's motives. Aggressive intent can be disguised in many ways (for example, intended harm can be made to look like an accident), and even apparent acts of kindness may serve aggressive ends (for example, giving tainted candy to trick-or-treaters on Halloween). Despite these shortcomings, many psychologists now favor the intentional definition of aggression, for the strict behavioral definition incorporates too many acts that most of us would not consider aggressive.

THE DISTINCTION BETWEEN HOSTILE AND INSTRUMENTAL AGGRESSION

Theorists who view aggression as stemming from internal forces (that is, instincts or drives) have made a distinction between hostile and instrumental aggression. Hostile aggression is said to result from one's motive to hurt others; if an actor's major goal is to harm a victim, then his or her behavior qualifies as hostile aggression. By contrast, instrumental aggression includes all acts in which one person inflicts injury or otherwise harms another *as a means to a nonaggressive end* (such as attaining possessions, power, or money). Clearly, the same overt act could be classified as either hostile or instrumental aggression depending on the circumstances. If a boy clobbered his sister and then teased her for crying, we would consider this hostile aggression. But these same actions could be labeled instrumentally aggressive (or a mixture of hostile and instrumental aggression) had the boy also grabbed a toy that his sister was using. Drive theorists are interested mainly in studying hostile aggression, which they view as the product of an aggressive drive. In fact, these researchers pay little attention to instrumental aggression, which they believe is more accurately characterized as assertiveness[1] or some other form of pseudo aggression (Feshbach, 1970).

Such a distinction seems preposterous to social-learning theorists, who note that most of the acts that people consider aggressive are examples of instrumental aggression (Bandura, 1973). For instance, virtually all wars are fought for political, economic, or religious purposes and may be considered examples of instrumental aggression. And it may make little difference to a "mugging" victim whether she was roughed up for the fun of it (hostile aggression) or for instrumental reasons such as the money in her purse; from her viewpoint, the act was aggressive and the hurt remains.

An example or two should illustrate the difficulty we face in determining whether an act is hostile or instrumental aggression. A neighborhood bully might appear to derive pleasure from beating up other children, but we can't be absolutely certain that his aggressiveness is purely hostile in character. Why? Because the bully may behave aggressively in order to maintain his high self-esteem or to preserve his status in the peer group—that is, for instrumental reasons. Bandura (1973) describes a teenage gang that routinely assaulted innocent victims on the street. But gang members did not necessarily attack others for kicks; they were required to rough up at least ten individuals in order to become full-fledged members of the group. So even behaviors that appear to be instances of hostile aggression may actually be controlled by hidden reinforcement contingencies.

In sum, the distinction between hostile and instrumental aggression is not as sharp as the drive theorists would have us believe. Even if we consider these forms conceptually distinct, we must still note that both are common and both have important consequences for victims and aggressors. Bandura (1973) reflects the sentiment of many in calling for a comprehensive theory that embraces both hostile and instrumental aggression.

AGGRESSION AS A SOCIAL LABEL

Although we have talked as if there were a class of intentional behaviors that almost everyone would label "aggressive," such a viewpoint is simply incorrect. Bandura and others (for example, Parke & Slaby, 1983) argue convincingly that "aggression" is really a social label that we apply to various acts, guided by our judgments about the meaning of those acts to us. Presumably, our interpretation of an act as aggressive or nonaggressive will depend on a variety of social, personal, and situational factors such as our own beliefs about aggression (which may vary as a function of our gender, culture, social class, and prior experiences), the context in which the response occurs, the intensity of the response, and the identities and reactions of the people involved, to name a few. Accordingly, a high-intensity response such as a hard right hand to someone's jaw is more likely to be labeled aggressive than a milder version of the same action, which we might interpret as a playful prompt or even as a sign of affection. Shooting a deer may be seen as much more violent and aggressive by a pacifist vegetarian than by a carnivorous card-carrying member of the National Rifle Association. Scuffles between children are more likely to be labeled aggressive if someone is hurt in the process. And as we see in Box 9-1, the identities of the people involved in a behavioral sequence can play a major role in determining our impressions of their aggressive intent.

In sum, aggression is to no small extent a *social judgment* that we make about the seemingly injurious or destructive behaviors that we observe or experience. Clearly, we can continue to think of aggression as behavior that is *intended* to harm or injure someone, as long as we recognize that the basis for inferring whether an actor has a harmful intent can vary dramatically across perceivers, perpetrators, victims, contexts, and situations, thereby ensuring that people will often disagree about what has happened and whether it qualifies as aggression.

THEORIES OF AGGRESSION

By now you may have guessed that each of the preceding definitions of aggression is based on a theory of some sort. In the pages that follow we will consider several theories that have been offered as explanations for human aggression.

INSTINCT THEORIES

Freud's psychoanalytic theory. Freud believed that we are all born with a death instinct (Thanatos) that seeks the cessation of life and underlies all acts of violence and destruction. His view was that energy derived from food is continually being converted to aggressive energy and that these aggressive urges must be discharged periodically to prevent them from building to dangerous levels. According to Freud, aggressive energy can be discharged in a socially acceptable fashion through vigorous work or play, or through less desirable activities such as insulting others, fighting, or destroying property. An interesting Freudian notion is that aggressive urges are occasionally directed inward, resulting in some form of self-punishment, self-mutilation, or perhaps even suicide.

Most contemporary psychoanalytic theorists continue to think of aggression as an instinctual drive but reject Freud's notion that we harbor a self-directed death instinct. Presumably, an instinctual tendency to aggress occurs whenever we are frustrated in our attempts at need satisfaction or face some other threat that hinders the functioning of the ego (Feshbach, 1970). Viewed in this way, aggressive drives are *adaptive*: they help the individual to satisfy basic needs and thus serve to promote life rather than self-destruction.

BOX 9-1   ADULT REACTIONS TO ROUGHHOUSING: BOYS WILL BE BOYS, BUT GIRLS ARE AGGRESSORS

Imagine you are walking down the street on a snowy winter afternoon and you happen to notice a child hitting, jumping on, and throwing snowballs at an age mate. How might you interpret this event? Would your judgment be affected by the identities of the actor and the recipient? What would you think if the children were both boys? Both girls? A boy and a girl?

Recently, John Condry and David Ross (1985) conducted an interesting experiment to determine how adults might interpret the rough-and-tumble activities of children they thought to be boys or girls. Subjects first watched a videotape in which two children, whose genders were concealed by snowsuits, played together in the snow. The play soon became quite rough as one child (the target) hit, jumped on, and hurled snowballs at the other (the recipient). Before watching the video, subjects were told that these children were both boys, both girls, a boy target and girl recipient, or a girl target and boy recipient. After the video was over, subjects were asked to rate the behavior of the target child along two dimensions: (1) the amount of aggression the target displayed toward the recipient and (2) the extent to which the target's behavior was merely active, playful, and affectionate.

The results were indeed interesting. As we see in scanning the figure, the rough-and-tumble behavior of the target child was much less likely to be interpreted as aggressive, and tended to be seen instead as a display of affection, when both the target child and the recipient were said to be boys. So if we see two children "roughhousing" and think that the two are boys, we say "Boys will be boys" and may fail to intervene. By contrast, boys' roughhousing with girls was definitely interpreted as aggressive behavior. And notice that the high-intensity antics of the girl targets were also seen as highly aggressive, regardless of whether the recipient of those actions was a boy or a girl! In summarizing these data, Condry and Ross say that "It may not be fair, and it certainly is not equal, but from the results of this study, it looks as if boys and girls really are judged differently in terms of what constitutes aggression" (p. 230).

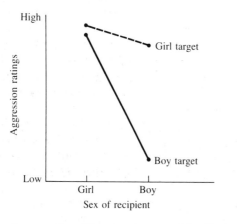
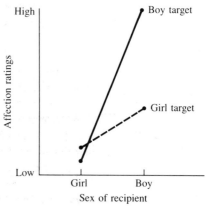

Average ratings of the aggressiveness and the affection of the target child's behavior as a function of the gender of the target and the recipient

Lorenz's ethological theory of aggression. A second instinct theory of aggression stems from the work of ethologist Konrad Lorenz. Lorenz (1966) argues that humans and animals have a basic fighting (aggressive) instinct that is directed against members of the same species. Like psychoanalytic theorists,

Lorenz views aggression as a hydraulic system that generates its own energy. But he believes that aggressive urges continue to build until relieved by an appropriate *releasing stimulus.*

What kinds of stimuli are likely to trigger aggressive behavior? What functions might these displays of aggression serve? According to Lorenz, all instincts, including aggression, serve a basic evolutionary purpose: to ensure the survival of the individual and the species. Thus, fights that occur when one animal enters another's territory are said to be adaptive; they disperse individuals over a wider area, thereby preventing large numbers of animals from congregating in the same locale, exhausting all sources of food, and starving. An animal may also fight off an intruder in order to protect its young, thereby allowing them to live, to mature, and eventually to reproduce. Finally, fighting among the males of a species determines which males will mate with available females. Since the stronger males usually win these battles, intraspecies aggression helps to ensure that the hardiest members of the lot will be the ones to reproduce.

From an ethological perspective, aggression can help most species survive because they have evolved various "instinctual inhibitions" that prevent them from killing members of their own kind. For example, many species of fish engage in "threat" displays or ritualized aggressive ceremonies in which one of the participants will "win" without seriously injuring an adversary. Birds of the same species could easily kill each other (or peck each other's eyes out) but rarely do so. Wolves normally refrain from killing each other when the loser of a battle "signals" that it has had enough by offering its unprotected throat to the teeth of the victor.

According to Lorenz, human beings kill members of their own species because their aggressive instinct is poorly controlled. Because *Homo sapiens* in prehistoric times lacked the innate equipment to kill (such as claws or fangs), there was little need for the evolution of instinctual inhibitions against maiming or killing other human beings. But humans did evolve intellectually, developed weapons of destruction, and, lacking innate inhibitions, showed little reluctance to use this lethal weaponry to defeat human adversaries. Lorenz points out that this lack of aggressive inhibitions, coupled with the recent development of doomsday weapons, presents a crucial challenge to humanity: we must now work very hard to channel our aggressive urges into socially acceptable pursuits or face the very real possibility of becoming an endangered species.

A critique of instinct theories. It is often argued that instinct theories of aggression are of limited explanatory value. For example, the notion that all aggression stems from inborn, instinctual forces cannot easily explain why some societies are more aggressive than others. Cultures such as the Arapesh of New Guinea, the Lepchas of the Himalayas, and the Pygmies of the Congo all use weapons to procure food but rarely show any kind of intraspecies aggression. When invaded by outsiders, these peace-loving people retreat to inaccessible regions rather than stand and fight (Gorer, 1968). Although these observations do not rule out the possibility of biological influences on aggression, they present a strong challenge to any theory that humans are *instinctively* aggressive.

To date, there is no neurophysiological evidence that the body generates or accumulates aggressive energy (Scott, 1966, 1972). John Scott believes that the instigation of aggression derives from external rather than internal forces. The mere fact that animals fight doesn't mean they are expending pent-up aggressive energy. To assume so is like assuming that "most people find the odor of roses pleasant [because] there is spontaneous internal stimulation to go out and smell the flowers" (Scott, 1966, p. 696).

Now recall one of the central arguments of instinct theory: human aggression is so widespread because it stems from recurring internal forces for which we have no inborn or instinctual inhibitions. Critics scoff at this assertion. It is true that human beings do not bare their throats or rely on other such signals of aggressive appeasement in exactly the same way that animals do. However, Bandura (1973) points out that these primitive gestures are unnecessary for humans, who have evolved a much more intricate system—namely, language—for controlling aggression.

Indeed, *human* ethologists are nowhere near as pessimistic about the prospect of controlling human aggression as Lorenz and Freud were. Ethological studies of children's play groups (Sluckin & Smith, 1977; Strayer, 1980) reveal that even 3- to 5-year-olds form reasonably stable dominance hierarchies (determined on the basis of who dominates whom in conflict situations) and know which of their playmates is likely to dominate or submit to them during a conflict. Strayer (1980) proposes that the function of these dominance hierarchies is to *minimize* aggression, just as similar hierarchies minimize fighting and promote the social adaptation of apes and other species. And apparently he is right. In play groups characterized by such dominance hierarchies, children who are attacked rarely counterattack or enlist the aid of teachers and peers. Instead, they generally submit to their more dominant classmates. One recent observational study of conflicts among 5-year-olds found that most disputes were quickly resolved as the "loser" simply stepped back and moved away from his or her adversary. And in a substantial percentage of these disputes, the nondominant child terminated conflict by making some sort of conciliatory gesture to the dominant one, such as offering to be his friend, offering to share a toy, or even touching the former adversary in a friendly manner (Sackin & Thelen, 1984). So not only can children successfully end most disputes before they escalate into violent, aggressive exchanges, but they are remarkably proficient at doing so at an early age.

And even if human beings were instinctively aggressive, it is likely that an individual's aggressive inclinations would soon be affected by social experiences. If we look at the animal literature, we find that cats will normally kill rats, a behavior that many people have called instinctive. In one ingenious experiment, Kuo (1930) raised kittens either by themselves, with rat-killing mothers, or with rats as companions. Of the kittens raised with rat-killing mothers, 85% became regular rat killers. But only 45% of the isolated kittens ever killed a rat, and few of those reared with rats (17%) became rat killers. When Kuo later exposed the pacifistic kittens to adult rat-killing models, 82% of the isolated pacifists became vigorous rat killers. However, only 7% of the pacifists that had been reared with rats followed the model's example and attacked rats. Kuo's study nicely illustrates the importance of environmental influences as determinants of aggressive behavior; it appears that aggressive responses that are often labeled instinctive can be modified substantially or even eliminated through social learning. Proponents of instinct theory could reply that all human beings have aggressive instincts and that any differences in their degree of aggressiveness are due to learning.

But Middlebrook (1974) points out that "such a response . . . only emphasizes the limited understanding of aggression that the instinct explanation offers. Human aggressive behaviors—whatever their basic origins—have been so modified by learning that it may not be helpful to spend much time on the extent to which their origins are instinctive" (p. 265).

NEO-HULLIAN THEORY: THE FRUSTRATION/AGGRESSION HYPOTHESIS

Perhaps the best-known explanation of human aggression was proposed by a group of psychologists and anthropologists at Yale University (Dollard, Doob, Miller, Mowrer, & Sears, 1939). Their theory, which came to be known as the frustration/aggression hypothesis, stated that frustration (the thwarting of goal-directed behavior) always produces some kind of aggression. A related claim was that aggression is always caused by frustration.

Were the Yale theorists proposing an innate link between frustration and aggression? Apparently not, for in an early review of the available literature, Neal Miller (1941) wrote that "no assumptions are made as to whether the frustration-aggression relationship is of innate or of learned origin" (p. 340). However, Robert Sears, another member of this neo-Hullian group, eventually concluded that the connection between frustration and aggression is learned. What seems to be innate, according to Sears (1958) and Feshbach (1964), is a relationship between frustration and *anger*. Angry children tend to throw tantrums and flail their limbs in an agitated manner, often striking other people, animals, or inanimate objects in the process. This observation led Feshbach (1964) to conclude that, during the first two years of life, "frustration produces an instigation to hit rather than to hurt" (p. 262). So how do children come to react aggressively when frustrated? Sears believes that a child learns to attack frustrators when he or she discovers that these attacks alleviate frustration. But the attacks have another important consequence: they produce signs of pain and suffering from the frustrator. If the child associates the frustrator's pain with the positive consequences arising from the removal of frustration, pain cues will assume the characteristics of secondary reinforcers, and the child will have acquired a motive to hurt others (a hostile-aggressive drive).[2]

Although there are many studies indicating that frustration may lead to aggression, *it does not always do so*. A now-classic experiment by Joel Davitz (1952) shows that a child's response to frustration can easily be modified by training. Davitz randomly assigned 7- to 9-year-olds to one of two experimental conditions. Children assigned to the *aggressive-training condition* were asked to play "rough and tumble" games and were rewarded for their aggressiveness. For example, one of the games, "scalp," required each child to protect a piece of cloth tied around his or her arm (the scalp) while trying to tear the scalps from the arms of playmates. Children assigned to the *constructive-training condition* were reinforced for constructive, cooperative activities (working together drawing pictures and assembling puzzles) and discouraged from behaving aggressively. After the training sessions, the children each received a candy bar and sat down to watch an interesting movie. At the climactic point of the movie, the experimenter frustrated the children by taking their candy and ushering them away from the film to play with some toys in another room.

Davitz found that the majority of the children in the aggressive-training condition responded to this frustration by becoming rather aggressive during the free-play period. By contrast, children who had been reinforced for cooperative activities were much less aggressively inclined and were more likely than their counterparts in the aggressive training group to play together constructively. One implication of these results is that a person's reaction to frustration is not necessarily aggression but, rather, whatever response the person most strongly associates with the setting in which he finds himself.

Now that we have seen that frustration does not always lead to aggression, we will consider a second question: Is aggression always caused by frustration? As you might imagine, the answer is no. In fact, an experiment by Russell Geen (1968) suggests that frustration may not even be the most potent cause of aggression!

Participants in Geen's experiment were first asked to assemble a jigsaw puzzle in the presence of an experimental confederate who posed as a second research participant. Subjects assigned to a *task frustration* condition worked on an insoluble puzzle that they believed to be a test of their intelligence. Other subjects experienced *personal frustration* when they failed to complete a solvable puzzle because of the confederate's repeated interruptions. A third group of subjects worked on a solvable puzzle, but they were subjected to what seemed to be arbitrary *verbal attacks* (insults) from the confederate. *Control* subjects were allowed to complete a solvable puzzle.

The second phase of the experiment required the subject to play the role of a teacher, presenting materials to the confederate, who was to play the role of a learner and attempt to master them. The subject sat in front of an impressive-looking electrical apparatus and was told by the experimenter that he should reward the confederate's correct responses by pushing a "correct" button and punish incorrect responses by pushing any of ten other buttons, each of which delivered a different level of electrical shock to the confederate (buttons with progressively higher numbers delivered progressively stronger shocks). The confederate proceeded to make 16 errors over the course of his 30 learning trials. Geen assumed that the stronger the shocks given the confederate on these error trials, the greater the subject's level of aggression toward this person.

Geen's results appear in Figure 9-1. As predicted by the frustration/aggression hypothesis, subjects in both frustration groups delivered stronger shocks to the confederate than subjects in the control group. However, we see that subjects who were verbally attacked by the confederate gave the strongest shocks of all. Not only is aggression sometimes caused by factors other than frustration, but verbal provocation seems to be a stronger stimulus for aggression than either task or personal frustration.

By now it should be apparent that the original version of the frustration/aggression hypothesis overstates the case. Frustration does not always lead to aggression, and aggression is not always caused by frustration. Problems with the original theory led Leonard Berkowitz to formulate a revised frustra-

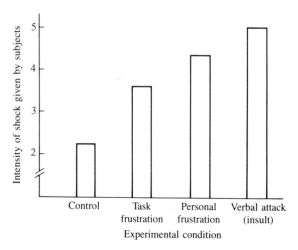

FIGURE 9-1 Average levels of aggression elicited by two kinds of frustration and verbal attack

tion/aggression hypothesis that he believes is better able to predict when frustration is likely to result in aggression.

BERKOWITZ'S REVISION OF THE FRUSTRATION/AGGRESSION HYPOTHESIS

Like Robert Sears, Berkowitz believes that frustration creates only a "readiness for aggressive acts," which we may think of as anger. However, he adds that a variety of other causes, such as *attack* and previously acquired *aggressive habits*, may also heighten a person's readiness to aggress. Finally, Berkowitz argues that an angered person who is "ready to aggress" will not necessarily commit an aggressive response!

> Aggressive responses will not occur, even given [a readiness to aggress], unless there are suitable cues, stimuli associated with the present or previous anger instigators. . . . These cues *evoke aggressive responses* from [a person who] is "primed" to make them. The strength of the aggressive response made to the [eliciting] cue is . . . a function of (1) the aggressive cue value of this stimulus—the strength of the association between the eliciting stimulus and the past or present determinants of aggression—and (2) the degree of aggression readiness [1965, p. 308; italics added].

So Berkowitz's theory makes a rather bold assertion—namely, that aggressive cues must be present before an aggressive act will occur. However, Berkowitz has recently modified his position somewhat to allow for the possibility that an extremely angry person may behave aggressively even when aggressive cues are not present (Berkowitz, 1974). A schematic representation of Berkowitz's theory appears in Figure 9-2.

Notice that Berkowitz's theory anticipates individual differences in aggression: when exposed to aggressive cues, children with well-ingrained aggressive habits should be more inclined to behave aggressively than those whose aggressive habits are not well established. But by far the most provocative of Berkowitz's ideas is the "aggressive cues" hypothesis, which implies that exposure to any object or event previously associated with aggression will serve a cuing function and increase the likelihood of aggressive exchanges among young children. Would toys such as guns, tanks, rubber soldiers, and other symbolic implements of destruction have such an effect?

Apparently so. In one study, Seymour Feshbach (1956) exposed 5- to 8-year-olds to structured play sessions in the classroom that revolved around *aggressive* themes such as pirates and soldiers or *neutral* themes such as circuses, farm activities, and running a store. Then, during periods of free play, an adult observer noted the aggressive interactions among these children and labeled each as *thematic aggression*—action that was appropriate in the context of earlier play, such as challenging an enemy pirate—or *inappropriate* aggression—verbal taunts or physical blows that were clearly outside the context of the previous play session. Not surprisingly, thematic aggression was highest for the children who had played with aggressive toys. However, those children were also involved in a greater number of inappropriate aggressive exchanges than classmates who had played with neutral toys. (See Turner & Goldsmith, 1976, for a similar pattern of results with preschool children.) So it appears that toys that encourage enactment of aggressive themes do increase the likelihood of hostile interactions in children's play groups.

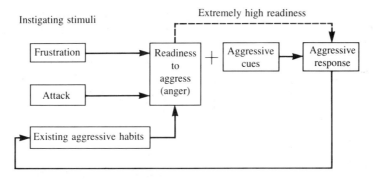

FIGURE 9-2 Berkowitz's revised frustration/aggression hypothesis

In sum, Berkowitz's revised frustration/aggression hypothesis views aggressive behavior as stemming from a combination of internal forces (anger) and external stimuli (aggressive cues). Although this theory may help to explain how aggressive responses are evoked from a person who is angry at the moment, it has little to say about the development of aggressive habits or about how various stimuli become "aggressive cues." Moreover, other theorists have criticized Berkowitz's model on the grounds that many aggressive acts are committed not out of a sense of anger or outrage but merely as a means to nonaggressive ends. And as we will see, the impact of aggressive cues on children's behavior seems to depend more on children's *interpretations* of those stimuli and events (cognitive factors) than on the mere presence of the cues themselves.

BANDURA'S SOCIAL-LEARNING THEORY

Bandura's (1973, 1977) social-learning theory of aggression is noteworthy in several respects. It is the first model to stress cognitive influences on aggression. It treats aggression as a class of social behaviors that are acquired through the same processes as any other type of social behavior. And whereas most theorists concentrate on factors that instigate aggression, Bandura proceeds a step further by explaining how aggressive behaviors are acquired and maintained.

According to Bandura, aggressive responses are acquired in either of two ways. The first and most

important method is *observational learning*—a cognitive process by which children attend to and retain in memory the aggressive acts that they see others commit. A study by Bandura, Ross, and Ross (1963) nicely illustrates the ease with which children can learn aggressive sequences from social models. In this experiment, nursery school children saw a television program in which a boy named Johnny refuses to share his toys with another boy named Rocky. Rocky then attacks Johnny with a baton, lassoes him with a Hula Hoop, shoots darts at his cars, and works him over. At the end of the show, Rocky is departing with Johnny's hobbyhorse under his arm and a sack of Johnny's toys over his shoulder. When the children were asked to evaluate Rocky's behavior, almost all of them disapproved, calling Rocky mean and nasty. Yet, when they were later placed in a similar situation, these children behaved much more aggressively than a control group that had not seen the aggressive television program. It seems clear that the children who had witnessed Rocky's aggressive behavior learned to make similar responses in a similar setting. In fact, one 4-year-old who had been horrified at Rocky's approach actually imitated many of Rocky's methods when she herself was placed in the test situation. After wresting the toys away from their original owner, this little girl turned to the experimenter and asked "Do you have a sack here?"

Children may also acquire aggressive responses (or aggressive habits) through *direct experience*. A child who is reinforced for aggressive behavior will

PHOTO 9-1 Although these young boys seem to be enjoying themselves, toys that encourage the enactment of aggressive themes do increase the likelihood of hostile interactions in children's play groups.

be more likely to resort to aggression in the future. In fact, a study by Ivar Lovaas (1961) shows how reinforcement of one type of aggression can make children more inclined to perform other, seemingly unrelated acts of aggression. Participants in Lovaas's study first played with dolls and were rewarded with trinkets for making either *aggressive, derogatory* statements (for example, "Bad doll"; "Dirty doll"; "This doll should be spanked") or *nonaggressive* statements as they played. At the end of this initial "training" session, each child was told that he or she could play with a crude pinball apparatus or with "striking dolls," an aggressive toy built so that pressing a lever would cause one doll to hit another with a stick. The number of times the child caused one doll to strike the other during a four-minute testing period served as a measure of the child's *nonverbal* aggression.

Lovaas found that he could easily increase the frequency of verbal aggression by simply reinforcing the hostile utterances of children in the aggressive-training group. Of greater interest was the finding that children who had been reinforced for verbal aggression were more likely than those in the nonaggressive-training group to play with the "striking

dolls" toy. The implication is clear: *children who are reinforced for one kind of aggression become more willing to display other (perhaps unrelated) forms of aggression in the future.*

Of course, participants in Lovaas's experiment were aggressing against inanimate objects (dolls). Could these results be replicated in a setting where the child has the opportunity to aggress against another child? The answer is yes. In one experiment, Slaby and Crowley (1977) asked nursery school teachers to reinforce verbal aggression by paying close attention to the hostile utterances of their students and then repeating these utterances in a friendly tone of voice. This treatment continued for one week, and the behavior of each child was carefully recorded. The results were clear. Reinforcement of verbal aggression not only increased the incidence of verbally aggressive statements but also increased the likelihood that a child's verbally aggressive utterance would be followed by a physically aggressive response!

How is aggression maintained? Bandura (1973) discusses a number of factors that are important in the maintenance of aggression. First, aggressive behavior often acquires *instrumental value* by serving as an efficient means to other ends. For example, a child may learn that attack is a quicker method of procuring desirable toys from a hoarding playmate than either negotiating or simply waiting for the hoarder to share.

Some types of aggression are maintained by *social rewards* or *societal approval.* Soldiers are decorated for their gallantry in battle. Football players win adulation for violent, aggressive play. Police officers are often commended for taking whatever measures they choose to break up demonstrations. Indeed, social approval of aggressive responses may often instigate counteraggression from the victims of such tactics, thereby providing even more approval for the use of aggression. For example, a club-swinging policeman who elicits an aggressive response from a Black South African protester is apt to be praised by his White Afrikaaner countrymen, who may view his actions as a necessary strategy for keeping "dangerous" elements of society in check. Thus, if legitimized by social approval, acts that victims consider "brutal" can become a perpetrator's self-defined altruism.

Aggressive responses may also be retained as a means of *self-protection*. The ghetto child who "grows up on the streets" knows that fighting back is often the most effective way to discourage attackers. Field studies of children's aggressive interactions (for example, Patterson, Littman, & Bricker, 1967) aptly demonstrate how aggressive behavior is acquired and maintained for protective purposes. Patterson et al. (1967) found that passive children who were frequently attacked adopted one of two methods of responding. Some children reacted by withdrawing, acquiescing to the aggressor's demands, or crying. These actions tended to reinforce the aggressor and increase the probability that he or she would attack these children again. Other children learned to counterattack, a strategy that was retained when it proved effective at influencing their tormentors to select other targets. An interesting sidelight is that passive children who learned to counterattack were soon initiating attacks of their own on other passive children. Could it be that the same is true of the many boys who receive boxing lessons from fathers eager to teach them to "defend" themselves?

Some people retain their aggressive habits because *they enjoy hurting others*. In the language of Bandura's theory, these individuals "have . . . adopted a *self-reinforcement* system in which aggressive actions are a source of personal pride" (1973, p. 208). A person may learn to enjoy hurting others by observing the satisfaction that extremely violent models derive from inflicting pain or by behaving aggressively and associating the victim's pain with positive consequences, such as the removal of frustration or the approval of one's peers. A passage from Toch (1969) provides an excellent illustration of the self-reinforcement of aggression:

> And he said . . . "F—— you man." And the dude got up and we were both on him, man. And we beat him to a pulp. . . . Once we got going we just wasted the dude. . . . Sent him on down to the hospital. And after that I felt like a king, man. I felt like you know, "I'm the man. You're not going to mess with me." . . . I felt like everybody looking up to me [pp. 91–92].

In sum, aggressive habits often persist because they are (1) instrumental to the satisfaction of nonaggressive goals, (2) socially sanctioned, (3) useful as a means of protection, or (4) intrinsically rewarding for the aggressor.

Internal states and aggressive behavior. Most theories of aggression assume that people are "driven" to aggress by internal forces such as instincts, acquired motives, frustrations, or anger. Bandura takes issue with all these theories by arguing that internal states such as frustration or anger may facilitate aggression but *are not necessary for its occurrence*.

Indeed, examples of nonangry or nonfrustrative aggression occur every day. People routinely swat cockroaches, not because these insects have angered or frustrated them (or because they have acquired a drive to kill cockroaches), but because they have learned to exterminate pests. Children snatch toys from one another for purely instrumental reasons. And one need not posit the existence of internal instigators to explain why an executioner destroys his victims: he does so to earn a paycheck.

According to Bandura, the role of internal arousal in human aggression is simply to increase the probability that a person will commit an aggressive response in situations where aggressive cues are present. Moreover, Bandura claims that *any* form of arousal can energize aggressive behavior, as long as the cues available in the situation cause the individual to *interpret* that arousal as frustration or anger. Several experiments conducted with adults support this line of reasoning: compared with subjects who are not aroused, people who have experienced arousal stemming from sources completely unrelated to aggression (for example, exercise, noise, rock music, and even erotica) are likely to reinterpret this arousal as anger and to display heightened aggression when exposed to insults or other provocations (Bryant & Zillmann, 1979; Rule, Ferguson, & Nesdale, 1980).

Controlling aggression. Bandura is optimistic about the possibility of reducing and controlling human aggression. He views aggressive habits as learned responses that can be modified if we work diligently at eliminating the conditions that maintain them. He proposes that people can be taught to respond nonaggressively to "negative" emotional states such as anger or frustration (Davitz's study supports this assertion). Of course, he realizes that the changes will not come easily and will require a concentrated effort on the part of society as a whole. And despite the fact that an undertaking of this magnitude has never been tried by any country, many of Bandura's strategies for reducing aggression have been tried and have proved effective with smaller groups. We will discuss some of these procedures later in the chapter.

DODGE'S SOCIAL INFORMATION-PROCESSING THEORY

Imagine that you are an 8-year-old carrying a heavy load when a classmate seated on a bench extends his leg into your path, tripping you and causing you to drop your cargo. As you fall to the sidewalk, you really have very little information about why this incident may have occurred, although you are already aroused. So how would you respond?

Social information-processing theorists believe that a person's reactions to frustration, anger, or an apparent provocation depend not so much on the social cues present in a situation as on the ways in which the person processes and interprets this information. Perhaps the best-known social-cognitive theory of aggression is that of Kenneth Dodge and his associates (Dodge, 1981, 1986; Dodge & Frame, 1982). Dodge assumes that children enter each social situation with a data base of past experiences (that is, a *memory store*) and a *goal* of some sort (for example, making friends, staying out of trouble, having fun, or even simply passing by without stopping to interact). Suddenly an event occurs that requires explanation (such as tripping over someone's leg). Dodge proposes that the child's response to this situation and the social cues it provides will depend on the outcomes of five cognitive "steps" or processes, which are illustrated in Figure 9-3.

The first step is a *decoding* process in which the child gathers information about the event from the environment. When tripped by a classmate, for ex-

ample, the victim searches for cues. Is there an expression of concern on the classmate's face? Does the classmate look away? Is he laughing? According to Dodge, the child's proficiency at gathering relevant information will affect his responses to such events.

Next comes the *interpretive* phase. Having gathered and focused on situational cues, the child will integrate them with information about similar events from the past, consider the goals that he was pursuing in this situation, and try to decide whether the act in question was accidental or intentional. Presumably, the information he has gathered, as well as his past interpretations of similar events, will influence his rendition of the present event.

Once the child has interpreted the situation, the next step is a *response search* process in which he considers alternative courses of action that he might pursue. Then comes the *response decision* phase: the child weighs the advantages and disadvantages of various response options and selects one that is viewed as "best" for this situation. Last comes the *encoding* phase, in which the child enacts his chosen response. However, Dodge points out that children may lack the ability to encode various response options. Thus, a child may decide to avoid further hostilities by merely admonishing an aggressor. But if he hasn't the verbal skills to do so without threatening his adversary, he may nevertheless end up in a fight.

Social information-processing theory clearly anticipates individual differences in aggression because children vary in both their past experiences (or memory stores) and their information-processing skills. According to Dodge (1981, 1986), highly aggressive children may be aggressive because they carry in memory an expectancy that "peers are hostile to me," which causes them to search for social cues compatible with that expectancy. Should they then experience truly ambiguous harmdoing, they may overattribute hostile intent to the harmdoer, which predisposes them to behave aggressively. The child's aggressive reaction may then trigger counteraggression from the harmdoing peer, which reinforces the aggressive child's impression that peers are hostile, thus starting the vicious cycle all over again (see Figure 9-4).

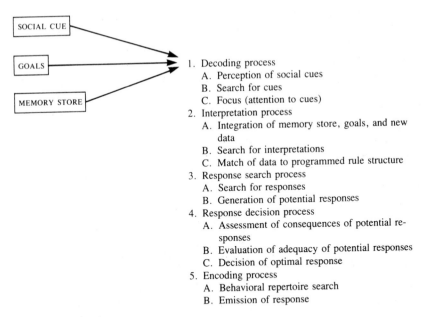

1. Decoding process
   A. Perception of social cues
   B. Search for cues
   C. Focus (attention to cues)
2. Interpretation process
   A. Integration of memory store, goals, and new data
   B. Search for interpretations
   C. Match of data to programmed rule structure
3. Response search process
   A. Search for responses
   B. Generation of potential responses
4. Response decision process
   A. Assessment of consequences of potential responses
   B. Evaluation of adequacy of potential responses
   C. Decision of optimal response
5. Encoding process
   A. Behavioral repertoire search
   B. Emission of response

FIGURE 9-3 A social information-processing model of aggression

Tests of the theory. Do aggressive youngsters distort ambiguous information about harmdoing? Are they more likely than nonaggressive children to interpret such information as implying a hostile intent? To test these hypotheses, Dodge (1980) had highly aggressive and nonaggressive boys from the second, fourth, and sixth grades each work on a jigsaw puzzle in one room while a peer worked on a similar puzzle in a second room. During a break when the boys had switched rooms to check on each other's progress, the subject heard a voice on the intercom. The voice (ostensibly that of the peer who was examining the subject's puzzle) then expressed either a *hostile* intent ("Gee, he's got a lot done—I'll mess it up"), a *benign* intent ("I'll help him—Oh, no, I didn't mean to drop it"), or an *ambiguous* intent ("Gee, he's got a lot done") just before a loud crash (presumably the subject's puzzle being scattered). How did the subjects respond? Dodge found that both aggressive and nonaggressive boys reacted much more aggressively (as measured by disassembling the harmdoer's puzzle or by verbal hostility) to a hostile intent than to a benign intent. Thus, aggressive boys did not distort social cues when the harmdoer's inten-

tions were obvious. But when the peer's intent was ambiguous, cue distortion was apparent: aggressive boys often retaliated as if the peer had acted with a hostile intent, whereas nonaggressive boys typically did nothing or said something positive, as if the peer's intentions were honorable ones.

In a second study measuring children's *verbal* responses to hypothetical episodes, Dodge (1980) found that aggressive and nonaggressive boys do differ in their attributions about "ambiguous" harmdoing. As expected, aggressive boys attributed hostile intentions to the harmdoer much more often than nonaggressive boys did—a pattern that has now been replicated with socially deviant children of both sexes (Dodge, Murphy, & Buchsbaum, 1984).

As it turns out, aggressive youngsters may have good reasons for attributing hostile intentions to their peers; not only do aggressive children provoke a large number of fights, but they are also more likely than nonaggressive children to become targets of aggression. In fact, *nonaggressive* children who are harmed under ambiguous circumstances are much more likely to retaliate *if the harmdoer has a reputation as an aggressive child* (Dodge & Frame, 1982).

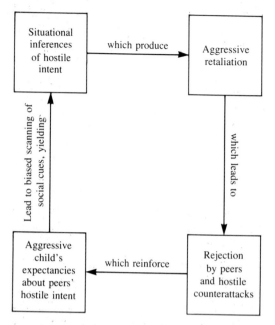

FIGURE 9-4 A social-cognitive model of the aggressive child's social information-processing biases and their behavioral consequences

So by virtue of their own hostile inclinations, highly aggressive children ensure that they will often be attacked by their peers.

A preliminary evaluation. Taken together, the studies we have reviewed provide impressive support for a social-cognitive theory of aggression. As predicted by the model, we've seen that children's behavioral responses to provocations depend more on their own *perceptions* of the harmdoer's intent than on the actual intentions portrayed by the harmdoer. Stated another way, the social cues present in a situation are not what determines whether a child will commit an aggressive response. What matters is how these cues are processed and interpreted.

The social information-processing approach is of very recent origin, and as is often true of new theories, it leaves many questions unanswered. For example, the model aptly describes variations in the information-processing skills of children already known to be aggressive or nonaggressive, but it does not as yet address the issues of how these children came to be aggressive or nonaggressive or why they

have different information-processing styles in the first place. Also unanswered are questions about how various emotional reactions (for example, anger) and personality characteristics (for example, impatience, frustration tolerance) might influence children's processing and interpretation of social cues in any given situation. In sum, the social-cognitive approach is an exciting new perspective that should continue to generate many insights about children's aggressive behavior. But as Parke and Slaby (1983) note, "The extent to which cognitive models of aggression [are able to] incorporate other dimensions such as affect [or emotional arousal] will determine their ultimate usefulness; it is unlikely that simple cognitive models alone will suffice" (p. 573).

DEVELOPMENTAL TRENDS IN AGGRESSION

Although children have served as subjects in many studies of aggression, very few of these studies are concerned with developmental issues. In this portion of the chapter we will examine what is known about the origins and changing character of children's aggressive behavior.

ORIGINS OF AGGRESSION

Although infants do get angry and may occasionally strike people, it is difficult to think of these actions as having an aggressive intent. Piaget (1952) describes an incident in which he frustrated 7-month-old Laurent by placing his hand in front of an interesting object that Laurent was trying to reach. The boy then smacked Piaget's hand as if to knock it out of the way. Although this looks very much like an example of instrumental aggression, it is unlikely that Laurent intended to frighten or harm his father. Instead, he seems to have been treating his father's hand as a simple obstruction that had to be removed. Even 12- to 15-month-olds will rarely look at each other as they struggle over a toy; their attention is usually riveted on the toy itself, and their goal seems to be to gain possession of the object rather than to intimidate or harm their adversary (Bronson, 1975).

Near the end of the second year, things begin to change. Dale Hay and Hildy Ross (1982) observed pairs of 20–23-month-olds at play, noting all instances of conflict. Unlike their younger counterparts, these toddlers began most of their tussles by communicating with an opponent (for example, "Mine," "No! Kenny have phone") rather than treating him or her as an inanimate obstacle. As these disputes wore on, they occasionally escalated into incidents of forcible contact—actions that might be interpreted as attempts to intimidate or to force an adversary to withdraw. Although sociable reactions such as sharing were actually more common than these "shows of force," it appears as if the seeds of instrumental aggression may have already been sown by the age of 20–23 months.

AGE-RELATED CHANGES IN THE NATURE OF AGGRESSION

It is very difficult to determine whether children become any more or less aggressive with the passage of time, because the aggressive acts of a 2-year-old are not directly comparable to those of an 8-year-old or an adolescent. As a result, researchers have studied age-related changes in both the *form* of aggressive behavior and the situations that elicit these responses.

Much of what we know about the aggressive behavior of preschool children comes from two studies. The first is a project conducted by Florence Goodenough (1931), who asked mothers of 2- to 5-year-olds to keep diaries recording each angry outburst displayed by their children, its apparent cause, and its consequences. The second is an observational study by Willard Hartup (1974), who analyzed the causes and consequences of aggressive acts that occurred over a five-week period in groups of children aged 4 to 6 and 6 to 7. These studies indicate the following:

1. Unfocused temper tantrums diminish during the preschool period and are uncommon after age 4. However, the total amount of aggression that children display increases over the preschool period, *peaking at about age 4.*
2. The tendency to retaliate in response to attack or frustration increases dramatically for children over age 3.

3. *The primary instigators of aggression vary with the age of the child.* At age 2–3, children are most often aggressive after parents have thwarted or angered them by exerting authority; older children are much more likely to aggress after conflicts with siblings or peers.
4. The *form* of aggression also changes over time. Children aged 2 or 3 are likely to hit or kick an adversary. Most of the squabbles among youngsters of this age concern toys and other possessions, so that their aggression is usually *instrumental* in character. Older nursery-schoolers (and young grade school children) show less and less physical aggression as they choose instead to tease, taunt, tattle, and call their victims uncomplimentary names. Although older children continue to fight over objects, an increasing percentage of their aggressive outbursts are *hostile* in character—designed primarily to harm another person.

Why are aggressive exchanges less common among 5-year-olds than 3- and 4-year-olds? One reason may be that parents and teachers are actively preparing older nursery-schoolers for kindergarten by refusing to tolerate aggressive acts and encouraging alternative responses such as cooperation and sharing (Emmerich, 1966). Of course, older children may have also learned from their own experiences that negotiation can be a relatively painless and efficient method of achieving the same objectives that they used to attempt through a show of force.

Although the overall incidence of aggression declines with age, hostile aggression shows a slight increase. Hartup (1974) attributes this finding to the fact that older children (particularly grade school children) are acquiring the social-cognitive skills that enable them to infer the intentions of other people and to retaliate when they believe that someone means to hurt them. "To the extent that hostile aggression is dependent upon attributions about [the aggressive *intent* of another person], this type of aggression should be less evident in younger than older children" (p. 338).

Research on children's perceptions of aggressive intent is consistent with Hartup's point of view. Although preschoolers may appropriately infer an

PHOTO 9-2   The squabbles of young children usually center around toys, candy, or other treasured resources and qualify as acts of instrumental aggression.

PHOTO 9-3   As children mature, an increasing percentage of their aggressive acts qualify as examples of hostile aggression.

actor's aggressive intentions if the relevant cues are clear and are made obvious to them, they are nowhere near as proficient at interpreting such information as older children or adults are (Nelson-LeGall, 1985). By kindergarten, children recognize that aggression aimed at harming someone is "naughtier" than that intended to teach the victim a lesson (Rule, Nesdale, & McAra, 1974). However, kindergartners are still not terribly proficient at inferring a harmdoer's hostile intent, compared with older grade school children. In one study (Dodge et al., 1984), kindergartners, second-graders, and fourth-graders were asked to judge the intentions of a child who had destroyed a peer's tower of blocks accidentally or while portraying either a hostile, a benign, or a prosocial intent. The results were clear: kindergartners correctly discriminated the actor's true intentions less than half the time (42%). Second-graders were more accurate (57% correct) but not nearly as skilled at detecting intentional cues as the fourth-graders (72% correct).

Are children's interpretations of an actor's intent the only factor that determines their *responses* to harmdoing? Probably not. It is likely that younger children will react aggressively to many provocations, even accidental ones, if they are incapable of inhibiting their anger or if they lack the skills to enact

a nonaggressive response. Consider a study by Shantz and Voydanoff (1973) in which 7-, 9-, and 12-year-old boys were asked how they would respond to a number of situations in which they had been harmed (either physically or verbally) by another child. Some of these incidents were described so as to suggest that they might have been accidental, whereas others appeared to be intentional. Seven-year-olds, who are generally proficient at discriminating accidents from blatantly intentional harmdoing, favored a highly aggressive form of retaliation regardless of whether the harm done to them was accidental or intentional. However, 9- and 12-year-olds responded much more aggressively to intentional attacks than to accidents. Although these findings do not establish that the "indiscriminate" aggression of the 7-year-olds stemmed from their inability to control their emotions or to encode nonaggressive responses, these are intriguing possibilities nevertheless—hypotheses that are certainly worthy of future research.

IS AGGRESSION A STABLE ATTRIBUTE?

We've seen that the kinds of aggression that children display will change over time. But what about aggressive dispositions? Do aggressive preschoolers remain highly aggressive throughout the grade school years, during adolescence, and as young adults?

Apparently aggression is a reasonably stable attribute from the preschool period through early adolescence. Not only are highly aggressive 3-year-olds likely to become aggressive 5-year-olds (Emmerich, 1966), but the amount of physical and verbal aggression that a child displays at ages 6 to 10 is a fairly good predictor of his or her tendency to threaten, insult, tease, and compete with peers at ages 10 to 14 (Kagan & Moss, 1962; Olweus, 1982).

On the basis of one longitudinal study of fewer than 100 individuals (Kagan & Moss, 1962), it has long been assumed that the stability of aggression from childhood to adulthood is greater for males than for females. However, later research has questioned this assertion. Rowell Huesmann and his associates (Huesmann, Eron, Lefkowitz, & Walder, 1984) tracked one sample of 600 subjects for 22 years and found, *for both males and females*, that childhood measures of aggression at age 8 were solid predictors of adult aggression at age 30 (as indexed by criminal behavior, spouse abuse, and self-reported physical aggression). Moreover, David Stevens and Carroll Truss (1985) used a personality inventory to measure aggression among two cohorts of 18–20-year-old college students and then followed up on these individuals at age 30 or age 40. As shown in Table 9-1, self-reported aggression was moderately stable for both men and women over a 12-year period for one cohort and a 20-year period for the other.

Of course, these findings reflect group trends and in no way imply that a highly aggressive individual

can't become relatively nonaggressive over time, and vice versa. However, we should not be surprised to find that aggression is a reasonably stable attribute for many children. Shortly we will see how some home settings can serve as early "training grounds" for the development of aggressive habits. And when children who have learned to react aggressively to conflicts at home later face similar problems at school, they may try their forceful tactics on classmates, thereby inviting counterattacks, which lead the child to assume that peers are hostile toward her. Before long, the child finds herself in the vicious cycle portrayed earlier in Figure 9-4—a pattern that seems likely to perpetuate her aggressive inclinations.

Are there also biological predispositions toward aggression that could help to explain its stability? Philippe Rushton and his associates (Rushton, Fulker, Neale, Nias, & Eysenck, 1986) think so. In their study, 296 pairs of identical twins and 277 pairs of fraternal twins completed a self-report measure of hostility and aggression. Even though these twins were adults, most of whom had presumably lived apart from their cotwins for many years, identical twin pairs were much more alike in self-reported aggression ($r = .40$) than pairs of fraternal twins ($r = .04$). Clearly some caution is warranted in interpreting these results, for the data are simply verbal reports that may or may not accurately reflect the twins' actual aggressive behaviors. Nevertheless, these findings imply that our aggressive inclinations may well be influenced to some extent by our genes.

How might one's genotype contribute to aggression and, specifically, to the stability of aggression over time? Perhaps in many ways. For example,

TABLE 9-1 Longitudinal Stability of Aggression from the College Years to Age 30 and Age 40

	Stability coefficient (correlation between college and adult aggression scores)	
Sex of subjects	30-year-olds	40-year-olds
Male	.44	.61
Female	.44	.51

Note: The 30-year-old and the 40-year-old samples were different people from different generations. The younger subjects' exposure to a number of significant events such as the Vietnam era and the turbulence of the late 1960s may help to explain why their aggression scores are slightly less stable than those of the 40-year-olds.

active and temperamentally difficult youngsters may regularly *elicit* negative reactions from other people, which, in turn, may engender hostility and aggression. And recall the concept of *active genotype/environment correlations* (discussed in Chapter 2)—that individuals create or select environmental niches that best suit their genotypes. Perhaps children who are genetically predisposed to be aggressive and who have begun to develop some aggressive habits will choose to associate with people like themselves (that is, aggressive peers). If so, they will have created an environment for themselves that could easily perpetuate their aggressive tendencies (Rushton et al., 1986).

SEX DIFFERENCES IN AGGRESSION

Although aggression appears to be a reasonably stable attribute for members of each sex, it turns out that males are more aggressive than females. Data from more than 100 studies conducted in countries all over the world reveal that boys and men are not only more physically aggressive than girls and women but more verbally aggressive as well (Maccoby & Jacklin, 1974, 1980; Tieger, 1980). Moreover, these sex differences in aggression are detectable by age 2 to 2½, when children first begin to behave in ways that fit our definitions of aggression, and they are more apparent in naturalistic-observational (that is, real-world) contexts than in contrived laboratory settings (Hyde, 1984; Maccoby & Jacklin, 1980).[3]

The probability of becoming a *target* of aggression also depends on one's gender. Aggressive conflicts occur far more often in boy/boy than in boy/girl or girl/girl dyads (Barrett, 1979; Smith & Green, 1974). And even though boys can be quite *verbally* abusive toward girls who have provoked them, it appears that both males and (to a lesser extent) females will reduce the intensity of their *physical* attacks on a harmdoer if that person is female (Barrett, 1979; Hoving, Wallace, & LaForme, 1976; Taylor & Epstein, 1967). Perhaps the simplest explanation for these findings is that children of both sexes are taught at an early age that "you don't hit little girls." However, it is also possible that signs of

pain and suffering are somehow more disturbing and more likely to elicit empathic concern if emitted by a female. Both hypotheses are worthy of future research.

Why do males and females differ in aggression? Let's consider three complementary points of view.

The biological viewpoint. According to Maccoby and Jacklin (1974, 1980), there are at least four reasons to suspect that biological factors contribute heavily to sex differences in aggression. First, males are more aggressive than females in almost every society that has been studied. Second, sex differences in aggression appear so early (about age 2) that it is difficult to attribute them solely to social learning or to parental child-rearing practices. Third, males tend to be the more aggressive gender among our closest phylogenetic relatives—species such as baboons and chimpanzees. Finally, there is evidence to suggest a link, in both animals and humans, between male hormones such as testosterone and aggressive behavior.[4] Although these observations imply that biological factors contribute in important ways to sex differences in aggression, they should *not* be interpreted to mean that social influences are unimportant.

The social viewpoint. Proponents of a social viewpoint suggest many ways that parents and other social agents contribute to sex differences in aggression. First, adults expect males to be more active and assertive than females. Even in the hospital nursery, parents of newborns are apt to call sons "big guy" or "tiger" while referring to daughters as "sugar" or "sweetie" (see MacFarlane, 1977). Parents engage in more physically active, rough-and-tumble play with sons than with daughters throughout infancy (Power & Parke, 1982), the preschool period (MacDonald & Parke, 1984), and the elementary school years (Tauber, 1979). The toys that parents buy for their children are revealing in themselves. Boys in North American culture receive ray guns, tanks, missile launchers, and other symbolic implements of destruction that encourage the enactment of aggressive themes, whereas girls are given dolls, doll houses, and dish sets to promote their adoption of a nurturant, caregiving role. Moreover, fathers are more likely to discourage fighting by their daughters than their sons (Block, 1978). And while few parents actively encourage sons to be physically aggressive (except perhaps to defend themselves), they may indirectly promote such behavior by adopting a "boys will be boys" attitude and downplaying the significance of scuffles among males (recall the results of Box 9-1). There are many more observations that could be cited here (see Parke & Slaby, 1983), but the point should be obvious—sex differences in aggression depend to no small extent on the sex-typing process and on sex differences in social learning.

The interactive viewpoint. Finally, proponents of an interactive viewpoint contend that sex-linked constitutional factors (biology) interact with social-environmental influences to promote sex differences in aggression. Consider some of the constitutional differences between infant males and females. Female infants tend to mature faster, to talk sooner, and to be more sensitive to pain than male infants, whereas males tend to be larger and more muscular, to sleep less, to cry more, and to be somewhat more active, more irritable, and harder to comfort than female infants (Bell, Weller, & Waldrip, 1971; Hutt, 1972; Maccoby, 1980; Moss, 1967). Clearly these (and other) sex-linked constitutional differences could have *direct* effects on a child's behavior; but a more likely possibility is that they have *indirect*, or interactive, effects by influencing the behavior of the child's companions (Tieger, 1980). For example, parents may find that they can play more vigorously with an active, muscular son who may be somewhat less sensitive to pain than with a docile, less muscular daughter who seems to enjoy these activities less. Or perhaps they are apt to become more impatient with irritable and demanding sons who are difficult to quiet or to comfort. In the first case, parents would be encouraging boys to partake in the kinds of fast-paced, vigorous activities from which aggressive outbursts often emerge. In the second case, parents' greater impatience or irritability with sons than with daughters could push males in the direction of becoming quicker to anger and/or somewhat more hostile or resentful toward other people. So it is unlikely that sex differences in aggression (or in any other

form of social behavior) are automatic or "biologically programmed." Instead it seems as if a child's biological predispositions are likely to affect the *behavior* of caregivers and other close companions, which, in turn, will elicit certain responses from the child and influence the activities and interests that the child is likely to display. The implication of this interactive model is that biological factors and social influences are complexly intertwined and that both nature and nurture are important contributors to sex differences in aggression.

SOCIAL INFLUENCES ON AGGRESSION

We have seen that genotype and other biological factors associated with gender can definitely affect one's propensity for aggressive behavior. However, Albert Bandura, Seymour Feshbach, and many other aggression theorists believe that a person's *absolute* level of aggression—that is, how aggressive an individual is likely to become—will depend very critically on social influences and the social environment in which he or she is raised. Thus, we will now focus on important social contributors to children's aggressive behavior.

CULTURAL AND SUBCULTURAL INFLUENCES

We have noted that some societies are more aggressive than others. The Arapesh of New Guinea and the Pygmies of central Africa are examples of passive, nonaggressive social orders. In marked contrast to these groups is the Ik tribe of Uganda, whose members live in small bands and will steal from, deceive, and even kill one another to ensure their own survival (Turnbull, 1972). Another aggressive society is the Mundugumor of New Guinea, who teach their children to be independent, combative, and emotionally unresponsive to the needs of others (Mead, 1935). These are values that serve the Mundugumor well, for during some periods of their history, the Mundugumor were cannibals who routinely killed human beings as prey and considered almost anyone other than close kinfolk to be fair game. The United States is also an aggressive society. On a percentage basis, the incidence of rape, assault, robbery, and homicide is higher in the United States than in any other stable democracy (National Commission on the Causes and Prevention of Violence, 1969).

Studies conducted in the United States and in England also point to social-class differences in aggression: children and adolescents from the lower socioeconomic strata (particularly males) exhibit more aggressive behavior and higher levels of delinquency than those from the middle class (see Feshbach, 1970, for a review). Although parents from the lower socioeconomic strata are no more permissive of aggression than their middle-class counterparts, they do tend to rely more on physical punishment as a means of discipline. This latter finding may help to explain the heightened aggression of lower-class children, for as Sears, Maccoby, and Levin (1957) have noted, "Lower-class parents, who frequently make use of physical punishment, are providing a living example of the use of aggression at the very moment they are trying to teach the child not to be aggressive" (p. 266).

Economic frustrations faced by members of the lower class may also contribute to antisocial conduct. In one study, it was found that crimes of larceny (minor theft) increased dramatically among poorer members of society soon after the introduction of television to their communities (Hennigan et al., 1982). The authors explained this finding by arguing that the poor felt a sense of frustration or "relative deprivation" after viewing mostly affluent people on television; consequently they turned to larceny to obtain some of the good things in life that they seemed to be lacking.

In sum, a person's tendencies toward aggression and antisocial conduct will depend, in part, on the extent to which the culture (or subculture) encourages and condones such behavior. Yet not all people in pacifistic societies are kind, cooperative, and helpful, nor are all members of aggressive societies prone to violence. One reason that there are dramatic individual differences in aggression within any social order is that individual children are raised in very

different families. In our next section, we will see how the home setting can sometimes serve as a breeding ground for hostile, antisocial conduct.

FAMILIAL INFLUENCES

How might one's family and the family setting contribute to violent and aggressive behavior? In the pages that follow, we will consider two interrelated avenues of influence: (1) the effects of particular child-rearing practices and (2) the more global impact of the family environment on children's aggressive inclinations.

Parental Child-Rearing Practices and Children's Aggressive Behavior

When investigators began to study the development of aggression, they operated under the assumption that parents' attitudes and child-rearing strategies play a major role in shaping children's aggressive behavior. Clearly, there is some truth to this assumption. Some of the most reliable findings in the child-rearing literature are that *cold* and *rejecting* parents who apply *power-assertive* discipline[5] (particularly physical punishment) in an *erratic* fashion and often *permit* their child to express aggressive impulses are likely to raise hostile, aggressive children (Eron, 1982; Olweus, 1980; Parke & Slaby, 1983). Surely these findings make good sense. Cold and rejecting parents are frustrating their children's emotional needs and modeling a lack of concern for others by virtue of their aloofness. By ignoring many of the child's aggressive outbursts, the permissive parent is legitimizing combative activities and failing to provide many opportunities for the child to control his or her aggressive urges. And when aggression escalates to the point where a permissive parent steps in and spanks the child, the results may be counterproductive for two reasons. First, the parent is now punishing a class of behavior that he or she has previously allowed to go unpunished, and both laboratory studies (Katz, 1971) and field research (Martin, 1975) suggest that behavior that is punished in an erratic, inconsistent fashion becomes extremely difficult to eliminate. This is especially true if the child's parents are themselves inconsistent in their treatment of aggression (that is, one parent punishes it while the other ignores or occasionally even encourages such behavior; see Parke & Slaby, 1983). Indeed, punishment that is mixed with an occasional reward may *increase* children's aggression: the child may feel that if I continue to aggress, it will eventually pay off! The second reason that forceful, power-assertive discipline may backfire is that the adult is serving as a model for the very behavior (aggression) that he or she is trying to suppress. So it is hardly surprising to find that parents who rely on physical punishment to discipline aggression have children who are highly aggressive outside the home setting in which the punishment normally occurs (Eron, 1982; Sears et al., 1957). Children who learn that they will be hit when they displease their parents will probably direct the same kind of response toward playmates who displease them.

Which of these child-rearing variables contributes most to children's aggressive behavior? A study by Olweus (1980) provides some clues. Olweus interviewed the parents of 13- to 16-year-old Swedish boys to determine what child-rearing practices they had used when raising their sons. Information about the boys' temperamental characteristics during childhood was also gathered. Finally, the aggressiveness of each boy in the sample was measured by ratings from his classmates. Four factors predicted children's aggression. The best predictor was the mother's permissiveness toward aggression, followed (in order of their importance as predictors) by the mother's cold and rejecting attitude toward her son, the boy's active, impetuous temperament, and the mother's and the father's use of power-assertive discipline.

Can the child be influencing the parent?

Although parental attitudes and child-rearing techniques may contribute to children's aggression, Olweus's findings reveal that the chain of influence also flows in the opposite direction, from child to parent. According to Olweus (1980), it is hardly an accident that a boy's temperament predicts his later aggressiveness, for the child's temperamental characteristics surely influence parental reactions to

PHOTO 9-4 Children who are hit when they displease others are likely to hit others when they displease them.

aggression. Olweus points out that "a boy with an active and impetuous temperament may . . . exhaust his mother, resulting in her becoming more permissive of aggression, which in turn may be conducive to a higher level of aggression in the boy" (p. 658). And should the child really anger his mother so that she simply cannot ignore his conduct, she may express her negative feelings openly or resort to power-assertive discipline as an expedient method of altering his behavior. The implication, then, is that children have a hand in creating the very environments that will influence their aggressive inclinations.

Parents as managers.

Another way that parents may indirectly influence their children's aggression is through their management and monitoring of the child's activities. For example, do the parents exert any control over the child's choice of friends? Do they monitor their child's activities and are they aware of the child's whereabouts?

Gerald Patterson and his associates (Patterson & Stouthamer-Loeber, 1984; Patterson, Stouthamer-Loeber, & Loeber, 1982) consistently find that *lack* of parental monitoring is associated with aggressive or delinquent adolescent behaviors such as fighting with peers, sassing teachers, destruction of property, and general rule breaking outside the home. According to Patterson and Stouthamer-Loeber (1984), "Parents of delinquents are indifferent trackers of their sons' whereabouts, the kinds of companions they keep, and the type of activities in which they engage. Perhaps this [lack of monitoring] constitutes an operational definition for what is meant by "the unattached parent'" (p. 1305).

However, not all parents who fail to monitor their children can be described as uncaring or unconcerned. Sanford Dornbusch and his associates (Dornbusch et al., 1985) have recently noted that a parent's ability to influence children depends in part on the composition of the family. Specifically, Dornbusch et al. found that the heads of mother-only households have a particularly difficult time managing the activities of adolescent sons and daughters without the support of a spouse or some other adult in the home. And given the association between lack of parental monitoring and deviant adolescent behavior in their own (and other) studies, Dornbusch et al. concluded that "the raising of adolescents is not a task that can easily be borne by a mother alone" (p. 340).

In sum, it appears that parental awareness of and control over a child's activities may be just as important in determining the child's aggressive inclinations as the particular child-rearing practices that parents use. Moreover, the finding that the structure of the family affects parental control suggests another interesting conclusion: to understand how aggression develops within the home setting, one must think of the family as a *social system* in which interactions among *all* family members (or the lack thereof) will affect the child's developmental outcomes. We will see just how true this conclusion is in the next several paragraphs.

The Home as a Breeding Ground for Aggression

There is now ample evidence that the emotional climate of the home can and often does influence children's behavior. For example, children from strife-ridden homes in which the parents often fight tend to display emotional difficulties and a variety of con-

duct problems, including aggression (Johnson & Lobitz, 1974; Porter & O'Leary, 1980). Proceeding from these correlational data, Mark Cummings and his associates (Cummings, Iannotti, & Zahn-Waxler, 1985) designed an interesting experiment to determine whether exposure to adult conflict would upset children and *cause* them to become more aggressively inclined. Two-year-olds seated together in a play area watched both angry and highly affectionate interactions between two adults in an adjacent room. The children's emotional reactions to these exchanges were recorded, as were their tendencies to fight or otherwise aggress against one another. The results were clear. Angry exchanges among adults had a much stronger effect on the children than affectionate ones. These angry interactions not only upset the toddlers but also increased their willingness to fight with each other as well (particularly for boys). Often these altercations were rather intense, and they seemed to be more closely related to the children's emotional distress than to any tendency to imitate the angry adults. Moreover, negative reactions to angry adult exchanges were even greater one month later when the children were exposed to a second such episode. So the results of this tightly controlled experiment provide good reason for believing that regular exposure to parental strife at home can place children on edge emotionally and thereby increase their likelihood of having hostile, aggressive interactions with siblings or peers.

We might also note that parents who rely on physical aggression to settle their own disputes tend to use similar kinds of power assertion on their children—often to the point of being abusive. So perhaps we should not be surprised to learn that physically abused children are quick to resort to the same physically coercive tactics as a means of resolving conflicts with both siblings (Steinmetz, 1977) and peers (Hoffman-Plotkin & Twentyman, 1984).

Families as Social Systems

Gerald Patterson (1981, 1982) has observed patterns of interaction among children and their parents in families that have at least one highly aggressive child. The aggressive children in Patterson's sample fought a lot at home and at school and were generally unruly and defiant. These families were then compared with other families of the same size and socioeconomic status that had no problem children.

Patterson found that his problem children were growing up in very atypical family environments. Unlike most homes, in which people frequently express approval and affection, the highly aggressive problem child usually lives in a setting in which family members are constantly struggling with each other: they are reluctant to initiate conversations, and when they do talk, they tend to needle, threaten, or otherwise irritate other family members rather than accentuating the positive. Patterson called these settings *coercive home environments* because a high percentage of interactions centered on one family member's attempts to force another to stop irritating him or her. He also noted that *negative reinforcement* was important in maintaining these coercive interactions: when one family member is making life unpleasant for another, the second will learn to whine, yell, scream, tease, or hit because these actions often force the antagonist to stop (and thus are reinforced). Consider the following sequence of events, which may be fairly typical in a coercive home environment:

1. A girl teases her older brother, who makes her stop teasing by yelling at her (yelling is negatively reinforced).
2. A few minutes later, the girl calls her brother a nasty name. The boy then chases and hits her.
3. The girl stops calling him names (which negatively reinforces hitting). She then whimpers and hits him back, and he withdraws (negatively reinforcing her hits). The boy then approaches and hits his sister again, and the conflict escalates.
4. At this point the mother intervenes. However, her children are too emotionally disrupted to listen to reason, so she finds herself applying punitive and coercive tactics to make them stop fighting.
5. The fighting stops (thus reinforcing the mother for using punitive methods). However, the children now begin to whine, cry, or yell at the mother. These countercoercive techniques are then rein-

forced if the mother backs off and accepts peace at any price. Unfortunately, backing off is only a temporary solution. The next time the children antagonize each other and become involved in an unbearable conflict, the mother is likely to use even more coercion to get them to stop. The children once again apply their own methods of countercoercion to induce her to "lay off," and the family atmosphere becomes increasingly unpleasant for everyone.

Patterson finds that mothers of problem children rarely use social reinforcement or social approval as a means of behavior control, choosing instead to rely almost exclusively on coercive tactics. And ironically, children who live in these highly coercive family settings eventually become resistant to punishment: not only have these youngsters learned to fight coercion with countercoercion, they often defy the parent and may *repeat the very act she is trying to suppress.* Why? Because this is one of the few ways that the child can be successful at commanding the attention of an adult who rarely offers praise or shows any signs of affection. No wonder Patterson calls these children "out of control"! By contrast, children from noncoercive families are apt to receive much more positive attention from siblings and parents, so that they don't have to irritate other family members to be noticed. Moreover, parents from noncoercive families are much more successful when they punish a child's undesirable behavior because they stand firm and will not "cave in" to countercoercion (Patterson, 1976).

So we see that the flow of influence in the family setting is multidirectional: coercive interactions between parents, parents and their children, and the children themselves will affect the behavior of all family members and may contribute to the development of a hostile family environment—a true breeding ground for aggression. Unfortunately, these problem families may never break out of this destructive pattern of attacking and counterattacking one another unless they receive help. In Box 9-2 we will look at one particularly effective approach to this problem—a method that necessarily focuses on the

BOX 9-2   *HELPING CHILDREN (AND PARENTS) WHO ARE "OUT OF CONTROL"*

How does one treat a problem child who is hostile, defiant, and "out of control"? Rather than focusing on the problem child, Gerald Patterson's (1976, 1981) approach is to work with the entire family. Patterson begins by carefully observing the family's interactions and determining just how family members are reinforcing one another's coercive activities. The next step is to describe the nature of the problem to parents and to teach them a new approach to managing their children's behavior. Some of the principles, skills, and procedures that Patterson stresses are the following:

1. Don't give in to the child's coercive behavior.
2. Don't escalate your own coercion when the child becomes coercive.
3. Control the child's coercion with the *time out* procedure—a method of punishment in which the child is sent to her room (or some other location) until she calms down and stops using coercive tactics.
4. Identify those of the child's behaviors that are most irritating and then establish a point system in which the child can earn credits (rewards, privileges) for acceptable conduct or lose them for unacceptable behavior. Parents with older problem children are taught how to formulate "behavioral contracts" that specify how the child is expected to behave at home and at school, as well as how deviations from this behavioral code will be punished. Whenever possible, children should have a say in negotiating these contracts.
5. Be on the lookout for occasions when you can respond to the child's prosocial conduct with warmth and affection. Although this is often difficult for parents who are accustomed to snapping at their children and accentuating the negative, Patterson believes that parental affection and approval will reinforce good conduct and eventually elicit displays of affection from the child—a clear sign that the family is on the road to recovery.

A clear majority of problem families respond quite favorably to these methods. Not only do problem children become less coercive, defiant, and aggressive, but the mother's depression fades as she gradually begins to feel better about herself, her child, and her ability to resolve family crises (Patterson, 1981). Some problem families show an immediate improvement. Others respond more gradually to the treatment and may require periodic "booster shots"—that is, follow-up treatments in which the clinician visits the family, determines why progress has slowed (or broken down), and then retrains the parents or suggests new procedures to correct the problems that are not being resolved. Clearly, this therapy works because it recognizes that "out of control" behavior stems from a *family system* in which both parents and children are influencing each other and contributing to the development of a hostile family environment. Therapies that focus exclusively on the problem child are not enough!

family as a social system rather than simply concentrating on the aggressive child who has been referred for treatment.

EFFECTS OF THE MASS MEDIA ON CHILDREN'S AGGRESSION

Earlier in the chapter, we learned that children can easily acquire violent, aggressive behaviors by merely observing the antics of aggressive models. This finding raises an interesting question: Do aggressive episodes portrayed in the movies or on television have systematic effects on the behavior of developing children?

As early as 1954, complaints raised by parents, teachers, and students of human development prompted Senator Estes Kefauver, then chairman of the Senate Subcommittee on Juvenile Delinquency, to question the need for violence in television programming. As it turns out, children in the United States, Canada, and several other Western nations can observe violent, aggressive episodes almost any time they care to by simply turning on their TV sets. In the United States, nearly 80% of prime-time television programs contain at least one incident of physical violence, with an average rate of 7.5 violent acts per hour (Gerbner, Gross, Morgan, & Signorielli, 1980). And it is estimated that the average child of 16, who has already spent more time watching TV than in school, will have witnessed more than 13,000 killings on television (Liebert & Schwartzberg, 1977). This remarkable statistic often shocks college students, particularly those who have young children of their own. Yet they would probably not be surprised by these figures were they to sit down and watch Saturday morning television. George Gerbner and his associates (Gerbner et al., 1980) report that the most violent programs on commercial television are those designed for children—especially Saturday morning cartoon shows, which contain nearly 25 violent incidents per hour. And despite many popular claims to the contrary, violence rates on commercial television have remained remarkably stable since the late 1960s (Parke & Slaby, 1983).

Theoretical Perspectives on Media Violence

Does a heavy exposure to media violence encourage spectators to behave aggressively? Here are two opposing points of view:

The catharsis hypothesis. The Greek philosopher Aristotle maintained that theatrical productions have a very beneficial effect on the audience: those who witness dramatic tragedies will be "purged" of any feelings of grief, fear, or anger through a process he called *Katharsis*. Psychoanalytic theorist Sigmund Freud (1920/1955) and aggressive-drive theorists Dollard et al. (1939) and Feshbach (1970) also believe in the tension-reducing properties of emotional expression. The catharsis hypothesis states that a person who commits an aggressive act reduces his or her aggressive drive (experiences catharsis) *and becomes less likely to commit another act of aggression in the immediate future*.

Feshbach (1970) contends that a person may experience catharsis by merely thinking aggressive thoughts (fantasy aggression). If this is the case, exposure to televised violence should *reduce* aggressive impulses by providing fantasy material that viewers can use for cathartic purposes.

The social-learning hypothesis. Bandura (1973) lists several reasons that media violence should *enhance* the aggressive inclinations of children who watch it. First, there is physiological evidence that children become *emotionally aroused*

when they see others fight (Cline, Croft, & Courrier, 1973; Osborn & Endsley, 1971)—arousal that might be reinterpreted as anger and thereby energize aggressive behavior if children should soon experience a situation that seems to suggest an aggressive response. Second, actors who portray violence on television serve as *aggressive models* who teach children a variety of violent acts that they may not know about or would not otherwise have considered performing. Robert Liebert and his associates (Liebert, Sprafkin, & Davidson, 1982) provide several dramatic illustrations of how children have acquired and performed unusual aggressive responses after watching similar actions on television. Here is one example:

> In Los Angeles, a housemaid caught a seven-year-old boy in the act of sprinkling ground glass into the family's lamb stew. There was no malice behind the act. It was purely experimental, having been inspired by curiosity to learn whether it would really work as well as it did on television [p. 72].

Finally, televised violence may reduce children's *inhibitions* about aggression if people in the story approve (or do not disapprove) of the actor's aggressive behavior. I am reminded of the "Thanks!" that townspeople typically shouted to the Lone Ranger as he rode into the sunset after shooting the villain of that particular episode or conspiring with Tonto to beat him to a pulp. If an actor's aggressive behavior is "legitimized" by social approval, observers may expect less risk of punishment or loss of self-respect should they engage in similar behavior.

In sum, Bandura's position on the effects of TV violence is diametrically opposed to that of Feshbach and other proponents of the catharsis hypothesis. Attempts to resolve this theoretical controversy include three types of research: (1) *correlational surveys* that assess the relationship between television viewing habits and aggressive behavior, (2) *laboratory investigations* in which subjects are exposed to aggressive films and then faced with a situation where they may choose to behave aggressively, and (3) *field experiments* in which the content of television programming is manipulated over a period of time in a real-world setting in order to measure the effects of the manipulation on viewers' aggressive habits. We will consider examples of each type of research as we evaluate the relative merits of the catharsis and the social-learning hypotheses.

Correlational Surveys

The vast majority of correlational studies conducted to date have found positive relationships between the amount of violence a child observes and his or her aggressiveness in naturalistic settings (Parke & Slaby, 1983). This relationship holds for preschool, grade school, high school, and adult subjects in the United States and has also been observed among grade school boys and girls in Australia, Finland, Poland, and Great Britain.

Despite the consistency of the findings, we face problems when we try to interpret them. A positive correlation between children's exposure to televised violence and their level of aggressiveness does not necessarily imply that violent television programming *causes* children to be aggressive. It may mean that *aggressive children* prefer violent programming or perhaps that some third variable underlies children's aggressive inclinations and their preferences for violent programming. Ordinarily, we would want to examine the results of well-controlled laboratory experiments to determine which of these possibilities is correct. Before we do, let's first consider the results of some rather sophisticated longitudinal surveys that have attempted to determine the direction of the relationship between televised violence and aggression in imaginative ways.

Longitudinal surveys. In 1963 Leonard Eron interviewed parents of third-graders to determine their children's TV viewing habits. In addition, each child in Eron's sample rated other children in his or her class on behaviors indicative of their aggressiveness: "Who takes other children's things without asking?" "Who starts a fight over nothing?" "Who says mean things?" Eron found a positive correlation between children's preferences for violent television programming and their aggressiveness, although this relationship was stronger for boys than for girls. Ten years later, these same people were asked to rate one another for aggressiveness and to describe their own

TV viewing habits. The results were clear (for boys, at least). Boys who had preferred highly violent and aggressive programming at age 8 were much more aggressive at age 18 than their classmates who had not preferred to watch violent shows (Eron, Huesmann, Lefkowitz, & Walder, 1972). So it appears that a heavy exposure to televised violence during early and middle childhood *may* promote the development of aggressive habits that persist over time. Indeed, Eron et al. (1972) reported that children's television preferences at age 8 predicted their aggression at age 18 better than any other factor they studied, including intelligence, social class, ethnicity, and parents' child-rearing practices!

Subsequent longitudinal surveys with different populations reveal that an earlier preference for televised violence predicts later aggression for both girls *and* boys (Eron, 1980, 1982). However, the data also reveal that children who are more aggressive are apt to watch more violent programs on television (Eron, 1982). So it is conceivable that the relationship between televised violence and children's aggression is a *reciprocal* one: exposure to TV violence may instigate aggressive behavior, which stimulates interest in violent programming, which promotes further aggression, and so on down the line.

One reason that televised violence may instigate aggression is that children younger than 8 or 9 cannot easily distinguish fantasy from reality and are likely to believe that much of what they see on television is quite realistic. A steady diet of violent programming may convince the child that the outside world is a violent place inhabited by people who typically rely on aggressive strategies when faced with interpersonal conflicts. Indeed, Leonard Eron and his associates (Eron, Huesmann, Brice, Fischer, & Mermelstein, 1983) found that 7- to 9-year-old boys and girls who were judged to be highly aggressive by their peers not only preferred violent television programs—they also believed that violent shows were an accurate portrayal of everyday life.

Intriguing as these survey results may be, let's keep in mind that they are correlational data that *do not demonstrate causality*. Let's now turn to other lines of inquiry that can tell us whether exposure to TV violence causes children to behave aggressively.

PHOTO 9-5 Heavy exposure to media violence may lead young children to believe that the world is a violent place populated mainly by hostile and aggressive people.

Laboratory Experiments

One method of determining whether violent films really do instigate (or reduce) aggression is to expose children to these materials and then give them an opportunity to commit aggressive responses. By 1972, 18 such experiments had been conducted, and 16 of them found that children became *more* aggressive after watching violent sequences on television (Liebert & Baron, 1972).

Representatives from the major television networks criticized much of this early research. Many of the studies had children aggressing against inanimate objects such as Bobo dolls. But would children really become more inclined to hurt another *human being* after watching violence on TV? And what would happen if you gave them a choice between helping and hurting that person? Liebert and Baron (1972) designed what is now regarded as a classic experiment to answer these questions.

In Liebert and Baron's experiment, children from two age groups (5–6 and 8–9) watched excerpts from one of two television programs. Half the children saw a 3½-minute sequence from a violent program, *The Untouchables*. This short clip contained a chase scene, two fistfights, two shootings, and a stabbing.

The remaining children saw 3½ minutes of a nonviolent but exciting track meet. Each child was then taken into another room and seated before a box that had wires leading into the adjoining room. On the box was a green button labeled HELP, a red button labeled HURT, and a white light positioned above the buttons. The experimenter noted that a child in the adjoining room would soon be playing a handle-turning game that would illuminate the white light. The subject was told that, by pushing the buttons when the light was lit, he or she could either help the other child by making the handle easy to turn or hurt the child by making the handle hot. When it was clear that the subject understood the instructions, the experimenter left the room, and the light came on 20 times. Thus, each subject had 20 opportunities to help or hurt another child. The total amount of time each subject spent pushing the HURT button served as a measure of his or her aggression toward the other child.

Liebert and Baron's results were clear: *despite the availability of an alternative helping response, boys and girls from both age groups were much more likely to hurt the other child if they had watched the violent television program.* However, children in the two experimental conditions did not differ in their willingness to push the HELP button. It appears that a mere 3½-minute exposure to televised violence increased children's willingness to hurt a peer, even though the aggressive acts they observed on television bore no resemblance to those they committed themselves (see Collins & Getz, 1976, for similar results with older children and adolescents).

Although the bulk of the laboratory evidence since 1972 indicates that televised violence instigates aggression (Parke & Slaby, 1983), this method of investigation has its shortcomings. It has been argued that laboratory experiments in which subjects give their undivided attention to a televised sequence is very dissimilar to the home setting, where parents may berate aggressors and where much of one's "viewing time" is spent talking to others, reading, playing with toys or pets, going to the refrigerator, and so on. Perhaps these exhortations and interruptions lessen the impact of televised violence in a naturalistic setting. We might also note that children at home rarely have a tailor-made opportunity to aggress immediately after watching violent programs. Is it possible that the instigating effects of TV violence are extremely short-lived and thus are a problem only in a laboratory setting where subjects are "encouraged" to be aggressive by the requirements of the task they face soon after observing violent programming? Liebert, Neale, and Davidson (1973) acknowledge these possibilities, noting that "we know from laboratory studies what type of relationship can exist between television violence and aggression, but cannot be wholly certain that this relationship *does* exist in the complex world of free-ranging behavior" (p. 69).

Field Experiments

The field experiment is probably the best method of assessing the impact of televised violence on children's behavior, because it combines the naturalistic approach of a correlational survey with the rigorous control of an experiment. In other words, well-conducted field experiments can determine whether real-life exposure to violent television increases the incidence of aggressive behavior in real-life settings.

An experiment with young children.   Stein and Friedrich (1972) assessed the impact of televised violence on the interpersonal behavior of nursery school children. The 97 children in their sample were observed for three weeks to establish a baseline level of "aggressiveness" for each child. The children were then randomly assigned to three experimental conditions. Those who watched *aggressive programming* saw one *Batman* or one *Superman* cartoon a day. Children exposed to *prosocial television* watched daily episodes of *Mister Rogers' Neighborhood*. The third group saw *neutral* (neither aggressive nor prosocial) films of circuses and farm scenes. After these month-long television diets, the children were observed daily for two additional weeks to measure the effects of the programming. Children who had watched aggressive programming were more aggressive in nursery school than children who had watched either prosocial or neutral programming. Although the impact of aggressive programming was significant only for those children who were above the

median in aggressiveness during the initial baseline period, these "initially aggressive" children were by no means extreme or deviant. They simply represented the more aggressive members of a normal nursery school peer group. Stein and Friedrich remind us that "these effects occurred in [a naturalistic setting] that was removed both in time and in environmental setting from the viewing experience. They occurred with a small amount of exposure . . . and they endured during the postviewing period" (1972, p. 247).

An experiment with adolescents.   The effects of violent and nonviolent movies on the interpersonal behavior of adolescent boys were the focus of a more recent field experiment (Leyens, Parke, Camino, & Berkowitz, 1975). The subjects were Belgian adolescents who lived together in cottages at a private institution for secondary school boys. Baseline observations suggested that the institution's four cottages could be divided into subgroups consisting of two cottages with relatively high aggressiveness and two with relatively low aggressiveness. For a period of one week, *aggressive* films such as *Iwo Jima, Bonnie and Clyde*, and *The Dirty Dozen* were shown to one of the two cottages in each subgroup, and *neutral films* such as *Lily, Daddy's Fiancée*, and *La Belle Américaine* were shown to the other. Instances of physical and verbal aggression among the residents of each cottage were recorded twice daily (at lunchtime and in the evenings after the movie) during the movie week and once daily (at lunchtime) during a posttreatment week.

Perhaps the most striking result of this research was the significant increase in *physical* aggression that occurred in the evenings among residents of *both* cottages assigned to the aggressive-film condition (see Figure 9-5). Since the violent movies contained a large number of physically aggressive incidents, it appears that they evoked similar responses from the boys who watched them. By contrast, boys who watched neutral films showed few signs of physical aggression after the movies. In fact, inhabitants of the high-aggressiveness cottage who saw neutral films showed a significant *decrease* in physical aggression compared with the baseline period.

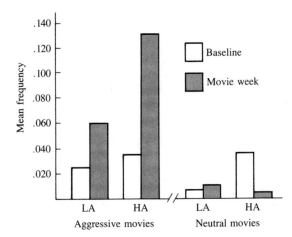

FIGURE 9-5   Mean physical aggression scores in the evening for highly aggressive (HA) and less aggressive (LA) boys under baseline conditions and after watching aggressive or neutral movies

There was also evidence of a generalization of aggressive responses over time. That is, boys in the high-aggressiveness cottage who watched violent movies became *more* verbally assaultive during the movie week and retained this level of verbal aggressiveness throughout the posttreatment period. Neutral films had the opposite effect: boys in the high-aggressiveness cottage who saw neutral films became *less* verbally aggressive during the movie week and remained low in verbal aggression during the posttreatment week. In sum, the experiment by Leyens et al. shows that (1) violent programming can instigate aggressive responses in naturalistic settings, especially among groups of viewers who are already high in interpersonal aggression, and (2) lighthearted, comical movies may actually reduce the incidence of aggression among a highly aggressive group of spectators. Other studies conducted recently in the United States have reported similar results (Parke, Berkowitz, Leyens, West, & Sebastian, 1977).

Although there are field experiments that have failed to find that violent programming increases children's aggression (see Freedman, 1984), most of the literature is consistent with the research we have reviewed. In commenting on these results, Parke and Slaby (1983) propose that "as a group, these field experiments have demonstrated the generalizability of previous laboratory findings to more naturalistic circumstances. . . . [Moreover], the individual viewer's predisposition toward aggression appears to play an important though poorly understood role in mediating this effect" (p. 601).

Media Violence as a Desensitizing Agent

In addition to instigating aggressive behavior, a steady diet of televised violence may increase children's *tolerance* for aggression, even aggression that takes place around them in the real world. Ronald Drabman and Margaret Thomas (1974) tested this *desensitization hypothesis* with 8- to 10-year-olds. Half the children watched a violent Hopalong Cassidy film that contained several gun battles and fistfights. The remaining children were assigned to a control condition and did not see a film. Each child was then asked to watch a television monitor in order to ensure that two kindergarten children who were playing in another room didn't get into any trouble while the experimenter was away at the principal's office. The experimenter took great care to explain to the child that he or she was to come to the principal's office for help should *anything* go wrong. Each child then observed the same videotaped sequence in which the two kindergartners got into an intense battle. The tape ended with a loud crash that occurred shortly after the video portion had gone dead.

The results of this study were straightforward: children who had watched the violent film reacted much more slowly to what they believed to be a real-world altercation than their classmates who had not seen a film. Drabman and Thomas concluded that an exposure to media violence may blunt viewers' emotional reactions to later aggressive episodes and perhaps even make them feel that aggressive acts are a part of everyday life that do not necessarily warrant a response.

In a second experiment, Thomas and her colleagues (Thomas, Horton, Lippincott, & Drabman, 1977) exposed 8- to 10-year-olds to either a *violent* film from the popular police series *S.W.A.T.* or a *nonviolent* but exciting film of a championship volleyball match. The viewers were hooked up to a physiograph that recorded their emotional reactions to the films (which were equally arousing). After the film was over, the experimenter switched channels and asked the child to monitor the play activities of two younger children who were playing in an adjacent room. At this point the experimenter departed, leaving the child hooked up to the physiograph. The child then observed the same videotaped altercation that was used in Drabman and Thomas's experiment, and his or her emotional reactions to these events were recorded.

Once again, the results were clear: children who had watched the violent programming were subsequently *less aroused* by the "real life" altercation than their classmates who had seen the nonviolent film. Here, then, is an explanation for children's tolerance of aggression in the first experiment: if exposure to media violence really lessens a viewer's emotional reactivity to later aggressive acts, then this emotionally desensitized person is unlikely to experience strong empathic distress for the victims of aggression. Consequently, he or she may be less inclined to do anything to help them.

A General Conclusion about the Effects of Media Violence

The different kinds of research we have reviewed rely on very different methods and yet converge to suggest one conclusion: heavy exposure to media violence can and often does encourage spectators to behave aggressively (or to passively accept the use of aggression by others). Not every one of the studies in the literature supports this conclusion, but the vast majority do. In fact, there is virtually no support for the notion that exposure to media violence leads to a reduction of viewers' aggressive impulses through catharsis.[6]

METHODS OF CONTROLLING AGGRESSION

How might parents and teachers control children's aggression? Over the years, a variety of solutions have been offered, including coaching strategies, the incompatible response technique, use of the time-out procedure to punish aggressive behavior, the creation of nonaggressive play environments, and the sug-

gestion that children be trained to empathize with the victims of aggression. But few solutions have been so highly touted as the recommendation that we offer children harmless ways to express their anger or frustrations. Let's consider this "popular" alternative first.

CATHARSIS: A DUBIOUS STRATEGY

Although we have seen that TV viewers are not "purged" of aggressive impulses by watching others commit violent aggressive acts, this does not mean that cathartic effects never occur. Maybe a person must actually commit an aggressive response to experience catharsis. Freud was a major proponent of this idea. He believed that people should be encouraged to express their aggressive impulses every now and then before they build to dangerous levels and trigger a truly violent or destructive outburst. The implications of this viewpoint are clear: presumably we could teach children to vent their anger or frustrations on inanimate objects such as Bobo dolls. In so doing, an angry child should experience catharsis and become less likely to commit aggressive acts against other people.

Popular as this cathartic technique has been, it does *not* work and *may even backfire*. In one study (Walters & Brown, 1963), children who had been encouraged to slap, punch, and kick an inflatable Bobo doll were found to be much more aggressive in their later interactions with peers than were classmates who had not had an opportunity to beat on the doll. Other investigators have noted that children who are first angered by a peer and then given an opportunity to aggress against an inanimate object become no less aggressive toward the peer who angered them in the first place (Mallick & McCandless, 1966). So cathartic techniques do not reduce children's aggressive urges. In fact, they may teach youngsters that hitting and kicking are acceptable methods of expressing their anger or frustrations.

ELIMINATING THE PAYOFFS FOR AGGRESSION

It is possible to reduce aggression by eliminating the rewards that sustain aggressive acts. However, this approach is not as simple as it sounds, for any number of objects and events may reinforce an act of aggression.

Suppose that 5-year-old Billy wrests an attractive toy away from his 3-year-old sister, Gail, causing her to cry. If Billy's aggression were motivated by the prospect of obtaining the toy, Billy's mother could simply return the toy to Gail and thus deny Billy his reward. Billy's tendency to attack should then wane, for this aggressive strategy has not "paid off" (Bandura, 1973).

Unfortunately, this solution wouldn't always work, for it is possible that Gail's submissive behavior is the "reward" that sustains Billy's aggression (Patterson, Littman, & Bricker, 1967). It is also possible that young Billy attacked his sister in order to obtain his mother's attention. If this were so, the mother would be reinforcing Billy's aggression if she attended to him at all. But we cannot recommend that the mother simply ignore Billy's aggressive outbursts, for Siegal and Kohn (1959) have shown that children may interpret an adult's nonintervention as tacit approval for their aggressive deeds. So what is an adult to do?

The incompatible response technique. One proven method of reducing children's aggression is to ignore their hostile outbursts *while reinforcing acts that are incompatible with aggression*. In a classic study of this "incompatible response" technique, Paul Brown and Rogers Elliot (1965) instructed nursery school teachers to turn their backs on all but the most severely aggressive exchanges among their pupils. At the same time, they were asked to reward all instances of prosocial behavior, such as sharing toys or playing together cooperatively. Within two weeks this treatment had significantly reduced the incidence of both physical and verbal aggression among the children, and the program was ended. A follow-up treatment given several weeks later brought about further reductions in aggressive behavior. In a second study, Ron Slaby (Slaby & Crowley, 1977) found that merely encouraging children to say nice things about one another produced an increase in prosocial behavior and a corresponding decrease in aggression. Clearly the reinforcement of responses that are incompatible with aggression can inhibit hostile behavior. The beauty of this nonpuni-

tive approach is that it does not reinforce children who seek attention through their hostile acts, it does not make children angry or resentful, and it does not expose them to a punitive or aggressive model. Thus, many of the negative side effects associated with punishment can be avoided.

The "time out" procedure. Obviously parents and teachers cannot rely exclusively on the incompatible response technique if their children are likely to do serious harm to one another. So how do they inhibit these very hostile acts without "reinforcing" them with their attention? One effective strategy is to use the "time out" technique (that is, time out from the opportunity to receive positive reinforcement), in which the adult "punishes" by disrupting or otherwise preventing the aggressive antics that the child finds reinforcing (for example, by sending the aggressor to his room until he is ready to behave appropriately). Although this technique may generate some resentment, the punitive agent is not physically abusing the child, is not serving as an aggressive model, and is not likely to unwittingly reinforce the child who misbehaves as a means of attracting attention. The time-out procedure is most effective at controlling children's hostilities when the adult in charge also reinforces cooperative, helpful interactions that are incompatible with aggression (Parke & Slaby, 1983).

MODELING AND COACHING STRATEGIES

Responses incompatible with aggression may also be instilled by modeling or by coaching strategies. When children see a model choose a nonaggressive solution to a conflict or are explicitly coached in the use of nonaggressive methods of problem solving, they become more likely to enact similar solutions to their own problems (Chittenden, 1942; Zahavi & Asher, 1978). Indeed, the coaching of effective methods of conflict resolution is particularly useful when working with chronically aggressive children, for these youngsters resort to aggressive tactics because they are not very skilled at generating adequate and amicable solutions for interpersonal problems on their own (Asher, Renshaw, & Geraci, 1980; Richard & Dodge, 1982).

Reducing children's exposure to aggressive models. Another method of decreasing children's aggression is to reduce their exposure to aggressive models. A useful first step might be to restrict the child's access to violent television programming while trying to interest him or her in shows that contain little or no violence. Anyone who would like a list of programs that the experts consider too violent for young children can get one by writing to Action for Children's Television, 46 Austin Street, Boston, Mass. 02160.

Of course, it would be next to impossible for parents to shield their children from televised violence, because violence is so widespread in the media, and curious youngsters who are not allowed to watch it at home may be eager to see what they are missing while watching TV at a community recreation center or in the homes of their friends. In recent years, organizations such as Action for Children's Television and the National Association for Better Broadcasting have campaigned against TV violence and recommended that concerned parents write to the commercial networks and local network affiliates to complain about the violent programming directed at their children. These protests have not always fallen on deaf ears, for several advertisers (for example, Best Foods, Miracle White, and Samsonite) have pledged to avoid sponsoring extremely violent television shows ("Cooling Off the Tube," 1976). So there is some evidence that organized protests and write-in campaigns can be effective at reducing the level of violence on TV—but only if enough concerned citizens become involved.

What do young children think when they see violence *punished* on television? Is such vicarious punishment apt to inhibit their own aggressive behavior? The research presented in Box 9-3 was designed to address these issues, and as we will see, it has produced some interesting results indeed.

Of course, campaigns aimed at reducing the amount of televised violence operate under the assumption that the medium itself (TV) is not to blame; presumably, the fault lies with its message (that is, the violent content of its programming). However, John Wright and Aletha Huston (1983) believe that the medium *is* partly to blame. To back their contention, they cite some of their own research in which children who watched programs containing many fast-paced action scenes and other attention-grabbing production features often became more aggressive in their play—*even when these programs contained no violence*! Clearly more research is needed to explain these intriguing findings. Nevertheless, we are probably safe in concluding that campaigns designed to lessen the amount of violence on television would prove more effective at achieving their ultimate goal of reducing children's aggression if steps were also taken to change the ways in which television producers use production features to "capture" young audiences.

Modifying children's understanding of violence and aggression. One reason that young children are so responsive to aggressive modeling influences is that they don't always interpret the violence they see in the same way adults do, often missing subtleties such as an aggressor's motives and intentions or the unpleasant consequences that perpetrators suffer as a result of their aggressive acts (Collins, Sobol, & Westby, 1981; see Box 9-3). Perhaps parents could help children to evaluate media violence by watching television with their children and making such information available to them. Indeed, researchers are beginning to find that when adults highlight subtle information about an aggressor's motives while strongly disapproving of his conduct, children gain a much better understanding of media violence and are less affected by what they have seen—particularly if the adult commentator also suggests how these perpetrators might have approached their problems in a more constructive way (Corder-Bolz & O'Bryant, 1977; Hicks, 1968; Horton & Santogrossi, 1978). Moreover, Leonard Eron and his associates (Eron & Huesmann, 1984) have been experimenting with a training program designed to teach heavy consumers of TV violence how to discriminate fantasy aggression from real-life events. The results are encouraging: two years later, children exposed to the training sessions were rated much less aggressive by their peers than were other heavy consumers of TV violence who had not received the training. So adults can play an important role in reducing children's aggression by helping youngsters to interpret the meaning and implications of the violence they see.

BOX 9-3 *PUNISHING AGGRESSION ON TV: DOES IT INHIBIT CHILDREN'S AGGRESSIVE BEHAVIOR?*

It is often assumed that children will be reluctant to imitate the antics of aggressive models if they see the aggressor punished for his behavior. Indeed, Bandura, Ross, and Ross (1963) report that children who had seen an aggressive model punished for his actions were subsequently less aggressive than children who had seen the aggressive model rewarded. But those who had seen the model punished were *no less aggressive* than a third group of children who had not been exposed to an aggressive model. The latter finding is important, for it suggests that we would be at least as successful at restraining children's aggression if we did not expose them to aggressive models at all.

An interesting experiment by Andrew Collins (1973) supports this contention. Third-, sixth-, and tenth-graders were given an aggression "test" and then, 18 days later, watched a TV program in which a criminal attacked federal agents and was punished for his actions (he was mortally wounded in a gunfight). The program was edited to yield two versions. In the *separation* version, four-minute commercials were inserted between the inciting incidents in the drama and the aggression and again between the aggression and its punishment. The *no-separation* version presented the entire aggressive scenario uninterrupted by commercials. About a third of the children from each grade level watched each version of the aggressive film. The remaining third saw a nonaggressive travelogue. After watching their film, the children took the aggression test a second time.

Children in all three experimental conditions showed an increase in aggression from the pretest to the posttest. However, there were two additional findings that are particularly noteworthy. First, an examination of the figure reveals that third-graders in the no-separation condition, who saw the model punished immediately, were not appreciably less aggressive on the posttest than their age mates who had watched a nonaggressive travelogue. Second—and of major importance to our discussion—*third-graders* became *much more* aggressive on the posttest if the filmed aggression and its negative consequences were separated by a commercial than if they occurred in sequence, uninter-

rupted by another event. Apparently, third-graders did not associate the aggression with its punishment when these two events were separated in time.

On television and in the real world, aggressors are seldom punished immediately after committing aggressive acts; usually hours, days, or weeks—or, on TV, numerous commercials—intervene before an aggressor gets his or her due. Collins's study suggests that exposing young children to aggressive models who are punished later—even a short time later—is *not* an effective means of reducing aggression. *Quite the contrary*: such an exposure appears to instigate aggression and may even foster the development of aggressive habits that are difficult to overcome.

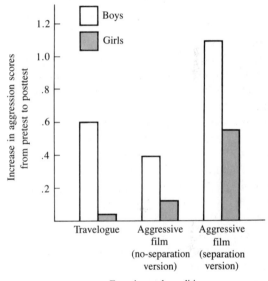

Average increase in the aggression scores of third-graders exposed to different versions of an aggressive film or to a nonaggressive travelogue

CREATING NONAGGRESSIVE ENVIRONMENTS

Yet another method that adults may use to reduce children's aggression is to create play areas that minimize the likelihood of interpersonal conflict. For

example, providing ample space for vigorous play helps to eliminate the kinds of accidental body contacts such as tripping and shoving that often provoke aggressive incidents (Hartup, 1974). Paul Gump (1975) points out that shortages in play materials also contribute to conflicts and hostilities. However, additional children can easily be assimilated into a play area without any increase in aggression if the number of slides, swings, and other toys is sufficient to prevent playmates from having to compete for scarce resources (Smith & Connolly, 1980).

Finally, we have seen that toys that suggest aggressive themes (guns, tanks, and so on) are likely to provoke hostile, aggressive incidents (Feshbach, 1956; Turner & Goldsmith, 1976). If our goal is to reduce the incidence of aggression, we may be better off in the long run to advise parents and teachers against making aggressive toys available to young children.

EMPATHY AS A DETERRENT TO AGGRESSION

A number of years ago, a very dear friend confessed to having recurring nightmares about the year he had spent as a combat infantryman in Vietnam. The event that triggered his discomfort would seem quite horrifying to most of us. He had once shot a man (a North Vietnamese) at close range and then watched this person suffer the agony of a slow, painful death. So distressed was my friend by this experience that he refused to bear arms any longer. He was granted a medical discharge from the armed services, but the nightmares remained.

Here is an example where pain cues emitted by a victim inhibited further aggression on the part of the perpetrator. This is not unusual: grade school children, adolescents, and adults will normally back off and stop attacking a victim who shows signs of pain or suffering (Baron, 1971; Perry & Bussey, 1977). However, many *preschool* children and *highly aggressive* grade school boys will continue to attack a suffering victim or one who denies that he has been hurt (Patterson et al., 1967; Perry & Perry, 1974). One possible explanation for this seemingly sadistic behavior is that young preschoolers and other highly aggressive individuals may not *empathize* with their victims. In other words, they may not feel bad or suffer themselves when they have harmed another person.

Does empathy inhibit aggression? Apparently so.

Grade school children who score high in empathy are rated low in aggression by their teachers, whereas classmates who test very low in empathy tend to be more aggressive (Bryant, 1982; Feshbach, 1978). Moreover, Michael Chandler (1973) found that highly aggressive 11–13-year-old delinquents who participated in a ten-week program designed to make them more aware of other people's feelings subsequently became less hostile and aggressive, compared with a second group of delinquents who had not participated in the program. (See also Feshbach & Feshbach, 1982, for similar results in an empathy-training program with 9- to 11-year-olds.)

In the home setting, adults can foster the development of empathy by modeling empathic concern (Zahn-Waxler, Radke-Yarrow, & King, 1979) and by using disciplinary techniques that (1) point out the harmful consequences of the child's aggressive actions while (2) encouraging the child to put himself in the victim's place and imagine how the victim feels. In the very next chapter, we will see that parents who rely mainly on these rational, nonpunitive disciplinary techniques tend to raise sympathetic children who seem genuinely concerned about the welfare of others.

SUMMARY

Human aggression is a pervasive phenomenon, so pervasive as to lead many theorists to believe that aggression is a part of human nature. Sigmund Freud proposed that we are driven by a destructive instinct, the Thanatos, which he considered responsible for the generation of hostile, aggressive impulses. Ethologists describe aggression as a fighting instinct triggered by certain eliciting cues in the environment. Although there are several important differences between psychoanalytic and ethological theories of aggression, both schools of thought contend that human beings are instinctively aggressive.

This view was challenged by neo-Hullian theorists, who argued that aggression is the result of frustration and that frustrating events invariably lead to aggression. This *frustration/aggression hypothesis* was soon amended when it became apparent that frustration could lead to outcomes other than aggression. Robert Sears, a neo-Hullian, came to view aggression as *an acquired drive to harm others.* Advocates of Sears's position are careful to distinguish between *hostile* and *instrumental* aggression. If an aggressor's major motivation is to harm a victim, his or her behavior qualifies as hostile aggression. Instrumental aggression includes those acts in which one person hurts another as a means to nonaggressive ends. Acquired-drive theorists are interested mainly in studying hostile aggression, which they believe to be motivated by an aggressive drive. Instrumental aggression is viewed by these theorists simply as a means to other ends (pseudo aggression).

Leonard Berkowitz has formulated a revised frustration/aggression hypothesis that emphasizes the interaction between an aggressor's internal emotional state and the environment. Berkowitz contends that frustration and a variety of other factors such as an attack or one's aggressive habits produce a *readiness to aggress* (anger). But aggressive responses will not occur unless *aggressive cues* are present in the environment, cues which have been associated with aggression in the past and which elicit aggressive responses from people who are "ready to aggress."

Bandura's social-learning theory treats aggression as a specific type of social behavior that is acquired by direct tuition or observational learning. Aggression is defined as *any behavior directed toward the goal of harming or injuring another organism.* Most theories of aggression assume that people are "driven" to aggress by some sort of internal motivation such as frustration or anger. Bandura takes issue with all these theories by arguing that internal states may facilitate aggression but are not necessary for its occurrence.

Dodge's social information-processing theory is an interesting new approach that emphasizes cognitive contributions to aggression. Presumably, a person's reaction to frustration, anger, or an apparent provocation depends not so much on the social cues actually present in the situation as on how the person *processes* and *interprets* this information. Support for the model comes from studies showing that highly aggressive youngsters distort ambiguous information about harmdoing, viewing it as implying an aggressive intent. Thus, compared with nonaggressive age mates, aggressive children are more likely to retaliate when harmed under ambiguous circumstances.

Aggression emerges during the second year as infants begin to quarrel with siblings and peers over toys and other possessions. During the preschool period, children become less likely to throw temper tantrums or to hit others and more likely to resort to verbally aggressive tactics such as name-calling or ridiculing. Although grade school children continue to fight over objects, an increasing percentage of their aggressive exchanges are person-directed hostile outbursts. Aggression is a reasonably stable attribute for both boys and girls: an aggressive 6-year-old is likely to be relatively high in aggression as an adolescent and a young adult.

Although aggression is equally stable for members of each sex, males are more physically and verbally aggressive than females and are more likely than females to become targets of aggression. These well-established sex differences in aggression reflect the interactive influence of biological and social forces.

A person's tendencies toward violence and aggression depend, in part, on the culture, subculture, and family setting in which he or she is raised. Cold and rejecting parents who rely on physical punishment and often permit aggression are likely to raise highly aggressive children. However, the "socialization" of aggression is a two-way street, for characteristics of the child (such as temperament or reactions to discipline) can affect parental attitudes and child-rearing practices. Strife-ridden homes appear to be breeding grounds for aggression. Highly aggressive youngsters who are "out of control" often live in coercive home environments where family members are constantly struggling with one another. In order to help these highly combative children, it is often necessary to treat the entire family.

Children who grow up in North America and several other Western cultures are frequently exposed to violence and aggression on television. Proponents of the *catharsis hypothesis* suggest that watching violent programs may *reduce* the incidence of aggression among viewers by providing an outlet for aggressive impulses. However, advocates of *social-learning theory* believe that violent television programs *instigate* aggression by (1) increasing the emotional arousal of viewers while (2) providing models for aggression who (3) are frequently rewarded. The vast majority of the evidence from correlational surveys, laboratory investigations, and field experiments indicates that exposure to violent movies and television often encourages spectators to behave aggressively and to become more tolerant (or accepting) of the use of aggression by others.

Proceeding in accordance with the catharsis hypothesis, the belief that children become less aggressive after behaving aggressively toward an inanimate object, is an ineffective control tactic that may instigate aggressive behavior. Some proven methods of controlling children's aggression are (1) the incompatible response technique, (2) use of the time-out procedure to punish aggressive behavior, (3) coaching and modeling nonaggressive solutions to conflict, (4) helping children to interpret the violence and aggression they see, (5) creating play environments that minimize the likelihood of conflict, and (6) encouraging children to recognize the harmful effects of their aggressive acts and to empathize with the victims of aggression.

when acting in a group where it is possible to diffuse personal responsibility for harmdoing among all who are present, females are just as aggressive as males (see Parke & Slaby, 1983).

4. The impact of sex hormones on the behavior of males and females will be discussed in some detail when we take up the topic of sex differences and sex-role development in Chapter 12.

5. Power assertion is a form of discipline in which the adult relies on his or her superior power (for example, by administering spankings or withholding privileges) to modify or control a child's behavior.

6. Feshbach and Singer (1971) conducted a field experiment that revealed that boys who watched a diet of violent programming for a six-week period were subsequently *less* aggressive than boys who were exposed to a like amount of nonviolent television. Although this finding was offered as support for the catharsis hypothesis, there are several reasons to question this interpretation. First, the boys who participated in this study preferred the violent television programs. Thus, subjects who were exposed to nonviolent programming might have become relatively aggressive because they were frustrated by their exposure to "dull" television. It should also be noted that boys who were exposed to nonviolent television protested until they were allowed to watch one extremely violent program, *Batman*. So it is certainly conceivable that these subjects showed higher levels of aggression because they had learned through their successful protests that the use of forceful assertive tactics is an effective means of accomplishing one's objectives. Finally, Wells (1972) replicated Feshbach and Singer's experiment, using adequate controls for some of its major methodological defects, and obtained exactly the opposite results: subjects who watched a diet of violent television programs became *more* physically aggressive than subjects who watched nonviolent programming.

NOTES

1. It is important to make a distinction between two terms that are often confused—*aggression* and *assertiveness*. As we have noted, aggression is behavior that is intended to harm or injure someone. By contrast, assertive behaviors are those intended to direct or control another person's actions without any accompanying intention to injure or to make the other person feel bad (Barrett & Yarrow, 1977).

2. Note that Sears's acquired-drive theory takes issue with one aspect of the original frustration/aggression hypothesis—namely, that aggression presupposes frustration. If inducing pain in others becomes pleasurable in itself, the implication is that not all aggressive acts need be preceded by frustration. This point is discussed in greater detail in the next few paragraphs.

3. There are situations, however, in which females approach or even equal males in aggression. For example, when they believe that no one will detect their actions, or

REFERENCES

ARDREY, R. (1967). *African genesis.* New York: Dell.

ARONSON, E. (1976). *The social animal.* New York: W. H. Freeman.

ASHER, S. R., Renshaw, P. D., & Geraci, R. L. (1980). Children's friendships and social competence. *International Journal of Psycholinguistics, 7,* 27–39.

BANDURA, A. (1973). *Aggression: A social learning analysis.* Englewood Cliffs, NJ: Prentice-Hall.

BANDURA, A. (1977). *Social learning theory.* Englewood Cliffs, NJ: Prentice-Hall.

BANDURA, A., Ross, D., & Ross, S. A. (1963). Vicarious reinforcement and imitative learning. *Journal of Abnormal and Social Psychology, 67,* 601–607.

BARON, R. A. (1971). Magnitude of victim's pain cues and level of prior anger arousal as determinants of adult aggressive behavior. *Journal of Personality and Social Psychology, 17,* 236–243.

BARON, R. A., & Byrne, D. (1984). *Social psychology: Understanding human interaction.* Boston: Allyn & Bacon.

BARRETT, D. E. (1979). A naturalistic study of sex differences in children's aggression. *Merrill-Palmer Quarterly, 25*, 193–203.

BARRETT, D. E., & Yarrow, M. R. (1977). Prosocial behavior, social inferential ability, and assertiveness in children. *Child Development, 48*, 475–481.

BELL, R. Q., Weller, G. M., & Waldrip, M. F. (1971). Newborn and preschooler: Organization of behavior and relations between periods. *Monographs of the Society for Research in Child Development, 36*(1–2, Serial No. 142).

BERKOWITZ, L. (1965). The concept of aggressive drive: Some additional considerations. In L. Berkowitz (Ed.), *Advances in experimental social psychology* (Vol. 2). Orlando, FL: Academic Press.

BERKOWITZ, L. (1974). Some determinants of impulsive aggression: Role of mediated association with reinforcement for aggression. *Psychological Review, 81*, 165–176.

BLOCK, J. H. (1978). Another look at sex differentiation in the socialization behaviors of mothers and fathers. In J. Sherman & F. L. Denmark (Eds.), *The psychology of women: Future directions of research*. New York: Psychological Dimensions.

BRONSON, W. C. (1975). Developments in behavior with age mates during the second year of life. In M. Lewis & L. A. Rosenblum (Eds.), *The origins of behavior: Friendship and peer relations*. New York: Wiley.

BROWN, P., & Elliot, R. (1965). Control of aggression in a nursery school class. *Journal of Experimental Child Psychology, 2*, 103–107.

BRYANT, B. K. (1982). An index of empathy for children and adolescents. *Child Development, 53*, 413–425.

BRYANT, J., & Zillmann, D. (1979). Effect of intensification of annoyance through unrelated residual excitation on substantially delayed hostile behavior. *Journal of Experimental Social Psychology, 15*, 470–480.

BUSS, A. H. (1961). *The psychology of aggression*. New York: Wiley.

CHANDLER, M. J. (1973). Egocentrism and antisocial behavior: The assessment and training of social perspective taking skills. *Developmental Psychology, 9*, 326–332.

CHITTENDEN, G. E. (1942). An experimental study in measuring and modifying assertive behavior in young children. *Monographs of the Society for Research in Child Development, 7*(Serial No. 31).

CLINE, V. B., Croft, R. G., & Courrier, S. (1973). Desensitization of children to television violence. *Journal of Personality and Social Psychology, 27*, 360–365.

COLLINS, W. A. (1973). Effect of temporal separation between motivation, aggression, and consequences: A developmental study. *Developmental Psychology, 8*, 215–221.

COLLINS, W. A., & Getz, S. K. (1976). Children's social responses following modeled reactions to provocation: Prosocial effects of a television drama. *Journal of Personality, 44*, 488–500.

COLLINS, W. A., Sobol, B. L., & Westby, S. (1981). Effects of adult commentary on children's comprehension and inferences about a televised aggressive portrayal. *Child Development, 52*, 158–163.

CONDRY, J. C., & Ross, D. F. (1985). Sex and aggression: The influence of gender label on the perception of aggression in children. *Child Development, 56*, 225–233.

COOLING OFF THE TUBE (1976, September 6). *Newsweek*, pp. 46–47.

CORDER-BOLZ, C. R., & O'Bryant, S. (1977, August). *Significant other modification of the impact of televised programming upon young children*. Paper presented at the annual meeting of the American Psychological Association, San Francisco.

CUMMINGS, E. M., Iannotti, R. J., & Zahn-Waxler, C. (1985). Influence of conflict between adults on the emotions and aggression of young children. *Developmental Psychology, 21*, 495–507.

DAVITZ, J. (1952). The effects of previous training on postfrustration behavior. *Journal of Abnormal and Social Psychology, 47*, 309–315.

DODGE, K. A. (1980). Social cognition and children's aggressive behavior. *Child Development, 51*, 162–170.

DODGE, K. A. (1981, April). *Behavioral antecedents of peer rejection and isolation*. Paper presented at the biennial meeting of the Society for Research in Child Development, Boston.

DODGE, K. A. (1986). A social information processing model of social competence in children. In M. Perlmutter (Ed.), *Minnesota Symposia on Child Psychology* (Vol. 18). Hillsdale, NJ: Erlbaum.

DODGE, K. A., & Frame, C. L. (1982). Social cognitive biases and deficits in aggressive boys. *Child Development, 53*, 620–635.

DODGE, K. A., Murphy, R. R., & Buchsbaum, K. (1984). The assessment of intention–cue detection skills in children: Implications for developmental psychopathology. *Child Development, 55*, 163–173.

DOLLARD, J., Doob, L. W., Miller, N. E., Mowrer, O. H., & Sears, R. R. (1939). *Frustration and aggression*. New Haven, CT: Yale University Press.

DORNBUSCH, S. M., Carlsmith, J. M., Bushwall, S. J., Ritter, P. L., Leiderman, H., Hastorf, A. H., & Gross, R. T. (1985). Single parents, extended households, and the control of adolescents. *Child Development, 56*, 326–341.

DRABMAN, R. S., & Thomas, M. H. (1974). Does media violence increase children's toleration of real-life aggression? *Developmental Psychology, 10*, 418–421.

EMMERICH, W. (1966). Continuity and stability in early social development: II. Teacher's ratings. *Child Development, 37*, 17–27.

ERON, L. D. (1963). Relationship of TV viewing habits and aggressive behavior in children. *Journal of Abnormal and Social Psychology, 67*, 193–196.

ERON, L. D. (1980). Prescription for the reduction of aggression. *American Psychologist, 35*, 244–252.

ERON, L. D. (1982). Parent-child interaction, television violence, and aggression of children. *American Psychologist, 37*, 197–211.

ERON, L. D., & Huesmann, L. R. (1984). The control of aggressive behavior by changes in attitudes, values and the conditions of learning. In R. J. Blanchard & C. Blanchard (Eds.), *Advances in the study of aggression* (Vol. 2). Orlando, FL: Academic Press.

ERON, L. D., Huesmann, L. R., Brice, P., Fischer, P., & Mermelstein, R. (1983). Age trends in the development of aggression, sex-typing, and related television habits. *Developmental Psychology, 19*, 71–77.

ERON, L. D., Huesmann, L. R., Lefkowitz, M. M., & Walder, L. O. (1972). Does television violence cause aggression? *American Psychologist, 27*, 253–263.

FESHBACH, N. (1978). Studies of the development of children's empathy. In B. Maher (Ed.), *Progress in experimental personality research*. Orlando, FL: Academic Press.

FESHBACH, N., & Feshbach, S. (1982). Empathy training and the regulation of aggression: Potentialities and limitations. *Academic Psychology Bulletin, 4*, 399–413.

FESHBACH, S. (1956). The catharsis hypothesis and some consequences of interaction with aggressive and neutral play objects. *Journal of Personality, 24*, 449–461.

FESHBACH, S. (1964). The function of aggression and the regulation of aggressive drive. *Psychological Review, 71*, 257–272.

FESHBACH, S. (1970). Aggression. In P. H. Mussen (Ed.), *Carmichael's manual of child psychology* (Vol. 2). New York: Wiley.

FESHBACH, S., & Singer, R. D. (1971). *Television and aggression: An experimental field study*. San Francisco: Jossey-Bass.

FREEDMAN, J. L. (1984). Effect of television violence on aggressiveness. *Psychological Bulletin, 96*, 227–246.

FREUD, S. (1955). Beyond the pleasure principle. In J. Strachey (Ed. and Trans.), *The standard edition of the complete psychological works of Sigmund Freud* (Vol. 18). London: Hogarth Press. (Original work published 1920)

GEEN, R. G. (1968). Effects of frustration, attack, and prior training in aggressiveness upon aggressive behavior. *Journal of Personality and Social Psychology, 9*, 316–321.

GERBNER, G., Gross, L., Morgan, M., & Signorielli, N. (1980). The mainstreaming of America. *Journal of Communication, 30*, 12–29.

GOODENOUGH, F. L. (1931). *Anger in young children*. Minneapolis: University of Minnesota Press.

GORER, G. (1968). Man has no "killer" instinct. In M. F. A. Montague (Ed.), *Man and aggression*. New York: Oxford University Press.

GUMP, P. V. (1975). Ecological psychology and children. In E. M. Hetherington (Ed.), *Review of child development research* (Vol. 5). Chicago: University of Chicago Press.

HARTUP, W. W. (1974). Aggression in childhood: Developmental perspectives. *American Psychologist, 29,* 336–341.

HAY, D. F., & Ross, H. S. (1982). The social nature of early conflict. *Child Development, 53,* 105–113.

HENNIGAN, K. M., Del Rosario, M. L., Heath, L., Cook, T. D., Wharton, J. D., & Calder, B. J. (1982). Impact of the introduction of television on crime in the United States: Empirical findings and theoretical implications. *Journal of Personality and Social Psychology, 42,* 461–477.

HICKS, D. J. (1968). Effects of co-observer's sanctions and adult presence on imitative aggression. *Child Development, 39,* 303–309.

HOFFMAN-PLOTKIN, D., & Twentyman, C. T. (1984). A multimodal assessment of behavioral and cognitive deficits in abused and neglected preschoolers. *Child Development, 55,* 794–802.

HORTON, R. W., & Santogrossi, D. A. (1978). The effect of adult commentary on reducing the influence of televised violence. *Personality and Social Psychology Bulletin, 4,* 337–340.

HOVING, K. L., Wallace, J. R., & LaForme, G. L. (1976). *The expression of interpersonal aggression in a competitive situation as a function of age, sex, amount and type of provocation.* Unpublished manuscript, Kent State University.

HUESMANN, L. R., Eron, L. D., Lefkowitz, M. M., & Walder, L. O. (1984). Stability of aggression over time and generations. *Developmental Psychology, 20,* 1120–1134.

HUTT, C. (1972). *Males and females.* Baltimore: Penguin Books.

HYDE, J. S. (1984). How large are gender differences in aggression? A developmental meta-analysis. *Developmental Psychology, 20,* 722–736.

JOHNSON, S. M., & Lobitz, C. K. (1974). The personal and marital adjustment of parents as related to observed child deviance and parenting behavior. *Journal of Abnormal Child Psychology, 2,* 193–207.

KAGAN, J., & Moss, H. A. (1962). *Birth to maturity.* New York: Wiley.

KATZ, R. C. (1971). Interactions between the facilitative and inhibitory effects of a punishing stimulus in the control of children's hitting behavior. *Child Development, 42,* 1433–1446.

KUO, Z. Y. (1930). The genesis of the cat's response to the rat. *Journal of Comparative and Physiological Psychology, 11,* 1–35.

LEYENS, J., Parke, R. D., Camino, L., & Berkowitz, L. (1975). Effects of movie violence on aggression in a field setting as a function of group dominance and cohesion. *Journal of Personality and Social Psychology, 32,* 346–360.

LIEBERT, R. M., & Baron, R. A. (1972). Some immediate effects of televised violence on children's behavior. *Developmental Psychology, 6,* 469–475.

LIEBERT, R. M., Neale, J. M., & Davidson, E. S. (1973). *The early window: Effects of television on children and youth.* New York: Pergamon Press.

LIEBERT, R. M., & Schwartzberg, N. S. (1977). Effects of mass media. In M. R. Rosenzweig & L. W. Porter (Eds.), *Annual review of psychology* (Vol. 28). Palo Alto, CA: Annual Reviews.

LIEBERT, R. M., Sprafkin, J. N., & Davidson, E. S. (1982). *The early window: Effects of television on children and youth* (2nd ed.). New York: Pergamon Press.

LORENZ, K. (1966). *On aggression.* New York: Harcourt, Brace & World.

LOVAAS, O. (1961). Interaction between verbal and nonverbal behavior. *Child Development, 32,* 329–336.

MACCOBY, E. E. (1980). *Social development: Psychological growth and the parent-child relationship.* San Diego, CA: Harcourt Brace Jovanovich.

MACCOBY, E. E., & Jacklin, C. N. (1974). *The psychology of sex differences.* Stanford, CA: Stanford University Press.

MACCOBY, E. E., & Jacklin, C. N. (1980). Sex differences in aggression: A rejoinder and reprise. *Child Development, 51,* 964–980.

MacDONALD, K., & Parke, R. D. (1984). Bridging the gap: Parent-child play interaction and peer interactive competence. *Child Development, 55,* 1265–1277.

MacFARLANE, A. (1977). *The psychology of childbirth.* Cambridge, MA: Harvard University Press.

MALLICK, S. K., & McCandless, B. R. (1966). A study of the catharsis of aggression. *Journal of Personality and Social Psychology, 4,* 591–596.

MARTIN, B. (1975). Parent-child relations. In F. D. Horowitz (Ed.), *Review of child development research* (Vol. 4). Chicago: University of Chicago Press.

MEAD, M. (1935). *Sex and temperament in three primitive societies.* New York: Morrow.

MIDDLEBROOK, P. N. (1974). *Social psychology and modern life.* New York: Knopf.

MILLER, N. E. (1941). The frustration-aggression hypothesis. *Psychological Review, 48,* 337–342.

MOSS, H. A. (1967). Sex, age, and state as determinants of mother-infant interaction. *Merrill-Palmer Quarterly, 13,* 19–36.

NATIONAL COMMISSION ON THE CAUSES AND PREVENTION OF VIOLENCE (1969). *To establish justice, to insure domestic tranquility.* New York: Award Books.

NELSON-LeGALL, S. A. (1985). Motive-outcome matching and outcome foreseeability: Effects on attribution of intentionality and moral judgments. *Developmental Psychology, 21,* 332–337.

OLWEUS, D. (1980). Familial and temperamental determinants of aggressive behavior in adolescent boys: A causal analysis. *Developmental Psychology, 16,* 644–660.

OLWEUS, D. (1982). Development of stable aggressive reaction patterns in males. In R. Blanchard & C. Blanchard (Eds.), *Advances in the study of aggression* (Vol. 1). New York: Academic Press.

OSBORN, D. K., & Endsley, R. C. (1971). Emotional reactions of young children to TV violence. *Child Development, 42,* 321–331.

PARKE, R. D., Berkowitz, L., Leyens, J., West, S., & Sebastian, R. J. (1977). Some effects of violent and nonviolent movies on the behavior of juvenile delinquents. In L. Berkowitz (Ed.), *Advances in experimental social psychology* (Vol. 10). Orlando, FL: Academic Press.

PARKE, R. D., & Slaby, R. G. (1983). The development of aggression. In E. M. Hetherington (Ed.), *Handbook of child psychology* (Vol. 4). New York: Wiley.

PATTERSON, G. R. (1976). The aggressive child: Victim and architect of a coercive system. In E. J. Mash, L. A. Hamerlynck, & L. C. Handy (Eds.), *Behavior modification and families.* Vol. 1: *Theory and research.* New York: Brunner/Mazel.

PATTERSON, G. R. (1981). Mothers: The unacknowledged victims. *Monographs of the Society for Research in Child Development, 45*(5, Serial No. 18b).

PATTERSON, G. R. (1982). *Coercive family processes.* Eugene, OR: Castilia Press.

PATTERSON, G. R., Littman, R. A., & Bricker, W. (1967). Assertive behavior in children: A step toward a theory of aggression. *Monographs of the Society for Research in Child Development, 32*(5, Serial No. 113).

PATTERSON, G. R., & Stouthamer-Loeber, M. (1984). The correlation of family management practices and delinquency. *Child Development, 55,* 1299–1307.

PATTERSON, G. R., Stouthamer-Loeber, M., & Loeber, R. (1982). *Parental monitoring and antisocial child behavior.* Unpublished manuscript, Oregon Social Learning Center.

PERRY, D. G., & Bussey, K. (1977). Self-reinforcement in high- and low-aggressive boys following acts of aggression. *Child Development, 48,* 653–657.

PERRY, D. G., & Perry, L. C. (1974). Denial of suffering in the victim as a stimulus to violence in aggressive boys. *Child Development, 45,* 55–62.

PIAGET, J. (1952) *The origins of intelligence in children.* New York: International Universities Press.

PORTER, B., & O'Leary, K. D. (1980). Marital discord and childhood behavior problems. *Journal of Abnormal Child Psychology, 8*, 287–295.

POWER, T. G., & Parke, R. D. (1982). Play as a context for early learning: Lab and home analyses. In I. E. Sigel & L. M. Laosa (Eds.), *The family as a learning environment.* New York: Plenum.

RICHARD, B. A., & Dodge, K. A. (1982). Social maladjustment and problem solving in school-aged children. *Journal of Consulting and Clinical Psychology, 50*, 226–233.

RULE, B. G., Ferguson, T. J., & Nesdale, A. R. (1980). Emotional arousal, anger, and aggression: The misattribution principle. In P. Pliner, K. Blankstein, & T. Spiegel (Eds.), *Advances in communication and affect.* Hillsdale, NJ: Erlbaum.

RULE, B. G., Nesdale, A. R., & McAra, M. J. (1974). Children's reactions to information about the intentions underlying an aggressive act. *Child Development, 45*, 794–798.

RUSHTON, J. P., Fulker, D. W., Neale, M. C., Nias, D. K. B., & Eysenck, H. J. (1986). Altruism and aggression: The heritability of individual differences. *Journal of Personality and Social Psychology, 50*, 1192–1198.

SACKIN, S., & Thelen, E. (1984). An ethological study of peaceful associative outcomes to conflict in preschool children. *Child Development, 55*, 1098–1102.

SCOTT, J. P. (1966). Agonistic behavior in mice and rats: A review. *American Zoologist, 6*, 683–701.

SCOTT, J. P. (1972). Hostility and aggression. In B. Wolman (Ed.), *Handbook of genetic psychology.* Englewood Cliffs, NJ: Prentice-Hall.

SEARS, R. R. (1958). Personality development in the family. In J. M. Seidman (Ed.), *The child.* New York: Holt, Rinehart and Winston.

SEARS, R. R., Maccoby, E. E., & Levin, H. (1957). *Patterns of child rearing.* New York: Harper & Row.

SHANTZ, D. W., & Voydanoff, D. A. (1973). Situational effects on retaliatory aggression at three age levels. *Child Development, 44*, 149–153.

SIEGAL, A. E., & Kohn, L. G. (1959). Permissiveness, permission, and aggression: The effect of adult presence or absence on aggression in children's play. *Child Development, 30*, 131–141.

SLABY, R. G., & Crowley, C. G. (1977). Modification of cooperation and aggression through teacher attention to children's speech. *Journal of Experimental Child Psychology, 23*, 442–458.

SLUCKIN, A. M., & Smith, P. K. (1977). Two approaches to the concept of dominance in preschool children. *Child Development, 48*, 917–923.

SMITH, P. K., & Connolly, K. J. (1980). *The ecology of preschool behavior.* New York: Cambridge University Press.

SMITH, P. K., & Green, M. (1974). Aggressive behavior in English nurseries and playgroups: Sex differences and response of adults. *Child Development, 45*, 211–214.

STEIN, A. H., & Friedrich, L. K. (1972). Television content and young children's behavior. In J. P. Murray, E. A. Rubinstein, & G. A. Comstock (Eds.), *Television and social behavior.* Vol. 2: *Television and social learning.* Washington, DC: U.S. Government Printing Office.

STEINMETZ, S. K. (1977). *The cycle of violence: Assertive, aggressive, and abusive family interaction.* New York: Praeger.

STEVENS, D. P., & Truss, C. V. (1985). Stability and change in adult personality over 12 and 20 years. *Developmental Psychology, 21*, 568–584.

STRAYER, F. F. (1980). Social ecology of the preschool peer group. In W. A. Collins (Ed.), *Minnesota Symposia on Child Psychology.* Vol. 13: *Development of cognition, affect, and social relations.* Hillsdale, NJ: Erlbaum.

TAUBER, M. (1979). Parental socialization techniques and sex differences in children's play. *Child Development, 50*, 225–234.

TAYLOR, S. P., & Epstein, S. (1967). Aggression as a function of the interaction of the sex of the aggressor and the sex of the victim. *Journal of Personality, 35*, 474–486.

THOMAS, M. H., Horton, R. W., Lippincott, E. C., & Drabman, R. S. (1977). Desensitization to portrayals of real-life aggression as a function of exposure to television violence. *Journal of Personality and Social Psychology, 35*, 450–458.

TIEGER, T. (1980). On the biological bases of sex differences in aggression. *Child Development, 51*, 943–963.

TOCH, H. (1969). *Violent men.* Hawthorne, NY: Aldine.

TURNBULL, C. M. (1972). *The mountain people.* New York: Simon & Schuster.

TURNER, C. W., & Goldsmith, D. (1976). Effects of toy guns and airplanes on children's antisocial free play behavior. *Journal of Experimental Child Psychology, 21*, 303–315.

WALTERS, R. H., & Brown, M. (1963). Studies of reinforcement of aggression: Transfer of responses to an interpersonal situation. *Child Development, 34*, 562–571.

WELLS, W. D. (1972). *Television and aggression: A replication of an experimental field study.* Unpublished manuscript, University of Chicago.

WRIGHT, J. C., & Huston, A. C. (1983). A matter of form: Potentials of television for young viewers. *American Psychologist, 38*, 835–843.

ZAHAVI, S., & Asher, S. R. (1978). The effect of verbal instructions on preschool children's aggressive behavior. *Journal of School Psychology, 16*, 146–153.

ZAHN-WAXLER, C., Radke-Yarrow, M., & King, R. A. (1979). Child rearing and children's prosocial initiations toward victims of distress. *Child Development, 50*, 319–330.

10

ALTRUISM AND PROSOCIAL DEVELOPMENT

WHAT ARE ALTRUISM AND PROSOCIAL BEHAVIOR?

A Motivational Definition of Altruism

A Behavioral Definition of Altruism

THEORIES OF PROSOCIAL DEVELOPMENT

*Biological Theories: Are We "Programmed" for
Prosocial Conduct?*

Psychoanalytic Theory: Let Your Conscience Be Your Guide

Social-Learning Theory: What's in It for Me?

Cognitive-Developmental Theory: Maturity Is the Medium

A Final Comment

DEVELOPMENTAL TRENDS IN ALTRUISM

Origins of Prosocial Behavior

Age Differences in Altruism

WHO HELPS WHOM? BENEFACTOR AND RECIPIENT CHARACTERISTICS THAT AFFECT ALTRUISM

Sex Differences in Altruism

Dependency: Does This Person Need My Help?

Getting By with a Little Help from My Friends

Feeling Good and Feeling Blue: Effects of Moods on Altruism

(continues)

COGNITIVE CONTRIBUTORS TO ALTRUISM

Role Taking and Altruism

Moral Reasoning and Altruistic Behavior

EMPATHY: AN AFFECTIVE CONTRIBUTOR TO ALTRUISM

BEHAVIORAL CONTRIBUTORS TO ALTRUISM

Direct Tuition and Reinforcement

Modeling Influences: Practicing and Preaching Altruism

METHODS OF PROMOTING CHILDREN'S ALTRUISM

Becoming a Prosocial Society

Implications from the Study of Prosocial Activists

Parental Discipline and Children's Altruistic Inclinations

Television as a Prosocial Instrument

SUMMARY

REFERENCES

At some point during the prehistoric era, humans became social animals. Groups of men, women, and children began to form collectives, or tribal units, which provided increased protection against common enemies and allowed individuals to share the many labors necessary for their survival. One rule of order that undoubtedly characterized these early cooperative social groupings was some version of what we now know as the *norm of social responsibility* (see Berkowitz & Daniels, 1963), which prescribes that *one should help others who need help*. This ideal is endorsed by most people in most cultures (Krebs, 1970), and its widespread acceptance has led many social philosophers to conclude that a concern for one's fellow human beings is a basic value of our species.

However, several psychoanalytic and social-learning theorists have not given prosocial behavior (behavior that benefits others) a prominent place in their overall view of personality development. They have traditionally stressed the self-serving side of human beings, depicting us as creatures who strive to attain power or self-advancement. Consequently, one individual is thought to help another only when he or she expects some personal gain or reward for doing so.

Surely this view of human nature is oversimplified. All of us can probably recall an occasion when one person has made a great personal sacrifice to help another without expecting anything in return. For example, what self-serving principle motivates the soldier who hurls himself on a live grenade in order to save his buddies? What personal gain could have possibly motivated the behavior of the many German citizens who *risked their lives* to save their Jewish countrymen during World War II? Many of these "rescuers" did not even know the names of the people they saved, much less receive rewards from them (Rosenhan, 1972a). In short, people often help others, even if this helping involves some cost to themselves and promises very little in the way of personal gain or reward.

In this chapter, we will explore the issue of how children acquire the capacity to give of themselves in order to benefit others. Our first task is to determine what psychologists mean by the terms *prosocial behavior* and *altruism*. We will then discuss several theoretical explanations for these interesting and often self-sacrificial forms of social behavior. Next we will chart the development of prosocial behavior from infancy to adolescence, noting who is most likely to benefit whom, and when. Finally, we will review the effects of many variables that are thought to influence the growth of prosocial inclinations and then conclude by discussing some strategies that adults might use to promote children's concern about the welfare of others.

WHAT ARE ALTRUISM AND PROSOCIAL BEHAVIOR?

Prosocial behavior is any *action that benefits other people*—such as sharing with someone less fortunate than oneself, comforting or rescuing a distressed person, cooperating with someone or helping him or her to achieve an objective, or even simply making others feel good by complimenting them on their appearance or accomplishments. Now before proceeding further, briefly scan the nine situations presented in Figure 10-1. Most of us would probably agree that these acts are examples of prosocial behavior. But would you consider each of them to be altruistic?

Were I to ask this question of 30 students, there would be some disagreement on whether several of the acts in Figure 10-1 qualify as altruism. Moreover, psychologists interested in prosocial behavior would debate the very same points, and for reasons that should become quite apparent as we discuss the two most common definitions of altruism.

A MOTIVATIONAL DEFINITION OF ALTRUISM

Those who favor a motivational definition of altruism focus on the motives, or intentions, that underlie prosocial acts. According to this motivational perspective, an act of kindness can be labeled "altruistic" if the actor's *primary* motive, or intent, is to provide positive consequences for another person. In other words, the true altruist acts more out of a

Situation	Altruistic?		
	Yes	Undecided	No
1. John S., a millionaire, makes a $50,000 contribution to the Heart Fund.	___	___	___
2. Sam P., a talented professional football player, agrees to donate his time to tape a commercial for the United Way.	___	___	___
3. Susie Q., an 8-year-old, freely chooses to spend Halloween night trick-or-treating for the March of Dimes.	___	___	___
4. Mary H. comforts a crying child who is lost in a large department store.	___	___	___
5. Fred W. intervenes to help a woman who is being mugged, and he is stabbed to death.	___	___	___
6. Tammy P., gives half of her 25¢ allowance to a friend who has no money.	___	___	___
7. John B. gives a pint of blood to a blood bank and receives $10 for his donation.	___	___	___
8. Bill K. repays Jim L. for a previous favor by offering to help Jim paint his garage.	___	___	___
9. Jack R., a used-car salesman, gives a quarter to the child of a customer when the child cries that she is thirsty for a soft drink.	___	___	___

You may want to compare your responses with those of your friends or other members of your class. Looking at the pattern of your own responses, do you favor a motivational or a behavioral definition of altruism?

FIGURE 10-1 When is a prosocial act altruistic?

concern for others than for the positive outcomes he or she may obtain as a result of helping, sharing with, or comforting them. Proponents of the motivational definition would classify a prosocial act as nonaltruistic if the actor hopes to reap significant personal gains from his or her benevolence or is simply repaying the recipient for a favor.

Although a majority of my students endorse a motivational definition of altruism, the more skeptical minority seriously doubt that any form of helping is motivated solely out of a concern for others without regard for the self. The minority may have a point, for it is often difficult to determine exactly what motivates a helping act. Consider Situation 1 of Figure 10-1. John S. could be considered altruistic if we conclude that his donation was prompted by a desire to help mankind solve the mysteries of heart disease. But we would probably label his act nonaltruistic if we learned that John suffers from heart disease or if we decided that his donation was intended as a tax write-off. Even Fred W. in Situation 5 could conceivably be seeking the adulation of the female victim or "doing the right thing" in order to maintain his own self-respect or ensure that he makes it to heaven. If so, his behavior does not qualify as altruism under a motivational definition. Consider one more example. Suppose that you found a wallet that contained a large sum of money, returned it to its owner, and subsequently declined a monetary offering with the statement "Your thanks is my reward." Is this "thank you" a sufficient reward to render your behavior nonaltruistic? The problems involved in inferring a helper's true intentions have led many psychologists to conclude that altruism is best defined behaviorally.

A BEHAVIORAL DEFINITION OF ALTRUISM

According to the behavioral perspective, the term *altruism* applies to an act that benefits another person or persons, *regardless of the actor's motives*. In other words, altruism and prosocial behavior are viewed as roughly synonymous concepts, so that any and all of the acts depicted in Figure 10-1 could be labeled "altruistic."

What kinds of behaviors do children view as altruistic? How do their views differ from those of adults? Lizette Peterson and Donna Gelfand (1984) addressed these issues by asking college students and first-, fourth-, and sixth-graders to rate the altruistic motivation of different children who had helped adults (1) out of empathy, (2) to obtain a tangible reward, (3) to win praise, (4) to repay a favor, or (5) to avoid criticism. Even the first-graders knew that an actor who helped in order to avoid criticism was not displaying an altruistic motive. However, they felt that all the other actors were about equally altruistic, regardless of the attributions they had received for the actors' helping. Surprisingly, perhaps, fourth- and sixth-graders showed roughly the same pattern of results—thus indicating that even 9–12-year-olds often fail to discriminate the motives underlying prosocial acts and seem to favor a behavioral definition of altruism. By contrast, the adults in this study clearly favored the motivational definition, for they attributed greater altruism to helpers who had empathized with the recipient than to those who were

simply repaying a favor or who had something to gain (praise or a tangible reward) from their assistance.

Like many developmentalists, I tend *not* to make sharp distinctions between altruism and prosocial behavior when referring to the benevolence of developing children. But in so doing, I do not wish to imply that the motivational bases for children's acts of kindness are unimportant or irrelevant. Some years ago, David Rosenhan (1972b) proposed a definition of altruism that distinguishes *autonomous altruism*, those prosocial acts motivated by a concern for others, from *normative altruism*, those acts of kindness given in expectation of receiving personal benefits or avoiding criticism for failing to act. This distinction appears to be a useful one, for we will see that these two kinds of prosocial conduct just may evolve along separate developmental paths.

THEORIES OF PROSOCIAL DEVELOPMENT

Several theorists have debated the issue of whether altruism is innate or learned. *Ethologists* and proponents of an emerging discipline known as *sociobiology* believe that altruism is a preadapted, genetically programmed attribute—a basic component of human nature—that helps to ensure the survival of the species. By contrast, *psychoanalytic* and *social-learning* theorists argue that a child's prosocial inclinations derive not from his or her genes or evolutionary history but, rather, from experiences with social agents (altruism is acquired). *Cognitive-developmental* theorists can certainly agree with this latter point of view. However, they would add that both the form and the frequency of a child's prosocial conduct will depend, in part, on his or her cognitive skills and level of intellectual development.

It will become apparent from our review that each of these theories has a particular focus that is not shared by the others, and as a result, no one of them provides a complete explanation of human altruism. Yet these models have stimulated a plethora of research from which we have gained important insights about the origins of children's altruistic concern.

BIOLOGICAL THEORIES: ARE WE "PROGRAMMED" FOR PROSOCIAL CONDUCT?

In 1965 Donald Campbell argued that altruism is, in part, instinctive—a basic component of human nature. His argument hinged on the assumption that individuals, be they animal or human, are more likely to receive protection from natural enemies and to satisfy their basic needs if they live together in cooperative social units. If this assumption is correct, then cooperative, altruistic individuals would be most likely to survive and to pass along "altruistic genes" to their offspring. Thus, over thousands of years evolutionary processes would favor the development of innate prosocial motives. Campbell aptly notes that "the tremendous survival value of being social makes innate social motives as likely on *a priori* grounds as self-centered ones" (1965, p. 301).

Of course, it could be argued that acting in behalf of others may be self-serving if the recipients of our benevolence tend to repay these acts of kindnes (Trivers, 1971). Moreover, sociobiologists such as Cunningham (in press) and Eberhard (1975) believe that we are more inclined to behave altruistically if the acts that we perform will help *our own* genes to survive. Accordingly, we should be more likely to help close relatives who share our genes (a process known as *kin selection*) than other people with whom we have no genes in common. Cunningham (in press) has recently tested this "kin selection" hypothesis in a study with adults. Subjects were given a long list of prosocial behaviors and were asked which of these acts they would be willing to perform for a number of recipients, ranging from close relatives to complete strangers. The results were clear: subjects' willingness to act in the interest of others was directly related to the degree of kinship between them and the prospective recipients. Close relatives were more likely to be helped than distant relatives, who, in turn, would receive more assistance than nonrelatives. Though consistent with the kin selection hypothesis, these data are obviously amenable to alternative interpretations. For example, one might argue that we have developed attachments to our relatives (particularly to close relatives) and that these emotional outgrowths of our social lives are

what really account for our heightened benevolence toward close kin.

If there is a genetic basis for altruism, then what exactly do we inherit that makes us prosocially inclined? Martin Hoffman (1981) proposes that a capacity for empathy—the tendency to become aroused by another person's distress—may be the biological mediator of altruistic concern. Indeed, we noted in Box 2-2 that newborn infants may be displaying a primitive empathic reaction when they become distressed at the sound of another infant's cries. And we also learned (in Chapter 2) that empathy is a heritable attribute, for identical twins are much more alike in empathic concern than fraternal twins (Matthews, Batson, Horn, & Rosenman, 1981). Later in this chapter, we will see that there is a meaningful relationship between a person's empathic sensitivities and his or her prosocial behavior. However, this does not necessarily imply that altruism is genetically programmed, for as Hoffman (1981) has argued, an inborn capacity for empathy is subject to environmental influence and may be fostered or dramatically inhibited by the social environments in which children are raised. With that comment in mind, let us turn to other theories that stress environmental contributions to children's prosocial development.

PSYCHOANALYTIC THEORY: LET YOUR CONSCIENCE BE YOUR GUIDE

Recall from our discussion of psychoanalytic theory (Chapter 2) that its originator, Sigmund Freud, described the young, unsocialized child as a self-serving creature constantly driven by id-based, hedonistic impulses. This characterization of human nature might seem to suggest that the concept of altruism offers a severe challenge to a psychoanalytic account of personality development: How is it possible for a selfish, egoistic child to acquire a sense of altruistic concern that will occasionally dictate that he or she make self-sacrificing responses to benefit others?

The challenge is not as formidable as it first appears. According to proponents of psychoanalytic theory, altruistic norms and principles—for example, the social responsibility norm and the Golden

Rule—are but a few of the many rules, regulations, and values that may be internalized during the period of childhood in which the superego develops. We will examine the process of superego development in some detail when we discuss moral development (see Chapter 11), but for the moment it should be noted that necessary conditions for the development of altruism include an exposure to altruistic values within the context of a warm, nurturant parent/child relationship. Once altruistic principles are internalized and become part of the ego-ideal, the child strives to help others in need so as to avoid punishment from the conscience (guilt, shame, self-degradation) for failing to render such assistance.

SOCIAL-LEARNING THEORY: WHAT'S IN IT FOR ME?

Altruism presents an interesting paradox for social-learning theory (Rosenhan, 1972a). A central premise of the social-learning approach is that people repeat behaviors that are reinforced and avoid repeating responses that prove costly or punishing. Yet many prosocial acts seem to defy this view of human nature: altruists often choose to take dangerous risks, forgo personal rewards, and donate their own valuable resources (thereby incurring a loss) in order to benefit others. The challenge for social-learning theorists is to explain how these self-sacrificial tendencies are acquired and maintained.

Responses to the challenge have been many and varied. On a conceptual level, several reinforcement theorists have taken the position that all prosocial acts, even those that prove extremely costly to the benefactor, are prompted by some form of subtle reward or self-gain. For example, we could argue that the German citizens who risked their lives to rescue Jews from their Nazi tormentors did so in order to increase their self-esteem, to win a favorable evaluation from future generations, or to reap the benefits afforded to morally righteous people in the afterlife. The major problem with this explanation is its circularity: it is assumed that, since helping behavior occurred, its consequences must have been reinforcing (Sigelman, 1984).

Although tangible rewards do not always follow altruistic responses, altruism may still be a function of social learning and reinforcement. Let's consider three ways in which children might learn that altruism "pays off."

Conditioning of empathic responses. Our capacity for empathy may help to explain why we might help, comfort, or share with others in situations where there are no obvious tangible rewards to sustain helping behavior. In Chapter 9 we defined empathy as the ability to recognize and experience the emotions of others. If an empathizer were to observe a happy or joyful person, she too might experience a pleasant, positive feeling and might be motivated to prolong the person's happiness as a means of sustaining her own good mood. Similarly, an empathizer should experience pain and suffering if exposed to a person who expresses these negative emotions. Assisting a suffering victim not only would relieve the victim's distress but might also reinforce the benefactor by relieving her vicarious distress. In sum, prosocial responses may often appear to be self-sacrificing when, in fact, they *reinforce* the helper by making her feel good or by relieving empathic discomfort.

How and when do children begin to associate their own empathic reactions with the performance of altruistic responses? According to Eleanor Maccoby (1980), the empathic mediation of altruism may develop through classical conditioning and begin very early in life:

> With empathic distress the process would work in the following way: A twelve-month-old has cried on hundreds of different occasions and the sound of crying has repeatedly been associated with the child's own distress. And so by a process of [classical conditioning], the sound of crying—anyone's crying—can now evoke feelings of distress . . . and even tears. If the young listener thinks of a way to make the other person stop crying, he or she will feel better. From the standpoint of simple self-interest, then, we should expect children to learn to perform such "altruistic" actions [p. 347].

Direct tuition of altruism. Neo-Hullian and operant-learning theorists argue that we may often behave altruistically without expecting immediate payoffs because previous rewards for similar acts of kindness have made such behavior intrinsically reinforcing. The process might work this way. Parents, teachers, Sunday school instructors, and other socializing agents often preach the virtues of prosocial conduct and reward children who behave accordingly. Over a period of time (and reinforcements), some of the positive affect stemming from these rewards becomes associated with the prosocial acts that are rewarded, so that altruistic gestures eventually become secondary reinforcers that, when enacted, make the child feel good. And because individuals in most cultures receive periodic praise, recognition, or other forms of extrinsic reinforcement for their benevolence, it is not hard to imagine how prosocial acts might retain their "satisfying" qualities and become extremely resistant to extinction.

Observational learning of altruism. While conceding that altruistic habits might be acquired through classical conditioning processes or direct tuition, Albert Bandura (1977) believes that the most pervasive influence on children's altruism is the behavior of other people—the social models to which they are exposed. And he may be right, for it is now apparent that children who witness the charitable acts of an altruistic model often become more altruistic themselves (see Rushton, 1976, or Radke-Yarrow, Zahn-Waxler, & Chapman, 1983, for a review). In one study, Rosenhan and White (1967) had fourth- and fifth-graders take turns playing a bowling game with an adult model. Each "winning" score of 20 attained by either the child or the adult earned the player two five-cent gift certificates that were redeemable at a local candy store. Children exposed to a *charitable* model saw the adult place one of his two gift certificates into a container labeled "Trenton Orphans' Fund" after each of his winning trials. In a *control* condition, the model did not donate any of his gift certificates to the orphans. At the conclusion of this "training" phase, the model pretended to have work to do elsewhere. The child was then left alone to play the bowling game. Before departing, the model told the child to return to the classroom after completing 20 plays. The outcomes for these 20 trials were rigged so that each child had four winning scores and thus four opportunities to donate gift certificates to needy children.

The results were clear. Of the children who had been exposed to a charitable model, 63% contributed to the orphans' fund during the training trials when the model was present. Perhaps these donations represent nothing more than normative altruism, for they may have been made in an attempt to win the approval of a charitable adult. Would these children behave in a similar fashion *when the model left the room*? Presumably, donations made in the model's absence are motivated by a concern for others (autonomous altruism) rather than a desire to win the model's approval. Rosenhan and White found that 47.5% of the children who witnessed the charitable model donated some of their gift certificates when the model was absent. However, not one of the children in the control group made a donation to the orphans' fund *at any time during the procedure*. So it appears that observation of a charitable model facilitates both normative and autonomous altruism in grade school children.

We have noted on many occasions that observers are especially willing to imitate a social model if the model's behavior is reinforced. Thus, it might seem that the influence of altruistic modeling presents a challenge for social-learning theory. Why should children follow the lead of prosocial models when these charitable individuals receive little or no tangible reinforcement for their exemplary behavior?

The answer may lie in the ways children process the relevant social information and interpret what they have seen. For example, Kohlberg (1969) argues that the model's behavior merely informs the child of what older, more competent people consider the "appropriate" or mature response under the circumstances. Presumably, the child then follows the model's example as part of his attempt to emulate the behavior of competent others; that is, imitating competent people is intrinsically reinforcing. A second possibility is that the model's prosocial acts simply remind children of the norm of social responsibility, which they have already internalized. Finally, children may learn that altruism is *self-reinforcing* if altruistic models reinforce themselves by expressing happiness or some other form of positive affect when they help others (Bandura, 1977). Indeed, Midlarsky and Bryan (1972) discovered that models who express positive affect while helping—for example,

PHOTOS 10-1   Children learn many prosocial responses by observing the behavior of altruistic models.

"Giving to the poor makes me feel *good*"—elicit more prosocial behavior from fourth- and fifth-grade children than equally charitable models who express positive affect that is unrelated to their acts of kindness (such as "This game is fun").

In sum, learning theorists have offered several plausible explanations for children's willingness to perform prosocial acts that promise few if any tangible rewards and may even be costly to themselves. In a later section of the chapter, we will follow up on these ideas by taking a closer look at the contributions of reinforcement, empathy, and social modeling influences to children's prosocial development.

COGNITIVE-DEVELOPMENTAL THEORY: MATURITY IS THE MEDIUM

Cognitive-developmental theorists assume that prosocial responses such as cooperation, sharing, giving reassurance and comfort, and volunteering to help others should become increasingly apparent over the course of childhood (see Eisenberg, Lennon, & Roth, 1983; Kohlberg, 1969). The basis for this prediction is straightforward: as children develop intellectually, they will acquire important cognitive skills that will affect both their reasoning about prosocial issues and their motivation to act in the interest of others.

Cognitive theorists have proposed that there are three broad stages of prosocial development. The first stage roughly coincides with Piaget's preoperational period (age 7 and younger). Presumably, young children are relatively egocentric, and their thinking about prosocial issues is often self-serving, or hedonistic: acts that benefit others are considered worth performing if those acts will also benefit the self. During middle childhood and preadolescence (or Piaget's concrete-operational stage), children are becoming less egocentric, are acquiring important role-taking skills, and should now begin to focus on the legitimate needs of others as a justification for prosocial behavior. This is the period when children begin to think that any act of kindness that most people would condone is probably "good" and should be performed. It is also the stage at which empathic or sympathetic responses should become an important mediator of altruism. Finally, adolescents who have reached formal operations have begun to understand and appreciate the implications of abstract prosocial norms—universal principles such as the norm of social responsibility or the Golden Rule that (1) would encourage them to direct their acts of kindness to a wider range of prospective recipients and (2) may also trigger feelings of guilt or self-condemnation should they violate these principles (Eisenberg et al., 1983).

Most cognitive-developmental researchers have

not looked for broad stages of prosocial development but have chosen instead to explore the relationship between the growth of particular cognitive skills (for example, role taking) and children's prosocial behavior. Yet in recent years, Nancy Eisenberg and her associates have begun to chart age-related changes in children's reasoning about prosocial issues, and her results are indeed interesting. We will review both these lines in inquiry in a later section of the chapter.

A FINAL COMMENT

It has only been within the past 15 to 20 years that researchers have begun to study the prosocial inclinations of developing children. And even though sociobiologists and behavior geneticists have recently proposed a number of intriguing ideas that are definitely worth pursuing, most of the existing work on prosocial development stems from either the social-learning or the cognitive-developmental approach. Although these two theories are often viewed as conflicting or contradictory, they clearly emphasize *different* aspects of development:

> The social learning approach emphasizes the role of antecedent and consequent environmental events (e.g., the presence or absence of a model or reinforcement), [whereas] the cognitive-developmental approach emphasizes the role of cognitive structures (stages) as measured, for example, by role-taking tasks and moral judgment stories [Rushton, 1976, p. 909].

I will simply add that predictions derived from both theories have received empirical confirmation, sometimes in the same experiment! For example, Rushton (1975) found that children exposed to charitable models were later more charitable themselves than age mates exposed to selfish models—a finding consistent with social-learning theory. However, closer inspection of the data revealed that children who had tested relatively high (that is, mature) in their levels of moral reasoning were much more charitable overall and were more likely to criticize the stinginess of a selfish model than those who had tested lower (or less mature) in their moral reasoning—findings that are clearly anticipated by cognitive-developmental theory. So in light of these results and other empirical evidence that we will examine, it seems wise to consider the social-learning and the cognitive-developmental perspectives as complementary, rather than contradictory, statements about the origins and development of altruism.

DEVELOPMENTAL TRENDS IN ALTRUISM

A genuine concern about the welfare of other people is a value that many adults hope their children will acquire. In fact, it is not at all unusual for parents to encourage prosocial responses such as sharing, cooperating, or helping while their children are still in diapers. Until very recently, most experts in child development would have claimed that these well-intentioned adults were wasting their time, for young, egocentric infants were thought to be incapable of considering the needs of anyone other than themselves. But in this case, the experts were wrong!

ORIGINS OF PROSOCIAL BEHAVIOR

Long before children receive any deliberate moral or religious training, they may act in ways that resemble the prosocial behavior of older people. At 12 months of age, infants are often "sharing" interesting experiences by pointing, and they will occasionally offer toys to their companions (Hay, 1979; Leung & Rheingold, 1981). By age 18 months, some children are already jumping in and trying to help with household chores such as sweeping, dusting, or setting the table (Rheingold, 1982). Moreover, a primitive type of reciprocity appears by the end of the third year. In one recent study (Levitt, Weber, Clark, & McDonnell, 1985), 29- to 36-month-old toddlers who had previously received a toy from a peer when they had had none of their own typically returned the favor (given a little maternal prompting) when they later found themselves with several toys to play with and the peer without any. But if that peer had earlier refused to share, the toddlers almost invariably hoarded the toys when it was their turn to control them. Finally, demonstrations of sympathy or compassion are not at all uncommon among young children (see Radke-Yarrow et al., 1983). Consider the reaction of 21-month-old John to his distressed playmate, Jerry:

> Today Jerry was kind of cranky; he just started . . . bawling and wouldn't stop. John kept coming over and handing Jerry toys, trying to cheer him up. . . . He'd say things like "Here Jerry," and I said to John "Jerry's sad; he doesn't feel good; he had a shot today." John would look at me with his eyebrows wrinkled together like he really understood that Jerry was crying because he was unhappy. . . . He went over and rubbed Jerry's arm and said "Nice Jerry," and continued to give him toys [Zahn-Waxler, Radke-Yarrow, & King, 1979, pp. 321–322].

Clearly John was concerned about his little playmate and did what he could to make him feel better.

Although some toddlers will often try to comfort distressed companions, others rarely do. In an attempt to document and explain these individual differences in compassionate behavior, Carolyn Zahn-Waxler and her associates (1979) asked mothers to keep records of (1) the reactions of their 1½- to 2½-year-olds to the distress of other children and (2) their own reactions when their child had been the cause of that distress. The results of this study were indeed interesting. Mothers of less compassionate toddlers tended to discipline acts of harmdoing with physical restraint ("I just moved him away from the baby"), physical punishment ("I swatted her a good one"), or unexplained prohibitions ("I said 'Stop that'"). By contrast, mothers of highly compassionate toddlers frequently disciplined harmdoing with *affective explanations* that helped the child to see the relationship between his or her own acts and the distress they had caused (for example, "You made Doug cry; it's not nice to bite"; "You must never poke anyone's eyes!"). According to Eleanor Maccoby (1980), these affective explanations may be a form of *empathy training*—that is, the mother's scolding will distress the child and simultaneously draw attention to the discomfort of another person. And once children begin to associate their own distress with that of their victims, the foundation for compassionate behavior has been laid. All that the child now needs to learn is that he can eliminate his own conditioned discomfort (or empathic distress) by relieving the distress of others.

AGE DIFFERENCES IN ALTRUISM

In addition to their occasional displays of compassion toward distressed companions, preschoolers will typically share cookies or toys with a peer if they are told to do so by an adult (Levitt et al., 1985) or if the peer should actively elicit sharing through a request or a threat of some kind, such as "I won't be your friend if you won't gimme some" (Birch & Billman, 1986). By contrast, *spontaneous* sharing of valuable resources is relatively uncommon among 3- to 5-year-olds, and aggressive acts actually outnumber expressions of prosocial concern in the day-to-day activities of nursery school children (Murphy, 1937; Yarrow & Waxler, 1976). Yet cooperation, sharing, and other forms of prosocial behavior do become more common between the ages of 3 and 6. One recent observational study revealed that 2½- to 3½-year-olds were more likely than their older nursery school classmates to perform acts of kindness during pretend play, whereas 4- to 6-year-olds performed more *real* helping acts and rarely "play-acted" the role of an altruist (Bar-Tal, Raviv, & Goldberg, 1982).

Children's willingness to share with others appears to increase rather dramatically between the ages of 6 and 12 (see Krebs, 1970; Rushton, 1976; Underwood & Moore, 1982, for reviews of the literature). The relationship between age and sharing is illustrated quite nicely in an early study of 291 Turkish children (Ugurel-Semin, 1952). Each child was asked to divide an odd number of nuts between himself and another known child of the same age. Children were classified as *altruistic* if they either gave more nuts than they kept or shared equally by refusing to assign the odd item and as *selfish* if they kept more than they gave. Sharing clearly increased with age. Only 33% of the 4–6-year-old children chose an altruistic division of resources, compared with 69% of the 6–7-year-olds, 81% of the 7–9-year-olds, and 96% of the 9–12-year-olds. Handlon and Gross (1959) performed a conceptual replication of Ugurel-Semin's study with American preschool, kindergarten, and fourth-, fifth-, and sixth-grade children. This study also revealed that children of preschool and kindergarten age are selfish in their allocation of resources to a peer and that generosity increases with age.

Green and Schneider (1974) sought to determine whether aspects of altruism other than sharing increase with age. Boys from four age groups—5–6, 7–8, 9–10, and 13–14—were given opportunities to (1) share candy with classmates who would not otherwise receive any, (2) help an experimenter who had "accidentally" dropped some pencils on the floor, and (3) volunteer to work on a project that would benefit poor children. The age trends for these three types of altruism appear in Table 10-1. The sharing data are consistent with previous literature indicating that generosity increases over the course of middle childhood. Further, this developmental increase in altruistic concern apparently generalizes to at least one measure of helping—picking up pencils for the experimenter. There were no age differences on the volunteering-to-work index; over 90% of the boys in each age group were willing to sacrifice some of their play time to help needy children. This lack of age differences may be due to an inability of younger children to anticipate or understand the costs that they would incur (giving up free time) as a result of their helpfulness.

Contributing factors.   Why might older children be more generous or helpful than younger ones? One possibility is that they are better *social information processors* and, thus, more likely than younger children to detect subtle cues that indicate the need for benevolent action. A recent study by Ruth Pearl (1985) is consistent with this interpretation. In Pearl's study, 4-year-olds and 9-year-olds watched a series of brief vignettes in which the central character needed some kind of assistance (in one vignette, for

PHOTO 10-2   Young children are not very altruistic and often must be coaxed to share.

example, a boy was struggling to open a cookie jar). The social cues reflecting the actor's distress ranged from very subtle (the boy gave up and looked sadly at the cookie jar) to very explicit (the boy gave up, saying "Rats! The top is stuck," and looked sadly at the cookie jar). After viewing the vignettes, children were questioned to determine whether they knew the central characters were distressed, and they were also asked to suggest a solution for each vignette. Pearl found that 4-year-olds were just as likely as 9-year-olds to notice the actors' distress and to suggest helpful solutions if the distress cues were very explicit. But when these cues were subtle, younger children were much less likely than older ones to per-

TABLE 10-1   Altruistic Behavior of Boys from Four Age Groups

	Age group			
Altruistic response	*5–6*	*7–8*	*9–10*	*13–14*
Average number of candy bars shared	1.36 (60%)	1.84 (92%)	2.88 (100%)	4.24 (100%)
Percentage of children who picked up pencils	48%	76%	100%	96%
Percentage of children who volunteered to work for needy children	96%	92%	100%	96%

Note: Figures in parentheses indicate percentage of children sharing at least one candy bar.

ceive an actor's need for help or to suggest a helpful response.

In addition to their greater ability to recognize others' needs for compassionate or helpful behavior, older children may also feel more *responsible* for helping others and more *competent* to render assistance. Lizette Peterson (1983) recently tested these hypotheses in an experiment with 4-, 7-, and 12-year-olds. Children were first trained at certain tasks (for example, opening a tricky lock) to establish their competence at these activities. Then the experimenter left the room, telling subjects to "watch over things" while she was gone (*responsibility focus* condition) or to simply wait until she returned (*control* condition). Shortly thereafter, a second adult entered the room and soon found herself needing assistance (1) with tasks at which the children were competent (for example, opening the lock) and (2) with other tasks on which children had not been trained (for example, tying a string around a package). The results were clear. Younger children were as likely as older children to help with the tasks at which they felt competent, particularly if responsibility for "watching over things" had been assigned to them. But on tasks at which children had not explicitly been made to feel competent, age differences were quite apparent: 12-year-olds were more helpful than 7-year-olds, who were more helpful than 4-year-olds. In sum, the latter findings do seem to imply that age-related increases in altruism may often reflect older children's greater feelings of responsibility for helping and, in particular, their impressions that they are sufficiently competent to help.

And some exceptions to the rule.   Although older children are often more likely to help or to share with others, it would be inappropriate to conclude that all forms of prosocial behavior increase with age or that older children are always more generous or helpful than younger children. For example, Marian Radke-Yarrow and her associates (1983) reviewed much of the available literature and found *no* consistent age trends for two kinds of prosocial conduct: demonstrations of compassionate behavior and willingness to cooperate with peers. In fact, several studies in this review found that American children actually become less cooperative and more competitive between the ages of 4 and 12.

A series of experiments by Ervin Staub (1970, 1974) shows just how complex the relation between age and altruism can become. In one experiment (Staub, 1970) children from kindergarten age through sixth grade were seated in one room when they heard a crash in the next room followed by a series of sobs and moans. Would these child bystanders help the victim by entering the room or informing the experimenter of the victim's distress? Much to his surprise, Staub found a curvilinear relation between age and helping: helpfulness increased from kindergarten through second grade (age 5 to 7) and then decreased from second through sixth grade (see Midlarsky & Hannah, 1985, for a similar pattern of results). When questioned about their inaction, the younger children often said they lacked the necessary competence to assist the injured victim (see Midlarsky & Hannah, 1985). However, the oldest children explained their inaction by saying that they feared disapproval from either the experimenter (for leaving their work) or the injured victim. Typical responses were "I thought I should stay here" or "If I went in there, I might get yelled at."

Were these concerns genuine? That is, will older children, who are often more altruistic than younger ones, actually allow vague, unstated "rules" of appropriate conduct to restrain their helpfulness? Staub (1974) tried to answer this question in the following way. Seventh-grade girls were taken to an experimental room and asked to complete a questionnaire. Before leaving the child alone in the room, the experimenter either said nothing (no-information condition), gave the child permission to play with some games in the next room (permission condition), or said that the girl in the next room was not to be bothered (prohibition condition). Ninety seconds later, subjects heard a crash followed by sounds of distress from the girl in the adjoining room. If seventh-grade children are greatly concerned about the possibility of violating *unstated* rules or prohibitions, then girls in the no-information condition should have been *less* helpful than girls who had permission to enter the next room and no more helpful than girls who were told that the person in the next room was not to be bothered. Staub's results confirmed these predictions; over 90% of the subjects who had permission to leave the room took some action to assist the victim, compared with 36% of the no-information subjects and 45% of the subjects in the prohibition group. Staub (1974) concluded that "the inhibitory effect of no information on children's helping behavior suggests that . . . socializing agents . . . may overemphasize the teaching of prohibitions against 'improper' behavior without sufficient emphasis on norms which prescribe prosocial behavior. . . . *The data suggest that behavior that manifests concern about others' welfare is relatively fragile, and easily yields to counterinfluences*" (p. 315; italics added).

Fortunately, older high school students and adults eventually become less concerned about violating unstated rules or prohibitions that conflict with the obvious needs of an injured victim (Midlarsky & Hannah, 1985; Staub, 1979). Nevertheless, even adolescents and adults may be very reluctant to help an injured party (or anyone else who could use some assistance) if they suspect that their benevolence will make the recipient feel embarrassed or incompetent (Midlarsky & Hannah, 1985).

Is altruism a consistent and stable attribute?　Although it appears that many kinds of prosocial behavior become more common as children mature, we might wonder just how consistent individuals are from situation to situation. Will a child who shares cookies with a playmate also share his bicycle with a visiting cousin? Will another youngster who refuses to cooperate or to play by the rules of a game later decline to comfort or share with one of her playmates should the opportunity present itself?

Several studies have found that there is a fair degree of consistency in children's prosocial inclinations from situation to situation. Not only are children who help or share in one situation more likely than their nonaltruistic age mates to help or share in similar situations (Rushton, 1980), but there is some consistency across different kinds of prosocial behavior as well. For example, sympathetic children are more cooperative than their nonsympathetic classmates (Murphy, 1937). And youngsters

who have often cared for other children tend to be more generous, helpful, and compassionate than those who have had few if any caregiving responsibilities (Radke-Yarrow et al., 1983; Whiting & Whiting, 1975).

Is altruism a stable attribute? Is an altruistic 2-year-old likely to become an altruistic 6-year-old, adolescent, or adult? Although few longitudinal studies of children's altruism have been conducted, the information we do have suggests that children's modes of altruistic expression are reasonably stable over time. For example, Radke-Yarrow and Zahn-Waxler (1983) found considerable variation among 2-year-olds in their responses to distressed companions. Some children were very emotional and tried to comfort whoever was distressed. Others adopted a more combative style of prosocial behavior (for example, "I'll hit the person who made you cry"), whereas a third group of toddlers tried to shut out others' distress signals by turning or running away from them. When these children were retested at age 7, about two thirds of them exhibited the *same general style* of response to distressed companions (that is, emotional, combative, or avoidant) as they had shown as 2-year-olds. Nevertheless, the fact that one third of the sample was now reacting in a *different* way to others' distress indicates that early patterns of altruistic expression can be modified. So for some children, development means change rather than consistency or stability.

WHO HELPS WHOM? BENEFACTOR AND RECIPIENT CHARACTERISTICS THAT AFFECT ALTRUISM

Children of any particular age level will differ considerably in their willingness to provide emotional support and comfort to distressed persons, to share their resources, and to volunteer their help. Moreover, not all unfortunate souls who could use some comforting or assistance are equally effective at eliciting altruistic responses from potential benefactors. In this section of the chapter we will consider several characteristics of benefactors and recipients that affect prosocial behavior.

SEX DIFFERENCES IN ALTRUISM

People often assume that girls are relatively compassionate, friendly, generous, and helpful, while boys tend to be more unsympathetic, selfish, and aggressive (see Shigetomi, Hartmann, & Gelfand, 1981; Zarbatany, Hartmann, Gelfand, & Vinciguerra, 1985). Yet several recent reviews of the literature dispute the notion that girls are more altruistic than boys (Radke-Yarrow et al., 1983; Rushton, 1976, 1980). When differences are found, females are likely to be the more helpful sex. However, the vast majority of studies find no sex differences in prosocial conduct, and boys are often more helpful than girls on some measures, such as active rescue behavior.

Does the sex of the person who needs help or comforting affect children's altruistic inclinations? Apparently so, at least for young children. Rosalind Charlesworth and Willard Hartup (1967) observed the interactions of nursery school children over a five-week period and found that these youngsters generally directed their acts of kindness to playmates of the same sex. However, the sex of a prospective recipient eventually becomes a less important consideration during the grade school years. In a recent laboratory study (Ladd, Lange, & Stremmel, 1983), kindergartners and first-, third-, and fourth-graders were given an opportunity to help other children complete some schoolwork. Some of these potential recipients clearly needed more help than others. Ladd et al. found that kindergartners and first-graders often disregarded recipients' apparent needs, choosing instead to help children of their own sex. However, this same-sex bias was much less apparent among third- and fourth-graders, who typically based their helping decisions on a recipient's need for help rather than his or her gender.

DEPENDENCY: DOES THIS PERSON NEED MY HELP?

One morning as I was about to enter my office building, I paused to allow the person in front of me to open the door. A few seconds passed before I noticed that he was carrying an armload of laboratory equipment that prevented him from turning the doorknob. I then stepped forward and opened the door for him. His burden had made me feel that he was somewhat dependent on me for assistance.

Children are also inclined to help those persons who seem to depend on them for assistance. In fact, we have just seen that third- and fourth-graders are more likely to assist someone who needs a lot of help than someone who needs very little (Ladd et al., 1983). Moreover, Elizabeth Midlarsky and Mary Hannah (1985) found that children between the ages of 6 and 16 are quicker to help a toddler who has been hurt than an age mate who has suffered the same injury, particularly when the injury appears to be severe. One interpretation of these findings is that children viewed toddlers as more dependent on them for assistance. Indeed, Midlarsky and Hannah's subjects indicated that they were much less concerned about lacking the competence to help or about embarrassing the victim if the injured party was a toddler who was apt to require their assistance.

Yet there are undoubtedly limits to these dependency effects, one of which is apparent in research with adults. When people see a man collapse on a subway, they are more likely to assist him if he is carrying a cane and appears to be sick than if he reeks of liquor and seems to be drunk (Piliavin, Dovidio, Gaertner, & Clark, 1981). Thus, if the dependency of a prospective recipient is perceived as illegitimate or personally caused, it may be less effective at eliciting prosocial responses.

GETTING BY WITH A LITTLE HELP FROM MY FRIENDS

To whom do you turn when you require aid or comfort? If you are like most people, you probably seek the attention of someone you feel close to, perhaps your spouse, a relative, or your best friend. Indeed, relationships between friends or relatives seem to imply a sense of mutual dependency or an obligation to help each other.

Are children more likely to comfort, assist, or share valuable resources with friends than acquaintances or strangers? The answer is yes, and this tendency to favor friends appears rather early. Even nursery school children (3- to 6-year-olds) are more likely to share favorite snacks or to make sacrifices for another child if the recipient of their benevolent act is a friend rather than a mere acquaintance (Birch & Billman, 1986; see also Box 10-1). Children are particularly generous or helpful toward a friend if they think that the friendship is threatened and view their acts of kindness as a way of solidifying or restoring the relationship (Staub & Noerenberg, 1981). However, if grade school children think that their relationship with a friend is *secure*, they are sometimes more generous with a stranger than with a *good* friend. Thus, when Wright (1942) asked 8-year-old boys to divide two toys that differed in attractiveness between a good friend and a stranger, many of them gave the attractive toy to the stranger. Those who favored the stranger often remarked that their generosity would help to eliminate the inequality between the friend, who knew he was liked, and the stranger. They also believed that they might win a new friend with their generosity and that the "deprived" friend would understand their actions.

Would children be more generous with friends than with strangers in *competitive* situations where the sharing of resources (such as a crayon) is necessary for both children to complete an assignment and/or win a prize? The evidence bearing on this issue is mixed. Diane Jones (1985) found that kindergartners, second-graders, and fourth-graders were more generous with friends than with acquaintances under these competitive circumstances. Even when they refused to share, children were more likely to explain to friends why they had done so, while often responding to the queries of acquaintances with a terse "No!" However, it is unfortunate that Jones did not conduct separate analyses for her male and female participants, because Thomas Berndt (1981) reports that grade school boys in competitive situations are likely to be *less* generous with friends than with acquaintances. Berndt's interpretation of this finding is straightforward: friendships among males are often quite competitive, so that the prospect of being upstaged by a friend (or receiving less for one's efforts than the friend does) may be sufficiently distasteful to inhibit altruism.

FEELING GOOD AND FEELING BLUE: EFFECTS OF MOODS ON ALTRUISM

Remarkable as it may seem, our willingness to help a person in need is often influenced by temporary fluctuations in mood. Suppose that you had just succeeded beyond your wildest expectations on an important exam, earning the highest grade in the class. Would you be any more willing under these circumstances to help or comfort someone than if you had only done about average on the test or had actually failed it?

Effects of Good Moods

It seems that good moods will clearly enhance the altruistic inclinations of both children and adults. Subjects who are feeling good after succeeding at a game or a test are typically more charitable and helpful than those whose performance was only average or below average (see Isen, 1970; Shaffer, 1986). And this "feel good–do good" effect is by no means limited to people who are experiencing the warm glow of success. For example, Isen and Levin (1972) reported that subjects who had found a dime in a telephone booth (good-mood condition) were more likely than those who had not found dimes (neutral-mood condition) to help a stranger who had dropped some papers. People who have been thinking happy thoughts or who have just received an unexpected gift are more charitable than people who are experiencing neutral affective states (Isen, Clark, & Schwartz, 1976; Shaffer & Smith, 1985). Even good weather can brighten our spirits and make us more prosocially inclined, for people leave waitresses larger tips and are more likely to volunteer as participants in research projects on bright and sunny days than on dull and dreary ones (Cunningham, 1979).

Why do positive moods promote altruism? Recent research by Michael Cunningham (1986) provides some strong clues. Cunningham finds that people experiencing positive moods are much more optimistic and self-confident and much less preoccupied about personal concerns than people experiencing neutral or negative moods. Moreover, good-mood subjects are more interested in partaking in a variety

BOX 10-1 *ME SACRIFICE FOR SOMEONE ELSE? WELL . . . THAT DEPENDS*

Recently, Frederick Kanfer and his associates (Kanfer, Stifter, & Morris, 1981) designed an interesting experiment to see whether 3½–6-year-olds would delay immediate gratification in order to produce a desirable outcome for somebody else. Each of Kanfer's young subjects first learned how to perform a dull chip-sorting task and earned five prize tokens that could be used later to purchase a toy. The child was then given a choice between playing with an array of attractive toys (small immediate incentive) and continuing to sort chips in order to earn more prize tokens with which to buy additional toys (larger delayed incentive). Some of the children were led to believe that they would be using their later "earnings" to buy *themselves* attractive toys. Others were told that their future earnings would be used to buy toys for (1) *another little boy or girl* (anonymous-other condition), (2) a *"classmate"* whom the experimenter would select as the recipient, or (3) a *"friend"* whom the child liked very much. Finally, children in the *control* condition were simply told that they could either play with the toys or sort chips if they wanted to but that no more prize tokens would be given for chip sorting. If the child began to sort chips (the delay choice), the experimenter left the room and observed the child's activities from an adjacent area for a maximum of 15 minutes. After

15 minutes had elapsed (or the child had quit working and started to play with the toys), the experimenter returned and praised the child for his or her work. The subject was then allowed to exchange the tokens earned at the beginning of the session for a toy.

The results of the experiment appear in the table. In evaluating these data, let's first note that not one child in the control condition chose to continue the chip-sorting task when his efforts would earn him no more tokens. Even preschool children won't work for nothing. And will they work for themselves? Yes, indeed, for 75% of those who could earn tokens to buy themselves additional toys chose to work rather than play, and most of these youngsters worked for the entire 15 minutes. Now for the question that stimulated this research: Will preschool children set aside personal pleasures in order to do something nice for somebody else? As we see in the table, the answer depends on who it is that they would be working for. The majority of these 3½–6-year-olds refused to do anything to benefit an anonymous child or a "classmate" whose identity was left unspecified. However, 55% of the children were willing to defer immediate gratification and perform the dull chip-sorting task when the person who would benefit from their sacrifice was a friend.

Number of Children Who Worked at the Dull Chip-Sorting Task for All, Part, or None of the 15-Minute Delay Interval

	Condition				
	Control (no tokens earned)	Self as recipient	Anonymous other as recipient	Classmate as recipient	Friend as recipient
No work	20 (100%)	5 (25%)	19 (95%)	15 (75%)	9 (45%)
Part-time work	0 (0%)	2 (10%)	1 (5%)	2 (10%)	1 (5%)
Maximum work	0 (0%)	13 (65%)	0 (0%)	3 (15%)	10 (50%)

of social activities (such as dancing or chatting with a new acquaintance) than subjects who are feeling "down" or depressed. Thus, positive moods may facilitate altruism because they (1) direct our attention outward toward other people, rather than inward on personal concerns, while (2) perhaps making us feel more confident or optimistic that we can successfully alleviate the distress of a person in need.

Effects of Bad Moods

Do negative moods, then, make one less altruistically inclined? To answer this question, Moore, Underwood, and Rosenhan (1973) asked 7- and 8-year-olds to recall events from their lives that had made them feel very happy (good-mood condition) or very sad (bad-mood condition). Children assigned to the control condition did not reminisce about prior experiences and were assumed to be in a neutral mood. After the mood manipulation, subjects were given an opportunity to donate some of the 25 pennies they had received for participating in the experiment to other children who would not have an opportunity to participate and earn pennies. Children were told that they could share their money if they wanted to but that they did not have to. The experimenter then left the room, thus providing each child an opportunity to make an anonymous donation to his or her less fortunate peers.

The results, summarized in Figure 10-2, reveal that subjects who had recalled happy events donated significantly more money to the children's fund than control subjects did. And subjects who had recalled unhappy events contributed significantly *less* than control subjects. Moore et al. (1973) concluded that "brief, even fleeting, affective experiences appear to have significant implications for behavior toward others. The transient experience of [mood-induced] positive affect makes children more generous to others, while the equally ephemeral experience of negative affect appears to make them more niggardly" (p. 102).

However, later research shows that negative moods do not always suppress altruism. Using a procedure similar to that of Moore et al. (1973), Robert Cialdini and Douglas Kenrick (1976) found that bad moods inhibited sharing among 6- to 8-year-olds but actually *enhanced* the generosity of older children and adolescents. Moreover, there is now a good deal of evidence to indicate that adults who are feeling "down" or depressed are often *more* prosocially inclined than those experiencing neutral moods (see Shaffer, 1986, for a review). How might we explain these inconsistent outcomes?

The "negative state relief" hypothesis. One possibility is that the effects of negative moods on altruism change with age. Indeed, Cialdini and Kenrick (1976) proposed that altruism eventually becomes *self-reinforcing* for an older child, who will have had many opportunities to associate prosocial responses with positive outcomes (such as praise and tangible reinforcement) and to learn that "helping

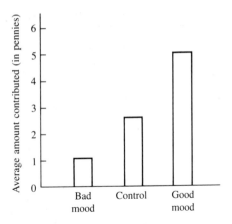

FIGURE 10-2 Average donations by children in the good-mood, bad-mood, and control conditions

makes *me* feel good." Thus, an older child who is feeling blue may be motivated to help others in order to make *himself* feel better and thereby overcome his negative mood. However, younger children who are feeling "down" should not be so prosocially inclined because they do not yet realize that altruism is self-reinforcing and can be used to brighten their spirits.

The "focus of attention" hypothesis. In contrast to Cialdini and Kenrick's developmental model, Mark Barnett and his associates (Barnett, King, & Howard, 1979) have proposed that a cognitive variable—focus of attention—determines whether a negative mood will enhance or inhibit altruism. After carefully reviewing the literature, these investigators concluded that, in studies showing that bad moods increase altruism, subjects were generally thinking about the misfortunes of others. By contrast, in studies showing that bad moods inhibit altruism, subjects were generally reflecting on their *own* misfortunes (for example, thinking about a sad personal experience or a personal failure). Thus, the implication is that people whose bad moods stem from an outward focus on the problems or misfortunes of other people are apt to be altruistically inclined, whereas an inward focus on one's own problems should heighten self-concern at the expense of one's concern for others.

Barnett et al. (1979) tested this "focus of attention" hypothesis by telling 7- to 12-year-old children to discuss a very sad incident that had happened to themselves or to another child. Children assigned to the control group provided information either about themselves or about another child that was essentially devoid of emotional content (data about the child's age, address, and so on). Soon thereafter, subjects were given an opportunity to anonymously donate some of the valuable prize chips they had received for their participation to a group of unfortunate children who would have no opportunity to earn prize chips. The results were clear: children who had been saddened by focusing outward on the misfortunes of another child shared significantly *more* prize tokens than their counterparts in the control group, whereas saddened children who focused on their own misfortunes were much *less* generous than those in the control group (see also Thompson, Cowan, & Rosenhan, 1980, for a similar set of findings with adult subjects). Because these "focusing" effects were apparent among even the youngest (7- to 8-year-old) subjects in Barnett's sample, it would appear to be one's attentional focus, rather than one's age or socialization history, that determines the effect of negative moods on altruism.

Summing up. Although Barnett's study seems to discredit some of the developmental implications of the negative state relief hypothesis, that theory may still be partly correct. People who are feeling sad and are focusing *inward* on their own concerns are often more altruistic than those experiencing neutral moods if (1) the needs of a prospective recipient are made obvious to them and (2) the type of prosocial response that is called for is not unpleasant or costly and thus offers some promise of improving their negative mood (see Shaffer, 1986, for a review of this literature). In other words, the prosocial behavior of these saddened and self-focused individuals has distinct *hedonistic* overtones: I'll help if it will make *me* feel better, but I'll decline if the act will do nothing to brighten my spirits. By contrast, people who are experiencing *positive* moods are much more concerned about the benefits accruing to the recipient than about the consequences of their actions for

themselves. In fact, happy people may even undertake very unpleasant or costly prosocial acts in the interest of others, whereas saddened and self-focused people routinely decline to help if the costs of their benevolence outweigh the benefits they can expect to receive (Cunningham, Shaffer, Barbee, & Smith, 1987; Shaffer & Graziano, 1983).

COGNITIVE CONTRIBUTORS TO ALTRUISM

Earlier we noted that generosity and other types of helping behavior become more frequent during middle childhood (ages 6 to 12). In addition, middle childhood is a period when children are becoming less egocentric, are becoming more proficient at role taking (that is, imagining themselves in the place of others), and are displaying some interesting changes in their moral reasoning. Proponents of cognitive-developmental theory believe that increases in altruism during middle childhood are linked to cognitive-developmental advances in role-taking abilities and moral judgments that also occur during this period. Let us see whether there is any support for this position.

ROLE TAKING AND ALTRUISM

It makes some sense to assume that proficient role takers might be more altruistic than poor role takers if their role-taking skills help them to recognize and appreciate the factors that contribute to another person's distress or misfortune. Indeed, we discussed a study in Chapter 7 that is consistent with this point of view. Recall that, when second-graders taught kindergartners how to make caterpillars from construction paper, both good and poor role takers were quite helpful if the younger children explicitly asked for help. But if the younger children's needs were subtle or their requests indirect, good role takers recognized them and offered assistance, whereas poor role takers simply smiled at their young charges and resumed their own activities (Hudson, Forman, & Brion-Meisels, 1982). Other studies paint a similar picture. Although role-taking skills have been measured in many different ways and do not invariably predict children's prosocial behavior, a recent review of 16 relevant studies suggests that (1) good role takers are often found to be more prosocially inclined than poor role takers, and (2) the link between role-taking skills and altruism becomes stronger with age (Underwood & Moore, 1982).

Unfortunately, the data we have reviewed are correlational patterns that do not necessarily imply that proficiency at role taking *causes* children to behave more altruistically. But if role taking truly mediates altruism, we might predict that children who receive training to further their role-taking skills should become more altruistic. Ronald Iannotti (1978) tested this hypothesis by exposing 6- and 9-year-old boys to either of two kinds of training experiences or to a control condition in which they received no training. Boys assigned to the *role-taking* condition met in groups of five for a 25-minute training session on ten successive days. Each boy assumed the role of a particular character as the subjects acted out stories involving aggressors, victims, helpers, and people in need. Boys assigned to the *role switching* condition met on the same schedule and acted out the same stories, except that each was required to assume a new role every five minutes. Finally, boys in the *control* condition merely listened to the stories without assuming roles and acting them out. After the final session, each boy took a role-taking test. The experimenter then gave him some treats (either raisins or candy), mentioned that he knew of a needy lad whose birthday was approaching, and left the room, giving the child an opportunity to donate some of his treats to the needy boy.

The results of this experiment were straightforward. First, boys assigned to the training conditions scored higher on the role-taking test than boys who received no training. Moreover, the 6-year-olds in the training conditions donated a larger number of treats to the needy child than their age mates in the control condition, suggesting that increases in role taking caused the children to become more altruistic (see Ahammer & Murray, 1979, for a similar training effect). Although 9-year-olds were generally more charitable than the younger children, the training did *not* affect their donations. Presumably, the role-

taking skills of the 9-year-olds were already sufficiently developed that the boys could easily recognize the recipient's needs and act accordingly.

MORAL REASONING AND ALTRUISTIC BEHAVIOR

In their recent review of the literature, Bert Underwood and Bill Moore (1982) concluded that there is a moderate relationship between the maturity of children's moral reasoning (as defined by their responses to moral-conflict stories) and their prosocial inclinations. Not only are mature moral reasoners quicker to help others who need help, but they are also more likely than immature moral reasoners to comfort distressed companions, to share, and to criticize selfishness after observing the miserly behavior of an uncharitable model.

One problem with this research is that the level of "maturity" of children's moral reasoning is often assessed from their reactions to conflicts involving a prohibition of some kind (for example, lawbreaking or defying an authority figure)[1] rather than from their judgments about prosocial issues and dilemmas. Recently, researchers have begun to chart the development of children's *prosocial* moral reasoning and its relationship to altruistic behavior. For example, Nancy Eisenberg and her colleagues have presented children with stories in which the central character has to decide whether or not to help or comfort someone when the prosocial act would be personally costly to the actor. The following story illustrates the kinds of dilemmas children were asked to think about (Eisenberg-Berg & Hand, 1979):

> One day a girl(boy) named Mary(Eric) was going to a friend's birthday party. On her way she saw a girl(boy) who had fallen down and hurt her/his leg. The girl asked Mary to go to her house and get her parents so that the parents could come and take her to a doctor. But if Mary did run and get the child's parents, she would be late to the birthday party and miss the ice cream, cake, and all the games.
> What should Mary(Eric) do? Why?

As illustrated in Table 10-2, reasoning about these prosocial moral dilemmas may progress through as many as five levels over the course of childhood and adolescence. Notice that the judgments of preschool children are frequently hedonistic: these youngsters often feel that Mary or Eric should go to the party so as not to miss out on the goodies. But as children mature, they tend to become increasingly responsive to the needs and wishes of others, so much so that some high school students feel that they could no longer respect themselves if they were to ignore the appeal of a person in need in order to pursue their own interests.

Does the level of a child's prosocial moral reasoning predict his or her altruistic inclinations? Yes, indeed! Eisenberg-Berg and Hand (1979) found that preschoolers who had begun to consider the needs of others when responding to the prosocial dilemmas later displayed more *spontaneous* sharing with peers in the nursery school setting than did their classmates whose moral judgments were more hedonistic. And in a later study of elementary and high school stu-

TABLE 10-2 Levels of Prosocial Reasoning

Level	Orientation	Description	Group
1	Hedonistic, self-focused	The individual is concerned with self-oriented consequences rather than moral considerations. Reasons for assisting or not assisting another include consideration of direct gain to self, future reciprocity, and concern for others whom the individual needs and/or likes (owing to the affectional tie).	Preschoolers and younger elementary school children
2	Needs of others	The individual expresses concern for the physical, material, and psychological needs of others even though the other's needs conflict with one's own needs. This concern is expressed in the simplest terms, without clear evidence of self-reflective role taking, verbal expressions of sympathy, or reference to internalized affect such as guilt.	Preschoolers and elementary school children
3	Approval and interpersonal and/or stereotype	Stereotyped images of good and bad persons and behaviors and/or considerations of others' approval and acceptance are used in justifying prosocial or nonhelping behaviors.	Elementary and high school students
4	a. Empathic	The individual's judgments include evidence of sympathetic responding, self-reflective role taking, concern with the other's humanness, and/or guilt or positive affect related to the consequences of one's actions.	Older elementary school and high school students
	b. Transitional (empathic and internalized)	Justifications for helping or not helping involve internalized values, norms, duties, or responsibilities or refer to the necessity of protecting the rights and dignity of other persons; these ideas, however, are not clearly stated.	Minority of people of high school age
5	Strongly internalized	Justifications for helping or not helping are based on internalized values, norms, or responsibilities, the desire to maintain individual and societal contractual obligations, and the belief in the dignity, rights, and equality of all individuals. Positive or negative affect related to the maintenance of self-respect for living up to one's own values and accepted norms also characterizes this stage.	Only a small minority of high school students and virtually no elementary school children

dents, Eisenberg (1983) noted that mature moral reasoners among the high school sample may even help someone they *dislike* if that person really needs their assistance, whereas immature moral reasoners are much more inclined to ignore the needs of a person they do not like.

Why are mature moral reasoners so sensitive to the needs of others—even disliked others? Perhaps this tendency to respond rather indiscriminately to others' *legitimate* needs simply reflects the subject's endorsement or internalization of important prosocial norms—such as the Golden Rule or the norm of social responsibility—which prescribe that one should assist or comfort *anyone* who might benefit from such acts of kindness, regardless of his or her identity. Another possibility is that morally mature individuals experience relatively strong empathic responses to the distress of other people and that these emotional reactions trigger some form of altruistic behavior. In the following section, we will take a closer look at the relationship between empathy and altruism.

EMPATHY: AN AFFECTIVE CONTRIBUTOR TO ALTRUISM

Empathy is a person's ability to experience the emotions of other people. According to Martin Hoffman (1981), empathy is a largely involuntary, vicarious reaction to emotional cues emitted by another person—a response capability that is inborn, has a neurological basis, and can be accentuated or inhibited by environmental influences. Indeed, we have already noted that "empathic concern" does seem to be a heritable attribute (Matthews et al., 1981) and that even newborn infants will react to the distress of another baby by becoming distressed themselves—a response that Hoffman interprets as a primitive form of empathy. Hoffman believes that empathy (or empathic arousal) will eventually become an important source of altruistic motivation—a true *mediator* of altruism—once children (1) recognize that someone else's distress or misfortune is the cause of their own empathic emotions and (2) learn

that they can reduce or eliminate this aversive empathic arousal by taking some action to relieve the other person's discomfort.

Although infants and toddlers do seem to recognize and will often react to the distress of their companions (Radke-Yarrow et al., 1983; Zahn-Waxler et al., 1979), their responses are not always helpful ones. In fact, the evidence for a link between empathy and altruism is weak at best for young children, though much stronger for preadolescents, adolescents, and adults (Underwood & Moore, 1982).

One possible explanation for these age trends is that younger children who empathize with a distressed companion may lack certain role-taking or social information-processing skills that would enable them to fully understand and appreciate why they too are feeling distressed. For example, when kindergartners see slides showing a boy becoming depressed after his dog runs away, they usually attribute his sadness to an external cause (the dog's disappearance) rather than to a more "personal," or internal, one, such as the boy's sadness or longing for his pet (Hughes, Tingle, & Sawin, 1981). And although kindergartners report that they too feel sad after seeing the slides, they usually provide egocentric explanations for this empathic arousal (for example, "I might lose my dog"). However, 7- to 9-year-olds are beginning to associate their own empathic emotions with those of the story character as they put themselves in his place and infer the *psychological* basis for his distress (for example, "I'm sad because he's sad . . . because if he really liked the dog, then . . ."). So as Hoffman had suggested, empathy may become an important mediator of altruism once children become more proficient at inferring others' points of view (role taking) and understanding the causes of their own empathic emotions.[2]

The relationship among role taking, empathy, and altruism is illustrated in a recent experiment by Mark Barnett and his associates (Barnett, Howard, Melton, & Dino, 1982). Sixth-graders rated high or low in empathy by their teachers were first asked to reminisce about something very sad. Half the children were asked to think about a sad event that had happened to someone else (other-focused, role-taking condition), and the other half were asked to think about a sad event that had happened to themselves (self-focused condition). A few minutes later, these youngsters were given an opportunity to make "color and activity" booklets to cheer up sick children who were hospitalized. The results were clear. As we see in the left-hand portion of Figure 10-3, a child's capacity for empathy, by itself, does not predict his willingness to do something nice for sick peers if he has been thinking about a personal misfortune. The only time that the highly empathic 12-year-olds were more helpful than their less empathic classmates was when they had been thinking about another person's misfortune—a form of role taking that apparently triggered strong emotional responses from high empathizers, which then increased their motivation to aid and comfort a group of unfortunate children (see also Coke, Batson, & McDavis, 1978, for a similar set of findings with adults).

Although the data we have reviewed seem to suggest that empathy promotes altruism, none of this work clearly demonstrates that subjects who have helped or comforted someone *actually empathized* with the persons they helped. Is there any direct evidence that empathic arousal mediates altruism?

Yes, indeed. Dennis Krebs (1975) used a physiograph to measure the empathic physiological responses (changes in skin conductance and heart rate) of adult males to another person's wins and losses at a game of roulette. The subjects were first informed that the person playing the game was either *very similar* or *very dissimilar* to themselves. Then half the subjects were told that the performer would receive varying amounts of money on winning trials and electrical shock on losing trials (high-empathy condition). The remaining subjects were not led to believe that the performer's outcomes would be rewarded or punished (low-empathy condition). Each subject then observed the performer win six times and lose six times at the roulette game. When the performer won, he gazed intently at the money dispenser as if he were trying to guess how much money he would receive on that trial. When he lost, the performer looked concerned and then flexed the muscles in his forearm, an act designed to convince subjects in the high-empathy condition that he had received an electrical shock.

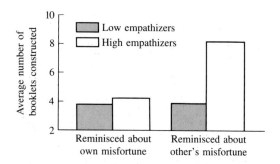

FIGURE 10-3 Average number of "color and activity" booklets constructed by high- and low-empathic 12-year-olds who had reminisced about a sad event that had happened to themselves or to another person

Following these "empathy" trials, subjects were given an opportunity to behave charitably toward the performer by determining the amount of money (between nothing and $2) he would receive for a win and the level of shock he would receive for a loss on a final try at the roulette wheel. The most altruistic response a subject could make was to assign $2 to the performer if he won and to allow him to escape all shock if he lost. But this would prove a costly response to the subject, for he would receive nothing if the performer won and would have to accept 100% of a maximally painful shock if the performer lost. The most selfish response a subject could make was to assign the performer nothing (and himself $2) for a win and 100% of the shock (and himself nothing) for a loss.

Krebs predicted that subjects in the high-empathy condition who observed a similar performer would show stronger empathic reactions to the performer's outcomes than subjects in the other three experimental conditions. The physiological data confirmed this hypothesis. Moreover, subjects in the high-empathy condition who observed a similar performer behaved much more altruistically toward the performer on the final trial than subjects in the other three conditions. In sum, it appears that empathy mediates altruism: the subjects who empathized most with the performer were most willing to help him, even though they had to incur personal costs (a loss of money or electrical shock) to do so. Krebs's data also suggest a reason that people are often most charitable toward family members, friends, and close associates: simply stated, we may be more inclined to empathize with people who are in some way similar to ourselves.

BEHAVIORAL CONTRIBUTORS TO ALTRUISM

According to social-learning theory, young children will often learn to share with and help others because their parents, teachers, and many other socializing agents tend to reward these acts of kindness. And earlier in the chapter, we reviewed data consistent with a second social-learning hypothesis—namely, that children who are exposed to altruistic models will frequently perform similar acts of charity, compassion, or helpfulness (Rosenhan & White, 1967). In this section we will take a closer look at the role played by direct tuition and the reinforcement of prosocial responses in the socialization of altruism. We will also see that the effectiveness of modeling as a means of promoting altruism depends on certain characteristics of the model and the kind of rationale that the model uses to justify acts of kindness.

DIRECT TUITION AND REINFORCEMENT

Perhaps the most obvious method of promoting altruism among young children is to insist that they show kindness toward other people and to reinforce them for their benevolent acts. In one study (Fischer, 1963), 4-year-olds were given material reinforcement (bubble gum) or social reinforcement (verbal approval) for sharing marbles with a child they did not know. Material reinforcement produced much more sharing than social reinforcement. Apparently a small amount of praise from an *unfamiliar* experimenter was simply not enough of a reinforcer to elicit self-sacrificing responses from these preschool children.

However, social reinforcement can promote altruistic behavior if it comes from a warm and charitable person whom children respect and admire

(Slaby & Crowley, 1977; Yarrow, Scott, & Waxler, 1973). Verbal reinforcement may be effective under these circumstances because children hope to live up to standards set by a liked and respected person, and praise that accompanies their kindly acts suggests a means of accomplishing that end. Indeed, youngsters may even come to view themselves as "kindly" or "helpful" individuals whose prosocial acts are *intrinsically* motivated if the person who praises their benevolence often makes reference to their prosocial *intentions* (for example, "It is kind of you to want to share your cupcake with Johnny").

Aversive approval: When reinforcement fails.
Can you think of an occasion when the reinforcement of prosocial responses will *inhibit* altruism? Paradoxical as this may seem, Elizabeth Midlarsky, James Bryan, and Phillip Brickman (1973) were able to imagine one such occasion.[3] They hypothesized that a child would become reluctant to share valuable resources with others if his or her charitable acts were reinforced by a *selfish* person. If we can assume that children disapprove of selfishness and dislike selfish people, then approval from a selfish person may lead the child to expect disapproval from other important people, who share a dislike for the selfish person. In other words, approval from a disliked source may prove "aversive" and actually inhibit, rather than strengthen, the behavior it was intended to reinforce (in this case, sharing behavior).

Midlarsky et al. conducted an interesting experiment to test this hypothesis. Twelve-year-old girls were exposed to an adult model who demonstrated how to play a pinball game. Some of the subjects saw the model behave in a *charitable* manner by donating a sizable portion of her winnings to a fund for needy children. Other children saw the model act *selfishly* by refusing to share any of her winnings with needy children. Each child then played the game several times and won 20 tokens that could be redeemed for valuable prizes. In the *social approval* condition, the adult model smiled and gave verbal praise—for example, "That's really sweet of you"—whenever the subject donated part of her winnings to needy children. Subjects assigned to a *no approval* condition were not praised for their charitable acts.

The results of this experiment appear in Figure 10-4. As we might expect, charitable models elicited larger donations than selfish models. But the effects of social approval depended on its source. Approval from a charitable model enhanced altruism, whereas approval from a selfish model appeared to *inhibit* it. A later experiment replicated this "aversive approval" effect among groups of 8- to 9-year-old children.

Why does approval from a selfish person inhibit altruism? The answer is not immediately obvious. When children rated the attractiveness of the adult models, the selfish model was rated *no less* attractive or well liked than the charitable model. This finding suggests that children who received social approval from a selfish model *did not* fear disapproval from others for accepting praise from an "unattractive" person. Perhaps the approving responses of a selfish model made the inconsistency between the model's actions and her verbal behavior obvious to the child. This inconsistency may then have prompted the child to think about the inequity of the situation and wonder "Why should I give when the model has not?"

The results Midlarsky et al. obtained have straightforward implications for parents and other socializing agents:

> This research indicates that an adult's inconsistency [between his actions and the behavior he reinforces] may cause him to lose the ability to exert positive influence in the domain of moral behavior . . . or to lose the ability to exercise one of the two most important means of [socializing a child], social reinforcement. . . . The parent who models selfishness may be better advised to do nothing than to attempt to reinforce altruism, if teaching altruism is his aim [1973, pp. 326–328].

Creating an altruistic self-concept. Would parents, teachers, and other social agents be more effective at promoting altruistic acts if they actively encouraged children to think of themselves as generous or helpful individuals? Joan Grusec and Erica Redler (1980) tried to answer this question by urging 5- and 8-year-olds to (1) donate marbles to poor children, (2) share colored pencils with classmates who hadn't any, and (3) help an experimenter with a dull and repetitive task. Once children had made an initial donation or had begun to work on the repetitive

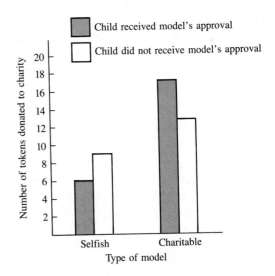

FIGURE 10-4 Average donations by girls who received or did not receive social approval for donating from charitable or selfish models

task, they were told that they were "nice" or "helpful" persons (self-concept training condition) or else nothing was said (control condition). One to two weeks later, the children were asked by another adult to give up some of their free time to make drawings and craft materials that might cheer up sick children at a local hospital.

Grusec and Redler found that self-concept training had a much greater effect on the 8-year-olds than on the 5-year-olds. The 8-year-olds who had been told that they must be "nice" and "helpful" persons were more likely than those in the control condition to share their possessions and to make drawings and craft materials for sick children. Why was the self-concept training so effective with 8-year-olds but not with 5-year-olds? The research we reviewed in Chapter 7 provides a very strong clue. Recall that 8-year-olds are just beginning to describe the self in psychological terms and to see these "traits" as relatively stable aspects of their characters. Thus, when told that they are "nice" or "helpful," older children will incorporate these "traitlike" attributions into their self-concepts and try to live up to their new self-image by sharing with or helping others.

Might we ever be effective at persuading younger children to view themselves as "helpers" and to make internal attributions for their acts of kindness? Probably so, but only if our self-concept training focuses directly on the helper's desirable intentions and is stated in *explicit behavioral terms*—precisely the kind of information that younger children use to describe the self (for example, "I hear that you are a nice boy who wants to share his toys [cookies, marbles] with other boys and girls"). Although the success of this kind of "behavioral" self-concept training has yet to be demonstrated for altruistic behavior, Fiona Ritchie and Ignatius Toner (1984) find that children only 3 years old will become *patient* (by forgoing immediate rewards to wait for a larger, delayed incentive) if the experimenter has labeled them as a boy or a girl who "can wait for nice things when you can't get them right away." So there is reason to believe that a form of self-concept training that is carefully tailored to the younger child's social information-processing capabilities might prove to be an effective means of altering self-perceptions and inducing prosocial behavior.

MODELING INFLUENCES: PRACTICING AND PREACHING ALTRUISM

Social-learning theorists have assumed that adults who encourage altruism and who practice what they preach will affect children in at least two ways. By practicing altruism, the adult model may induce the child to perform similar acts of kindness. In addition, regular exposure to a model's *altruistic exhortations* (that is, verbal encouragements to help, comfort, share, or cooperate with others) provides the child with opportunities to internalize principles such as the norm of social responsibility that should contribute to the development of an altruistic orientation.

When young children observe charitable or helpful models, they generally become more altruistic themselves—particularly if they know and respect the model and have established a warm and friendly relationship with this benevolent companion (Rushton, 1980; Yarrow et al., 1973). Moreover, several child-rearing studies (for example, Hoffman, 1975; Rutherford & Mussen, 1968) indicate that warm, nurturant parents tend to raise altruistic children. Perhaps we should not be surprised to learn that

warm, nurturant relationships with socializing agents are an important contributor to children's prosocial behavior. As Yarrow et al. (1973) have argued, an adult's nurturance has "a special relevance for the child's acquisition of altruistic responses when one considers that nurturance [given to the child] is itself an example or model of altruism" (p. 242).

Modeling and the development of altruistic dispositions. Do the modeling effects so often seen in laboratory studies of altruism stand the test of time? Will a child who sees a model act charitably in one context become more inclined to help or to share with needy persons at a later date in situations outside the experimental setting? If so, we might conclude that prosocial modeling influences contribute to the development of altruistic habits or dispositions.

Apparently the changes in behavior prompted by exposures to altruistic models are both durable and generalizable. Elizabeth Midlarsky and James Bryan (1972) found that a model who donated valuable tokens to a charity increased children's willingness to donate a *different* commodity (candy) to the same charity, even though the candy donations were solicited ten days later in a different setting by a person the children had never seen before (see Yarrow et al., 1973, for a similar set of findings with preschool children). Other investigators have noted that children who observe charitable models are more generous than those who observe selfish models, even when they are tested *two to four months later* (Rice & Grusec, 1975; Rushton, 1975). Taken together, these findings suggest that encounters with altruistic models may indeed foster the development of altruistic habits and values.

The importance of "practicing what you preach." Although most parents encourage their children to be kind, generous, or helpful to others, they don't always practice what they preach. How do children respond to these inconsistencies? James Bryan and his associates (Bryan & Schwartz, 1971; Bryan & Walbek, 1970) addressed this issue by exposing grade school children to models who *behaved* either charitably or selfishly while *preaching* either charity ("It's good to donate to poor children") or greed ("Why should I give my money to other people?"). When children were later given an opportunity to donate some of their own valuable resources to charity, the size of their donations was influenced by the model's behavior but not his exhortations. In other words, children who saw a model refuse to donate while preaching charity (or greed) showed a low level of altruism themselves, while those who observed a charitable model who exhorted greed (or charity) gave sizable amounts to charity. These findings appear to have important implications for child rearing: parents would be well advised to back up their verbal exhortations with altruistic deeds if they hope to instill a strong sense of altruistic concern in their children.

Are altruistic exhortations ever effective?   Although a model's actions may speak louder than his or her words, it would be inappropriate to conclude that words are wasted on children. Midlarsky and Bryan (1972) suspected that the charitable exhortations of previous studies were weak—at best, doing little more than reminding children of the norm of social responsibility. By contrast, parents often provide their children with meaningful cognitive rationales for sharing with, comforting, or helping others. Perhaps stronger exhortations that justify acts of kindness on the basis of their impact on recipients would prove more successful at eliciting prosocial responses from children.

Midlarsky and Bryan tested this hypothesis by exposing children to an adult model who took ten turns at a game, winning five times and losing five times. On winning trials, the model either behaved *charitably*, by donating some of his winnings to a needy children's fund, or *selfishly*, by keeping all of his winnings for himself. On losing trials, the model either preached *charity* and emphasized the positive impact of charitable acts on recipients ("I know that I don't have to give, but it would make some children very happy") or preached *greed* and stressed the undesirable aspects of charity ("I could really use some spending money this week; it makes some children feel bad to get charity"). The child then played the game, won five times, and thus had five opportunities to donate money to needy children.

Table 10-3 summarizes the results. As expected, children who observed a charitable model donated a larger percentage of their winnings (35.8%) than children who observed a selfish model (14%). Furthermore, the model's verbal exhortations had a significant effect; models who exhorted charity elicited larger donations from the children (30.8%) than models who exhorted greed (19%). So charitable exhortations can increase children's generosity if they are strongly stated and justified in terms of the needs of prospective recipients. However, the relatively large donations prompted by the charitable model who preached charity serve as a reminder that our altruistic exhortations are most effective when we practice what we preach.

METHODS OF PROMOTING CHILDREN'S ALTRUISM

Our society is one of contrasts. People are often very helpful to one another in certain situations but display an amazing lack of prosocial concern in others. This point is aptly illustrated by the two newspaper stories of Figure 10-5, which appeared recently on Christmas Eve and Christmas Day. Although the first story is heartwarming, the second illustrates that there is too little helping in our society. Can anything be done to prevent people from adopting the apathetic or even sadistic attitudes of the patrons who watched Mr. Romero bleed to death? Perhaps something can. But in adopting an optimistic outlook for the future, I am

TABLE 10-3   Average Percentage of Winnings Donated by Children Exposed to Charitable or Selfish Models Who Preached Charity or Greed

	Model's verbal preaching		
Model's behavior	Charity	Greed	Row averages
Charitable	44.0	27.5	35.8
Selfish	17.5	10.5	14.0
Column averages	30.8	19.0	

Child's Letter To Santa Stirs Hearts

SEATTLE (AP) — A haphazardly-spelled letter to Santa, signed "Craig" and bearing no return address, has prompted gifts of food, toys, and money from all over the country — and even a song.

"I think parents are using this as an example of what Christmas is about — sharing," said Shirley Martin, who organized a holiday drive for needy families after the letter was accidentally delivered to a restaurant here.

"Dear Santa," the letter said. "Moma said you got lost last year and couldin't find your way to our house. we wrilly mist you aspechely my little sisters. pleas come this year santa."

To assure a visit from St. Nick, the boy said he was enclosing a map to his house. But he forgot to include the map, and the envelope bore no return address.

A postscript said, "ps. don't leav any thing for dady becuse he isn't hear anymore."

Employees at Francisco's restaurant started a food and toy drive, hoping that if they helped enough needy families in the area they might accidentally help Craig's.

"We have checks coming in from all over the country," said Mrs. Martin, who volunteered to help wrap gifts and has since taken over the drive. "We get calls from out of state from people who know needy families we could help. We tell them we will try, but that they should try to take care of that family, too."

So far, more than $1,500 in cash has come in, along with several tricycles and bicycles and piles of toys.

"When those trucks pull out of the parking lot, I think I'm gonna break down and cry," Mrs. Martin said.

A woman in Houston read an Associated Press story about Craig's letter and wrote a song for him.

"Don't put prezunts in our sox, Santa,

"Our sox and our shooz ain't got no toze — " the lyrics say.

"I feel so much empathy for the little guy," the woman said in a letter to The AP. "I was a poor kid, too — but never so poor that Santa got totally 'lost' on Christmas."

Meanwhile, the search for Craig goes on.

Patrons laugh
as man dies

SAN FRANCISCO (UPI) — Patrons of the Tic Tock drive-in did not let their hamburgers and french fries get cold Thursday night — even though a man lay on the pavement in front of them bleeding to death.

Witnesses said the customers stood around munching their food and watching Joseph Romero, 53, cry and die "as if it were a sideshow."

Romero and his wife, Camella, had steak sandwiches at the drive-in and then Romero went back to get apple pie and coffee. He was accosted by three men as he started back to his car. A struggle ensued and Romero was shot in the back, possibly with his own gun.

The three men fled and Romero fell to the pavement, fatally wounded.

Mrs. Romero rushed to her husband's side but the other customers, who had scattered for cover at the gunshot, stood around finishing their meals during the 30 minutes Romero lay crying and bleeding.

"They stood around like it was a sideshow," said cook Carol Peppars. "They were laughing."

Romero died in surgery at San Francisco General Hospital.

FIGURE 10-5 These two stories illustrate that people in our society are often inconsistent in their responses to victims who need help. Why do you suppose the little boy received help while the man who lay dying was ignored?

assuming that most parents hope to raise altruistic children and would make some attempt to employ child-rearing practices that serve this end.

In this section of the chapter, we will briefly consider some of the child-rearing practices that seem to foster a sense of altruistic concern in young children.

We will also examine the evidence indicating that television can play a very important role in the socialization of altruism.

BECOMING A PROSOCIAL SOCIETY

Although most people in most cultures would be willing to verbally endorse altruistic values such as the norm of social responsibility, there are major differences across cultures in the emphasis placed on prosocial activities. In one interesting cross-cultural study, Beatrice and John Whiting (1975) observed the altruistic behavior of 134 children aged 3 to 10 in six cultures—Kenya, Mexico, the Philippines, Okinawa, India, and the United States. As we see in Table 10-4, the cultures in which children were most altruistic were the less industrialized societies where people tend to live in large families and everyone contributes to the family welfare. The Whitings concluded that children who are assigned important responsibilities, such as producing and processing food or caring for infant brothers and sisters, are likely to develop a cooperative, prosocial orientation at an early age.

One possible explanation for the low altruism scores among children from industrialized nations is that many Westernized societies place a tremendous emphasis on *competition* and stress individual rather than group goals. By contrast, Native American and Mexican children are taught to cooperate with others and to avoid interpersonal conflicts. The impact of

TABLE 10-4 Prosocial Behavior in Six Cultures: Percentages of Children in Each Culture Who Scored above the Median Altruism Score for the Cross-Cultural Sample as a Whole

Type of society	Percentage scoring high in altruism
Nonindustrialized	
Kenya	100
Mexico	73
Philippines	63
Industrialized	
Okinawa	29
India	25
United States	8

these cultural teachings can be seen when children are asked to play games in which they may choose to cooperate or compete, but cooperation is necessary to earn scores high enough to win prizes. Under these circumstances, Mexican children, who are taught to cooperate, clearly outperform their more competitive Mexican-American and Anglo-American age mates (Kagan & Masden, 1971, 1972). In fact, many 7- to 9-year-old American children are so competitive at these games that they will attempt to lower their partners' outcomes even though they will receive no tangible benefits for doing so (Kagan & Masden, 1972). Apparently this competitive orientation can be acquired very early and may interfere with prosocial activities, such as sharing. In a study of nursery school children, Eldred Rutherford and Paul Mussen (1968) found that boys who were judged to be highly competitive by their teachers were less likely than other preschoolers to share a bag of candy with their friends.

Although few adults from Westernized societies would favor retraining our children to subordinate all their individual goals to those of the group (or the state), many would undoubtedly prefer a little more emphasis on cooperation, so that children would be quicker to adopt cooperative strategies in situations that call for them. One way that adults might accomplish this aim is to structure play activities so that children are likely to discover the benefits of cooperating and helping one another. In Box 10-2 we will see how one investigator has used this strategy to increase both the cooperativeness and the generosity of preschool children.

IMPLICATIONS FROM THE STUDY OF PROSOCIAL ACTIVISTS

Might we learn more about the encouragement of altruism by studying prosocial activists to determine why they are so altruistically inclined? David Rosenhan (1970) thought so. Rosenhan's strategy was to conduct extensive interviews with people who had participated in the civil rights movement in the southern part of the United States during the early to mid-1960s. His interviews suggested that these

"freedom riders" could be divided into two groups: (1) *fully committed* activists who had given up their homes, jobs, and educations to participate extensively in the civil rights movement and (2) *partially committed* activists who had limited their involvement to one or two freedom rides without altering the course of their lives in a significant way.

The two groups held similar attitudes about racial equality and civil rights. But there were two striking differences between fully and partially committed activists, both involving events that had taken place in childhood. First, the fully committed subjects had parents who themselves had been prosocial activists for other causes in an earlier era. For example, one member of the fully committed group noted that his mother "felt close to Jesus and . . . [had] devoted her entire life to Christian education." By contrast, the partially committed activists had parents who had often preached but rarely practiced altruism.

The second difference between the two groups centered on their emotional relationships with their parents. Fully committed activists had generally maintained a warm, cordial relationship with at least one parent, whereas the partially committed activists described their parental relations as hostile during childhood and rather cool at the time they were interviewed.

It seemed to Rosenhan (1972b) that the behavior of the fully committed activists qualified as autonomous altruism, for these people had ignored their present or future careers to advance the cause of others. The antecedents of their deep sense of altruistic commitment appeared to be a *warm, nurturant relationship with parents who were good altruistic models*. These findings are reminiscent of the laboratory evidence we have reviewed, which indicates that altruistic models who are warm and nurturant are especially likely to elicit prosocial responses from children.

Partially committed activists did not incur many personal costs and were only minimally committed to the cause. Rosenhan suspected that their participation was prompted by group *esprit* or social conformity and thus qualified as normative altruism. Recall that these individuals had experienced rather cool relations with parents who had often failed to practice what they preached. The literature we have reviewed

BOX 10-2   PROMOTING ALTRUISM THROUGH COOPERATIVE GAMES

Teaching children to get along well, to share, and to cooperate are important goals of preschool educational programs. How might we accomplish these objectives? Terry Orlick (1981) has been experimenting with a "cooperative activities" program in which children must join forces in order to meet a challenge or achieve the goals of various games. In a game called "bridges," for example, children are instructed to band together in groups of two or three to make bridges with their bodies. They then connect their bridges until the whole group forms one long bridge. Orlick compares the behavior of these youngsters with that of children in a "traditional activities" group who are encouraged to undertake individual pursuits. When children in the traditional program play "bridges," the objective is for each child to make his or her own unique bridge.

Preschool children who participate in a "cooperative activities" program do become more cooperative with their peers, both in the training environment and during unstructured free-play sessions in the gym and the classroom (Orlick & Foley, 1979; Orlick, McNally, & O'Hara, 1978). But does this cooperative training stimulate other altruistic acts such as sharing?

To find out, Orlick (1981) had one group of kindergarten children play cooperative games four times a week for 18 weeks. Children in a traditional games group spent the same amount of time playing very similar but individualized games that did not require a partner. At both the beginning and the end of the 18-week training period, each child received a bag containing five candies to keep or to share with other kindergartners (the afternoon class) who would otherwise not receive any candy. All children thus had an opportunity to donate some of their candies anonymously to their less fortunate peers in the other class. The table summarizes the results. Note that 11 of the children

from the "cooperative games" program became more generous as a result of their training, while only 5 children became less willing to share. The pattern was reversed in the "traditional games" program, where 17 children became less willing to donate candy to others and only 5 showed an increase in sharing.

In sum, a program designed to teach young children to cooperate not only accomplishes that objective but may also promote completely different forms of altruism, such as sharing. This finding is even more impressive when we recall that the recipients of the children's generosity were not familiar playmates but, rather, peers from another kindergarten class.

Gerald Sagotsky and his colleagues report that normally competitive American schoolchildren can be taught to cooperate at games that require cooperation in order for participants to win prizes (Sagotsky, Wood-Schneider, & Konop, 1981). In fact, Sagotsky et al. report that 7–8-year-olds who learn to work together while playing one set of games will usually adopt cooperative strategies for new games introduced *seven weeks later*. If our goal is to increase our children's prosocial behavior, we should probably be spending much more time teaching youngsters to play cooperative games and persuading them to pull together to achieve important objectives.

Number of Children Showing Change in Willingness to Share after Participating in a "Cooperative Activities" or a "Traditional Activities" Program

Training condition	Change in generosity	
	Increase	Decrease
Cooperative games	11	5
Traditional games	5	17

does indeed suggest that a cool relationship with a relatively nonaltruistic (or hypocritical) model is not conducive to the development of a strong sense of altruistic concern.

Unfortunately, one disadvantage of interview data such as Rosenhan's is that they could well be inaccurate. For example, were the parents of the fully committed participants really that altruistic; or, rather, were these altruistic activists simply being charitable in their memories of their parents? One way to assess

the merits of Rosenhan's ideas about the antecedents of altruism would be to identify groups of people who had had the same kinds of childhood experiences as Rosenhan's fully committed and partially committed activists and then see whether the former group was *subsequently* more altruistic than the latter group. The research described in Box 10-3 relied on this type of prospective methodology, and as we will see, its results provide striking support for Rosenhan's earlier conclusions.

BOX 10-3 DO CHILDHOOD EXPERIENCES PREDICT ADULT ALTRUISM?

Gil Clary and Jude Miller (1986) have conducted an important replication of Rosenhan's study that differs from the civil rights project in one very crucial way. These investigators first obtained reports of subjects' childhood experiences with parents. They then observed these subjects over a period of time to determine whether the kinds of experiences subjects reported having had with their parents would *predict* the subjects' future altruistic behaviors.

The participants in this study were adult volunteers at a crisis counseling agency in Minneapolis, Minnesota. During the period when the volunteers were trained, each of them completed an extensive questionnaire about his or her childhood experiences. On the basis of their responses (and Rosenhan's earlier classification scheme), subjects were classified as "autonomous altruists" (that is, those who reported having had warm relations with altruistic parents who practiced what they preached) or "normative altruists" (those reporting cooler relations with parents who had rarely modeled altruism). As the volunteers were being trained, the cohesiveness, or *esprit de corps*, of their training group was also measured and was classified as high or low. All trained volunteers were expected to fulfill a six-month commitment to the crisis counseling agency—a commitment requiring them to work one four-hour shift each week. The dependent variable in this study was a measure of *sustained* altruism—that is, did the volunteer actually complete his or her six-month commitment to the agency?

The results of this study were quite interesting. The table reveals that a majority of subjects classified as normative altruists completed their obligations to the agency *if their training group happened to be a cohesive one*; however, 70% of the normative altruists *failed* to fulfill their commitments if their groups were less cohesive. So, consistent with Rosenhan's earlier results, the pleasantness of the social context, or *group esprit*, was critical in determining

the sustained altruism of subjects classified as normative altruists. By contrast, a clear majority of volunteers who had been classified by their childhood experiences as autonomous altruists followed through to complete their commitments to the agency, *regardless of the level of cohesiveness of their training groups*. Apparently social benefits stemming from the volunteer experience itself were less important to these individuals than the services they might provide to clients who needed crisis counseling. In other words, the motivation for their helpfulness did seem to come from within and to reflect a sense of *autonomous* altruism.

So here, then, is important converging evidence for Rosenhan's proposition that different childhood experiences can promote different kinds of altruism. Parents who are not particularly nurturant or altruistic are likely to raise children whose prosocial inclinations are situationally determined and will depend to a large extent on the benefits they can expect to receive. By contrast, nurturant parents who frequently encourage and display altruism are more likely to raise children whose prosocial acts are internally motivated and reflect a genuine concern for the welfare of other people.

Percentages of Subjects Completing Their Obligation to a Crisis Counseling Agency as a Function of Their Prior Childhood Experiences and the Cohesiveness of Their Training Groups

	Group cohesiveness	
Childhood experiences	Low	High
Normative (cool relations with nonaltruistic parents)	30	60
Autonomous (warm relations with altruistic parents)	57	62

PARENTAL DISCIPLINE AND CHILDREN'S ALTRUISTIC INCLINATIONS

Parental reactions to a child's harmdoing may also play a significant role in the development of altruism. Martin Hoffman (1975) has argued that *power-assertive* discipline, such as spankings, or *love-oriented* discipline, such as the withdrawal of affec-

tion, is likely to (1) arouse resentment or anxiety and focus the child's attention on his own negative consequences, (2) contribute nothing to the child's understanding of another person's distress, and (3) expose the child to a punitive, rather than an altruistic, model. By comparison, *inductive* (or *victim-centered*) discipline relies on reasoning rather than punitive consequences to alter children's behavior. The goal of an inductive disciplinarian is to inform the child of the harm he has caused, encourage the child to imagine himself in the victim's place, and urge the child to direct some sort of comforting or helpful response toward the victim. Hoffman believes that children are likely to develop a strong altruistic orientation if their parents often rely on these victim-centered disciplinary techniques.

Hoffman tested his hypothesis by interviewing 80 fifth-grade children and their parents. Children were asked to nominate three boys or girls in their class who were most likely to (1) care about other children and try not to hurt their feelings and (2) stick up for a child whom others were making fun of. The number of nominations received by each child defined his or her altruism score. Parents were asked how they would respond to each of three situations in which their child had caused another person some distress. The responses of each parent were scored for the number and type of victim-centered techniques that were mentioned. Hoffman found that the children's altruism scores were positively correlated with the amount of victim-centered discipline used by the parent of the other sex (rs = about $+.50$). In other words, the greater a mother's use of victim-centered discipline, the higher her son's altruism score; the greater a father's use of victim-centered discipline, the higher his daughter's altruism score.

Although other investigators have not always found the "cross-sex" effect reported by Hoffman, their results are generally consistent with Hoffman's views on the effectiveness (or ineffectiveness) of various forms of discipline. Parents who rely mainly on inductive discipline do tend to raise children who are relatively sympathetic, self-sacrificing, and concerned about the welfare of other people, whereas frequent use of power assertion or love withdrawal appears to inhibit altruism and lead to the development of self-centered values (Brody & Shaffer, 1982; Dlugokinski & Firestone, 1974).

If we think about it, there are several reasons that inductive discipline might inspire children to become more altruistic. First, it encourages the child to assume another person's perspective (role taking) and to experience that person's distress (empathy training). It also communicates standards of appropriate conduct while urging the child to perform helpful or comforting "acts of reparation" that are

likely to make both the child and the other person feel better. And last but not least, these reparative responses may help to convince older (grade school) children that they can be "nice" or "helpful" people, a positive self-image that they may try to perpetuate by performing other acts of kindness in the future (Grusec & Redler, 1980).

TELEVISION AS A PROSOCIAL INSTRUMENT

In Chapter 9 we cast a wary eye at television, speaking of its capacity to instigate aggression and to desensitize children to violence in the real world. Yet, there is now reason to believe that television could become a most effective means of teaching prosocial lessons if its content were altered to reflect these principles. Let's examine some of the evidence to support this claim.

Prosocial effects of commercially broadcast programs. Although network programming designed for children is often violent, each of the commercial networks has made an attempt to broadcast some programs with prosocial themes (Liebert, Sprafkin, & Davidson, 1982). For example, CBS consulted with educators and child psychologists to develop *Fat Albert and the Cosby Kids*, a program designed to teach elementary school children how to deal effectively with a host of social issues, such as divorce, the arrival of a new baby, discrimination, being honest, and being helpful or compassionate. Moreover, several commercial series such as *Lassie* and *The Waltons* occasionally present episodes that revolve around one character's predicament and the helpful acts of a protagonist. Do young children learn these prosocial lessons? If so, are they likely to put them into practice?

The answer to both questions is a qualified yes. In the formative stages of *Fat Albert and the Cosby Kids*, the Columbia Broadcasting System (1974) reported that about 90% of the children who watched the pilot episode were able to verbalize its prosocial themes. Soon thereafter, investigators began to study the effects of such programming on children's behavior. For example, Joyce Sprafkin and her associates (Sprafkin, Liebert, & Poulos, 1975) found that fourth-graders who had watched a *Lassie* episode containing a dramatic rescue scene were later more inclined than subjects in a control condition to leave a game (and thereby give up the chance of winning a nice prize) to attend to some puppies that were apparently distressed. In a similar study (Baran, Chase, & Courtright, 1979), 8- to 10-year-olds who had watched an episode from *The Waltons* that portrayed a cooperative solution to a conflict later behaved more cooperatively while playing a game than their age mates who had seen a noncooperative film or no film. Finally, Sprafkin and Rubinstein (1979) discovered that children who prefer and often watch prosocial programming tend to behave more prosocially at school than their classmates who rarely watch such shows. Although no one has yet studied the persistence of these effects over time, the data are nevertheless encouraging and suggest that "it is possible to produce [commercial] programming that features action and adventure, appeals to child and family audiences, and still has a salutary rather than a negative social influence on viewers" (Sprafkin et al., 1975, p. 125).

Educational television and children's prosocial behavior. A number of programs broadcast on the Public Broadcasting System are designed to supplement the everyday learning experiences of preschool children. For example, *Sesame Street* was created to entertain children while fostering their intellectual and social development. A typical episode combines fast action and humorous incidents with a carefully planned educational curriculum designed to teach the letters of the alphabet, numbers, counting, and vocabulary. Another program, *Mister Rogers' Neighborhood*, is designed to facilitate the child's social and emotional development. To accomplish these objectives, Mister Rogers talks directly to his audience about things that may interest or puzzle children (for example, crises such as the death of a pet); he reassures them about common fears such as riding in airplanes; he encourages viewers to learn from and to cooperate with children of different races and social backgrounds; and he helps children to see themselves in a positive light by repeatedly emphasizing that "there is only one person in the whole world like you, and I like you just the way you are."

Both of these programs seem to have a positive influence on the social behavior of young viewers. When preschool children watch either program over a long period, they often become more affectionate, considerate, cooperative, and helpful toward their nursery school classmates (Coates, Pusser, & Goodman, 1976; Friedrich & Stein, 1973, 1975; Paulson, 1974). However, it is important to note that merely parking nursery schoolers in front of the tube to watch *Sesame Street* or *Mister Rogers* is not an effective training strategy, for this programming has few if any lasting effects unless adults encourage children to rehearse and enact the prosocial lessons they have learned (Friedrich & Stein, 1975; Friedrich-Cofer, Huston-Stein, Kipnis, Susman, & Clewett, 1979). Furthermore, children who are exposed to prosocial programming and encouraged to follow up on the themes they have witnessed may well become more prosocially inclined *without becoming any less aggressive* (Friedrich-Cofer et al., 1979). This puzzling finding may simply reflect the fact that children who watch prosocial programming typically become more outgoing and thus will have more opportunities to argue with their peers.

In sum, it would appear that the positive effects of prosocial programming on educational television greatly outweigh the negatives, particularly if adults are willing to watch some of this material with their children and to encourage them to verbalize, rehearse, and enact the principles that the shows have portrayed. Unfortunately, only about 200 stations in the United States regularly broadcast educational programs, and many families either live in rural areas where educational programming is unavailable or do not own television sets that are equipped to receive the UHF (or cable) channels that carry these offerings in the local area. Parents in the United States could help to remedy this situation if they were to encourage their elected representatives to support legislation calling for the financing of educational television on VHF channels in areas that do not currently enjoy this arrangement.

There are several methods that parents might try in an attempt to alter the content of commercial television. These include (1) boycotting products made by sponsors of violent programming, (2) informing sponsors and network executives of the reasons for this action, and (3) working cooperatively with groups such as Action for Children's Television that are organized to bring about changes in the content of children's shows. There is little doubt that commercial television has the potential to increase the incidence of prosocial behavior in our society. Whether or not this potential is realized will depend in part on the efforts of concerned citizens to bring about a change in the kind of material presented for our viewing pleasure.

SUMMARY

Most people in most cultures endorse the *norm of social responsibility*, which prescribes that one should help others who need help. The widespread acceptance of this principle has sparked a controversy about human nature. One school of thought contends that all prosocial behavior—behavior that benefits others—is motivated by expectations of self-gain or self-reinforcement; other theorists argue that such behavior often follows from concern for the welfare of others.

Altruism, a form of prosocial behavior, is usually defined in one of two ways. Proponents of a *motivational* definition contend that an act is altruistic if it benefits others and if the helper is acting more out of a concern for others than for the positive outcomes he or she might obtain. Advocates of a *behavioral* definition note that it is often difficult to infer a helper's true intentions. As a result, they define altruism as an act that provides assistance to others, regardless of the helper's motives.

Several theoretical explanations of altruism have been proposed. Evolutionary theorists argue that altruism is a preadapted, genetically programmed motive that evolved because it promotes the survival of the individual and the species. By contrast, proponents of psychoanalytic, social-learning, and cognitive-developmental theories believe that children must *acquire* a sense of altruistic concern. Psychoanalytic theorists assume that altruistic values are internalized and become a part of one's superego. Social-learning theorists believe that altruistic habits are acquired and maintained because children learn that prosocial behavior is rewarding. Cognitive-developmental theorists argue that the growth of altruistic concern depends on fundamental cognitive changes that occur during childhood; these changes include a decline in egocentrism, the development of role-taking skills, and advances in moral reasoning.

Although infants and toddlers will occasionally offer toys to playmates, try to help their parents with household chores, and try to soothe distressed companions, examples of altruism become increasingly common over the first 10–12 years of life. By middle childhood there is a fair degree of consistency in children's prosocial inclinations: those who help or share in one situation are likely to behave in a helpful or kindly manner in related situations. Contrary to popular belief, females are not more altruistic than males, although there is some evidence that young children are more inclined to assist or comfort members of their own sex. By middle childhood, the sex of a prospective recipient is less important in determining children's willingness to help than the recipient's apparent need for help. Generally speaking, children are more likely to comfort, assist, or share valuable resources with friends than acquaintances or strangers. And a child's prosocial behavior may be influenced by his or her mood. Children are more prosocially inclined if they are experiencing positive emotions, whereas the effects of negative moods are quite complex. If one's negative affect stems from personal misfortunes, it is likely to inhibit altruism. However, blue moods stemming from a consideration of someone else's misfortunes may increase altruism, in both children and adults.

A child's role-taking abilities and level of moral reasoning will affect his or her altruistic behavior. Children with good role-taking skills are often found to be more prosocially inclined than poor role takers, and the link between role taking and altruism becomes stronger with age. Mature moral reasoners are more generous and helpful than immature moral reasoners. In fact, mature moral reasoners may often help someone they dislike, whereas immature moral reasoners are much more inclined to ignore the needs of such a person.

Although young children may often empathize with a person in need, their behavioral responses to the person's distress are not always helpful ones. In fact, the evidence for a link between empathy and altruism is very weak for young children, though much stronger for preadolescents, adolescents, and adults. Empathy eventually becomes an important mediator of altruism once children acquire the role-taking or social information-processing skills that will enable them (1) to understand that the distress or misfortune of others is the cause of their own empathic emotions and (2) to realize that they can eliminate their own empathic arousal by taking some action to relieve a victim's distress.

One method of promoting children's altruism is to insist on kindly behavior and to reinforce them for their benevolent acts. Social reinforcement can be quite effective in this regard as long as the praise is administered by someone children like and respect. However, social approval may actually inhibit altruism if it comes from selfish, hypocritical people. Parents, teachers, and other socializing agents may also promote altruism by persuading children to think of themselves as "kindly" or "helpful" persons. School-age children are likely to incorporate these "traitlike" attributions into their self-concepts and try to live up to this new self-image by being more helpful or kindly in the future.

Children who are exposed to altruistic models often become more altruistic themselves, particularly if they know and respect the model and have previously established a warm and friendly relationship with this benevolent companion. Although a model's actions speak louder than his or her words, it is inappropriate to conclude that words are wasted on children. Verbal exhortations will facilitate altruism if they are strongly stated and provide the child with a meaningful cognitive rationale for sharing with, comforting, or helping others.

There are several strategies that adults might use to increase the incidence of prosocial behavior in our society. Structuring play activities so that children will discover the benefits of cooperating and helping one another (together with a little less emphasis on the competitive pursuit of individual goals) seems to be a step in the right direction. Parents who maintain a warm and affectionate relationship with their children, who frequently model altruistic behavior, and who rely on inductive (or victim-centered) techniques to discipline harmdoing tend to raise children who are relatively sympathetic, self-sacrificing, and concerned about the welfare of other people. Finally, the evidence indicates that both commercial and educational television could become an effective means of teaching prosocial lessons, particularly if adults will watch some of this material with their children and encourage them to verbalize, rehearse, and enact the principles that the shows have portrayed.

NOTES

1. The development of this kind of moral reasoning is described in detail in Chapter 11.

2. Of course, empathy can and often does mediate altruism among children as young as toddlers if the reasons for a companion's distress are obvious to them (see Denham, 1986; Zahn-Waxler et al., 1979). The point, however, is that empathic arousal will become a much more consistent or reliable source of altruistic motivation once children become better role takers and are more proficient at inferring the causes of their *own* empathic emotions.

3. According to attribution theory, extrinsic reinforcement should inhibit prosocial behavior if the child decides her acts of kindness are motivated by the promise of a reward rather than by her intrinsic motivation to help or comfort the recipient. However, extrinsic reward does not ordinarily have this inhibiting effect on the prosocial conduct of young children, probably because their intrinsic motivation for "self-sacrifice in the interest of others" *is not terribly high in the first place*. Recall from Chapter 8 that external reinforcement will typically promote or strengthen those activities that children are *not* intrinsically motivated to perform. Thus, praise or other social reinforcers are likely to foster, rather than inhibit, the self-sacrificial responses of young children.

REFERENCES

AHAMMER, I. M., & Murray, J. P. (1979). Kindness in the kindergarten: The relative influence of role playing and prosocial television in facilitating altruism. *International Journal of Behavioral Development, 2,* 133–157.

BANDURA, A. (1977). *Social learning theory.* Englewood Cliffs, NJ: Prentice-Hall.

BARAN, S. J., Chase, L. J., & Courtright, J. A. (1979). Television drama as a facilitator of prosocial behavior: "The Waltons." *Journal of Broadcasting, 23,* 277–284.

BARNETT, M. A., Howard, J. A., Melton, E. M., & Dino, G. A. (1982). Effect of inducing sadness about self or other on helping behavior in high- and low-empathic children. *Child Development, 53*, 920–923.

BARNETT, M. A., King, L. M., & Howard, J. A. (1979). Inducing affect about self or other: Effects on generosity in children. *Developmental Psychology, 15*, 164–167.

BAR-TAL, D., Raviv, A., & Goldberg, M. (1982). Helping behavior among preschool children: An observational study. *Child Development, 53*, 396–402.

BERKOWITZ, L., & Daniels, L. (1963). Responsibility and dependence. *Journal of Abnormal and Social Psychology, 66*, 429–436.

BERNDT, T. J. (1981). Effects of friendship on prosocial intentions and behavior. *Child Development, 52*, 636–643.

BIRCH, L. L., & Billman, J. (1986). Preschool children's food sharing with friends and acquaintances. *Child Development, 57*, 387–395.

BRODY, G. H., & Shaffer, D. R. (1982). Contributions of parents and peers to children's moral socialization. *Developmental Review, 2*, 31–75.

BRYAN, J. H., & Schwartz, T. H. (1971). The effects of filmed material upon children's behavior. *Psychological Bulletin, 75*, 50–59.

BRYAN, J. H., & Walbek, N. (1970). Preaching and practicing self-sacrifice: Children's actions and reactions. *Child Development, 41*, 329–353.

CAMPBELL, D. T. (1965). Ethnocentric and other altruistic motives. In D. Levine (Ed.), *Nebraska Symposium on Motivation* (Vol. 13). Lincoln: University of Nebraska Press.

CHARLESWORTH, R., & Hartup, W. W. (1967). Positive social reinforcement in the nursery school peer group. *Child Development, 38*, 993–1002.

CIALDINI, R. B., & Kenrick, D. T. (1976). Altruism as hedonism: A social development perspective on the relationship of negative mood state and helping. *Journal of Personality and Social Psychology, 34*, 907–914.

CLARY, E. G., & Miller, J. (1986). Socialization and situational influences on sustained altruism. *Child Development, 57*, 1358–1369.

COATES, B., Pusser, H. E., & Goodman, I. (1976). The influence of "Sesame Street" and "Mister Rogers' Neighborhood" on children's social behavior in the preschool. *Child Development, 47*, 138–144.

COKE, J. S., Batson, C. D., & McDavis, K. (1978). Empathic mediation of helping: A two-stage model. *Journal of Personality and Social Psychology, 36*, 752–766.

COLUMBIA BROADCASTING SYSTEM. (1974). *A study of messages received by children who viewed an episode of* Fat Albert and the Cosby Kids. New York: Broadcast Group.

CUNNINGHAM, M. R. (1979). Weather, mood, and helping behavior: Quasi-experiments with the sunshine Samaritan. *Journal of Personality and Social Psychology, 37*, 1947–1956.

CUNNINGHAM, M. R. (1986). *What do you do when you're feeling blue? Mood, cognition, and compensatory behavior.* Manuscript submitted for publication.

CUNNINGHAM, M. R. (in press). Levites and brother's keepers: A sociobiological perspective on prosocial behavior. *Humboldt Journal of Social Relations.*

CUNNINGHAM, M. R., Shaffer, D. R., Barbee, A., & Smith, J. D. (1987). *Dual process mechanisms in the relationship of mood to altruism: Helping for you and for me.* Manuscript submitted for publication.

DENHAM, S. A. (1986). Social cognition, prosocial behavior, and emotion in preschoolers: Contextual validation. *Child Development, 57*, 194–201.

DLUGOKINSKI, E. L., & Firestone, I. J. (1974). Other centeredness and susceptibility to charitable appeals: Effects of perceived discipline. *Developmental Psychology, 10*, 21–28.

EBERHARD, M. T. W. (1975). The evolution of social behavior by kin selection. *Quarterly Review of Biology, 50*, 1–33.

EISENBERG, N. (1983). Children's differentiations among potential recipients of aid. *Child Development, 54*, 594–602.

EISENBERG, N., Lennon, R., & Roth, K. (1983). Prosocial development: A longitudinal study. *Developmental Psychology, 19*, 846–855.

EISENBERG-BERG, N., & Hand, M. (1979). The relationship of preschoolers' reasoning about prosocial moral conflicts to prosocial behavior. *Child Development, 50*, 356–363.

FISCHER, W. F. (1963). Sharing in pre-school children as a function of the amount and type of reinforcement. *Genetic Psychology Monographs, 68*, 215–245.

FRIEDRICH, L. K., & Stein, A. H. (1973). Aggressive and prosocial television programs and the natural behavior of preschool children. *Monographs of the Society for Research in Child Development, 38*(4, Serial No. 51).

FRIEDRICH, L. K., & Stein, A. H. (1975). Prosocial television and young children: The effect of verbal labeling and role-playing on learning and behavior. *Child Development, 46*, 27–38.

FRIEDRICH-COFER, L. K., Huston-Stein, A., Kipnis, D. M., Susman, E. J., & Clewett, A. S. (1979). Environmental enhancement of prosocial television content: Effects on interpersonal behavior. *Developmental Psychology, 15*, 637–646.

GREEN, F. P., & Schneider, F. W. (1974). Age differences in the behavior of boys on three measures of altruism. *Child Development, 45*, 248–251.

GRUSEC, J. E., & Redler, E. (1980). Attribution, reinforcement, and altruism: A developmental analysis. *Developmental Psychology, 16*, 525–534.

HANDLON, B. J., & Gross, P. (1959). The development of sharing behavior. *Journal of Abnormal and Social Psychology, 59*, 425–428.

HAY, D. F. (1979). Cooperative interactions and sharing among very young children and their parents. *Developmental Psychology, 15*, 647–653.

HOFFMAN, M. L. (1975). Altruistic behavior and the parent-child relationship. *Journal of Personality and Social Psychology, 31*, 937–943.

HOFFMAN, M. L. (1981). Is altruism part of human nature? *Journal of Personality and Social Psychology, 40*, 121–137.

HUDSON, L. M., Forman, E. R., & Brion-Meisels, S. (1982). Role-taking as a predictor of prosocial behavior in cross-age tutors. *Child Development, 53*, 1320–1329.

HUGHES, R., Jr., Tingle, B. A., & Sawin, D. B. (1981). Development of empathic understanding in children. *Child Development, 52*, 122–128.

IANNOTTI, R. J. (1978). Effect of role-taking experiences on role-taking, empathy, altruism, and aggression. *Developmental Psychology, 14*, 119–124.

ISEN, A. M. (1970). Success, failure, attention, and reaction to others: The warm glow of success. *Journal of Personality and Social Psychology, 15*, 294–301.

ISEN, A. M., Clark, M., & Schwartz, M. F. (1976). Duration of the effect of good mood on helping: "Footprints on the sands of time." *Journal of Personality and Social Psychology, 34*, 385–393.

ISEN, A. M., & Levin, P. F. (1972). Effects of feeling good on helping: Cookies and kindness. *Journal of Personality and Social Psychology, 21*, 384–388.

JONES, D. C. (1985). Persuasive appeals and responses to appeals among friends and acquaintances. *Child Development, 56*, 757–763.

KAGAN, S., & Masden, M. C. (1971). Cooperation and competition of Mexican, Mexican-American, and Anglo-American children of two ages and four instructional sets. *Developmental Psychology, 5*, 32–39.

KAGAN, S., & Masden, M. C. (1972). Rivalry in Anglo-American and Mexican children of two ages. *Journal of Personality and Social Psychology, 24*, 214–220.

KANFER, F. H., Stifter, E., & Morris, S. J. (1981). Self-control and altruism: Delay of gratification for another. *Child Development, 47*, 51–61.

KOHLBERG, L. (1969). Stage and sequence: The cognitive-developmental approach to socialization. In D. A. Goslin (Ed.), *Handbook of socialization theory and research*. Skokie, IL: Rand McNally.

KREBS, D. L. (1970). Altruism—an examination of the concept and a review of the literature. *Psychological Bulletin, 73,* 258–302.

KREBS, D. L. (1975). Empathy and altruism. *Journal of Personality and Social Psychology, 32,* 1134–1146.

LADD, G. W., Lange, G., & Stremmel, A. (1983). Personal and situational influences on children's helping behavior: Factors that mediate compliant helping. *Child Development, 54,* 488–501.

LEUNG, E. H. L., & Rheingold, H. L. (1981). Development of pointing as a social gesture. *Developmental Psychology, 17,* 215–220.

LEVITT, M. J., Weber, R. A., Clark, M. C., & McDonnell, P. (1985). Reciprocity of exchange in toddler sharing behavior. *Developmental Psychology, 21,* 122–123.

LIEBERT, R. M., Sprafkin, J. N., & Davidson, E. S. (1982). *The early window: Effects of television on children and youth.* New York: Pergamon Press.

MACCOBY, E. E. (1980). *Social development.* San Diego, CA: Harcourt Brace Jovanovich.

MATTHEWS, K. A., Batson, C. D., Horn, J., & Rosenman, R. H. (1981). "Principles in his nature which interest him in the fortune of others . . .": The heritability of empathic concern. *Journal of Personality, 49,* 237–247.

MIDLARSKY, E., & Bryan, J. H. (1972). Affect expressions and children's imitative altruism. *Journal of Experimental Research in Personality, 6,* 195–203.

MIDLARSKY, E., Bryan, J. H., & Brickman, P. (1973). Aversive approval: Interactive effects of modeling and reinforcement on altruistic behavior. *Child Development, 44,* 321–328.

MIDLARSKY, E., & Hannah, M. E. (1985). Competence, reticence, and helping by children and adolescents. *Developmental Psychology, 21,* 534–541.

MOORE, B. S., Underwood, B., & Rosenhan, D. L. (1973). Affect and altruism. *Developmental Psychology, 8,* 99–104.

MURPHY, L. B. (1937). *Social behavior and child personality: An exploratory study of some roots of sympathy.* New York: Columbia University Press.

ORLICK, T. D. (1981). Positive socialization via cooperative games. *Developmental Psychology, 17,* 426–429.

ORLICK, T. D., & Foley, C. (1979). Pre-school cooperative games: A preliminary perspective. In M. J. Melnick (Ed.), *Sport sociology: Contemporary themes* (2nd ed.). Dubuque, IA: Kendall/Hunt.

ORLICK, T. D., McNally, J., & O'Hara, T. (1978). Cooperative games: Systematic analysis and cooperative impact. In F. Smoll & R. Smith (Eds.), *Psychological perspectives in youth sports.* Washington, DC: Hemisphere.

PAULSON, F. L. (1974). Teaching cooperation on television: An evaluation of *Sesame Street*'s social goals and programs. *AV Communication Review, 22,* 229–246.

PEARL, R. (1985). Children's understanding of others' need for help: Effects of problem explicitness and type. *Child Development, 56,* 735–745.

PETERSON, L. (1983). Influence of children's age, task competence, and responsibility focus on children's altruism. *Developmental Psychology, 19,* 141–148.

PETERSON, L., & Gelfand, D. M. (1984). Causal attributions of helping as a function of age and incentives. *Child Development, 55,* 504–511.

PILIAVIN, J., Dovidio, J., Gaertner, S., & Clark, R. (1981). *Emergency intervention.* Orlando, FL: Academic Press.

RADKE-YARROW, M., & Zahn-Waxler, C. (1983). Roots, motives, and patterns in children's prosocial behavior. In J. Reykowski, T. Karylowski, D. Bar-Tal, & E. Staub (Eds.), *Origins and maintenance of prosocial behaviors.* New York: Plenum.

RADKE-YARROW, M., Zahn-Waxler, C., & Chapman, M. (1983). Children's prosocial dispositions and behavior. In E. M. Hetherington (Ed.), *Handbook of child psychology* (Vol. 4). New York: Wiley.

RHEINGOLD, H. L. (1982). Little children's participation in the work of adults, a nascent prosocial behavior. *Child Development, 53,* 114–125.

RICE, M. E., & Grusec, J. E. (1975). Saying and doing: Effects on observer performance. *Journal of Personality and Social Psychology, 32,* 584–593.

RITCHIE, F. K., & Toner, I. J. (1984). Direct labeling, tester expectancy, and delay maintenance behavior in Scottish preschool children. *International Journal of Behavioral Development, 7,* 333–341.

ROSENHAN, D. L. (1970). The natural socialization of altruistic autonomy. In J. Macaulay & L. Berkowitz (Eds.), *Altruism and helping behavior.* Orlando, FL: Academic Press.

ROSENHAN, D. L. (1972a). Learning theory and prosocial behavior. *Journal of Social Issues, 28,* 151–163.

ROSENHAN, D. L. (1972b). Prosocial behavior of children. In W. W. Hartup (Ed.), *The young child* (Vol. 2). Washington, DC: National Association for the Education of Young Children.

ROSENHAN, D. L., & White, G. M. (1967). Observation and rehearsal as determinants of prosocial behavior. *Journal of Personality and Social Psychology, 5,* 424–431.

RUSHTON, J. P. (1975). Generosity in children: Immediate and long term effects of modeling, preaching, and moral judgment. *Journal of Personality and Social Psychology, 31,* 459–466.

RUSHTON, J. P. (1976). Socialization and the altruistic behavior of children. *Psychological Bulletin, 83,* 898–913.

RUSHTON, J. P. (1980). *Altruism, socialization, and society.* Englewood Cliffs, NJ: Prentice-Hall.

RUTHERFORD, E., & Mussen, P. H. (1968). Generosity in nursery school boys. *Child Development, 39,* 755–765.

SAGOTSKY, G., Wood-Schneider, M., & Konop, M. (1981). Learning to cooperate: Effects of modeling and direct instruction. *Child Development, 52,* 1037–1042.

SHAFFER, D. R. (1986). Is mood-induced altruism a form of hedonism? *Humboldt Journal of Social Relations, 13,* 195–216.

SHAFFER, D. R., & Graziano, W. G. (1983). Effects of positive and negative moods on helping tasks having pleasant or unpleasant consequences. *Motivation and Emotion, 7,* 269–278.

SHAFFER, D. R., & Smith, J. E. (1985). Effects of preexisting moods on observers' reactions to helpful and nonhelpful models. *Motivation and Emotion, 9,* 101–122.

SHIGETOMI, C. C., Hartmann, D. P., & Gelfand, D. M. (1981). Sex differences in children's altruistic behavior and reputations for helpfulness. *Developmental Psychology, 17,* 434–437.

SIGELMAN, C. K. (1984). Prosocial behavior. In K. Deaux & L. S. Wrightsman, *Social Psychology in the 80s* (4th ed.). Monterey, CA: Brooks/Cole.

SLABY, R. G., & Crowley, C. G. (1977). Modification of cooperation and aggression through teacher attention to children's speech. *Journal of Experimental Child Psychology, 23,* 442–458.

SPRAFKIN, J. N., Liebert, R. M., & Poulos, R. W. (1975). Effects of a prosocial televised example on children's helping. *Journal of Experimental Child Psychology, 20,* 119–126.

SPRAFKIN, J. N., & Rubinstein, E. A. (1979). A field correlational study of children's television viewing habits and prosocial behavior. *Journal of Broadcasting, 23,* 265–276.

STAUB, E. (1970). A child in distress: The influence of age and number of witnesses on children's attempts to help. *Journal of Personality and Social Psychology, 14,* 130–140.

STAUB, E. (1974). Helping a distressed person: Social, personality, and stimulus determinants. In L. Berkowitz (Ed.), *Advances in experimental social psychology* (Vol. 7). Orlando, FL: Academic Press.

STAUB, E. A. (1979). *Positive social behavior and morality* (Vol. 2). Orlando, FL: Academic Press.

STAUB, E. A., & Noerenberg, H. (1981). Property rights, deservingness, reciprocity, friendship: The transactional character of children's sharing behavior. *Journal of Personality and Social Psychology, 40,* 271–289.

THOMPSON, W. C., Cowan, C. L., & Rosenhan, D. L. (1980). Focus of attention mediates the impact of negative mood on altruism. *Journal of Personality and Social Psychology, 38,* 291–300.

TRIVERS, R. L. (1971). The evolution of reciprocal altruism. *Quarterly*

Review of Biology, 46, 35–57.

UGUREL-SEMIN, R. (1952). Moral behavior and moral judgment of children. *Journal of Abnormal and Social Psychology, 47,* 463–474.

UNDERWOOD, B., & Moore, B. (1982). Perspective-taking and altruism. *Psychological Bulletin, 91,* 143–173.

WHITING, B. B., & Whiting, J. W. M. (1975). *Children of six cultures.* Cambridge, MA: Harvard University Press.

WRIGHT, B. A. (1942). Altruism in children and perceived conduct of others. *Journal of Abnormal and Social Psychology, 37,* 218–233.

YARROW, M. R., Scott, P. M., & Waxler, C. Z. (1973). Learning concern for others. *Developmental Psychology, 8,* 240–260.

YARROW, M. R., & Waxler, C. Z. (1976). Dimensions and correlates of prosocial behavior in young children. *Child Development, 47,* 118–125.

ZAHN-WAXLER, C., Radke-Yarrow, M., & King, R. A. (1979). Childrearing and children's prosocial initiations toward victims of distress. *Child Development, 50,* 319–330.

ZARBATANY, L., Hartmann, D. P., Gelfand, D. M., & Vinciguerra, P. (1985). Gender differences in altruistic reputation: Are they artifactual? *Developmental Psychology, 21,* 97–101.

11

MORAL DEVELOPMENT

A DEFINITION OF MORALITY

How Psychologists Look at Morality

Moral Maturity and Its Measurement

PSYCHOANALYTIC EXPLANATIONS OF MORAL DEVELOPMENT

Freud's Theory of Oedipal Morality

Neo-Freudian Explanations of Moral Development

Attempts to Verify Psychoanalytic Theory

COGNITIVE-DEVELOPMENTAL THEORY: THE CHILD AS A MORAL PHILOSOPHER

Piaget's Theory of Moral Development

Tests of Piaget's Theory

Kohlberg's Theory of Moral Development

Tests of Kohlberg's Theory

(continues)

Suppose that a large sample of parents were asked "What is the most important aspect of a child's social development?" Surely this is a question that could elicit any number of responses. However, it's a good bet that many parents would hope above all that their children would acquire a strong sense of morality—right and wrong—to guide their everyday exchanges with other people.

The moral development of each successive generation is of obvious significance to society. One of the reasons that people can live together in peace is that they have evolved codes of ethics that sanction certain practices and prohibit others. Although moral standards may vary from culture to culture (Garbarino & Bronfenbrenner, 1976), every society has devised rules that its constituents must obey in order to remain members in good standing. Thus, the moral education of each succeeding generation serves two important functions: (1) to maintain the social order while (2) making it possible for the individual to function appropriately within his or her culture (or subculture).

Sigmund Freud once argued that moral education is the largest hurdle that parents face when raising a child, and many of his contemporaries agreed. In one of the first social psychology texts, William McDougall (1908) said:

> The fundamental problem of social psychology is the moralization of the individual into the society into which he was born as an amoral and egoistic infant. There are successive stages, each of which must be traversed by every individual before he can attain the next higher: (1) the stage in which . . . [innate] impulses are modified by the influence of rewards and punishments, (2) the stage in which conduct is controlled . . . by social praise or blame, and (3) the highest stage in which conduct is regulated by an ideal that enables a man to act in a way that seems to him right regardless of the praise or blame of his immediate social environment [p. 6].

The third stage in McDougall's theory suggests that children do not go through life submitting to society's moral dictates because they expect rewards for complying or fear punishments for transgressing. Rather, they eventually internalize the moral principles that they have learned and will behave in accordance with these ideals even when authority figures are not present to enforce them. As we will see, many contemporary theorists consider *internalization* to be a very important part of the development of moral controls.

A DEFINITION OF MORALITY

Virtually all adults have some idea of what morality is, although the ways they define the term will depend, in part, on their general outlooks on life. A theologian, for example, might mention the relationship between human beings and their Creator. A philosopher's definition of morality may depend on the assumptions that he or she makes about human nature. Psychologists are generally concerned with the feelings, thoughts, and actions of people who are facing moral dilemmas. But most adults would probably agree that morality implies *a set of principles or ideals that help the individual to distinguish right from wrong and to act on this distinction.*

HOW PSYCHOLOGISTS LOOK AT MORALITY

Psychological research has focused on three basic components of morality: the *affective*, or emotional, component, the *cognitive* component, and the *behavioral* component. Psychoanalytic theorists emphasize the emotional aspects of moral development. According to Freud, the kind of emotional relationships a child has with his or her parents will determine the child's willingness to internalize the parents' standards of right and wrong. Freud also believed that a child who successfully internalizes the morality of his parents will experience negative emotions such as shame or guilt—that is, *moral affect*—if he violates these ethical guidelines. Cognitive-developmental theorists have concentrated on the cognitive aspects of morality, or *moral reasoning*, and have found that the ways children think about right and wrong may change rather dramatically as they mature. Finally, the research of social-learning and social information-processing (or attribution) theorists has helped us to understand how children learn to resist temptation and to practice *moral be-havior*, inhibiting actions such as lying, stealing, and cheating that violate moral norms.

MORAL MATURITY AND ITS MEASUREMENT

Like McDougall, most contemporary researchers be-lieve that moral development proceeds toward the internalization of a set of ethical principles or norms against which the appropriateness of various feel-ings, thoughts, and actions is evaluated. Thus, "mor-al maturity" implies an ability and a willingness to abide by one's chosen (internalized) ethical stan-dards, even when authority figures are not around to approve of praiseworthy conduct or to punish transgressions.

By contrast, those whose conduct is controlled by the expectation of rewards for acceptable behaviors and/or fear of punishment for prohibited acts are said to have an *external* moral orientation. These persons have not selected and internalized a set of ethical principles to guide their conduct and, thus, could be considered "morally immature."[1]

Over the years, researchers have devised several methods of assessing moral maturity. The most com-mon measure of moral affect is some index of the amount of guilt, shame, or self-criticism that children associate with the commission of prohibited acts. The typical procedure presents subjects with an in-complete story in which a child of the same age and sex has committed a transgression that is unlikely to be detected. The subject is asked to complete the story by telling what the protagonist thinks or feels and what will happen as a result of these feelings. Of course, the assumption is that children will project onto the story character the reactions that they them-selves experience after a transgression. If a child says the protagonist runs away to avoid punishment, his answer is interpreted as a sign of an external moral orientation (and moral immaturity). A more mature, or "internal," response would be one in which the child expresses remorse, guilt, shame, or some other self-critical reaction.

The cognitive component of morality, or moral reasoning, is typically measured by (1) questioning subjects about the meaning of rules and having them make judgments about the naughtiness of different rule violations or (2) asking them to think about moral dilemmas that require a choice between obeying a rule, law, or authority figure and endorsing an action that conflicts with this rule while serving a human need. The purpose of these procedures (which will be described in much greater detail later in the chapter) is to determine how children think about moral issues and the extent to which their moral reasoning centers on external sanctions for harm-doing.

Traditionally, moral conduct has been assessed in either of two ways: (1) by tempting the child to cheat or to violate other prohibitions when there is no one around to detect this transgression or (2) by measur-ing (through projective stories or parental interview) the child's tendency to confess or accept responsi-bility for deviant behavior when the possibility of its detection is remote. Of course, the child's willingness to share, comfort, or help others is also a behavioral indicator of morality—the posi-tive side of morality (prosocial concern), discussed in Chapter 10.

Although different theories emphasize different aspects of morality and moral development, in real life these moral components are obviously interre-lated—at least to some extent. For example, a child's confession of wrongdoing (moral conduct) may be driven by her intense feelings of guilt (moral affect). Another child's willingness to violate a prohibition in the absence of external surveillance (moral conduct) may stem from a belief (or moral reasoning) that violations that go undetected and unpunished are really not all that harmful.

In this chapter, we will be discussing the develop-ment of all three aspects of moral character. We will begin by examining each of the major theories of moral development and the research it has generated. After we have seen how each theory approaches the topic of moral growth and development, we will take a closer look at the relations among moral affect, moral reasoning, and moral behavior. This informa-tion should help us to decide whether a person really has a unified "moral character" that is stable over time and across situations. Finally, we will consider how various child-rearing practices may affect a child's moral development and, in so doing, will attempt to integrate much of the information that we have reviewed.

PSYCHOANALYTIC EXPLANATIONS OF MORAL DEVELOPMENT

According to Freud (1935/1960), the personality consists of three basic components—the id, the ego, and the superego. Recall from Chapter 2 that the id is impulsive and hedonistic. Its purpose is to gratify the instincts. The function of the ego is to restrain the id until realistic means for satisfying needs can be worked out. The superego is the final component of the personality to develop. Its role is to determine whether id impulses and the means of impulse satisfaction produced by the ego are acceptable or unacceptable (moral or immoral).

Freud believed that infants and toddlers are basically amoral and hedonistic because they are dominated by their ids. Before the superego has formed, parents must reward behaviors that they consider acceptable and punish those that they consider unacceptable if they hope to restrain the child's hedonistic impulses. Once the superego develops, it will monitor the child's thoughts and actions and become an *internal* censor. Indeed, Freud argued that a well-developed superego is a harsh master that will punish the ego for moral transgressions by producing feelings of guilt, shame, or a loss of self-esteem. Presumably, the morally mature child will then resist temptation to violate moral norms in order to avoid these dreaded forms of negative moral affect.

FREUD'S THEORY OF OEDIPAL MORALITY

According to Freud, the superego develops during the phallic stage (age 3–6), when children were said to experience a hostile rivalry with the same-sex parent that stemmed from their incestuous desire for the other-sex parent (that is, an Oedipus complex for males and an Electra complex for females). Freud proposed that hostilities arising from the Oedipus complex would build until a boy came to fear his father and would be forced to identify with him in order to reduce this fear. By identifying with the father, the boy should internalize many of his father's attributes, including the father's moral standards. In other words, Freud assumed that the male superego would emerge during the preschool period and mature by the age of 6 to 7, when most boys would have resolved their oedipal conflicts.

Girls were assumed to experience similar conflicts during the phallic stage as they began to compete with their mothers for the affection of their fathers. But Freud argued that girls are never quite as afraid of their mothers as boys are of their fathers, because in the worst of all imaginable circumstances, their mothers could never castrate them. The implication is that a young girl might find it difficult to resolve her Electra complex because she experiences no overriding fear that would absolutely force her to identify with her mother. For this reason, Freud believed that females develop weaker superegos than males do!

As you might expect, Freud's rather chauvinistic views on female morality have made him a frequent target of feminist groups. However, it may be some consolation to women that Freud was unable to convince many of his own disciples that his explanation of moral development was correct.

NEO-FREUDIAN EXPLANATIONS OF MORAL DEVELOPMENT

Many psychoanalytic theorists (such as Erikson, 1963; Ferenczi, 1927; Hartmann, 1960) have largely rejected Freud's theory of oedipal morality and argued that children internalize the moral principles of *both* parents. According to the neo-Freudians, moral development can be traced to *social* (rather than sexual) conflicts that begin during the second year, when the child begins to submit to parental authority (literally, the parents' superegos) in order to avoid losing their love (or to avoid feeling shameful). The preschool period is viewed as a trying time for children. Presumably, 2- to 5-year-olds very much resent parental attempts to restrict and control their behavior. They would love to find a way of getting back at (or getting even with) their dominating and controlling parents, but they realize that if they retaliate they could lose mom's and dad's love. In order to resolve this social dilemma, children repress their hostilities and seek parental affection by internalizing the parents' moral standards. This identification with one's parents is a kind of insurance for *both boys and girls*, who believe that "if I become like mom and dad, they'll have to love me."

Unlike Freud, the neo-Freudians believe that both the *ego* and the superego play important roles in moral development. The superego dictates to the ego the kinds of behavior that are morally acceptable and unacceptable. But unless the ego is strong enough to inhibit the id's undesirable impulses, the child will be unable to resist the id, regardless of the strength of the superego. In other words, the neo-Freudians assume that morality is a product of both the internalized rules of the superego and the restraining forces of the ego that enable the child to obey these rules.

ATTEMPTS TO VERIFY PSYCHOANALYTIC THEORY

Both the Freudian and the neo-Freudian theories of moral development offer several testable hypotheses. Because these theories make different predictions, we will evaluate the evidence pertaining to each.

Tests of Freudian theory. Three hypotheses flow directly from Freud's explanation of moral development:

Hypothesis 1. If the superego develops out of the child's fear of the same-sex parent, then children whose same-sex parents are relatively punitive or threatening should develop relatively strong superegos.

Hypothesis 2. Boys, who have an especially good reason to fear their fathers (castration anxiety), should develop stronger superegos than girls.

Hypothesis 3. Children should be morally mature by the end of the phallic period (age 6 to 7), when the formation of the superego is completed.

Studies of moral development provide very little support for any of Freud's hypotheses. Cold, threatening parents do not raise children who are morally mature. Quite the contrary; parents who rely on punitive forms of discipline, such as spankings, tend to have youngsters who often misbehave and who rarely express feelings of guilt, remorse, shame, or self-criticism (Brody & Shaffer, 1982; Hoffman, 1970). Furthermore, there is simply no evidence that males develop stronger superegos than females. In fact, investigators who have left children alone so that they are tempted to violate a prohibition usually find no sex differences in moral behavior, or they find differences favoring females (Hoffman, 1975b). Finally, there is little evidence that children are morally mature at age 6 or 7, when they have supposedly resolved their oedipal conflicts. As we will see later in the chapter, at least one aspect of morality—moral reasoning—continues to develop well into young adulthood. In view of the repeated failures to confirm these and other Freudian hypotheses, many developmentalists now believe that it is time to lay Freud's theory of oedipal morality to rest.

Tests of neo-Freudian theory. If neo-Freudian theory is correct, parents who use *love-oriented* disciplinary techniques—for example, by scolding the child or withholding affection, thereby generating anxiety over a loss of love—should raise children who develop stronger superegos than would children whose parents use *power-assertive* discipline, such as spankings or withholding privileges. Moreover, the neo-Freudian (particularly, Erik Erikson's) emphasis on the role of the ego in moral development suggests that children with strong egos (as measured by their ability to defer immediate gratification in the service of long-range goals) should be more morally mature than those with weaker egos.

As we will see later in the chapter, there is little evidence that parents' use of love-oriented disciplinary techniques contributes to children's moral maturity (see Brody & Shaffer, 1982). However, there are data to support Erikson's "ego strength" hypothesis. For example, Walter Mischel (1974) reports that children who tested high in the ability to delay immediate gratification were rated more "socially responsible" by adults and were better able to resist the temptation to cheat at an experimental game than subjects who scored low on this attribute. Moreover, Podd (1972) reported a positive correlation between ego strength and maturity of moral reasoning in a sample of male college students, and Campagna and Harter (1975) found that sociopathic children—who are thought to have weak egos—exhibited lower levels of moral reasoning than their nonsociopathic age mates.

Although this "ego" research is consistent with neo-Freudian theory, it is also easily interpreted within the framework of other theories, most notably the cognitive approach. Since the ego is the rational component of the personality—the seat of all higher intellectual functions—the neo-Freudians are arguing that moral development depends, in part, on intellectual development. The cognitive-developmentalists definitely agree.

COGNITIVE-DEVELOPMENTAL THEORY: THE CHILD AS A MORAL PHILOSOPHER

Cognitive-developmentalists study morality by looking at the development of *moral reasoning*—that is, the thinking that children display when deciding whether various acts are right or wrong. The most basic assumption of the cognitive approach is that moral development depends to a large extent on the child's cognitive development. Moral reasoning is said to progress through an *invariant sequence* of "stages," each of which is a consistent way of thinking about moral issues that is different from the stages preceding and following it. Presumably each moral stage evolves from and replaces its immediate predecessor, so that there can be no skipping of stages. If these assumptions sound familiar, they should, for they are the same ones that Piaget made about his stages of intellectual development.

In this section of the chapter we will consider two cognitive-developmental theories of moral reasoning—Jean Piaget's (1932/1965) model and Lawrence Kohlberg's (1969, 1981, 1984) revision and extension of Piaget's approach.

PIAGET'S THEORY OF MORAL DEVELOPMENT

According to Piaget (1932/1965), moral maturity implies both a respect for rules and a sense of social justice—that is, a concern that all people be treated fairly and equitably under the socially defined rules

of order. Piaget studied the development of a respect for rules by rolling up his sleeves and playing marbles with a large number of Swiss children. As he played with children of different ages, Piaget would ask them questions about the rules of the game—questions such as "Where do these rules come from? Must everyone obey a rule? Can these rules be changed?" Once he had identified developmental stages in the understanding and use of rules, he proceeded to study children's conceptions of social justice by presenting them with moral dilemmas in the form of stories. Here is one example:

> *Story A.* A little boy who is called John is in his room. He is called to dinner. He goes into the dining room. But behind the door there was a chair, and on the chair there was a tray with 15 cups on it. John couldn't have known that there was all this behind the door. He goes in, the door knocks against the tray, bang go the 15 cups, and they all get broken.

> *Story B.* Once there was a little boy whose name was Henry. One day when his mother was out he tried to reach some jam out of the cupboard. He climbed onto a chair and stretched out his arm. But the jam was too high up, and he couldn't reach it. . . . While he was trying to get it, he knocked over a cup. The cup fell down and broke [Piaget, 1932/1965, p. 122].

Having heard the stories, subjects were asked "Are these children equally guilty?" and "If not, which child is naughtier? Why?" Subjects were also asked how the naughtier child should be punished. Through the use of these research techniques, Piaget formulated a theory of moral development that includes a premoral period and two moral stages.

The Premoral Period

According to Piaget, preschool children show little concern for or awareness of rules. In a game of marbles, these "premoral" children do not play systematically with the intent of winning. Instead, they seem to make up their own rules, and they think the point of the game is to take turns and have fun. Toward the end of the premoral period (ages 4 to 5), the child becomes more aware of rules by watching older children and imitating their rule-bound behavior. But the premoral child does not yet understand that rules represent a cooperative agreement about how a game should be played.

The Stage of Moral Realism, or Heteronomous Morality

Between the ages of 6 and 10, the child develops a strong respect for rules and a belief that they must be obeyed at all times. Children at this "heteronomous" stage assume that rules are laid down by authority figures such as God, the police, or their parents, and they think these regulations are sacred and unalterable. Try breaking the speed limit with a 6-year-old at your side and you may see what Piaget was talking about. Even if you are rushing to the hospital in a medical emergency, the young child may note that you are breaking a "rule of the road" and consider your behavior unacceptable conduct that deserves to be punished. In sum, heteronomous children think of rules as *moral absolutes*. They believe that there are a "right" side and a "wrong" side to any moral issue, and right always means following the rules.

Children at this first moral stage are apt to judge the naughtiness of an act by its objective consequences rather than the actor's intent. For example, Piaget found that many 6–10-year-olds judged John, who accidentally broke 15 cups while performing a well-intentioned act, to be naughtier than Henry, who broke one cup while stealing jam. Perhaps this focus on objective harm done, or "moral realism," stems from the fact that young children may be punished if and when their behavior produces harmful consequences. For example, a girl who bumps into a table without doing any harm is less likely to be reprimanded for her clumsiness than a second youngster who nudges the table and knocks over a number of her mother's plants in the process.

Heteronomous children favor *expiatory punishment*—punishment for its own sake with no concern for its relation to the nature of the forbidden act. For example, a 6-year-old might favor spanking a boy who had misbehaved and broken a window rather than making the boy pay for the window from his allowance. Moreover, the heteronomous child believes in *immanent justice*—the idea that violations of social rules will invariably be punished in one way or another. So if a 6-year-old boy were to fall and skin his knee while stealing cookies, he might conclude that this injury was the punishment he deserved for his transgression. (Indeed, parents may often pro-mote such beliefs by telling their children things like "If you hadn't been naughty, you wouldn't have hurt yourself" or "If you are bad this year, Santa won't stop at our house").

The Stage of Moral Relativism, or Autonomous Morality

By age 10 or 11 most children are entering Piaget's second moral stage—the stage of moral relativism, or "autonomous morality." Older, autonomous children now realize that social rules are arbitrary agreements that can be challenged and even changed with the consent of the people they govern. They also feel that rules may be violated in the service of human needs. Thus, a driver who speeds during a medical emergency will no longer be considered a wrongdoer, even though she is breaking the law. Judgments of right and wrong now depend more on the actor's *intent* to deceive or to violate social rules than on the objective consequences of the act itself. For example, 10-year-olds reliably say that Henry, who broke one cup while stealing some jam (bad intent), is naughtier than John, who broke 15 cups while coming to dinner (good or neutral intent).

When deciding how to punish a transgression, the morally autonomous person usually favors *reciprocal punishments*—that is, treatments that shape the punitive consequences to the "crime" so that the rule breaker will understand the implications of a transgression and perhaps be less likely to repeat it. For example, an autonomous child may decide that the boy who deliberately breaks a window should pay for it out of his allowance (and learn that windows cost money) rather than simply submitting to a spanking. Children at this higher stage of moral reasoning no longer believe in immanent justice, because they have learned from experience that violations of social rules often go undetected and unpunished.

Moving from Heteronomous to Autonomous Morality

Piaget believes that two cognitive deficits contribute to the young child's rigid and absolutistic moral reasoning. The first is *egocentrism*—a difficulty in recognizing perspectives other than one's own. The second is *realism*—the tendency to confuse subjective experience (one's own thoughts) with external reality. Perhaps you can see how these cognitive shortcomings might lead to a sense of moral realism. When parents or other authority figures enforce a rule, the young child assumes that this dictate must be sacred and unalterable, particularly since it comes from a powerful person who can make the rule stick (realism). And since the child at this age assumes that other people see things as she does (egocentrism), she will conclude that various rules must be "absolutes" that apply to everyone.

According to Piaget, both cognitive maturation and social experience play a role in the transition from heteronomous to autonomous morality. The cognitive advances that are necessary for this shift are a general decline in egocentrism and the development of role-taking skills that will enable the child to view moral issues from several perspectives. The kind of social experience that Piaget considers important is *equal status* contact with peers. Beginning at about age 6, the child spends four to six hours a day at school surrounded by other children of approximately the same age. In a group of peers, conflicts will often arise because the members of the group will not always agree on how they should play games or solve problems. Since everyone has roughly equal status, children will soon learn that they must compromise on a course of action, often without any assistance from adults, if they are to play together cooperatively or accomplish other group goals. While settling disputes, each child will assume the roles of "governor" and "governed" and see that rules are merely social contracts that derive their power from the consent of the group members rather than from an external authority figure. In sum, Piaget believes that equal-status contacts with peers lead to a more flexible morality because they (1) lessen the child's unilateral respect for adult authority, (2) increase his or her self-respect and respect for peers, and (3) illustrate that rules are arbitrary agreements that can be changed with the consent of the people they govern.

And what role do parents play? According to Piaget, parents may actually slow the progress of moral development by reinforcing the child's unilateral respect for authority figures. If, for example, a parent enforces a demand with a threat or a statement such as "Do it because I told you to," it is easy to see

how the young moral realist might conclude that rules are "absolutes" that derive their "teeth" from the parent's power to enforce them. Although Piaget believes that the peer group plays the greater role in the development of autonomous morality, he suggests that parents could help by relinquishing some of their power to establish a more egalitarian relationship with their children.

TESTS OF PIAGET'S THEORY

Many researchers have used Piaget's methods in an attempt to replicate his findings, and much of the data they have collected are consistent with his theory. In Western cultures, there is a clear relationship between children's ages and stages of moral reasoning: younger children are more likely than older children to think of rules as moral absolutes, to believe in immanent justice, and to consider the objective consequences of an act rather than the actor's intent when making moral judgments (Hoffman, 1970; Lickona, 1976). Apparently the child's level of moral reasoning does depend, in part, on his or her level of cognitive development. For example, IQ and moral maturity are positively correlated (Lickona, 1976), and children who score high on tests of role taking tend to make more advanced moral judgments than age mates whose role-taking skills are less well developed (Ambron & Irwin, 1975; Selman, 1971).

Finally, there is even some support for Piaget's peer participation hypothesis: popular children who often take part in social activities and who assume positions of leadership in the peer group tend to make mature moral judgments (Keasey, 1971). Moreover, 5- to 7-year-olds who have had a hand in formulating the rules of a new game are later more flexible about changing these rules than their age mates who simply learned the same rules from an adult (Merchant & Rebelsky, 1972).

Yet in spite of this supportive evidence, there is reason to believe that Piaget's theory has some serious shortcomings. Let's take a closer look.

Do Heteronomous Children Ignore an Actor's Intentions?

Recent research indicates that younger children can and often do consider an actor's intentions when evaluating his behavior. One problem with Piaget's moral-decision stories is that they confounded intentions and consequences by asking the child whether a person who caused a small amount of harm in the service of bad intentions was naughtier than one who caused a larger amount of damage while serving good intentions. Since younger children give more weight to concrete evidence that they can see than to abstract information that they must infer (Surber, 1982), it is hardly surprising that they would consider the person who did more damage to be the naughtier of the two.

Sharon Nelson (1980) unconfounded information about an actor's motives and intentions in an interesting experiment with 3-year-olds. Each child listened to stories in which a character threw a ball to a playmate. The actor's motive was described as *good* (his friend had nothing to play with) or *bad* (the actor was mad at his friend), and the consequences of his act were described as *positive* (the friend caught the ball and was happy to play with it) or *negative* (the ball hit the friend in the head and made him cry). To ensure that these young subjects would understand the actor's motives, the experimenter showed some of them drawings such as Figure 11-1, which happens to depict a negative intent. The remaining subjects simply had the actor's motives described to them in words. The children were then asked to evaluate the "goodness" or "badness" of the actor's behavior.

The results were rather interesting. As we see in Figure 11-2, Nelson's 3-year-olds did consider acts that had positive consequences to be more favorable than those having negative consequences. Yet the more interesting finding was that the good-intentioned actor who had wanted to play was evaluated much more favorably than the actor who intended to hurt his friend, *regardless of the consequences of his actions*. In a later study using a very similar methodology (Nelson-Le Gall, 1985), 3- to 4-year-olds judged negative consequences that the actor could have *foreseen* to be more intentional and naughtier than the same consequences produced by an actor who could not have foreseen them. Finally, 5-year-olds believe that harmful acts stemming from carelessness or negligence are more blameworthy than those that are purely accidental (Shultz, Wright, & Schleifer, 1986). Taken together, these findings are clearly inconsistent with Piaget's view of younger

FIGURE 11-1 Example of drawings used by Nelson to convey an actor's intentions to preschool children

children as "moral realists" who focus exclusively on objective harm done to assign moral responsibility. Apparently preschool children can and often do use intentions when making moral judgments if this information is clear to them.

Why do younger children not appear more "intentional" on Piaget's moral-decision stories? Probably because (1) intentional information was not made explicit by Piaget (while consequences were), and (2) young children may generally assume that motives and outcomes are logically related. Indeed, Nelson (1980) found that, if intentions are not made clear, 3-year-olds assume that actors who produce negative consequences must have had a negative intent. Their problem is not that they fail to consider an actor's intentions but, rather, that they are less proficient than older children at discriminating intentions from consequences and using these separate pieces of information to make moral judgments. When do children first recognize that intentions and consequences are distinctly different kinds of information? Colleen Surber (1982) finds that many youngsters reach this milestone by age 5—several years earlier than Piaget had assumed.

Do Heteronomous Children Respect All Rules (and Adult Authority)?

According to Piaget, young children think of rules as sacred and obligatory prescriptions that are laid down by respected authority figures and are not to be questioned or changed. However, Elliot Turiel (1978, 1983) notes that children actually encounter two kinds of rules: (1) *moral rules*, which focus on the rights and privileges of individuals, and (2) *social-conventional rules*, which are determined by consensus and serve to govern interpersonal behavior within

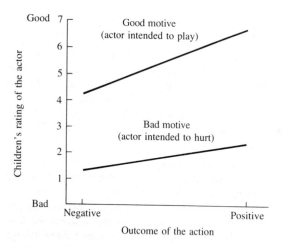

FIGURE 11-2   Average ratings of an actor's behavior for actors who produced positive or negative outcomes while serving either good or bad intentions

a particular social setting. The procedures followed while playing marbles are examples of social-conventional rules, whereas prescriptions such as "Thou shalt not steal [shove, hit, lie]" are examples of moral rules. Do children treat these two kinds of rules as equivalent?

Apparently not. In a recent observational study conducted on ten playgrounds, Larry and Maria Nucci (1982) noted the reactions of younger (age 7–10) and older (age 11–14) children to violations of moral and social-conventional rules. Social-conventional transgressions included acts such as spitting or eating grass—deviations from social norms. Moral transgressions consisted of acts such as throwing sand at smaller children or snatching away a child's playthings—violations of individual rights. Nucci and Nucci found that children from both age groups were much more likely to react to moral than to social-conventional violations. Moreover, children's responses clearly depended on the nature of the transgression. Moral breaches elicited comments about the injury or loss that the victim had suffered, comments about the unfairness of the transgressor's behavior, and retaliatory acts. By contrast, social-conventional violations were greeted with statements that admonished the actors for deviating ("You're not supposed to spit") or ridiculed them in some way ("Bobby and Allison sitting in a tree, K-I-S-S-I-N-

G"). Clearly, these 7–14-year-olds showed some respect for both moral and social-conventional rules, although they did not treat them as one and the same.

Judith Smetana (1981, 1985) finds that even 2½–6-year-olds make important distinctions between moral and social-conventional rules. Moral transgressions such as hitting, stealing, or refusing to share are considered much more serious and deserving of punishment than social-conventional violations such as not staying in one's seat at nursery school or not saying grace before eating. When asked whether a violation would be OK if there were no rule against it, children said that moral transgressions are always wrong but that social-conventional violations are OK in the absence of any explicit prohibitions. So not only did these preschoolers fail to see social-conventional rules as sacred and unalterable, they actually showed a strong respect for the moral prescriptions at 2½ to 3—much sooner than Piaget had assumed they would.

Do heteronomous children show a special reverence for adults and adult authority? Once again, the answer is apparently not! Six- to 11-year-olds typically acknowledge that their parents are justified in making and enforcing rules about *moral* issues such as stealing; but they feel that parents are often behaving in an inappropriate and unjustified way should they enforce rules that restrict their choice of friends or that arbitrarily require them to perform various household chores (Tisak, 1986). Moreover, Marta Laupa and Elliot Turiel (1986) recently found that 7- to 11-year-olds were more likely to obey the commands of a peer "authority" (for example, a playground monitor) than those of an adult "nonauthority" (for example, a woman who lived across the street from the playground). So heteronomous children do have ideas about what constitutes legitimate authority, and those ideas are not based solely on a special respect for the size, age, and power of adults as Piaget had assumed.

Finally, Piaget argues that, by rigidly enforcing rules and by punishing a child's transgressions on the basis of the amount of objective harm done, parents may typically *inhibit* the development of mature moral reasoning. Yet the research presented in Box 11-1 provides a very serious challenge to this point of view.

BOX 11-1 PARENTS AS MORAL PHILOSOPHERS: DO THEY AFFECT THEIR CHILDREN?

Might we alter children's moral reasoning by exposing them to adult models (such as parents) whose moral judgments are more sophisticated than their own? Piaget says no. He expects a young child's moral judgments to be very difficult to modify because (1) they are based on the child's underlying thought structures (which depend on the child's level of cognitive development), and (2) young premoral, or heteronomous, children are simply too intellectually immature to understand and appreciate autonomous moral reasoning.

Despite Piaget's claims to the contrary, several investigators have found that children's moral reasoning is subject to modeling influences (see Bandura & McDonald, 1963; Dorr & Fey, 1974; Harvey & Liebert, 1979). In fact, Schleifer and Douglas (1973) reported that 3-year-olds, who should be at Piaget's premoral level, can be trained to reason at Piaget's *autonomous* level! However, it is not entirely clear whether the youngsters in these experiments were actually adopting a new moral orientation from their relatively brief exposures to social models. Indeed, cognitive theorists have argued that social models merely teach children "conforming" responses that are likely to be displayed in the short run to win the model's approval but are unlikely to persist over time.

If children's moral judgments are not readily amenable to social influence, as the cognitive theorists have proposed, then the moral reasoning of 6- to 7-year-old "heteronomous" youngsters should bear little resemblance to that of their parents. But if moral judgments are truly subject to modeling influences, as social-learning theorists (for example, Bandura, 1977) have argued, then there ought to be at least some correspondence between the moral reasoning of young children and that of their parents. Recently, Manuel Leon (1984) conducted an interesting experiment to compare the moral decisions of 6- to 7-year-old boys with those of their mothers. The boys were tested first while their mothers were off in an adjacent room. Each boy listened to nine stories in which boys like himself had done no damage, a little damage, or lots of damage (consequences information) by accident, out of displaced anger, or with malice (intentions information). After listening to each story, the boy indicated the amount of punishment (from

none to severe) that the actor deserved. When the boy had finished, he was dismissed and his mother summoned to listen to the same stories and to recommend punishments for the same actors her son had evaluated.

Leon found that different mothers used different "rules" in assigning punishments to the story characters. The three types of reasoning that mothers used were as follows:

1. *Intent + damage linear rule.* These mothers (N = 18) combined intentions and consequences information when making punishment decisions. Thus, the most severe punishment was assigned to actors who did a lot of damage with malicious intent, whereas the least punishment was assigned when the actor did no damage in an accident.
2. *Accident-configural rule.* These mothers (N = 10) also combined intentions and consequences information if the story character had acted out of displaced anger or with a malicious intent. However, they always assigned mild punishment, regardless of the damage done, when the act in question was accidental.
3. *Damage-only rule.* These mothers (N = 4) ignored the actors' intentions and assigned punishment solely on the basis of the amount of damage the actors had caused.

From a Piagetian perspective, the damage-only rule is pure "heteronomous" moral reasoning, whereas the linear rule and especially the configural rule (in which accidents are viewed as totally unintentional and hence not blameworthy) are more characteristic of autonomous moral reasoning.

How did the boys' moral judgments compare with those of their mothers? Remarkable as it may seem, the rules used by the majority of these 6- to 7-year-olds to assign punishments to the story characters were *virtually identical* to those of their own mothers. Recall that the boys had been tested first and, thus, were not merely "imitating" their mothers' judgments. The implication, then, is that the moral reasoning of young children is much more amenable to social influence than Piaget had thought. Moreover, the finding that 6- to 7-year-olds use a relatively mature configural rule if their mothers do suggests that parents may often *foster* (rather than inhibit) the growth of children's moral reasoning.

Piaget was among the first to suggest that children's moral reasoning may develop in stages. His early work stimulated an enormous amount of research and several new insights, some of which were

inconsistent with his original theory. One theorist who was profoundly influenced by Piaget and who has contributed many of these new insights is Lawrence Kohlberg of Harvard University.

KOHLBERG'S THEORY OF MORAL DEVELOPMENT

Kohlberg (1969, 1981, 1984) has refined and extended Piaget's theory of moral development by asking 10-, 13-, and 16-year-old boys to resolve a series of "moral dilemmas." Each dilemma challenged the respondent by requiring him to choose between (1) obeying a rule, law, or authority figure and (2) taking some action that conflicts with these rules and commands while serving a human need. The following story is the best known of Kohlberg's moral dilemmas:

> In Europe, a woman was near death from a special kind of cancer. There was one drug that doctors thought might save her. It was a form of radium that a druggist in the same town had recently discovered. The drug was expensive to make, but the druggist was charging $2000, or 10 times the cost of the drug, for a small (possibly life-saving) dose. Heinz, the sick woman's husband, borrowed all the money he could, about $1000, or about half of what he needed. He told the druggist that his wife was dying and asked him to sell the drug cheaper or let him pay later. The druggist replied "No, I discovered the drug, and I'm going to make money from it." Heinz then became desperate and broke into the store to steal the drug for his wife.
> Should Heinz have done that?

Kohlberg was actually less interested in the subject's decision (that is, what Heinz should have done) than in the underlying rationale, or "thought structures," that the subject used to justify his decision. To determine the "structure" of a subject's moral reasoning, Kohlberg asked probing questions. Should Heinz be punished for stealing the drug? Did the druggist have a right to charge so much? Would it be proper to charge the druggist with murder? If so, should his punishment be greater if the woman who died was an important person? And so on.

Kohlberg soon discovered some interesting discrepancies between his data and the findings reported earlier by Piaget. First, he noted that the adherence to rules shown by his younger subjects stemmed from a *fear of punishment* rather than a "unilateral respect" for rules or the authority figures who proposed them. Second, Kohlberg found that moral development was far from complete when the child reached age 10 to 12, or Piaget's autonomous stage. Indeed, moral reasoning seemed to evolve and become progressively more complex throughout adolescence and into young adulthood. Careful analyses of his subjects' responses to several dilemmas led Kohlberg to conclude that moral growth progresses through an *invariant sequence* of three moral levels, each of which is composed of two distinct moral stages. According to Kohlberg, the order of these moral levels and stages is invariant because each depends on the development of certain cognitive abilities that evolve in an invariant sequence. Like Piaget, Kohlberg assumes that each succeeding stage evolves from and replaces its predecessor; once the individual has attained a higher stage of moral reasoning, he or she should never regress to earlier stages.

Before looking at Kohlberg's sequence of stages, it is important to emphasize that each stage represents a particular perspective, or *method of thinking* about moral dilemmas, rather than a particular type of moral decision. Decisions are not very informative in themselves, because subjects at each moral stage might well endorse either of the alternative courses of action when resolving one of these ethical dilemmas.

The basic themes and defining characteristics of Kohlberg's three moral levels and six stages are described in Box 11-2.

Examples of how subjects at each stage might respond to the Heinz dilemma appear in Box 11-3. Although these particular responses were constructed for illustrative purposes, they represent precisely the kinds of logic that Kohlberg's subjects used to justify stealing or not stealing the drug.

TESTS OF KOHLBERG'S THEORY

The data from which Kohlberg fashioned his theory of moral development came from his doctoral research, in which boys aged 10, 13, and 16 each spent up to two hours resolving nine moral dilemmas. In analyzing the data, Kohlberg found that each child showed a fairly consistent pattern of reasoning when justifying his answers to different dilemmas. The kinds of judgments that these boys made seemed to fall into six general categories, which became Kohlberg's six moral stages.

BOX 11-2   AN OVERVIEW OF KOHLBERG'S LEVELS AND STAGES OF MORAL REASONING

Level 1: Preconventional Morality

At this level, morality is truly external. The child conforms to rules imposed by authority figures in order to avoid punishment or to obtain personal rewards. The preconventional level consists of two stages:

Stage 1: Punishment-and-obedience orientation. At this stage, the child determines the goodness or badness of an act on the basis of its consequences. The child will defer to authority figures and obey their commands in order to avoid punishment. There is no true conception of rules, however; if the child can "get away with" an act, it is not considered bad. The seriousness of a violation depends on the magnitude of its consequences (that is, the amount of punishment received or the amount of objective harm done).

Stage 2: Naive hedonism, or instrumental orientation. A person at the second stage of moral development conforms to rules in order to gain rewards or to satisfy personal needs. Doing things for others is "right" if the actor will benefit in the long run. This low-level reciprocity is quite pragmatic; "You scratch my back and I'll scratch yours" is the guiding philosophy of the individual at Stage 2. The seriousness of a violation now depends, in part, on the actor's intent.

Level 2: Conventional Morality

At this level, the individual strives to obey the rules set forth by others (such as parents, peers, and social groups) in order to win praise and recognition for virtuous conduct or to maintain social order.

Stage 3: "Good boy" or "good girl" orientation. Moral behavior is that which pleases, helps, or is approved of by others. Actions are evaluated on the basis of the actor's intent. "He means well" is a common expression of moral approval at this stage. A primary objective of a Stage 3 respondent is to be thought of as a "nice" person.

Stage 4: Authority and social-order-maintaining morality. At this stage, one accepts and conforms to social rules and conventions in order to avoid censure by legitimate authorities. The reason for conformity is not so much a fear of punishment as a belief that rules and laws maintain a social order that is worth preserving. Thus, behavior is judged as "good," or moral, to the extent that it conforms to rules that maintain social order.

Level 3: Postconventional Morality, or the Morality of Self-Accepted Moral Principles

The individual who has attained this third level of moral reasoning is personally committed to a set of principles that are often shared with others and yet transcend particular authority figures. In other words, moral standards are internalized and become the person's own.

Stage 5: Morality of contract, individual rights, and democratically accepted law. There is a flexibility in moral judgments at this stage. Moral actions are those that express the will of the majority or maximize social welfare. To be acceptable, rules must be arrived at by democratic procedures and must be impartial. Laws that are imposed or that compromise the rights of the majority are considered unjust and worthy of challenge. By contrast, the person at Stage 4 will not ordinarily challenge an established law and may be suspicious of those who do. This fifth stage of moral reasoning represents the official morality of the United States Constitution.

Stage 6: Morality of individual principles of conscience. At this "highest" stage of moral reasoning, the individual defines right and wrong on the basis of the self-chosen ethical principles of his or her own conscience. These principles are not concrete rules such as the Ten Commandments. They are abstract moral guidelines or principles of universal justice (and respect for individual rights) that are to be applied in all situations. Deviations from one's self-chosen moral standards produce feelings of guilt or self-condemnation; for example, the Stage 6 conscientious objector may refuse to conform to a draft law that violates his pacifist beliefs. To comply would bring self-degradation, a punishment that may be much more aversive to the conscientious objector than a short prison sentence.

Age Trends in the Use of Kohlberg's Moral Stages

If Kohlberg's stages represent a true developmental sequence, then we might expect that the use of Stage 1 and Stage 2 reasoning will decline with age, while judgments at stages 3 through 6 will become more frequent. Figure 11-3 (on page 328) shows age trends in the use of Kohlberg's stages for a sample of American males. Note that preconventional reasoning (stages 1 and 2) declines sharply with age: 80% of the moral

BOX 11-3 EXAMPLES OF HOW SUBJECTS AT EACH OF KOHLBERG'S SIX MORAL STAGES MIGHT RESPOND TO THE HEINZ DILEMMA

Stage 1: Punishment-and-Obedience Orientation

Protheft. It isn't really bad to take it—he did ask to pay for it first. He wouldn't do any other damage or take anything else and the drug he'd take is only worth $200, not $2000.

Antitheft. Heinz doesn't have permission to take the drug. He can't just go and break through a window. He'd be a bad criminal doing all that damage. That drug is worth a lot of money, and stealing anything so expensive would be a big crime.

Note. Both these answers disregard Heinz's intentions and judge the act in terms of its consequences. The "pro" answer minimizes the consequences while the "con" answer maximizes them. The implication is that big crimes warrant severe punishment.

Stage 2: Instrumental Hedonism

Protheft. Heinz isn't really doing any harm to the druggist, and he can always pay him back. If he doesn't want to lose his wife, he should take the drug.

Antitheft. The druggist isn't wrong, he just wants to make a profit like everybody else. That's what you're in business for, to make money.

Note. Heinz's intentions are apparent in the pro answer, while the intentions of the druggist come out in the con answer. Both Heinz and the druggist are "right" for satisfying their own needs or goals.

Stage 3: "Good Boy" or "Good Girl" Morality

Protheft. Stealing is bad, but this is a bad situation. Heinz is only doing something that it is natural for a good husband to do. You can't blame him for doing something out of love for his wife. You'd blame him if he didn't save her.

Antitheft. If Heinz's wife dies, he can't be blamed. You can't say he is heartless for failing to commit a crime. The druggist is the selfish and heartless one. Heinz tried to do everything he really could.

Note. Both the pro and con answers seek to resolve the dilemma by doing what others would approve of under the circumstances. In either case, Heinz is described as a well-intentioned person who is doing what is right.

Stage 4: Authority and Social-Order-Maintaining Morality

Protheft. The druggist is leading the wrong kind of life if he just lets somebody die; so it's Heinz's duty to save her.

judgments of 10-year-olds were preconventional (stages 1 and 2), as opposed to about 18% at age 16–18 and only 3% at age 24. Use of conventional reasoning (stages 3 and 4) increased until about age 22 and then stabilized at roughly 90% of all moral statements. Postconventional reasoning also increased with age. Whereas the 10- to 16-year-olds in this sample never used Stage 5 or Stage 6 reasoning, approximately 10% of the moral judgments of the 24-year-olds were at the postconventional level (Stage 5). Finally, a few of the 16–24-year-old subjects made statements that Kohlberg had originally interpreted as examples of Stage 6. However, a careful analysis of the rationales underlying these judgments suggested that they were more appropriately classified at Stage 3, 4, or 5 (Colby, Kohlberg, Gibbs, & Lieberman, 1983).[2]

Similar age trends have been reported in Mexico, the Bahamas, Taiwan, Turkey, Central America, India, Kenya, and Nigeria (Edwards, 1981; Kohlberg, 1969; Magsud, 1979; Parikh, 1980; Turiel, Edwards, & Kohlberg, 1978). In all these cultures, adolescents and young adults typically reason about moral issues at a higher level than children do. So it seems that Kohlberg's levels and stages of moral reasoning are "universal"—as we would expect if they represent a true developmental sequence based, in part, on one's intellectual development.

Although Kohlberg has argued that his stages represent an invariant developmental sequence, he be-

BOX 11-3 *continued*

But Heinz can't just go around breaking laws—he must pay the druggist back and take his punishment for stealing.

Antitheft. It's natural for Heinz to want to save his wife, but it's still always wrong to steal. You have to follow the rules regardless of your feelings or the special circumstances.

Note. The obligation to the law transcends special interests. Even the pro answer recognizes that Heinz is morally wrong and must pay for his transgression.

Stage 5: Morality of Contract, Individual Rights, and Democratically Accepted Law

Protheft. Before you say stealing is wrong, you've got to consider this whole situation. Of course the laws are quite clear about breaking into a store. And even worse, Heinz would know that there were no legal grounds for his actions. Yet it would be reasonable for anybody in this kind of situation to steal the drug.

Antitheft. I can see the good that would come from illegally taking the drug, but the ends don't justify the means. You can't say that Heinz would be completely wrong to steal the drug, but even these circumstances don't make it right.

Note. The judgments are no longer black and white. The pro answer recognizes that theft is legally wrong but that an emotional husband may be driven to steal the drug—and that is understandable (although not completely moral). The con answer recognizes exactly the same points. Heinz would be committing an immoral act in stealing the drug, but he would do so with good intentions.

Stage 6: Morality of Individual Principles of Conscience

Protheft. When one must choose between disobeying a law and saving a human life, the higher principle of preserving life makes it morally right to steal the drug.

Antitheft. With many cases of cancer and the scarcity of the drug, there might not be enough to go around to everybody who needs it. The correct course of action can only be the one that is "right" by all people concerned. Heinz ought to act, not on emotion or the law, but according to what he thinks an ideally just person would do in this case.

Note. Both the pro and con answers transcend the law and self-interest and appeal to higher principles (individual rights, the sanctity of life) that all "reasonable" persons should consider in this situation. The pro answer is relatively straightforward. However, it is difficult to conceive of a "con" Stage 6 response unless the drug was scarce and Heinz would be depriving other equally deserving people of life by stealing the drug to save his wife.

---

lieves that only a small minority of any group will actually reach Stage 5 or 6—the postconventional level. In fact, the dominant level of moral reasoning among adults from virtually all societies is conventional morality (Stage 3 or 4), and it is not at all unusual to find that people from rural villages in underdeveloped countries show absolutely no evidence of postconventional reasoning (Harkness, Edwards, & Super, 1981; Kohlberg, 1969; Tietjen & Walker, 1985). Kohlberg suggests that fixation (or arrested development) may occur at any stage if the individual is not exposed to persons or situations that force a reevaluation of current moral concepts. And what kinds of experiences might have such an effect? Apparently education does. People who have a university education reason at higher stages than those who do not, and the differences in moral reasoning between high school graduates and college students become greater with each successive year of school that the college students complete (Rest & Thoma, 1985). Moreover, having a position of leadership or responsibility is an experience that seems to promote the growth of moral reasoning. Even in underdeveloped societies, tribal leaders who must often resolve interpersonal conflicts tend to reason at higher levels (typically Stage 3 or 4) than their followers (Harkness et al., 1981; Tietjen & Walker, 1985). So the implication is that people in many societies will not reason at the postconventional level because they are never exposed to the kinds of judgments and

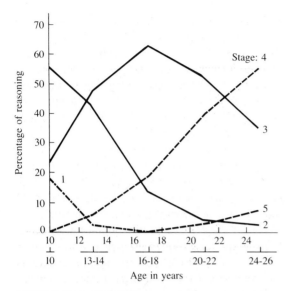

FIGURE 11-3 Use of Kohlberg's moral stages by male subjects aged 10 through 26 years

Are Kohlberg's Stages an Invariant Sequence?

Although Kohlberg's early research and the cross-cultural studies are generally consistent with his developmental scheme, they do not establish that his moral stages develop in a fixed, or invariant, sequence. The major problem with the cross-sectional studies is that subjects at each age level were *different* children, and we cannot be certain that a 24-year-old at Stage 5 has progressed through the various moral levels and stages in the order specified by Kohlberg's theory. How can we evaluate the invariant-sequence hypothesis? By examining two important sources of evidence: (1) experimental attempts to modify children's moral judgments and (2) longitudinal studies of the moral development of individual children.

The experimental evidence. If Kohlberg's stages represent an invariant sequence, as he has proposed, then children should be influenced by models who reason about moral issues at one stage higher than their own. However, reasoning that is less advanced should be rejected as too simplistic, and moral judgments that are two stages higher should be too difficult for subjects to comprehend.

Most of the available evidence is consistent with these hypotheses. When exposed to moral reasoning that is one stage above (+ 1) or one stage below (− 1) their own, children generally favor and are more influenced by the more sophisticated set of arguments (Arbuthnot, 1975; Rest, 1983; Turiel, 1966). And yet Lawrence Walker (1982) found that the moral judgments of 10- to 13-year-olds can be influenced by arguments that are *two stages higher* than their own—a level that Kohlberg assumes to be too difficult for them to understand. Does this finding invalidate Kohlberg's invariant-sequence hypothesis? Not necessarily. Walker's subjects were a very select sample of children who had already achieved all the cognitive prerequisites for the next higher (+ 1) stage of moral development, even though they were not yet reasoning at that level. By contrast, children who are not ready to move to the next moral stage are generally not influenced by moral arguments two stages higher than their own (Turiel, 1966).

experiences that might enable them to progress beyond a sense of conventional morality.

We can illustrate this point by contrasting life in an urban, industrialized society with that in a small village in a nonindustrialized country. In industrialized societies consisting of many political, religious, racial, and ethnic groups, people are often governed by a system of justice that transcends these subgroups and is designed (in theory, at least) to maximize the welfare of all social factions. This is precisely the type of sociopolitical climate in which Stage 5 reasoning (the social-contract orientation) could evolve (Harkness et al., 1981). By contrast, people in many rural, nonindustrialized societies are governed at the village or the tribal level, and they need to be concerned only with the laws and customs of their immediate social group. These individuals have little if any experience with the kinds of political compromise and governmental control on which Stage 5 reasoning seems to depend, so that they may never reason about moral issues at the postconventional level. Nevertheless, their conventional reasoning (stages 3 and 4) is perfectly adaptive and hence "mature" within their own social systems (Harkness et al., 1981).

Other researchers (for example, Berkowitz, Gibbs, & Broughton, 1980; Maitland & Goldman, 1974) have found that adolescents who are asked to discuss moral issues and reach a consensus show greater increases in their own moral reasoning (particularly those subjects who scored lower than their peers before the discussions) than age mates who thought about the same issues and made individual moral judgments. It is important to note that the advance in moral reasoning shown by the "changers" in these discussions is not merely a modeling effect. Berkowitz and Gibbs (1983) report that change is unlikely to occur unless the discussions are characterized by *transactive interactions*—that is, exchanges among participants in which each party performs mental operations on the reasoning of his or her partner (for example, "Your reasoning misses an important distinction"; "Here is an elaboration of your position"; "We can combine our positions into a common view"). This latter finding is important, for it reinforces Kohlberg's conclusion that social experiences promote moral growth by introducing *cognitive* challenges (or disequilibriums) to one's current position—challenges to which the *less mature* individual will adapt by assimilating and accommodating to the other person's logic. Why do the more mature discussants not move in the direction of their less mature partners? Because the challenges introduced by their less mature counterparts are based on reasoning that they have already rejected. Indeed, their lack of change in the face of such logic provides additional support for Kohlberg's invariant-sequence hypothesis.

The longitudinal evidence. Clearly the most compelling evidence for Kohlberg's invariant-sequence hypothesis would be a demonstration that individual children progress through the moral stages in precisely the order that Kohlberg says they should. Ann Colby and her associates (1983) have recently reported the results of a 20-year longitudinal study of 58 American males who were 10, 13, or 16 years old at the beginning of the project. These boys responded to nine of Kohlberg's moral dilemmas when the study began and again in five follow-up sessions adminis-

tered at three- to four-year intervals. Colby et al. found that subjects proceeded through the stages in the order Kohlberg predicted and that no subject ever skipped a stage between testings. Furthermore, the answers a subject gave during any single testing were remarkably consistent in that about 70% fell within the subject's dominant moral stage, the remainder falling either one stage higher or one stage lower. Similar results have been reported in a nine-year longitudinal study of adolescents in Israel (Snarey, Reimer, & Kohlberg, 1985) and a twelve-year longitudinal project conducted in Turkey (Nisan & Kohlberg, 1982). So it would appear that Kohlberg's moral stages do represent a true developmental sequence.

However, regression from higher to lower stages is not unknown, particularly when subjects are retested over very short intervals. The most common reversal is for people who have attained Stage 5 to regress to Stage 4 (or to a point intermediate between stages 4 and 5) (Gilligan & Murphy, 1979; Holstein, 1976). Although these reversals may be true developmental regressions (which would discomfirm Kohlberg's invariant-sequence hypothesis), they could also represent the minor fluctuations in performance that people often show when taking the same test twice over a brief interval. Indeed, the "test-retest" explanation is supported by a short-term longitudinal study (Kohlberg & Kramer, 1969) in which the few subjects who had seemed to regress from Stage 4 in high school to a lower stage of moral reasoning in college were later reasoning at either Stage 4 or Stage 5 when retested during their midtwenties.

Finally, the only way we can consider movement from Stage 5 to Stage 4 to be a true developmental regression is if we assume that stages 5 and 6 are somehow better or more "mature" than Stage 4 reasoning. It may be that Kohlberg is only partly correct—that stages 1–4 represent an invariant developmental sequence but that stages 5 and 6 will require a very special kind of environment to ever emerge (Gibbs, 1979; Harkness et al., 1981; Saltzstein, 1983). At one point, Kohlberg himself suggested that stages 4, 5, and 6 may be "alternative types of mature [reasoning] rather than an invariant sequence" (1969, p. 385). Additional research is needed to clarify this point. Yet it is worth noting that whenever Stage 5 reasoning first appears, it has always evolved from the subject's Stage 4 reasoning—a finding that supports Kohlberg's invariant-sequence hypothesis (Colby et al., 1983; Snarey et al., 1985).

The Relationship of Kohlberg's Stages to Cognitive Development

According to Kohlberg (1969), the young, preconventional child reasons about moral issues from an egocentric point of view. At Stage 1 the child thinks that certain acts are bad because they are punished. At Stage 2 the child shows a limited awareness of the needs, thoughts, and intentions of others but still judges self-serving acts as "right," or appropriate. However, conventional reasoning clearly requires an ability to role-take, or assume the perspective of others. For example, a person at Stage 3 must necessarily recognize others' points of view before she will evaluate intentions that would win their approval as "good" or morally acceptable. Furthermore, postconventional, or "principled," morality would seem to require much more than a decline in egocentrism and a capacity for reciprocal-role taking: the person who bases moral judgments on abstract principles must be able to reason abstractly rather than simply adhering to concrete moral norms. In other words, Kohlberg believes that the highest level of cognitive development, *formal operations*, is necessary for principled moral reasoning (stages 5 and 6).

Much of the available research is consistent with Kohlberg's hypotheses. For example, John Moir (1974) administered Kohlberg's "dilemmas test" and several measures of role taking to a group of 11-year-old girls, many of whom showed a mixture of Stage 2 (preconventional) and Stage 3 (conventional) reasoning on the moral dilemmas. Moir found a very substantial positive correlation between role-taking abilities and moral maturity; girls who were more proficient at role taking were more likely to reason at Kohlberg's conventional level (Stage 3). In another study of 10–13-year-olds, Lawrence Walker (1980) found that the only subjects who had reached Kohlberg's third stage of moral reasoning ("good boy/good girl" morality) were those who were quite proficient at reciprocal-role taking. However, not all the proficient role takers had reached Stage 3 in their moral reasoning. So Walker's results imply that reciprocal-role-taking skills are *necessary but not sufficient* for the development of conventional morality.

Carol Tomlinson-Keasey and Charles Keasey (1974) administered Kohlberg's moral dilemmas and three tests of cognitive development to sixth-grade girls (age 11–12) and to college women. An interesting pattern emerged. All the subjects who reasoned at the postconventional level (Stage 5) on the dilemmas showed at least some formal-operational thinking on the cognitive tests. But not all the formal operators reasoned at the postconventional level on the dilemmas test. This same pattern also emerged in a later study by Deanna Kuhn and her associates (Kuhn, Kohlberg, Langer, & Haan, 1977). So it seems that formal operations are *necessary but not sufficient* for the development of postconventional morality.

In sum, Kohlberg's moral stages are clearly related to one's level of cognitive development. Proficiency at role taking may be necessary for the onset of conventional morality, and formal operations appear to be necessary for postconventional, or "principled," morality. Yet it is important to emphasize that intellectual growth does not guarantee moral development, for a person who has reached Piaget's highest stages of intellect may continue to reason at the preconventional level about moral issues. The implication, then, is that both *intellectual growth* and *relevant social experiences* (exposure to persons or situations that force a reevaluation of one's current moral concepts) are necessary before children can progress from preconventional morality to Kohlberg's higher stages.

Some Lingering Questions about Kohlberg's Approach

The relationship between moral reasoning and moral behavior. One common criticism of Kohlberg's theory is that it is based on subjects' responses to hypothetical and somewhat artificial dilemmas that they do not have to face themselves (Baumrind, 1978). Would children reason in the same way about the moral dilemmas they actually encounter? Would a person who said that Heinz should steal the drug actually do so if he were in Heinz's shoes? Can we ever predict a person's moral behavior from a knowledge of his or her stage of moral reasoning?

Many researchers have found that the moral judgments of young children do *not* predict their actual behavior in situations where they are induced to cheat or violate other moral norms (Nelson, Grinder, & Biaggio, 1969; Santrock, 1975; Toner & Potts, 1981). However, studies of older grade school children, adolescents, and young adults often find at least some consistency between moral reasoning and moral conduct (see Blasi, 1980, 1983, for reviews of the evidence). Kohlberg (1975), for example, found that only 15% of the students who reasoned at the postconventional level actually cheated when given an opportunity, compared with 55% of the "conventional" students and 70% of those at the preconventional level. Moreover, subjects at Kohlberg's Stage 4 were more likely to refuse to shock an experimental confederate who seemed to be in pain than were their age mates at Kohlberg's Stage 3 (Kohlberg & Candee, 1984). Yet Kohlberg is hardly surprised that moral reasoning often fails to predict moral behavior; after all, he has argued that subjects at any of his moral stages may favor either course of action when resolving an ethical dilemma. It is the *structure* of their reasoning that sets them apart into different "stages" of moral development, not the decisions they reach.[3]

In sum, Kohlberg expects a significant but imperfect relationship between moral reasoning and moral behavior, and this is precisely what the data seem to show (Blasi, 1980). A person who reasons at Stage 5 will often act differently in moral situations than one who reasons at Stage 4, Stage 3, or Stage 2. However, the correlations between moral reasoning and moral conduct that are reported in this research are based on *group* trends, and it is not always possible to specify how an *individual* will behave from a knowledge of his or her stage of moral reasoning.

Situational influences on moral reasoning.
One interesting aspect of Kohlberg's research is that subjects are fairly consistent in the type (or stage) of reasoning that they use to resolve different moral issues. Does this coherence simply reflect the fact that all Kohlberg's dilemmas are abstract and hypothetical? Would subjects be so consistent when reacting to more common moral issues—ones that they may often face? Apparently not, for Leming (1978) found that adolescents use lower levels of moral reasoning when asked to resolve practical dilemmas that could have negative consequences *for them.*

The impact of negative consequences on moral reasoning is nicely illustrated in a recent study by William Sobesky (1983). High school and college students read and resolved a version of the Heinz dilemma in which the consequences of stealing the drug were described as rather severe (Heinz would definitely be caught and sent to prison) or quite mild (Heinz could take such a small amount of the drug that it would not be missed). Subjects were asked to imagine themselves in Heinz's position and to describe what they would do and why. Sobesky found that, when the consequences were severe, people were less likely to advocate stealing the drug, and the levels of moral reasoning used to justify their decisions were lower. We see, then, that both the content and the structure of moral reasoning depend to some extent on the situation. Subjects reason at a higher level when resolving hypothetical dilemmas (or those without serious personal consequences) than when thinking about practical moral issues that could have negative implications for themselves.

The question of sex differences. Some investigators have reported an interesting sex difference in moral reasoning: adult females in these studies are typically at Stage 3 of Kohlberg's stage sequence, while adult males are usually at Stage 4 (Holstein, 1976; Kohlberg, 1969; Parikh, 1980). Does this mean that females are less morally mature than males (as Freud assumed)? Carol Gilligan (1977, 1982) says no, arguing that Kohlberg's moral stages were derived from interviews with males and that they may

BOX 11-4   *GILLIGAN'S THEORY OF FEMALE MORAL DEVELOPMENT*

Do females have a different orientation to moral issues than males do? Are there fundamental differences between the sexes in the character of moral reasoning? Carol Gilligan (1977, 1982) believes that males and females do adopt different perspectives on moral issues and that these sex differences in moral reasoning stem from the ways in which boys and girls are raised. Gilligan suggests that boys learn to be independent, assertive, and achievement-oriented—experiences that encourage them to consider moral dilemmas as inevitable conflicts of interest between two or more parties that laws and other social conventions are designed to resolve (a perspective that represents Stage 4 reasoning in Kohlberg's scheme). By contrast, girls are taught to be nurturant, empathic, and concerned about the needs of others—in short, to define their sense of "goodness" in terms of their relationships with other people. These experiences should encourage females to think of moral dilemmas as conflicts between one's own selfishness and the needs or desires of others (a perspective that approximates Stage 3 in Kohlberg's scheme). According to Gilligan, the interpersonal orientation that women adopt when thinking about moral issues is neither more nor less mature than the rule-bound morality of men. Instead, she views these moralities as "separate but equal" and suggests that females go through a different series of moral stages than males do.

Gilligan's next step was to study the moral development of females by asking pregnant women to discuss an important dilemma that they were currently facing—should they continue their pregnancies or have abortions? After analyzing the responses of her 29 subjects, Gilligan proposed that women's moral judgments progress through a sequence of three levels (and two transitions between levels), where each level represents a more complex understanding of the relationship between one's own perspective and the rights and concerns of others. These moral levels (and transitions) are described as follows.

Level I: Orientation to Individual Survival

At this first level, a woman's thinking about abortion centers on her own needs and desires. The issue is individual survival, and the needs of others are largely ignored. For example, one 18-year-old, when asked what she thought when she found herself pregnant, replied: "I really didn't think anything except that I didn't want it . . . I wasn't ready for it, and next year will be my last year and I want to go to school" (Gilligan, 1977, p. 492).

The first transition: From selfishness to responsibility. According to Gilligan, there is a transitional period between Level I and Level II reasoning when women first recognize that there may be a clash between their own desires and the responsible course of action—a conflict between "doing something for oneself" and "doing the right thing." For example, one young woman stated: "What I want to do is to have the baby, . . . but what I feel I should do is to have an abortion right now. . . . Sometimes what is necessary comes before what you want, because [what you want] might not always lead to the right thing" (Gilligan, 1977, p. 494). Gilligan believes that females must experience this transitional conflict between selfishness and responsibility before they can move to the second level of moral reasoning.

Level II: Goodness as Self-Sacrifice

At this level, women have adopted many traditional feminine values and have come to evaluate themselves in terms of their interpersonal relationships. Now the orientation is to do right by others and to avoid hurting them if at all possible—even if one's decision represents a personal sacrifice. Clearly, the issue of hurting others is of primary concern when women reason about an abortion. When there is no decision that she can make that seems in the best interests of everyone, a female finds it exceedingly difficult to choose the "right" course of action. For example, a woman who feels protective toward her unborn fetus, and yet knows that her mate wishes her to abort it, is clearly in a

not capture the essence of feminine moral reasoning. In Box 11-4 we consider the basis for Gilligan's provocative claim as we examine the kinds of moral judgments that her female subjects displayed when deciding whether to have abortions.

Summing Up

Kohlberg's theory is an important statement about children's moral growth. Kohlberg has identified a sequence of moral stages that does seem to be related to cognitive development. Yet the theory applies

BOX 11-4 *continued*

no-win situation. If she aborts, she does the "right" thing in terms of the father's wishes but ignores her own feelings and the rights of the child. However, a decision not to abort might be construed as doing right by the fetus while ignoring the father's wishes. When forced to choose between two things she loves, the woman feels that she must make a large personal sacrifice, regardless of whether she serves the needs of her mate by aborting or those of her fetus by continuing the pregnancy.

The second transition: From goodness to truth. Between Level II and Level III comes a transitional period in which women begin to question the logic of moral self-sacrifice. Once again, the issue of selfishness versus responsibility comes to the forefront, but this time the woman also considers the "rightness" of hurting oneself as well as the issue of hurting others. She strives to be responsible to others and thus "good" but also to be responsible to herself and, thus, truthful or "honest." One Catholic woman illustrated this transitional logic by stating "I am doing it [abortion] because I have to do it. I'm not doing it the least bit because I want to. . . . Keeping the child . . . was impractical" (Gilligan, 1977, p. 500). This woman went on to state that, in the beginning, she had decided to have an abortion not so much for herself as for her parents (that is, to be good to others). But in the final analysis, she admitted to herself that she honestly didn't want to be a mother and that it is not always right to hurt oneself in the name of morality. *Didn't consider the baby*

Level III: The Morality of Nonviolence

At this third level, women have largely rejected the notion of moral self-sacrifice as immoral in its power to hurt the self. The principle of nonviolence—an injunction against hurting—becomes the basic premise underlying all moral judgments. Looking after the welfare of people is now a self-chosen and *universal* obligation that permits the woman to recognize a moral equality between herself and others that must be considered when making moral judg-

ments. This morality of nonviolence is apparent in the justification that one 25-year-old gave for having an abortion: "I would not be doing myself or the child a favor by having this child . . . I don't need to pay off my imaginary debts to the world through this child, and I don't think that it is right to bring a child into the world and use it for that purpose" (Gilligan, 1977, p. 505). Note that the concern here is to hurt neither oneself nor the baby. Although the decision to terminate the pregnancy was described as a "very heavy thing" that obviously compromised the woman's principles of nonviolence, she felt that the ultimate harm to herself and to an unwanted child could be greater had she decided to continue her pregnancy. Gilligan concludes that this Level III moral reasoning is every bit as abstract and "postconventional" as Kohlberg's highest stages, even though Kohlberg's scheme places it at Stage 3 (and hence less mature) because of its focus on personal and interpersonal obligations.

Wouldn't have murdered it. is it?

Evaluating Gilligan's Approach

Although Gilligan's theory represents an exciting new perspective on female moral development, many questions remain to be answered. For example, will men who are affected by an abortion decision show similar patterns of moral reasoning when thinking about this issue? Gilligan's theory seems to suggest that they will not. Will females reason in the same ways about practical dilemmas other than abortion (for example, mercy killing or capital punishment)? Do Gilligan's moral levels and transitions represent an invariant developmental sequence that is related to cognitive development in the same way that Kohlberg's stages seem to be? And how might Gilligan explain the fact that the vast majority of studies using the Kohlberg scheme find no sex differences in moral reasoning? (See Walker, 1984, 1986, for reviews.) These are some of the issues that must now be resolved before we will know whether Gilligan's model is a more accurate account of female moral development than the sequence of moral levels and stages described earlier by Lawrence Kohlberg.

most directly to the cognitive aspects of morality—specifically, to the reasoning that people use to justify moral decisions that they make when resolving hypothetical dilemmas. There is some question whether the theory applies equally well to males and

females. We've also seen that moral reasoning does not always predict moral behavior and that both these components of morality depend to some extent on the situation that one faces. In the next section, we will examine a third theory—the social-learning approach—that attempts to specify some of the important social and situational influences on a child's moral development.

MORALITY AS A PRODUCT OF SOCIAL LEARNING (AND SOCIAL INFORMATION PROCESSING)

Unlike psychoanalytic theorists, who assume that the development of the superego implies a consistent moral orientation, social-learning theorists argue that morality (especially moral conduct) is *situation specific*. The implications of these opposing viewpoints can be seen in the following example. Suppose we expose a young girl to two tests of moral conduct. In the first test, the child is told not to play with some attractive toys and is then left alone with them. The second test is one in which the child is left to play a game that is "rigged" in such a way that she must cheat in order to win a valuable prize. Each situation requires the child to resist the temptation to do something she is not supposed to do before we would label her behavior morally responsible. If morality is a general attribute, as psychoanalytic theorists contend, our subject should either resist temptation on both of the tests or transgress on both. However, if morality is specific to the situation, the child might resist temptation on both tests, transgress on both, or resist on one and transgress on the other.

Prominent social-learning theorists such as Justin Aronfreed (1976) and Albert Bandura (1977) think of moral behavior as a class of "socially acceptable" responses that are self-reinforcing (for example, it feels good to help) or instrumental for avoiding guilt, anxiety, or punishment. Bandura argues that specific moral responses or habits are acquired in much the same way as any other type of social behavior—through direct tuition and observational learning. Thus, if the girl in our example had often been punished for violating verbal prohibitions (or rewarded for following instructions) and had been reinforced in the past for her honesty (or exposed to honest models), she might well resist temptation on both of the "moral conduct" tests. But inconsistent

behavior could occur if one of these moral habits (for example, complying with verbal instructions) had been established while the other (honesty) had not.

HOW CONSISTENT IS MORAL BEHAVIOR?

Perhaps the most extensive study of children's moral conduct is one of the oldest—the Character Education Inquiry reported by Hugh Hartshorne and Mark May (1928–1930). The purpose of this five-year project was to investigate the moral "character" of nearly 11,000 children (aged 8–16) by tempting them to lie, cheat, or steal in a variety of situations. The most noteworthy finding of this massive investigation was that children tended *not* to be consistent in their moral behavior; a child's willingness to cheat in one situation did not predict his or her willingness to lie, cheat, or steal in other situations. Of particular interest was the finding that children who cheated in a particular setting were just as likely as those who did not to state that cheating was wrong! Hartshorne and May concluded that "honesty" is largely specific to the situation rather than a stable character trait.

This "doctrine of specificity" has been questioned by other researchers. Roger Burton (1963, 1984) reanalyzed the reliable measures from Hartshorne and May's study, using new and more sophisticated statistical techniques. His analyses provide some support for behavioral consistency. For example, the child's willingness to cheat or not cheat in one context (on tests in the classroom) is reasonably consistent, although the same child might behave very differently in highly unrelated contexts (for example, while playing competitive games on the playground). A similar conclusion was drawn by Nelson, Grinder, and Mutterer (1969), who tempted sixth-grade children to violate six different prohibitions and found that "temptation behavior is at least moderately consistent across a variety of tasks" (p. 265). Finally, Philippe Rushton (1980) reports some consistency in children's altruistic behavior: those who are most helpful in one particular context are likely to provide assistance in other, related contexts. So we see that moral behavior of a particular type (for example, cheating on exams; helping needy others) is not nearly so "situationally specific" as Hartshorne and May had thought. However, these results do not minimize the importance of the setting, for a child's willingness to lie, cheat, or violate other moral prohibitions is definitely influenced by a variety of situational factors such as the importance of the goal that can be achieved by transgressing, the probability of being detected, and the amount of encouragement provided by peers for deviant behavior (Burton, 1984).

THE SCOPE OF SOCIAL-LEARNING RESEARCH

Several theorists have argued that there are two classes of moral conduct. Some moral acts are "acts of commission" such as comforting, helping, or sharing, whereas others are "acts of omission" in which one behaves appropriately by *inhibiting* an inclination to cheat, lie, steal, or violate other moral norms. In Chapter 10, we discussed the development of prosocial habits, or moral acts of commission. We will now review the efforts of social-learning theorists to determine the origins of moral prohibitions, or acts of omission. Two classes of moral behavior will be considered: reactions to transgression and resistance to temptation.

REACTIONS TO TRANSGRESSION

Imagine that you have just stolen some money from your mother, an act that is blatantly inconsistent with the well-known Biblical exhortation "Thou shalt not steal." If you believe that stealing is wrong, you may well be experiencing some sort of negative emotional reaction such as guilt or shame as a result of your transgression. As a matter of fact, you may feel so bad that you criticize yourself severely and are eventually driven to confess and make some sort of restitution for your actions—perhaps by volunteering to give up your allowance until your debt is repaid. Like Freud, social-learning theorists have assumed that learning to feel guilty or ashamed when one has transgressed is an important aspect of moral development. Presumably these negative emotional reactions to transgression will (1) induce transgressors to atone for their sins and (2) reduce the likelihood that they will commit a similar act in the future.

PHOTO 11-1   Sometimes it is difficult to tell whether children are working together, helping each other, or using each other's work. Although there is some consistency to moral behavior, a child's conduct in any particular situation is likely to be influenced by factors such as the importance of a goal that might be achieved by breaking a moral rule and the probability of getting caught should he or she commit a transgression.

How do children come to criticize themselves for inappropriate behavior and to experience guilt or shame? Let's consider two points of view.

The operant-learning, or conditioning, viewpoint.   Young children are often criticized for their transgressions and frequently describe themselves or their unacceptable acts with a self-critical label. For example, a 3-year-old who is punished and told that he is "bad" for pulling the cat's tail may describe himself as a "bad boy" should he later repeat this act. Now, most of us find criticism aversive, and it is not immediately obvious why young children would want to criticize themselves. According to Justin Aronfreed (1964), children learn to criticize themselves or their transgressions because self-critical remarks are *self-reinforcing*—that is, they reduce the anxiety associated with the performance of prohibited acts! Let's explore this idea further.

Aronfreed proposes that, when parents punish a transgression, they often voice their criticisms at or near the *end* of the punitive episode. And because any transgression is likely to be detected, punished, and criticized on several occasions, the child should eventually (1) associate the performance of the prohibited act with punishment and hence with *anxiety* and (2) associate the critical remarks of his or her parents with the termination of punishment and the *reduction* of anxiety. In other words, transgressions themselves eventually come to elicit anxiety, and critical remarks have become conditioned stimuli for anxiety reduction. At this point, the child should begin to criticize his or her own unacceptable behavior in order to "signal" an end to the anxiety aroused by a transgression (see Figure 11-4).

Aronfreed (1964) tested his theory by inducing 9- to 10-year-old girls to commit incorrect responses while playing a game and then punishing these errors by sounding an aversive buzzer and taking away some of the candy they had received for participating. Some of the girls heard the experimenter voice his criticisms *at the beginning* of each punitive episode, whereas others heard the criticism *as the punishment was ending*. After this training phase, each girl played the game alone. As predicted by Aronfreed's theory, girls who had heard the experimenter's critical remarks at the end of the punitive episodes were much more likely to criticize their later errors than girls in the other condition. It appears that the former group made such frequent use of self-critical labels because they had associated these remarks with the *termination* of punishment and the reduction of anxiety it had produced. Thus, whenever they erred, these subjects could easily "terminate" whatever uneasiness they were experiencing by criticizing themselves.

Are these self-critical remarks truly "moral" behaviors—the precursors of guilt and shame? Probably not. Although the experience of powerful emotions such as guilt certainly includes a self-evaluative component, it is by no means obvious how self-critical responses that *reduce* anxiety are related to the self-evaluative aspects of guilt, which *increase* one's feelings of uneasiness. In sum, few parents would hope to raise a child who easily dismisses the unpleasant aspects of immoral conduct by uttering a few simple self-critical remarks. Most parents want their children to feel genuine guilt, shame, and re-

morse over their transgressions—truly *internal* reactions that might induce the child to make reparative responses and/or decrease the likelihood of repeating the prohibited act. How, then, do children come to experience such emotions?

Hoffman's cognitive-attributional hypothesis.

Martin Hoffman (1977) proposes that people experience guilt because they (1) empathize with another person's distress and (2) recognize that they (or their inappropriate acts) are the cause of these negative emotions. Thus, a young child is unlikely to feel guilty over a transgression unless he empathizes with the person who is disapproving of his behavior and understands that it was indeed *his own conduct* that is responsible for the other person's distress *and* the uneasiness he is feeling.

According to Hoffman (1977, 1984), punitive disciplinary techniques such as spankings should *not* promote the development of guilt, shame, or self-criticism. The problem with punitive discipline is that it focuses the child's attention on her *own* negative consequences and leads her to assume that the cause of any uneasiness or discomfort she is experiencing is attributable to the punishment that she has received (an external attribution). Consequently, this child may experience only a vague sense of anxiety or a fear of being detected should she transgress again, and she may be quite willing to repeat the prohibited act when external agents are not present to detect and punish such behavior. By contrast, a rational, nonpunitive discipline such as induction (or victim-centered reasoning) should promote the development of guilt, shame, and remorse by making children aware of how *their* actions have made others feel. As the child empathizes with the victim (or the disciplinarian) and recognizes that it is she who is responsible for that person's distress, she should make an internal attribution for her own uneasiness, experience guilt, and become less inclined to repeat her inappropriate conduct.

Later in the chapter, we will take a closer look at the effects of parental discipline on children's moral development. For now let's simply note that there are data consistent with Hoffman's cognitive-

Events

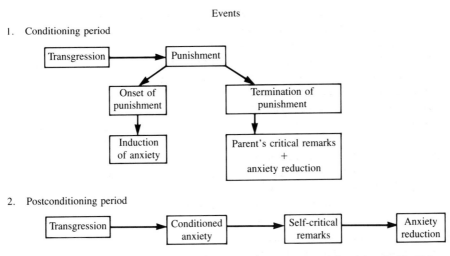

1. Conditioning period

2. Postconditioning period

FIGURE 11-4 A schematic representation of Aronfreed's explanation of the origins of self-criticism

attributional analysis of moral self-evaluation. For example, when children are asked to explain how a story character feels after committing a serious transgression, those whose parents rely on inductive discipline often say that the character feels guilty or ashamed (an internal orientation), whereas their age mates whose parents favor more punitive disciplinary strategies are much more inclined to say that the transgressor is worried about getting caught and punished (an external orientation) (see Hoffman, 1970).

RESISTANCE TO TEMPTATION

From society's standpoint the most important index of morality is the extent to which an individual is able to resist pressures to violate moral norms *even when the possibility of detection and punishment is remote* (Hoffman, 1970). A person who resists temptation in the absence of external surveillance not only has learned a moral rule but is also internally motivated to abide by that rule. How do children acquire moral standards, and what motivates them to obey these learned codes of conduct? Social-learning theorists have tried to answer these questions by studying the effects of reinforcement, punishment, and social modeling on children's moral behavior.

The Resistance-to-Temptation Paradigm

When studying children's resistance to temptation, an experimenter will first establish a prohibition of some sort and then leave the child alone so that he is tempted to violate that edict. A common procedure is to tell children that they are not to touch certain attractive toys but that they are free to play with any number of other, unattractive objects. Once a child has learned the prohibition and refrains from playing with the attractive items, the experimenter leaves the room and thereby tempts the child to violate the rule. As we will see, this *"forbidden toy"* paradigm has proved quite useful at determining whether various forms of praise, punishment, and other disciplinary techniques affect the child's willingness to comply with rules and regulations.

Reinforcement as a Determinant of Moral Conduct

We have seen on several occasions that the frequency of many behaviors can be increased if these acts are reinforced. Moral behaviors are certainly no exception. For example, sharing among preschool children becomes more common when adults reinforce these acts of kindness with bubble gum (Fischer, 1963). But the role played by external reward in establishing and maintaining *inhibitory* controls is difficult to determine, because parents, teachers, and peers will often fail to recognize that the child has *resisted* a temptation and is deserving of praise. By contrast, people may be quick to inform the child of his or her misdeeds by punishing moral transgressions!

Does punishment play a larger role than reinforcement in the establishment of moral controls? Although many children would probably say yes, it appears that reinforcement may be a very important part of a child's moral education. David Perry and Ross Parke (1975) found that children were more likely to obey a prohibition against touching attractive toys if they had been reinforced for playing with other, unattractive items. Thus, rewarding alternative behaviors that are incompatible with prohibited acts can be an effective method of instilling moral controls. In addition, physical punishment administered by a warm, loving (socially reinforcing) parent is more effective at producing resistance to temptation than the same punishment given by a cold, rejecting parent (Sears, Maccoby, & Levin, 1957). Although adults may often use punishment as a means of establishing moral prohibitions, the effectiveness of this strategy will depend, in part, on their past history as reinforcing agents.

The Role of Punishment in Establishing Moral Prohibitions

Parents often assume that the best way to restrain a child's undesirable antics is to punish them. Yet many psychologists believe that punishment produces anger, resentment, and at best a temporary suppression of the behavior it is designed to eliminate. Their point is that a fear of aversive consequences can never be a totally effective deterrent, because the child will simply inhibit unacceptable conduct until it is unlikely to be detected and punished.

Both arguments have some merit. Parents who are severely punitive do tend to raise hostile, antisocial children (Bandura & Walters, 1959), and few contemporary theorists believe that a person's internal morality, or capacity for *self*-control, is based on a fear that unacceptable behavior will be detected and punished. Yet punishment can contribute to the establishment of moral controls if it is not overly harsh and

if it helps children to view their misconduct (and/or the prohibited act) in a negative light. In other words, fear of detection and punishment is not enough; children must wish to avoid the prohibited act itself before they are likely to inhibit that response when there is no one around to oversee their activities.

Early research on the effects of punishment. Working initially from an operant-learning, or "conditioning," framework, Ross Parke and his associates have used the "forbidden toy" paradigm to study the effects of punishment on children's resistance to temptation. The conditioning viewpoint is that (1) punishment makes children anxious, (2) this anxiety becomes conditioned to the act that is punished, and (3) children will eventually learn to inhibit that act in order to avoid the feelings of anxiety that they would experience were they to perform it. Thus, moral inhibitions were conceptualized as conditioned avoidance responses.

During the first phase of a typical experiment, subjects are punished (usually by hearing a loud verbal rebuke or a noxious buzzer) whenever they touch an attractive toy; however, nothing happens when they play with unattractive toys. Once the child has learned the prohibition (that is, "Don't touch attractive toys"), the experimenter leaves the room. The child is then surreptitiously observed to determine whether he or she will play with the forbidden objects.

Parke (1972, 1977) found that not all punishments are equally effective at promoting the development of moral controls. Table 11-1 briefly summarizes the conditions under which punishment was most likely to inhibit undesirable conduct in this early program of research.

Effects of verbal rationales. One problem with the research presented in Table 11-1 is that it is somewhat unrealistic: adult authority figures were making arbitrary rules and punishing deviations from these edicts without explaining their actions. Yet when adults discipline a child in a naturalistic setting, they frequently explain to the child why they are punishing him and why it is important to obey rules and to inhibit undesirable conduct. Ross Parke (1977) now believes that virtually any form of punishment becomes more effective if it is accompanied by a *cognitive rationale* that provides the child with reasons for inhibiting a forbidden act. Even a simple statement such as "Don't touch these toys because I don't have any others like them" may be effective with young children. In fact, Parke (1972, 1977) found that, when rationales accompany punishment, (1) mild forms of punishment become just as effective at producing resistance to temptation as strong punishment, (2) delayed punishment becomes as effective as early punishment, and (3) punishment from an aloof, impersonal adult becomes as effective as that administered by a warm and rewarding adult. Parke also noted that resistance to temptation is much more stable over time if children are told why their deviant acts are inappropriate when they receive their punishment. This finding is extremely important, for it suggests that the establishment of long-term (internalized) moral controls "may *require* the use of cognitively oriented training procedures. Punishment techniques that rely solely on anxiety induction, such as the noxious noises employed . . . in many experiments . . . or the more extreme forms of physical punishment sometimes used by parents, may be effective mainly in securing only short-term inhibition" (Parke, 1972, p. 274).

Do rationales alone produce any resistance to temptation? Indeed they do. In fact, Parke reports that rationales are more effective than mild punish-

TABLE 11-1   Characteristics of Punishment and the Punitive Context That Influence a Child's Resistance to Temptation

Timing of punishment	Punishment administered as children initiate deviant acts is more effective than punishment given after the acts have been performed. Early punishment makes children apprehensive as they prepare to commit a transgression, so that they are less likely to follow through. By contrast, late punishment makes children apprehensive *after* the act is completed, so that they may perform the act again and only then feel anxious.
Intensity of punishment	High-intensity punishment (a loud buzzer or a forceful *No!*) is more effective at inhibiting undesirable conduct than milder forms of the same punitive consequences. However, a caution is in order. Although the high-intensity punishments used in this research were certainly discomforting, they were probably a lot less aversive than a forceful spanking or a week's restriction to one's room. If high-intensity punishments are perceived as "cruel and unusual," children may become hostile toward the punitive agent and/or concerned only about not getting caught—hence they may be willing to commit the prohibited acts, perhaps "out of spite," when the disciplinarian is not around to oversee their activities.
Consistency of punishment	To be effective, punishment must be administered *consistently.* As most prohibited acts are themselves satisfying to the child, he or she will experience positive outcomes on those occasions when transgressions are not punished. In other words, inconsistent punishment may result in the *partial reinforcement* of unacceptable behavior, which strengthens these responses and makes them extremely resistant to extinction—even after the disciplinarian begins to punish them on a regular basis.
Relationship to the punitive agent	Punishment is more effective in establishing moral prohibitions when administered by someone who has previously established a warm and friendly (rewarding) relationship with the child. Children who are punished by a warm, caring person may perceive the reprimand as a loss of affection and may inhibit the punished act as a means of regaining approval. However, children who are punished by a cold, rejecting adult should not be highly motivated to inhibit forbidden acts, because they have no expectation of reestablishing a warm relationship with this cool or aloof disciplinarian.

ment at persuading children not to touch attractive toys. However, let's not conclude that parents should abandon punishment in favor of rationales, for a combination of a punishment and a rationale is much more effective than either of these treatments by itself (Parke, 1977).

On picking the right rationale.

Parke (1974, 1977) finds that not all rationales are equally effective at producing resistance to temptation. Preschool children are much more responsive to concrete, *object-oriented* rationales such as "Don't touch the toy; it's fragile and might break" than to abstract rationales based on ownership (for example, "Don't touch the toy; it belongs to someone else"). By contrast, older children tend to be more responsive to abstract, *person-oriented* rationales that indicate ownership or justify response inhibition in terms of the negative effects that a transgression would have on others (for example, "I'll be sad if you touch the toy"). So it appears that rationales are most effective when they are consistent with the ways in which children normally think about moral rules and issues: young, morally realistic children seem to require concrete rationales, whereas older, morally autonomous children are affected more by reasoning that focuses on the rights, privileges, and feelings of other people.

Why are rationales important for the establishment of moral controls? Justin Aronfreed (1976), a conditioning theorist, suggests two reasons. First, he proposes that any anxiety stemming from the aversive aspects of a disciplinary encounter may become conditioned to both the deviant act *and the cognitive rationale*, particularly if the disciplinary agent has stressed the child's intentions when punishing a transgression (for example, "You shouldn't have wanted to touch that toy because it might break"). Once this conditioning occurs, the child should become rather anxious or apprehensive at the *mere thought* of committing the deviant act. Second, the rationale provides the child with a *good reason* for inhibiting undesirable behavior, so that he or she can reduce anxiety by refusing to deviate and, at the same time, feel good about this "mature and responsible" conduct.

Now let's contrast this point of view with the more recent attributional (or social information-processing) perspective on resistance to temptation.

The attributional perspective on punishment, cognitive rationales, and resistance to temptation.

According to attribution theorists, the role played by punishment in the establishment of moral controls is simply to increase children's *emotional arousal* when they are later tempted to perform an act for which they have previously been punished. But attribution theorists contend that it is not the amount of arousal or apprehension that the child experiences that determines whether he will deviate—the critical determinant of his conduct is the *causal attribution* he makes for the uneasiness he is experiencing. Here is where the reasoning that has accompanied punishment comes into play. Presumably, children who have often heard rationales that stress why prohibited acts are wrong or why *they* should not perform them will learn to make *internal* attributions for their emotional arousal (for example, "I'd feel guilty if I were to deviate"; "I'd violate my positive self-image")—attributions that should help them to resist many temptations, even in the absence of external surveillance. By contrast, children who receive no rationales or who have been exposed to reasoning that focuses their attention on the punitive consequences they might receive for deviating should tend to make *external* attributions for the arousal they are experiencing (for example, "I'm worried about getting caught and punished")—attributions that might induce compliance with moral norms in the presence of authority figures but should increase the likelihood of deviant behavior if there is no one around to detect and punish a transgression.

Richard Dienstbier and his associates (Dienstbier, Hillman, Lehnhoff, Hillman, & Valkenaar, 1975) conducted an interesting experiment to test these attributional hypotheses. The children in this study had each promised to perform a dull and tedious task for an adult. At one point during the experiment, the adult mentioned that he had to run an errand and then left the room after instructing the child to keep working at the boring task. Soon thereafter, some very attractive toys in the room were activated by remote control, thereby persuading children to break their promise by leaving the work to go and play with these objects. The experimenter then returned, caught the children goofing off, and criticized them for their inappropriate behavior. Half the children heard a critique in which it was suggested that they were now feeling upset because they had done something *they had known to be wrong* (internal attribution condition). The remaining children were told that they were probably feeling upset because they had been *caught and scolded* for doing something they had been told not to do (external attribution condition). So the groups heard the same scolding, although they received different explanations for the arousal they were experiencing.

Soon thereafter, the children were left alone once again to work on the boring task after learning that it was unlikely that anyone would be looking in on them as they worked (of course, their behavior was surreptitiously observed). As predicted by attribution theory, children in the internal attribution condition were much less likely to stop working and go and play with the toys than their counterparts in the external attribution condition. So it appears that the rationales adults use when punishing transgressions will affect the causal attributions that children make when tempted to violate a prohibition, which, in turn, will influence the likelihood that they will resist this temptation.

Is punishment truly the answer? Although parents, teachers, and other authority figures often succeed in inhibiting children's undesirable conduct through the use of punishment, we should not assume that punitive tactics are the most efficient or effective way to establish moral controls. One major problem with punitive techniques is that they frequently have undesirable side effects that can limit their usefulness. For example, we have noted on several occasions that children often resent and will generally avoid punitive adults and that the anxiety generated by severe punishments may prevent the child from learning the lesson (or appreciating the rationale) that the disciplinarian intended to convey. Moreover,

punitive disciplinarians often serve as aggressive models whose actions may "legitimize" coercive, antisocial methods of conflict resolution. Finally, punitive strategies could easily backfire when administered to children who misbehave as a means of attracting attention. For these youngsters, the negative attention that accompanies punishment may be preferable to no attention at all.

Let's now consider some alternative techniques that adults might use to facilitate children's resistance to temptation while avoiding many of the undesirable side effects associated with punishment.

Nonpunitive Methods of Promoting Self-Control

Three nonpunitive strategies that appear to promote self-restraint or self-control are those that (1) alter children's thinking about the forbidden acts or forbidden goal objects, (2) provide children with a strategy or a "blueprint for action" that will help them to maintain their resolve in the face of temptation, or (3) work on children's self-concepts by convincing them that they are "good" or "honest" people who are intrinsically motivated to resist temptations and to comply with rules.

Reconceptualizing the forbidden fruit. Suppose you have just baked a batch of cookies, have placed them on the kitchen table to cool, and now wish to find a way to keep your children (who have gathered around the table) from ruining their dinner by snitching a cookie or two while your back is turned. Might you be successful by communicating this prohibition and then telling children to think about how good the cookies will taste later when they receive some for dessert (consummatory ideation)? Or might a better strategy be to direct their attention away from the cookies' desirable attributes by telling the children to think of them not as cookies but as nonedible objects such as lumps of stone or seashells (abstract ideation)?

Walter Mischel (1974; Mischel & Mischel, 1983) has addressed this issue in an interesting series of experiments with 3- to 12-year-olds. Mischel finds that, when children are face to face with a tempting object (such as a cookie), they are often over-whelmed with desire for that object, and thinking about the object's desirable attributes (consumma-tory ideation) only makes matters worse. By con-trast, children who are told to reconceptualize the goal object in a way that downplays its desirable attributes (for example, thinking about a tempting cookie as a flat rock) are better able to inhibit the desire to have that object right away. So one way to help a child resist the temptation to commit undesir-able acts is to get him or her to think about forbidden objects or activities in ways that reduce their inherent attractiveness. As Mischel (1976) has noted, self-restraint is largely under *cognitive* control: ability to resist temptation depends on "what is in the chil-dren's heads—not what is physically in front of them" (p. 447).

Self-instructional strategies. Unfortunately, many forbidden objects and activities are so tempting that children simply cannot help thinking about their desirable qualities. But if a child's willingness to resist temptation is truly under cognitive control, as Mischel has argued, then it should be possible to teach young children how to instruct themselves to follow rules and to resist temptation. To test this hypothesis, Walter Mischel and Charlotte Patterson (1976) asked preschool children to work on a dull task in the presence of a talking "clown box" that tried to persuade these youngsters to stop working and come play with him. Children who had been taught to say to themselves "I'm not going to look at Mr. Clown box . . . when Mr. Clown box says to look at him" were better able than those who had received no self-instructional strategy to resist this tempting distraction and keep on working.

In another study of children's self-control (Toner & Smith, 1977), preschool girls played a "waiting" game in which they received one piece of candy for every 30 seconds that they continued to wait. The rules were simple. As long as the child continued to wait, candies would accumulate in front of her. But if she told the experimenter to stop so that she could enjoy her treats, the game was over and could not be restarted. As the game began, the young subjects were either (1) given no further instructions, (2) told

to talk about how good the candy would taste, or (3) told to instruct themselves "It is good if I wait." The results were clear. Children who instructed them-selves that it was a good idea to wait did in fact wait much longer before ending the game than their peers who either received no further instructions or talked about how good the candy would be.

When first- and second-grade girls were tested, the results were similar—with one notable exception. If these older girls had not been instructed to say any-thing to themselves while waiting, they waited quite a while before ending the game. It appeared as if the older subjects were better able to resist temptation because they knew that they must distract themselves from the candy's positive qualities in order to main-tain their resolve. By contrast, the preschool children apparently preferred to focus on the candy itself and were unable to resist temptation unless they were specifically *instructed* to think distracting thoughts (see also Toner, 1981).

In sum, we see that the plans or "blueprints for action" that children have available for use in the face of temptation will clearly affect their ability to follow rules and to delay immediate gratification. And one reason that preschool children often seem so lacking in self-control is that these youngsters do not *spon-taneously* produce the kinds of self-instructions that would enable them to inhibit their own immediate impulses so that they can comply with rules.

Instilling a "moral" self-concept. If the attribu-tional analysis of resistance to temptation is correct, then we should be able to increase children's com-pliance with moral rules by convincing them that they are "good" or "honest" people who are inhibiting the temptation to lie, cheat, or steal because *they* want to (an internal attribution). Children who incorporate attributions of "goodness," "honesty," or "strength of character" into their self-concepts may strive very hard to live up to these positive self-images and could become highly self-critical or remorseful should they subsequently violate a moral rule.

Apparently this kind of moral self-concept training does have the desired effect on children's self-images and their subsequent moral conduct. In one study, William Casey and Roger Burton (1982) found that

7- to 10-year-olds became much more honest while playing games if "honesty" was stressed and the players had learned to remind themselves to follow the rules. Yet when honesty was *not* stressed, the players were likely to cheat—even when they had been taught to periodically tell themselves how they were supposed to be playing. Moreover, David Perry and his associates (Perry, Perry, Bussey, English, & Arnold, 1980) found that 9- to 10-year-olds who were told that they were especially good at carrying out instructions and following rules (moral self-concept training) behaved very differently after succumbing to a nearly irresistible temptation (leaving a boring task to watch an exciting TV show) than their counterparts who had not been told they were especially good. Specifically, children who had heard positive attributions about themselves were much more inclined than control subjects to punish their transgressions by giving back many of the valuable prize tokens that they had been paid for working at the boring task. So it appears that labeling children as "good" or "honest" not only increases the likelihood that they will resist temptations but also contributes to children's feelings of regret or remorse should they behave inappropriately and violate their positive self-images. Indeed, Perry et al. (1980) suggest that the expectation of feeling guilty or remorseful over deviant conduct may be what often motivates children with positive self-concepts to resist temptations in the first place.

Summing up. We see, then, that adults can promote children's resistance to deviation by teaching them to reconceptualize forbidden objects and activities, by helping them to develop self-instrumental plans, or "blueprints for action," that will enable them to maintain their resolve when tempted to deviate, and by encouraging them to think of themselves as "good," "truthful," or "honest" persons who can take pride in *their* ability to live up to their positive self-images. Unlike punishment, which is easily applied after a transgression, these nonpunitive strategies will require a substantial amount of planning of the adult. But despite the effort that one must expend, the potential advantages of these alternatives to punishment are many. For example, a parent who is obviously concerned about helping the child to *prevent future transgressions* is apt to be perceived as a caring and loving person—an impression that should increase the child's motivation to comply with parental requests. Moreover, self-concept training and the use of self-instruction may help to convince the child that "I'm resisting this temptation because *I* want to" and thus lead to the development of truly internalized controls rather than response inhibition based on a fear of detection and punishment. And last but certainly not least, these three strategies have few if any of the undesirable side effects that often accompany punishment.

Of course, there may be a time and place for the use of punishment: adults may occasionally have to resort to forceful or punitive strategies to command the attention of an unruly child. Yet parents and teachers who make a serious effort to try these nonpunitive training techniques may find that they rarely have to rely on punishment in order to control the behavior of their children.

Effects of Social Models on Children's Moral Conduct

Social-learning theorists have generally assumed that modeling influences play an important role in the child's moral development. And they are undoubtedly correct, for as we have seen, young children often imitate the compassionate and helpful acts of altruistic models. But helpful acts are *active* responses that will capture a child's attention. Will children learn *inhibitory controls* from models who exhibit socially desirable behavior in a "passive" way by failing to commit forbidden acts?

Apparently they will, as long as they recognize that the "passive" model is actually resisting the temptation to violate a moral norm. Nace Toner and his associates (Toner, Parke, & Yussen, 1978) exposed preschool and second-grade boys to rule-following models and found that this experience did indeed promote resistance to temptation. In fact, some of the children who had been exposed to the rule-following models were still following the rule when retested a week later. In a similar study, Joan Grusec and her associates (Grusec, Kuczynski, Rushton, & Simutis, 1979) found that a model who resists temptation can be particularly effective at inspiring children to behave in kind if he clearly verbalizes that he is following a rule and states a rationale for not committing the deviant act. Finally, the type of rationale that the model provides to justify his resistance to temptation is important. Rule-following models whose rationales match the child's customary level of moral reasoning are more influential than models whose rationales are beyond that level (Toner & Potts, 1981).

Of course, a model who violates a moral norm may *disinhibit* observers by giving them reason to think that they too can break the rule, particularly if the model is not punished for his deviant acts (Rosenkoetter, 1973; Walters & Parke, 1964). Thus, social models play two roles in a child's moral development, sometimes leading the child to resist temptation and at other times serving as "bad influences" who encourage inappropriate conduct.

Resistance to temptation also seems to be enhanced by *serving* as a model of moral restraint. An experiment by Nace Toner and his associates produced a very interesting outcome: 6- to 8-year-olds who were persuaded to serve as models of moral restraint for other children became more likely than age mates who had not served as exemplary models to obey rules during later tests of resistance to temptation (Toner, Moore, & Ashley, 1978). It was almost as if serving as a model had produced a change in the children's self-concepts, so that they now defined themselves as "people who follow rules." The implications for child rearing are obvious: perhaps parents could succeed in establishing inhibitory controls in their older children by appealing to their maturity and persuading them to serve as models of self-restraint for their younger brothers and sisters.

IS MORALITY A STABLE AND UNITARY ATTRIBUTE?

Earlier in the chapter, we saw that psychoanalytic theorists think of morality as a reasonably stable attribute that is controlled by the superego, whereas social-learning theorists argue that morality is unstable, or situation-specific. Can you guess where the cognitive-developmentalists stand on this issue? As it turns out, they side with the psychoanalysts; moral reasoning is said to be reasonably consistent across situations and a strong determinant of both moral affect and moral behavior.

If morality is a stable and *unitary* attribute, we should find that the three basic components of moral character—affect, reasoning, and behavior—bear some meaningful relationship to one another. Yet we've already learned that the moral reasoning of young children often does not predict their moral conduct and that a child's willingness to lie, cheat, or steal in one situation is not a very good indicator of how he or she will behave in unrelated contexts.

However, studies of adolescents and young adults often find that (1) the moral behavior of these older subjects is more consistent across situations and (2) there is some consistency between their moral reasoning and their moral behavior. And at least one study of young adults (MacKinnon, 1938) found a link between moral affect (guilt) and moral behavior: subjects who did not cheat on a problem-solving task reported that they would have felt guilty if they had, whereas those who cheated and denied their transgression said that they would not have felt guilty about cheating.

So we see that morality is neither a unified whole, as envisioned by the psychoanalytic and the cognitive-developmental theorists, nor totally specific to the situation, as the social-learning theorists argue. It is possible that moral affect, moral reasoning, and moral behavior emerge as three separate "moralities" that older children eventually integrate *to some extent* as they reach that point in their intellectual development when they are able to recognize the basic commonalities or interrelationships among these three moral components. However, it is unlikely that the "moral character" of even the most mature of adults is perfectly consistent across all settings and situations.

WHO RAISES CHILDREN WHO ARE MORALLY MATURE?

Several years ago, Martin Hoffman (1970) carefully reviewed the child-rearing literature to determine whether parents' disciplinary techniques have any effect on the moral development of their children.

Much of the research that he reviewed was designed to test the hypothesis that *love-oriented discipline* (withdrawing affection or approval), which generates anxiety over a loss of love, would prove more effective at furthering the child's moral development than *power-assertive discipline* (physical punishment or withholding privileges), which generates anger or resentment.

Hoffman discovered that neither love withdrawal nor power assertion is particularly effective at promoting moral development. In fact, parents who often rely on power-assertive techniques have children who can be described as morally immature. The one disciplinary strategy that seems to foster the development of moral affect (guilt, shame), moral reasoning, and moral behavior is an approach called *induction*. Induction

> includes techniques in which the parent gives explanations or reasons for requiring the child to change his behavior. Examples are pointing out physical requirements of the situation or the harmful consequences of the child's behavior for himself or others. These techniques are . . . an attempt to . . . convince the child that he should change his behavior in the prescribed manner. Also included are techniques that appeal to conformity-inducing agents that already exist within the child. Examples are appeals to the child's pride, strivings for mastery and to be "grown up," and concern for others [Hoffman, 1970, p. 286].

Hoffman noted that inductive parents who regularly stress the needs and emotions of others as part of their discipline have children who show the highest levels of moral maturity. This *"other-oriented"* induction is accomplished by

> directly pointing out the nature of the consequence (e.g., If you throw snow on their walk, they will have

to clean it up all over again; Pulling the leash like that can hurt the dog's neck; That hurts my feelings); pointing out the relevant needs or desires of others (e.g., he is afraid . . . , so please turn the light back on); or explaining the motives underlying the other person's behavior toward the child (e.g., Don't yell at him. He was only trying to help) [Hoffman, 1970, p. 286].

Table 11-2 summarizes the relationships among the three patterns of parental discipline (power assertion, love withdrawal, and induction) and various measures of children's moral development. Clearly these data confirm Hoffman's conclusion: parents who rely on inductive discipline tend to have children who are morally mature, whereas frequent use of power assertion may actually inhibit the child's moral development.

Do these findings apply to infants, toddlers, and preschool children? It is often argued that parents may have to resort to more forceful and punitive techniques to control the behavior of infants, toddlers, and nursery school children; after all, very young children are notoriously impulsive and may be too cognitively immature to appreciate and understand the inductive component of a disciplinary encounter. Indeed, in reviewing the literature summarized in Table 11-2, Brody and Shaffer (1982) found that parents' use of inductive discipline was not consistently related to measures of moral maturity for children less than 6 years old.

However, it now appears that earlier conclusions about the effectiveness or ineffectiveness of various disciplinary practices with very young children may have to be modified. Recently, Thomas Power and

TABLE 11-2 Relationships between Parents' Use of Three Disciplinary Strategies and Children's Moral Development

Direction of relationship (between parent's use of a disciplinary strategy and children's moral maturity)	Type of discipline		
	Power assertion	Love withdrawal	Induction
+ (positive correlation)	7	8	38
− (negative correlation)	32	11	6

Note: Table entries represent the number of occasions on which a particular disciplinary technique was found to be associated (either positively or negatively) with a measure of children's moral affect, reasoning, or behavior.

Lynn Chapieski (1986) found that 19–22-month-old infants whose mothers had earlier relied on physical force to punish transgressions were much more likely to touch forbidden objects and to display other forms of misconduct than age mates whose mothers had rarely or only occasionally resorted to power-assertive tactics. Mothers of the compliant infants made many demands for impulse control and consistently enforced these demands—but they did not need to rely on physical punishment to ensure that their children complied!

Moreover, there is now evidence to suggest that inductive reasoning which is backed up with the occasional use of power assertion (to command the child's attention to the reasoning) can be highly effective with infants and toddlers. Recall from Chapter 10 that mothers who discipline harmdoing with *affective explanations* (in which they clearly voice their displeasure with the child's conduct while telling the child why that conduct is wrong) tend to have highly compassionate toddlers who are concerned about the welfare of others (Zahn-Waxler, Radke-Yarrow, & King, 1979). By contrast, mothers who disciplined harmdoing with forceful techniques (physical punishment) or by simply preventing the child from misbehaving without explaining the implications of these unacceptable acts had toddlers who showed less compassion for others and less self-control.

Finally, Mary Parpal and Eleanor Maccoby (1985) have recently reported that preschool children become much more compliant with their mothers' demands if mothers have been trained to be more responsive to the child's requests and to comply more frequently with the child's directives during their playful interactions. The lesson to be learned from these observations is a very simple one: preschool children are quite capable of behavioral reciprocity and are generally willing to cooperate with a "responsive" parent who has previously demonstrated a willingness to cooperate with them.

In sum, there is every reason to believe that rational, nonpunitive discipline administered by a responsive and generally cooperative parent can be an effective means of inhibiting the undesirable conduct of young children while fostering their prosocial inclinations. By contrast, a heavy reliance on power assertion is not an effective means of establishing self-control or willingness to comply with rules—even for young and highly impulsive toddlers and preschool children.

Why is induction effective? Hoffman's integrative overview. Hoffman believes there are several reasons that parents who rely on inductive discipline will tend to raise children who are morally mature. First, the inductive diciplinarian provides *cognitive standards* (or rationales) that children can use to evaluate their actions. And when inductive discipline is other-oriented, parents are furnishing their child with the kinds of experiences that should foster the development of empathy and reciprocal-role taking—two cognitive abilities that contribute to the growth of mature *moral reasoning*. Second, use of inductive discipline allows parents to talk about the *affective* components of morality, such as guilt and shame, that are not easily discussed with a child who is made emotionally insecure by love-oriented discipline or angry by power-assertive techniques. Finally, parents who use inductive discipline are likely to explain to the child (1) what he or she *should have done* when tempted to violate a prohibition and (2) what he or she *can now do* to make up for a transgression. So it appears that induction is an effective method of moral socialization because it clearly illustrates the affective, cognitive, and behavioral aspects of morality and may help the child to integrate them. Moreover, the primary focus of inductive techniques is inward, on the child's thoughts and feelings, rather than outward, on the external consequences that the child can expect to receive should a transgression be detected by others. Thus, induction should foster *internal* explanations for one's uneasiness when tempted to deviate (for example, "I'm feeling ashamed for considering this action") or for one's decision to abide by rules ("I'm resisting this temptation because I want to")—precisely the kinds of attributions that contribute to truly internalized moral controls (or moral maturity).

Does induction promote moral maturity—or, rather, do morally mature children elicit more inductive forms of discipline from their parents? Since

' IF YOU'RE TRYIN' TO GET SOMETHING INTO MY
HEAD, YOU'RE WORKIN' ON THE WRONG END!"

DENNIS THE MENACE, ® AND © BY FIELD ENTERPRISES, INC.

the child-rearing studies are correlational in nature, either of these possibilities could explain Hoffman's findings.

Recent research suggests that the discipline that parents use in any given situation does depend to some extent on (1) what the child has done and (2) how he or she has reacted to previous disciplinary encounters. When trying to gain *long-term* compliance or when dealing with transgressions such as lying or ridiculing others that have caused someone *psychological* harm, parents are apt to use inductive techniques. By contrast, if parents are trying to gain *short-term* compliance with a directive or to immediately inhibit acts of disobedience such as fighting or obstinacy, they are more likely to use forceful strategies such as spankings or the withdrawal of privileges or affection (Grusec & Kuczynski, 1980; Kuczynski, 1984). Moreover, the child's reactions to discipline will affect the way he or she is treated. For example, Ross Parke (1977) found that children who had ignored a disciplinarian or who had pleaded for mercy were dealt with much more forcefully

during the next disciplinary encounter than those who had reacted to the earlier discipline by offering to undo the harm they had done (see also Brunk & Henggeler, 1984).

Although he acknowledges that children can have meaningful effects on the disciplinary practices of their parents, Hoffman (1975a) contends that parents exert far more constraints on their children's behavior than children exert on parents. In other words, he believes that parental use of inductive discipline promotes moral maturity rather than the other way around. As we see in Box 11-5, there is some experimental support for Hoffman's argument that inductive discipline fosters mature, responsible conduct. Nevertheless, it is likely that moral socialization in the home setting is a two-way street and that children who respond more favorably to discipline are the ones who are apt to be treated in a rational, nonpunitive manner by their parents.

Finally, it is important to remember that few if any parents are totally inductive, love-oriented, or power-assertive in their approach to discipline; most make at least some use of all three disciplinary techniques. Although parents classified as "inductive" frequently use inductive methods, they occasionally take punitive measures whenever punishment is necessary to command the child's attention or to discipline repeated transgressions. So the style of parenting that Hoffman calls induction may be very similar to the "rationale + mild punishment" treatment that is so effective at producing resistance to temptation in the laboratory.

A child's-eye view of discipline. What do you suppose children think about various disciplinary strategies? Do they feel (as many developmentalists do) that physical punishment and love withdrawal are likely to be ineffective methods of promoting self-control? Would they favor inductive techniques? Or is it conceivable that children would prefer their parents to adopt a more permissive attitude and not be so quick to discipline transgressions?

Recently, Michael Siegal and Jan Cowen (1984) addressed these issues by asking 100 children and adolescents between the ages of 4 and 18 to listen to stories describing different kinds of inappropriate

BOX 11-5 AN EXPERIMENTAL DEMONSTRATION OF THE EFFECTIVENESS OF INDUCTIVE DISCIPLINE

Do inductive procedures make children more willing to obey rules or to comply with the requests of an authority figure? Leon Kuczynski (1983) attempted to answer this question in a recent experiment with 9–10-year-olds. Each child took part in a project in which he or she was asked to evaluate the merits of a highly attractive group of toys. After ten minutes of play, the child was informed that it was now time to put these toys aside and test the desirability of a simple crank-turning device. Each subject was then seated at a table with his or her back to the attractive items and was told to keep turning the toy crank. The experimenter gave one of three sets of instructions to keep the child working and to prohibit him or her from even looking at the attractive toys:

1. *Unelaborated prohibition* (a form of power assertion): "Listen, don't look at those toys again until I let you!"
2. *Self-oriented induction*: Don't look at those other toys. "You'll be unhappy if you look at them. . . . If you don't work hard enough you'll have to do some of this work later and you'll have little time to play with those toys."
3. *Other-oriented induction*: Don't look at those other toys. "You'll make me unhappy if you look at them now. If you don't work hard enough, I'll have to do some of this work later and I'll have little time to do what I want to do."

The child's willingness to comply with the experiment-er's request was then observed in three contexts: (1) a two-minute period while the experimenter remained in the room, (2) a seven-minute period while the experimenter was out of the room making a phone call, and (3) a second seven-minute period after the experimenter had returned, said that he would be away for a while longer and that he would not be angry if the child looked at the toys (disinhibi-tion instructions), and then departed once again. The mea-sures of compliance were (1) the rate at which the child worked at the dull crank-turning chore and (2) the amount of time that the child spent looking at (or playing with) the attractive toys.

The results were clear. As we see in the first graph, other-oriented induction was more effective than either self-oriented induction or the unelaborated prohibition at persuading children to keep working at the crank-turning task. Note that children in the other-oriented condition, who believed that they would be hurting the experimenter by not working, were willing to keep working hard, even after the experimenter had implied that it was OK to look at the toys.

How long did the children spend looking at the attractive toys? As we see in the second graph, subjects who had received an other-oriented rationale spent much less time gazing at the prohibited items than did those who had received a self-oriented rationale or unelaborated prohibi-tion. In fact, the experimenter's statement that he would not

conduct and to evaluate several strategies that mothers had used in response to these antics. Five kinds of transgressions were described: (1) simple disobedience (the child refused to clean up his or her room), (2) causing physical harm to others (the child punched a playmate), (3) causing physical harm to oneself (ignoring an order not to place one's hand on a hot stove), (4) causing psychological harm to others (making fun of a person with a physical disability), and (5) causing physical harm to objects (breaking a lamp while roughhousing indoors). The four disci-plinary techniques on which mothers were said to have relied were *induction* (reasoning with the culprit by pointing out the harmful consequences of his or her actions for self and others), *physical punishment* (hitting or spanking the child), *love withdrawal* (tell-ing the culprit she wanted nothing more to do with him or her), or *permissive nonintervention* (ignoring the incident and assuming the child would learn im-portant lessons on his or her own). Each participant heard 20 stories that resulted from pairing each of the four maternal strategies with each of the five trans-gressions. After listening to or reading each story, the subject indicated whether the mother's approach to the problem was "very wrong," "wrong," "half right–half wrong," "right," or "very right."

The results of this study were indeed interesting. Although the perceived appropriateness of each dis-ciplinary technique varied somewhat across trans-gressions, the most interesting findings overall were

BOX 11-5 *continued*

be angry if they looked only increased the looking time of the "other-oriented" subjects to the level that the other children had already shown before receiving these disinhibiting instructions.

So inductive reasoning can increase children's motivation to comply with the wishes or demands of an authority figure. And as Hoffman had found in his review of the child-rearing literature, the type of reasoning that was most effective at gaining compliance was an *other-oriented* induction in which children were informed of the negative consequences that their noncompliant acts would have on someone other than themselves.

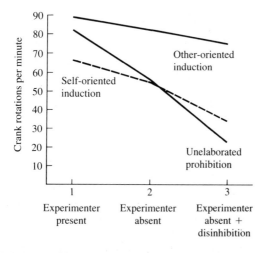

Average rate of work as a function of the type of rationale children received and the context in which they were observed

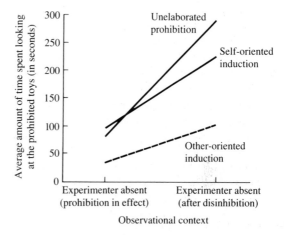

Average amount of time spent looking at prohibited toys as a function of the type of rationale given for not looking and the context in which the observations occurred

that (1) induction was the most preferred disciplinary strategy for subjects of all ages (even preschoolers), and (2) physical punishment was the next most favorably evaluated technique. In other words, participants of all ages seemed to prefer a rational disciplinarian who relies heavily on reasoning that is occasionally backed by power assertion. By contrast, love withdrawal and permissiveness were favorably evaluated by no age group. However, it is interesting to note that the youngest children in the sample (that is, the 4- to 9-year-olds) favored *any* form of discipline, even love withdrawal, over a permissive attitude on the mother's part (which they viewed as "wrong" or "very wrong"). Apparently, young children see the need for adults to step in and control their

inappropriate conduct, for they were quite bothered by a scenario in which youngsters were generally free to do their own thing, largely unencumbered by adult constraints.

Finally, we see that the disciplinary style that children evaluate most favorably (induction backed by the occasional use of power assertion) is the one that is most closely associated with measures of moral maturity in the child-rearing studies and with resistance to temptation in the laboratory. So another reason that inductive discipline promotes moral maturity may be that children view this approach as the "right" way to deal with transgressions and they may be highly motivated to accept influence from a disciplinarian whose "world view" matches their own. By contrast, children who favor induction but are usually disciplined in other ways may see little justification for internalizing the values and exhortations of a disciplinarian whose very methods of inducing compliance seem unwise, unjust, and hardly worthy of their respect.

SUMMARY

The present chapter focuses on what many theorists consider a critical aspect of social and personality development: morality and the growth of moral controls. Morality has been defined in many ways, although almost everyone agrees that it implies *a set of principles or ideals that help the individual to distinguish right from wrong and to act on this distinction*. Morality has three basic components: *moral affect, moral reasoning*, and *moral behavior*.

Psychoanalytic theorists emphasize the affective, or "emotional," aspects of morality. According to Freud, the character of the parent/child relationship largely determines the child's willingness to internalize the moral standards of the same-sex parent. This internalization is said to occur during the phallic stage and results in the development of the superego. Once formed, the superego functions as an internal censor that will reward the child for virtuous conduct and punish moral transgressions by making the child feel anxious, guilty, or ashamed.

Neo-Freudians have proposed a theory of moral development that differs from Freud's version in two important respects. First, the superego is said to result from social (rather than sexual) conflicts that cause the child to internalize the moral standards of *both* parents in order to avoid losing their love and affection. Second, both the ego and the superego are said to play important roles in determining the child's moral conduct and character. Many tests of Freudian theory have now been conducted, and most of the evidence does *not* support Freud's explanation of moral development. Neo-Freudian theory fares better, although the evidence cited to support this model can also be explained by other theories.

Cognitive-developmental theorists have emphasized the cognitive component of morality by studying the development of moral reasoning. Jean Piaget was the pioneer. He formulated a two-stage model of moral development based on changes that occur in children's conceptions of rules and their sense of social justice. Although Piaget did identify some important processes and basic trends in the development of moral reasoning, recent research suggests that his two-stage theory is too simple. Lawrence Kohlberg believes that moral development progresses through an invariant sequence of three moral levels, each composed of two distinct stages. According to Kohlberg, the order of progression through the levels and stages is invariant because each of these modes of thinking depends, in part, on the development of certain cognitive abilities that evolve in a fixed sequence. Each successive stage represents a reorganization of previous stages; and once the individual has attained a higher stage of moral reasoning, he or she will not regress to earlier stages.

Attempts to verify the cognitive theories reveal that moral reasoning is related to cognitive development. Moreover, children progress through the first four of Kohlberg's six stages in the order that Kohlberg specifies. Yet most people never reach Kohlberg's highest moral stages, which seem to require a special kind of environmental support in order to develop. Moreover, the cognitive theories apply most directly to the cognitive aspects of morality—specifically, to the reasoning that people use when resolving hypothetical dilemmas. Finally, one's level of moral reasoning does not always predict one's moral conduct—both of these components of morality depend to some extent on the situation one faces.

Social-learning theorists emphasize the behavioral component of morality, and their research has helped us to understand how children are able to resist temptation and to inhibit acts that violate moral norms. Among the processes that are important in establishing inhibitory controls are reinforcing the child for acceptable behavior and punishing unacceptable conduct. However, some punishments are more effective than others. Among the factors that determine the effectiveness of punishment are its timing, intensity, consistency, and accompanying rationale, as well as the emotional warmth of the punitive agent. Nonpunitive techniques such as teaching the child how to reconceptualize forbidden objects and activities or how to instruct himself to avoid temptation are also quite effective at promoting self-control, as is the practice of convincing the child that he is a "good" or "honest" person. Indeed, any technique that induces children to make *internal attributions* for their uneasiness in the face of temptation or for their compliance with rules is apt to contribute to their moral development. Children may also acquire inhibitory controls by observing models who show moral restraint or by serving as rule-following models for other children.

Measures of moral affect, moral reasoning, and moral behavior are not highly interrelated, even among adults. Moreover, people are sometimes inconsistent in their moral behavior from situation to situation. So morality is neither a "unified whole," as envisioned by psychoanalytic and cognitive theorists, nor is it totally specific to the situation, as argued by social-learning theorists.

Martin Hoffman has looked at the relationship between parental disciplinary practices and children's moral development. His findings indicate that warm and loving parents who rely mainly on inductive discipline tend to raise children who are morally mature. Induction is an effective method of moral socialization because it often illustrates and may help the child to integrate the affective, cognitive, and behavioral aspects of morality. And because children generally prefer induction to other disciplinary techniques, viewing it as the wise choice for handling most transgressions, they may be highly motivated to accept influence from an "inductive" adult whose methods they can respect.

NOTES

1. Robert Liebert (1979) objects to the labeling of some forms of moral affect, reasoning, or behavior as more "mature" than others. He notes that there is little if any evidence for the existence of universal ethical principles and suggests that standards of right and wrong are socially defined "value judgments" that vary considerably both within and across cultures. Moreover, he argues that the designation of certain types of moral functioning as "better" simply because individuals develop in those directions

rests on the tenuous assumption that development presupposes improvement. Clearly these arguments are not without merit. But at the risk of appearing value-laden to some, I have chosen to talk about moral "maturity" and "immaturity" in the same way that most developmental researchers do when studying moral growth and development.

2. Because Stage 6 reasoning is so rare and virtually no one functions consistently at that level, Kohlberg now treats it as a theoretical construct—that is, the stage to which people would progress if they were to develop beyond Stage 5. In fact, the latest version of Kohlberg's scoring system no longer contains guidelines for assessing Stage 6 reasoning (Colby & Kohlberg, 1984).

3. Another reason that moral judgments often fail to predict moral behavior is that researchers have used *global* measures of moral reasoning (the person's average stage score across several dilemmas) to try to predict *specific* kinds of conduct (for example, cheating). It is likely that the correlations between moral reasoning and moral behavior would be much higher if subjects were asked to reason about the kind of moral conduct that one is trying to predict (Ajzen & Fishbein, 1977). If you wanted to predict a child's willingness to play baseball at the school picnic, you would be better off asking her whether she likes baseball (specific measure) rather than asking her whether she likes outdoor activities or sports (global measures). Likewise, if you hoped to predict someone's willingness to cheat, the most effective strategy would be to assess the stage at which that person reasoned while resolving an ethical dilemma concerning a decision to cheat or not to cheat (specific moral judgment) rather than asking him to reason about lying, stealing, or hurting others and then averaging these responses (global measure of moral reasoning).

REFERENCES

AJZEN, I., & Fishbein, M. (1977). Attitude-behavior relations: A theoretical analysis and review of empirical research. *Psychological Bulletin, 84*, 888–918.

AMBRON, S. R., & Irwin, D. M. (1975). Role-taking and moral judgment in five- and seven-year-olds. *Developmental Psychology, 11*, 102.

ARBUTHNOT, J. (1975). Modification of moral judgment through role-playing. *Developmental Psychology, 11*, 319–324.

ARONFREED, J. (1964). The origin of self-criticism. *Psychological Review, 71*, 193–218.

ARONFREED, J. (1976). Moral development from the standpoint of a general psychological theory. In T. Lickona (Ed.), *Moral development and behavior.* New York: Holt, Rinehart and Winston.

BANDURA, A. (1977). *Social learning theory.* Englewood Cliffs, NJ: Prentice-Hall.

BANDURA, A., & McDonald, F. J. (1963). Influence of social reinforcement and the behavior of models in shaping children's moral judgments. *Journal of Abnormal and Social Psychology, 67*, 274–281.

BANDURA, A., & Walters, R. H. (1959). *Adolescent aggression.* New York: Ronald Press.

BAUMRIND, D. (1978). A dialectical materialist's perspective on knowing social reality. In W. Damon (Ed.), *New directions for child development* (No. 2): *Moral development*. San Francisco: Jossey-Bass.

BERKOWITZ, M. W., & Gibbs, J. C. (1983). Measuring the developmental features of moral discussion. *Merrill-Palmer Quarterly, 29*, 399–410.

BERKOWITZ, M. W., Gibbs, J. C., & Broughton, J. M. (1980). The relation of moral judgment stage disparity to developmental effects of peer dialogues. *Merrill-Palmer Quarterly, 26*, 341–357.

BLASI, A. (1980). Bridging moral cognition and moral action: A critical review of the literature. *Psychological Bulletin, 88*, 1–45.

BLASI, A. (1983). Moral cognition and moral action: A theoretical perspective. *Developmental Review, 3*, 178–210.

BRODY, G. H., & Shaffer, D. R. (1982). Contributions of parents and peers to children's moral socialization. *Developmental Review, 2*, 31–75.

BRUNK, M. A., & Henggeler, S. W. (1984). Child influences on adult controls: An experimental investigation. *Developmental Psychology, 20*, 1074–1081.

BURTON, R. V. (1963). The generality of honesty reconsidered. *Psychological Review, 70*, 481–499.

BURTON, R. V. (1984). A paradox in theories and research in moral development. In W. M. Kurtines & J. L. Gewirtz (Eds.), *Morality, moral behavior, and moral development*. New York: Wiley.

CAMPAGNA, A. F., & Harter, S. (1975). Moral judgment in sociopathic and normal children. *Journal of Personality and Social Psychology, 31*, 199–205.

CASEY, W. M., & Burton, R. V. (1982). Training children to be consistently honest through verbal self-instructions. *Child Development, 53*, 911–919.

COLBY, A., & Kohlberg, L. (1984). Invariant sequence and internal consistency in moral judgment stages. In W. M. Kurtines & J. L. Gewirtz (Eds.), *Morality, moral behavior, and moral development*. New York: Wiley.

COLBY, A., Kohlberg, L., Gibbs, J., & Lieberman, M. (1983). A longitudinal study of moral judgment. *Monographs of the Society for Research in Child Development, 48*(Nos. 1–2, Serial No. 200).

DIENSTBIER, R. A., Hillman, D., Lehnhoff, J., Hillman, J., & Valkenaar, M. C. (1975). An emotion-attribution approach to moral behavior: Interfacing cognitive and avoidance theories of moral development. *Psychological Bulletin, 82*, 299–315.

DORR, D., & Fey, S. (1974). Relative power of adult and peer models in the modification of children's moral choice behavior. *Journal of Personality and Social Psychology, 29*, 335–341.

EDWARDS, C. P. (1981). The development of moral reasoning in cross-cultural perspective. In R. H. Munroe, R. L. Munroe, & B. B. Whiting (Eds.), *Handbook of cross-cultural human development*. New York: Garland Press.

ERIKSON, E. H. (1963). *Childhood and society* (2nd ed.). New York: Norton.

FERENCZI, S. (1927). Psychoanalysis of sexual habits. *Further contributions to the theory and technique of psychoanalysis*. London: Hogarth Press.

FISCHER, W. F. (1963). Sharing in pre-school children as a function of the amount and type of reinforcement. *Genetic Psychology Monographs, 68*, 215–245.

FREUD, S. (1960). *A general introduction to psychoanalysis*. New York: Washington Square Press. (Original work published 1935)

GARBARINO, J., & Bronfenbrenner, U. (1976). The socialization of moral judgment and behavior in cross-cultural perspective. In T. Lickona (Ed.), *Moral development and behavior*. New York: Holt, Rinehart and Winston.

GIBBS, J. (1979). Kohlberg's moral stage theory: A Piagetian revision. *Human Development, 22*, 89–112.

GILLIGAN, C. (1977). In a different voice: Women's conceptions of self and morality. *Harvard Educational Review, 47*, 481–517.

GILLIGAN, C. (1982). *In a different voice: Psychological theory and women's development*. Cambridge, MA: Harvard University Press.

GILLIGAN, C., & Murphy, J. M. (1979). Development from adolescence to adulthood: The philosopher and the dilemma of the fact. In D. Kuhn (Ed.), *New directions for child development* (No. 5): *Intellectual development beyond childhood*. San Francisco: Jossey-Bass.

GRUSEC, J. E., & Kuczynski, L. (1980). Direction of effect in socialization: A comparison of the parent's versus the child's behavior as determinants of disciplinary techniques. *Developmental Psychology, 16*, 1–9.

GRUSEC, J. E., Kuczynski, L., Rushton, J. P., & Simutis, Z. (1979). Learning resistance to temptation through observation. *Developmental Psychology, 15*, 233–240.

HARKNESS, S., Edwards, C. P., & Super, C. M. (1981). Social roles and moral reasoning: A case study in a rural African community. *Developmental Psychology, 17*, 595–603.

HARTMANN, H. (1960). *Psychoanalysis and moral values*. New York: International Universities Press.

HARTSHORNE, H., & May, M. S. (1928–1930). *Studies in the nature of character*. Vol. 1: *Studies in deceit*. Vol. 2: *Studies in self-control*. Vol. 3: *Studies in the organization of character*. New York: Macmillan.

HARVEY, S. E., & Liebert, R. M. (1979). Abstraction, interference, and acceptance in children's processing of an adult model's moral judgments. *Developmental Psychology, 15*, 552–558.

HOFFMAN, M. L. (1970). Moral development. In P. H. Mussen (Ed.), *Carmichael's manual of child psychology* (Vol. 2). New York: Wiley.

HOFFMAN, M. L. (1975a). Moral internalization, parental power, and the nature of parent-child interaction. *Developmental Psychology, 11*, 228–239.

HOFFMAN, M. L. (1975b). Sex differences in moral internalization and values. *Journal of Personality and Social Psychology, 32*, 720–729.

HOFFMAN, M. L. (1977). Moral internalization: Current theory and research. In L. Berkowitz (Ed.), *Advances in experimental social psychology* (Vol. 10). Orlando, FL: Academic Press.

HOFFMAN, M. L. (1984). Empathy, its limitations, and its role in a comprehensive moral theory. In W. M. Kurtines & J. L. Gewirtz (Eds.), *Morality, moral behavior, and moral development*. New York: Wiley.

HOLSTEIN, C. (1976). Irreversible, stepwise sequence in the development of moral judgment: A longitudinal study of males and females. *Child Development, 47*, 51–61.

KEASEY, C. B. (1971). Social participation as a factor in the moral development of preadolescents. *Developmental Psychology, 5*, 216–220.

KOHLBERG, L. (1969). Stage and sequence: The cognitive-developmental approach to socialization. In D. A. Goslin (Ed.), *Handbook of socialization theory and research*. Skokie, IL: Rand McNally.

KOHLBERG, L. (1975, June). The cognitive-developmental approach to moral education. *Phi Delta Kappan*, pp. 670–677.

KOHLBERG, L. (1981). *Essays on moral development*. Vol. 1: *The philosophy of moral development*. New York: Harper & Row.

KOHLBERG, L. (1984). *Essays on moral development*. Vol. 2: *The psychology of moral development*. New York: Harper & Row.

KOHLBERG, L., & Candee, D. (1984). The relationship of moral judgment to moral action. In W. M. Kurtines & J. L. Gewirtz (Eds.), *Morality, moral behavior, and moral development*. New York: Wiley.

KOHLBERG, L., & Kramer, R. (1969). Continuities and discontinuities in childhood and adult moral development. *Human Development, 12*, 93–120.

KUCZYNSKI, L. (1983). Reasoning, prohibitions, and motivations for compliance. *Developmental Psychology, 19*, 126–134.

KUCZYNSKI, L. (1984). Socialization goals and mother-child interaction: Strategies for long-term and short-term compliance. *Developmental Psychology, 20*, 1061–1073.

KUHN, D., Kohlberg, L., Langer, J., & Haan, N. (1977). The development of formal operations in logical and moral judgment. *Genetic Psychology Monographs, 95*, 97–188.

LAUPA, M., & Turiel, E. (1986). Children's conceptions of adult and peer authority. *Child Development, 57*, 405–412.

LEMING, J. (1978). Intrapersonal variation in stage of moral reasoning among adolescents as a function of situational context. *Journal of Youth and Adolescence, 7*, 405–416.

LEON, M. (1984). Rules mothers and sons use to integrate intent and damage information in their moral judgments. *Child Development, 55*, 2106–2113.

LICKONA, T. (1976). Research on Piaget's theory of moral development. In T. Lickona (Ed.), *Moral development and behavior*. New York: Holt, Rinehart and Winston.

LIEBERT, R. M. (1979). Moral development: A theoretical and empirical analysis. In G. J. Whitehurst & B. J. Zimmerman (Eds.), *The functions of language and cognition*. Orlando, FL: Academic Press.

MacKINNON, D. W. (1938). Violation of prohibitions. In H. W. Murray (Ed.), *Explorations in personality*. New York: Oxford University Press.

MAGSUD, M. (1979). Resolution of moral dilemmas by Nigerian secondary school pupils. *Journal of Moral Education, 7*, 40–49.

MAITLAND, K. A., & Goldman, J. R. (1974). Moral judgment as a function of peer group interaction. *Journal of Personality and Social Psychology, 30*, 699–704.

McDOUGALL, W. (1908). *An introduction to social psychology*. London: Methuen.

MERCHANT, R. L., & Rebelsky, F. (1972). Effects of participation in rule formation on the moral judgment of children. *Genetic Psychology Monographs, 85*, 287–304.

MISCHEL, H. N., & Mischel, W. (1983). The development of children's knowledge of self-control strategies. *Child Development, 54*, 603–619.

MISCHEL, W. (1974). Processes in the delay of gratification. In L. Berkowitz (Ed.), *Advances in experimental social psychology* (Vol. 7). Orlando, FL: Academic Press.

MISCHEL, W. (1976). *Introduction to personality*. New York: Holt, Rinehart and Winston.

MISCHEL, W., & Patterson, C. J. (1976). Substantive and structural elements of effective plans for self-control. *Journal of Personality and Social Psychology, 34*, 942–950.

MOIR, J. (1974). Egocentrism and the emergence of conventional morality in preadolescent girls. *Child Development, 45*, 299–304.

NELSON, E. A., Grinder, R. E., & Biaggio, A. M. B. (1969). Relationships between behavioral, cognitive-developmental, and self-report measures of morality and personality. *Multivariate Behavioral Research, 4*, 483–500.

NELSON, E. A., Grinder, R. E., & Mutterer, M. L. (1969). Sources of variance in behavioral measures of honesty in temptation situations: Methodological analyses. *Developmental Psychology, 1*, 265–279.

NELSON, S. A. (1980). Factors influencing young children's use of motives and outcomes as moral criteria. *Child Development, 51*, 823–829.

NELSON-LE GALL, S. A. (1985). Motive-outcome matching and outcome foreseeability: Effects on attribution of intentionality and moral judgments. *Developmental Psychology, 21*, 332–337.

NISAN, M., & Kohlberg, L. (1982). Universality and variation in moral judgment: A longitudinal and cross-sectional study in Turkey. *Child Development, 53*, 865–876.

NUCCI, L. P., & Nucci, M. S. (1982). Children's responses to moral and social conventional transgressions in free-play settings. *Child Development, 53*, 1337–1342.

PARIKH, B. (1980). Moral judgment development and its relation to family factors in Indian and American families. *Child Development, 51*, 1030–1039.

PARKE, R. D. (1972). Some effects of punishment on children's behavior. In W. W. Hartup (Ed.), *The young child* (Vol. 2). Washington, DC: National Association for the Education of Young Children.

PARKE, R. D. (1974). Rules, roles, and resistance to deviation: Explorations in punishment, discipline, and self-control. In A. Pick (Ed.), *Minnesota Symposia on Child Psychology* (Vol. 8). Minneapolis: University of Minnesota Press.

PARKE, R. D. (1977). Some effects of punishment on children's behavior—revisited. In E. M. Hetherington & R. D. Parke (Eds.), *Con-temporary readings in child psychology*. New York: McGraw-Hill.

PARPAL, M., & Maccoby, E. E. (1985). Maternal responsiveness and subsequent child compliance. *Child Development, 56*, 1326–1334.

PERRY, D. G., & Parke, R. D. (1975). Punishment and alternative response training as determinants of response inhibition in children. *Genetic Psychology Monographs, 91*, 257–279.

PERRY, D. G., Perry, L. C., Bussey, K., English, D., & Arnold, G. (1980). Processes of attribution and children's self-punishment following misbehavior. *Child Development, 51*, 545–551.

PIAGET, J. (1965). *The moral judgment of the child*. New York: Free Press. (Original work published 1932)

PODD, M. H. (1972). Ego identity status and morality: The relationship between two developmental constructs. *Developmental Psychology, 6*, 497–507.

POWER, T. G., & Chapieski, M. L. (1986). Childrearing and impulse control in toddlers: A naturalistic observation. *Developmental Psychology, 22*, 271–275.

REST, J. R. (1983). Morality. In J. Flavell & E. Markman (Eds.), *Handbook of child psychology* (Vol. 3). New York: Wiley.

REST, J. R., & Thoma, S. J. (1985). Relation of moral development to formal education. *Developmental Psychology, 21*, 709–714.

ROSENKOETTER, L. I. (1973). Resistance to temptation: Inhibitory and disinhibitory effects of models. *Developmental Psychology, 8*, 80–84.

RUSHTON, P. L. (1980). *Altruism, socialization, and society*. Englewood Cliffs, NJ: Prentice-Hall.

SALTZSTEIN, H. D. (1983). Commentary: Critical issues in Kohlberg's theory of moral reasoning. In A. Colby, L. Kohlberg, J. Gibbs, & M. Lieberman, A longitudinal study of moral judgment. *Monographs of the Society for Research in Child Development, 48*, Nos. 1–2(Serial No. 200).

SANTROCK, J. W. (1975). Moral structure: The interrelations of moral behavior, moral judgment, and moral affect. *Journal of Genetic Psychology, 127*, 201–213.

SCHLEIFER, M., & Douglas, V. I. (1973). Effects of training on the moral judgment of young children. *Journal of Personality and Social Psychology, 28*, 62–68.

SEARS, R. R., Maccoby, E. E., & Levin, H. (1957). *Patterns of child rearing*. New York: Harper & Row.

SELMAN, R. L. (1971). The relation of role-taking to the development of moral judgment in children. *Child Development, 42*, 79–91.

SCHULTZ, T. R., Wright, K., & Schleifer, M. (1986). Assignment of moral responsibility and punishment. *Child Development, 57*, 177–184.

SIEGAL, M., & Cowen, J. (1984). Appraisals of intervention: The mother's versus the culprit's behavior as determinants of children's evaluations of discipline techniques. *Child Development, 55*, 1760–1766.

SMETANA, J. G. (1981). Preschool children's conceptions of moral and social rules. *Child Development, 52*, 1333–1336.

SMETANA, J. G. (1985). Preschool children's conceptions of transgressions: Effects of varying moral and conventional domain-related attributes. *Developmental Psychology, 21*, 18–29.

SNAREY, J. R., Reimer, J., & Kohlberg, L. (1985). Development of social-moral reasoning among kibbutz adolescents: A longitudinal cross-cultural study. *Developmental Psychology, 21*, 3–17.

SOBESKY, W. (1983). The effects of situational factors on moral judgments. *Child Development, 54*, 575–584.

SURBER, C. F. (1982). Separable effects of motives, consequences, and presentation order on children's moral judgments. *Developmental Psychology, 18*, 257–266.

TIETJEN, A. M., & Walker, L. J. (1985). Moral reasoning and leadership among men in a Papua New Guinea society. *Developmental Psychology, 21*, 982–992.

TISAK, M. S. (1986). Children's conceptions of parental authority. *Child Development, 57*, 166–176.

TOMLINSON-KEASEY, C., & Keasey, C. B. (1974). The mediating role of cognitive development in moral judgment. *Child Development, 45*, 291–298.

TONER, I. J. (1981). Role involvement and delay maintenance behavior in preschool children. *Journal of Genetic Psychology, 138*, 245–251.

TONER, I. J., Moore, L. P., & Ashley, P. K. (1978). The effect of serving as a model of self-control on subsequent resistance to deviation in children. *Journal of Experimental Child Psychology, 26*, 85–91.

TONER, I. J., Parke, R. D., & Yussen, S. R. (1978). The effect of observation of model behavior on the establishment and stability of resistance to deviation in children. *Journal of Genetic Psychology, 132*, 283–290.

TONER, I. J., & Potts, R. (1981). Effect of modeled rationales on moral behavior, moral choice, and level of moral judgment in children. *Journal of Psychology, 107*, 153–162.

TONER, I. J., & Smith, R. A. (1977). Age and overt verbalization in delay maintenance behavior in children. *Journal of Experimental Child Psychology, 24*, 123–128.

TURIEL, E. (1966). An experimental test of the sequentiality of developmental stages in the child's moral judgments. *Journal of Personality and Social Psychology, 3*, 611–618.

TURIEL, E. (1978). The development of concepts of social structure: Social convention. In J. Glick & A. Clarke-Stewart (Eds.), *The development of social understanding*. New York: Gardner Press.

TURIEL, E. (1983). *The development of social knowledge: Morality and convention*. Cambridge: Cambridge University Press.

TURIEL, E., Edwards, C. P., & Kohlberg, L. (1978). Moral development in Turkish children, adolescents, and young adults. *Journal of Cross-Cultural Psychology, 9*, 75–86.

WALKER, L. J. (1980). Cognitive and perspective-taking prerequisites for moral development. *Child Development, 51*, 131–139.

WALKER, L. J. (1982). The sequentiality of Kohlberg's stages of moral development. *Child Development, 53*, 1330–1336.

WALKER, L. J. (1984). Sex differences in the development of moral reasoning: A critical review. *Child Development, 55*, 677–691.

WALKER, L. J. (1986). Sex differences in the development of moral reasoning: A rejoinder to Baumrind. *Child Development, 57*, 522–526.

WALTERS, R. H., & Parke, R. D. (1964). Influences of response consequences to a social model on resistance to deviation. *Journal of Experimental Child Psychology, 1*, 269–280.

ZAHN-WAXLER, C., Radke-Yarrow, M., & King, R. A. (1979). Child rearing and children's prosocial initiations toward victims of distress. *Child Development, 50*, 319–330.

12

SEX DIFFERENCES AND SEX-ROLE DEVELOPMENT

(continues)

How important is a child's gender to his or her eventual development? The answer seems to be "Very important." Often the first bit of information parents receive about their child is its sex, and the question "Is it a boy or a girl?" is the very first one that most friends and relatives ask when proud new parents telephone to announce the birth of their baby (Intons-Peterson & Reddel, 1984). Indeed, the ramifications of this gender labeling are normally swift in coming and rather direct. In the hospital nursery or delivery room, parents often call an infant son things like "big guy" or "tiger," and they are apt to comment on the vigor of his cries, kicks, or grasps. By contrast, female infants are more likely to be labeled "sugar" or "sweetie" and described as soft, cuddly, and adorable (Maccoby, 1980; MacFarlane, 1977). A newborn infant is usually blessed with a name that reflects his or her sex, and in many Western societies children are immediately adorned in either blue or pink. Mavis Hetherington and Ross Parke (1975, pp. 354–355) describe the predicament of a developmental psychologist who "did not want her observers to know whether they were watching boys or girls":

> Even in the first few days of life some infant girls were brought to the laboratory with pink bows tied to wisps of their hair or taped to their little bald heads. . . . When another attempt at concealment of sex was made by asking mothers to dress their infants in overalls, girls appeared in pink and boys in blue overalls, and "Would you believe overalls with ruffles?"

This gender indoctrination continues during the first year as parents provide their children with "sex-appropriate" clothing, toys, and hairstyles. Moreover, they often play differently with and expect different reactions from their young sons and daughters. Clearly, gender is an important attribute that frequently determines how other people will respond to an infant.

Why do people react differently to males and females—especially *infant* males and females? One explanation centers on the biological differences between the sexes. Recall that fathers determine the gender of their offspring. A zygote that receives an X chromosome from each parent is a genetic (XX) female that will develop into a baby girl, whereas a zygote that receives a Y chromosome from the father is a genetic (XY) male that will normally assume the appearance of a baby boy. Could it be that this basic genetic difference between the sexes is ultimately responsible for *sex differences in behavior*—differences that might explain why parents often do not treat their sons and daughters alike? We will explore this interesting idea in some detail in a later section of the chapter.

However, there is more to sex differences than biological heritage. Virtually all societies expect males and females to behave differently and to assume different roles. In order to conform to these expectations, the child must understand that he is a boy or that she is a girl and must incorporate this information into his or her self-concept. In this chapter we will concentrate on the interesting and controversial topic of *sex typing*—the process by which children acquire not only a gender identity but also the motives, values, and behaviors considered appropriate in their culture for members of their biological sex.

We begin the chapter by summarizing what people generally believe to be true about sex differences in personality and social behavior. As it turns out, some of these stereotypes appear to be reasonably accurate, although many others are best described as fictions or fables that have no basis in fact. We will then look at developmental trends in sex typing and see that youngsters are often well aware of sex-role stereotypes and are displaying sex-typed patterns of behavior long before they are old enough to go to kindergarten. And how do children learn so much about the sexes and sex roles at such an early age? We will address this issue by reviewing several influential theories of sex typing—theories that indicate how biological forces, social experiences, and cognitive development might combine or interact to influence the sex-typing process. Next we will look at sex typing in the nontraditional family and see that factors such as a mother's employment or the absence of a father figure can influence a child's sex-role development. Finally, we will consider a new perspective on sex typing and learn why many theorists now believe that traditional sex roles have outlived their usefulness in the more egalitarian social climate of the 1980s.

CATEGORIZING MALES AND FEMALES: SEX-ROLE STANDARDS

Most of us have learned a great deal about males and females by the time we enter college. In fact, if you and your classmates were asked to jot down ten psychological dimensions on which men and women are thought to differ, it is likely that every member of the class could easily generate such a list. Here's a head start: Which gender is most likely to display emotions? to be tidy? to be competitive? to use harsh language?

A sex-role standard is a value, a motive, or a class of behavior that is considered more appropriate for members of one sex than the other. Taken together, a society's sex-role standards describe how males and females are expected to behave, thereby reflecting the stereotypes by which we categorize and respond to members of each sex.

The female's role as childbearer is largely responsible for the sex-role standards that characterize many societies, including our own. Girls are typically encouraged to assume a nurturant, *expressive role*, for as a wife and mother, the female often takes on the tasks of raising the children she has borne and keeping the family functioning on an even keel. To serve this end, girls are expected to become warm, friendly, cooperative, and sensitive to the needs of others (Parsons, 1955). By contrast, boys are encouraged to adopt an *instrumental* orientation, for as a husband and father, the male faces the tasks of providing for the family and protecting it from harm. Thus, young boys are expected to become dominant, independent, assertive, and competitive—in short, to acquire those attributes that will prepare them to make a living and to serve as intermediaries between the family and society. Roger Brown (1965) describes how this sexual "division of labor" has affected the sex-role stereotypes of American society:

> In the United States, a *real* boy climbs trees, disdains girls, dirties his knees, plays with soldiers, and takes blue for his favorite color. A real girl dresses dolls, jumps rope, plays hopscotch, and takes pink as her favorite color. When they go to school, real girls

PHOTO 12-1 Sex-role socialization begins very early as parents provide their infants and toddlers with "gender-appropriate" clothing, toys, and hairstyles.

like English, music, and "auditorium"; real boys prefer manual training, gym, and arithmetic. In college, the boys smoke pipes, drink beer, and major in engineering or physics; the girls chew gum, drink cokes, and major in fine arts. The real boy matures into a "man's man" who plays poker, goes hunting, drinks brandy, and dies in the war; the real girl becomes a "feminine" woman who loves children, embroiders handkerchiefs, drinks weak tea, and "succumbs" to consumption [p. 161].

Needless to say, these traditional standards of masculinity and femininity have become rather controversial in recent years. At this writing, the Equal Rights Amendment to the United States Constitution is soon to be reintroduced in the U.S. Congress, and advocates of women's rights have fought for and won major legal concessions (such as the Equal Opportunity Employment Act) that allow women more freedom to assume the instrumental role so long enjoyed by American males. But in spite of these important (and long overdue) advances, a homogenization of the sex roles is not likely in the foreseeable future. Several recent studies (see Ruble, 1983; Shaffer & Johnson, 1980; Werner & LaRussa, 1983) indicate that young adults of both sexes still endorse many traditional standards of masculinity and femininity and prefer members of their own and the other sex who conform to these stereotypes. Table 12-1 illustrates the traits and characteristics that U.S. college students and mental health professionals assign to "typical" men and women. Note that most desirable feminine characteristics reflect warmth and emotional expressiveness, whereas the desirable masculine attributes seem to signify a competent or instrumental orientation.

Cross-cultural studies (Best et al., 1977; D'Andrade, 1966) reveal that a large number of societies endorse the sex-role standards and stereotypes shown in Table 12-1. In one rather ambitious project, Her-bert Barry, Margaret Bacon, and Irvin Child (1957) analyzed the sex-typing practices of 110 nonindustrialized societies. Two judges rated each society for sex differences in the socialization of five basic attributes: nurturance, obedience, responsibility, achievement, and self-reliance. The results are summarized in Table 12-2. Note that achievement and self-reliance were more often expected of young boys, while young girls were encouraged to become nurturant, responsible, and obedient. The societies that placed the greatest emphasis on this pattern of sex typing were (1) those in which people live in large, cooperative family units where a division of

TABLE 12-1   Common Stereotypes of Men and Women

Competency cluster (masculine descriptions are considered more desirable)

Feminine descriptions	*Masculine descriptions*
Not at all aggressive	Very aggressive
Not at all independent	Very independent
Does not hide emotions at all	Almost always hides emotions
Very subjective	Very objective
Very submissive	Very dominant
Very passive	Very active
Not competitive	Very competitive
Very home-oriented	Very worldly
Very sneaky	Very direct
Not adventurous	Very adventurous
Has difficulty making decisions	Can make decisions easily
Not at all self-confident	Very self-confident

Warmth-expressive cluster (feminine descriptions are considered more desirable)

Feminine descriptions	*Masculine descriptions*
Doesn't use harsh language	Uses very harsh language
Very tactful	Very blunt
Very gentle	Very rough
Very aware of others' feelings	Not at all aware of others' feelings
Very quiet	Very loud
Very neat	Very sloppy
Very strong need for security	Very little need for security
Enjoys art and literature	Does not enjoy art and literature
Easily expresses tender feelings	Does not easily express tender feelings

PHOTO 12-2 In many societies throughout the world, girls are encouraged to be warm and nurturant.

labor is absolutely necessary and (2) those that depend on strength or physical prowess (for example, in hunting or herding large animals) as a means of obtaining food and earning a living.

Of course, these findings do not necessarily imply that self-reliance in females is frowned on or that disobedience by young males is somehow acceptable; in fact, all five of the attributes that Barry et al. studied are encouraged of *both* boys and girls, but

TABLE 12-2 Sex Differences in the Socialization of Five Attributes

Attribute	Percentage of societies in which socialization pressures were greater for:	
	Boys	*Girls*
Nurturance	0	82
Obedience	3	35
Responsibility	11	61
Achievement	87	3
Self-reliance	85	0

Note: The percentages for each attribute do not add to 100, because some of the societies did not place differential pressures on boys and girls with respect to that particular attribute. For example, 18% of the societies for which pertinent data were available did not differentiate between the sexes in the socialization of nurturance.

with different emphases on different attributes depending on the sex of the child (Zern, 1984). So it appears that the first goal of socialization is to encourage children to acquire those traits that will enable them to become well-behaved, contributing members of society. A second goal (but one that adults apparently view as important nevertheless) is to "sex-type" the child by stressing the importance of group-oriented (or expressive) attributes for females and individualistic (or instrumental) ones for males.

Children in modern industrialized societies also face strong sex-typing pressures, even though most people in these countries neither live in extended families nor depend on hunting and herding skills for their livelihood. Although parents may play a major role in this sex-typing process, they hardly stand alone. As we will see, other significant adults (for example, teachers), peers, and even the television set are important in shaping children's attitudes about the sexes and encouraging them to adopt culturally prescribed sex roles.

SOME FACTS AND FICTIONS ABOUT SEX DIFFERENCES

The old French maxim *"Vive la différence"* reflects a fact that we all know to be true: males and females are anatomically different. Adult males are typically taller, heavier, and more muscular than adult females, while females may be hardier in the sense that they live longer and are less susceptible to many diseases. But although these physical variations are fairly obvious, the evidence for sex differences in psychological functioning is not as clear as most of us might think.

Eleanor Maccoby and Carol Jacklin (1974) have conducted a major review of the literature and concluded that very few of the stereotyped views of men and women are accurate. Maccoby and Jacklin place traditional sex-role standards into the following three basic categories: (1) those that are probably correct, (2) open questions (stereotypes that may be overstated), and (3) those that qualify as "cultural myths" having no basis in fact. Let's begin with the stereotypes that seem to be correct.

SEX DIFFERENCES THAT APPEAR TO BE REAL

After reviewing more than 1500 studies, Maccoby and Jacklin state that only four common sex-role stereotypes are reasonably accurate. First, females seem to have greater *verbal ability* than males. Girls develop verbal skills at an earlier age than boys, although differences between the sexes are very small until adolescence, when female superiority in verbal ability becomes increasingly apparent. However, males outperform females on tests of *visual/spatial ability* (spatial perception; identifying the same figure from different angles) and *arithmetic reasoning*—particularly at subjects such as geometry or trigonometry that depend, in part, on visual/spatial skills. Although sex differences in visual/spatial abilities are detectable throughout the life span (see Linn & Petersen, 1985), males do not begin to outperform females in mathematics until early adolescence (ages 12 to 13). Finally, Maccoby and Jacklin conclude that males are more physically and verbally *aggressive* than females.

Since the publication of Maccoby and Jacklin's influential work, researchers have identified a few additional sex-role stereotypes that seem to be accurate. For example, males are usually found to be more active than females (Eaton & Keats, 1982; Phillips, King, & Dubois, 1978), more willing to take risks (Ginsburg & Miller, 1982), more receptive to bouts of nonaggressive rough-and-tumble play (DiPietro, 1981), and more vulnerable to problems such as reading disabilities, speech defects, emotional disorders, and certain forms of mental retardation (Hutt, 1972; Wittig & Petersen, 1979). From about age 5 onward, girls and women appear to be more interested in and more responsive to infants than boys and men are (Berman, 1985; Berman & Goodman, 1984; Blakemore, 1981). Girls are also less demanding than boys (Martin, 1980) and are more likely to respond playfully to parents' social overtures and to comply with their requests (Gunnar & Donahue, 1980; Hetherington, Cox, & Cox, 1976). After reviewing many of these recent studies, Maccoby (1980) suggests that perhaps there is some truth to the old wives' tale that boys are harder to raise than girls.

However, let's keep in mind that these sex differ-

PHOTO 12-3 Rough-and-tumble play is more common among boys than girls.

ences reflect *group averages* that may or may not characterize the behavior of any particular individual. For example, some males are as interested in infants as the most nurturant of females, and many girls and women are just as mathematically inclined as the best-performing boys and men. So even though one *group* may differ from another on certain attributes, there are many people within a group who do not fit the pattern. Stated another way, it is impossible to predict the aggressiveness, the mathematical skill, or the verbal ability of any individual simply by knowing his or her gender. Only when group averages are computed do the sex differences emerge.

ATTRIBUTES THAT MAY DIFFERENTIATE THE SEXES

The evidence for sex differences on several other social attributes is suggestive at best. As we review these findings, keep in mind that more research will be necessary before we will be able to draw any firm conclusions.

People commonly assume that females are more timid, fearful, anxious, and emotional than males, although the data on these issues are mixed. Observational studies of children who are exposed to a variety of stressful situations usually find no sex differences in timidity or fearful behavior. However, females are more likely than males to *report* feeling timid, anxious, and fearful and tend to characterize their emotional reactions as deeper and more intense than males do (Diener, Sandvik, & Larsen, 1985; Maccoby & Jacklin, 1974). Studies of dominance and competitive behavior often find no sex differences, although males tend to be the more dominant or competitive gender when differences are found. In childhood, girls appear to be more compliant with the demands of parents, teachers, and other authority figures. But girls are no more compliant than boys with the demands and directives of age mates. And although there are data to indicate that 6- to 10-year-old girls are more nurturant than their male counter-

parts (and perhaps more empathic as well), the findings reviewed in Chapter 10 indicate that girls are no more altruistic than boys.

CULTURAL MYTHS

Several popular sex-role stereotypes are best described as unfounded opinions or "cultural myths" that have no basis in fact. Among the most widely accepted of these "myths" are those in Table 12-3.

Why do these inaccuracies persist? Maccoby and Jacklin (1974) propose that

a . . . likely explanation for the perpetuation of "myths" is the fact that stereotypes are such powerful things. An ancient truth is worth restating here: if a

TABLE 12-3   Some Unfounded Beliefs about Sex Differences

Belief	Facts
1. Girls are more "social" than boys.	Research indicates that the two sexes are equally interested in social stimuli, equally responsive to social reinforcement, and equally proficient at learning through the imitation of social models. At certain ages, boys, actually spend more time than girls with playmates.
2. Girls are more "suggestible" than boys.	Most studies of children's conformity find no sex differences. However, some researchers have found that boys are more likely than girls to accept peer-group values that conflict with their own.
3. Girls have lower self-esteem than boys.	The sexes are highly similar in their overall self-satisfaction and self-confidence throughout childhood and adolescence. However, men and women differ in the areas in which they have their greatest self-confidence: girls rate themselves higher in social competence, while boys see themselves as dominant or potent. Thus, males and females apply questionable sex-role stereotypes to themselves.
4. Girls are better at simple repetitive tasks, whereas boys excel at tasks that require higher-level cognitive processing.	The evidence does not support these assertions. Neither sex is superior at rote learning, probability learning, or concept formation.
5. Boys are more "analytic" than girls.	Overall, boys and girls do not differ on tests of analytic cognitive style or logical reasoning, although boys do excel if the task requires visual/spatial abilities.
6. Girls lack achievement motivation.	Under "neutral" conditions girls actually score higher than boys on tests of achievement motivation. Under competitive conditions, the achievement motivation of boys increases to about the level that girls have already attained. Perhaps the myth of lesser achievement motivation for females has persisted because males and females have generally directed their achievement strivings toward different goals.

generalization about a group of people is believed, whenever a member of the group behaves in the expected way the observer notes it and his belief is confirmed and strengthened; when a member of the group behaves in a way that is not consistent with the observer's expectations, the instance is likely to pass unnoticed, and the observer's generalized belief is protected from disconfirmation. We believe that this well-documented [selective attention] process occurs continually in relation to the expected and perceived behavior of males and females, and results in the perpetuation of myths that would otherwise die out under the impact of negative evidence [p. 355].

In other words, sex-role stereotypes are well-ingrained cognitive schemata that we use to interpret (or misinterpret) the behavior of males and females (Martin & Halverson, 1981; see Box 12-1). People even use these schemata to classify the behavior of infants. In one study (Condry & Condry, 1976), college students watched a videotape of a 9-month-old child who was introduced as either a girl ("Dana") or a boy ("David"). As the students observed the child at play, they were asked to interpret his or her reactions to toys such as a teddy bear or a jack-in-the-box. The resulting impressions of the child's behavior clearly depended on his or her presumed sex. For example, a strong reaction to the jack-in-the-box was labeled "anger" when the child was presumed to be a male and "fear" when the child had been introduced as a female. Later research indicates that even 3- to 5-year-olds are using sex-role stereotypes to interpret the play activities of infants described as boys or girls (Haugh, Hoffman, & Cowan, 1980).

As it turns out, the persistence of unfounded or inaccurate sex-role stereotypes has important consequences for both males and females. Some of the more negative implications of these cultural myths are discussed in the following section.

EVALUATING THE ACCOMPLISHMENTS OF MALES AND FEMALES

In 1968 Phillip Goldberg asked female college students to judge the merits of several professional articles that were attributed to a male author ("John McKay") or to a female author ("Joan McKay"). Although these manuscripts were identical in every other respect, subjects perceived the articles osten-sibly written by a male to be of higher quality than those by a female.

This tendency to undervalue the accomplishments of females is apparent even when males and females are asked to explain their *own* successes. Kay Deaux (1977) has reviewed several studies in which males and females have succeeded at *unfamiliar* tasks and finds that "it is far more common for the female to explain her performance on the basis of luck, whether the outcome is a good or a bad one. Males, on the other hand, are much more likely to claim that ability was responsible for their successes" (p. 467).

Even when luck is not a plausible explanation, people are reluctant to attribute a female's accomplishments to her abilities. Consider the following example. Shirley Feldman-Summers and Sara Kiesler (1974) asked subjects to explain the achievements of either a male or a female physician who had established a highly successful practice after years of work. Luck was seldom used to explain the success of either the male or the female physician. But subjects did tend to attribute the male's success to ability and the female's success to effort. In other words, people believe that women must try harder in order to accomplish the same feats as men. This attitude may explain the finding that employers who must choose between equally qualified male and female applicants will frequently offer a more advanced position or a higher starting salary to the male (Forisha & Goldman, 1981; Terborg & Ilgen, 1975).

In Chapter 8, we noted how adults may contribute to these sexist attitudes by encouraging boys and girls to draw different conclusions about their abilities from *equivalent* achievement experiences. For example, parents tend to believe that math and science courses are harder and less enjoyable for daughters than for sons. By attributing their daughters' academic accomplishments to "hard work" and their sons' to "high ability," parents seem to be conveying an impression that girls are less competent than boys (Parsons, Adler, & Kaczala, 1982).

Teachers may also reinforce these sex-typed attitudes if they react differently to the accomplishments of their male and female students. Recall Carol Dweck's finding that elementary school teachers often react to academic successes by praising girls for their perserverance or hard work (that is, high effort)

BOX 12-1   DO SEX STEREOTYPES COLOR CHILDREN'S INTERPRETATIONS OF COUNTERSTEREOTYPIC INFORMATION?

Maccoby and Jacklin (1974) proposed that once people learn sex stereotypes, they are more likely to attend to and remember events that are consistent with these beliefs than events that would disconfirm them. Carol Martin and Charles Halverson (1981) agree. Martin and Halverson argue that gender stereotypes are well-ingrained schemata or naive theories that people use to organize and represent experience. Once established, these gender schemata should have at least two important effects on a child's (or an adult's) cognitive processes: (1) an *organizational* effect on memory, such that information consistent with the schemata will be easier to remember than counterstereotypic events, and (2) a *distortion* effect, such that counterstereotypic information will tend to be remembered as much more consistent with one's gender schemata than the information really is. For example, it should be easier for people to remember that they saw a girl at the stove cooking (sex-consistent information) than a boy partaking in the same activity (sex-inconsistent information). And if people were to witness the latter event, they might distort what they had seen to make it more consistent with their stereotypes—perhaps by remembering the actor as a girl rather than a boy or by reconstruing the boy's activities as *fixing* the stove rather than cooking.

Martin and Halverson (1983) tested their hypotheses in an interesting study with 5- to 6-year-olds. During a first session, each child was shown 16 pictures, half of which depicted a child performing *gender-consistent* activities (for example, a boy playing with a truck) and half showing children displaying *gender-inconsistent* behaviors (for example, a girl chopping wood). One week later, children's memory for what they had seen was assessed. The children were first asked whether they had seen each of the activities (for example, chopping wood) that had been presented in the first session (other activities that they hadn't seen were also mentioned as a way of determining whether children were merely guessing or were likely to say "Yes, I saw it" when asked about any activity). Then children were asked whether the person who had performed each of the recalled activities was a male or a female and to state how confident they were ("not sure at all," "fairly sure," "pretty sure," or "very sure") about the actor's sex.

The results of the experiment were indeed interesting. Children easily recalled the sex of the actor for scenes in which actors had performed gender-consistent activities. But when the actor's behavior was gender-inconsistent, these youngsters often distorted the scene by saying that the actor's sex was consistent with the activity they recalled (for example, they were apt to say that it had been a boy rather than a girl who had chopped wood). As predicted, children's *confidence* about the sex of the actors was greater for gender-consistent scenes than for gender-inconsistent ones, suggesting that counterstereotypic information is harder to remember. But it was interesting to note that, when children distorted a gender-inconsistent scene, they were just as confident about the sex of the actor (which, of course, they had recalled incorrectly) as they were for the gender-consistent scenes in which they had correctly re-called the actor's sex. So it appears that children are likely to distort counterstereotypic information to be more consistent with their stereotypes and that these memory distortions are as "real" to them as stereotypical information that has not been distorted (see Cann & Newbern, 1984, for a similar set of results with 6- to 8-year-olds).

Why, then, do inaccurate sex stereotypes persist? Because we find disconfirming evidence harder to recall and, in fact, will often distort that information in ways that will confirm our initial (and inaccurate) beliefs.

and boys for their problem-solving strategies (that is, high ability). By contrast, teachers are more inclined to attribute failures to poor problem-solving strategies (that is, low ability) when criticizing their female students (Dweck & Elliott, 1983). Moreover, Jacquelynne Parsons and her associates (Parsons, Kaczala, & Meese, 1982) found that some elementary school teachers are more likely to praise girls whom they expect to do poorly than girls whom they expect to do well. But just the opposite is true for boys, who are likely to receive more praise when the teacher expects them to achieve. So the praise received by female students may not reflect the teacher's true expectations about their future academic accomplishments. Perhaps you can see how a star female student who is rarely praised for her achievements might eventually conclude that she must lack ability or that academic success is not very important for girls, particularly when both the star male students and her less competent female classmates receive far more praise from the teacher than she does.

Will the picture become brighter for females as they become increasingly prominent in business and the professions? Almost certainly, although the prospects of immediate change are not terribly encouraging. In one interesting experiment, John Touhey (1974) asked males and females to rate the prestige and desirability of five high-status occupations—architect, professor, lawyer, physician, and scientist—after receiving information that the proportion of women entering these fields was either increasing or unchanged. Both male and female subjects rated these professions *lower* in prestige when they were led to believe that the proportion of women practitioners was increasing. The implication is clear: when women are likely to make significant contributions to a high-status profession, people tend to reassess the value of these contributions (or the value of the profession) rather than the competencies of women. Sex-role stereotypes are very powerful indeed.

When do children first begin to think that males are more competent than females? Very early, or so it seems. Susan Haugh and her colleagues (1980) asked 3- and 5-year-olds to watch two infants on film, one of whom was presumed to be a male. When told to point to the baby who was "smart," these preschool children typically chose whichever infant had been labeled the boy. Nick Pollis and Donald Doyle (1972) found that first-grade boys were judged by their male and female classmates to be more competent at a number of unfamiliar tasks and more worthy of leadership roles than first-grade girls. Finally, Claire Etaugh and Barry Brown (1975) asked 10-, 13-, 16-, and 18-year-olds to explain the performance of a male or a female who had either succeeded or failed at some mechanical tasks. The female's success at mechanics was attributed to her untiring efforts to succeed, while the male's success was attributed to his mechanical abilities. However, failure at mechanics was more likely to be attributed to a definite *lack of ability* when the person who had failed was a female. There were no age or "sex of subjects"

effects in these studies. So it appears that the tendency to underestimate the abilities and accomplishments of females is well established in both boys and girls by the age of 6 to 10 and possibly much sooner.

DEVELOPMENTAL TRENDS IN SEX TYPING

Sex-typing research has traditionally focused on three separate but interrelated topics: (1) the development of *gender identity*, or the knowledge that one is either a boy or a girl and that gender is an unchanging attribute, (2) the development of *sex-role stereotypes*, or ideas about what males and females are supposed to be like, and (3) the development of *sex-typed* patterns of *behavior*—that is, the child's tendency to favor same-sex activities over those usually associated with the other sex. Let's look first at the child's understanding of gender and its implications.

DEVELOPMENT OF THE GENDER CONCEPT

Children initially discriminate "maleness" from "femaleness" on the basis of clothing and hairstyles rather than body types and other morphological characteristics (Katcher, 1955; Thompson & Bentler, 1971). Spencer Thompson (1975) found that some 2-year-olds can readily identify the sex of people shown in pictures, even if the females are wearing short hair or pants. However, these toddlers are often uncertain about their own gender identities. By age 2½ to 3, almost all children can accurately label themselves as either boys or girls, although they have not yet developed a sense of *gender constancy*—a form of conservation in which they recognize that biological sex is unchanging. Indeed, it is not at all uncommon for 3- to 5-year-olds to think that boys can become mommies and girls daddies or that a person who alters his or her appearance (by changing hairstyle and clothing) has become a member of the other sex (Marcus & Overton, 1978; Slaby & Frey, 1975). Children normally begin to conserve gender between the ages of 5 and 7, precisely the time that they are beginning to conserve physical quantities such as liquids and mass (Marcus & Overton, 1978). Apparently 5- to 7-year-olds will apply gender constancy to themselves before they recognize that the gender of other people is invariant (Gouze & Nadelman, 1980). The sequence that youngsters seem to follow is (1) gender constancy for self, (2) gender constancy for same-sex others, (3) gender constancy for members of the other sex (Eaton & Von Bargen, 1981).

ACQUIRING SEX-ROLE STEREOTYPES

Remarkable as it may seem, toddlers begin to acquire sex-role stereotypes at roughly the same time as or shortly after they first become aware of their gender identities (see Huston, 1983; Weinraub et al., 1984). Deanna Kuhn and her associates (Kuhn, Nash, & Brucken, 1978) showed a male doll ("Michael") and a female doll ("Lisa") to 2½–3½-year-olds and then asked each child which of the two dolls would engage in sex-stereotyped activities such as cooking, sewing, playing with dolls, trucks, or trains, talking a lot, giving kisses, fighting, and climbing trees. Almost all the 2½-year-olds had some knowledge of sex-role stereotypes. For example, boys and girls agreed that girls talk a lot, never hit, often need help, like to play with dolls, and like to help their mothers with chores such as cooking and cleaning. By contrast, these young children felt that boys like to play with cars, like to help their fathers, like to build things, and are apt to make statements such as "I can hit you." Children who knew the most about sex-role stereotypes were the older ones (that is, 3½-year-olds), particularly those who had some idea that gender is a stable attribute.

Over the next several years, children learn much more about the behavior of males and females and eventually begin to differentiate the sexes on *psychological* dimensions. In a well-known cross-cultural study, Deborah Best and her colleagues (1977) found that fourth- and fifth-graders in England, Ireland, and the United States generally agree that women are weak, emotional, soft-hearted, sophisticated, and affectionate, while men are ambitious, assertive, aggressive, dominating, and cruel. However, the stereotypes held by older grade school children are far more flexible than those of their younger counterparts. For example, a 7-year-old might say that carpentry is a masculine occupation that is not appropriate for a woman, while an 11- to 13-year-old is more likely to argue that females can and perhaps should pursue a "masculine" occupation such as carpentry if they really want to (Carter & Patterson, 1982; Meyer, 1980).

DEVELOPMENT OF SEX-TYPED BEHAVIOR

The most common method of assessing the "sex appropriateness" of children's behavior is to observe whom and what they like to play with. Sex differences in toy preferences develop very early—even before the child has established a clear gender identity or can correctly label various toys as "boy things" or "girl things" (Blakemore, LaRue, & Olejnik, 1979; Fagot, Leinbach, & Hagan, 1986; Weinraub et al., 1984). Boys aged 14 to 22 months usually prefer trucks and cars to other objects, while girls of this age would rather play with dolls and soft toys (Smith & Daglish, 1977). By the time children enter nursery school, they generally play at sex-typed or gender-neutral activities, and they have often segregated into male and female play groups (Hartup, 1983).

Apparently children's preferences for same-sex playmates also develop very early. In the nursery school setting, 2-year-old girls already prefer to play with other girls rather than with their more boisterous male classmates (La Freniere, Strayer, & Gauthier, 1984), and by age 3, boys are reliably selecting boys rather than girls as companions (Charlesworth & Hartup, 1967). Might these same-sex affiliative preferences reflect a basic incompatibility in the play behaviors of young boys and girls? To find out, Jacklin and Maccoby (1978) dressed pairs of 33-month-old toddlers in gender-neutral clothing (T-shirts and pants) and placed them together in a laboratory playroom that contained several interesting toys. Some of these dyads were same-sex pairs (two boys or two girls), and others were mixed-sex pairs (a boy and a girl). As the children played, an adult observer recorded the frequency with which they engaged in solitary activities and in socially directed play. As we see in Figure 12-1, social play varied as a function of

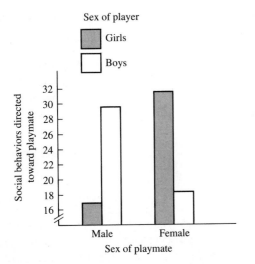

Sex of player

■ Girls

□ Boys

FIGURE 12-1 Do toddlers prefer playmates of their own sex? Apparently so, for boys are much more sociable with boys than with girls, whereas girls are more outgoing with girls than with boys.

the sex of one's playmate: boys directed more social responses to boys than to girls, while girls were more sociable with girls than with boys. In the same-sex dyads, interactions between playmates were lively and basically positive in character. By contrast, girls tended to withdraw from boys in the mixed-sex dyads, while boys continued playing on their own. Jacklin and Maccoby suggested that there is something about boys' behavior that may scare other children and cause girls to shy away from them. Of course, an alternative interpretation for these results is that 2- to 3-year-old boys and girls have already developed interests in different kinds of toys and games and, as a result, will respond more positively to same-sex companions, who are likely to share those interests.

Sex Differences in Sex-Typed Behavior

Many cultures, including our own, assign greater status to the male role (D'Andrade, 1966; Rosenblatt & Cunningham, 1976), and boys face stronger pressures than girls to adhere to sex-appropriate codes of conduct. Consider that fathers of baby girls are generally willing to offer a truck to their 12-month-old daughters, while fathers of baby boys are likely to

withhold dolls from their sons (Snow, Jacklin, & Maccoby, 1983). Moreover, parents of 2- to 9-year-olds (particularly fathers) express more concern about their child's cross-sex play activities if the child is a male (Fagot, 1978; Langlois & Downs, 1980; Tauber, 1979b), and they perceive a wider range of behaviors as appropriate for girls than for boys (Fagot, 1978). Perhaps it can be argued that we live in a male-oriented society where "tomboys" are at least tolerated while "sissies" are ridiculed and rejected. In other words, the male role is more clearly defined than the female role, and boys, who face stronger sex-typing pressures than girls, will soon learn what is or is not expected of them as they are criticized for deviating from approved sex-role standards. Walter Emmerich (1959) has suggested that the major accomplishment for young girls is to learn how not to be babies, while young boys must learn how not to be girls.

Indeed, males are quicker than females to adopt sex-typed preferences and patterns of behavior. Judith Blakemore and her associates (Blakemore et al., 1979) found that 2-year-old boys already favor sex-appropriate toys while 2-year-old girls do not. Even at age 3, many girls will not prefer feminine to masculine toys unless they are first reminded that the feminine toys are more "appropriate" for them (Blakemore et al., 1979). Finally, 3- to 4-year-old boys are more likely than 3- to 4-year-old girls to say that they dislike opposite-sex toys (Eisenberg, Murray, & Hite, 1982).

Between the ages of 4 and 10, both males and females are becoming more aware of what is expected of them and conforming to these cultural prescriptions (Huston, 1983). However, girls are more likely than boys to retain an interest in cross-sex toys, games, and activities. For example, John Richardson and Carl Simpson (1982) recorded the toy preferences of 750 children aged 5 to 9 years as expressed in their letters to Santa Claus. Although their requests were clearly sex-typed, we see in Table 12-4 that more girls than boys asked for "opposite sex" items. With respect to their actual sex-role preferences, young girls often wish they were boys, but it is unusual for a boy to wish he were a girl (Brown, 1957; Nash, 1975).

There are probably several reasons that girls are drawn to male activities and the masculine role during middle childhood. For one thing, they are becoming increasingly aware that masculine behavior is more highly valued, and perhaps it is only natural that girls would want to be what is "best" (or at least something other than a second-class citizen). And as we have noted, girls are much freer than boys to engage in cross-sex pursuits. Finally, it is conceivable that fast-moving masculine games and "action" toys are simply more interesting than the playthings and pastimes (dolls, dollhouses, dish sets, cleaning and caretaking activities) often imposed on girls to encourage their adoption of a nurturant, expressive orientation. Consider the reaction of Gina, a 5-year-old who literally squealed with delight when she received an "action garage" (complete with lube racks, gas pumps, cars, tools, and spare parts) from Santa one Christmas. At the unveiling of this treasure, Gina and her three female cousins (aged 3, 5, and 7) immediately ignored their dolls, dollhouses, and other unopened gifts to cluster around and play with this unusual and intriguing toy.

"Please don't bring me anything that requires my acting out traditional female roles!"

BERRY'S WORLD, REPRINTED BY PERMISSION OF NEWSPAPER ENTERPRISE ASSOCIATION, INC.

TABLE 12-4 Percentages of Boys and Girls Who Requested Popular "Masculine" and "Feminine" Items from Santa Claus

	Percentage of boys requesting	Percentage of girls requesting
Masculine items		
Vehicles	43.5	8.2
Sports equipment	25.1	15.1
Spatial-temporal toys (construction sets, clocks, and so on)	24.5	15.6
Race cars	23.4	5.1
Real vehicles (tricycles, bikes, motorbikes)	15.3	9.7
Feminine items		
Dolls (adult female)	.6	27.4
Dolls (babies)	.6	23.4
Domestic accessories	1.7	21.7
Dollhouses	1.9	16.1
Stuffed animals	5.0	5.4

In spite of their earlier interest in masculine activities, most girls come to prefer the feminine role as they reach puberty, become preoccupied with their changing body images, and face strong pressures to be more "ladylike" (Brown, 1957; Kagan & Moss, 1962).

Social-Class Differences in Sex Typing

Patterns of sex typing differ somewhat for children from the lower and the middle classes. In 1950 Meyer Rabban found that youngsters from lower-class backgrounds were more likely than middle-class age mates to prefer sex-appropriate toys and activities. Lower-class boys indicated a strong preference for masculine activities by age 4 or 5. Lower-class girls and middle-class boys were firmly sex-typed by age 7. However, middle-class girls did not clearly prefer feminine pastimes until age 9. These class differences in sex typing are still apparent today. In both England and the United States, children from the lower socioeconomic strata usually show stronger preferences for sex-typed behaviors and hold a more stereotyped view of males and females than middle-class children (Angrist, Mickelson, & Penna, 1977; Morgan, 1982; Nadelman, 1970, 1974).

There may be several factors contributing to social-class differences in sex typing. For example, we know that parents from the lower socioeconomic strata are more likely than middle-class parents to accept traditional, nonegalitarian sex-role standards (Meyer, 1980; Thompson, 1975) and to stress different achievement goals for their sons and daughters (Barnett, 1979). Moreover, working-class and middle-class parents may serve as very different kinds of models for their children. Many working-class fathers are employed as heavy laborers, mechanics, or construction workers—occupations that are generally regarded as highly masculine. By contrast, middle-class fathers are often employed at white-collar jobs that may not be perceived as exclusively masculine, and they are more likely than lower-class fathers to take part in "feminine" activities such as housekeeping and child care. Although a large percentage of women from each social class have entered the labor force, mothers from the lower socioeconomic strata tend to work at traditionally feminine jobs such as waitressing or clerking, while middle-class mothers may work at occupations such as business, law, and medicine that are not exclusively feminine. In sum, it appears that many children from working-class backgrounds are more firmly sex-typed than those from the middle class because their parents are more likely than middle-class parents to *encourage* and to *display* sex-typed patterns of behavior.

Stability of Sex-Typed Behaviors

Are highly sex-typed children likely to become highly sex-typed adults? The Fels longitudinal project attempted to answer this question by measuring the stability of several types of behavior in a group of middle-class children who were studied from birth to early adulthood (Kagan & Moss, 1962). Seven classes of behavior were examined: passivity, dependence, behavior disorganization (for example, angry outbursts, aggression), heterosexual activity, spontaneity, achievement, and sex-typed activities (for example, interest in mechanics for boys and cooking for girls). Figure 12-2 summarizes the rela-

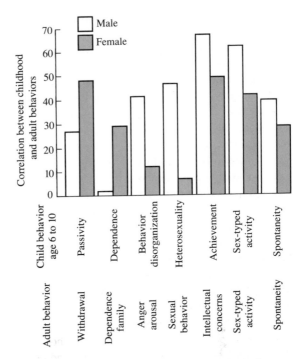

FIGURE 12-2 Stability of seven classes of behavior between childhood and early adulthood

tionships between childhood and adult measures for each of these attributes. In examining the figure, we see that certain behaviors—namely, achievement, sex-typed activity, and spontaneity—were found to be reasonably stable over time for members of each sex. By contrast, aggression and heterosexual activities were stable for males but not for females, whereas passivity and dependence were much more stable for females than males.

How can we account for this pattern of results? Kagan and Moss (1962) suggest that a particular class of behavior will remain stable over time if these actions are consistent with culturally prescribed sex roles. In the United States, achievement and sex-typed activities are encouraged in both boys and girls, so that these attributes should remain stable over time for members of each sex. However, aggression and the initiation of heterosexual activities are generally considered more appropriate for (or characteristic of) males, and these attributes were stable only for males. Finally, passivity and dependence, which many people think of as "feminine" attributes, were stable for females but not for males. So it appears that childhood behaviors that match traditional sex-role standards are encouraged and will remain stable over time, while behaviors that conflict with these cultural prescriptions are apt to be discouraged and will not predict similar behaviors in adulthood.

Although highly sex-typed 6- to 10-year-olds often become highly sex-typed adults, an adult's sex-role behavior is hardly "set in stone." Recently, investigators have been finding that the birth of a baby heralds a change in sex roles: fathers become more concerned about their breadwinner (instrumental) function, whereas mothers become more nurturant and "expressive" (Cowan & Cowan, 1987). And as adults reach middle age (and beyond), sex roles continue to evolve: males now become more compassionate and expressive and females more autonomous (Feldman, Biringen, & Nash, 1981). So we see that sex typing is really a continuous process and that an adult's enactment of traditional sex-role behaviors may depend more on the utility of these responses at any given point in time than on any overriding personal desire to be "masculine" or "feminine."

THEORIES OF SEX TYPING AND SEX-ROLE DEVELOPMENT

Several theories have been proposed to account for sex differences and the development of sex roles. On the one hand, theorists who stress biological processes suggest that genetic, anatomical, and hormonal variations between the sexes are largely responsible for sex-linked behavioral differences, which, in turn, will predispose males and females to adopt gender-consistent sex roles. On the other hand, many developmentalists believe that *social* factors are crucial in determining both sex differences in behavior and the outcomes of the sex-typing process. Historically, the most influential of these "social" theories have been Freud's psychoanalytical model, social-learning theory, Kohlberg's cognitive-developmental theory, and (more recently) Martin and Halverson's gender schema (or social information-processing)

theory. In this section of the chapter, we will briefly review these approaches and discuss the strengths and weaknesses of each.

THE BIOLOGICAL APPROACH

From a biological perspective, males and females differ in five important respects:

1. *Sex chromosomes*—XY for males, XX for females.
2. *Hormonal balance*—for example, males higher in androgen; females higher in estrogen.
3. *Composition of gonads*—testicular tissue for males; ovarian tissue for females.
4. *Internal reproductive system*—testes, seminal vesicles, and prostate for males; vagina, uterus, ovaries, and fallopian tubes for females.
5. *External genitalia*—penis and scrotum for males; labia and clitoris for females.

How do these physical variations affect sex typing? Some theorists have argued that genetic and hormonal differences between the sexes are responsible for several sex-linked characteristics that are apparent at birth or shortly thereafter. For example, female infants are said to be hardier, to mature faster, to talk sooner, and to be more sensitive to pain than male infants, while males tend to be larger and more muscular, to sleep less, to cry more, and to be somewhat more active, more irritable, and harder to comfort than female infants (see Bell, Weller, & Waldrip, 1971; Hutt, 1972; Maccoby, 1980; Moss, 1967). If these sex differences are constitutionally based, it might seem that males and females are biologically programmed for certain activities that are congruent with the masculine or the feminine role. Could boys, for example, be predisposed toward activities such as aggression, assertiveness, and rough-and-tumble play by virtue of their higher pain thresholds, heightened activity, irritable or demanding dispositions, and muscular physiques? Could docile, undemanding, and highly verbal females be ideally suited for adoption of a nurturant, cooperative, expressive orientation?

People often assume that most sex differences are biologically determined, since biology is responsible for some (namely, the five physical characteristics listed above). A more likely possibility is that sex-linked constitutional factors *interact* with environmental events to produce sex-typed patterns of behavior (Huston, 1983). In Chapter 9, for example, we noted that parents may play more vigorously with active, muscular sons than with docile, less muscular daughters. Or perhaps they become more impatient with irritable and demanding sons who are difficult to quiet or comfort. In the first case, adults would be encouraging young boys to partake in the kinds of fast-paced, vigorous activities from which aggressive outbursts may emerge. In the second case, a parent's irritability with an agitated son could have the effect of making the child hostile or resentful toward the parent. So sex differences in aggression or any other form of sex-typed behavior may not be automatic, or "biologically programmed." Indeed, it appears that the child's biological predispositions are likely to affect the behavior of caregivers and other close companions, which, in turn, will elicit certain reactions from the child and influence the activities and interests that the child is likely to display. The implication of this interactive model is that biological factors and social influences are completely intertwined and that both nature and nurture are important contributors to a child's sex-role development.

In the pages that follow, we will first consider some of the biological factors that contribute to sex differences and sex-typed patterns of behavior. Then we will take a look at the research suggesting that biology is not destiny.

Chromosomal Differences between the Sexes

Corinne Hutt (1972) believes that genetic differences between the sexes may account for the finding that boys are more vulnerable to problems such as reading disabilities, speech defects, various emotional disorders, and certain forms of mental retardation. Since genetic (XY) males have but one X chromosome, they are necessarily more susceptible to any X-linked recessive disorder for which their mother is a carrier (genetic [XX] females would have to inherit a recessive gene from each parent to have the same disorder). And since males have more genetic information (by virtue of having some genes that appear only on a Y chromosome), they show a wider variety of attributes, including some negative ones.

Although it was once thought that gender variations in visual/spatial and verbal skills might be directly attributable to genetic (or chromosomal) differences between the sexes, recent reviews of the behavior genetics literature provide little support for this point of view (see Huston, 1983; Linn & Petersen, 1985). Nevertheless, Hutt's chromosomal hypothesis should be investigated further, for psychological theories of sex typing cannot easily explain why males face greater risks of developmental disorders than females do.

Hormonal Influences

Hormones are powerful chemicals that play an important role in the development of bodily structures, the regulation of growth, and the functioning of organ systems. During the prenatal period,[1] hormones trigger the development of the genitals and other organs and may have an effect on the organization and functioning of the central nervous system, most notably the brain (see Hines, 1982; Hoyenga & Hoyenga, 1979). Male hormones such as androgen and female hormones such as estrogen and progesterone are present in different concentrations in both males and females—in other words, they are biological *correlates* of gender and gender differences. But to what extent do they influence sex typing or *cause* sex differences in behavior?

Some sex differences are at least partly attributable to the uneven distribution of sex hormones between males and females. The clearest evidence comes from animal studies which reveal that changes in a developing organism's hormonal balance are likely to have both anatomical and behavioral effects. For example, one team of investigators injected pregnant rhesus monkeys with the male hormone testosterone and noted that the female offspring showed malelike external genitalia and a pattern of social behaviors that is normally more characteristic of males (Young, Goy, & Phoenix, 1964). These masculinized females often threatened other monkeys, engaged in rough-and-tumble play, and would try to "mount" a partner as males do at the beginning of a sexual encounter.

Frank Beach (1965) reports that female rat pups that received testosterone injections in the first three days of life frequently displayed masculine sexual responses such as "mounting" as adults. The reverse was true for males. That is, castrated pups, which could not produce testosterone, exhibited feminine sexual characteristics such as receptive posturing as adults. Similar cross-sex mating behaviors occur among female hamsters that receive injections of the male hormone androgen as infants (Doty, Carter, & Clemens, 1971).

Although the evidence is limited, it appears that human beings may be subject to the same kinds of hormonal influences. For example, a small percentage of males are affected by a genetic anomaly called *testicular feminization syndrome*. A male fetus who inherits this trait is insensitive to the male hormone androgen and will develop external genitalia that resemble those of a female.

John Money and his associates (Ehrhardt & Baker, 1974; Money, 1965; Money & Ehrhardt, 1972) call our attention to the reverse effect in females. Occasionally a female fetus will be exposed to much higher than normal levels of androgen, owing either to a glandular malfunction of her own or to androgen-like drugs that were once prescribed for pregnant women to prevent miscarriage. This overexposure to androgen has the effect of masculinizing female fetuses: if it occurs during the period when the genitals are developing, a genetic (XX) female will be born with a female internal reproductive system and external organs that resemble those of a male (for example, a large clitoris that looks like a penis and fused labial folds that resemble a scrotum).

Money and Ehrhardt (1972; Ehrhardt & Baker, 1974) have followed several of these *androgenized females* whose external organs were surgically altered and who were then raised as girls. Compared with their sisters and other female age mates, many of the androgenized girls were little tomboys who preferred to dress in slacks and shorts, showed almost no interest in jewelry and cosmetics, and clearly favored vigorous athletic activities (and male playmates) over traditionally feminine pastimes. Moreover, their attitudes toward sexuality and achievement were similar to those of males. They expressed some interest in

marriage and motherhood but thought in terms of a late marriage with few children—events that should be delayed until they had established themselves in a career (they were clearly heterosexual, however, choosing males as sex partners in real life and in their fantasies). Although it could be argued that other family members had reacted to the girls' abnormal genitalia and treated them more like boys, interviews with the girls' parents suggested that they had not (Ehrhardt & Baker, 1974). So we must seriously consider the possibility that prenatal exposure to male hormones affects the attitudes, interests, and activities of human females.[2]

Sex differences in aggression appear so early (about age 2) in so many cultures that it is difficult to attribute them solely to parental child-rearing practices (Maccoby & Jacklin, 1980). It has been suggested that males are more aggressive than females because of their higher levels of androgen and testosterone—activating male sex hormones that are thought to promote aggressive behavior. Indeed, Dan Olweus and his associates (Olweus, Mattsson, Schalling, & Low, 1980) found that 16-year-old boys who label themselves as physically and verbally aggressive do have higher testosterone levels than boys who view themselves as nonaggressive. And in their study of androgenized females, Ehrhardt and Baker (1974) report that, in the majority of families, it was the androgenized sibling who started fights with her nonandrogenized sister, rather than the other way around. However, we must be cautious in interpreting these findings, for a person's hormone level may depend on his or her experiences. For example, Irwin Bernstein and his associates (Rose, Bernstein, & Gordon, 1975) found that the testosterone levels of male rhesus monkeys rose after they had won a fight and fell after they had been defeated. So it appears that higher concentrations of the male sex hormones may be either a cause or an effect of aggressive behavior (Maccoby & Jacklin, 1980).

The "Timing of Puberty" Effect

In recent years, investigators have found a relationship between the timing of puberty and children's performance on tests of visual/spatial abilities: both males and females who mature late perform better on spatial tests than those who mature early (Meyer-Bahlberg et al., 1985; Sanders & Soares, 1986; Waber, 1977). Since boys reach puberty some two years later than girls, this "timing of puberty" effect may help to explain why males outperform females on tests of spatial reasoning.

Why should the timing of puberty affect spatial abilities? A knowledge of the organization of the brain and brain functions may provide some clues. The highest brain center, or cerebrum, consists of a left and a right hemisphere, each of which serves different functions and becomes increasingly specialized (or lateralized) until puberty. Thus, one explanation for the "timing of puberty" effect is that the lateralization of spatial functions in the right cerebral hemisphere will continue until the onset of puberty, so that those who mature early will be less specialized for spatial abilities than those who mature late (Waber, 1977). Although this is an interesting (and highly controversial) idea, the available evidence is far too limited to allow any firm conclusions.

Why Biology Is Not Destiny

Even though biological factors may predispose males and females toward different patterns of behavior, many developmentalists believe that these "forces of nature" can be modified by social experience. There are at least three lines of evidence to support this contention: John Money's work with androgenized females, Margaret Mead's cross-cultural studies of sex typing, and Nora Newcombe's recent research on the "timing of puberty" effect.

Recall that Money's androgenized females were born with the internal reproductive organs of a normal female even though their external genitalia resembled a penis and scrotum. These children are sometimes labeled boys at birth and raised as such until their abnormalities are detected. Money (1965; Money & Ehrhardt, 1972) reports that the discovery and correction of this condition (by surgery and gender reassignment) presented few if any adjustment problems for the child, provided that the sex change took place *before the age of 18 months*. But after age 3, sexual reassignment was exceedingly difficult because these genetic females had experienced prolonged masculine sex typing and had already labeled

themselves as boys. These data led Money to conclude that there is a "critical period" between 18 months and 3 years of age for the establishment of gender identity. It is probably more accurate to call the first three years a *sensitive* period, for at least one group of West Indian males who had been raised from birth as females were able to accept a masculine identity at *puberty*, once their bodies assumed a more malelike appearance (Imperato-McGinley, Peterson, Gautier, & Sturla, 1979). Nevertheless, Money's findings (see also Box 12-2) indicate that social labels and sex-role socialization play a prominent and perhaps crucial role in determining a child's sex-role preferences and behaviors.

Margaret Mead's (1935) observations of three primitive tribes lead to the same conclusion. Mead noted that both males and females of the Arapesh tribe were taught to be cooperative, nonaggressive, and sensitive to the needs of others. This behavioral profile would be considered "expressive" or "feminine" in most Western cultures. By contrast, both men and women of the Mundugumor tribe were expected to be hostile, aggressive, and emotionally unresponsive in their interpersonal relationships—a masculine pattern of behavior by Western standards. Finally, the Tchambuli displayed a pattern of sex-role development opposite to that of Western societies: males were passive, emotionally dependent, and socially sensitive, whereas females were dominant, independent, and aggressive. In sum, members of these three tribes developed in accordance with the sex roles prescribed by their culture—even when these roles were quite inconsistent with sex-linked biological predispositions.

Nora Newcombe and Mary Bandura (1983) have recently found a "timing of puberty" effect for 11- and 12-year-old girls: those who mature late perform better on tests of spatial abilities than those who mature early. But in this study, measures of hemispheric lateralization of the brain were *unrelated* to either the timing of puberty or spatial performance. The factors that did predict the spatial abilities of these normal, nonandrogenized females were (1) timing of puberty, of course (a biological variable), and (2) measures of the girls' desire to be boys and their interest in masculine activities—interests that

BOX 12-2   A CASE STUDY IN SEXUAL REASSIGNMENT

The impact of socialization on sex-role development is readily apparent in a case study reported by Money and Tucker (1975). The patient was a male identical twin whose penis was damaged beyond repair during circumcision. After seeking medical advice and considering the alternatives, the parents subjected their 21-month-old child to a surgical procedure designed to make him female.

After the operation, the child's mother began to actively sex-type her new daughter by changing the child's hairstyle and dressing her in pink slacks, frilly blouses, dresses, and the like. The child soon learned many sex-appropriate attitudes and behaviors such as aspiring to motherhood and sitting to urinate, and within a year or two people could easily determine which of the identical twins was female. By age 5, the girl had developed strong preferences for feminine toys, activities, and apparel. Unlike her brother, she was neat and dainty. If similar cases of early gender reassignment provide any guidelines, this young girl will retain her preference for feminine interests and activities and will lead a reasonably satisfying life as a female.

The implications are obvious. Here is a circumstance in which a *normal* genetic male was sexually reassigned and socialized into the feminine role. The male twin was very dissimilar in his sex-role orientation, preference, and pattern of sex-typed behaviors, even though his genetic constitution was identical to that of his sister. Thus, biology alone does not determine the course of sex typing. Assigned sex and sex-role socialization are important factors that in this case overcame biological predispositions.

---

appear to be *socially* transmitted. Finally, timing of puberty itself was not related to the girls' preferences for the male role or masculine activities. The investigators concluded that

> the sexes differ not only in timing of puberty but also in possession of masculine personality traits and interests. . . . Since timing of puberty and [measures of masculine interest] were found to be independently related to spatial ability, either factor could potentially explain sex-differences in spatial ability. . . . Both possibilities need investigation [p. 222].

In sum, the evidence we have reviewed indicates that biology is not destiny; sex-linked biological predispositions can be modified and possibly even reversed by social and cultural influences. John Money and Anke Ehrhardt (1972) take note of this fact in their recent biosocial theory of sex typing. This theory is appropriately labeled *bio*social because it emphasizes the biological factors that determine how other people will respond to the child.

Money and Ehrhardt's Biosocial Theory

Money and Ehrhardt (1972) propose that there are a number of critical episodes or events that will affect a person's eventual preference for the masculine or the feminine sex role. The first critical event occurs at conception as the child inherits either an X or a Y chromosome from the father. Over the next six weeks, the developing embryo has only an undifferentiated gonad, and the sex chromosomes determine whether this structure will become the male testes or the female ovaries. If a Y chromosome is present, the embryo develops testes; otherwise ovaries will form.

These newly formed gonads then determine the outcome of episode 2. The testes of a male embryo secrete two hormones—*testosterone*, which stimulates the development of a male internal reproductive system, and *mullerian inhibiting substance* (MIS), which inhibits the development of female organs. In the absence of these hormones, the embryo develops the internal reproductive system of a female.

At choice point 3, three to four months after conception, testosterone secreted by the testes leads to the development of a penis and scrotum. If testosterone is absent (as in normal females) or if the male fetus is insensitive to the male sex hormones, the female external genitalia will form. This is the point at which a female fetus may develop the external genitalia of a male if exposed to a heavy dose of male sex hormones through drugs that the mother is taking or because of a genetic dysfunction of her own adrenal glands (of course, these androgenized females have no testes; their saclike "scrotums" are empty). Money and Ehrhardt also believe that testosterone alters the development of the brain and the nervous system, thereby suppressing the production of female sex hormones in males, which will eventually prevent males from experiencing menstrual cycles at puberty.

The next major development occurs during the first three years after birth. Parents and other social agents label and begin to sex-type the child on the basis of the appearance of his or her genitals. In addition, the child will become more aware of his or her body type and learn how males and females are supposed to look. By age 3, most children have established a basic gender identity and are now well aware that they are boys or girls. Money considers this a critical development because he has found that children who undergo gender reassignment after age 3 usually experience serious adjustment problems and may never feel comfortable with their newly assigned sex.

Later, at puberty, changes in hormonal functioning are responsible for the growth of the reproductive system, the appearance of secondary sex characteristics, and the development of sexual urges. These events, in combination with one's earlier self-concept, provide the basis for an adult gender identity and sex-role preference (see Figure 12-3).

Although Money and Ehrhardt believe that social forces play an important role in the sex-typing process, their theory emphasizes the early biological developments that people are responding to when deciding how to raise a child. Other theorists have focused more intently on the socialization process itself, trying to identify the kinds of experiences that will convince children that they are boys who should adopt a masculine orientation or girls who should favor feminine pursuits. The first of these "social" theories was Sigmund Freud's psychoanalytic approach—a highly controversial perspective on sex typing to which we will now turn.

FREUD'S PSYCHOANALYTIC THEORY

Freud's explanation of psychosexual development acknowledges the contributions of both social and biological factors. Recall from our discussion of psychoanalytic theory in Chapter 2 that sexuality (the sex instinct) was said to be innate. Freud also believed that everyone is constitutionally bisexual, having inherited, in varying proportions, the biological attributes of both sexes. What, then, is responsible for the child's adoption of a sexual identity consistent with his or her (predominant) biological sex?

Freud's answer was that sex typing occurs through the process of *identification*. Recall that identification is the child's tendency to emulate another person, usually the parent of the same sex. Freud argued that a 3- to 6-year-old boy will internalize masculine attitudes and behaviors when he is forced to identify with his father (the aggressor) as a means of renouncing his incestuous desires for his mother, reducing his castration anxiety, and thus resolving the Oedipus complex. According to Freud, a boy may show inadequate sex typing or homosexual tendencies later in life if his father is inadequate as a masculine model, often absent from the home, or not sufficiently threatening to foster a strong identification; if the boy inherited a relatively strong feminine constitution; or if some combination of these factors is operating.

Freud argued that sex typing is somewhat more difficult for girls. During the oedipal period, a young girl's affectional ties to her mother are normally weakened because the mother is now perceived as a competitor for the father's love. But unlike her brother, the girl does not fear castration for her rivaling conduct; indeed, there is no analogue of castration anxiety that would compel a daughter to identify with her mother and resolve her Electra complex.

Why, then, would a girl ever develop a preference for the feminine role? For two reasons: (1) the mother retains some of her attractiveness from the pre-oedipal period, when she had served as the girl's benevolent caretaker, and (2) the father is likely to reinforce his daughter for "feminine" behavior—an act that increases the attractiveness of the mother, who serves as the girl's model of femininity. Freud believed that a girl could become a tomboy or perhaps even a lesbian later in life if she failed to identify with her mother (or overidentified with her father), if she had inherited a relatively strong masculine constitution, or if her mother proved inadequate as a feminine model.

Some of the evidence we have reviewed is generally consistent with Freudian theory. Recall that young

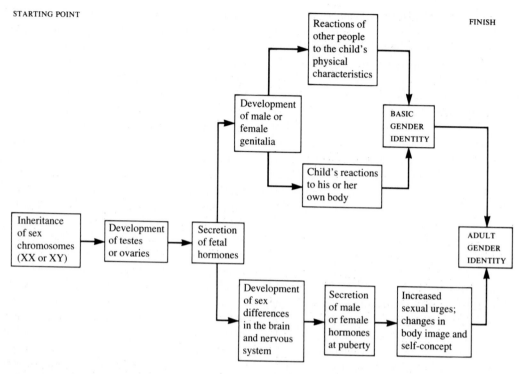

FIGURE 12-3 Schematic representation of Money and Ehrhardt's biosocial theory of sex typing

children are rapidly acquiring sex-role stereotypes and developing sex-typed behaviors at roughly the age that Freud says they will (3 to 6). And the finding that sex typing takes a little longer for girls than for boys is also in line with Freudian theory. Finally, the notion that fathers play an important role in the sex typing of their daughters has now been confirmed (Hetherington, 1967; Lamb, 1981; Langlois & Downs, 1980; Snow et al., 1983).

However, the results of several other studies are very damaging to psychoanalytic theory. The idea that young children experience an Oedipus complex including castration anxiety for boys and penis envy for girls assumes that 3- to 6-year-olds are well aware of the differences between the male and female genitalia. Yet, as we saw in Chapter 2, 4- to 5-year-olds are inept at assembling dolls so that the genitals match other parts of the doll's body (Katcher, 1955). These oedipal-aged children, who knew that they were boys or girls, made mistakes that showed they

were ignorant about sex differences in genital anatomy (see also McConaghy, 1979). So it is hardly plausible that 3- to 6-year-olds would experience an Oedipus (or Electra) complex with castration anxiety or penis envy.

Other investigators have found that boys show a stronger identification with their fathers and heightened masculinity when the fathers are warm and nurturant rather than overly punitive or threatening (Hetherington & Frankie, 1967; Mussen & Rutherford, 1963). These data are clearly inconsistent with the Freudian notion that a boy's sex-role development is furthered by experiencing a hostile relationship with a threatening father.

In sum, Freud's explanation of sex typing has not received much empirical support, even though children begin to develop sex-role preferences at about the time that he specified. Let's now consider the social-learning interpretation of sex typing to see whether this approach looks any more promising.

SOCIAL-LEARNING THEORY

Prominent social-learning theorists (Bandura, 1977; Mischel, 1970) have argued that children acquire their gender identities, sex-role preferences, and sex-typed behaviors in two ways: through direct tuition and through observational learning. *Direct tuition* refers to the tendency of parents, teachers, and other social agents to reinforce the child's sex-appropriate responses and to punish or otherwise discourage those behaviors that they consider more appropriate for members of the other sex. Thus, boys are urged to be tough, assertive, and competitive and to play with action toys such as trucks or guns; girls are encouraged to be gentle and cooperative and to play with toys such as dolls or dish sets that require them to assume a nurturant, caretaking role. In addition, every child learns a variety of sex-typed attitudes and behaviors by observing the activities of same-sex models, including peers, teachers, older siblings, and media personalities, as well as the mother or the father. Walter Mischel (1970) has noted that children do not necessarily identify with (that is, hope to emulate) all the models who contribute to their sex-role development. Indeed, imitative responses that psychoanalysts call "identification" are just as easily described as examples of observational learning.

Direct Tuition of Sex Roles

Are parents actively involved in the sex typing of their children? Yes, indeed, and the shaping of sex-typed behaviors begins rather early. Beverly Fagot (1978) studied 24 families, each of which consisted of two parents and a single child between the ages of 20 and 24 months. Each family was observed in the home for five one-hour periods, during which the child's behaviors and the reactions of the parents were carefully recorded. Fagot noted that parental responses to certain classes of behavior *clearly depended on the sex of the toddler*. On the one hand, parents reinforced their daughters for dancing, dressing up (as women), following them around, asking for assistance, and playing with dolls. Daughters were discouraged from manipulating objects, running, jumping, and climbing. On the other hand,

boys were punished for "feminine" activities (playing with dolls, seeking help) and encouraged to play with "masculine" items such as blocks, trucks, and push-and-pull toys that require large-muscle activity. Parents perceived aggression and rough-and-tumble play as more appropriate for boys than for girls, although they did not encourage their sons to display these behaviors. Fagot also noted that boys were more likely to be punished for feminine behaviors than girls were for masculine behaviors.

Perhaps an even more basic strategy that parents use to encourage sex-typed interests is to select gender-consistent toys for their infants and toddlers (Eisenberg, Wolchik, Hernandez, & Pasternack, 1985). A glance at the bedrooms of young boys and girls is revealing in itself: boys' rooms are likely to contain outer-space toys, construction sets, sporting equipment, and vehicles, whereas girls' rooms will typically contain dolls, domestic toys, floral furnishings, and ruffles (MacKinnon, Brody, & Stoneman, 1982). Given this early "channeling" of sex-typed interests, parents may find that additional pressures (such as differential reinforcement) are often unnecessary—unless, of course, the child's play patterns and interests seem "inappropriate" to them (Eisenberg et al., 1985).

Do parents react strongly to cross-sex play? To find out, Judith Langlois and Chris Downs (1980) compared the reactions of mothers, fathers, and peers to 3- to 5-year-old children who were asked (by the experimenter) to play with either same-sex or cross-sex toys. Fathers showed the clearest pattern by rewarding their children for playing with same-sex items and punishing cross-sex play. Mothers showed this same pattern with their daughters but tended to reward their sons for playing with either masculine or feminine toys. Finally, peers were especially critical of children who played with cross-sex toys, often ridiculing the offender or disrupting this "inappropriate" play. Indeed, Beverly Fagot (1985) finds that peer pressure for "sex-appropriate" play begins very early: even before establishing a basic gender identity, 21- to 25-month-old boys would belittle or disrupt each other for playing with feminine toys or with a girl, and girls of this same age were critical of other girls who chose to play with boys.

In sum, it appears that the child's earliest preferences for sex-typed toys and activities may result from the tendency of parents (particularly fathers) to actively encourage sex-appropriate behavior and to discourage acts that they consider sex-inappropriate. As the child grows older, other people, such as teachers, Scout leaders, and especially peers, will become increasingly important as sources of reinforcement for sex-typed attitudes and behaviors (Roopnarine, 1984).

Observational Learning

According to Albert Bandura (1977), children acquire a large percentage of their sex-typed attributes by observing and imitating same-sex models. Bandura believes that there are two reasons a child might pay particular attention to models of his or her own sex. First, young children may often be reinforced for imitating same-sex siblings or parents. Indeed, you have probably heard a proud parent make statements such as "That's my little man; you're just like daddy!" or "You're as pretty as your mommy when you dress up like that!" As the child acquires a firm gender identity, a second factor comes into play. Same-sex models are now more worthy of attention because children perceive them as *similar* to themselves.

One problem with Bandura's hypothesis is that children do *not* pay more attention to same-sex models until relatively late—about 6 to 7 years of age (Ruble, Balaban, & Cooper, 1981; Slaby & Frey, 1975). In fact, John Masters and his associates (Masters, Ford, Arend, Grotevant, & Clark, 1979) found that preschool children are much more concerned about the sex-appropriateness of the *behavior* they are observing than the sex of the model who displays it. For example, 4- to 5-year-old boys will play with new objects labeled "boys' toys" even after they have seen a girl playing with them. However, these youngsters are reluctant to play with objects labeled "girls' toys" that boy models have played with earlier. In other words, children's toy choices are affected more by the labels attached to the toys than by the sex of the child who served as a model. But once children recognize that gender is an unchanging aspect of their personalities (at age 6 to 7), they do begin to attend selectively to same-sex models and are now likely to avoid toys and activities that members of the other sex seem to enjoy (Ruble et al., 1981).

A central tenet of social-learning theory is that a large number of same-sex models will contribute to the child's sex-role development. If this is so, we might expect that the child will become less like the father or the mother as he or she matures and is frequently exposed to same-sex teachers, peers, media personalities, and the like. Indeed, studies of parent/child similarities reveal that school-age children and adolescents are not notably similar to either parent (Maccoby & Jacklin, 1974). One investigator (Tolar, 1968) found that college males actually resembled their mothers more than their fathers! Surely these findings are damaging to any theory (particularly the psychoanalytic approach) that claims that children acquire important personality traits by identifying with the same-sex parent.

The family as a social system. The number of children in a family and their distribution by age and sex affect the sex-role behaviors of *all* family members (Rosenberg & Sutton-Smith, 1964; Sutton-Smith & Rosenberg, 1970; Tauber, 1979a). For example, fathers who have two daughters tend to portray a more "masculine" image than fathers who have a son and a daughter. At first, this finding seems puzzling. But it is conceivable that fathers in girl/girl families must spend a large amount of time playing the complementary (masculine) role in order to successfully encourage the femininity of *two* girls.

The impact of siblings on sex typing is not well understood. It might seem as if both boys and girls would be more traditionally sex-typed if they had one or more same-sex siblings (particularly older ones) to encourage and model gender-consistent behavior. Indeed, studies of two-child families find that children are more traditionally sex-typed if they have a same-sex rather than an other-sex sibling (see Brim, 1958; Sutton-Smith & Rosenberg, 1970). However, the findings from studies of larger families tell another story. Margaret Tauber (1979a) reports that school-age girls who have older sisters and boys from all-boy families are the children who are most likely to enjoy *cross-sex* games and activities. Moreover, Harold Grotevant (1978) found that adolescent girls who have sisters develop a less "feminine" pattern of interests than girls who have brothers. These latter findings make some sense if children are concerned about establishing a personal niche within the family. A child with other-sex sibs could easily achieve such an individual identity by behaving in a traditionally "masculine" or "feminine" manner. However, a child who is surrounded by same-sex sibs may have to engage in cross-sex activities in order to distinguish the self from brothers (or sisters) and avoid being categorized as one of the "boys" (or "girls").

Although we are only beginning to understand how the structure of the family affects children's sex typing, this much is clear: the child's sex-role socialization within the home depends more on the total family environment than on the influence of the same-sex parent.

Media influences.   For the most part, males and females are portrayed in a highly stereotyped fashion in children's storybooks and on television. The majority of children's readers feature males as the central characters, and it is almost invariably a male who responds to emergencies, makes important decisions, and assumes a position of leadership. In contrast, females are usually depicted as passive, dependent, excitable, and lacking in ability (Brooks-Gunn & Matthews, 1979; Kolbe & LaVoie, 1981). Sex roles on television are similar to those found in children's books: males are dominant characters who work at a profession, whereas females are passive, emotional creatures who usually manage a home or work at "feminine" occupations such as nursing (Liebert, Sprafkin, & Davidson, 1982). Even TV commercials are sex-stereotyped; males are more often portrayed as experts on the advertised product, while females are typically the ones who are "convinced" by demonstrations of the product's superiority (McArthur & Resko, 1975).

Do these media models affect the sex-role development of young children? Indeed they do if the child is frequently exposed to these stereotyped portrayals of men and women. For example, 5- to 11-year-olds who watch more than 25 hours of television a week are more likely to choose sex-appropriate toys and to hold stereotyped views of males and females than their classmates who watch little television

(Frueh & McGhee, 1975; Leary, Greer, & Huston, 1982; Rothschild, 1979). Even adolescents are quite susceptible to the media typing of sex roles, particularly those aspects of masculinity and femininity portrayed in advertising (Tan, 1979). In one recent longitudinal study of young adolescents, Michael Morgan (1982) found that the youngsters who are affected most by watching sex-role stereotypes on television are girls of above-average intelligence from middle-class homes—precisely the group that is otherwise least likely to hold traditionally sexist attitudes. In recent years, steps have been taken to design TV programming aimed at reducing the sex-role stereotyping of children and adolescents. We will evaluate the effectiveness of these programs when we return to the topic of media influences in Chapter 14.

KOHLBERG'S COGNITIVE-DEVELOPMENTAL THEORY

Lawrence Kohlberg (1966, 1969) has proposed a cognitive theory of sex typing that is strikingly different from the other theories we have considered. Recall that both psychoanalytic theory and social-learning theory specify that boys initially learn to do "boy things" and girls learn to do "girl things" because their companions encourage these activities and discourage cross-sex behavior. Presumably children will eventually begin to identify with (or habitually imitate) same-sex models, thereby acquiring a stable gender identity and sex-appropriate attitudes and behaviors.

The cognitive theory of sex typing turns this sequence upside down. Kohlberg suggests that a child's gender identity is a cognitive judgment about the self that *precedes* his or her selective attention to (or identification with) same-sex models. Furthermore, the child's conception of gender, which is of central importance to the sex-typing process, will depend on his or her level of cognitive development. Kohlberg believes that children progress through the following three stages as they acquire an understanding of gender and its implications:

1. *Basic gender identity.* The child recognizes that he or she is a male or a female. Three-year-olds have usually reached this stage, although they fail to realize that gender is an unchanging attribute.

2. *Gender stability.* Gender is now perceived as stable over time. The child at this stage knows that boys invariably become men and that girls grow up to be women.

3. *Gender consistency.* The gender concept is now complete, for the child realizes that gender is stable over time *and* across situations. Children of 6 to 7 who have reached this stage are no longer fooled by appearances. They know, for example, that one's gender cannot be altered by superficial changes such as dressing up as a member of the other sex or partaking in cross-sex activities.

According to Kohlberg, a child's basic interests and values will begin to change once he or she acquires a *mature* gender identity. For example, a boy who realizes that he will always be a male should come to value male attributes and the masculine role. At this point, he will begin to seek out male models and imitate their mannerisms in order to learn sex-appropriate patterns of behavior. The encouragement that he receives for successfully imitating males informs him that he is behaving the way boys should behave and thereby strengthens his masculine self-concept. Thus, Kohlberg's model is a cognitive-consistency theory: children are motivated to acquire values, interests, and behaviors that are consistent with their cognitive judgments about the self. It is worth repeating that, for Kohlberg, a child's conservation of gender (gender consistency) is the *cause*, rather than the consequence, of attending to same-sex models.

Support for Kohlberg's Viewpoint

The results of several experiments are consistent with various aspects of Kohlberg's theory. For example, studies of 3- to 7-year-olds indicate that children's understanding of gender develops gradually and is clearly related to other aspects of their cognitive development, such as the conservation of mass and liquids (DeVries, 1974; Marcus & Overton, 1978). Ron Slaby and Karin Frey (1975) have also noted that the gender concept develops *sequentially*, progressing through the three stages Kohlberg describes (see also Wehren & De Lisi, 1983, and particularly Munroe, Shimmin, & Munroe, 1984, for evidence that

children in other cultures pass through this same sequence in their understanding of gender concepts). And there was a second interesting finding in Slaby and Frey's experiment: children who were at the higher stages of gender constancy were more likely to attend to same-sex models in a movie than children whose gender concepts were less well developed (see also Ruble et al., 1981). Finally, the research presented in Box 12-3 suggests that a child's understanding of gender may affect his or her interpretation of sex-role stereotypes and expectations.

Limitations of Kohlberg's Theory

The one major problem with Kohlberg's cognitive approach is that sex typing is already well underway before the child acquires a mature gender identity. As we have noted, 2-year-old boys prefer masculine toys before they are even aware that these playthings are more appropriate for boys than for girls (Blakemore et al., 1979). Moreover, 3-year-olds of both sexes have learned many sex-role stereotypes and already prefer same-sex activities and playmates long before they begin to attend more selectively to same-sex models (Kuhn et al., 1978; Maccoby, 1980). And let's not forget the work of John Money (Money & Ehrhardt, 1972), who found that gender reassignment is exceedingly difficult once children have reached the age of 3 (or Kohlberg's basic identity stage) and have *tentatively* categorized themselves as boys or girls. In sum, it appears that Kohlberg overstates the case in arguing that a mature understanding of gender is necessary for sex typing and sex-role development.

MARTIN AND HALVERSON'S GENDER SCHEMA THEORY

Carol Martin and Charles Halverson (1981) have recently proposed a schematic-processing model of sex typing that appears quite promising. Like Kohlberg, Martin and Halverson believe that children are intrinsically motivated to acquire values, interests, and behaviors that are consistent with their cognitive judgments about the self. However, they contend that this "self-socialization" begins as soon as the child acquires a *basic* gender identity and, thus, is well underway by age 6 or 7 when the child achieves gender constancy. Let's take a closer look.

Martin and Halverson propose that the establishment of a basic gender identity is the cornerstone of sex typing. Having reached this point, children will begin to acquire *gender schemata* (or stereotypes)—that is, organized sets of beliefs and expectations about males and females that will influence the kinds of information they will attend to, elaborate, and remember. Two kinds of gender schemata are thought to be important. Initially, children acquire a relatively superficial "in-group/out-group" schema as they learn which objects, behaviors, and roles are characteristic of males and females (for example, cars are for boys; girls can cry, boys shouldn't). This is the kind of information that investigators normally tap when studying children's knowledge of sex-role stereotypes. In addition, children are said to acquire an *own-sex* schema, which consists of detailed plans of action that one will need to perform various gender-consistent behaviors and to enact one's sex role. Thus, a young girl who has acquired a basic gender identity will first learn to make distinctions between the sexes, such as "girls sew" and "boys build model airplanes" (in-group/out-group schema). And because she is a girl and wants to act consistently with her own self-concept, she will attend carefully to the actions involved in sewing, making them part of her own-sex schema, while paying little attention to "sex-inappropriate" behaviors, such as those involved in building model airplanes.

Once formed, gender schemata "structure" experience by providing an organization for processing social information. The idea here is that people are likely to encode and remember information consistent with their schemata and to either forget schema-inconsistent information or transform it so that it becomes consistent with their stereotypes. Support for this latter proposition was presented in Box 12-1; recall that children who heard stories in which actors performed cross-sex behavior (for example, a girl chopping wood) tended to recall the action but to alter the scene to conform to their gender stereotypes (saying a boy had been doing the chopping). Moreover, children do seem to be more interested in acquiring and remembering information about objects or activities that match their "own-sex" schemata. In one recent study (Bradbard, Martin, Endsley, & Halverson, 1986), 4- to 9-year-olds were given boxes of gender-neutral objects (for example, hole punches, burglar alarms, pizza cutters) and were told that these objects were all "girl" items or "boy" items. They were then allowed several minutes to explore the objects and, one week later, were tested to determine whether they (1) remembered the gender label assigned to the objects and (2) could recall the specific information the experimenter had provided when describing the objects' functions. The findings were clear. During the initial session, boys explored more than girls if the objects had been labeled "boy" items, whereas just the reverse was true when the objects were described as things that girls enjoy. Apparently these gender labels were incorporated into children's "in-group/out-group" schemata, for they were easily recalled in the second session one week later. However, boys recalled more in-depth information about "boy" items than girls did, whereas girls recalled more than boys about these *same* objects if they had been labeled "girl" items. Finally, some of the children had been offered an incentive (a toy from a "treasure chest") for correct recall, but this inducement did *not* affect the accuracy with which they recalled the characteristics of "gender-inconsistent" items. So we see that the information-processing biases associated with gender schemata are very powerful indeed.

In sum, Martin and Halverson's gender schema theory is an interesting "new look" at the sex-typing process. Not only does this model describe how sex stereotypes might originate and persist over time, but it also indicates how these emerging "gender schemata" might contribute to the development of strong sex-role preferences and sex-typed patterns of behavior—even before the child realizes that gender is an unchanging attribute.

AN ATTEMPT AT INTEGRATION

Perhaps some combination of the biosocial, social-learning, cognitive-developmental, and gender schema approaches provides the most accurate explanation

BOX 12-3 CHILDREN'S CONCEPTIONS OF SEX-ROLE STEREOTYPES

What do young children think about the sex-role standards and stereotypes that they have learned? Must they conform to these expectations; or, rather, do they feel free to do their own thing?

According to Lawrence Kohlberg, the answers to these questions will depend on the child's understanding of gender. Until they realize that gender is unchanging, young, egocentric children may feel that cross-sex behaviors are acceptable as long as a child really wants to partake in these activities. But once the child achieves gender constancy, at age 6 to 7, he or she should become something of a chauvinist and interpret sex-role standards as absolute laws or moral imperatives that everyone should follow. Finally, Kohlberg proposes that older children who are approaching formal operations will be capable of thinking more abstractly and thus seeing the arbitrary nature of many sex-role stereotypes. In other words, preadolescents should become more flexible about sex-role standards, viewing them more as social conventions than as moral absolutes that everyone must obey.

William Damon (1977) has tested Kohlberg's hypotheses in an interesting study of 4- to 9-year-olds. Each child was told a story about a little boy named George who insists on playing with dolls, even though his parents have told him that dolls are for girls and that boys should play with other toys. The children were then asked a series of questions about this story—questions designed to assess their own impressions of sex-role stereotypes. For example:

1. Why do people tell George not to play with dolls? Are they right?
2. Is there a rule that boys shouldn't play with dolls? Where does it come from?
3. What should George do?
4. What if George wanted to wear a dress to school? Can he do that?

Damon's findings were generally consistent with Kohlberg's cognitive explanation of stereotyping. Four-year-olds (who do not conserve gender) believe that doll play and other cross-sex behaviors are OK if that is what George really wants to do. Here are some of the answers provided by a 4-year-old named Jack:

(Is it ok for boys to play with dolls?) Yes. *(Why?)* Because they wanted to. . . . *(So what should George do?)* Play with dolls. *(Why?)* Because it's up to him. . . . *(Can boys have dresses?)* No. *(Why not?)* Because boys don't wear them. *(Does George have the right to wear a dress to school if he wants to?)* Yes, but he didn't want to. *(Is it ok if he wanted to?)* It's up to him [Damon, 1977, p. 249; italics added].

By age 6, about the time that they acquire gender constancy, children become extremely intolerant of a person who violates traditional standards of masculinity or femininity. Consider the reaction of 6-year-old Michael to George's doll play:

(Why do you think people tell George not to play with dolls?) Well, he should only play with things that boys play with.

---

of sex differences and the sex-typing process. Money and Ehrhardt (1972) have contributed to our understanding of sex typing by describing the important biological developments that people use to label the child as a boy or a girl and treat him or her accordingly. Yet their biosocial model is not very explicit about the psychological determinants of sex differences and sex-role development.

Kohlberg's cognitive-developmental theory and Martin and Halverson's gender schema approach emphasize the importance of cognitive milestones and information-processing biases that occur sometime after age 3, when the child acquires a basic gender identity. However, an integrative theorist

would surely point out that these cognitive approaches largely ignore the important events of the first three years, when a boy, for example, develops a preference for masculine toys and activities because parents, siblings, and even his young peers frequently remind him that he is a boy, reinforce him for doing "boy things," and discourage those of his behaviors that they consider feminine. In other words, it appears that the social-learning theorists have accurately described early sex-typing: very young children display gender-consistent behaviors *because other people encourage these activities.*

As a result of this early socialization (and the growth of some basic categorization skills), children

BOX 12-3 *continued*

The things that he is playing with now is girls' stuff. . . . (*Can George play with Barbie dolls if he wants to?*) No sir! . . . (*What should George do?*) He should stop playing with girls' dolls and start playing with G. I. Joe. (*Why can a boy play with G. I. Joe and not a Barbie doll?*) Because if a boy is playing with a Barbie doll, then he's just going to get people teasing him . . . and if he tries to play more, to get girls to like him, then the girls won't like him either [Damon, 1977, p. 255; italics added].

The oldest children in Damon's sample were only 9, but these youngsters were already less chauvinistic about sex-role standards and sex-typed activities. Note how 9-year-old James makes a distinction between moral rules that imply a sense of obligation and sex-role standards that are customary but nonobligatory:

(*What do you think his parents should do?*) They should . . . get him trucks and stuff, and see if he will play with those. (*What if . . . he kept on playing with dolls? Do you think they would punish him?*) No. (*How come?*) It's not really doing anything bad. (*Why isn't it bad?*) Because . . . if he was breaking a window, and he kept on doing that, they could punish him, because you're not supposed to break windows. But if you want to you can play with dolls. (*What's the difference . . . ?*) Well, breaking windows you're not supposed to do. And if you play with dolls, you can, but boys usually don't [Damon, 1977, p. 263; italics added].

Now consider a set of observations that Kohlberg's theory does not anticipate: 12- to 13-year-olds, who should be attaining formal operations, once again become very intolerant of cross-sex behaviors (such as a male wearing nail polish), even though they continue to be quite flexible about the occupations that males and females might pursue (see Carter & McCloskey, 1983–1984; Carter & Patterson, 1982; Stoddart & Turiel, 1985). How can we account for this second round of gender chauvinism?

One possibility is that youngsters may tend to exaggerate sex-role stereotypes in order to "get them cognitively clear" during those developmental epochs when gender and gender-related issues are particularly salient to them (Maccoby, 1980). The early grade school years (age 6 to 7) are one such period, for this is when children first realize that gender is truly invariant—a *permanent* part of their personalities. And given the many gender-linked physical and physiological changes that occur at puberty, a young adolescent's sudden intolerance with what seem to be deviant cross-sex *behaviors* may simply reflect a second attempt to clarify sex-role standards in his or her own mind as a prelude to establishing a mature *personal/social* (or *heterosexual*) identity. One implication of this point of view is that older adolescents and young adults should again become more flexible in their thinking about sex-role stereotypes once they have resolved their identity crises and now feel more comfortable with their masculine or feminine self-concepts. Support for this prediction comes from a study by Urberg (1979), who found that the sex-role stereotypes of adults were indeed much less rigid than those of high school students.

acquire a basic gender identity. This is an important development, for Money's research suggests that as soon as a child first labels himself or herself as a boy or a girl, this self-concept is difficult to change (even though children do not yet recognize that gender itself is invariant). At this point, children begin (1) to actively seek information about sex differences, (2) to organize this information into in-group/out-group gender schemata, and (3) to learn more about those behaviors that they consider appropriate for members of their *own* sex. Although social-learning processes such as differential reinforcement are still implicated in the development of sex-typed behavior, the child is now *intrinsically motivated* to perform those acts that

match his or her "own-sex" gender schema and to avoid activities that are more appropriate for the other sex. Thus, 4- to 5-year-old boys, for example, will play with objects labeled "boys' toys" even if they have seen girls playing with and enjoying them (Masters et al., 1979). Their gender schemata tell them that "boy" toys are sex-appropriate, and they are inclined to approach these objects. The model's sex is of lesser importance, for these youngsters do not yet realize that her gender is invariant, and besides, they may simply distort what they have seen to match their gender schemata (for example, recalling that it was a boy rather than a girl who had enjoyed these "boy" toys).

Once children achieve gender constancy, at age 6 to 7, their strategies for incorporating sex-typed characteristics begin to change. Rather than focusing almost exclusively on gender schemata to define what is "appropriate" or "inappropriate" for them, older children now pay closer attention to the *sex* of the models who display various attributes. Thus, a 7-year-old girl will typically select females as her models because she recognizes (1) that *she will always be a female* and (2) that she can make her own behavior more consistent with this firm, future-oriented self-image by selectively attending to other people like her (females) and then "doing what girls and women do."

In sum, biological characteristics and social-learning mechanisms such as direct tuition and observational learning play a central role in the sex-typing process. However, these factors clearly interact with one's cognitive structuring abilities and information-processing biases (gender schemata) to determine the course and outcome of sex-role development (see Table 12-5 for a brief summary of this integrative viewpoint).

SEX TYPING IN THE NONTRADITIONAL FAMILY

Much of the work we have reviewed is based on studies of children growing up in a traditional family setting—that is, an intact home where the father is the primary breadwinner. But in today's rapidly changing society, the so-called traditional family is becoming less and less common. Economic realities have forced many mothers to work full-time, and in some families where the mother's earning capacity is substantial, it is the father who remains at home and assumes the role of "househusband." One issue that has intrigued developmental psychologists is the impact of changing parental roles on sex-role development of young children. In this section of the chapter, we will consider the effects of one type of role reversal: the case in which the mother could be described as the dominant parent.

Fatherless homes are now rather common. Recent statistics reveal that nearly 50% of U.S. marriages

TABLE 12-5   An Overview of the Sex-Typing Process from the Perspective of an Integrative Theorist

Developmental period	Events and outcomes
Prenatal period	The fetus develops the morphological characteristics of a male or a female, which others will react to once the child is born.
Birth to 3 years	Parents and other companions label the child as a boy or a girl, frequently remind the child of his or her gender, and begin to encourage gender-consistent behavior while discouraging cross-sex activities. As a result of these social experiences and the development of very basic classification skills, the young child acquires some sex-typed behavioral preferences and the knowledge that he or she is a boy or a girl (basic gender identity).
3 to 6 years	Once children acquire a basic gender identity, they begin to seek information about sex differences, form gender schemata, and become intrinsically motivated to perform those acts that are viewed as "appropriate" for their own sex. When acquiring gender schemata, children attend to both male and female models. And once their "own sex" schemata are well established, these youngsters are apt to imitate behaviors considered appropriate for their sex, regardless of the gender of the model who displays them.
Age 6 to 7 and beyond	Children finally acquire a sense of gender consistency—a firm, future-oriented image of themselves as boys who must necessarily become men or girls who will obviously become women. At this point they begin to rely less exclusively on gender schemata and more on the behavior of same-sex models to acquire those mannerisms and attributes that are consistent with their firm categorization of self as a male or female.

end in divorce, and about 40% of all children born in the United States during the 1970s will spend an average of six years living in a single-parent home (Hetherington, 1979; MacKinnon et al., 1982). At the beginning of this decade, about 20% of American families were currently headed by a single parent, nearly always the mother ("One-Parent Families," 1980). In view of the important role that fathers play in the sex-typing process, it seems legitimate to wonder whether children from fatherless homes will show an atypical pattern of sex-role development.

We know much less about the effects of mother absence because motherless homes are still relatively uncommon. Mothers are usually awarded custody of their children in divorce proceedings, and should a mother die or lose a custody hearing, the father often remarries or hires a female caretaker, thereby providing his children with a mother surrogate (Santrock & Warshak, 1979). However, an increasing number of young mothers are taking jobs that render them unavailable to their children for several hours of a typical workday. By 1982, almost 50% of mothers with preschool children and nearly two thirds of those with school-age youngsters were employed outside the home (Klein, 1985; Select Committee on Children, Youth, and Families, 1983). In the pages that follow, we will look at some of the research that seeks to determine whether a mother's work activities and her temporary absences from the home have any systematic effects on the sex-role development of her children.

EFFECTS OF MOTHER DOMINANCE

The balance of power between mothers and fathers varies considerably from family to family. In the United States, the father tends to be the dominant parent (Lavine, 1982), although mother-dominant households are not particularly uncommon. The obvious question is "What happens if the mother is clearly the dominant parent?" Will her daughters be less feminine and her sons less masculine than girls and boys from father-dominant homes?

Mavis Hetherington (1965) attempted to answer these questions in a study of 4- to 11-year-old chil-

dren and their parents. The sex-role preferences of each child were measured by the *It scale*, a test in which the child projects his or her own toy and activity preferences by guessing the choices that a sexually ambiguous stick figure, "It," would make when presented with pairs of masculine and feminine items (for example, a dress versus a pair of trousers, cosmetics versus shaving implements, a doll versus a ball). In addition, children took an "identification" test that measured their willingness to imitate each parent. Finally, the child's parents were asked to work out mutually agreeable solutions to 12 hypothetical child-rearing problems, such as "Your son/daughter loses his/her temper while playing with a toy and intentionally breaks it." The dominant parent was determined by noting which spouse spoke first, which spoke the most, and which tended to accept the other's influence as they worked out their cooperative solutions.

Hetherington found that boys from mother-dominant households made significantly fewer masculine choices on the It test than boys from father-dominant homes. Furthermore, the identification test revealed that boys from father-dominant homes imitated their fathers more than their mothers, while boys from mother-dominant homes *imitated their mothers more than their fathers*. It appears that a dominant mother clearly affects the sex typing of her son, for boys from mother-dominant homes were apparently reluctant to identify with their passive fathers (for additional evidence see Biller & Borstelmann, 1967; Lynn, 1974).

Mother dominance did not seem to affect the sex typing of daughters; that is, girls from mother-dominant homes were no less feminine on the It test than girls from father-dominant households. This result may come as a surprise, since a dominant mother would seem to offer her daughter a rather "unfeminine" role model. But Hetherington (1965) notes that "the measure of maternal dominance in this study was one of dominance relative to the spouse and not to other members of her own sex. Thus a mother could be more dominant than a passive husband and still not be dominant or unfeminine relative to other women" (p. 90).

A recent article by Linda Lavine (1982) suggests that dominant mothers may have at least one effect on the sex typing of their daughters. In her study of 7- to 11-year-olds, Lavine found that girls from mother-dominant or egalitarian families were more likely than those from father-dominant homes to aspire to traditionally masculine occupations such as law or medicine. Apparently a girl feels more comfortable about accepting the challenges of a "male-dominated" occupation if she has seen her mother make important decisions or demonstrate an ability to influence an adult male (namely, her father).

EFFECTS OF FATHER ABSENCE

Fatherless homes resemble mother-dominant households in that the mother is, by necessity, the parent who exerts more influence over her children. Therefore, we might expect that the absence of a father (or father figure) would hinder the sex-role development of sons who haven't an adequate masculine role model in the home. However, fatherless daughters should show fewer disruptions in sex typing, for their mothers are present to serve as models of femininity. The data are generally consistent with these hypotheses.

Effects on Sons

Boys who are separated from their fathers early in life tend to be more emotionally dependent, less aggressive, less achievement-oriented, and less masculine in their sex-role preferences than boys from homes where the father is present (Biller, 1974; Drake & McDougall, 1977; Hetherington, 1966; Levy-Shiff, 1982). Sons of military personnel who are separated from their fathers for long periods during the first five years may find it particularly difficult to incorporate various aspects of the masculine role. Many of these boys are considered "sissies" by their fathers, and they often remain somewhat effeminate in their overt behavior (for example, submissive and unassertive) even after their fathers have returned to the home (Leichty, 1960; Stolz, 1954).

An interesting study by Mavis Hetherington (1966) indicates that the age at which father separation occurs is an important consideration. Hetherington's subjects were 9- to 12-year-old boys who were rated on a number of sex-typed dimensions by recreation directors who knew the boys well. In addition, the sex-role preferences of each boy were assessed by means of the It test. Hetherington found few differences between boys from intact homes and boys who had been separated from their fathers *after age 6.* But boys who had been separated from their fathers *before age 4* were less masculine on the It test, more dependent, less aggressive, and less willing to engage in rough-and-tumble play than boys from intact homes.

Why are boys from fatherless homes often less "sex-typed" than those from intact families? Certainly the boy's lack of a masculine role model during the early years is one contributing factor (Hetherington, 1966). Indeed, fatherless boys who happen to have older brothers do tend to be more masculine in their sex-role behaviors than their counterparts who have no elder masculine models (Wohlford, Santrock, Berger, & Leiberman, 1971). However, we should also note that father absence has *indirect* effects that could influence a son's sex typing. For example, mothers in fatherless homes are often found to be more punitive, more restrictive, and less likely to encourage independence than mothers who have a male around to assist them with child rearing (Hetherington, Cox, & Cox, 1978; Levy-Shiff, 1982; Santrock, 1975). So part of the impact of "father absence" on young boys may be attributable to the attitudes and child-rearing practices of their mothers.

Finally, it would be inappropriate to conclude that most boys from fatherless homes are "effeminate," for their mannerisms and sex-role preferences tend to be much more similar to those of other boys than to those of girls. And mothers in fatherless homes do not invariably behave in ways that would disrupt a boy's sex typing. Indeed, Hetherington et al. (1978) found that sons of divorcees are apt to show a quite normal pattern of masculine attributes if their mothers actively encourage them to be independent, to explore, and to display sex-typed patterns of behavior.

Effects on Daughters

It appears that the absence of the father from the home has little if any effect on the sex-role development of preadolescent daughters (Hetherington, 1972; Santrock, 1970). In fact, some researchers have reported that father-absent girls are actually more "feminine" in certain respects (for example, more dependent on the mother) than girls from intact homes (Baggett, 1967; Lynn & Sawrey, 1959).

Although father absence does not disrupt a girl's sex typing, it may affect the way she relates to males in later life. Mavis Hetherington (1972) has studied a group of lower- to lower-middle-class adolescent females who fell into three categories: (1) girls from intact homes, (2) girls from homes where the father was absent because of divorce, and (3) girls whose fathers had died. None of the father-absent families had had any males living in the home since the father's departure. Hetherington collected several pieces of information about each girl, including her performance on tests of sex typing, observations of her behavior at a community recreation center, and data from interviews with the girl and her mother.

The results were interesting. As noted earlier, the father-absent girls did not differ from the father-present group on traditional measures of sex typing: girls in all three groups clearly preferred female activities and the feminine role. However, many of the father-absent girls reacted to males in one of two ways that distinguished them from the father-present group.

The *daughters of widows* tended to be shy and noticeably discomforted in the presence of males. At recreation center dances, these girls assumed the role of "wallflowers," clustering at one end of the room away from the boys and remaining there unless asked to dance. When interviewed by a male experimenter, the daughters of widows often sat in an upright (uptight?) posture with their legs together and their arms crossed. They frequently chose to sit in the chair farthest from the interviewer, and they maintained little eye contact with him. These girls were generally described by their mothers as very outgoing with the girls but shy and retiring around boys and men.

By contrast, *daughters of divorcees* tended to be rather assertive and uninhibited in their interactions with males. They regularly initiated contacts with boys and often asked them to dance at recreation center socials. When interviewed by a male, the daughters of divorcees frequently sat near the interviewer and assumed a sprawling posture, leaning forward with their legs apart and their arms hooked around the back of the chair. They seemed quite receptive to the male interviewer, smiling and maintaining more eye contact with him than girls from intact homes or daughters of widows.

Apparently the differences between daughters of widows and daughters of divorcees were not attributable to variations in their mothers' child-rearing practices or affection for their daughters. Both groups of mothers loved their daughters and held positive attitudes toward men in general. But the divorcees were often anxious and unhappy. Their attitudes toward their former husbands and their memories of marriage were negative, and they usually felt that they had received little support from other people during the crisis of divorce and the times of stress they had experienced while trying to raise a child by themselves. By contrast, widows expressed favorable attitudes toward marriage and their departed husbands, and they frequently reported that they had received the emotional support of friends and relatives during the period since the death of their spouses. Hetherington suggests that the daughters of divorcees are well aware of their mothers' unhappiness and are likely to conclude that men are essential for a happy life. As a result, these girls may feel that they must do whatever it takes to secure a man. However, daughters of widows may have an aggrandized image of their fathers that prompts them to avoid males for either of two reasons: (1) they believe that few men can compare favorably with their fathers, or (2) they have come to regard all males as superior and as objects of deference and apprehension.

Hetherington has followed up on these girls, noting that the daughters of divorcees married younger than daughters of widows (several of whom were not yet married) and were more often pregnant at the time of their marriages. The daughters of divorcees tended to marry immature and inconsiderate husbands who were poorly educated and had unstable work histories, whereas the daughters of widows were more likely to marry nurturant, ambitious, and somewhat inhibited men who were characterized by one interviewer as "repulsively straight." When asked to select adjectives from an adjective checklist that best described the men in their lives, daughters from father-absent homes tended to report more similarities between their husbands and fathers than daughters from intact homes. According to Hetherington, father-absent girls seemed to be selecting mates who matched their images of their fathers, whereas girls from intact homes were much less constrained by father-fantasies when choosing (and later evaluating) their husbands (Hetherington & Parke, 1986).

Surely not all girls from father-absent homes will show the extreme reactions to males that characterized the father-absent females in Hetherington's sample. We must remember that Hetherington's father-absent subjects were atypical in that they had had *no* males living in the home from the day that father separation occurred. In other words, they were not only father-deprived but male-deprived. In a more recent study, Louise Hainline and Ellen Feig (1978) report that, among a sample of *middle class* college students, neither daughters of widows nor daughters of divorcees were radically different in their reactions to males from female students who came from intact homes. What these data may indicate is that father-absent girls (at least older girls from middle-class backgrounds) are likely to overcome whatever social deficiencies they have had once they "have the opportunity to engage in social interactions of varying intensities with males" (Hainline & Feig, 1978, p. 42). Nevertheless, Hetherington's research does point to some problems that *young* adolescent girls may face if they are denied an opportunity to establish a stable relationship with a father or father figure.

EFFECTS OF MATERNAL EMPLOYMENT

There are several reasons that we might expect maternal employment to influence the sex-role development of young children. First, working mothers expend a sizable amount of time and effort at job-related activities outside the home. As a result, they are less available to serve as models of femininity for their daughters and may have less energy to do so when they are home. And if both parents are employed, the child may find it more difficult to discriminate the mother's role from the father's; both parents share the instrumental function traditionally assigned to males, and fathers may often assist working mothers with household chores and child-rearing responsibilities that are usually associated with the feminine role. So it seems reasonable to assume that children of working mothers (especially daughters) will be less traditional in their sex-role attitudes and behaviors than children of nonworking mothers.

Most of the available evidence is consistent with this hypothesis. By age 2 to 3, toddlers whose mothers work are already making fewer distinctions between "boy" toys and "girl" toys than their age mates whose mothers are rarely absent from the home (Weinraub et al., 1984). And by age 7 to 11, daughters of employed mothers perceive fewer *psychological* differences between the sexes than daughters of homemakers (Marantz & Mansfield, 1977). Apparently traits such as competence, independence, and competitiveness that are normally associated with working fathers are likely to be attributed to working mothers as well. In a study of 10-year-olds, Delores Gold and David Andres (1978) found that both sons and daughters of working mothers (particularly mothers who were satisfied with their work roles) had more egalitarian sex-role concepts than children of homemakers. However, daughters' perceptions of sex-role standards were influenced more by maternal employment than sons' were (see Vogel, Broverman, Broverman, Clarkson, & Rosenkrantz, 1970, for a similar set of findings with American college students).

Other investigators have found that daughters of working mothers are more independent, have fewer feminine interests, and are less likely than daughters of homemakers to devalue the competence or achievements of women (Baruch, 1972; Hoffman, 1979; Stein, 1973). Adolescent daughters of working mothers view work as something they will want to do when they are mothers; in fact, they are more likely to have jobs already than adolescent daughters of nonworking mothers (Etaugh, 1974). There is even some evidence that maternal employment contributes positively to a girl's personal adjustment and self-esteem, particularly if her mother enjoys her work or is a professional (Hoffman, 1984; Kappel & Lambert, 1972).

In sum, children of working mothers do grow up with a less stereotyped view of men and women than children whose mothers remain at home and provide a "sex-typed" contrast to the role played by working fathers. Is this a positive sign? Lois Hoffman (1979) thinks so. She notes that maternal employment is a part of modern family life—a pattern that may be

> better suited to socializing the child for the adult roles that he or she will occupy. This is particularly true for the daughter, but for the son too, the broader range of emotions and skills that each parent [displays] are more consistent with his adult role. Just as his father shares his breadwinning role and the child-rearing role with his mother, so the son too, will be likely to share these roles. The rigid sex-role stereotyping perpetuated by the division of labor in the traditional family is not appropriate for the demands children of either sex will have made on them as adults [p. 864].

PSYCHOLOGICAL ANDROGYNY: A NEW LOOK AT SEX ROLES

Throughout this chapter, we have used the term *sex-appropriate* to describe the mannerisms and behaviors that societies consider more suitable for members of one sex than the other. Today many psychologists believe that these rigidly defined sex-role standards are actually harmful or maladaptive because they constrain the behavior of both males and females. Indeed, Sandra Bem (1978) has stated that her major purpose in studying sex roles is "to help free the human personality from the restrictive prison of sex-role stereotyping and to develop a conception of mental health that is free from culturally imposed definitions of masculinity and femininity."

Psychologists have traditionally assumed that masculinity and femininity are at opposite ends of a single dimension: masculinity supposedly implies the absence of femininity, and vice versa. Bem challenges this assumption by arguing that a person can

be *androgynous*—that is, both masculine and feminine, instrumental and expressive, assertive and nonassertive, competitive or noncompetitive, depending on the utility or situational appropriateness of these attributes. The underlying assumption of Bem's model is that masculinity and femininity are *two separate dimensions*. A person who has many masculine and few feminine characteristics is defined as a *masculine sex-typed individual*. One who has many feminine and few masculine characteristics is said to be *feminine sex-typed*. Finally, the *androgynous* individual is a person who has a large number of both masculine and feminine characteristics (see Figure 12-4).

Do androgynous people really exist? To find out, Bem (1974, 1979) and other investigators (Spence & Helmreich, 1978) have developed sex-role inventories that contain both a masculinity and a femininity scale. One testing of a large sample of college students (Spence & Helmreich, 1978) revealed that roughly 33% of the test takers were sex-typed, 27–32% were androgynous, and the remaining subjects were either "undifferentiated" (low in both masculinity and femininity) or "sex-reversed" (masculine sex-typed females or feminine sex-typed males). Judith Hall and Amy Halberstadt (1980) have constructed a similar sex-role inventory for grade school children and found that 27–32% of their 8- to 11-year-olds could be classified as androgynous. So androgynous individuals do indeed exist, and in sizable numbers.

IS ANDROGYNY A DESIRABLE ATTRIBUTE?

Bem (1975, 1978) has argued that androgynous people are "better off" than their sex-typed counterparts because they are not constrained by rigid sex-role concepts and are freer to respond effectively to a wider variety of situations. Seeking to test this hypothesis, Bem exposed masculine, feminine, and androgynous men and women to situations that called for independence (a masculine attribute) or nurturance (a feminine attribute). The test for masculine independence assessed the subject's willingness to resist social pressure by refusing to agree with peers who gave bogus judgments when rating cartoons for

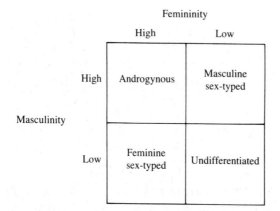

FIGURE 12-4 Categories of sex-role orientation (masculinity and femininity are conceptualized as separate and independent dimensions)

funniness (for example, several peers might say that a very funny cartoon was unfunny or that unfunny cartoons were hilarious). Nurturance, or feminine expressiveness, was measured by observing the behavior of the subject when left alone for ten minutes with a 5-month-old baby. The results confirmed Bem's hypotheses. Both the masculine sex-typed and the androgynous subjects were more independent (less conforming) on the independence test than feminine sex-typed individuals. Furthermore, both the feminine sex-typed and the androgynous subjects were more nurturant than the masculine sex-typed individuals when interacting with the baby. Thus, the androgynous subjects were quite flexible; they performed as masculine subjects did on the "masculine" task and as feminine subjects did on the "feminine" task.

If androgynous people are truly "better off," as Bem has argued, then we might expect them to be popular and to score higher on measures of self-esteem than traditional males and females do. As a matter of fact, recent research indicates that androgynous adolescents and college students do enjoy higher self-esteem and are perceived by peers to be more likeable and better adjusted than classmates who are traditionally sex-typed (Major, Carnevale, & Deaux, 1981; Massad, 1981; Spence, 1982). Moreover, androgynous females are more likely than sex-typed females to attribute their achievements to ability

(rather than effort or luck), their failures to factors other than lack of ability, and to show little if any decrement in performance (helplessness) after initially failing at an achievement task (R. L. Welch, cited in Huston, 1983). Clearly these data seem to imply that androgyny is a desirable attribute.

However, a caution is in order as we try to interpret these results. Since the androgynous person has a large number of masculine and feminine traits, we might wonder whether it is the masculine or the feminine component of androgyny that is primarily responsible for the higher levels of self-esteem and personal adjustment that seem to characterize androgynous people. Those who have researched the question find that it is the masculine component of androgyny that contributes most heavily to self-esteem; the feminine component has a much smaller effect (Lamke, 1982; Whitley, 1983). Perhaps this finding makes good sense when we recall that both males and females perceive masculine attributes and activities as more desirable and socially prestigious than feminine qualities and pastimes.

WHO RAISES ANDROGYNOUS OFFSPRING?

Although the data are sketchy at this point, we are beginning to get some idea of how androgyny originates. There is some evidence that androgynous adolescents and college students come from homes in which the parents are androgynous themselves (Orlofsky, 1979; Spence & Helmreich, 1978). Moreover, parents who are *nurturant* and *highly involved* with their children and who encourage them to develop close relations with the parent of the other sex tend to foster the development of both masculine and feminine attributes (Hetherington, Cox, & Cox, 1978; Orlofsky, 1979). Finally, daughters of working mothers are more likely to be androgynous than daughters of nonworking mothers (Hansson, Chernovetz, & Jones, 1977). So it appears that adults who value both "masculine" instrumentality and "feminine" expressiveness and who make these feelings known are the ones who are most likely to raise androgynous offspring.

Do androgynous adults make better parents than those who are traditionally sex-typed? At first glance

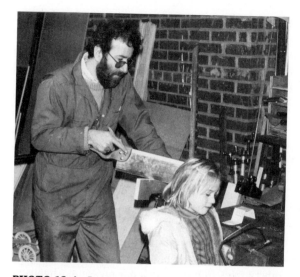

PHOTO 12-4 Parents who maintain a close relationship with their children and who are themselves androgynous are likely to raise androgynous sons and daughters.

it may seem so if androgynous parents raise androgynous children, who, in turn, enjoy high self-esteem and are perceived as likable and well adjusted by their peers. Yet in one recent study (Baumrind, 1982), 9-year-old daughters of androgynous parents were actually found to be somewhat *less* competent than their female classmates whose parents were traditionally sex-typed.

Do these findings imply that traditional adults make better parents than those who are androgynous? Diana Baumrind (1982) thinks so, although other interpretations are possible. For example, it may be that the benefits of having androgynous parents are minimal until adolescence, when teenagers (1) become more interested in close interpersonal relationships (in which nurturance and a concern for others are adaptive attributes) and (2) are planning and preparing for a career (so that independence, assertiveness, and other "masculine" attributes might be advantageous). In fact, there is some evidence that the benefits of being androgynous oneself are much more apparent for adolescents and young adults than for grade school children (see Perry & Bussey, 1984). So at this point, whether androgynous parents are any more or less effective than traditional parents is an open question—one that developmentalists will be trying to answer in the years ahead.

IMPLICATIONS AND PRESCRIPTIONS FOR THE FUTURE

The androgyny concept has generated an enormous amount of research within a brief time, and these early returns are fascinating. Perhaps the major implication of this work is that the notion of masculine superiority is a myth; androgynous persons of each sex seem to be adaptable to a wide variety of situations, and they need not fear rejection from either same-sex or other-sex peers for having incorporated both masculine and feminine attributes into their personalities. Advocates of the women's movement have long argued that women should be freer to become more like men, and many of us may have barely noticed their support for the opposite premise—namely, that men might be "better off" if they became a little more like women. Although some people react quite negatively to the androgyny concept, thinking that it implies that a drab, unisex society is "best," it is worth repeating that the androgynous females are perceived as no less feminine, nor are androgynous males perceived as any less masculine, simply because they have characteristics traditionally associated with the other sex (Major et al., 1981). In other words, the research to date provides little or no evidence of any disadvantage associated with being androgynous, and it illustrates that androgynous people are adaptive, well-adjusted individuals who are liked and respected by their peers.[3]

Recently, Bem (1981) has changed her views on androgyny. She now argues that the adaptability shown by androgynous people stems not so much from having incorporated both masculine and feminine traits as from being relatively unconstrained by the implications of sex-role stereotypes. In fact, Bem believes that androgynous people are neither "masculine" nor "feminine" (nor both) but, instead, are *gender aschematic*. Unlike sex-typed persons (or "gender schematics") who have defined various beliefs, values, mannerisms, and behaviors as "appropriate" or "inappropriate" for members of their sex, gender aschematic persons rarely think about sex-related labels or prescriptions when pursuing an interest, picking a friend, or deciding how to behave in any given situation. In short, they are free of the restrictions of gender—a state of affairs that Bem (1975) has suggested will someday come to define "a new and more human standard of psychological health."

Other theorists are not so sure that society would ever consider gender totally irrelevant or would define someone who does as a model of psychological well-being (indeed, a colleague once called Bem's ideas "gender anarchy" theory, even though he acknowledges that it is probably beneficial for members of each sex to incorporate some of the most desirable attributes of the other sex). In her chapter on sex typing in the *Handbook of Child Psychology*, Aletha Huston (1983) suggests that gender can never be totally irrelevant to children's social and personality development, the reason being that only females can bear children and that this biological "fact of life" has clear implications for many aspects of men's and women's lives. One problem with strong and largely untested pronouncements such as Bem's is that they could lead to a significant decline in interest in sex typing and gender-related issues—a possibility that Huston thinks undesirable in that we are only beginning to understand how genetic, hormonal, and other biological variables may affect the behavior of males and females. At the risk of sounding stodgy and

conservative to some, I too think it important to continue to study sex typing and to seek a better understanding of why males and females behave as they do. Nevertheless, provocative viewpoints such as Bem's can serve a most useful function by helping "to guide the field in directions that challenge old theories and assumptions and to produce research findings with real social importance" (Huston, 1983, p. 45).

SUMMARY

Males and females differ in several respects. Some sex differences are biological in origin, whereas others stem from socialization pressures. Interests, activities, and attributes that are considered more appropriate for members of one sex than the other are called sex-role standards (or sex-role stereotypes). Sex typing is the process by which children acquire a gender identity and assimilate the motives, values, and behaviors considered appropriate in their culture for members of their biological sex.

Some sex-role stereotypes are more accurate than others. Males tend to be more active and aggressive than females and to outperform them on tests of spatial abilities and arithmetic reasoning; females are less irritable and demanding than males, more compliant with parents' requests, and somewhat more responsive to infants, and they tend to outperform males on tests of verbal abilities. But on the whole, males and females are more similar than they are different. Among the stereotypes that have *no* basis in fact are the notions that females are more sociable, suggestible, and illogical and less analytical and achievement-oriented than males. The persistence of these "cultural myths" is particularly damaging to women. For example, members of both sexes tend to devalue women's accomplishments by attributing them to luck or hard work rather than competence. This tendency to degrade the achievements of females is well established among boys and girls by middle childhood.

Sex typing begins very early. By age 2½, most children know whether they are boys or girls, they tend to favor sex-typed toys and activities, and they are already aware of several sex-role stereotypes. By the time they enter school (or shortly thereafter), they know that gender is an unchanging aspect of their personalities, and they have learned most of the sex-role standards of their society. Boys face stronger sex-typing pressures than girls do, and consequently males are quicker to develop a preference for sex-appropriate patterns of behavior. In Western societies such as the United States and Canada, children from the lower socioeconomic strata are more firmly sex-typed than children from the middle class.

Several theories have been proposed to account for sex differences and the sex-typing process. Money and Ehrhardt's biosocial theory emphasizes the biological developments that occur before a child is born—developments that parents and other social agents will react to when deciding how to socialize the child. Other theorists have focused more intently on the socialization process itself. Psychoanalytic theorists suggest that sex typing is one result of the child's identification with the same-sex parent. Social-learning theorists offer two mechanisms to explain how children acquire sex-typed attitudes and behaviors: (1) direct tuition (reinforcement for sex-appropriate behaviors and punishment for sex-inappropriate ones) and (2) observational learning. Cognitive-developmental theorists point out that the course of sex-role development will depend, in part, on the child's cognitive development. And proponents of gender schema theory have shown how children's emerging conceptions of sex-role stereotypes color their interpretations of social events and contribute to the development of sex-typed interests, attitudes, and patterns of behavior.

Family structure affects the sex typing of both boys and girls. A boy may have difficulties incorporating certain aspects of the masculine role if his mother is the dominant parent. Boys whose fathers are absent from the home during the first five years are often less aggressive, more dependent, and less masculine in their sex-role preferences than boys from intact families. Father absence has a lesser effect on daughters, although girls from fatherless homes may experience some difficulties in their relationships with males during adolescence and young adulthood. Maternal

employment has no disruptive effects on sex typing. However, children of working mothers, particularly daughters, develop less traditional views of men and women and more favorable impressions of the feminine role.

The psychological attributes "masculinity" and "femininity" are generally considered to be at opposite ends of a single dimension. However, one "new look" at sex roles proposes that masculinity and femininity are two separate dimensions and that the *androgynous* person is someone who possesses a fair number of masculine *and* feminine characteristics. Recent research indicates that androgynous people do exist, are relatively popular and well adjusted, and may be adaptable to a wider variety of environmental demands than people who are traditionally sex-typed.

NOTES

1. The prenatal period refers to the roughly 266 days between conception and birth when an unborn child is developing in the mother's uterus.

2. Indeed, it has been argued that prenatal exposure to male hormones causes the female fetus's brain to be organized like that of a male fetus, which, in turn, accounts for her heightened activity, tomboyishness, and interest in "masculine" pursuits. However, Huston (1983) points out that many of these androgenized females received cortisone therapy to control their androgen levels and prevent further masculinization of their bodies and that one side effect of cortisone is to dramatically increase a person's activity level. Thus, there is some doubt whether these girls' preferences for masculine activities are really attributable to their prenatal exposure to androgen or to its effects on the organization of the central nervous system. A plausible alternative interpretation is that their behavior was influenced by the cortisone treatments they received.

3. Of course, it is important to remember that the behavioral patterns that are considered adaptive or nonadaptive depend to a large extent on the culture in which one is raised. In the two countries where androgyny has been studied most extensively—the United States and Canada—there are some advantages associated with being "androgynous." Yet, it is likely that an androgynous person would feel very uncomfortable indeed (and be viewed as foolhardy or maladjusted) if he or she were a citizen of a

conservative Islamic society or any other culture in which the public expression of "cross-sex" attitudes and behaviors is not sanctioned and is apt to be punished.

REFERENCES

ANGRIST, S. S., Mickelson, R., & Penna, A. N. (1977). Sex differences in sex-role conceptions and family orientation of high school students. *Journal of Youth and Adolescence, 6*, 179–186.

BAGGETT, A. T. (1967). The effect of early loss of father upon the personality of boys and girls in late adolescence. *Dissertation Abstracts, 28*(1-B), 356–357.

BANDURA, A. (1977). *Social learning theory.* Englewood Cliffs, NJ: Prentice-Hall.

BARNETT, R. C. (1979, March). *Parent child-rearing attitudes: Today and yesterday.* Paper presented at the biennial meeting of the Society for Research in Child Development, San Francisco.

BARRY, H., III, Bacon, M. K., & Child, I. L. (1957). A cross-cultural survey of some sex differences in socialization. *Journal of Abnormal and Social Psychology, 55*, 327–332.

BARUCH, G. K. (1972). Maternal influences upon college women's attitudes toward women and work. *Developmental Psychology, 6*, 32–37.

BAUMRIND, D. (1982). Are androgynous individuals more effective persons and parents? *Child Development, 53*, 44–75.

BEACH, F. A. (1965). *Sex and behavior.* New York: Wiley.

BELL, R. Q., Weller, G. M., & Waldrip, M. F. (1971). Newborn and preschooler: Organization of behavior and relations between periods. *Monographs of the Society for Research in Child Development, 36*(1–2, Serial No. 142).

BEM, S. L. (1974). The measurement of psychological androgyny. *Journal of Consulting and Clinical Psychology, 42*, 155–162.

BEM, S. L. (1975). Sex-role adaptability: One consequence of psychological androgyny. *Journal of Personality and Social Psychology, 31*, 634–643.

BEM, S. L. (1978). Beyond androgyny: Some presumptuous prescriptions for a liberated sexual identity. In J. A. Sherman & F. L. Denmark (Eds.), *The psychology of women: Future directions in research.* New York: Psychological Dimensions.

BEM, S. L. (1979). Theory and measurement of androgyny: A reply to the Podhazer-Tetenbaum and Locksley-Colten critiques. *Journal of Personality and Social Psychology, 37*, 1047–1054.

BEM, S. L. (1981). Gender schema theory: A cognitive account of sex-typing. *Psychological Bulletin, 88*, 354–364.

BERMAN, P. W. (1985). Young children's responses to babies: Do they foreshadow differences between maternal and paternal styles? In A. Fogel & G. F. Melson (Eds.), *Origins of nurturance.* Hillsdale, NJ: Erlbaum.

BERMAN, P. W., & Goodman, V. (1984). Age and sex differences in children's responses to babies: Effects of adults' caretaking requests and instructions. *Child Development, 55*, 1071–1077.

BEST, D. L., Williams, J. E., Cloud, J. M., Davis, S. W., Robertson, L. S., Edwards, J. R., Giles, H., & Fowles, J. (1977). Development of sex-trait stereotypes among young children in the United States, England, and Ireland. *Child Development, 48*, 1375–1384.

BILLER, H. B. (1974). *Paternal deprivation.* Lexington, MA: Heath.

BILLER, H. B., & Borstelmann, L. J. (1967). Masculine development: An integrative review. *Merrill-Palmer Quarterly, 13*, 253–294.

BLAKEMORE, J. E. O. (1981). Age and sex differences in interaction with a human infant. *Child Development, 52*, 386–388.

BLAKEMORE, J. E. O., LaRue, A. A., & Olejnik, A. B. (1979). Sex-appropriate toy preference and the ability to conceptualize toys as sex-role related. *Developmental Psychology, 15*, 339–340.

BRADBARD, M. R., Martin, C. L., Endsley, R. C., & Halverson, C. F. (1986). Influence of sex stereotypes on children's exploration and memory: A competence versus performance distinction. *Developmental Psychology, 22*, 481–486.

BRIM, O. G. (1958). Family structure and sex-role learning by children: A further analysis of Helen Koch's data. *Sociometry, 21*, 1–16.

BROOKS-GUNN, J., & Matthews, W. S. (1979). *He and she.* Englewood Cliffs, NJ: Prentice-Hall.

BROVERMAN, I. K., Vogel, S. R., Broverman, D. M., Clarkson, F. E., & Rosenkrantz, P. S. (1972). Sex-role stereotypes: A current appraisal. *Journal of Social Issues, 28*, 59–78.

BROWN, D. G. (1957). Masculinity-femininity development in children. *Journal of Consulting Psychology, 21*, 197–202.

BROWN, R. (1965). *Social psychology.* New York: Free Press.

CANN, A., & Newbern, S. R. (1984). Sex stereotype effects in children's picture recognition. *Child Development, 55*, 1085–1090.

CARTER, D. B., & McCloskey, L. A. (1983–1984). Peers and the maintenance of sex-typed behavior: The development of children's conceptions of cross-gender behavior in their peers. *Social Cognition, 2*, 294–314.

CARTER, D. B., & Patterson, C. J. (1982). Sex roles as social conventions: The development of children's conceptions of sex-role stereotypes. *Developmental Psychology, 18*, 812–824.

CHARLESWORTH, R., & Hartup, W. W. (1967). Positive social reinforcement in the nursery school peer group. *Child Development, 38*, 993–1002.

CONDRY, J., & Condry, S. (1976). Sex differences: A study in the eye of the beholder. *Child Development, 47*, 812–819.

COWAN, C. P., & Cowan, P. A. (1987). A preventive intervention for couples becoming parents. In C. F. Z. Boukydis (Ed.), *Research on support for parents and infants in the postnatal period.* New York: Ablex.

DAMON, W. (1977). *The social world of the child.* San Francisco: Jossey-Bass.

D'ANDRADE, R. G. (1966). Sex differences and cultural institutions. In E. E. Maccoby (Ed.), *The development of sex differences.* Stanford, CA: Stanford University Press.

DEAUX, K. (1977). The social psychology of sex roles. In L. Wrightsman, *Social psychology.* Monterey, CA: Brooks/Cole.

DeVRIES, R. (1974). Relationship among Piagetian, IQ, and achievement assessments. *Child Development, 45*, 746–756.

DIENER, E., Sandvik, E., & Larsen, R. J. (1985). Age and sex effects for emotional intensity. *Developmental Psychology, 21*, 542–546.

DiPIETRO, J. A. (1981). Rough and tumble play: A function of gender. *Developmental Psychology, 17*, 50–58.

DOTY, R. L., Carter, C. S., & Clemens, L. G. (1971). Olfactory control of sexual behavior in male and early-androgenized female hamsters. *Hormones and Behavior, 2*, 325–335.

DRAKE, C. T., & McDougall, D. (1977). Effects of the absence of the father and other male models on the development of boys' sex-roles. *Developmental Psychology, 13*, 537–538.

DWECK, C. S., & Elliott, E. S. (1983). Achievement motivation. In E. M. Hetherington (Ed.), *Handbook of child psychology* (Vol. 4). New York: Wiley.

EATON, W. O., & Keats, J. G. (1982). Peer presence, stress, and sex differences in the motor activity levels of preschoolers. *Developmental Psychology, 18*, 534–540.

EATON, W. O., & Von Bargen, D. (1981). Asynchronous development of gender understanding in preschool children. *Child Development, 52*, 1020–1027.

EHRHARDT, A. A., & Baker, S. W. (1974). Fetal androgens, human central nervous system differentiation, and behavioral sex differences. In R. C. Friedman, R. M. Richard, & R. L. Van de Wiele (Eds.), *Sex differences in behavior.* New York: Wiley.

EISENBERG, N., Murray, E., & Hite, T. (1982). Children's reasoning regarding sex-typed toy choices. *Child Development, 53*, 81–86.

EISENBERG, N., Wolchik, S. A., Hernandez, R., & Pasternack, J. F. (1985). Parental socialization of young children's play: A short-term longitudinal study. *Child Development, 56*, 1506–1513.

EMMERICH, W. (1959). Parental identification in young children. *Genetic Psychology Monographs, 60*, 257–308.

ETAUGH, C. (1974). Effects of maternal employment on children: A review of recent research. *Merrill-Palmer Quarterly, 20*, 71–98.

ETAUGH, C., & Brown, B. (1975). Perceiving the causes of success and failure of male and female performers. *Developmental Psychology, 11*, 103.

FAGOT, B. I. (1978). The influence of sex of child on parental reactions to toddler children. *Child Development, 49*, 459–465.

FAGOT, B. I. (1985). Beyond the reinforcement principle: Another step toward understanding sex-role development. *Developmental Psychology, 21*, 1097–1104.

FAGOT, B. I., Leinbach, M. D., & Hagan, R. (1986). Gender labeling and the adoption of sex-typed behaviors. *Developmental Psychology, 22*, 440–443.

FELDMAN, S. S., Biringen, Z. C., & Nash, S. C. (1981). Fluctuations of sex-typed self-attributions as a function of stage of family life cycle. *Developmental Psychology, 17*, 24–35.

FELDMAN-SUMMERS, S., & Kiesler, S. B. (1974). Those who are number two try harder: The effect of sex on attribution of causality. *Journal of Personality and Social Psychology, 30*, 846–855.

FORISHA, B. L., & Goldman, B. H. (1981). *Outsiders on the inside: Women and organizations*. Englewood Cliffs, NJ: Prentice-Hall.

FRUEH, T., & McGhee, P. H. (1975). Traditional sex-role development and the amount of time spent watching television. *Developmental Psychology, 11*, 109.

GINSBURG, H. J., & Miller, S. M. (1982). Sex differences in children's risk-taking behavior. *Child Development, 53*, 426–428.

GOLD, D., & Andres, D. (1978). Developmental comparisons between ten-year-old children with employed and nonemployed mothers. *Child Development, 49*, 75–84.

GOLDBERG, P. (1968). Are women prejudiced against women? *Trans/Action, 5*, 28–30.

GOUZE, K. R., & Nadelman, L. (1980). Constancy of gender identity for self and others in children between the ages of three and seven. *Child Development, 51*, 275–278.

GROTEVANT, H. D. (1978). Sibling constellations and sex-typing of interests in adolescence. *Child Development, 49*, 540–542.

GUNNAR, M. R., & Donahue, M. (1980). Sex differences in social responsiveness between six months and twelve months. *Child Development, 51*, 262–265.

HAINLINE, L., & Feig, E. (1978). The correlates of childhood father absence in college-aged women. *Child Development, 49*, 37–42.

HALL, J. A., & Halberstadt, A. G. (1980). Masculinity and femininity in children: Development of the Children's Personal Attributes Questionnaire. *Developmental Psychology, 16*, 270–280.

HANSSON, R. O., Chernovetz, M. E., & Jones, W. H. (1977). Maternal employment and androgyny. *Psychology of Women Quarterly, 2*, 76–78.

HARTUP, W. W. (1983). The peer system. In E. M. Hetherington (Ed.), *Handbook of child psychology* (Vol. 4). New York: Wiley.

HAUGH, S. S., Hoffman, C. D., & Cowan, G. (1980). The eye of the very young beholder: Sex-typing of infants by young children. *Child Development, 51*, 598–600.

HETHERINGTON, E. M. (1965). A developmental study of the effects of sex of the dominant parent on sex-role preference, identification, and imitation in children. *Journal of Personality and Social Psychology, 2*, 188–194.

HETHERINGTON, E. M. (1966). Effects of paternal absence on sex-typed behaviors in Negro and white preadolescent males. *Journal of Personality and Social Psychology, 4*, 87–91.

HETHERINGTON, E. M. (1967). The effects of familial variables on sex-typing, on parent-child similarity, and on imitation in children. In J. P. Hill (Ed.), *Minnesota Symposia on Child Psychology* (Vol. 1). Minneapolis: University of Minnesota Press.

HETHERINGTON, E. M. (1972). Effects of father absence on personality development in adolescent daughters. *Developmental Psychology, 7*, 313–326.

HETHERINGTON, E. M. (1979). Divorce: A child's perspective. *American Psychologist, 34*, 851–858.

HETHERINGTON, E. M., Cox, M., & Cox, R. (1976). Divorced fathers. *Family Coordinator, 25*, 417–428.

HETHERINGTON, E. M., Cox, M., & Cox, R. (1978). The aftermath of divorce. In J. H. Stevens & M. Matthews (Eds.), *Mother-child, father-child relations*. Washington, DC: National Association for the Education of Young Children.

HETHERINGTON, E. M., & Frankie, G. (1967). Effect of parental dominance, warmth, and conflict on imitation in children. *Journal of Personality and Social Psychology, 6*, 119–125.

HETHERINGTON, E. M., & Parke, R. D. (1975). *Child psychology: A contemporary viewpoint*. New York: McGraw-Hill.

HETHERINGTON, E. M., & Parke, R. D. (1986). *Child psychology: A contemporary viewpoint* (3rd ed.). New York: McGraw-Hill.

HINES, M. (1982). Prenatal gonadal hormones and sex differences in human behavior. *Psychological Bulletin, 92*, 56–80.

HOFFMAN, L. W. (1979). Maternal employment: 1979. *American Psychologist, 34*, 859–865.

HOFFMAN, L. W. (1984). Work, family, and the socialization of the child. In R. D. Parke (Ed.), *Review of child development research*. Vol. 7: *The family*. Chicago: University of Chicago Press.

HOYENGA, K. B., & Hoyenga, K. T. (1979). *The question of sex differences*. Boston: Little, Brown.

HUSTON, A. C. (1983). Sex-typing. In E. M. Hetherington (Ed.), *Handbook of child psychology* (Vol. 4). New York: Wiley.

HUTT, C. (1972). *Males and females*. Baltimore: Penguin Books.

IMPERATO-McGINLEY, J., Peterson, R. E., Gautier, T., & Sturla, E. (1979). Androgyns and the evolution of male gender identity among male pseudohermaphrodites with 5a-reductase deficiency. *New England Journal of Medicine, 300*, 1233–1237.

INTONS-PETERSON, M., & Reddel, M. (1984). What do people ask about a neonate? *Developmental Psychology, 20*, 358–359.

JACKLIN, C. N., & Maccoby, E. E. (1978). Social behaviors at 33 months in same-sex and mixed-sex dyads. *Child Development, 49*, 557–569.

KAGAN, J., & Moss, H. A. (1962). *Birth to maturity*. New York: Wiley.

KAPPEL, B. E., & Lambert, R. D. (1972). *Self worth among children of working mothers*. Unpublished manuscript, University of Waterloo.

KATCHER, A. (1955). The discrimination of sex differences by young children. *Journal of Genetic Psychology, 87*, 131–143.

KLEIN, R. P. (1985). Caregiving arrangements by employed women with children under 1 year of age. *Developmental Psychology, 21*, 403–406.

KOHLBERG, L. (1966). A cognitive-developmental analysis of children's sex-role concepts and attitudes. In E. E. Maccoby (Ed.), *The development of sex differences*. Stanford, CA: Stanford University Press.

KOHLBERG, L. (1969). Stage and sequence: The cognitive-developmental approach to socialization. In D. A. Goslin (Ed.), *Handbook of socialization theory and research*. Chicago: Rand McNally.

KOLBE, R., & LaVoie, J. C. (1981). Sex-role stereotyping in preschool children's picture books. *Social Psychology Quarterly, 44*, 369–374.

KUHN, D., Nash, S. C., & Brucken, L. (1978). Sex-role concepts of two- and three-year-olds. *Child Development, 49*, 445–451.

LA FRENIERE, P., Strayer, F. F., & Gauthier, R. (1984). The emergence of same-sex affiliative preferences among preschool peers: A developmental/ethological perspective. *Child Development, 55*, 1958–1965.

LAMB, M. E. (1981). *The role of the father in child development*. New York: Wiley.

LAMKE, L. K. (1982). The impact of sex-role orientation on self-esteem in early adolescence. *Child Development, 53*, 1530–1535.

LANGLOIS, J. H., & Downs, A. C. (1980). Mothers, fathers, and peers as socialization agents of sex-typed play behaviors in young children. *Child Development, 51*, 1237–1247.

LAVINE, L. O. (1982). Parental power as a potential influence on girls' career choice. *Child Development, 53*, 658–663.

LEARY, M. A., Greer, D., & Huston, A. C. (1982, April). *The relation between TV viewing and gender roles*. Paper presented at the meeting of the Southwestern Society for Research in Human Development, Galveston, TX.

LEICHTY, M. M. (1960). The effect of father absence during early childhood upon the oedipal situation as reflected in young adults. *Merrill-Palmer Quarterly, 6*, 212–217.

LEVY-SHIFF, R. (1982). Effects of father absence on young children in mother-headed families. *Child Development, 53*, 1400–1405.

LIEBERT, R. M., Sprafkin, J. N., & Davidson, E. S. (1982). *The early window: Effects of television on children and youth*. New York: Pergamon Press.

LINN, M. C., & Petersen, A. C. (1985). Emergence and categorization of sex differences in spatial ability: A meta-analysis. *Child Development, 56*, 1479–1498.

LYNN, D. B. (1974). *The father: His role in child development*. Monterey, CA: Brooks/Cole.

LYNN, D. B., & Sawrey, W. L. (1959). The effects of father absence on Norwegian boys and girls. *Journal of Abnormal and Social Psychology, 59*, 258–262.

MACCOBY, E. E. (1980). *Social development*. San Diego, CA: Harcourt Brace Jovanovich.

MACCOBY, E. E., & Jacklin, C. N. (1974). *The psychology of sex differences*. Stanford, CA: Stanford University Press.

MACCOBY, E. E., & Jacklin, C. N. (1980). Sex differences in aggression: A rejoinder and reprise. *Child Development, 51*, 964–980.

MacFARLANE, A. (1977). *The psychology of childbirth*. Cambridge, MA: Harvard University Press.

MacKINNON, C. E., Brody, G. H., & Stoneman, Z. (1982). The effects of divorce and maternal employment on the home environments of preschool children. *Child Development, 53*, 1392–1399.

MAJOR, B., Carnevale, P. J. D., & Deaux, K. (1981). A different perspective on androgyny: Evaluations of masculine and feminine personality characteristics. *Journal of Personality and Social Psychology, 41*, 988–1001.

MARANTZ, S. A., & Mansfield, A. F. (1977). Maternal employment and the development of sex-role stereotyping in five- to eleven-year-old girls. *Child Development, 48*, 668–673.

MARCUS, D. E., & Overton, W. F. (1978). The development of cognitive gender constancy and sex-role preferences. *Child Development, 49*, 434–444.

MARTIN, C. L., & Halverson, C. F., Jr. (1981). A schematic processing model of sex typing and stereotyping in children. *Child Development, 52*, 1119–1134.

MARTIN, C. L., & Halverson, C. F., Jr. (1983). The effects of sex-typing schemas on young children's memory. *Child Development, 54*, 563–574.

MARTIN, J. A. (1980). A longitudinal study of the consequences of early mother-infant interaction: A microanalytic approach. *Monographs of the Society for Research in Child Development, 46*(3, Serial No. 190).

MASSAD, C. M. (1981). Sex-role identity and adjustment during adolescence. *Child Development, 52*, 1290–1298.

MASTERS, J. C., Ford, M. E., Arend, R., Grotevant, H. D., & Clark, L. V. (1979). Modeling and labeling as integrated determinants of children's sex-typed imitative behavior. *Child Development, 50*, 364–371.

McARTHUR, L. Z., & Resko, B. G. (1975). The portrayal of men and women in American television commercials. *Journal of Social Psychology, 97*, 209–229.

McCONAGHY, M. J. (1979). Gender permanence and the genital basis of gender: Stages in the development of constancy of gender identity. *Child Development, 50*, 1223–1226.

MEAD, M. (1935). *Sex and temperament in three primitive societies*. New York: Morrow.

MEYER, B. (1980). The development of girls' sex-role attitudes. *Child Development, 51*, 508–514.

MEYER-BAHLBERG, H. F. L., Bruder, G. E., Feldman, J. F., Ehrhardt, A. A., Healey, J. M., & Bell, J. (1985). Cognitive abilities and hemispheric lateralization in females following idiopathic precocious puberty. *Developmental Psychology, 21*, 878–887.

MISCHEL, W. (1970). Sex-typing and socialization. In P. H. Mussen (Ed.), *Carmichael's manual of child psychology* (Vol. 2). New York: Wiley.

MONEY, J. (1965). Psychosexual differentiation. In J. Money (Ed.), *Sex research: New developments*. New York: Holt, Rinehart and Winston.

MONEY, J., & Ehrhardt, A. (1972). *Man and woman, boy and girl*. Baltimore: Johns Hopkins University Press.

MONEY, J., & Tucker, P. (1975). *Sexual signatures: On being a man or a woman*. Boston: Little, Brown.

MORGAN, M. (1982). Television and adolescents' sex-role stereotypes: A longitudinal study. *Journal of Personality and Social Psychology, 43*, 947–955.

MOSS, H. A. (1967). Sex, age, and state as determinants of mother-infant interaction. *Merrill-Palmer Quarterly, 13*, 19–36.

MUNROE, R. H., Shimmin, H. S., & Munroe, R. L. (1984). Gender understanding and sex-role preferences in four cultures. *Developmental Psychology, 20*, 673–682.

MUSSEN, P. H., & Rutherford, E. (1963). Parent-child relations and parental personality in relation to young children's sex-role preferences. *Child Development, 34*, 589–607.

NADELMAN, L. (1970). Sex identity in London children: Memory, knowledge, and preference tests. *Human Development, 13*, 28–42.

NADELMAN, L. (1974). Sex identity in American children: Memory, knowledge, and preference tests. *Developmental Psychology, 10*, 413–417.

NASH, S. C. (1975). The relationship among sex-role stereotyping, sex-role preference, and the sex difference in spatial visualization. *Sex Roles, 1*, 15–32.

NEWCOMBE, N., & Bandura, M. M. (1983). Effect of age at puberty on spatial ability in girls: A question of mechanism. *Developmental Psychology, 19*, 215–224.

OLWEUS, D., Mattsson, A., Schalling, D., & Low, H. (1980). Testosterone, aggression, physical and personality dimensions in normal adolescent males. *Psychosomatic Medicine, 42*, 253–269.

ONE-PARENT FAMILIES AND THEIR CHILDREN: The school's most significant minority. (1980). *Principal, 60*, 31–37.

ORLOFSKY, J. L. (1979). Parental antecedents of sex-role orientation in college men and women. *Sex Roles, 5*, 495–512.

PARSONS, J. E., Adler, T. F., & Kaczala, C. M. (1982). Socialization of achievement attitudes and beliefs: Parental influences. *Child Development, 53*, 310–321.

PARSONS, J. E., Kaczala, C. M., & Meese, J. L. (1982). Socialization of achievement attitudes and beliefs: Classroom influences. *Child Development, 53*, 322–339.

PARSONS, T. (1955). Family structure and the socialization of the child. In T. Parsons & R. F. Bales (Eds.), *Family socialization and interaction processes*. New York: Free Press.

PERRY, D. G., & Bussey, K. (1984). *Social development*. Englewood Cliffs, NJ: Prentice-Hall.

PHILLIPS, S., King, S., & Dubois, L. (1978). Spontaneous activities of female versus male newborns. *Child Development, 49*, 590–597.

POLLIS, N. P., & Doyle, D. C. (1972). Sex role, status, and perceived competence among first-graders. *Perceptual and Motor Skills, 34*, 235–238.

RABBAN, M. (1950). Sex-role identification in young children in two diverse social groups. *Genetic Psychology Monographs, 42*, 81–158.

RICHARDSON, J. G., & Simpson, C. H. (1982). Children, gender, and social structure: An analysis of the contents of letters to Santa Claus. *Child Development, 53*, 429–436.

ROOPNARINE, J. L. (1984). Sex-typed socialization in mixed-aged preschool classrooms. *Child Development, 55*, 1078–1084.

ROSE, R. M., Bernstein, I. S., & Gordon, T. P. (1975). Consequences of social conflict on plasma testosterone levels in rhesus monkeys. *Psychosomatic Medicine, 37*, 50–61.

ROSENBERG, B. G., & Sutton-Smith, B. (1964). Ordinal position and sex-role identification. *Genetic Psychology Monographs, 70*, 297–328.

ROSENBLATT, P. C., & Cunningham, M. R. (1976). Sex differences in cross-cultural perspective. In B. Lloyd & J. Archer (Eds.), *Exploring sex differences*. London: Academic Press.

ROTHSCHILD, N. (1979). *Group as a mediating factor in the cultivation process among young children*. Unpublished master's thesis, Annenberg School of Communications, University of Pennsylvania.

RUBLE, D. N., Balaban, T., & Cooper, J. (1981). Gender constancy and the effects of sex-typed televised toy commercials. *Child Development, 52*, 667–673.

RUBLE, T. L. (1983). Sex stereotypes: Issues of change in the 1970s. *Sex Roles, 9*, 397–402.

SANDERS, B., & Soares, M. P. (1986). Sexual maturation and spatial ability in college students. *Developmental Psychology, 22*, 199–203.

SANTROCK, J. W. (1970). Paternal absence, sex-typing, and identification. *Developmental Psychology, 2*, 264–272.

SANTROCK, J. W. (1975). Father absence, perceived maternal behavior, and moral development in boys. *Child Development, 46*, 753–757.

SANTROCK, J. W., & Warshak, R. A. (1979). Father custody and social development in boys and girls. *Journal of Social Issues, 35*, 112–125.

SELECT Committee on Children, Youth, and Families. (1983, May). *U.S. children and their families: Current conditions and recent trends. A report*. Washington, DC: U.S. Government Printing Office.

SHAFFER, D. R., & Johnson, R. D. (1980). Effects of occupational choice and sex-role preferences on the attractiveness of competent men and women. *Journal of Personality, 48*, 505–519.

SLABY, R. G., & Frey, K. S. (1975). Development of gender constancy and selective attention to same-sex models. *Child Development, 46*, 849–856.

SMITH, P. K., & Daglish, L. (1977). Sex differences in parent and infant behavior in the home. *Child Development, 48*, 1250–1254.

SNOW, M. E., Jacklin, C. N., & Maccoby, E. E. (1983). Sex-of-child differences in father-child interaction at one year of age. *Child Development, 54*, 227–232.

SPENCE, J. T. (1982). Comment on Baumrind's "Are androgynous individuals more effective persons and parents?" *Child Development, 53*, 76–80.

SPENCE, J. T., & Helmreich, R. L. (1978). *Masculinity and femininity: Their psychological dimensions, correlates, and antecedents*. Austin: University of Texas Press.

STEIN, A. H. (1973). The effects of maternal employment and educational attainment on the sex-typed attributes of college females. *Social Behavior and Personality, 1*, 111–114.

STODDART, T., & Turiel, E. (1985). Children's conceptions of cross-gender activities. *Child Development, 56*, 1241–1252.

STOLZ, L. M. (1954). *Father relations of war-born children*. Stanford, CA: Stanford University Press.

SUTTON-SMITH, B., & Rosenberg, B. G. (1970). *The sibling*. New York: Holt, Rinehart and Winston.

TAN, R. S. (1979). TV beauty ads and role expectations of adolescent female viewers. *Journalism Quarterly, 56*, 283–288.

TAUBER, M. A. (1979a). Parental socialization techniques and sex differences in children's play. *Child Development, 50*, 225–234.

TAUBER, M. A. (1979b). Sex differences in parent-child interaction styles during a free-play session. *Child Development, 50*, 981–988.

TERBORG, J. R., & Ilgen, D. R. (1975). A theoretical approach to sex discrimination in traditionally masculine occupations. *Organizational Behavior and Human Performance, 13*, 352–376.

THOMPSON, S. K. (1975). Gender labels and early sex-role development. *Child Development, 46*, 339–347.

THOMPSON, S. K., & Bentler, P. M. (1971). The priority of cues in sex discrimination by children and adults. *Developmental Psychology, 5*, 181–185.

TOLAR, C. J. (1968). An investigation of parent-offspring relationships. *Dissertation Abstracts, 28*(8-B), 3465.

TOUHEY, J. C. (1974). Effects of additional women professionals on ratings of occupational prestige and desirability. *Journal of Personality and Social Psychology, 29*, 86–89.

URBERG, K. A. (1979). Sex-role conceptualization in adolescents and adults. *Developmental Psychology, 15*, 90–92.

VOGEL, S. R., Broverman, I. K., Broverman, D. M., Clarkson, F. E., & Rosenkrantz, P. S. (1970). Maternal employment and perception of sex roles among college students. *Developmental Psychology, 3*, 384–391.

WABER, D. P. (1977). Sex differences in mental abilities, hemispheric lateralization, and rate of physical growth at adolescence. *Developmental Psychology, 13*, 29–38.

WEHREN, A., & De Lisi, R. (1983). The development of gender understanding: Judgments and explanations. *Child Development, 54*, 1568–1578.

WEINRAUB, M., Clemens, L. P., Sockloff, A., Ethridge, T., Gracely, E., & Myers, B. (1984). The development of sex-role stereotypes in the third year: Relationships to gender labeling, gender identity, sex-typed toy preferences, and family characteristics. *Child Development, 55*, 1493–1503.

WERNER, P. D., & LaRussa, G. W. (1983). *Persistence and change in sex-role stereotypes*. Unpublished manuscript, California School of Professional Psychology.

WHITLEY, B. E., Jr. (1983). Sex-role orientation and self-esteem: A critical meta-analytic review. *Journal of Personality and Social Psychology, 44*, 765–778.

WITTIG, M. A., & Petersen, A. C. (1979). *Sex-related differences in cognitive functioning: Developmental issues*. Orlando, FL: Academic Press.

WOHLFORD, P., Santrock, J. W., Berger, S. E., & Leiberman, D. (1971). Older brothers' influence on sex-typed aggressive and dependent behavior in father absent children. *Developmental Psychology, 4*, 124–134.

YOUNG, W. C., Goy, R. W., & Phoenix, C. H. (1964). Hormones and sexual behavior. *Science, 143*, 212–218.

ZERN, D. S. (1984). Relationships among selected child-rearing variables in a cross-cultural sample of 110 societies. *Developmental Psychology, 20*, 683–690.

13

THE FAMILY

(continues)

SOCIAL-CLASS DIFFERENCES IN PARENTING
Social-Class Differences in Attitudes, Values, and Lifestyles
Patterns of Child Rearing in High-SES and Low-SES Families

EFFECTS OF SIBLINGS AND THE FAMILY CONFIGURATION
The Nature of Sibling Interactions
Origins and Determinants of Sibling Rivalry
Positive Effects of Sibling Interaction
Characteristics of First-Born and Later-Born Children

THE IMPACT OF DIVORCE
The Immediate Effects
The Crisis Phase
Long-Term Reactions to Divorce
Delinquency among Children from Single-Parent Homes
Children in Reconstituted Families

EFFECTS OF MATERNAL EMPLOYMENT

(continues)

WHEN PARENTING BREAKS DOWN: THE PROBLEM OF CHILD ABUSE

Who Is Abused?

Who Are the Abusers?

Social-Situational Triggers: The Ecology of Child Abuse

How Can We Help Abusive Parents and Their Children?

SUMMARY

REFERENCES

Have humans always been social animals? Although no one can answer this question with absolute certainty, the archeological record provides some strong clues. Apparently our closest evolutionary ancestors (dating back before the Neanderthals) were already living in small bands, or tribal units, that provided increased protection against common enemies and allowed individuals to share the many labors necessary for their survival (Weaver, 1985). Of course, there are no written records of social life among these early collectives. But it is clear that, at some point during the prehistoric era, early human societies (and perhaps even the protohuman aggregations) evolved codes of conduct that defined the roles of various tribal members and sanctioned certain motives and practices while prohibiting others. Once a workable social order was established, it then became necessary to "socialize" each succeeding generation.

Socialization is the process by which children acquire the beliefs, values, and behaviors deemed significant and appropriate by the older members of their society. The socialization of each generation serves society in at least three ways. First, it is a means of regulating children's behavior and controlling their undesirable or antisocial impulses. Second, the socialization process helps to promote the personal growth of the individual. As children interact with and become like other members of their culture, they acquire the knowledge, skills, motives, and aspirations that should enable them to adapt to their environment and function effectively within their communities. Finally, socialization perpetuates the social order. Socialized children become socialized adults who will impart what they have learned to their own children.

All societies have developed various mechanisms, or institutions, for socializing their young. Examples of these socializing institutions are the family, the church, the educational system, children's groups (for example, Boy and Girl Scouts), and the mass media.

Central among the many social agencies that impinge on the child is that institution we call the family. More than 99% of children in the United States are raised in a family of one kind or another (U.S. Department of Commerce, 1979), and most children in most societies grow up in a home setting with at least one biological parent or other relative. Often children have little exposure to people outside the family for several years until they are placed in day care or nursery school or until they reach the age at which they will begin formal schooling. So it is fair to say that the family has a clear head start on other institutions when it comes to socializing a child. And since the events of the early years are very important to the child's social, emotional, and intellectual development, it is perhaps appropriate to think of the family as society's most important instrument of socialization.

Our focus in this chapter is on the family as a social system—an institution that both influences and is influenced by its young. What is a family, and what functions do families serve? How does the birth of a child affect other family members? Do the existing (or changing) relationships among other members of the family have any effect on the care and training that a young child receives? Are some patterns of child rearing better than others? Do parents decide how they will raise their children—or might children be influencing their parents? Does the family's socioeconomic status affect parenting and parent/child interactions? Do siblings play an important part in the socialization process? How do children react to divorce, maternal employment, or a return to the two-parent family when a single parent remarries? And why do some parents mistreat their children? These are the issues we will consider as we look at the important roles that families play in the cognitive, social, and emotional development of their children.

BASIC FEATURES AND FUNCTIONS OF THE FAMILY

The characteristics of a family are difficult to summarize in a sentence or two. Many family sociologists prefer to think of the family unit as a social system consisting of three basic roles: wife/mother, husband/father, and child/sibling. Of course, there are many variations on this traditional *nuclear family*. In the United States, for example, there are nearly as many childless married couples as there are families with children, and about 40–50% of American children will spend some time in a *single-parent home*

(Clarke-Stewart, 1982; Glick, 1984). Although the nuclear family is the norm in contemporary Western society, people in many cultures (and subcultures) live in *extended families*—an arrangement in which grandparents, parents and their children, aunts, uncles, nieces, and nephews may live under the same roof and share responsibility for maintaining the household. Indeed, the extended family is a common arrangement for Black Americans—and an adaptive one in that large numbers of economically disadvantaged Black mothers must work, are often supporting their offspring without the father, and can surely use the assistance they receive from grandparents, siblings, uncles, aunts, and cousins who may live with them (or nearby) and serve as surrogate parents for young children (Wilson, 1986). Until recently, family researchers have largely ignored extended families or looked upon them as unhealthy contexts for child rearing. Yet that view is now changing, thanks in part to research showing how support from members of extended families (for example, grandparents) can help disadvantaged single mothers to establish secure attachments with their infants and toddlers (see Egeland & Sroufe, 1981). Indeed, it would not be surprising to see an explosion of research on the extended family in the years ahead, for the high incidence of divorce and the ever-increasing numbers of children born out of wedlock are making the extended family arrangement more and more common among all segments and strata of American society (Wilson, 1986).

THE FUNCTIONS OF A FAMILY

Families serve society in many ways. They produce and consume goods and services, thereby playing a role in the economy. Traditionally, the family has served as an outlet for the sexual urges of its adult members and as the means of replacing the elements of society who succumb to illness, accidents, or old age. Indeed, few societies sanction the birth of "illegitimate" children (that is, those born out of wedlock), who are often treated as second-class citizens and called uncomplimentary names such as "bastard." Historically, families have cared for their elderly, although this function is now less common in Western societies with the advent of institutions such

as Social Security, socialized medical care, and nursing homes. But perhaps the most widely recognized functions of the family—those that are served in all societies—are the caregiving, nurturing, and training that parents and other family members provide for young children.

THE GOALS OF PARENTING

After studying the child-rearing practices of many diverse cultures, Robert LeVine (1974, p. 230) concluded that families in all societies have three basic goals for their children:

1. The *survival goal*—to promote the physical survival and health of the child, ensuring that the child will live long enough to have children of his or her own.
2. The *economic goal*—to foster the skills and behavioral capacities that the child will need for economic self-maintenance as an adult.
3. The *self-actualization goal*—to foster behavioral capabilities for maximizing other cultural values (for example, morality, religion, achievement, wealth, prestige, and a sense of personal satisfaction).

According to LeVine, these universal goals of parenting form a hierarchy. Parents and other caregivers are initially concerned about maximizing the child's chances of survival, and higher-order goals such as teaching the child to talk, count, or abide by moral rules are placed on the back burner until it is clear that the youngster is healthy and is likely to survive. When physical health and security can be taken for granted, then parents begin to encourage those characteristics that are necessary for economic self-sufficiency. Only after survival and the attributes necessary for economic productivity have been established do parents begin to encourage the child to seek status, prestige, and self-fulfillment.

LeVine's ideas stem from his observations of child-rearing practices in societies where infants often die before their second birthday. Regardless of whether one is observing African Bushmen, South American Indians, or Indonesian tribes, parents in societies where infant mortality is high tend to maintain close contact with their infants 24 hours a day,

PHOTO 13-1 In many cultures, parents increase their babies' chances of survival by keeping them close at all times.

often carrying them on their hips or their backs in some sort of sling or cradleboard. LeVine suggests that these practices increase the infants' chances of survival by reducing the likelihood of their becoming ill or dehydrated, crawling into the river or the campfire, or ambling off to be captured by a predator. Although infants are kept close at all times, their parents rarely chat with or smile at them and may seem almost uninterested in their future psychological development. Could this pattern of psychologically aloof yet competent physical caregiving be a defensive maneuver that prevents parents from becoming overly attached to an infant who could well die? Perhaps so, for many cultures in which infant mortality is high still institutionalize practices such as not speaking to neonates as if they were human beings or not naming them until late in the first year, when it is more probable that they will survive (Brazelton, 1979).

The next task that parents face is to promote those characteristics and competencies that will enable children to care for themselves and their own future families. Anthropologist John Ogbu (1981) points out that the economy of a culture (that is, the way in which people support themselves, or subsist) will determine how families socialize their young. To illustrate his point, he cites a well-known cross-cultural study by Herbert Barry and his associates (Barry, Child, & Bacon, 1959), which we discussed in Chapter 8. Recall the findings of that study: Societies that depended on an agricultural or pastoral economy (those that accumulate food) trained their children to be obedient and cooperative and to work for the greater good of the group. By contrast, groups that do not accumulate food (hunting, trapping, and fishing societies) encouraged their children to be independent and assertive and to pursue individual goals. So both types of society were simply emphasizing the values, competencies, and attributes that are necessary to maintain their way of life.

Even in industrialized societies such as the United States, a family's social position or socioeconomic status affects the child-rearing practices that parents will use. For example, parents from the lower socioeconomic strata, who typically work for a boss and must defer to his or her authority, tend to stress obedience, neatness, cleanliness, and respect for power—attributes that should enable their children to function effectively within a blue-collar economy. By contrast, middle-class parents, particularly those who work for themselves or who are professionals, are more likely to stress ambition, curiosity, creativity, and independence when raising their children (Hess, 1970; Kohn, 1979). The latter finding would hardly surprise LeVine, who would argue that middle-class parents who have the resources to promote their child's eventual economic security are freer to encourage his or her initiative, achievement, and personal self-fulfillment (the third set of parenting goals) at a very early age.

SOME CAUTIONARY COMMENTS ABOUT THE STUDY OF FAMILIES

As we progress through the chapter, looking at the ways families influence and are influenced by the development of their young, there are several important points to keep in mind. First, there is no "best way" to study families; each of the methods that investigators have used has very definite strengths and weaknesses (see Box 13-1), and the most convincing information that we have about family effects

BOX 13-1 *METHODS OF STUDYING THE FAMILY*

Investigators who study family relationships have traditionally used one of three research strategies: the *interview* or *questionnaire* technique, *direct observation* of family interactions, or *laboratory analogue studies* (that is, experimental simulations of parent/child interactions). Although these approaches have generated a lot of very useful information about families, it is important to understand the strengths and weaknesses of each.

Interview and Questionnaire Studies

In an interview or questionnaire study, parents are asked to recall and describe the child-rearing practices they have used and to indicate the ways their children have acted at different times and in a variety of situations. The major advantage of this approach is that one can collect an enormous amount of information about a parent and his or her children in a short time.

Unfortunately, the interview/questionnaire method can generate inaccurate and misleading data if parents cannot recall how they or their child behaved earlier or if they confuse the child-rearing practices they used while raising different children. When asked to describe the previous behavior of any one of their children, parents are likely to become confused about which child did what and when, and thus they may end up providing a composite description of all their children. Finally, most parents have heard noted authorities express opinions about "proper" child-rearing practices, and often the practices advocated by experts differ from those that the parent has used. If even a small percentage of parents say that they relied on these "socially desirable" practices rather than the ones that they actually used, this response bias could obscure any real relationships that may exist between parenting styles and behavior of young children.

Today few investigators rely exclusively on the interview or questionnaire technique when studying family relations. Perhaps the most common research strategy is to observe family members interacting with one another at home or in the laboratory and to supplement these observations with questionnaire data or interviews.

Observational Methodologies

One excellent method of studying family relations and learning how family members influence one another is to observe them interacting at home or in the laboratory. Researchers who conduct observational studies are able to look at *behavioral sequences* among various family members and determine who did what to whom with what effect. By focusing on behavioral sequences, the investigator can answer questions such as: What does the mother typically do when her son ignores her? Does she raise her voice to ensure that he listens; threaten to take away a cherished privilege; spank him? How does the child respond to his mother's influence attempts? Does he comply; argue with her; cry? Does the father become involved in these exchanges; how; when? Of course, use of an observational methodology requires the researcher to assess the *reliability* of his or her observations (see Chapter 1 for a discussion of the reliability issue). And unfortunately the mere presence of an observer making notes and recording data can

consists of findings that have been replicated using several methods.

In addition, much of the research that we will review assumes that the child-rearing practices that parents use largely determine how their children will behave. But as we will see, this unidirectional model of family effects is much too simple. Not only do children seem to influence the behavior and child-rearing strategies of their parents, but there is also reason to believe that a family is a complex social system in which each family member influences the thinking and behavior of every other family member.

Finally, some of the research that we will examine might seem to suggest that certain patterns of parent-

ing are better or "more competent" than others. Now let's see why many family researchers are reluctant to endorse this conclusion.

THE MIDDLE-CLASS BIAS

Much of the data that we will review were collected from White, middle-class samples in Western cultures and apply most directly to the development of White, middle-class children. Should we assume that the patterns of child rearing that are most effective for these youngsters are "better" or more appropriate than other parenting techniques? If we do, we may be making a serious mistake, for as John Ogbu (1981)

BOX 13-1 *continued*

affect the ways family members relate to one another. For example, Leslie Zegoib and her associates (Zegoib, Arnold, & Forehand, 1975) report that mothers are warmer, more patient, and more involved with their children when they know they are being observed. Moreover, siblings and peer playmates are less likely to issue commands or to tease, quarrel, or threaten each other when observers are present (Brody, Stoneman, & Wheatley, 1984). Some investigators have tried to minimize these "observer effects" by capturing family interactions on videotape recorders placed in unobtrusive locations in the lab or the home. Another strategy is to mingle with the family for a few days before any data are collected so the family members will gradually become accustomed to the observer's presence and behave more naturally.

The Analogue Experiment

In a laboratory analogue, an adult experimenter behaves in a way that simulates a particular pattern of child rearing and then observes the effect of this experimental manipulation on the child's behavior. For example, we've seen in Chapter 11 how Ross Parke and his associates used the analogue technique to study the impact of various forms of punishment on children's resistance to temptation.

One problem with this approach is that the sequential complexities of parent/child interactions are difficult if not impossible to simulate in a situation where the child interacts on a *single occasion* with a *strange* adult. Moreover, the experimental tasks that children face in an analogue and the rules they must follow are often very dissimilar to those they encounter at home, at school, or on the playground. Consider that children are often required to play with unattractive objects and to refrain from touching attractive toys in laboratory tests of resistance to temptation. Such a "prohibition" may seem arbitrary or irrational to youngsters whose experience in the home and at school suggests that it is acceptable to play with whatever toys are present in their play areas. Finally, prevailing ethical standards prevent experimenters from exposing children to the kinds of *intense* child-rearing practices (for example, spanking, ridicule, name-calling, and rejection) that may occur in the home setting. So laboratory simulations of a particular child-rearing strategy are often rather weak approximations of their naturalistic referents, and they may have very different effects on the behavior of young children (Brody & Shaffer, 1982).

In spite of these limitations, the laboratory analogue serves an important "sufficiency" function by demonstrating that various child-rearing practices can (and often do) have immediate effects on children's behavior. Clearly, the observational and interview methodologies are invaluable because they provide data on the relations between the patterns of child rearing that *parents* use and the behavior of *their* children. Once these relations are known, the experimental analogue can then be used to tease apart the effects of the many child-rearing practices that make up a general style or pattern of parenting and thus allow us to draw meaningful conclusions about the ways parents and children are likely to influence each other.

aptly notes, what passes as "competent parenting" for middle-class youngsters may fall far short of the mark if applied to children in other sociocultural groups.

Consider the case of disadvantaged children who grow up in urban ghettos in the United States. According to Ogbu (1981), these youngsters are encouraged to look upon conventional jobs as indications of success. However, they may also have to acquire a very different set of competencies than those learned by middle-class age mates if they are to function effectively within the "street economy" of their subculture. Thus, while Johnny from the suburbs may strive to perfect skills such as reading and math that will prepare him for a traditional job, Johnny from the ghetto may come to view academics as somewhat less important and choose instead to pursue other "survival strategies" such as fighting, hustling, becoming a respected member of a neighborhood street gang, or even working on his jump shot. It is not that ghetto youngsters are less interested than middle-class age mates in being successful and attaining power, money, or self-esteem; they simply differ in the means they choose to achieve these ends—often pursuing strategies suggested to them by the subculture in which they live.

Ogbu notes that ghetto parents are extremely warm and affectionate toward their infants but tend to use harsh and inconsistent punishment with their pre-school and school-age children. Although the latter practices tend to be frowned on by middle-class parents (and researchers), they may be very functional within the ghetto environment. If applied regularly, harsh, inconsistent discipline and a generally confrontive parental style should foster the development of assertiveness, self-reliance, and a mistrust of authority figures—precisely the attributes that ghetto youngsters may need in order to make it within their street culture. Of course, Ogbu is not implying that ghetto children will grow up to be deviant or abnormal by anyone's standards. His point is simply that the practices that qualify as "competent parenting" will depend on the particular skills and abilities that children will need for success within any given culture or subculture. So let's keep this point in mind and not automatically assume that deviations from middle-class patterns of child rearing are somehow "deficient" or "pathological."

THE DIRECTIONALITY ISSUE

Until very recently, social scientists have assumed that influence within families was a one-way street—from parents, who did the shaping, to their children, whose personalities were molded by the caregiving practices and disciplinary techniques used by their elders. Indeed, much of the work that we will discuss has attempted to determine the correspondence between various patterns of parenting and the development of young children. When relationships were found, it was generally assumed that the behavior of parents determined the behavior of their children.

Today we have reason to believe that the pattern of influence in most, if not all, social relationships is *reciprocal*. Parents do indeed influence the behavior of their children. But at the same time, children play an important role in shaping the child-rearing practices used by their parents.

An excellent example of how children influence their parents comes from a study by David Buss (1981). Buss measured the activity level of 117 children at age 3 and again at age 4. When these children were 5 years old, they were placed in an experimental setting in which either their mothers or their fathers watched as they performed a battery of four cognitive

tasks. The parent was encouraged to provide whatever assistance might be necessary to enable the child to complete the problems. Buss found that parents of active children often got into power struggles with their youngsters, tended to intrude physically and to become somewhat hostile, and had a difficult time establishing good working relationships with the children. By contrast, interactions between parents and less active children were much more peaceful and harmonious. Since activity level is a moderately heritable component of temperament, one could argue that active children have active parents and that interactions between two reasonably active individuals are bound to lead to power struggles. But even if this is so, the data clearly indicate that the child's activity level is contributing in an important way to the treatment that he or she receives from parents. And as we have noted on several occasions, the techniques that parents use to discipline transgressions depend to a large extent on (1) the particular act that the *child* committed and (2) the *child's reactions* to previous disciplinary encounters (Grusec & Kuczynski, 1980; Holden, 1983; Mulhern & Passman, 1981). So influence in parent/child interactions is a two-way street: children may have nearly as much effect on the behavior of their parents as parents have on the behavior of their children.

RECONCEPTUALIZING FAMILY EFFECTS: THE FAMILY AS A SOCIAL SYSTEM

Another limitation of the early research on families is that investigators concentrated on mother/child and father/child interactions and failed to treat the family as a true social system. Jay Belsky (1981) notes that the family consisting of a mother, a father, and a first-born child is a complex entity. Not only does the infant enter into a reciprocal relationship when alone with each parent, but the presence of *both* parents "transforms the mother-infant dyad into a *family system* [comprising] a husband-wife as well as mother-infant and father-infant relationships" (p. 17). As it turns out, the mere presence of the second parent does affect the way the first parent interacts with a child. For example, fathers talk less to their toddlers when the mother is present (Stoneman & Brody,

1981), and mothers are less likely to play with or hold their youngsters when the father is around (Belsky, 1981). In early adolescence, mother/son interactions are less conflict-ridden in the presence of the father, whereas the entry of the mother into father/son interactions often erodes the quality of that contact by causing the father to withdraw and become less involved in the boy's activities (Gjerde, 1986). Finally, the quality of the marriage (that is, the husband/wife relationship) can affect parent/child interactions, which, in turn, can have an effect on the quality of the marriage. So the patterns of influence in even the simplest of nuclear families are a whole lot more complex than researchers have generally assumed (see Figure 13-1). Of course, the social system becomes much more intricate with the birth of the second child and the addition of sibling/sibling and sibling/parent relationships.

We should also recognize that families exist within a larger cultural or subcultural setting and that the ecological niche that a family occupies (for example, the family's religion, its social class, and the values that prevail within a subculture or even a neighborhood) can affect family interactions and the development of a family's children (Bronfenbrenner, 1979). According to Belsky (1981), future advances in the study of family relations will stem from interdisciplinary efforts in which developmentalists, family sociologists, and community psychologists pool their expertise to gain a better understanding of how families (within particular social contexts) influence and are influenced by their young. Belsky argues:

> It is no longer acceptable to focus narrowly on parent-infant interaction. Such experience must be examined from the perspective of the family system, and thus, the marital relationship (as well as sibling relations) must be considered. The family too . . . needs to be examined within the wider ecology in which it is embedded. . . . Such [interdisciplinary research] should . . . thoroughly revitalize the study, and enhance our understanding of [the family and its impact on developing children] [1981, p. 19].

THE CHANGING AMERICAN FAMILY

To date, most family research is based on traditional nuclear families consisting of a mother, a father, and one or more children. And perhaps this emphasis is

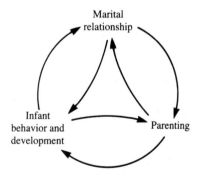

FIGURE 13-1 A model of the family as a social system. As implied in the diagram, a family is bigger than the sum of its parts. Parents affect infants, who affect each parent and the marital relationship. Of course, the marital relationship may affect the parenting the infant receives, the infant's behavior, and so on. Clearly, families are complex social systems. As an exercise, you may wish to rediagram the patterns of influence within a family after adding a sibling or two.

understandable in that the nuclear family remains the dominant living arrangement in modern industrialized societies. In the United States, for example, nearly 80% of children live in an intact family setting with their parents, stepparents, or legal guardians such as foster parents or grandparents (U.S. Bureau of the Census, 1982). The major changes in the American nuclear family are that (1) more mothers are working outside the home and (2) people are having fewer children.

Although most children live in nuclear families, the number of single-parent households is steadily increasing. Mavis Hetherington (1981) reports that the number of children living in single-parent homes doubled between 1960 and 1978 (rising from 5.8 million to 11.7 million), and it is worth repeating that 40–50% of all children born in the 1980s will spend some time living in a single-parent family. Two trends are responsible for this dramatic increase in the number of single-parent households: (1) the increasing number of children born out of wedlock and (2) the large number of divorces. Of these two factors, divorce is by far the major contributor. Only 16% of single-parent homes are the result of an illegitimate birth. However, the divorce rate in the United States doubled between 1965 and 1978 (Hetherington,

1981). It is now estimated that nearly 50% of marriages between young adults will end in divorce, a sizable majority of these divorces involving children under age 18 (Glick, 1984).

As these statistics clearly indicate, marital disruptions and restructuring of family ties are experiences that many children are now facing or will face in the years ahead. How do they cope? Does a divorce leave permanent emotional scars on the developing child? Is it possible that children may be better off in a single-parent home than in a strife-ridden nuclear family where the parents are constantly bickering? These are issues that family researchers are currently exploring as they study the impact of divorce on both parents and children.

Although recent research has increased our knowledge about the effects of divorce and family dissolution, much less is known about how children are affected by a common by-product of divorce: the remarriage of the custodial parent. Over 6 million children now live in stepparent homes, and these *reconstituted families* form about 11% of all American households (Santrock, Warshak, Lindbergh, & Meadows, 1982). Later in the chapter, we will take a closer look at the reconstituted family and see whether there is any evidence for the Cinderella syndrome—the notion that many stepparents are cool, aloof caregivers who tend to favor their own biological offspring and may even abuse a stepchild.

The ways researchers think about and study family relations are changing almost as fast as the families themselves. Our upcoming review of the literature is a blend of (1) the old unidirectional research in which parents were assumed to mold the character of their children and (2) the "new look" at the family as a complex social system in which each family member interacts with and thereby influences every other family member. The older research is definitely worth reviewing, for it gives us some idea of how various patterns of child rearing contribute to positive or negative developmental outcomes. But as we discuss this work, let's keep in mind that children are active participants in the socialization process who play a major role in determining the character of the home environment to which they are exposed.

INTERACTIONS BETWEEN PARENTS AND THEIR INFANTS

A child begins to influence the behavior of other family members long before he or she is born. Adults who have hoped to conceive and who eagerly anticipate their baby's arrival will often plan for the blessed event by selecting names for the infant, buying or making baby clothes, moving to larger quarters, decorating a nursery, changing or leaving jobs, and preparing older children in the family for the changes that are soon to come (Grossman, Eichler, Winickoff, & Associates, 1980). Of course, the impact of an unborn child may be far less pleasant for an unwed mother or a couple who do not want their baby, who cannot afford a child, or who receive very little encouragement and support from friends, relatives, and other members of the community (David & Baldwin, 1979).

How is the birth of a child likely to influence the mother, the father, and the marital relationship? Do the changes that parents experience affect their reactions to the baby? Are some parents more capable than others of coping with a difficult infant? Is there any truth to the claim that shaky marriages can be strengthened by having a child? In exploring these questions, we will see why researchers like to think of families as complex entities that they are only now beginning to understand. However, this much is certain: the arrival of an infant transforms the marital dyad into a rather intricate social system that can influence the behavior and emotional well-being of all family members.

THE TRANSITION TO PARENTHOOD

The birth of a baby is a highly significant event that alters the behavior of both mothers and fathers and may affect the quality of their marital relationship. As noted in Chapter 12, the onset of parenthood often results in a change in sex roles. Even among egalitarian couples who have previously shared household tasks, new mothers typically become more "expressive," will partake in more traditionally feminine activities, and now feel more "feminine," whereas new fathers are apt to focus more intently on their role as a provider (Cowan & Cowan, 1987). If both parents previously worked, it is nearly always the mother who stays home to look after the baby. However, it is interesting to note that new fathers often report feeling more "feminine" after the birth of a baby, owing perhaps to the increased nurturance and affection they display while interacting with their infants (Feldman & Aschenbrenner, 1983).

How does the birth of a child affect the marital relationship? Many family sociologists believe that the advent of parenthood is a "crisis" of sorts for a marriage. Couples must now cope with greater financial responsibilities, a possible loss of income, changes in sleeping habits, and less time to themselves—events that may be perceived as aversive and could well disrupt the bond between husbands and wives (Miller & Sollie, 1980). Yet the research on this issue is mixed: some investigators find that the birth of a first child leads to a reduction in spousal intimacy and affection, while others report that the adjustment to parenthood is only mildly stressful (Belsky, 1981).

How do we explain these inconsistencies? After reviewing the available literature, Belsky (1981) concluded that the impact of a new baby on the marital relationship tends to be less severe or disruptive when parents are older, conceive after the marriage ceremony, and have been married longer before conceiving. Moreover, the parents' own family histories have an effect. If both husband and wife had been treated in a warm and accepting manner by their own parents, their marriage is unlikely to suffer as they make the transition to parenthood. Yet if either the husband or wife had been raised in an aloof or rejecting manner, the couple are apt to experience some marital discord after their child is born (Belsky & Isabella, 1985).

Of course, the behavior of the infant can also influence the couple's adjustment to parenthood. Parents of temperamentally difficult infants who cry a lot, have feeding problems, and are often "on the move" report more disruption of normal activities and greater dissatisfaction in their marital relationships than parents of "quiet" or "easy" babies (Levitt, Weber, & Clark, 1986; Russell, 1974). Moreover, many parents of infants who require special care (for example, babies with Down's syndrome or those with illnesses that demand constant monitoring) have problems with their spouses and believe that rearing a "special" child has made their marriages worse (Cain, Kelly, & Shannon, 1980; Gath, 1978). But for every set of parents who experience marital disharmony as a result of caring for a special child, there is at least one other couple who say that their abnormal infant has brought them closer together! So it appears that the arrival of a baby who requires special attention may disrupt the balance of a vulnerable marriage without shaking the foundation of one that is already on firm ground (Gath, 1978).

EFFECTS OF PARENTS ON THEIR INFANTS (AND EACH OTHER)

In recent years, investigators have begun to collect longitudinal data on parent/child interactions to determine how parents affect the social, emotional, and intellectual development of their infants and toddlers. The results of these studies are remarkably consistent: warm and sensitive mothers who often talk to their infants and try to stimulate their curiosity are contributing to the establishment of secure emotional attachments (Ainsworth, 1979) as well as to the child's exploratory competence (Belsky, Garduque, & Hrncir, 1984; Cassidy, 1986) and intellectual growth (Bradley, Caldwell, & Elardo, 1979; Cohen & Beckwith, 1979). Jay Belsky (1981) notes that the importance of warm and responsive mothering is

> underscored by several studies indicating that one of the products of maternal sensitivity, a secure attachment to the caregiver, forecasts skill in problem-solving and peer competence when the child is 2 and 5 years of age. . . . Block and Block . . . have also shown that the kinds of skills assessed by Sroufe and his students during the preschool years are . . . related to [the competencies children display] during the

elementary school years. These findings strengthen the argument that sensitivity is *the* influential dimension of mothering in infancy: It not only fosters healthy psychological functioning during this developmental epoch, but it also lays the foundation on which future experience will build [pp. 7–8].

Recently, Christoph Heinicke and his associates (Heinicke, Diskin, Ramsey-Klee, & Given, 1983) have found that it is possible to predict who is likely to become a sensitive, responsive mother even before the child is born. A testing of 46 mothers at midpregnancy revealed that those who were warm and outgoing, high in ego strength (a measure of adaptive functioning and self-esteem), and confident in visualizing themselves as mothers were later found to be highly sensitive and responsive to their infants' needs throughout the first year.

Father/Infant Interactions

Until very recently, investigators have concentrated on mother/infant interactions and all but ignored the influence of fathers. One reason for this emphasis is that mothers attend more to their infants than fathers do, even when the fathers are home from work (Clarke-Stewart, 1978). Several years ago, Freda Rebelsky and Cheryl Hanks (1971) attached microphones to ten infants and recorded how often their fathers spoke to them between the ages of 2 weeks and 3 months. On an average day, the fathers in this study addressed their infants only 2.7 times for a total of approximately 40 seconds. However, these results are somewhat deceiving. One reason that American fathers in earlier reports may have seemed so detached from or unresponsive to their newborns is that very few fathers were allowed in delivery rooms to greet their neonates and become involved with them. Today, birthing practices have changed so that fathers are often encouraged to be present for the baby's arrival. These changes are largely due to the finding that fathers who are present in the nursery or delivery room often appear to be just as intrigued, or engrossed, by their neonates as mothers are (Greenberg & Morris, 1974; Parke, 1981).

And even when fathers have had very little contact with their neonates, they will typically become much more involved with them over the next several months (Easterbrooks & Goldberg, 1984). Unlike mothers, who are likely to hold, soothe, care for, or play quietly with their infants, fathers are much more boisterous, choosing to initiate physically stimulating, rough-and-tumble activities that infants seem to enjoy (Lamb, 1981). In assuming the role of "special playmate," the father is in a unique position to influence the activities and preferences of his children. Indeed, fathers of 12-month-old infants are already beginning to encourage their children (particularly their sons) to play with sex-typed toys and to avoid playful activities that are considered more appropriate for children of the other sex (Snow, Jacklin, & Maccoby, 1983). However, let's note that fathers are more than mere playmates; they are often successful at soothing or comforting a distressed infant, and they may also serve as a "secure base" from which their infant will venture to explore the environment. Finally, a secure attachment to the father can help to offset the social deficiencies and emotional disturbances that could otherwise result when an infant is insecurely attached to the mother (Main & Weston, 1981).

Indirect Effects

Parents may also have "indirect" effects on their infants by virtue of their ability to influence the behavior of their spouses. For example, marital tension following the birth of a baby can disrupt a mother's caretaking routines and interfere with her ability to enjoy her infant (Belsky, 1981). Indeed, Frank Pedersen and his associates (Pedersen, Anderson, & Cain, 1977) found that both mothers and fathers were likely to be unresponsive or negative toward their 5-month-old infants in families characterized by marital strife. So it would seem that unhappily married couples are ill advised to have children as a means of solidifying a shaky marriage. Not only is this practice unlikely to strengthen the marital bond, but it is almost guaranteed to lead to poor parent/child relations.

Of course, the indirect effects of either parent may

often be positive ones. For example, fathers tend to be much more involved with their infants when mothers believe that the father should play an important role in the child's life (Palkowitz, 1984) and when the two parents talk frequently about the baby (Belsky, Gilstrap, & Rovine, 1984; Lamb & Elster, 1985). In these studies, it appeared that mothers (who served as the infants' primary caregivers) were exerting an indirect influence on father/infant interactions by encouraging fathers to become more knowledgeable and concerned about the development of their children. Apparently the influence of parents on each other is often reciprocal, for mothers who have a close, supportive relationship with their husbands tend to be more patient with their infants and more sensitive to their needs than mothers who receive little support from their spouses and feel that they are raising their children on their own. In fact, intimate support from the husband seems to be more important to a mother's life satisfaction than any other kind of social support that she might receive—particularly if her infant is temperamentally difficult (Levitt et al., 1986). The picture that emerges, then, is that happily married couples seem to function as sources of *mutual* support and encouragement, so that many child-rearing problems are easier to overcome (Crnic, Greenberg, Ragozin, Robinson, & Basham, 1983). Indeed, parents of babies who are at risk for later emotional problems (as noted by the child's sluggish and disorganized performance on the Brazelton Neonatal Behavioral Assessment Scale) will typically establish "synchronous" and satisfying relationships with their infants *unless they are unhappily married* (Belsky, 1981).

After examining the data on parent/infant interactions, we see that even the simplest of families is a true social system that is bigger than the sum of its parts. Not only does each family member influence the behavior of every other family member, but the relationship that any two family members have can indirectly affect the interactions and relationships among all other members of the family. Clearly, socialization within the family setting is not merely a two-way street—it is more accurately described as the busy intersection of many avenues of influence.

PARENTAL EFFECTS ON PRESCHOOL AND SCHOOL-AGE CHILDREN

During the second and the third years, parents spend less time caring for and playing with their child as they begin to impose restrictions on the child's activities and try to teach him or her how to behave (or how not to behave) in a variety of situations. According to Erik Erikson (1963), this is the period when socialization begins in earnest. Parents must now limit the child's autonomy in the hope of instilling a sense of social propriety and self-control, while taking care not to undermine the child's curiosity, initiative, and feelings of personal competence. Erikson believed that two aspects of parenting are especially important during the preschool and school-age years: parental warmth and parental control (that is, permissiveness/restrictiveness).

TWO MAJOR DIMENSIONS OF CHILD REARING

A number of studies suggest that parents do differ on the two attributes that Erikson thought to be so important. Let's first consider the dimension of parental control.

Permissiveness/restrictiveness refers to the amount of autonomy that parents allow their children. Restrictive parents limit their children's freedom of expression by imposing many demands and actively surveying their children's behavior to ensure that these rules and regulations are followed. Permissive parents are much less controlling. They make relatively few demands of their children and allow them considerable freedom in exploring the environment, expressing their opinions and emotions, and making decisions about their own activities. A common finding is that parents become less restrictive as their children mature, although some parents are more likely to loosen the reins than others (Schaefer & Bayley, 1963).

Parental warmth (or *warmth/hostility*) refers to the amount of affection and approval that an adult displays toward his or her children. Parents described as warm and nurturant are those who often smile at, praise, and encourage their child while limiting their criticisms, punishments, and signs of disapproval. By contrast, the hostile or rejecting parent is one who is quick to criticize, belittle, punish, or ignore a child while limiting his or her expressions of affection and approval. It is important to note that measures of parental warmth reflect the character of an adult's reactions to the child *across a large number of situations*. For example, a parent who is cool and critical when a child misbehaves but generally warm and accepting in other contexts would be classified as high in parental warmth. One who is warm and nurturant whenever her child praises her but critical, punitive, or indifferent in most other situations would be considered a more aloof or rejecting parent.

These two dimensions of child rearing are reasonably independent, so that we find parents who are warm and restrictive, warm and permissive, cool (rejecting) and restrictive, and cool and permissive. Are these aspects of parenting related in any meaningful way to the child's social, emotional, and intellectual development?

PATTERNS OF PARENTAL CONTROL

Perhaps the best-known research on the effects of parental control is that of Diana Baumrind (1967, 1977). Baumrind's sample consisted of 134 preschool children and their parents. Each child was observed on several occasions in nursery school and at home. These data were used to rate the child on several behavioral dimensions (for example, sociability, self-reliance, achievement, moodiness, and self-control). Parents were also interviewed and observed while interacting with their children at home. When Baumrind analyzed the parental data, she found that individual parents generally used one of three patterns of parental control, which were described in some detail in Chapter 8. By way of review, these patterns were:

1. *Authoritarian parenting*. A very restrictive pattern of parenting in which adults impose many rules on their children, expect strict obedience, will rarely if ever explain to the child why it is necessary to comply with all these regulations, and will often rely on forceful tactics to gain compliance.
2. *Authoritative parenting*. A more flexible style of parenting in which adults allow their children considerable freedom but are careful to provide rationales for the restrictions they impose and will ensure that the children follow these guidelines. Authoritative parents are responsive to their children's needs and points of view. However, they expect the child to comply with the spirit of the restrictions they impose and will use both power (if necessary) and reason to assure that he does.
3. *Permissive parenting*. A lax pattern of parenting in which adults make relatively few demands, encourage their children to express their feelings and impulses, and rarely exert firm control over their behavior.

On the basis of her observations in the nursery school setting, Baumrind identified three groups of preschool children: *energetic-friendly*, *conflicted-irritable*, and *impulsive-aggressive*. As shown in Table 13-1, these patterns of child behavior were closely related to parents' patterns of control. Authoritative parents generally had friendly-energetic youngsters who were cheerful, socially responsive, self-reliant, achievement-oriented, and cooperative with adults and peers. By contrast, children of authoritarian parents tended to fall into the conflicted-irritable category: they were moody and seemingly unhappy much of the time, easily annoyed, relatively aimless, and not very pleasant to be around. Finally, permissive parents often had children classified as impulsive-aggressive. These youngsters (particularly the boys) tended to be bossy and self-centered, rebellious, aggressive, rather aimless, and quite low in independence and achievement.

Although Baumrind's findings seem to favor the authoritative pattern of control, one might legitimately wonder whether the children of authoritarian or permissive parents might eventually "outgrow" the emotional conflicts and behavioral disturbances they displayed as preschoolers. Seeking to answer this question, Baumrind (1977) observed her subjects (and their parents) once again when the children were 8 to 9 years old. As we see in Table 13-2, children of authoritative parents were still relatively high in both *cognitive competencies* (that is, shows originality in thinking, has high achievement motivation, likes intellectual challenges) and *social skills* (for example, is sociable and outgoing, participates actively and shows leadership in group activities), whereas children of permissive parents were relatively unskilled in both areas. Baumrind also reported an interesting sex difference in the effects of authoritarian parenting: among children whose parents had remained highly authoritarian during the school-age years, boys were more likely than girls to lose interest in achievement and to withdraw from social contacts. Finally, Baumrind's latest follow-up on these youngsters suggests that the patterns of cognitive and social competencies that they displayed as grade school children tend to persist into adolescence (see Maccoby & Martin, 1983).

One limitation of Baumrind's research is that almost all the parents in her sample were reasonably warm and accepting. As it turns out, the effects of either restrictive or permissive parenting will depend, in part, on the extent to which the parent displays warmth and affection toward the child (Becker, 1964). Children of *restrictive and rejecting* parents are often found to be extremely withdrawn and inhibited, and they may even show masochistic or suicidal tendencies. By contrast, children of *permissive and rejecting* parents tend to be very hostile and rebellious toward authority figures and prone to engage in delinquent acts such as alcohol and drug abuse, sexual misconduct, truancy, and a variety of criminal offenses (Patterson & Stouthamer-Loeber, 1984; Pulkkinen, 1982). What these findings seem to suggest is that the undesirable effects of either extremely restrictive (authoritarian) or extremely permissive parenting are exaggerated when parents are also cool and aloof toward their children or unconcerned about their welfare.

PARENTAL WARMTH/HOSTILITY

Although most parents are typically warm and loving, a small minority in any sample are clearly rejecting—expressing a lack of concern or feelings of dislike for their youngsters, who are often perceived as burdensome (Maccoby, 1980). Throughout this text, we have taken care to note the relationships between parental warmth and various aspects of children's social, emotional, and intellectual development. Here are but a few of the attributes that characterize the children of warm and accepting parents:

- They are securely attached at an early age. Of course, secure attachments are an important contributor to the growth of curiosity, exploratory competence, problem-solving skills, and positive social relations with both adults and peers (see Chapters 6 and 7).
- They are relatively altruistic, especially when their parents preach altruistic values and practice what they preach (see Chapter 10).

TABLE 13-1 Patterns of Parental Control and Corresponding Patterns of Children's Behavior

Parental classification	Children's behavioral profile
Authoritative parenting	Energetic-friendly Self-reliant Self-controlled Cheerful and friendly Copes well with stress Cooperative with adults Curious Purposive Achievement-oriented
Authoritarian parenting	Conflicted-irritable Fearful, apprehensive Moody, unhappy Easily annoyed Passively hostile Vulnerable to stress Aimless Sulky, unfriendly
Permissive parenting	Impulsive-aggressive Rebellious Low in self-reliance and self-control Impulsive Aggressive Domineering Aimless Low in achievement

- They are generally obedient, noncoercive youngsters who get along reasonably well with parents and peers (see Chapter 9).
- They tend to be high in self-esteem and role-taking skills, and when they are disciplined, they usually feel that their parents' actions are justified (Brody & Shaffer, 1982; Coopersmith, 1967).
- They are satisfied with their gender identities and are likely to be firmly sex-typed or androgynous (Mussen & Rutherford, 1963; see Chapter 12).
- They will often refer to internalized norms rather than fear of punishment as a reason for complying with moral rules (Brody & Shaffer, 1982).

Now compare this behavioral profile with that of a group of "unwanted" Czechoslovakian children whose mothers had tried repeatedly to gain permission to abort them during the prenatal period. Compared with a group of "wanted" Czech children from similar family backgrounds, the unwanted children had less stable ties to their mothers and fathers and were described by the researchers as anxious, emotionally frustrated, and irritable (Matejcek, Dytrych, & Schuller, 1979). Although they were all physically healthy at birth, the unwanted children were more likely than those in the "wanted" group to have spotty medical histories that had required them to be hospitalized. Children in the unwanted group made significantly poorer grades at school even though they were comparable in intelligence to their "wanted" classmates. Finally, the unwanted children were less well integrated into the peer group and more likely to require psychiatric attention for serious behavior disorders. (For another look at the long-term consequences of cool, aloof parenting, see Box 13-2.)

Is parental warmth alone likely to lead to positive developmental outcomes? Probably not, for we've seen that children of warm but permissive parents tend to be low in both cognitive and social competencies (Baumrind, 1967, 1977). Nevertheless, warmth and affection are clearly important components of effective parenting. As Eleanor Maccoby (1980) has noted,

> Parental warmth binds children to their parents in a positive way—it makes children responsive and more willing to accept guidance. If the parent-child relationship is close and affectionate, parents can exercise what control is needed without having to apply heavy disciplinary pressure. It is as if parents' responsiveness, affection, and obvious commitment to their children's welfare have earned them the right to make decisions and exercise control [p. 394].

PATTERNS OF PARENTAL DISCIPLINE

In earlier chapters we saw that parents differ in the strategies they use to enforce their demands and to discipline transgressions. Both *power-assertive* discipline (use of forceful commands, physical punishment, and control over valuable resources) and *love withdrawal* (expressions of ridicule, disliking, or withdrawing affection) may threaten the child. Children whose parents rely heavily on these disciplinary practices are motivated to comply with parental demands in order *to avoid negative consequences*. By

TABLE 13-2 Patterns of Parental Control during the Preschool Period and Children's Cognitive and Social Competencies during the Grade School Years

Pattern of parenting during preschool period	Children's competencies at age 8–9	
	Girls	*Boys*
Authoritative	Very high cognitive and social competencies	High cognitive and social competencies
Authoritarian	Average cognitive and social competencies	Average social competencies; low cognitive competencies
Permissive	Low cognitive and social competencies	Low social competencies; very low cognitive competencies

BOX 13-2 PARENTAL REJECTION AS A CONTRIBUTOR TO ADULT DEPRESSION

Recently, Thomas Crook, Allen Raskin, and John Eliot (1981) proposed that adults who are clinically depressed and view themselves as inferior or worthless are often the product of a home environment in which they were clearly rejected by one or both parents. To evaluate their hypothesis, Crook et al. asked 714 adults who were hospitalized for depression to describe their childhood relationships with their mothers and fathers by indicating whether each of 192 statements characterized the behavior of either or both parents—for example, Did your mother [father] worry about you when you were away? Threaten not to love you if you misbehaved? Often make you feel guilty? Set firm standards? Consistently enforce her [his] rules? Often ridicule you? As a comparison group, 387 nondepressed adults answered the same questions. Since an adult's self-reports of childhood experiences may be distorted and unreliable, the investigators also interviewed siblings, other relatives, and long-time friends of the subjects as a check on the accuracy of their recollections. Data collected from these "independent sources" were then used to rate each subject's mother and father on the warmth/hostility and the autonomy/control (permissiveness/restrictiveness) dimensions.

The results of this study were straightforward. Subjects hospitalized for depression rated *both their mothers and their fathers* as less accepting and more hostile, detached, and rejecting than nondepressed adults in the comparison sample. Although the parents of depressed patients were not rated as any more restrictive or controlling than parents of nondepressed adults, they were perceived as exercising control in a more derisive way, often choosing to ridicule,

belittle, or withdraw affection from their children. So even the guidance and discipline that depressed adults received during childhood were administered in a hostile, rejecting manner.

Data collected from the "independent sources" were quite consistent with the subjects' own reports. Both the mothers and fathers of the depressed patients were described as less affectionate and less involved with their children than the parents of nondepressed adults.

Recently, Monroe Lefkowitz and Edward Tesiny (1984) conducted a *prospective* study to determine whether parental rejection measured *during childhood* would predict a person's depressive tendencies in adolescence. Mothers and fathers of 8-year-old females completed a child-rearing questionnaire containing items designed to assess their satisfaction with their child and her behavior (extremely low scores were taken as indications of parental rejection). Ten years later, these girls (who were now 18-year-old adolescents) completed the Depression scale of the Minnesota Multiphasic Personality Inventory, a well-known diagnostic test. The results were clear: girls whose mothers and fathers were rejecting during childhood scored significantly higher on the depression scale as adolescents than did their counterparts whose parents were not so rejecting.

In sum, it appears that a primary contributor to adult depression is a family setting in which one or both parents treat the child as if he or she were unworthy of their love and affection. Perhaps it is fair to say that parents who blatantly reject their children are committing an extremely powerful form of child abuse—one that could leave emotional scars that will last a lifetime.

contrast, *induction* is a relatively nonpunitive form of discipline in which parents try to reason with their children. The goal of the inductive disciplinarian is to make children understand (1) why they need to follow various rules and regulations, (2) why their transgressions are wrong, and (3) how they might alter their behavior to prevent future transgressions or undo whatever harm they may have done.

In one recent review of the literature, Gene Brody and David Shaffer (1982) found that parents who rely on power assertion to enforce their demands are likely to have extremely self-centered children who score low on tests of moral development. By contrast,

parents who use inductive discipline, particularly those who also have a *warm, affectionate* relationship with their children, have youngsters who are highly altruistic and who score above average on tests of moral development. Note that the inductive disciplinarian who is warm and accepting and who appeals to reason in order to enforce his or her demands sounds very much like Baumrind's authoritative parent. In contrast, adults who use arbitrary forms of punishment such as spankings or withdrawal of affection are in some ways similar to Baumrind's authoritarian parent. So the research on parental discipline dovetails nicely with the earlier work on other aspects of child rearing. The implication is that parents who are warm, controlling, and inductive in their role as disciplinarians are likely to raise children who are quite friendly, outgoing, intellectually competent, and morally mature.

What do children think of the parenting they receive? What do they view as competent or effective parenting? As we see in Box 13-3, the answers to these questions depend, in part, on the child's developmental level.

SOCIAL-CLASS DIFFERENCES IN PARENTING

Social class (or *socioeconomic status*) refers to one's position within a society that is stratified according to status or power (Maehr, 1974). In many countries (such as India) a person's social standing is determined at birth by the status of his or her parents. If you were to grow up in this kind of society, you would be compelled by virtue of your origins to pursue one of a limited number of occupations, to live in a designated neighborhood, and to marry someone who occupies a similar position in the social hierarchy.

This scenario sounds rather dismal to those of us who live in Western industrialized societies, where the most common measures of social class—family income, prestige of father's occupation, and parents' educational level—are indications of the family's achievements. In the United States, we are fond of saying that virtually anyone can rise above his or her origins if that person is willing to work extremely hard toward the pursuit of success. Indeed, this proverb is the cornerstone of the American dream.

However, sociologists tell us that the "American dream" is a belief that is more likely to be endorsed by members of the middle and upper classes—those elements of society that have the economic resources to maintain or improve on their lofty economic status (Hess, 1970). As we will see, many people from the lower and working classes face very different kinds of problems, pursue different goals, and often adopt different values. In short, they live in a different world than middle-class people do, and these ecological considerations may well affect the methods and strategies that they use to raise their children.

SOCIAL-CLASS DIFFERENCES IN ATTITUDES, VALUES, AND LIFESTYLES

Perhaps the most obvious differences between middle- and lower-class families are economic: middle-class families usually have more money and material possessions. A more subtle difference between *high SES* (middle- and upper-class) and *low SES* (lower- and working-class) families centers on their feelings of power and influence. People from the lower socioeconomic strata often believe that, without material resources, they have few opportunities to get ahead and no direct access to those in power, and consequently they feel that their lives are largely controlled by the "advantaged" members of society. In order to qualify for housing, financial, or medical assistance, they must often live where the bureaucrats tell them to live or otherwise do as the bureaucrats say. Many low-SES parents cannot afford the luxury of health or disability insurance, and their resources are likely to be insufficient to cope with problems such as an accident, an extended illness, or the loss of a job. Is it any wonder, then, that many lower- and working-class adults feel relatively insecure or helpless and are apt to develop an external locus of control (Hess, 1970; Phares, 1976)?

A low income may also mean that living quarters are crowded, that family members must occasionally make do without adequate food or medical care, and that parents are constantly tense or anxious about living under these marginal conditions. Eleanor Maccoby (1980) suggests that low-income living is probably more *stressful* for parents and that stress affects the ways parental functions are carried out. Recently, John Zussman (1980) has studied the impact of stress on parent/child interactions in an interesting analogue experiment. Either mothers or fathers were asked to perform a distracting cognitive activity (a mental anagram task) in the presence of their two young children (in this study, families with one nursery school child and one toddler were recruited). The room in which the experiment took place in-

BOX 13-3   WHY "MOM IS THE GREATEST"

After reviewing the literature, many people would undoubtedly conclude that "great parents" are those who are generally warm, accepting, and authoritative in their approach to child rearing. Do children agree? To find out, John Weisz (1980) analyzed the contents of letters submitted by 7–17-year-olds to a newspaper contest entitled "Why Mom Is the Greatest." If children and developmental researchers see eye to eye on the determinants of effective parenting, then youngsters should stress maternal attributes such as nurturance and a willingness to give praise, to be supportive, and to grant some autonomy as their reasons for thinking that "mom is the greatest."

Weisz found that young grade school children clearly value the *physical nurturance* that their mothers provide (that is, the mother's willingness to attend to the child's physical needs—to provide toys, clothes, meals, and transportation). One 7-year-old named April wrote that her mom was the greatest because "she cooks the best chili and she kisses me every day on the nose." Older children and adolescents also valued their mothers' physical nurturance, but they were more likely than younger children to stress their mothers' *psychological nurturance* (for example, willingness to listen to problems, counsel, and give emotional support) and to think highly of her for "*just being there*" (a form of security in knowing that mom is always there when she is needed). For example, a 15-year-old named Bill wrote "She teaches me right from wrong even though it may hurt. She's very heart warming when your down in the

blues [*sic*]." The older child's emphasis on psychological nurturance seems to reflect the development of important role-taking skills—namely, the ability to recognize that mom makes an active attempt to understand his or her point of view. Indeed, many adolescents said mom is the greatest because "she always seems to know how I feel" or "when I'm sad, she knows what's on my mind."

How did children feel about parental control over their activities? Younger children generally valued mothers who gave them lots of autonomy. Ten-year-old Melissa wrote "My mother is the greatest because she lets us do almost anything." However, older children and adolescents seemed to favor a little more control. They apparently recognized that maternal restraints reflect love and concern about their welfare, whereas extreme permissiveness may indicate laxity or lack of interest.

Although Weisz's findings are based on only 244 letters that were written by children who had obviously established good relationships with their mothers, it is interesting to note that these youngsters stressed the very attributes that child developmentalists consider important dimensions of effective parenting. In fact, statements indicative of aloof, authoritarian parenting almost never appeared in the letters of these young respondents. Since the data apply only to mothers, it would be interesting to see whether children mention the same attributes and child-rearing practices when they tell us "why Dad is the greatest."

---

cluded toys that were difficult to operate without the parent's assistance as well as attractive nuisances such as a filled ashtray and stacks of papers and index cards. Parent/child interactions were observed during two ten-minute periods: one in which the parent was instructed simply to observe the play of his or her children (low-stress condition) and one in which the parent was preoccupied with the distracting cognitive activity (high-stress condition). Zussman found that the stress created by trying to concentrate on the cognitive task while keeping one's children out of mischief had a dramatic effect on the quantity and quality of parent/child interactions. Under the stressful conditions, parents became much less responsive

and helpful toward their nursery school children. And although they continued to show as much attention to their toddlers under the stressful circumstances, the character of their interactions changed as the parents became more critical, restrictive, and punitive toward the younger child.

In sum, Zussman's study shows that even very mild and temporary forms of stress can affect the ways adults react to their children. When we consider that low-SES families are more likely to experience major and prolonged life stresses such as inadequate housing, losses of employment due to economic uncertainties, anxieties about being able to pay bills or put food on the table, and family disruptions because of divorce or desertion, we have good reason to believe that low-SES parents may end up raising their children differently than middle- and upper-class parents do. Indeed, Rand Conger and his associates (Conger, McCarty, Yang, Lahey, & Kropp, 1984) have recently found a rather strong association between the number of environmental stresses that a family experiences (for example, lesser education of parents, low income, many children, being a single parent, relying on welfare payments) and the treatment that children receive from their mothers. Specifically, the greater the number of environmental stressors the family was experiencing, the less supportive mothers were when interacting with their children, the more likely they were to make derogatory statements about their youngsters or to threaten, slap, push, or grab them, and the more authoritarian they became when expressing their views on child rearing.

PATTERNS OF CHILD REARING IN HIGH-SES AND LOW-SES FAMILIES

Eleanor Maccoby (1980) has reviewed the child-rearing literature and concluded that high-SES parents differ from low-SES parents in at least four respects:

1. Low-SES parents tend to stress obedience and respect for authority, neatness, cleanliness, and staying out of trouble. Higher-SES parents are more likely to stress happiness, curiosity, independence, creativity, ambition, and self-control.
2. Lower-SES parents are more restrictive and authoritarian, often setting arbitrary standards and enforcing them with power-assertive forms of discipline. Higher-SES parents tend to be either permissive or authoritative, and they are more likely to use inductive forms of discipline.
3. Higher-SES parents talk more with their children, reason with them more, and may use somewhat more complex language than lower-SES parents.
4. Higher-SES parents tend to show more warmth and affection toward their children.

According to Maccoby, these relationships seem to be true in many cultures and across racial and ethnic groups within the United States. However, there is some evidence that differences between high-SES and low-SES parenting are much more pronounced for boys than for girls. For example, John Zussman (1978) found that lower-class parents were more likely than middle-class parents to use power assertion with their sons, although parents from both social classes used very low levels of power assertion with their daughters.

Of course, we should keep in mind that these class-linked differences in parenting represent *group averages* rather than absolute contrasts: some middle-class parents are highly restrictive, power-assertive, and aloof in their approach to child rearing, whereas many lower- and working-class parents function more like their counterparts in the middle class (Laosa, 1981). But on the average, it appears that lower- and working-class parents are somewhat more critical, more punitive, and more intolerant of disobedience than parents from the middle and upper socioeconomic strata.

There are undoubtedly many factors that contribute to social-class differences in child rearing. Earlier we saw that the stresses associated with low-income living may cause parents to become more punitive and less responsive to a child's needs—in short, to seem somewhat aloof or uninvolved with their children. And as John Ogbu (1981) and others have noted, the way a family earns its livelihood may affect the strategies that parents use to raise their children. Low-SES parents may emphasize respect, obedience, neatness, and staying out of trouble because these are precisely the attributes that they view as critical for success in the blue-collar economy. By contrast, high-SES parents may reason or negotiate more with their children while emphasizing individual initiative and achievement because these are the skills, attributes, and abilities that high-SES parents find necessary in their own roles as businesspersons, white-collar workers, or high-salaried professionals. Finally, let's note that the children themselves may contribute to social-class differences in child rearing. Low-SES mothers, who are often younger and may receive less adequate prenatal care, are more likely than middle-class mothers to deliver prematurely or to experience other complications of childbirth (Kessner, 1973). In other words, low-SES families are more likely to have irritable, unresponsive, or otherwise difficult babies who may be harder to care for and love.

When we look at the data, it may seem that high-SES parenting is somehow "better" or more competent. After all, the responsive, authoritative parenting often observed in middle-class families produces highly sociable children who are curious, outgoing, intellectually capable, and morally mature. Yet there is another side to this issue—one that researchers in Western societies sometimes fail to consider. Perhaps middle-class parenting is "better" for children who are expected to grow up to become productive members of a middle-class subculture. However, a middle-class pattern of parenting that stresses individual initiative, intellectual curiosity, and competitiveness may actually represent "incompetent" parenting among the Temne of Sierra Leone, a society in which everyone must pull together and suppress individualism if the community is to successfully plant, harvest, and ration the meager crops on which its livelihood absolutely depends (Berry, 1967). And since many children from Western, industrialized societies will choose a career within the so-called blue-collar economy, it hardly seems reasonable to conclude that a pattern of child rearing that prepares them for this undertaking is in some way deficient or "incompetent."

The closest thing to a general law of parenting is that warm, sensitive, and responsive caregiving seems to be associated with positive developmental outcomes in virtually all the cultures and subcultures that social scientists have studied. But people are being somewhat *ethnocentric*[1] when they suggest that a particular pattern or style of child rearing (for example, authoritative parenting) that produces favorable outcomes in one culture (middle-class Western societies) is the optimal pattern for children in all other cultures and subcultures. Louis Laosa (1981, p. 159) makes this same point, noting that "indigenous patterns of child care throughout the world represent largely successful adaptations to conditions of life that have long differed from one people to another. Women are 'good mothers' by the only relevant standards, those of their own culture."

EFFECTS OF SIBLINGS AND THE FAMILY CONFIGURATION

Perhaps the one aspect of family socialization that we know least about is the effects that siblings have on one another. The vast majority of American children grow up with siblings, and there is certainly no shortage of speculation about the roles that brothers and sisters play in a child's life. For example, parents are often concerned about the fighting and bickering that their youngsters display, and they may wonder whether this rivalrous conduct is good for their children. At the same time, the popular wisdom is that "only" children are likely to be lonely, overindulged "brats" who would profit both socially and emotionally from having siblings to teach them that they are not nearly so "special" or important as they think they are.

Although our knowledge about sibling influences is not extensive, we will see that brothers and sisters may often play an important role in a child's life. Moreover, it appears that the influence that siblings are likely to have will depend, in part, on whether they are older or younger than the child.

THE NATURE OF SIBLING INTERACTIONS

Do children respond differently to siblings than to parents? Linda Baskett and Stephan Johnson (1982) tried to answer this question by visiting with 47 families in their homes. Each family was observed for 45 minutes on five occasions. The children in these two- or three-child families ranged from 4 to 10 years of age.

Baskett and Johnson found that interactions between children and their parents were much more positive in character than those that occurred between siblings. Children often laughed with, talked to, and showed affection toward their parents, and they were more likely to comply with parental commands. By contrast, hitting, yelling, and other annoying physical antics were more often directed toward siblings. Although positive social responses outnumbered negative ones in both parent/child and sibling/sibling interactions, brothers and sisters were more coercive than parents and tended to respond less positively to a child's social overtures.

Other observational studies (for example, Abramovitch, Corter, Pepler, & Stanhope, 1986; Berndt & Bulleit, 1985) reveal that there are reliable differences in the behavior of older and younger siblings. Older siblings are generally more domineering and aggressive, whereas younger siblings are more compliant. However, older siblings also initiate more helpful, playful, and other prosocial behaviors, a finding that may reflect the pressure parents place on older children to demonstrate their maturity by looking after a younger brother or sister.

ORIGINS AND DETERMINANTS OF SIBLING RIVALRY

Sibling rivalry, a spirit of competition, jealousy, or resentment among siblings, often begins rather early, while the younger child is still in diapers. Carol Kendrick and Judy Dunn (1980) found that older toddlers and preschool children receive less attention from their mothers after the birth of a baby, and they are likely to respond to this "neglect" by demanding attention or doing something naughty while the mother is caring for the infant. By the time the younger child is 8 months of age, older siblings will occasionally harass him or her by hitting, poking, pinching, or taking away objects that the infant is playing with (Dunn & Kendrick, 1981b). Quarrels are usually initiated by the older sibling, and they are likely to become more frequent and intense once the younger child reaches 18 to 24 months of age and is better able to retaliate by hitting or teasing the older child or by directing a parent's attention to the older sib's misconduct (Dunn & Munn, 1985). Several investigators have found that *same sex* siblings tend to display more positive social behaviors (such as smiling, sharing, and showing affection) and fewer negative behaviors and are more inclined to feel close to each other than cross-sex siblings (see Abramovitch et al., 1986; Furman & Buhrmester, 1985a, 1985b; Dunn & Kendrick, 1981b). Apparently this "sex of sibling" effect can appear very early and may be indirectly attributable to the behavior of mothers.

PHOTO 13-2 Coercive and rivalrous conduct between siblings is a normal aspect of family life.

In their study of 14-month-old infants and their older siblings, Dunn and Kendrick (1981b) reported that mothers spent much more time playing with the younger child when he or she *differed* in gender from the older sibling. Thus, an infant sibling of the other sex may represent a greater threat to the older child's security, which, in turn, leads him or her to resent the other-sex sib and to respond less positively to this little intruder.

Additional evidence that mothers influence sibling interactions comes from a second study by Dunn and Kendrick (1981a). In this project, the investigators found that older girls who had received lots of attention during the weeks after a baby was born were the ones who played *least* with and were *most negative* toward their baby brother or sister 14 months later. The older children who were most positive toward their infant brothers or sisters were those whose mothers had not permitted them to brood or respond negatively toward the baby. Although parents should set some time aside for their older children to let them know that they are still loved and considered important, it appears that this practice can promote rivalrous conduct if a mother becomes *overly* attentive or solicitous toward her older children.

Conflict among siblings is commonplace, particularly among those who are nearly the same age (Furman & Buhrmester, 1985a; Minnett, Vandell, & Santrock, 1983). And there is some evidence that sibling rivalries may intensify over the course of childhood, for John Santrock and Ann Minnett (1981) found that interactions between older female sibs (for example, an 8-year-old and a 12-year-old) were more negative in tone and included fewer positive acts than interactions between pairs of younger sisters (for example, a 4-year-old and an 8-year-old).

In some ways, sibling relationships are rather paradoxical. For example, Furman and Buhrmester (1985a, 1985b) found that siblings who are similar in age report more warmth and closeness than other sibling pairs but, at the same time, more friction and conflict (conflict being especially prevalent among opposite-sex sibs who are close in age). Moreover, grade school children view their sibling relations as more conflict-ridden and less satisfying than their relations with either parent, their grandparents, or their friends. Yet when children were asked to rate the *importance* of different social relationships and the *reliability* of their various social alliances, siblings were viewed as more important and more reliable than friends! So older grade school children clearly view siblings as significant people in their lives— people to whom they may turn for support and companionship, even though their relations with them have often been rather stormy.

Perhaps these seemingly paradoxical data make perfectly good sense if we carefully reexamine the findings on the nature of sibling/sibling interactions. Yes, rivalrous conduct and conflicts among siblings are a very normal part of family life. However, the observational record consistently shows that brothers and sisters often do nice things for one another and that these acts of kindness and affection are typically much more common than hateful or rivalrous conduct (see, for example, Abramovitch et al., 1986; Baskett & Johnson, 1982).

POSITIVE EFFECTS OF SIBLING INTERACTION

One recent survey of child-rearing practices in 186 societies found that older children were the principal caregivers for infants and toddlers in 57% of the groups studied (Weisner & Gallimore, 1977). Even in industrialized societies such as the United States, older siblings (particularly females) are often asked to look after and care for their younger brothers and sisters (Cicirelli, 1982). So there is reason to believe that older children may play a major role in the lives of younger siblings, often serving as their teachers, playmates, and advocates and occasionally as their disciplinarians.

Siblings as Attachment Objects

Do infants become attached to their older brothers and sisters? To find out, Robert Stewart (1983) exposed 10–20-month-old infants to a variation of Ainsworth's "strange situations" test. Each infant was left with a 4-year-old sibling in a strange room that a strange adult soon entered. The infants typically showed signs of distress as their mothers departed, and they were wary in the company of the stranger. Stewart noted that these distressed infants would often approach their older brother or sister, particularly when the stranger appeared. Moreover, a majority of the 4-year-olds offered some sort of comforting or caregiving to their baby brothers and sisters. In a later study, Stewart and Marvin (1984) replicated these results and showed that the preschoolers who were most inclined to comfort an infant sibling were those who had developed the role-taking skills to understand and appreciate the basis for the infant's distress. So it appears that older preschool children can become important sources of emotional support who help younger siblings to cope with uncertain situations when their parents are not around. Moreover, infants are likely to venture much farther away to explore a strange environment if a sensitive and attentive older sibling is nearby to serve as a "secure base" for exploration (Samuels, 1980; Stewart & Marvin, 1984).

Siblings as Social Models

In addition to providing a sense of security and facilitating the child's exploratory competencies, older siblings serve as models for their younger brothers and sisters. As early as 12 to 20 months of age, infants are already becoming very attentive to their older sibs, often choosing to imitate their actions or to take over toys that the older children have abandoned (Abramovitch, Corter, & Pepler, 1980; Samuels, 1977). By contrast, an older child will typically focus on parents as social models and will pay little attention to the behavior of a younger sib, unless they happen to be playing together or the younger sibling is interfering with the older child's activities (Baskett, 1984; Samuels, 1977).

Siblings as Teachers

Recently, Gene Brody and his associates (Brody, Stoneman, & MacKinnon, 1982) asked 8- to 10-year-olds to play a popular board game with (1) a younger (4½–7-year-old) sibling, (2) an 8–10-year-old peer, and (3) a younger sib and a peer. As the children played, observers noted how often each child assumed the following roles: *teacher*, *learner*, *manager* (child requests or commands an action), *managee* (child is the target of management), and *equal-status playmate*. Brody et al. found that older children dominated the sibling/sibling interactions by assuming the teacher and manager roles much more often than younger sibs did. Yet when playing with a peer, these 8- to 10-year-olds took the role of equal-status playmate and rarely tried to dominate their friends. When all three children played together, it was the older sibling rather than the peer who assumed responsibility for "managing" the younger child, although neither the older sib nor the peer did much teaching in this situation. So older siblings are likely to make an active attempt to instruct their younger brothers and sisters, particularly when they are playing alone with them. Although the teaching that older sibs performed in this study may seem rather trivial, other research indicates that younger siblings who experience little difficulty in learning to read are likely to have older brothers and sisters who played "school" with them and who taught them important lessons such as the ABCs (Norman-Jackson, 1982).

Do older children benefit from teaching their younger siblings? Indeed they may. Studies of peer tutoring, in which older children teach academic lessons to younger pupils, consistently find that the tutors show significant gains in academic achieve-ment—bigger gains than those posted by age mates who have not had an opportunity to tutor a younger child (Feldman, Devin-Sheehan, & Allen, 1976). Moreover, Robert Zajonc and his associates (Zajonc, Markus, & Markus, 1979) report that first-born children with younger sibs tend to score higher on tests of intelligence and academic achievement than "only" children who have no younger siblings to tutor. Finally, Delroy Paulhus and David Shaffer (1981) found that the greater the number of younger siblings (up to three) that college women have had an opportunity to tutor, the higher these women score on the Scholastic Aptitude Test (SAT).

So it appears that the teacher/learner roles that siblings often assume at play are beneficial to all parties involved: older siblings learn by tutoring their younger brothers and sisters, while the young tutees seem to profit from the instruction they receive.

CHARACTERISTICS OF FIRST-BORN AND LATER-BORN CHILDREN

For more than 100 years social scientists have specu-lated that a child's ordinal position within the family will affect his or her personality (Henderson, 1981). One popular notion was that first-born children, who initially enjoy an exclusive relationship with their parents, will remain forever closer to their mothers and fathers than later-borns. Another was that later-borns will eventually become more likable and popu-lar than first-borns because they have had to acquire important social skills in order to negotiate with their older and more powerful siblings. Do these claims have any merit? Do first-borns reliably differ from later-borns, and if so, why?

Characteristics of First-Borns

In Chapter 8, we noted that first-borns are overrepre-sented among populations of eminent people and that they tend to score higher than later-borns on tests of intelligence, academic achievement, and achieve-ment motivation. And in Chapter 7, we learned that first-born toddlers, nursery school children, and col-lege students are more sociable than their later-born age mates. However, it is interesting to note that first-borns tend to be less confident in social situations than later-borns, and first-born males are more likely than later-borns to exhibit behavior disorders and to be rated by teachers as anxious and aggressive toward their peers (Lahey, Hammer, Crumrine, & Forehand, 1980; Schachter, 1959). As a result, many first-borns are not terribly popular, even though they may be outgoing and seem to enjoy being around other people.

First-born children (particularly females) tend to be more obedient and somewhat more socially responsible than later-borns. Brian Sutton-Smith and B. G. Rosenberg (1970) propose that this obedience may stem from the special and exclusive early relationship that first-borns have had with their parents. Parents seem to expect more of their first-borns and are often critical of their behavior (Baskett, 1985; Rothbart, 1971). However, they also appear to be more attentive and affectionate toward their first-born children (Jacobs & Moss, 1976), a finding that may help to explain why first-borns often feel closer to their parents than later-borns do (Sutton-Smith & Rosenberg, 1970).

Characteristics of Later-Borns

It is difficult to characterize later-borns because they occupy many different sibling statuses (for example, second-born female in a family of two; fourth-born and male in a family with three elder sisters) and are not really a homogeneous group. In two-child families, the behavior of the later-born child is clearly influenced by the sex of his or her sibling. For example, a boy who has an older sister is likely to develop more "feminine" interests than a boy with an older brother (Sutton-Smith & Rosenberg, 1970).

As a group, later-borns seem to establish better relations with peers than first-borns do. In one study of 1750 first-born, middle-born, and last-born schoolchildren (Miller & Maruyama, 1976), the investigators found that the "babies of the family" (that is, last-borns) were most popular with their classmates, while middle-borns enjoyed intermediate popularity, and first-borns were least popular. Only children were similar in popularity to the first-borns in this study, although other investigators have reported that only children are more self-centered and less popular than their classmates who have one or

more siblings (Jiao, Ji, & Jing, 1986). Let's keep in mind that these "ordinal position" effects represent group averages. Many first-borns and only children are extremely popular with their peers, just as many later-borns are highly obedient, socially responsible, and motivated to achieve. Only when group averages are compared do the differences between first-borns and later-borns emerge.

Explaining Birth-Order Effects

It appears that parents contribute to ordinal-position effects by treating first-borns differently than later-borns. Many investigators believe that first-time (primiparous) parents will devote more attention to first-borns because they feel unpracticed at child rearing and are especially concerned about whether they are raising their child appropriately. But after raising one child successfully, parents gain considerable self-confidence and are not so apprehensive about the development of later-borns (Lasko, 1954; Schachter, 1959). Indeed, parents do have higher expectations for first-borns than for later-borns (Baskett, 1985), and they exert greater pressures on first-borns to be responsible and to work to the best of their ability (Lasko, 1954; Rothbart, 1971). In one study of children's achievement behavior (Hilton, 1967), mothers of first-borns were more likely than mothers of later-borns to stress achievement and to tailor their reactions to the child's performance. That is, mothers of first-borns were *extremely* warm and affectionate when their 4-year-olds succeeded on a cognitive task but were also more likely than mothers of later-borns to act peeved and to *withhold affection* if their child performed poorly on a task. Perhaps this pattern helps to explain why first-borns are so obedient and interested in pleasing their parents and are also higher in achievement motivation than later-borns.

Why are first-borns *more sociable* and yet *less popular* than later-borns? Many researchers believe that these findings are attributable to the character of sibling interactions. If you grew up with brothers and sisters, you know very well that power is unequally distributed among siblings. We have already seen that older sibs will try to dominate younger brothers and sisters in order to achieve their objectives—a tendency that may suppress the affiliative tendencies of later-borns and make them somewhat cautious and concerned about interacting with others (Abramovitch et al., 1986; Brody et al., 1982). Indeed, there is some evidence that older siblings who reliably use their greater power to impose their will on a younger brother or sister tend to employ these same tactics with peers (Berndt & Bulleit, 1985)—a move that is not likely to enhance their popularity or status in the peer group. Moreover, socially cautious later-borns may eventually become more popular than first-borns because

> if later-born children are to obtain . . . a fair share of positive outcomes, they must develop their interpersonal skills—powers of negotiation, accommodation, tolerance, and a capacity to accept less favorable outcomes—to a degree not found in first-born children . . . who may simply take or achieve what they want quite arbitrarily. . . . The acquisition of [these] interpersonal skills should facilitate social interactions with peers and thereby increase a [later-born] child's popularity [Miller & Maruyama, 1976, pp. 123–124].

THE IMPACT OF DIVORCE

Earlier in the chapter, we saw that nearly 50% of contemporary American marriages will end in divorce and about 40–50% of American children born in the 1980s will spend some time in a single-parent household—usually one headed by the mother. Only recently have investigators begun to conduct longitudinal studies to determine how children cope with a divorce and whether this disruption of the nuclear family is likely to have long-term effects on their social, emotional, and intellectual development. Let's see what they have learned.

THE IMMEDIATE EFFECTS

In her review of the literature, Mavis Hetherington (1981) notes that divorce is a stressful and painful event for many children. At first, these youngsters are likely to feel angry, fearful, depressed, or guilty about a divorce, and these initial reactions may strike hardest at young, relatively egocentric preschoolers, who are likely to perceive themselves as somehow

responsible for the dissolution of their parents' marriages. Although adolescents may experience considerable pain and anger when their parents divorce, they are better able to infer why the divorce has occurred, to resolve any loyalty conflicts that may arise, and to understand and cope with the financial and other practical problems that the family now faces. Yet it may be as long as a year after the divorce before the children of any age recover from the initial shock and begin to feel more positive about themselves and their new living arrangements (Hetherington, 1981).

THE CRISIS PHASE

Hetherington (1981) proposes that most children go through two phases when adjusting to a divorce: the *crisis phase*, which often lasts a year or more, and the *adjustment phase*, in which they settle down and begin to adapt to life in a single-parent home.

The emotional upheaval that accompanies the crisis phase is likely to affect the relationship that children have with their custodial parent. Hetherington and her associates (Hetherington, Cox, & Cox, 1982) find that the parenting practices of divorced mothers frequently deteriorate in the first year after the divorce, typically becoming much more coercive. Divorced mothers are apt to feel overburdened with the tasks of providing for their families and fulfilling all the responsibilities of homemaking and child rearing—almost as if they were shouldering the burden of two adults (indeed, they often are) with little or no time for themselves. Consequently, they are likely to become edgy, impatient, less sensitive to their children's needs, and more forceful and punitive in their approach to child rearing. And the children, who may already be emotionally devastated by dissolution of their family, will frequently react to their mother's coercive parenting by becoming cranky, disobedient, and downright disrespectful. The low point in mother/child relations often comes about a year after the divorce. One divorced mother described her family's ordeal as a "struggle for survival," while another characterized her experiences with her children as like "getting bitten to death by ducks" (Hetherington, Cox, & Cox, 1982, p. 258). Not surprisingly, the stresses resulting from a divorce and this new coercive lifestyle will often disrupt a child's relations with peers and undermine the quality of his or her work at school (Hetherington et al., 1982; Zill & Peterson, 1982).

The Question of Sex Differences

According to Hetherington (1981; Hetherington et al., 1982), the effects of marital disharmony and divorce are much more powerful and enduring for boys than for girls. At least two longitudinal studies found that girls had largely recovered from their social and emotional disturbances two years after a divorce (Hetherington et al., 1982; Wallerstein & Kelly, 1980). Although boys improved dramatically over this same period, many of them continued to show signs of emotional distress and problems in their relationships with parents, siblings, teachers, and peers.

However, other investigators have found no sex differences in children's short-term or long-term reactions to divorce (Kurdek, Blisk, & Siesky, 1981; J. A. Powell, personal communication, November 1983). One factor that does seem to predict children's postdivorce relations with their parents is the quality of their relations with each parent during the year *preceding* the divorce (Fine, Moreland, & Schwebel, 1983). Perhaps boys who show a very poor adjustment to divorce are those who were very close to their fathers. Separation from the father is undoubtedly quite stressful and frustrating for these youngsters, who may then express their anger and resentment toward the closest available targets—namely, their mothers, siblings, and peers. However, this hypothesis has not been tested, and it remains for future research to specify the conditions under which boys and girls are likely to differ in their reactions to divorce.

On Staying Together for the Good of the Children

The conventional wisdom used to be that unhappily married couples should remain together for the good of the children. Yet recent research suggests that, after the first year, children in single-parent homes are usually better adjusted than those who remain in conflict-ridden nuclear families (Hetherington et al., 1982; Wallerstein & Kelly, 1980, 1982; Zill & Peterson, 1982). Hetherington (1981) believes that an eventual escape from conflict may be the most positive outcome of divorce for many children. Judith Wallerstein and Joan Kelly (1980) definitely agree, adding that "today's conventional wisdom holds . . . that an unhappy couple might well *divorce* for the good of the children; that an unhappy marriage for the adults is also unhappy for the children; and that a divorce that promotes the happiness of the adults will benefit the children as well" (p. 67).

Coping with a Divorce: The Role of the Noncustodial Parent

Though no longer present in the home, divorced fathers often continue to play an important role in their children's development. In fact, Hetherington (1981) believes that the quality of the child's eventual adjustment to a divorce depends to a large extent on how much support the family receives from the noncustodial parent.

Let's first consider the *financial* support. After a divorce, mother-headed families must often get by on a fraction of the income they had when the father was present. This often necessitates a move to more modest housing in a poorer neighborhood and thus may take the family away from important sources of social support such as friends and neighbors. And if the mother begins to work at the time of the divorce or soon thereafter, she may have much less time to devote to her children than ever before. Of course, this apparent withdrawal of attention and affection often comes during a period of intense emotional strife, when children are in greatest need of parental support. Moreover, the lack of monetary resources for trips, toys, treats, and other pleasantries to which children may be accustomed can be a significant contributor to family quarrels and bickering. So it should hardly come as a surprise that children who adjust well to a divorce often live in homes where the family finances and level of economic support are not seriously undermined by marital separation (Desimone-Luis, O'Mahoney, & Hunt, 1979; Hodges, Wechsler, & Ballantine, 1979).

The amount of *emotional* support that the non-custodial parent provides is perhaps the most important contributor to the child's eventual adjustment. If parents continue to squabble after a divorce and are generally hostile toward each other, the quality of the mother's parenting is apt to suffer. This is the circumstance under which children of divorce are most likely to show serious disruptions in their academic performance and interpersonal relationships, particularly if a disruptive father visits his children on a regular basis. By contrast, children from divorced families may experience few if any long-term problems in adjusting when their parents maintain reasonably warm and friendly relations. Mothers who have cordial ex-husbands tend to be more involved with their children and more sensitive to their needs, particularly when the parents agree on child-rearing strategies and disciplinary issues (Berg & Kelly, 1979; Hetherington et al., 1982). Regular visits from *supportive* fathers also help children (particularly sons) to make a positive adjustment to their new life in a single-parent home (Hess & Camara, 1979; Rosen, 1979). In summarizing this research, Hetherington (1981, p. 50) suggests that "a continued, mutually supportive relationship including involvement of the father with the child is the most effective support system for divorced mothers in their parenting role."

How do children react to a divorce when the father is the custodial parent? In recent years, investigators have tried to answer this question by comparing the behavior of children growing up in father-headed and mother-headed single-parent homes. In Box 13-4, we will look at this research and see that fathers may be more competent as single parents than many people (and the legal system) have generally assumed.

LONG-TERM REACTIONS TO DIVORCE

Recently, Lawrence Kurdek and his associates (1981) asked 8- to 17-year-olds how they felt about their parents' divorce at four years and again at six years after the marriage was dissolved. They found that many children still had negative feelings about the divorce, even though the youngsters now understood that they had not been personally responsible for the break-up. Children generally described their parents

in positive or neutral terms (thus harboring few grudges), and most of them felt that the divorce had not adversely affected their peer relationships. In fact, those who had shown positive changes in their feelings about the divorce during the interval between the fourth and sixth years often reported that having friends whose parents were also divorced had helped them to cope with their earlier feelings of bitterness and resentment. Finally, Kurdek et al. found that the older children in their sample had made the most positive adjustments to divorce, particularly those youngsters who tested high in interpersonal understanding (that is, role-taking skills) and who had an internal locus of control.

In sum, a divorce is an unsettling experience—one that few children feel very positive about some four to six years after the fact. But despite their sentiments, it seems that a conflict-ridden nuclear family is often more detrimental to the child's development than the absence of a divorced parent. Indeed, the children of divorce may actually benefit in the long run if the dissolution of a bad marriage leads to an overall reduction in stress that enables either or both parents to be more sensitive and responsive to their needs (Hetherington, 1981; Wallerstein & Kelly, 1982).

DELINQUENCY AMONG CHILDREN FROM SINGLE-PARENT HOMES

Although the vast majority of children who are raised by their mothers adapt to single parenting and turn out to be reasonably well adjusted, at least one study of a representative sample of adolescents from all over the United States found that delinquent behavior is much more common among *both* male and female teenagers from single-parent homes (Dornbusch et al., 1985). The survey also suggested a possible explanation for this outcome: compared with parents from intact families, single parents exerted less influence over teenagers' choices of friends, their activities, and the hours they kept. This is an important finding, for we learned in Chapter 9 that lack of parental monitoring of an adolescent's activities is an important contributor to deviant and antisocial conduct. The survey by Dornbusch et al. produced another interesting outcome: the presence of any

BOX 13-4   *THE FATHER AS A CUSTODIAL PARENT*

Although the overwhelming majority of children from broken homes live with their mothers, about 10% of custody hearings now award children to the father, and joint custody is becoming more and more common (National Center for Health Statistics, 1980). How do fathers fare as custodial parents? Are they able to cope with the emotional distress that their children may be experiencing? Do they establish good relations with their children? Are children in father-custody homes any different from those living in mother-headed families?

Fathers who have custody of their children report many of the same problems thgat divorced mothers do: they feel overburdened with responsibilities, are somewhat depressed, and are concerned about their competence as parents and their ability to cope with their children's emotional needs (Hetherington, 1981). As a group, custodial fathers are more likely than custodial mothers to make use of alternative caregiving and support systems such as babysitters, relatives, day-care facilities, or even the noncustodial parent (Santrock & Warshak, 1979). Single-parent fathers typically demand more help with household tasks and more independence from their children than custodial mothers do. But most fathers in single-parent households perceive their relationships with their children to be reasonably sound (Hetherington, 1981), and they are more likely than

custodial mothers to report that their children are well behaved (Ambert, 1982).

As for the children, it appears that both boys and girls react differently to the parenting they receive when the father is the custodial parent. For boys, the differences are positive ones. John Santrock and Richard Warshak (1979) report that boys are much less coercive and demanding with custodial fathers than in mother-headed families. Moreover, boys in father-custody homes are more independent than girls, while just the reverse is true when the mother is the custodial parent. If there is a weakness in the father-custody arrangement, it concerns the father/daughter relationship. Custodial fathers are often quite concerned about their ability to cope with the problems and emotional needs of their daughters and the fact that their daughters have no feminine role model in the home (Mendes, 1976; Santrock & Warshak, 1979). And they have reason to be concerned, for at least one study has found that girls in families where the father has custody are less well adjusted than girls who live with their divorced mothers (Santrock & Warshak, 1979). However, boys in homes where the father has custody were found to be better adjusted than boys who were living with their mothers. As Hetherington (1981, p. 50) points out, "These findings need to be replicated and will have important implications for custody assignments if they are confirmed."

other adult (for example, a grandparent) in a mother-headed household was associated with greater parental control over the adolescent's activities and low levels of delinquent behavior. Clearly, these findings suggest "that there are functional equivalents of two-parent families—non-traditional groupings that can do the job of parenting—and that the raising of *adolescents* is not a task that can easily be borne by a mother alone" (Dornbusch et al., 1985, p. 340).

CHILDREN IN RECONSTITUTED FAMILIES

Within three to five years of a divorce, about 75% of all children from broken homes will experience yet another major change in their lives: a return to the

nuclear family when the custodial parent remarries and they suddenly acquire a stepparent (Glick, 1984). Apparently children from divorced families want to live in two-parent homes, even if it means having their mothers marry someone other than their fathers (Santrock et al., 1982). But are children happy with their new living arrangements once the custodial parent remarries? Do they prosper in these reconstituted families; or, rather, are they more likely to experience problems with their stepparent that could affect their cognitive, social, and emotional development?

Most studies of reconstituted families have compared the progress of children from *stepfather* homes to that of age mates in single-parent or intact families. The bulk of this research suggests that boys may make a slightly better adjustment to life with a stepfather than girls do. Compared with boys in single-parent homes, boys with stepfathers are less likely to show personality disorders or deficiencies in cognitive development (Chapman, 1977; Santrock, 1972).[2] Moreover, boys in stepfather families feel closer to their surrogate father, are less anxious and/or angered about this living arrangement, and seem to enjoy higher self-esteem than girls do (Clingempeel, Ievoli, & Brand, 1984; Santrock et al., 1982). Much less is known about children's reactions to *stepmothers* because stepmother families are relatively uncommon (recall that biological fathers receive custody of their children in only 10% of all custody hearings). However, the data that are available suggest that the transition from a father-headed single-parent home to a two-parent stepmother family is also more difficult for girls than for boys, particularly if the biological mother maintains frequent contact with her daughter (Clingempeel & Segal, 1986; Furstenberg & Seltzer, 1983). Yet the emotional disruption that daughters may initially experience in stepmother families is often short-lived, for "over time, the relative childrearing roles of biological mother and stepmother [are] effectively negotiated, and girls may [actually] benefit from a support system augmented by a second mother figure" (Clingempeel & Segal, 1986, p. 482).

Apparently these sex differences in children's responses to remarriage are not solely attributable to the behavior of stepparents, for these substitute caregivers are no less attentive and authoritative with their stepdaughters than with stepsons. Part of the stepdaughters' anxiety in *stepfather* homes may result from the behavior of their biological mothers, who are somewhat less attentive and authoritative than mothers in intact homes (Santrock et al., 1982). And what kind of parenting do *stepfathers* provide? The parenting behavior of stepfathers in Santrock's sample was at least as competent (by middle-class standards) as that given by biological fathers to their daughters and somewhat more competent than that given by biological fathers to their sons (Santrock et al., 1982). Finally, the often transitory problems in *stepmother*/stepdaughter relations stem not from an indifferent treatment of daughters by stepmothers but, rather, from the stepmothers' intrusive and somewhat premature attempts to establish good motherly relations with these girls, who are often closely attached to their biological mothers and may now be experiencing rather intense loyalty conflicts (Clingempeel & Segal, 1986).

On the basis of very limited evidence, then, it appears that boys in stepparent families may actually fare rather well, whereas girls are probably no worse and possibly better off (in the long run) than they would be in a single-parent home. Finally, there is little or no support for the notion that most stepparents are cool, aloof disciplinarians who are unconcerned about their stepchildren. On the contrary, the stepparents who have been studied to date seem to be competent parents who are involved with their stepchildren and sensitive to their needs.

A final note: Although the overwhelming majority of children in reconstituted families successfully adapt to this arrangement and become well-adjusted young men and women, there is some evidence that the incidence of deviant or delinquent behavior is higher among adolescents from stepparent homes than among age mates living with both biological parents (see Dornbusch et al., 1985; Garbarino, Sebes, & Schellenbach, 1984). Some theorists have speculated that stepparents are prone to become more coercive and rejecting toward an unruly teenager with whom they have no genetic connection, although alternatives to this sociobiological interpretation are many. For example, it could be argued that adolescents, who are becoming increasingly independent, simply view rules imposed by a stepparent as more intrusive or unwarranted than those coming from a natural parent. Indeed, the adolescent may even feel bitter and resentful toward a biological parent (and more inclined to deviate) if this lifelong advocate lends support to any unpleasant restrictions imposed by "that outsider" in their home. Clearly, the issue of deviant conduct among adolescents from reconstituted families is a topic that begs for additional research. Yet it is important to emphasize that most adolescents who are raised by stepparents are perfectly normal teenagers who are unlikely to display any psychopathological tendencies.

EFFECTS OF MATERNAL EMPLOYMENT

We have previously seen that a majority of young mothers now work outside the home and that this arrangement need not disrupt the emotional development or the sex typing of their children. Infants and toddlers are likely to become securely attached to their working mothers if they have quality day care and receive responsive caregiving when their mothers return home from work (Belsky, 1985; Hoffman, 1979). Moreover, children of working mothers (particularly daughters) hold higher educational and occupational aspirations and less stereotyped views of men and women than children whose mothers are not employed (Hoffman, 1979). Recent research suggests that children of working mothers are at least as outgoing and adaptable to social situations as children of homemakers. Frances Schachter (1981) studied a group of 20- to 36-month-old toddlers, about half of whom had mothers who were employed outside the home. She found no differences between the two groups in maturity of emotional development. However, children with employed mothers were more self-sufficient, less dependent on adults, and more sociable with peers. In a similar vein, studies of nursery school children, grade school children, and adolescents consistently indicate that both sons and daughters of working mothers show more independence and tend to score higher on tests of social and personal adjustment than children whose mothers remain at home (Gold & Andres, 1978a, 1978b; Gold, Andres, & Glorieux, 1979).

Does maternal employment have any effect on a child's cognitive development? The answer to this question is by no means clear at present. In her review of the literature, Lois Hoffman (1979) noted that most studies find no differences in either cognitive or scholastic performance between children of homemakers and those whose mothers work. However, at least two recent studies of infants and toddlers suggest that the *very young* children of working mothers perform at lower levels on developmental tests and score lower on standardized measures of intelligence than children of homemakers (Cohen, 1978; Schachter, 1981). Other recent work has found that mothers' working outside the home is associated with lower academic achievement for middle-class boys but not for girls (Bronfenbrenner & Crouter, 1982; Hoffman, 1984). But perhaps most sobering of all is a report published by the U.S. Department of Education (Ginsburg, cited in "Study: Children with Working Mothers," 1983) indicating that high school students from two-parent families in which the mother works score significantly lower on tests of academic achievement than their classmates whose mothers have never worked. This latter study is particularly important because it is based on a large national sample, and the findings seem to hold in every region of the country for families from all racial and socioeconomic backgrounds.

Clearly, these are provocative results that we should interpret cautiously until they are replicated in other large, national samples. But even if these findings are confirmed in future research, it may make little sense to advise working mothers that they should abandon their careers in order to stay home with their children. Economic realities have forced many mothers to work, and in one survey the vast majority of working women (76%) stated that they would continue to work even if they did not have to (Dubnoff, Veroff, & Kulka, 1978). One implication of the latter finding is that many women might resent a life of full-time mothering if they were pressured to assume that role, and it is possible that they would vent their frustrations on their children. Indeed, Francine Stuckey and her associates (Stuckey, McGhee, & Bell, 1982) found that the amount of complaining and criticism expressed among mothers, fathers, and their preschool children was significantly greater in families with *unemployed mothers who wanted to work* than in families where the mothers either were unemployed and preferred it that way or were employed and happy about it. Moreover, later research has consistently indicated that when mothers are satisfied with their working (or nonworking) statuses, they express predominantly favorable impressions of their children and have pleasant interactions with them (Alvarez, 1985; Lerner & Galambos, 1985). But if mothers are dissatisfied with their roles (either as homemakers or as working parents), they are apt to be aloof, impatient, and intolerant with their children, which, in turn, makes the children more cranky and temperamentally difficult (Lerner & Galambos, 1985). So it seems that family interactions are most likely to be amiable and conducive to the child's development when the mother's employment status matches her attitudes about working.

In sum, maternal employment is an integral part of modern family life—a role that often satisfies a mother's personal needs as well as providing for the economic welfare of the family. Although most children are not adversely affected by a mother's working outside the home, additional research is needed to discover exactly how, why, and under what circumstances maternal employment is likely to have any detrimental effects. Once these parameters are known, it should then be possible to help working mothers to adjust their caregiving routines or obtain outside support (day care, tutoring, and the like) so that they can promote their children's social and academic competencies while continuing in the careers that they must or desperately hope to pursue.

WHEN PARENTING BREAKS DOWN: THE PROBLEM OF CHILD ABUSE

In recent years, researchers and child-care professionals have coined terms such as *the mistreated child* or *the battered child syndrome* to describe those youngsters who are burned, bruised, beaten, starved, suffocated, neglected, sexually abused, or otherwise mistreated by their caregivers. Child abuse is a very serious problem in the United States—one that seems to be increasing at an alarming rate. Between 1968 and 1972, the number of *reported* cases of seriously battered children rose from 721 to 30,000 in the state of Michigan and from 4000 to nearly 40,000 in California (Kempe & Kempe, 1978). Since many cases of child abuse are neither detected nor reported, these statistics may be the tip of the iceberg. Raymond Starr (1979) estimates that every year, in the United States, as many as 1.4–1.9 *million* children are sub-

jected to forms of violence or neglect that could cause them serious physical or emotional harm.

Clearly, there are many factors that contribute to a problem as widespread as child abuse. To date, researchers have attempted to understand the battered-child syndrome by seeking answers for three basic questions: (1) Who gets abused? (2) Who are the abusers? and (3) Under what circumstances is abuse most likely to occur?

WHO IS ABUSED?

Although just about any child could become a target of neglect or abuse, some youngsters are more vulnerable than others. For example, children who react to discipline by defying or ignoring an adult are likely to elicit even stronger forms of punishment from the disciplinarian. And if these high-intensity tactics are reinforced by inhibiting the undesirable antics of a defiant child, they are likely to become the disciplinarian's preferred method of behavior control. This is indeed unfortunate, for reliance on physically coercive forms of discipline is often the first step along the road to child abuse (Parke & Lewis, 1981).

Children of all ages can contribute to their own abuse—even tiny infants! Babies who are emotionally unresponsive, hyperactive, irritable, or ill face far greater risks of being abused than quiet, healthy, and responsive infants who are easy to care for (Egeland & Sroufe, 1981; Sherrod, O'Connor, Vietze, & Altemeier, 1984). Indeed, *premature* babies, who are often active, irritable, and unresponsive, represent nearly 25% of the population of battered children—even though only 8% of the total infant population is born prematurely (Klein & Stern, 1971). Of course, this does not mean that 25% of all premature infants are abused but, rather, that the premature baby is more likely than a full-term infant to display certain characteristics that may trigger abusive responses from *some* caregivers. The emphasis on "some" caregivers is important, for the vast majority of difficult children are not mistreated by their parents or guardians, while other seemingly normal and happy children do become targets of abuse. Thus, the implication is that certain people may be "primed" to become abusive when their children irritate or anger them.

WHO ARE THE ABUSERS?

Strange as it may seem, only about 1 child abuser in 10 has a serious mental illness that is difficult to treat (Kempe & Kempe, 1978). The fact is that people who abuse their children come from all races, ethnic groups, and social classes, and many of them appear to be rather typical, loving parents—except for their tendency to become extremely irritated with their children and to do things they will later regret.

However, overt appearances can be very deceiving. Recently, Ann Frodi and Michael Lamb (1980) presented videotapes of smiling and crying infants to groups of abusive and nonabusive mothers who were matched for age, marital status, and the number of children they had had. While the subjects watched the tapes, their physiological responses were monitored. Afterward, each subject described the emotional reactions that she had experienced while observing the infants. Frodi and Lamb reported that their nonabusive parents showed increases in physiological arousal to the infant's cries but not to his or her smiles; cries were described as unpleasant, while smiles generally made the nonabusers feel happy. By contrast, the abusive parents had much stronger physiological reactions to both cries and smiles, and they felt less happy and less willing to interact with a smiling infant than nonabusers. Frodi and Lamb suggest that child abusers may find all of an infant's social signals aversive. Thus, even a smile might trigger a hostile response from an abusive caregiver.

Some child abusers may react very negatively to their infants because they themselves were abused, neglected, or unloved as children and may never have learned how to give and receive affection (Belsky, 1980; Steele & Pollack, 1974). Byron Egeland (1979; Egeland, Sroufe, & Erickson, 1983) found that abusive mothers in his sample, many of whom had been neglected or abused by their own parents, were likely to misinterpret their babies' behavior. For example, when the infant cried to communicate needs such as hunger, nonabusive mothers treated these vocalizations as a sign of discomfort (correct interpretation), whereas abusive mothers often inferred that the baby was criticizing or rejecting them! Although such an interpretation may be understandable given the abusive mothers' own histories of being rejected or abused during childhood, perhaps you can see how their misreading of an infant's emotional signals might contribute to further distress and irritability on the part of the baby, whose "nasty temperament" may then elicit abusive responses. You may recall from Chapter 6 that Harry Harlow and his associates observed a similar phenomenon among rhesus monkeys: Female monkeys who were either abused as infants or raised without caregivers later became indifferent or abusive toward their own offspring (Harlow, Harlow, Dodsworth, & Arling, 1966; Suomi, 1978). Not only did they push their babies away, refusing to let them nurse, but some of the reluctant caregivers even killed their infants by biting off their fingers and toes. Apparently these abusive mother monkeys who had never received love from a caregiver simply did not know how to attend to an infant or how to respond to its signals. They treated infants as if they were irritants.

Indeed, this tendency to misinterpret emotional signals and to respond inappropriately to others' distress can already be observed in abused infants and toddlers. In a recent study of day-care children, Mary Main and Carol George (1985) observed the reactions of abused and nonabused 1- to 3-year-olds to the fussing and crying of classmates. As shown in Figure 13-2, nonabused toddlers typically reacted to a peer's distress by attending carefully to the other child and/ or by displaying concern. By contrast, not one abused toddler showed any concern in response to the distress of an age mate. Instead, the abused toddlers were likely to emit disturbing patterns of behavior, often becoming angry at this fussing and then *physically attacking* the crying child. So it seems that abused children are apt to be abusive companions who have apparently learned from their own experiences that distress signals are particularly irritating to others and will typically elicit angry responses rather than displays of sympathy and compassion.

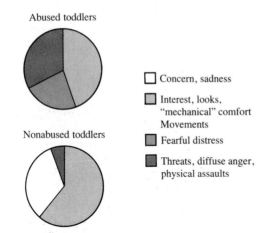

Abused toddlers

Nonabused toddlers

☐ Concern, sadness

◻ Interest, looks, "mechanical" comfort Movements

◼ Fearful distress

◼ Threats, diffuse anger, physical assaults

FIGURE 13-2 Responses to the distress of peers observed in abused and nonabused toddlers in the day-care setting. (The figures show the mean proportion of responses falling in each category for the nine abused and nine nonabused toddlers.)

Fortunately, many human beings who were abused or neglected during childhood learn how to respond appropriately to other people long before they have children of their own. In fact, recent research indicates that people who were mistreated or emotionally deprived as children are likely to become abusive parents *only* if they are currently experiencing other kinds of social or environmental stresses (Conger, Burgess, & Barrett, 1979). Let's now consider some of the social and situational factors that can contribute to child abuse.

SOCIAL-SITUATIONAL TRIGGERS: THE ECOLOGY OF CHILD ABUSE

Child abuse is most likely to occur in families under stress. Consider, for example, that battered children often come from a large family in which overburdened caregivers have many small children to attend to (Light, 1973). The probability of abuse under these stressful circumstances is further compounded if the mother is relatively young, is poorly educated, and receives little child-rearing assistance from the father, a friend or relative, or some other member of her social network (Egeland et al., 1983). Other significant life changes such as the death of a family

member, the loss of a job, or moving to a new home can disrupt social and emotional relationships within a family and thereby contribute to abusive and neglectful parenting (Conger et al., 1979; Steinberg, Catalano, & Dooley, 1981). Finally, children are much more likely to be abused or neglected if their parents are unhappily married (Belsky, 1980; Kempe & Kempe, 1978).

Of course, families are embedded in a broader social context (for example, a neighborhood, a community, and a culture) that may well affect a child's chances of being abused. Some neighborhoods can be labeled "*high risk*" areas because they have much higher rates of child abuse than other neighborhoods of the same demographic and socioeconomic backgrounds. What are these high-risk areas like? According to James Garbarino and Deborah Sherman (1980), they tend to be deteriorating neighborhoods in which families "go it alone" without interacting much with their neighbors or making use of community services such as Scouting or recreation centers. Unlike mothers in low-risk areas, those in high-risk areas take very little pride in their neighborhoods and see them as poor places to raise children. Garbarino and Sherman (1980) describe the high-risk neighborhood as a physically unattractive and socially impoverished setting in which parents not only are struggling financially but also are isolated from formal and informal support systems (for example, friends, relatives, the church, and a sense of "community"). Although the quality of a neighborhood will depend, in part, on the people who live there, let's also note that the actions of government and industry can have an effect. For example, a decision to rezone a low-risk area or to locate a highway there can lead to destruction of play areas, declining property values, a loss of pride in the neighborhood, and the eventual isolation of families from friends, community services (which may no longer exist), and other bases of social support. James Garbarino (1982) is one of many theorists who believe that large numbers of American children are likely to be mistreated because of political or economic decisions that have undermined the health and stability of low-risk, family-oriented neighborhoods.

Some researchers have argued that child abuse is

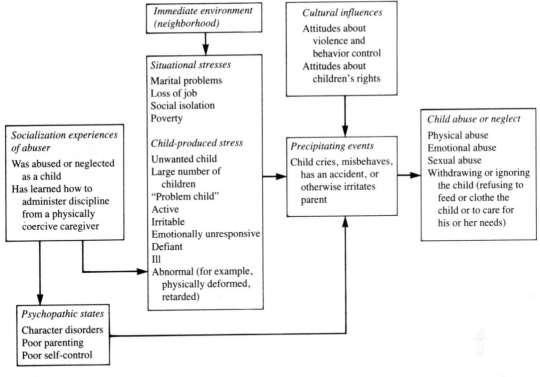

FIGURE 13-3 A social-ecological model of child abuse

rampant in the United States because people in this society (1) have a permissive attitude about violence and (2) generally sanction the use of physical punishment as a means of controlling children's behavior. Indeed, there may be some truth to these assertions, for cross-cultural studies reveal that children are rarely abused in societies that discourage the use of physical punishment (see Belsky, 1980).

In sum, child abuse is a very complex phenomenon that has many causes and contributing factors. An examination of Figure 13-3 indicates that we have come a long way from those early theories that focused almost exclusively on the abusive parent (and his or her personality) as the primary contributor to the battered-child syndrome. But despite our better understanding of the causes of child abuse, we are still a long way from solving the problem. Rather than conclude on that depressing note, let's look at some of the methods that have been used to assist the abused child and his or her abusers.

HOW CAN WE HELP ABUSIVE PARENTS AND THEIR CHILDREN?

A number of strategies have been devised in an attempt to prevent or control the problem of child abuse. For example, Kempe and Kempe (1978) report that a large percentage of abusive parents will stop physically mistreating their children if they can be persuaded to use certain services, such as 24-hour "hotlines" or crisis nurseries, that will enable them to discuss their hostile feelings with a volunteer or to get away from their children for a few hours when they are about to lose control. However, these are only stopgap measures that will probably not work for long unless the abuser also takes advantage of other services—such as *Parents Anonymous* or family therapy—that are designed to help the caregiver to understand his or her problem while providing the friendship and emotional support that an abusive parent so often lacks.[3]

Babies who are at risk for later emotional difficulties can be identified through neonatal assessment programs, and their parents can be taught how to make these infants respond more favorably to their caregiving. Indeed, we have already seen that Brazelton testing and training programs (see Box 5-2) are effective methods of preventing the "miscommunications" between infants and caregivers that could lead to child abuse. The Kempes (1978) also note that potential child abusers can often be identified in the delivery room by their reluctance to look at, touch, hold, or cuddle their infants. However, many of these reluctant caregivers will never abuse their child if they are visited regularly by a child care professional who provides them with emotional support and encouragement, as well as the information and guidance they will need to establish a sound relationship with their baby (Kempe & Kempe, 1978).

Although its potential is largely untapped, television could become an effective ally in our efforts to prevent child abuse (Parke & Lewis, 1981). Thirty-second public service announcements might be an excellent method of publicizing formal support systems (for example, Parents Anonymous or crisis nurseries) that are locally available to abusive parents. Programming could be developed to teach parents effective, nonpunitive child care techniques that would minimize social conflicts within the family and decrease the probability of child abuse (see McCall, Gregory, & Murray, 1984). Finally, television could be used to modify our attitudes about the rights of parents and their children. In the United States, the courts and welfare agencies are often hesitant to take children from their abusive parents, even when there is a history of repeated physical abuse (Rosenheim, 1973). One reason for their reluctance is that, historically, children have been treated as their parents' possessions. Another is that abused children and their parents are often firmly attached to each other, so that neither the abusive adult nor the battered child wishes to be separated. However, it is essential that we carefully weigh the child's rights against the rights and wishes of the parents in cases of child abuse, for some abusive

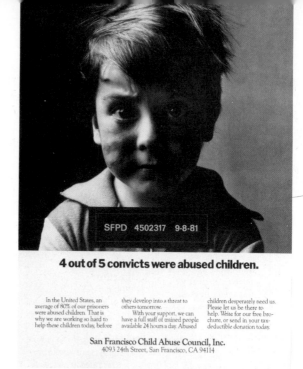

4 out of 5 convicts were abused children.

In the United States, an average of 80% of our prisoners were abused children. That is why we are working so hard to help these children today, before they develop into a threat to others tomorrow.

With your support, we can have a full staff of trained people available 24 hours a day. Abused children desperately need us. Please let us be there to help. Write for our free brochure, or send in your tax-deductible donation today.

San Francisco Child Abuse Council, Inc.
4093 24th Street, San Francisco, CA 94114

PHOTO 13-3   A number of programs and services have been created in an attempt to prevent or control the problem of child abuse.

adults will continue to seriously harm and occasionally even kill their battered children, regardless of the counseling they receive (Fontana, 1973; Kempe & Kempe, 1978).

Clearly, no caregiver has the right to abuse a child. In cases of severe abuse or neglect, our first priority must be to provide for the health and safety of mistreated children, even if that means terminating the abusers' legal rights of parenthood and placing their children in foster care or adoptive homes.

SUMMARY

The family is the primary agent of socialization—the setting in which children begin to acquire the beliefs, attitudes, and values of their society. The most common arrangement in Western societies is the *nuclear family*, a social system that consists of three basic roles—wife/mother, husband/father, and child/sibling—although adaptive alternatives, such as the *extended family*, are quite common in many cultures and subcultures. Parents in all societies pursue three goals in raising their children: (1) ensuring the child's survival, (2) preparing the child for economic self-sufficiency, and (3) training the child to maximize other cultural values such as morality, religion, intellectual achievement, and personal satisfaction.

Traditionally, researchers have assumed that the flow of influence within a family was from parents, who did the shaping, to children, whose characters were molded by the child-rearing strategies of their elders. Today we recognize that families are complex social systems: parents influence each other and each of their children, who, in turn, may influence one another, each parent, and the parents' marital relationship. Families also live within a broader social context (for example, a particular neighborhood, community, and society) that may affect family interactions and ultimately the development of the children within a family. To understand the influence of the family on developing children, one must treat the family as a social system rather than focusing exclusively on the ways parents may influence the child.

The birth of a child is a highly significant event that alters the behavior of both parents and may change the character of their marital relationship. The transition to parenthood tends to be less severe or disruptive when parents are older and have been married for some time before the child is conceived. Warm, responsive parenting during infancy contributes to the establishment of secure parent/child attachments and promotes the child's exploratory competence and intellectual growth. Although fathers interact less with their very young infants than mothers do, they soon become more involved with their children and begin to play a very special role in the child's life. The quality of the marital relationship is very important. Unhappily married couples often establish shaky emotional relations with their children, whereas parents who are happily married provide the mutual support and encouragement that usually enables them to establish good relations with their infants, even those who require special care or are temperamentally difficult.

Two important aspects of parenting are warmth/hostility and permissiveness/restrictiveness (parental control). These two parental dimensions are independent, so that we find parents who are warm and restrictive, warm and permissive, cool (rejecting) and restrictive, and cool and permissive. Generally speaking, warm and restrictive parents who appeal to reason in order to enforce their demands are likely to raise cheerful, friendly children who are intellectually curious, self-confident, and morally mature.

Parents from different social classes have different values, concerns, and outlooks on life that influence their child-rearing strategies. Lower- and working-class parents stress obedience, respect, neatness, cleanliness, and staying out of trouble—precisely the characteristics that their children will need to adapt to a position in the blue-collar economy. In contrast, middle-class parents are less restrictive and authoritarian and more likely than low-SES parents to stress independence, creativity, ambition, and self-control—the attributes that their children will need for success in business or the professions. Thus, parents from all socioeconomic strata tend to emphasize the characteristics that contribute to success *as they know it*, and it is inappropriate to conclude that one particular style of parenting is somehow "better" or more competent than all others.

Interactions between siblings are generally more negative than those between children and their parents. But even though sibling rivalries are a normal aspect of family life, there is a positive side to having a sibling. Older sibs serve as attachment objects who may comfort their distressed brothers and sisters and provide a "secure base" for exploration. Moreover, the teacher/learner roles that siblings often assume at play are beneficial to all parties: older siblings learn by tutoring their younger brothers and sisters, while the younger tutees appear to profit from the instruction they receive. First-born children, who receive more attention and achievement training from their parents, tend to be more obedient, anxious, and achievement-oriented than later-borns. However, later-borns, who must acquire important social skills in order to negotiate with older, more powerful sibs, tend to establish better relations with peers than first-borns do.

Divorce represents a drastic change in family life

that is stressful and unsettling for many children. Their initial reactions often include anger, fear, depression, and guilt—feelings that may last more than a year. The emotional upheaval that follows a divorce may influence the parent/child relationship. Children often become cranky, disobedient, or otherwise difficult, while the custodial parent may suddenly become more punitive and controlling. The stresses resulting from a divorce and this new coercive lifestyle often affect the child's peer relations and schoolwork. But after the first year, children of divorce are usually better adjusted than those who remain in conflict-ridden nuclear homes. Moreover, children from divorced homes may experience few if any long-term problems in adjustment when their parents are cordial and can agree on child-rearing strategies and when the noncustodial parent continues to provide financial assistance.

Maternal employment does not seem to disrupt children's social and emotional development; in fact, children of working mothers are often found to be more independent and more sociable and to have less stereotyped views of men and women than children whose mothers are not employed. Although the data are scanty at this point, there is some evidence that children of working mothers score lower on tests of academic achievement than their classmates whose mothers have never worked. If this finding proves to be reliable, we will need to learn why maternal employment affects academic achievement so that working mothers can take the steps necessary to prevent these problems while continuing in the careers that they must (or very much hope to) pursue.

Child abuse is a serious problem that is becoming more common. Just about any child could become the target of abuse, although defiant children and those who are active, irritable, emotionally unresponsive, or ill are more vulnerable than happy, healthy children who are easy to care for. Child abusers come from all social strata, but many of them were themselves victims of abuse as children. Child abuse is more likely in families under social, financial, or environmental stress. Programs designed to assist abused children and their abusive parents have achieved some success. However, we are still a long way from solving the problem.

NOTES

1. Ethnocentrism is a prejudicial tendency to view one's own culture as "best" and to use one's own cultural standards as a basis for evaluating other cultures.

2. Girls show little distinct improvement in cognitive functioning upon moving from a single-parent to a stepfather home. However, they function better than boys do in single-parent homes and have less room for improvement.

3. Fortunately these services are often free. Chapters of Parents Anonymous are now located in many cities and towns in the United States (for the location of a nearby chapter, one can consult a telephone directory or write to Parents Anonymous, 2230 Hawthorne Blvd., Suite 93102, Torrance, Calif. 90505). In addition, many cities and counties provide free family therapy to abusive parents. Often the therapists are lay volunteers who have been trained to serve in this capacity and who do so quite effectively.

REFERENCES

ABRAMOVITCH, R., Corter, C., & Pepler, D. J. (1980). Observations of mixed-sex sibling dyads. *Child Development, 51,* 1268–1271.

ABRAMOVITCH, R., Corter, C., Pepler, D. J., & Stanhope, L. (1986). Sibling and peer interaction: A final follow-up and a comparison. *Child Development, 57,* 217–229.

AINSWORTH, M. D. S. (1979). Attachment as related to mother-infant interaction. In J. S. Rosenblatt, R. A. Hinde, C. Beer, & M. Busnel (Eds.), *Advances in the study of behavior* (Vol. 9). Orlando, FL: Academic Press.

ALVAREZ, W. F. (1985). The meaning of maternal employment for mothers and their perceptions of their three-year-old children. *Child Development, 56,* 350–360.

AMBERT, A. (1982). Differences in children's behavior toward custodial mothers and custodial fathers. *Journal of Marriage and the Family, 44,* 73–86.

BARRY, H., Child, I. L., & Bacon, M. K. (1959). The relation of child training to subsistence economy. *American Anthropologist, 61,* 51–63.

BASKETT, L. M. (1984). Ordinal position differences in children's family interactions. *Developmental Psychology, 20,* 1026–1031.

BASKETT, L. M. (1985). Sibling status effects: Adult expectations. *Developmental Psychology, 21,* 441–445.

BASKETT, L. M., & Johnson, S. M. (1982). The young child's interaction with parents versus siblings: A behavioral analysis. *Child Development, 53,* 643–650.

BAUMRIND, D. (1967). Child care practices anteceding three patterns of preschool behavior. *Genetic Psychology Monographs, 75,* 43–88.

BAUMRIND, D. (1977, March). *Socialization determinants of personal agency.* Paper presented at the biennial meeting of the Society for Research in Child Development, New Orleans.

BECKER, W. C. (1964). Consequences of different kinds of parental discipline. In M. L. Hoffman & L. W. Hoffman (Eds.), *Review of child development research* (Vol. 1). New York: Russell Sage Foundation.

BELSKY, J. (1980). Child maltreatment: An ecological integration. *American Psychologist, 35,* 320–335.

BELSKY, J. (1981). Early human experience: A family perspective. *Developmental Psychology, 17,* 3–23.

BELSKY, J. (1985). Two waves of day-care research: Developmental effects and conditions of quality. In R. Ainslie (Ed.), *The child and the day care setting*. New York: Praeger.

BELSKY, J., Garduque, L., & Hrncir, E. (1984). Assessing performance, competence, and executive capacity in infant play: Relations to home environment and security of attachment. *Developmental Psychology, 20*, 406–417.

BELSKY, J., Gilstrap, B., & Rovine, M. (1984). The Pennsylvania Infant and Family Development Project, I: Stability and change in mother-infant and father-infant interaction in a family setting at one, three, and nine months. *Child Development, 55*, 692–705.

BELSKY, J., & Isabella, R. A. (1985). Marital and parent-child relationships in family of origin and marital change following the birth of a baby: A retrospective analysis. *Child Development, 56*, 342–349.

BERG, B., & Kelly, R. (1979). The measured self-esteem of children from broken, rejected, and accepted families. *Journal of Divorce, 2*, 363–370.

BERNDT, T. J., & Bulleit, T. N. (1985). Effects of sibling relationships on preschoolers' behavior at home and at school. *Developmental Psychology, 21*, 761–767.

BERRY, J. W. (1967). Independence and conformity in subsistence-level societies. *Journal of Personality and Social Psychology, 7*, 415–418.

BRADLEY, R. H., Caldwell, B. M., & Elardo, R. (1979). Home environment and cognitive development in the first 2 years: A cross-lagged panel analysis. *Developmental Psychology, 15*, 246–250.

BRAZELTON, T. B. (1979). Behavioral competence of the newborn infant. *Seminars in Perinatology, 3*, 35–44.

BRODY, G. H., & Shaffer, D. R. (1982). Contributions of parents and peers to children's moral socialization. *Developmental Review, 2*, 31–75.

BRODY, G. H., Stoneman, Z., & MacKinnon, C. E. (1982). Role asymmetries in interactions among school-aged children, their younger siblings, and their friends. *Child Development, 53*, 1364–1370.

BRODY, G. H., Stoneman, Z., & Wheatley, P. (1984). Peer interaction in the presence and absence of observers. *Child Development, 55*, 1425–1428.

BRONFENBRENNER, U. (1979). Contexts of child rearing: Problems and prospects. *American Psychologist, 34*, 844–850.

BRONFENBRENNER, U., & Crouter, A. C. (1982). Work and family through time and space. In S. Kamerman & C. D. Hayes (Eds.), *Families that work: Children in a changing world*. Washington, DC: National Academy Press.

BUSS, D. M. (1981). Predicting parent-child interactions from children's activity level. *Developmental Psychology, 17*, 59–65.

CAIN, L., Kelly, D., & Shannon, D. (1980). Parents' perceptions of the psychological and social impact of home monitoring. *Pediatrics, 66*, 37–40.

CASSIDY, J. (1986). The ability to negotiate the environment: An aspect of infant competence as related to quality of attachment. *Child Development, 57*, 331–337.

CHAPMAN, M. (1977). Father absence, stepfathers, and the cognitive performance of college students. *Child Development, 48*, 1155–1158.

CICIRELLI, V. G. (1982). Sibling influence throughout the life-span. In M. E. Lamb & B. Sutton-Smith (Eds.), *Sibling relationships*. Hillsdale, NJ: Erlbaum.

CLARKE-STEWART, K. A. (1978). And daddy makes three: The father's impact on the mother and young child. *Child Development, 49*, 466–478.

CLARKE-STEWART, K. A. (1982). *Daycare*. Cambridge, MA: Harvard University Press.

CLINGEMPEEL, W. G., Ievoli, R., & Brand, E. (1984). Structural complexity and the quality of stepparent-stepchild relationships. *Family Process, 23*, 547–560.

CLINGEMPEEL, W. G., & Segal, S. (1986). Stepparent-stepchild relationships and the psychological adjustment of children in stepmother and stepfather families. *Child Development, 57*, 474–484.

COHEN, S. E. (1978). Maternal employment and mother-child interaction. *Merrill-Palmer Quarterly, 24*, 189–197.

COHEN, S. E., & Beckwith, L. (1979). Preterm infant interaction with the caregiver in the first year of life and competence at age two. *Child Development, 50*, 767–776.

CONGER, R. D., Burgess, R., & Barrett, C. (1979). Child abuse related to life change and perceptions of illness: Some preliminary findings. *Family Coordinator, 28*, 73–78.

CONGER, R. D., McCarty, J. A., Yang, R. K., Lahey, B. B., & Kropp, J. (1984). Perception of child, child-rearing values, and emotional distress as mediating links between environmental stressors and observed maternal behavior. *Child Development, 55*, 2234–2247.

COOPERSMITH, S. (1967). *The antecedents of self-esteem*. New York: W. H. Freeman.

COWAN, C. P., & Cowan, P. A., (1987). A preventive intervention for couples becoming parents. In C. F. Z. Boukydis (Ed.), *Research on support for parents and infants in the postnatal period*. New York: Ablex.

CRNIC, K. A., Greenberg, M. T., Ragozin, A. S., Robinson, N. M., & Basham, R. B. (1983). Effects of stress and social support on mothers and premature and full-term infants. *Child Development, 54*, 209–217.

CROOK, T., Raskin, A., & Eliot, J. (1981). Parent-child relationships and adult depression. *Child Development, 52*, 950–957.

DAVID, H. P., & Baldwin, W. P. (1979). Childbearing and child development: Demographic and psychosocial trends. *American Psychologist, 34*, 866–871.

DESIMONE-LUIS, J., O'Mahoney, K., & Hunt, D. (1979). Children of separation and divorce: Factors influencing adjustment. *Journal of Divorce, 3*, 37–42.

DORNBUSCH, S. M., Carlsmith, J. M., Bushwall, S. J., Ritter, P. L., Leiderman, H., Hastorf, A. H., & Gross, R. T. (1985). Single parents, extended households, and the control of adolescents. *Child Development, 56*, 326–341.

DUBNOFF, S. J., Veroff, J., & Kulka, R. A. (1978, August). *Adjustment to work: 1957–1976*. Paper presented at the meeting of the American Psychological Association, Toronto.

DUNN, J., & Kendrick, C. (1981a). Interaction between young siblings: Association with the interaction between mother and firstborn child. *Developmental Psychology, 17*, 336–343.

DUNN, J., & Kendrick, C. (1981b). Social behavior of young siblings in the family context: Differences between same-sex and different-sex dyads. *Child Development, 52*, 1265–1273.

DUNN, J., & Munn, P. (1985). Becoming a family member: Family conflict and the development of social understanding in the second year. *Child Development, 56*, 480–492.

EASTERBROOKS, M. A., & Goldberg, W. A. (1984). Toddler development in the family: Impact of father involvement and parenting characteristics. *Child Development, 55*, 740–752.

EGELAND, B. (1979). Preliminary results of a prospective study of the antecedents of child abuse. *International Journal of Child Abuse and Neglect, 3*, 269–278.

EGELAND, B., & Sroufe, L. A. (1981). Attachment and early maltreatment. *Child Development, 52*, 44–52.

EGELAND, B., Sroufe, L. A., & Erickson, M. (1983). The developmental consequences of different patterns of maltreatment. *International Journal of Child Abuse and Neglect, 7*, 459–469.

ERIKSON, E. H. (1963). *Childhood and society* (2nd ed.). New York: Norton.

FELDMAN, R. S., Devin-Sheehan, L., & Allen, V. L. (1976). Children tutoring children: A critical review of research. In V. L. Allen (Ed.), *Children as teachers: Theory and research on tutoring*. Orlando, FL: Academic Press.

FELDMAN, S. S., & Aschenbrenner, B. (1983). Impact of parenthood on various aspects of masculinity and femininity: A short-term longitudinal study. *Developmental Psychology, 19*, 278–289.

FINE, M. A., Moreland, J. R., & Schwebel, A. I. (1983). Long-term effects of divorce on parent-child relationships. *Developmental Psychology, 19*, 703–713.

FONTANA, V. J. (1973). *Somewhere a child is crying: Maltreatment—causes and prevention.* New York: Macmillan.

FRODI, A. M., & Lamb, M. E. (1980). Child abusers' responses to infant smiles and cries. *Child Development, 51*, 238–241.

FURMAN, W., & Buhrmester, D. (1985a). Children's perceptions of the personal relationships in their social networks. *Developmental Psychology, 21*, 1016–1024.

FURMAN, W., & Buhrmester, D. (1985b). Children's perceptions of the qualities of sibling relationships. *Child Development, 56*, 448–461.

FURSTENBERG, F. F., & Seltzer, J. A. (1983, April). *Divorce and child development.* Paper presented at the meeting of the Orthopsychiatric Association, Boston.

GARBARINO, J. (1982). The human ecology of school crime. In B. Emrich (Ed.), *Theoretical perspectives on school crime.* Davis, CA: National Council on Crime and Delinquency.

GARBARINO, J., Sebes, J., & Schellenbach, C. (1984). Families at risk for destructive parent-child relations in adolescence. *Child Development, 55*, 174–183.

GARBARINO, J., & Sherman, D. (1980). High-risk neighborhoods and high-risk families: The human ecology of child maltreatment. *Child Development, 51*, 188–198.

GATH, A. (1978). *Down's syndrome and the family: The early years.* Orlando, FL: Academic Press.

GJERDE, P. F. (1986). The interpersonal structure of family interaction settings: Parent-adolescent relations in dyads and triads. *Developmental Psychology, 22*, 297–304.

GLICK, P. C. (1984). Marriage, divorce, and living arrangements: Prospective changes. *Journal of Family Issues, 5*, 7–26.

GOLD, D., & Andres, D. (1978a). Developmental comparisons between adolescent children with employed and nonemployed mothers. *Merrill-Palmer Quarterly, 24*, 243–254.

GOLD, D., & Andres, D. (1978b). Developmental comparisons between 10-year-old children with employed and nonemployed mothers. *Child Development, 49*, 75–84.

GOLD, D., Andres, D., & Glorieux, J. (1979). The development of Francophone nursery-school children with employed and nonemployed mothers. *Canadian Journal of Behavioral Science, 11*, 169–173.

GREENBERG, M., & Morris, N. (1974). Engrossment: The newborn's impact upon the father. *American Journal of Orthopsychiatry, 44*, 520–531.

GROSSMAN, F. K., Eichler, L. S., Winickoff, S. A., & Associates. (1980). *Pregnancy, birth, and parenthood: Adaptations of mothers, fathers, and infants.* San Francisco: Jossey-Bass.

GRUSEC, J. E., & Kuczynski, L. (1980). Direction of effect in socialization: A comparison of the parent's versus the child's behavior as determinants of disciplinary techniques. *Developmental Psychology, 16*, 1–9.

HARLOW, H. F., Harlow, M. K., Dodsworth, R. O., & Arling, G. L. (1966). Maternal behavior of rhesus monkeys deprived of mothering and peer associations as infants. *Proceedings of the American Philosophical Society, 110*, 88–98.

HEINICKE, C. M., Diskin, S. D., Ramsey-Klee, D. M., & Given, K. (1983). Pre-birth parent characteristics and family development in the first year of life. *Child Development, 54*, 194–208.

HENDERSON, R. W. (1981). Home environment and intellectual performance. In R. W. Henderson (Ed.), *Parent-child interaction: Theory, research, and prospects.* Orlando, FL: Academic Press.

HESS, R. D. (1970). Social class and ethnic influences upon socialization. In P. H. Mussen (Ed.), *Carmichael's manual of child psychology* (Vol. 2). New York: Wiley.

HESS, R. D., & Camara, K. A. (1979). Post divorce family relationships as mediating factors in the consequences of divorce for children. *Journal of Social Issues, 35*, 79–96.

HETHERINGTON, E. M. (1981). Children and divorce. In R. W. Henderson (Ed.), *Parent-child interaction: Theory, research, and prospects.* Orlando, FL: Academic Press.

HETHERINGTON, E. M., Cox, M., & Cox, R. (1982). Effects of divorce on parents and children. In M. E. Lamb (Ed.), *Nontraditional families.* Hillsdale, NJ: Erlbaum.

HILTON, I. (1967). Differences in the behavior of mothers toward first and later born children. *Journal of Personality and Social Psychology, 7*, 282–290.

HODGES, W. F., Wechsler, R. C., & Ballantine, C. (1979). Divorce and the preschool child: Cumulative stress. *Journal of Divorce, 3*, 55–68.

HOFFMAN, L. W. (1979). Maternal employment: 1979. *American Psychologist, 34*, 859–865.

HOFFMAN, L. W. (1984). Work, family, and the socialization of the child. In R. D. Parke (Ed.), *Review of child development research.* Vol. 7: *The family.* Chicago: University of Chicago Press.

HOLDEN, G. W. (1983). Avoiding conflict: Mothers as tacticians in the supermarket. *Child Development, 54*, 233–240.

JACOBS, B. S., & Moss, H. A. (1976). Birth order and sex of siblings as determinants of mother-infant interaction. *Child Development, 47*, 315–322.

JIAO, S., Ji, G., & Jing, Q. (1986). Comparative study of behavioral qualities of only children and sibling children. *Child Development, 57*, 357–361.

KEMPE, R. S., & Kempe, C. H. (1978). *Child abuse.* Cambridge, MA: Harvard University Press.

KENDRICK, C., & Dunn, J. (1980). Caring for the second baby: Effects on interaction between mother and firstborn. *Developmental Psychology, 16*, 303–311.

KESSNER, D. M. (1973). *Infant death: An analysis by maternal risk and health care.* Washington, DC: National Academy of Sciences.

KLEIN, M., & Stern, L. (1971). Low birth weight and the battered child syndrome. *American Journal of Diseases of Childhood, 122*, 15–18.

KOHN, M. L. (1979). The effects of social class on parental values and practices. In D. Reiss & H. A. Hoffman (Eds.), *The American family: Dying or developing?* New York: Plenum.

KURDEK, L. A., Blisk, D., & Siesky, A. E., Jr. (1981). Correlates of children's long-term adjustment to their parents' divorce. *Developmental Psychology, 17*, 565–579.

LAHEY, B. B., Hammer, D., Crumrine, P. L., & Forehand, R. L. (1980). Birth order × sex interactions in child behavior problems. *Developmental Psychology, 16*, 608–615.

LAMB, M. E. (1981). *The role of the father in child development.* New York: Wiley.

LAMB, M. E., & Elster, A. B. (1985). Adolescent mother-infant-father relationships. *Developmental Psychology, 21*, 768–773.

LAOSA, L. M. (1981). Maternal behavior: Sociocultural diversity in modes of family interaction. In R. W. Henderson (Ed.), *Parent-child interaction: Theory, research, and prospects.* Orlando, FL: Academic Press.

LASKO, J. K. (1954). Parent behavior towards first and second children. *Genetic Psychology Monographs, 49*, 96–137.

LEFKOWITZ, M. M., & Tesiny, E. P. (1984). Rejection and depression: Prospective and contemporary analyses. *Developmental Psychology, 20*, 776–785.

LERNER, J. V., & Galambos, N. L. (1985). Maternal role satisfaction, mother-child interaction, and child temperament: A process model. *Developmental Psychology, 21*, 1157–1164.

LeVINE, R. A. (1974). Parental goals: A cross-cultural view. *Teachers College Record, 76*, 226–239.

LEVITT, M. J., Weber, R. A., & Clark, M. C. (1986). Social network relationships as sources of maternal support and well-being. *Developmental Psychology, 22*, 310–316.

LIGHT, R. J. (1973). Abused and neglected children in America: A study of alternative policies. *Harvard Educational Review, 43*, 556–598.

MACCOBY, E. E. (1980). *Social development.* San Diego, CA: Harcourt Brace Jovanovich.

MACCOBY, E. E., & Martin, J. A. (1983). Socialization in the context of the family: Parent-child interaction. In E. M. Hetherington (Ed.), *Handbook of child psychology* (Vol. 4). New York: Wiley.

MAEHR, M. L. (1974). *Sociocultural origins of achievement.* Monterey, CA: Brooks/Cole.

MAIN, M., & George, C. (1985). Responses of abused and disadvantaged toddlers to distress in agemates: A study in the day-care setting.

Developmental Psychology, 21, 407–412.

MAIN, M., & Weston, D. R. (1981). The quality of the toddler's relationship to mother and to father: Related to conflict and the readiness to establish new relationships. *Child Development, 52*, 932–940.

MATEJCEK, Z., Dytrych, Z., & Schuller, V. (1979). The Prague study of children born from unwanted pregnancies. *International Journal of Mental Health, 7*, 63–74.

McCALL, R. B., Gregory, T. G., & Murray, J. P. (1984). Communicating developmental research results to the general public through television. *Developmental Psychology, 20*, 45–54.

MENDES, H. A. (1976). Single fathers. *Family Coordinator, 25*, 439–440.

MILLER, B. C., & Sollie, D. L. (1980). Normal stresses during the transition to parenthood. *Family Relations, 29*, 459–465.

MILLER, N., & Maruyama, G. (1976). Ordinal position and peer popularity. *Journal of Personality and Social Psychology, 33*, 123–131.

MINNETT, A. M., Vandell, D. L., & Santrock, J. W. (1983). The effects of sibling status on sibling interaction: The influence of birth order, age spacing, sex of child and sex of sibling. *Child Development, 54*, 1064–1072.

MULHERN, R. K., & Passman, R. H. (1981). Parental discipline as affected by sex of parent, sex of child, and the child's apparent responsiveness to discipline. *Developmental Psychology, 17*, 604–613.

MUSSEN, P. H., & Rutherford, E. (1963). Parent-child relations and parental personality in relation to young children's sex-role preferences. *Child Development, 34*, 589–607.

NATIONAL CENTER FOR HEALTH STATISTICS. (1980). *Provisional statistics* (Monthly Vital Statistics Report). Washington, DC: U.S. Department of Health, Education and Welfare.

NORMAN-JACKSON, J. (1982). Family interactions, language development, and primary reading achievement of Black children in families of low income. *Child Development, 53*, 349–358.

OGBU, J. U. (1981). Origins of human competence: A cultural-ethological perspective. *Child Development, 52*, 413–429.

PALKOWITZ, R. (1984). Parental attitudes and fathers' interactions with their 5-month-old infants. *Developmental Psychology, 20*, 1054–1060.

PARKE, R. D. (1981). *Fathers*. Cambridge, MA: Harvard University Press.

PARKE, R. D., & Lewis, N. G. (1981). The family in context: A multilevel interactional analysis of child abuse. In R. W. Henderson (Ed.), *Parent-child interaction: Theory, research, and prospects*. Orlando, FL: Academic Press.

PATTERSON, G. R., & Stouthamer-Loeber, M. (1984). The correlation of family management practices and delinquency. *Child Development, 55*, 1299–1307.

PAULHUS, D., & Shaffer, D. R. (1981). Sex differences in the impact of number of older and number of younger siblings on scholastic aptitude. *Social Psychology Quarterly, 44*, 363–368.

PEDERSEN, F., Anderson, B., & Cain, R. (1977, March). *An approach to understanding linkages between parent-infant and spouse relationships*. Paper presented at the biennial meeting of the Society for Research in Child Development, New Orleans.

PHARES, E. J. (1976). *Locus of control in personality*. Morristown, NJ: General Learning Press.

PULKKINEN, L. (1982). Self-control and continuity from childhood to adolescence. In P. Baltes & O. G. Brim (Eds.), *Life-span development and behavior* (Vol. 4). Orlando, FL: Academic Press.

REBELSKY, F., & Hanks, C. (1971). Father verbal interaction with infants in the first three months of life. *Child Development, 42*, 63–68.

ROSEN, R. (1979). Some crucial issues concerning children of divorce. *Journal of Divorce, 3*, 19–26.

ROSENHEIM, M. K. (1973). The child and the law. In B. M. Caldwell & H. N. Ricciuti (Eds.), *Review of child development research* (Vol. 3). Chicago: University of Chicago Press.

ROTHBART, M. K. (1971). Birth order and mother-child interaction in an achievement situation. *Journal of Personality and Social Psychology, 17*, 113–120.

RUSSELL, C. (1974). Transitions to parenthood: Problems and gratifications. *Journal of Marriage and the Family, 36*, 294–301.

SAMUELS, H. R. (1977, March). *The sibling in the infant's social environment*. Paper presented at the biennial meeting of the Society for Research in Child Development, New Orleans.

SAMUELS, H. R. (1980). The effect of older sibling on infant locomotor exploration of a new environment. *Child Development, 51*, 607–609.

SANTROCK, J. W. (1972). The relations of type and onset of father absence to cognitive development. *Child Development, 43*, 455–469.

SANTROCK, J. W., & Minnett, A. M. (1981, April). *Sibling interaction: An observational study of sex of sibling, age spacing, and ordinal position*. Paper presented at the biennial meeting of the Society for Research in Child Development, Boston.

SANTROCK, J. W., & Warshak, R. A. (1979). Father custody and social development in boys and girls. *Journal of Social Issues, 35*, 112–125.

SANTROCK, J. W., Warshak, R. A., Lindbergh, C., & Meadows, L. (1982). Children's and parents' observed social behavior in stepfather families. *Child Development, 53*, 472–480.

SCHACHTER, F. F. (1981). Toddlers with employed mothers. *Child Development, 52*, 958–964.

SCHACHTER, S. (1959). *The psychology of affiliation*. Stanford, CA: Stanford University Press.

SCHAEFER, E. S., & Bayley, N. (1963). Maternal behavior, child behavior, and their intercorrelations from infancy through adolescence. *Monographs of the Society for Research in Child Development, 28*(3, Serial No. 87).

SHERROD, K. B., O'Connor, S., Vietze, P. M., & Altemeier, W. A., III. (1984). Child health and maltreatment. *Child Development, 55*, 1174–1183.

SNOW, M. E., Jacklin, C. N., & Maccoby, E. E. (1983). Sex-of-child differences in father-child interaction at one year of age. *Child Development, 54*, 227–232.

STARR, R. H., Jr. (1979). Child abuse. *American Psychologist, 34*, 872–878.

STEELE, B. F., & Pollack, C. B. (1974). A psychiatric study of parents who abuse infants and small children. In R. E. Helfer & C. H. Kempe (Eds.), *The battered child*. Chicago: University of Chicago Press.

STEINBERG, L. D., Catalano, R., & Dooley, D. (1981). Economic antecedents of child abuse and neglect. *Child Development, 52*, 975–985.

STEWART, R. B. (1983). Sibling attachment relationships: Child-infant interactions in the strange situation. *Developmental Psychology, 19*, 192–199.

STEWART, R. B., & Marvin, R. S. (1984). Sibling relations: The role of conceptual perspective-taking in the ontogeny of sibling caregiving. *Child Development, 55*, 1322–1332.

STONEMAN, Z., & Brody, G. H. (1981). Two's company, three makes a difference: An examination of mothers' and fathers' speech to their young children. *Child Development, 52*, 705–707.

STUCKEY, M. F., McGhee, P. E., & Bell, N. J. (1982). Parent-child interaction: The influence of maternal employment. *Developmental Psychology, 18*, 635–644.

STUDY: Children with working mothers score lower on tests. (1983, June 26). *Atlanta Journal*, p. 4-A.

SUOMI, S. J. (1978). Maternal behavior by socially incompetent monkeys: Neglect and abuse of offspring. *Journal of Pediatric Psychology, 3*, 28–34.

SUTTON-SMITH, B., & Rosenberg, B. G. (1970). *The sibling*. New York: Holt, Rinehart and Winston.

U.S. BUREAU OF THE CENSUS. (1982). *Characteristics of American children and youth: 1980* (Current Population Reports, Series P-23, No. 114). Washington, DC: U.S. Government Printing Office.

U.S. DEPARTMENT OF COMMERCE. (1979). *Marital status and living arrangements: March 1978* (Current Population Reports, Series P-20, No. 338). Washington, DC: U.S. Government Printing Office.

WALLERSTEIN, J. S., & Kelly, J. B. (1980, January). California's children of divorce. *Psychology Today*, pp. 67–76.

WALLERSTEIN, J. S., & Kelly, J. B. (1982). *Surviving the breakup: How children and parents cope with divorce*. New York: Basic Books.

WEAVER, K. F. (1985). Stones, bones, and early man: The search for our ancestors. *National Geographic, 168*, 561–623.

WEISNER, T. S., & Gallimore, R. (1977). My brother's keeper: Child and sibling caretaking. *Current Anthropology, 18*, 169–190.

WEISZ, J. R. (1980). Autonomy, control, and other reasons why "Mom is the greatest": A content analysis of children's Mother's Day letters. *Child Development, 51*, 801–807.

WILSON, M. N. (1986). The Black extended family: An analytical consideration. *Developmental Psychology, 22*, 246–258.

ZAJONC, R. B., Markus, H., & Markus, G. B. (1979). The birth order puzzle. *Journal of Personality and Social Psychology, 37*, 1325–1341.

ZEGOIB, L. E., Arnold, S., & Forehand, R. (1975). An examination of observer effects in parent-child interactions. *Child Development, 46*, 509–512.

ZILL, N., & Peterson, J. L. (1982, January). *Trends in the behavior and emotional well-being of U.S. children: Findings from a national survey*. Paper presented at the meeting of the American Association for the Advancement of Science, Washington, D.C.

ZUSSMAN, J. U. (1978). Relationship of demographic factors to parental disciplinary techniques. *Developmental Psychology, 14*, 685–686.

ZUSSMAN, J. U. (1980). Situational determinants of parental behavior: Effects of competing cognitive activity. *Child Development, 51*, 792–800.

14

EXTRAFAMILIAL INFLUENCES

THE EARLY WINDOW: EFFECTS OF TELEVISION ON CHILDREN AND YOUTH

Children's Use of Television

Some Potentially Undesirable Effects of Television

Television as an Educational Instrument

Should Television Be Used to Socialize Children?

THE SCHOOL AS A SOCIALIZATION AGENT

Does Schooling Promote Cognitive Development?

Determinants of Effective and Ineffective Schooling

The Teacher's Influence

The School as a Middle-Class Institution: Effects on Disadvantaged Youth

(continues)

THE SECOND WORLD OF CHILDHOOD: PEERS AS SOCIALIZATION AGENTS

Who or What Is a Peer?

Peers as Promoters of Social Competence and Personal Adjustment

Determinants of Peer Acceptance

Children and Their Friends

Mechanisms of Peer (and Peer-Group) Influence

Peer versus Adult Influence: The Question of Cross-Pressures

SUMMARY

REFERENCES

In Chapter 13 we focused on the family as an instrument of socialization, looking at the ways parents and siblings affect developing children. Although families have an enormous impact on their young throughout childhood and adolescence, it is only a matter of time before other societal institutions begin to exert their influence. For example, infants and toddlers are often exposed to alternative caregivers and a host of new playmates when their working parents place them in some kind of day care. Even those toddlers who remain at home will soon begin to learn about the outside world once they develop an interest in television. Between the ages of 2 and 5, many American children spend several hours of every weekday away from home as they attend nursery school. And by the age of 6 to 7, virtually all children in Western societies are going to elementary school, a setting that requires them to interact with other little people who are similar to themselves and to adjust to the rules and regulations of a new world—one that may be very dissimilar to the home environment from which they came.

So as they mature, children are becoming increasingly familiar with the outside world and will spend much less time under the watchful eyes of their parents. How do these experiences affect their lives? This is the issue to which we will now turn as we consider the impact of three "extrafamilial" agents of socialization: television, schools, and children's peer groups.

THE EARLY WINDOW: EFFECTS OF TELEVISION ON CHILDREN AND YOUTH

It seems almost incomprehensible that only 40 years ago the average person in the United States could not have answered the question "What is a television?" When first introduced in the late 1940s, television was an expensive luxury for the wealthy—one that made the children of well-to-do parents immensely popular with their peers. Today a television occupies a prominent location in virtually all American homes, and 70% of American families have more than one set. Robert Liebert and his associates (Liebert, Sprafkin, & Davidson, 1982) believe that television has changed our daily lives more than any other technological innovation of the 20th century. And they may be correct, for the average TV set in the United States runs more than six hours a day, and it is not all uncommon for people to alter their sleeping habits or plan their meals and leisure activities to accommodate television (Steinberg, 1980).

CHILDREN'S USE OF TELEVISION

In the United States, children between the ages of 3 and 11 watch an average of three to four hours of television a day. As we see in Figure 14-1, time spent in front of the television gradually increases until about age 12 and then declines somewhat during adolescence. A recent survey of television use in Australia, Canada, and several European countries reported virtually the same developmental trends in children's viewing habits (Murray, 1980). To place these findings in perspective, we need only note that by age 18 a child born today will have spent more time watching television than in any other single activity except sleeping (Liebert et al., 1982). Is it any wonder, then, that parents, educators, and those who study children are curious and often concerned about the possible effects of this incredible exposure to the electronic media?

What Do Children Watch?

It is often assumed that children spend most of their TV time watching programs designed for children. In fact, many 7–8-year-olds are already watching programs intended for adults at least half the time (Brown, 1976). The production features that are most likely to capture a young child's attention are fast-paced action sequences, special effects, zooms, and segments in which there are rapid changes in the scenery or the number of characters (Anderson, Lorch, Field, & Sanders, 1981). Shows containing a lot of violence typically incorporate all these attention-grabbing features. However, it appears that 2–11-year-olds actually prefer situation comedies to violent programming, even though they end up watching a lot of violence on television (Huston & Wright, 1982).

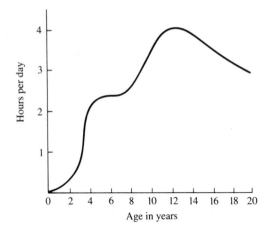

FIGURE 14-1 Average number of hours per day that American children and adolescents spend watching television

Has Television Changed Family Life?

The presence of a television in the home has a significant impact on parents, children, and the structuring of family life. One survey found that a majority of families altered their sleeping patterns and mealtimes once they had purchased a television (Johnson, 1967). The introduction of television also had the effect of decreasing the amount of time parents spent with their youngsters in non-TV-related leisure activities (that is, games and family outings), and most parents at least occasionally used television as an "electronic babysitter." Although parents and children may spend many hours in close proximity as they watch television together, many critics believe that this form of family interaction is not very meaningful for the younger set—particularly if they are often told to sit still or keep their mouths shut until the commercials come on. Urie Bronfenbrenner (1970b) has argued:

> The primary danger of . . . television . . . lies not so much in the behavior that it produces—although there is danger there—as in the behavior that it prevents: the talks, games, the family festivities and arguments through which much of the child's learning takes place and through which his character is formed. Turning on the television set can turn off the process that transforms children into people.

Does television really transform children into social isolates who are so captivated by their visual experiences that they become less interested in playing games, making friends, or doing their homework? The answer to this question is a qualified no. Children who live in remote areas without television do spend significantly more time reading comics, going to movies, or listening to the radio than age mates who live in similar communities served by television (Huston & Wright, 1982; Schramm, Lyle, & Parker, 1961). But when television comes to an isolated area, children simply substitute TV viewing for these other roughly equivalent forms of entertainment. Apparently the availability of television does not affect the amount of time children spend on leisure reading, if we exclude comic books. Moreover, popular children who partake in many sports and extracurricular activities tend to read a lot and to watch a lot of TV (Lyle & Hoffman, 1972). So it is clearly inappropriate to argue that television viewing has replaced valuable pastimes and activities such as reading or playing with one's peers.

The impact of television on academic achievement is not well understood. At least one researcher found that the reading comprehension of elementary school students declined once television was introduced to an isolated community (Williams, 1977, cited in Huston & Wright, 1982). However, a recent study published by the U.S. Department of Education suggests that students in the lower grades may actually learn a great deal of useful information by watching television—particularly educational programming ("Study: Children with Working Mothers," 1983). It may be that the effects of television on academic performance depend largely on what the children are watching. An educational program such as *The Electric Company*, which is designed to teach reading concepts, may well reinforce the elementary school curriculum and have a positive effect on academic achievement, whereas popular programs such as *The Three Stooges* or *Magnum P.I.* have little educational value and could undermine academic achievement if they keep children from their lessons. Indeed, the authors of the Department of Education study reported that high school students perform better on standardized achievement tests when they spend more time on homework and watch less commercial television.

SOME POTENTIALLY UNDESIRABLE EFFECTS OF TELEVISION

Aside from its potential for distracting children from schoolwork, there are several other undesirable lessons that TV could teach young viewers. In Chapter 9, for example, we saw that regular and prolonged exposure to violent TV programming seems to instigate aggression and may lead to the development of aggressive habits (or aggressive modes of resolving conflicts). Moreover, heavy consumption of media violence may blunt children's emotional reactions to real-life aggression (a desensitization effect) and lead them to believe that the world is a violent place populated mainly by violent and aggressive people (see Eron, Huesmann, Brice, Fischer, & Mermelstein, 1983). Now let's consider some other possible concomitants of children's TV viewing that seem to annoy or even anger many adults.

Television as a Source of Social Stereotypes

Television is often the young child's first exposure to the outside world and the people who live there. Indeed, many children have had little or no contact with police officers, lawyers, teachers, people from different racial and ethnic groups, or the elderly, and their "knowledge" of these individuals is likely to consist of what they have seen on television.

In Chapter 12, we noted that sex-role stereotyping is common on television and that children who watch a lot of commercial TV (and are often exposed to these stereotyped portrayals) are more likely to hold conventional views of males and females than their classmates who watch little television. In fact, the youngsters who are affected most by exposure to sex-role stereotypes on television are girls of above-average intelligence from middle-class homes—precisely the group that is otherwise least likely to hold traditionally sexist attitudes (Morgan, 1982).

Stereotyping of minorities. Until the middle to late 1970s, ethnic minorities other than Blacks were practically ignored on television. When foreigners or non-Black minorities did appear, they were presented in an unfavorable light, often cast in the roles of swindlers or villains (Liebert et al., 1982). Blacks were almost always placed in minor roles, and the one Black show that appeared in the early days of television—*Amos and Andy*—presented such an unfavorable image of Black Americans that the National Association for the Advancement of Colored People (NAACP) demanded that CBS take it off the air. Today the representation of minorities on television has increased to approximate their proportions in the population. Yet compared with Whites, a greater percentage of non-White characters are depicted as very poor people who work at menial occupations, are prone to violence, or are involved in illegal activities (Liebert et al., 1982).

A study by Sheryl Graves (1975) suggests that these media stereotypes may affect children's racial attitudes. In Graves's experiment, both Black and White children watched a series of cartoons in which Black people were portrayed either positively (as competent, trustworthy, and hardworking) or negatively (as inept, lazy, and powerless). On a later test of racial attitudes, both Black and White children became more favorable toward Blacks if they had seen the positive portrayals. But when the depictions of Blacks were negative, an interesting racial difference emerged: Black children once again became more favorable in their racial attitudes, while Whites became much *less* favorable. So the way Blacks are portrayed on television may have a striking effect on the racial attitudes of White viewers, whereas the mere presence of Black TV characters may be sufficient to produce more favorable attitudes toward Blacks among a young Black audience.

Countering stereotypes on television. In recent years, attempts have been made to design programs for the younger set that counter inaccurate racial, sexual, and ethnic stereotypes while fostering goodwill among children from different backgrounds. In 1969 *Sesame Street* led the way with positive portrayals of Blacks and Hispanics. Indeed, one study (Gorn, Goldberg, & Kanungo, 1976) found that White preschool children became more willing to include non-Whites in their play activities after watching episodes of *Sesame Street* that depicted minority youngsters as cheerful companions. Among the other shows that have been effective at fostering international awareness and reducing children's ethnic stereotypes are *Big Blue Marble*, a program designed to teach children about people in other countries, and *Vegetable Soup*, a show that portrays many ethnic groups in a favorable light (Liebert et al., 1982).

In 1975 the National Institute of Education funded a program named *Freestyle*, designed to counter sex-role stereotypes and to make grade school children more aware of various career options that may be available to them. *Freestyle* is

> a television intervention aimed at 9 to 12-year-olds . . . a carefully articulated package designed to influence the attitudes and behaviors of this age group in a way that would reduce sex-role stereotypes and expand the "career awareness" of children, especially girls, in non-traditional ways. The task was to be accomplished by focusing on non-traditional possibilities in the 9 to 12-year-old's own world. . . . Its purpose would be to have children relate non-traditional childhood interests to educational and ultimately to occupational choices [Johnston, Ettema, & Davidson, 1980].

Although it is too early to tell whether *Freestyle* will accomplish its long-term objectives, the early returns are encouraging. For example, one group of grade school children showed the following changes after viewing 13 episodes of the program (Johnston et al., 1980):

1. Boys became more tolerant of girls who attempted sporting or mechanical activities, and girls became much more interested in these endeavors.
2. Both boys and girls became more accepting of boys who engage in "feminine" activities such as housework or caring for younger children.
3. Both boys and girls became more accepting of men and women who have nontraditional jobs.
4. Both boys and girls became less traditional and more egalitarian in their views about family roles such as who should cook, clean, or repair the house.

So we see that television can either reinforce or reduce inaccurate and potentially harmful social stereotypes, depending, of course, on the type of programming to which people are exposed. Unfortunately, the stereotyped depictions of gender, race, and ethnicity that often appear on commercial TV are presently far more numerous than the nonstereotyped portrayals, which are largely limited to selected programs that appear on public (educational) television.

Children's Reactions to Commercial Messages

In the United States, the average child is exposed to nearly 20,000 television commercials each year—many of which extol the virtues of various toys, fast-food products, and sugary treats that adults may not wish to purchase. Nevertheless, young children continue to ask for products that they have seen advertised on television, and conflicts often ensue when parents refuse to honor their requests (Atkin, 1978). In one study, 4- and 5-year-olds saw a program that had either no commercials or two commercials for a particular toy. The children were later shown photographs of a father and son and were told that the father had refused to buy the advertised toy after his son had requested it. More than 60% of the youngsters who had seen the commercials, but fewer than 40% of those who had not, felt that the boy would be resentful and would not want to play with his father (Goldberg & Gorn, 1977, as cited in Liebert et al., 1982).

In addition to making children angry or resentful toward adults who refuse to buy advertised products, commercials may have an indirect effect on a child's peer relations. In the experiment by Goldberg and Gorn described above, children were asked whether they would rather play with the advertised toy or with friends in a sandbox. Those who had seen the commercials for the toy were much more likely to choose the toy over their friends than children who had not seen the commercials. When asked whether they would rather play with a "nice boy" without the toy or a "not-so-nice boy" with the toy, 65% of the commercial viewers chose the "not-so-nice boy" who possessed the advertised item, compared with only 30% of those in the no-commercial group. Is it any wonder, then, that parents are often concerned about the impact of commercials on their children? Not only do children's ads often push products that are unsafe or of poor nutritional value, they could also contribute to coercive family interactions and poor peer relations.

TELEVISION AS AN EDUCATIONAL INSTRUMENT

Thus far, we've cast a wary eye at television, talking mostly about its capacity to do harm. Yet there is now reason to believe that this "early window" could become a most effective means of teaching a variety of valuable lessons if only its content were altered to convey such information. In the pages that follow, we will examine some of the evidence to support this claim.

Television as a Contributor to Prosocial Behavior

In Chapter 10, we saw that regular exposure to prosocial television programming such as *Sesame Street* and *Mister Rogers' Neighborhood* can have very positive effects on young viewers: preschoolers who regularly watch these offerings often become more affectionate, considerate, cooperative, and helpful toward their nursery school classmates. We also noted that youngsters who prefer and who often watch prosocial programming on commercial television tend to behave more prosocially at school than their classmates who rarely watch such shows. Yet it is important to emphasize that mere exposure to such prosocial television fare is not enough, for the data indicate that this programming will have few if any lasting effects unless *adults* encourage children to rehearse and enact the prosocial lessons they have learned (see Friedrich-Cofer, Huston-Stein, Kipnis, Susman, & Clewett, 1979).

Promoting Good Nutrition on Television

An overwhelming majority of food advertisements currently aired on children's television are for high-calorie foods containing large amounts of sugar and fat and few beneficial nutrients (Barcus, 1978; Stoneman & Brody, 1981). Since a diet containing too much of these foods has been established as a risk factor in a number of diseases (for example, high blood pressure) and dental problems, investigators

have hoped to counter the influence of such advertising by producing pronutritional educational messages and commercials for high-nutrition foods. Do these attempts to promote healthful eating practices affect children's dietary habits?

The evidence on this issue is somewhat mixed. Polly Peterson and her colleagues (Peterson, Jeffrey, Bridgwater, & Dawson, 1984) exposed 6-year-olds to pronutritional programming from shows such as *Mulligan Stew* (a PBS series) and *Captain Kangaroo* and found that children (1) *learned* the pronutrition information presented in the programs and (2) showed an increased *verbal preference* for more nutritious foods. But when given a choice between nutritious and nonnutritious snacks, these youngsters were no more likely to select nutritious foods than they had been before viewing the programs. However, Joan Galst (1980) found that 3- to 6-year-olds who had watched pronutritional programming tended to choose nutritious rather than nonnutritious snacks if they had heard an adult comment on an ad for the nonnutritious snacks by stressing these products' poor nutritional value and threats to one's dental health. So there is reason to believe that regular exposure to pronutritional television programming could be effective in teaching pronutritional concepts and perhaps even in altering children's dietary habits. Yet the success of such programming in achieving its objectives may depend very critically on having an adult present to help children interpret the implications of what they have seen and to translate those lessons into action.

Television as a Contributor to Cognitive Development

In 1968 the U.S. government and a number of private foundations contributed the funding to create the *Children's Television Workshop (CTW)*, an organization committed to producing TV programs that would hold children's interest and facilitate their intellectual development. CTW's first production, *Sesame Street*, became the world's most popular children's TV series—one that now reaches about 85% of the 3–5-year-olds in the United States and is broadcast to nearly 70 other countries around the world (Liebert et al., 1982; Wright & Huston, 1983).

***The objectives of* Sesame Street.** As noted above, production artists, educators, and experts in child development worked together to design a program for preschool children that would foster important cognitive skills such as recognizing and discriminating numbers and letters, counting, ordering and classifying objects, and solving simple problems. It was hoped that children from disadvantaged backgrounds would be much better prepared for school after viewing this programming on a regular basis. In In 1969 *Sesame Street* was unveiled and became an immediate hit. But was it accomplishing its objectives?

The evaluations. During the first season that *Sesame Street* was broadcast, its impact was assessed by the Educational Testing Service. About 950 children from five areas of the United States participated in the study. At the beginning of the project, children took a pretest that measured their cognitive skills and determined what they knew about letters, numbers, and geometric forms. At the end of the season, they took this test again to see what they had learned. Originally the sample had been divided into an experimental group that was encouraged to watch *Sesame Street* and a control group that received no such encouragement. However, the program proved so popular that the control children ended up watching nearly as often as the experimental group. As a result, the sample was divided into quartiles (a quartile equals 25% of the viewers) on the basis of the frequency of viewing. Children in Q_1 rarely watched *Sesame Street*; those in Q_2 watched two or three times a week; Q_3 watched about four or five times a week; and Q_4 watched more than five times a week.

When the data were analyzed, it was clear that *Sesame Street* was achieving its objectives. In Figure 14-2, we see that the children who watched *Sesame Street* the most (Q_3 and Q_4) were the ones who showed the biggest improvements in their total test scores (panel A), their scores on the alphabet test (panel B), and their ability to write their names (panel C). The 3-year-olds posted bigger gains than the 5-year-olds, probably because the younger children knew less to begin with.

During the second year a new sample of urban disadvantaged youngsters was selected from cities where *Sesame Street* had not been available during the first year. The investigators also followed up on 283 of the disadvantaged children from the original sample, many of whom were now in kindergarten or the first grade. The results of the second-year evaluation paralleled those of the original study—children who often watched *Sesame Street* posted larger cognitive gains than those who watched infrequently (Bogatz & Ball, 1972). In addition, the heavy viewers from the original sample were rated by their teachers as better prepared for school and more interested in school activities than their classmates who rarely watched the program.

The Electric Company. In 1970 CTW consulted with reading specialists to create *The Electric Company*, a TV series designed to teach reading skills to young elementary school children. The programming was heavily animated, and to interest children in the content, well-known personalities such as Bill Cosby often appeared. The curriculum attempted to teach children the correspondence between letters (or letter combinations) and sounds—knowledge that should help them to decode words. Reading for meaning and syntax were also taught (Liebert et al., 1982).

The success of *Electric Company* was evaluated by administering a battery of reading tests to first- through fourth-grade children. Although home viewing had little or no effect on children's reading skills, those who watched the program at school attained significantly higher scores on the reading battery than nonviewers (Ball & Bogatz, 1973). In other words, *Electric Company* was achieving many of its objectives when children watched it *with an adult*, in this case the teacher, who could help them to apply what they had learned. *The Electric Company* is now used in many elementary schools in the United States, and in some ways the program is quite a bargain: while a typical Saturday morning children's show costs about $70,000 to produce, an average episode of *Electric Company* costs only about $32,000 (Liebert et al., 1982).

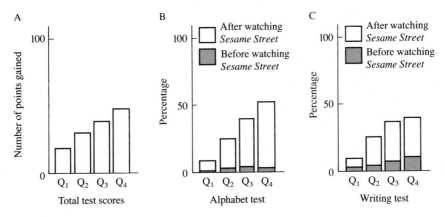

FIGURE 14-2   Relationship between amount of viewing of *Sesame Street* and children's abilities. Children were grouped into quartiles according to amount of viewing: A, improvement in total test scores; B, percentage of children who recited the alphabet correctly; C, percentage of children who wrote their first names correctly.

Other educational programs.   In recent years, CTW and other noncommercial producers have created children's programs designed to teach subjects such as math (*Infinity Factory*; *Square One*), logical reasoning (*Think About*), science (*3-2-1 Contact*), and social studies (*Big Blue Marble*), to name a few. Most of these offerings have been quite popular in the areas where they are broadcast, although it remains to be seen whether they are achieving their stated objectives.

Limitations of educational programming.
One criticism of educational television is that it is essentially a one-way medium in which the pupil is a passive recipient rather than an active processor of information. Indeed, we've seen that programs such as *The Electric Company* (or, indeed, pronutritional programming and programs stressing cooperation and prosocial behavior) are unlikely to achieve their stated objectives unless children watch *with an adult* who then encourages them to apply what they have learned. Perhaps John Wright and Aletha Huston (1983) are correct in arguing that television will soon be a much more powerful teaching device as it becomes computer-integrated and interactive, allowing the viewer to be more actively involved in the learning process.

Even the highly successful educational programs are not without their critics. Some have argued that the fast-paced *Sesame Street* will shorten the attention spans of frequent viewers and make the classroom seem a boring place. Yet the evidence available to date suggests that habitual consumers of *Sesame Street* are actually rated by their teachers as better adjusted to the school environment than their classmates who rarely watch the show (Bogatz & Ball, 1972).

Although *Sesame Street* was primarily targeted at disadvantaged preschoolers in an attempt to narrow the intellectual gap between these youngsters and their advantaged peers, it seems that children from advantaged backgrounds are the ones who are more likely to watch the program. As a result, *Sesame Street* may actually end up *widening* the intellectual and academic gaps between advantaged and disadvantaged youth (Cook et al., 1975). Yet it seems fruitless to blame the program itself, for disadvantaged youngsters who watch it regularly learn just as much as their more advantaged classmates (Bogatz & Ball, 1972). In other words, *Sesame Street* is *potentially* a valuable resource for all preschool children. The formidable task lies ahead—that being to convince parents that episodes of *Sesame Street* (and other educational programs) are indeed rewarding and valuable experiences, ones that they and their children should not be missing.

SHOULD TELEVISION BE USED TO SOCIALIZE CHILDREN?

Although television is often criticized as an instigator of violence or an "idiot box" that undermines the intellectual curiosity of our young, we have seen that the medium can have many positive effects on children's social, emotional, and intellectual development. Should we now work at harnessing television's potential—at using this "early window" as a means of socializing our children? Many developmentalists think so, although not everyone agrees, as we see in the following newspaper account of a conference on behavioral control through the media. To set the stage, the conference participants were reacting to the work of Dr. Robert M. Liebert, a psychologist who had produced some 30-second TV spots to teach children cooperative solutions to conflicts. Here is part of the account that appeared in the *New York Times*:

> The outburst that followed Liebert's presentation flashed around the conference table. Did he believe that he had a right to . . . deliberately impose values on children? Should children . . . be taught cooperation? Did ghetto kids perhaps need to be taught to slug it out in order to survive in this society? Was it not . . . immoral to create a TV advertisement . . . to influence kids' behavior? Liebert was accused of . . . manipulation and even brainwashing. One would have thought he had proposed setting up Hitler Youth Camps on Sesame Street. . . .
>
> However, I understand why the hackles had gone up around the . . . table. I am one of those people who [are] terrified of manipulation. A Skinnerian world filled with conditioned people scares the daylights out of me—even if those people do hate war and . . . love their fellow man. [Behavior control through technology may come] . . . at the cost of our freedom [Rivers, 1974, as cited in Liebert et al., 1982, pp. 210–211].

The concern of those conference participants is perhaps understandable, for television is often used as a means of political indoctrination in many countries. And is the use of television for socialization not a subtle form of brainwashing? Perhaps it is. However, one could argue that television in this country is already serving as a potent agent of socialization and that much of what children see in the media helps to create attitudes and to instigate actions that the majority of us may not condone. Perhaps the question we

should be asking is "Can we somehow alter television to make it a more effective agent of socialization—one that teaches attitudes, values, and behaviors that more accurately reflect the mores of a free society?" Surely we can, although it remains to be seen whether we will.

THE SCHOOL AS A SOCIALIZATION AGENT

Of all the formal institutions that children encounter in their lives away from home, few have as much of an opportunity to influence their behavior as the schools they attend. Starting at age 6, the typical child in the United States spends about five hours of each weekday at school. And children are staying there longer than ever before. In 1870 there were only 200 public high schools in the United States, and only half of all American children were attending during the three to five months that school was in session. Today the school term is about nine months long (180 school days); more than 75% of American youth are still attending high school at age 17; and nearly 50% of U.S. high school graduates enroll in some form of postsecondary education (Coleman & Selby, 1983). Yet these figures are somewhat unusual even in the Western world. For example, only 29% of all Australians and 47% of Belgians complete the final year of high school (Copperman, 1978).

If asked to characterize the mission of the schools, we are likely to think of them as the place where children acquire basic knowledge and academic skills: reading, writing, arithmetic, and, later, computer skills, foreign languages, social studies, higher math, and science. But schools seem to have an *informal curriculum* as well. Children are expected to obey rules, to cooperate with their classmates, to respect authority, to learn about the American way of life, and to become upstanding citizens. Today we see the schools providing information and moral guidance in an attempt to combat social problems such as racism, teenage sex, and drug abuse. Although many social critics believe that educators should stick to academics and leave other forms of socialization to the church and the family, it is in-

teresting to note that the push for compulsory education in the United States arose from the need to
"Americanize" an immigrant population—to teach
them the values and principles on which this country
was founded so that they could be assimilated into the
mainstream of American society and become productive citizens. Ironically, the need to train an uneducated work force was of only secondary importance,
for most people earned a living from unskilled labor
or farming—occupations that required little or no
formal schooling (Boocock, 1976; Rudolph, 1965).

So it is proper to think of the school as a socializing
agent—one that is likely to affect children's social
and emotional development as well as imparting
knowledge and helping to prepare students for a job
and economic self-sufficiency.

In this section of the chapter, we will take a closer
look at the ways in which schools influence children.
First, we will consider whether formal classroom
experiences are likely to promote children's intellectual development. Then we will see that schools
clearly differ in "effectiveness"—that is, the ability
to accomplish both curricular goals and noncurricular
objectives that contribute to what educators often call
"good citizenship." After reviewing the characteristics of effective and less effective schools, we will
examine some of the ways in which teachers influence the social behavior and academic progress of
their pupils. Finally, we will discuss a few of the
problems that disadvantaged youth may encounter as
they enter the middle-class environment of the
schools.

DOES SCHOOLING PROMOTE
COGNITIVE DEVELOPMENT?

If you have completed the first two years of college, it
is likely that you know far more biology, chemistry,
or physics than many of the brightest college professors of only 100 years ago. Clearly, students acquire
a vast amount of knowledge about their world from
the classes they attend. But when developmentalists
ask "Do schools promote cognitive growth?," they
want to know whether formal education hastens intellectual development or encourages modes of thinking
and methods of problem solving that are less likely to
develop in the absence of schooling.

To address these issues, investigators have typically studied the intellectual growth of children from
developing countries where schooling is not yet
available throughout the society. Studies of this type
generally find that children who attend school are
quicker to reach a number of Piagetian milestones
(for example, conservation) and will perform better
on tests of memory and categorization skills than age
mates from similar backgrounds who do not go to
school (see Rogoff, 1981; Sharp, Cole, & Lave,
1979). And at least one study of very bright U.S.
college students found a positive relationship between the amount of higher education the students
had completed and their proficiency at solving problems requiring formal-operational reasoning (Commons, Richards, & Kuhn, 1982). So it appears that
schooling may indeed promote cognitive growth by
teaching children general rules, strategies, and problem-solving skills that they can apply to many different kinds of information. Yet it is important to note
that the differences between educated and uneducated subjects are likely to be small on any cognitive
test (for example, recognition memory or nonverbal
IQ) that does not depend on the use of cognitive
strategies that are taught in school (Sharp et al.,
1979).

DETERMINANTS OF EFFECTIVE AND
INEFFECTIVE SCHOOLING

One of the first questions that parents often ask when
searching for a residence in a new town is "What are
the schools like here?" or "Where should we live
so that our children will get the best education?"
These concerns reflect the common belief that some
schools are "better" or "more effective" than others.
But are they?

Michael Rutter (1983) is one theorist who thinks
so. According to Rutter, *effective schools* are those
that promote academic achievement, social skills,
polite and attentive behavior, positive attitudes toward learning, low absenteeism, continuation of
education beyond the age at which attendance is
mandatory, and acquisition of skills that will enable
students to find and hold a job. Rutter argues that
some schools are more successful than others at
accomplishing these objectives, regardless of the stu-

dents' racial, ethnic, or socioeconomic backgrounds. Let's examine some of the evidence for this claim.

In one study, Rutter and his associates (Rutter, Maughan, Mortimore, Ouston, & Smith, 1979) conducted extensive interviews and observations in 12 secondary schools serving lower- to lower-middle-class populations in London, England. As the students entered these schools, they were given a battery of achievement tests to measure their prior academic accomplishments. At the end of the secondary school experience, they took another major exam to assess their academic progress. Other information such as attendance records and teacher ratings of classroom behavior was also available. When the data were analyzed, Rutter et al. found that the 12 schools clearly differed in "effectiveness": students from the "better" schools exhibited fewer problem behaviors, attended school more regularly, and made more academic progress than students from the less effective schools. We get some idea of the importance of these "schooling effects" from Figure 14-3. The "bands" on the graph refer to the pupils' academic accomplishments *at the time they entered* the secondary schools (band 3, low achievers; band 1, high achievers). In all three bands, students attending the "more effective" schools outperformed those in the "less effective" schools on the final assessment of academic achievement. Even more revealing is the finding that the initially poor students (band 3) who attended the "better" school ended up scoring just as high on this final index of academic progress as the initially good (band 1) students who attended the least effective schools. Similar findings were obtained in a large study of elementary schools in the United States. Even after controlling for potentially important variables such as the racial composition and socioeconomic backgrounds of the student bodies and the type of communities served, some elementary schools were found to be much more "effective" than others (Brookover, Beady, Flood, Schweitzer, & Wisenbaker, 1979; see also Rutter, 1983).

So the school that children attend can make a difference. And although the evidence is sketchy at this point, we are beginning to understand why some schools are able to accomplish many of their objectives while others are not. In the pages that follow, we

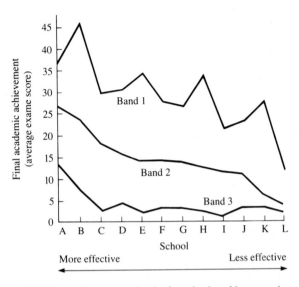

FIGURE 14-3 Average level of academic achievement in secondary school as a function of initial achievement at the time of entry (bands 1–3) and the school that pupils were attending (schools A–L). Note that pupils in all three bands performed at higher levels on this final academic assessment if they attended the more effective schools. Moreover, students in band 2 performed like band 1 students in the more effective schools but like band 3 students in the least effective schools.

will first consider some of the variables that are thought to contribute to an effective school environment and then try to determine how individual teachers might influence their students.

Monetary Resources and the Physical Plant

Surprising as it may seem, factors such as the amount of money spent per pupil, the number of books in the school library, teachers' salaries, and teachers' academic credentials play only a minor role in determining student outcomes (Rutter, 1983). In two studies of secondary schools in England, the investigators found that neither the age nor the physical appearance of the school buildings predicted children's conduct or their academic accomplishments (Reynolds, Jones, St. Leger, & Murgatroyd, 1980; Rutter et al., 1979). Similar studies in the United States indicate that the level of "personnel support" (that is, teacher credentials and salaries) is positively related to student achievement only in the predominantly Black, inner-city schools where resources in some school districts are marginal at best (Brookover et al., 1979). The latter finding implies that there is some basic minimum level of support that is required for effective schooling but that increases in monetary support beyond that level seem to be of limited importance in determining pupil outcomes (Rutter, 1983).

School and Class Size

Is the size of the school that children attend in any way important? It may well be. Roger Barker and Paul Gump (1964) tried to determine whether students from small high schools are more likely than those in larger schools to participate in extracurricular activities. Schools ranging from fewer than 100 to more than 2000 students participated in the study. Although the larger schools offered more extracurricular activities to their students, it was the pupils in the smaller schools who were more heavily involved in these activities. Moreover, students in smaller schools were more likely than those in larger schools to say that they enjoyed the challenge of working in and contributing to their extracurricular groups. Finally, there were few "isolates" in the small schools, where almost everyone was encouraged to join in one or more activities. By contrast, the marginal student in larger schools felt few pressures to participate and could easily get lost in the crowd. To the extent that a sense of belonging is an important aspect of schooling, these findings suggest that there may be some advantages to attending smaller schools.[1]

Does the size of one's school have any effects on academic achievement? Those who have studied this issue focus on *average class size* rather than the size of the institution, and the results of their research are not always consistent. One recent review of the literature concluded that, in classes ranging from 20 to 40 students, class size has little if any effect on academic achievement (Rutter, 1983). However, there are some exceptions to this very general rule. It appears that smaller classes are advantageous to students in the primary grades who are just learning to read and to do arithmetic (Educational Research Service, 1978). Smaller classes also seem to aid the academic progress of economically disadvantaged students and those who are handicapped.

These findings may have important policy implications. Clearly, an across-the-board decrease in class size—say, from 35 to 24 students—is unlikely to have any major effects on academic standards. So if a school district were to have the money to hire additional instructors, the wisest course might be to devote these "personnel resources" to the primary grades, to remedial instruction, or to classes for the handicapped—precisely the settings in which smaller classes seem to enhance children's academic achievement (Rutter, 1983).

Organizational Structure of the School and the Classroom

Ability tracking. If you attended high school within the past 30 years, you may well have experienced *ability tracking*—a procedure in which students are placed in categories based on IQ scores or academic achievement and then taught in classes with pupils of comparable academic or intellectual standing. The pros and cons of this practice have been debated for years. Some theorists argue that students learn best when surrounded by peers of comparable ability. Others believe that ability tracking undermines the self-esteem of low-ability students and actually contributes to their poor academic achievement and high dropout rate.

In his recent review of the literature, Rutter (1983) found that neither ability tracking nor mixed-ability teaching has decisive advantages: both procedures are common in highly effective and less effective schools. A closer inspection of the data suggested that mixed-ability instruction may be advantageous with younger children and that ability tracking makes more sense in secondary schools, where it is difficult to teach advanced subjects to students who vary considerably in their background knowledge. However, ability tracking is occasionally found to have negative effects on the self-esteem and academic achievement of low-ability students. After reviewing the tracking systems of effective and ineffective schools, Rutter (1983) concluded that *effective* ability tracking—

1. Categorizes students on the basis of their *tested abilities* in *particular subjects* rather than using an

across-the-board assignment based on teachers' ratings or IQ scores.

2. Ensures that students in *all* ability groups will have some exposure to the more experienced, popular, or "effective" teachers rather than simply assigning the best teachers to the high-ability groups.

3. Takes steps to integrate the bottom-track students into the nonacademic aspects of schooling such as music, sports, and extracurricular activities. By taking part in these activities and occasionally being picked for positions of responsibility, bottom-track students are less likely to be stigmatized in a negative way or to suffer a loss of self-esteem.

Open versus traditional classrooms.

Although it may be difficult to remember your elementary school days, chances are you were educated in "traditional classrooms" where the seats were arranged in neat rows facing the teacher, who lectured and gave demonstrations at a desk or a blackboard. In a traditional classroom, the curriculum is highly structured. Normally, everybody will be studying the same subject at a given moment, and students are expected to interact with the teacher rather than with one another. One interesting aspect of this classroom arrangement is that teachers end up interacting with some students more than others. As we see in Figure 14-4, children who sit in the front or the center of the class are more likely to catch the teacher's eye and participate in classroom discussions than their classmates who sit outside this "zone of activity" (Adams & Biddle, 1970).

In recent years, many American classrooms have become much less formal or structured. "Open" education is a philosophy based on the premise that children are curious explorers who will achieve more by becoming actively involved in the learning process than by simply listening to a teacher recite facts, figures, and principles. In an "open classroom," all the children are rarely doing the same thing at once. A more typical scenario is for students to distribute themselves around the room, working individually or in small groups. For example,

Two youngsters may be stretched out on a rug reading library books. The teacher is at the math table, show-

FIGURE 14-4 In a traditional classroom, the students in the shaded area are more likely to capture the teacher's attention and to participate in classroom activities than their classmates who sit outside this "zone of activity."

ing four children how to use scales to learn about weights. Two children in the writing corner play a word game. Another takes notes about the nursing behavior of the class guinea pig. A sense of purpose pervades the room [Papalia & Olds, 1979, p. 401].

Is the open classroom more effective than the highly structured setting? This question is difficult to answer because students who attend open nursery and elementary schools often come from different (usually more affluent) backgrounds than those who receive traditional instruction. It does appear that students generally prefer an "open" atmosphere, are more cooperative in that kind of setting, and are apt to create fewer disciplinary problems than students in traditional classrooms (Minuchin & Shapiro, 1983). Moreover, the open classroom may be effective in helping elementary school children to develop novel ideas and concepts (Rutter, 1983; Thomas & Berk, 1981), and one recent study found that boys who had attended relatively unstructured nursery schools at age 4 were later performing at higher levels in reading and math during the sixth, seventh, and eighth grades than their classmates who had attended structured preschools (Miller & Bizzell, 1983). This latter finding is particularly intriguing, for the children who participated in the research had been randomly assigned to the structured or the unstructured nursery schools, and the two groups did not initially differ in either intelligence or socioeconomic background.

However, open education is hardly the answer for all instructional problems. Many investigators find no differences in the performance (or the conduct) of students in open and traditional classrooms; others have concluded that students will actually learn more in a structured classroom whenever the subject matter requires teachers to illustrate very difficult concepts or transmit a lot of factual information (Good, 1979; Good, Biddle, & Brophy, 1975; Rutter, 1983). Finally, a particular instructional format will not affect all children in the same way. Students who are restless, distractible, and low in achievement motivation seem to do better in a highly structured setting, while those who are less fidgety and more achievement-oriented may do rather well in an open classroom (Grimes & Allinsmith, 1961; Peterson, 1977). Michael Rutter (1983) is probably correct in arguing that "the debates on whether 'open classrooms' are better than traditional approaches . . . or whether 'formal' methods are preferable to 'informal' methods . . . are probably misplaced. Neither system has an overall superiority, but both include elements of good practice" (p. 21).

Other Contributors to an "Effective" School Environment

In his review of the literature, Rutter (1983) lists several additional values and practices that seem to characterize "effective" schools. For example:

• *Academic emphasis.* Effective schools have a clear focus on academic goals. Children are regularly assigned homework, which is checked, corrected, and discussed with them. Teachers expect a lot of their students and devote a high proportion of their time to active teaching and to planning lessons so that their expectations can be met. Instructors often plan their curriculum in groups and then monitor one another to ensure that they are doing what they can to achieve their objectives.

• *Classroom management.* In effective schools, teachers spend little time setting up equipment, handing out papers, and dealing with disciplinary problems. Lessons begin and end on time. Pupils are told exactly what is expected of them and receive clear and unambiguous feedback about their academic performance. The classroom atmosphere is comfortable;

PHOTO 14-1 Students at work in an open classroom.

all students are actively encouraged to work to the best of their abilities, and ample praise is given to acknowledge good work.

• *Discipline.* In effective schools, the staff is firm in enforcing rules and does so on the spot rather than sending offenders off to the principal's office. Rarely do instructors resort to physical punishment. In fact, several studies suggest that corporal punishment and unofficial physical sanctions (slapping, cuffing) contribute to truancy, disobedient behavior, delinquency, and the establishment of a tense, negative atmosphere that is hardly conducive to effective learning.

• *Staff organization and teacher morale.* Student conduct and academic achievement are better in schools where both the curriculum and approaches to discipline are agreed on by the staff working together as a team. Although it may be necessary for administrators to make decisions that individual instructors don't like, pupil outcomes are best in schools where all teachers feel that their points of view are taken seriously, even if they are not adopted.

In sum, we see that effective schools are those in which staff members work together to achieve well-defined educational objectives based on what children want and need to know. Teachers are encouraged to offer helpful guidance and discouraged from commanding, ridiculing, or punishing their pupils. The emphasis in effective schools is on successes rather than failures, and ample praise and recognition are given to students for a job well done. In other words, the effective school environment is a comfortable but businesslike setting in which students are *motivated* to learn. After reviewing the literature, Michael Rutter (1983) concluded that the task of motivating students was of critical importance, for "in the long run, good pupil outcomes were [nearly always] dependent on pupils *wanting* to participate in the educational process" (p. 23).

And whose job is it to motivate students? Traditionally we have assigned this responsibility to the classroom instructor.

THE TEACHER'S INFLUENCE

Once they reach school age, many children spend nearly as much time around their teachers as they do around their parents or guardians. Indeed, teachers are often the first adults outside the immediate family to play a major role in a child's life, and children's reactions to school usually depend on how well they like their teachers. Generally speaking, children like instructors who are kind, patient, fair, and interested in them as persons; they dislike teachers who ridicule, scold, or punish them, as well as those who are rigid or ill-tempered or who assign too much homework (Jersild, 1968).

The Changing Role of the Classroom Instructor

The roles played by classroom instructors will change as children progress through the educational system (Minuchin & Shapiro, 1983). Nursery school and kindergarten classes are in some ways similar to home life: teachers function as companions and substitute caregivers who provide reassurance if needed while striving to help individual children achieve the objectives of the preschool curriculum. Elementary school classrooms are more structured and complex. Teachers are now focusing mainly on curricular goals, and grade school children are apt to perceive their instructors as evaluators and authority figures rather than pals. During the adolescent years, teachers continue to serve as evaluators and authority figures. But since high school and college students change classes hourly and are exposed to many different teachers, it is less likely that any particular

instructor will exert so much influence over their lives as was true during the earlier years. Instead, high school students tend to think of school as a complex social organization; their orientation is now more diffuse, centering on the school as a whole—peer groups, extracurricular activities, sports, and, yes, even curricular matters—rather than on a particular classroom or classroom instructor.

Much of the research on teacher influences has focused on two very broad topics: (1) influences stemming from the teacher's evaluation of students and (2) the effects of teaching styles and instructional techniques on pupil outcomes.

Teachers as Appraisers and Evaluators

In Chapter 8, we learned that teachers form distinct impressions of their students' scholastic capabilities and that these expectancies often influence students' subsequent academic progress. Recall that students who are expected to succeed are apt to live up to these positive expectancies, whereas those who are expected to perform rather poorly often do earn lower grades and score lower on standardized tests than peers of comparable ability for whom the teacher has no negative expectancies (Rosenthal & Jacobson, 1968; Seaver, 1973). Indeed, these "teacher expectancy" effects are quite understandable when we consider how a teacher's evaluation of a particular pupil affects his or her behavior toward the child (Brophy, 1983; Minuchin & Shapiro, 1983). Teachers often demand better performances from "high expectancy" students and are more likely to praise these youngsters for answering questions correctly (perhaps leading the high-expectancy students to infer that they have high abilities). By contrast, "low expectancy" students are more likely to be criticized for incorrect responses (for example, "Wrong again, Henry"), a practice that may convince them that their failures reflect a lack of ability. And when "high expectancy" students do answer incorrectly, they often hear the question rephrased so that they can get it right (thus implying that failures can be overcome by trying harder). So teachers treat and evaluate "high expectancy" students in ways that promote a mastery orientation in the classroom, whereas "low expectancy" students often receive a pattern of evaluation that could undermine achievement motivation or even contribute to learned helplessness (Dweck & Elliott, 1983).

Teachers often hear remarks such as "I knew the material but froze during the test" or "I worried so much about finishing that I made stupid mistakes." Are these kinds of statements merely rationalizations for poor marks? Probably not. A sizable minority of any group of students will become highly anxious during tests, and this "test anxiety" can interfere with their academic performance, particularly if the test is timed. In one study (Hill & Eaton, 1977), highly anxious and less anxious grade-schoolers took an arithmetic test under one of two conditions. Some of the children had all the time they needed to complete the test, whereas the remaining youngsters had a time limit imposed on them—one ensuring that they would fail to finish. The results were clear. On the timed test, highly anxious children made three times as many errors and spent twice as much time per problem as their low-anxious classmates. But if time pressures were removed, the highly anxious students worked just as quickly and performed just as well on the test as their less anxious peers. We see, then, that the ways teachers structure their evaluative procedures can have a major impact on the academic performance of students high in test anxiety. Although any test has the potential to elicit some concern about being evaluated, it appears that teachers who favor and use highly stressful evaluative techniques may inadvertently underrate the scholastic abilities and perhaps undermine the achievement motivation of their more anxious pupils.

Teaching Styles and Instructional Techniques

Earlier we saw that teachers in "effective" schools will typically set clear-cut standards for their students to achieve, emphasize successes more than failures, firmly enforce rules without derogating an offender or becoming overly punitive, and use praise rather than threats to encourage each child to work to the best of his or her ability. Perhaps you have noticed that these managerial characteristics are in some ways similar to the pattern of control that Diana Baumrind calls authoritative parenting. Indeed, Baumrind (1972) believes that the three major patterns of control that characterize parent/child interactions are also found in the classroom. Teachers who use an *authoritarian* style tend to dominate their pupils, relying on power-assertive methods to enforce their demands. The *authoritative* teacher is also controlling but will rely on reason to explain his or her demands, encourage verbal give-and-take, and value autonomy and creative expression so long as the child is willing to live within the rules that the teacher has established. Finally, the *laissez faire* (or permissive) instructor makes few demands of students and provides little or no active guidance. Baumrind believes that teachers who use an authoritative style will contribute to children's intellectual curiosity, their academic achievement, and their social and emotional development.

A classic study by Kurt Lewin and his associates (Lewin, Lippitt, & White, 1939) is certainly relevant. The subjects were 11-year-old boys who met in groups after school to partake in hobby activities (such as making papier-mâché theater masks). Each group was led by an adult who behaved in one of three ways. The *authoritarian* leaders assigned jobs and work partners to each boy, dictated policy, frequently criticized the boys' work, remained somewhat aloof, and gave little or no explanation of the reasons for their policies. By contrast, *democratic* leaders talked about long-range goals, allowed the boys to participate in policy making, permitted them to select their own work partners, evaluated them honestly, and remained open and receptive to all questions. (The "democratic" leadership in this study represents a pattern of control roughly equivalent to what Baumrind calls the authoritative style.) Finally, *laissez faire* leaders gave their groups free rein—they provided the necessary equipment and would answer questions if any were asked, but they remained noncommittal for the most part.

Lewin et al. found that boys responded very differently to these three supervisory styles. Authoritarian leadership produced tension, restlessness, aggressive outbursts, damage to play materials, and a general dissatisfaction with the group experience. Productivity (as indexed by the number of theater masks the groups constructed) was high under authoritarian leadership while the leader was present. But when the leader left the room, work patterns disintegrated. Democratic leadership was more effective; the boys were much less hostile and generally happier with the leader and their group. Although the boys did not produce as many masks under democratic leadership, they continued to work when the leader left the room. Moreover, the work they did complete was of higher quality than that produced under authoritarian or laissez-faire leaders. Finally, the "permissive," laissez-faire approach generally resulted in an apathetic group atmosphere and very low productivity. All but 1 of the 20 boys in this experiment clearly favored democratic supervision.

These findings also seem to hold in the school setting. Students prefer a democratic atmosphere in the classroom (Rosenthal, Underwood, & Martin, 1969), and it appears that a flexible, nondictatorial instructional style is conducive to academic achievement (Brookover et al., 1979; Prather, 1969). But a word of caution is in order, for the instructional techniques that a teacher uses will not affect all children in the same way. For example, Brophy (1979) notes that teachers get the most out of high-ability students by moving at a quick pace and requiring high standards of performance. In other words, brighter students perform best when they are challenged. By contrast, low-ability and disadvantaged children respond much more favorably to slow-paced instruction from a teacher who is warm and encouraging rather than intrusive and demanding.

In sum, authoritative instruction does seem to increase academic achievement. Yet there are many ways that authoritative instructors might try to motivate their pupils, and the techniques that work best will depend, in part, on the type of student they are trying to reach.

THE SCHOOL AS A MIDDLE-CLASS INSTITUTION: EFFECTS ON DISADVANTAGED YOUTH

Public schools in the United States are middle-class institutions largely staffed by middle-class instructors who preach middle-class values. Some theorists have argued that this particular emphasis places children from lower-class or minority subcultures at an immediate disadvantage. After all, these youngsters must adjust to an environment that may seem altogether foreign and somewhat foreboding to them—a problem with which middle-class students do not have to contend.

Many lower-class and minority students do have problems at school. They are more likely than middle-class youngsters to make poor marks, to be disciplined by the staff, to be "held back" in one or more grades, and to drop out before completing high school. Among the factors thought to contribute to these sociocultural differences in scholastic achievement are (1) the nature of the educational materials that schools provide, (2) the attitudes of parents about the importance of schooling, and (3) the tendency of teachers to respond differently to students from different social backgrounds.

Educational Materials and Academic Achievement

The textbooks that children read are clearly centered on the lives and experiences of middle-class people. These characters live in suburban homes, work at white-collar jobs, ride in fancy cars, take airplane trips, go on picnics, give parties, and are never unhappy—experiences that may seem unimportant or irrelevant to many disadvantaged children. But does the use of "irrelevant" instructional materials have any effect on their will to achieve?

Maybe so. Spencer Kagan and Lawrence Zahn (1975) compared groups of Anglo-American and Mexican-American children on two measures of academic achievement: math and reading proficiency. Although Anglo students performed better than Mexican-Americans on both achievement tests, the cultural gap was much wider on the reading measure. Furthermore, the reading deficit of Mexican-American children was not attributable to differences between the groups in IQ or cognitive style, to teacher prejudices, or to the use of English in the classroom (almost all these children were third-generation Mexican-Americans who spoke only English). Kagan and Zahn believe that Mexican-American students may simply lack the motivation to master traditional reading materials that adequately represent the White culture but are largely irrelevant to their own experiences and values. According to this line of reasoning, the Mexican-American students showed much less deficiency in mathematics because math texts contain less culturally irrelevant information. If Kagan and Zahn are correct in their interpretation, then perhaps we should be using more "culturally relevant" educational materials in school systems heavily populated by underachieving ethnic minorities.

Parents' Attitudes and Values

In Chapter 8 we saw that many lower- and working-class parents encourage their children to "get by" in school, while middle- and upper-class parents are more likely to stress "doing well" and "getting ahead." Parents from the lower socioeconomic strata are generally less knowledgeable about the school system and less involved in school activities, and this lack of participation may convince their children that school is really not all that important. Yet when lower-class parents are interested and involved in school activities, their children do well in school (Brookover et al., 1979; Laosa, 1982). So it appears that parental encouragement and involvement can make a big difference.

Teachers' Reactions to Disadvantaged Students

In a book entitled *Dark Ghetto*, Kenneth Clark (1965) argues that the classroom represents a "clash of cultures" in which adults who have adopted middle-class values fail to appreciate the difficulties faced by students from different subcultural and socioeconomic backgrounds. According to Clark, teachers in schools serving lower-income minority populations make nearly three times as many negative comments to their students as their colleagues in middle-income schools. Teachers often have lower expectancies for children from low-income families (Minuchin & Shapiro, 1983). Even before they have any academic information about their students, many instructors are already placing them into "ability groups" on the basis of their grooming, the quality of their clothing, and their use or misuse of standard English (Rist, 1970). In one study (Gottlieb, 1966), teachers were asked to select from a checklist those attributes that best described their lower-class pupils. Middle-class respondents consistently checked adjectives such as *lazy, fun-loving,* and *rebellious.* Clearly, these instructors did not expect much of their disadvantaged

students—an attitude that undoubtedly contributes to social-class differences in achievement.

Ironically, disadvantaged children may be convinced that they are doing well if their teachers assign them passing marks and routinely promote them from grade to grade, regardless of their actual accomplishments (Plummer, Hazzard-Lineberger, & Graziano, 1984). Indeed, Katherine Fulkerson and her associates (Fulkerson, Furr, & Brown, 1983) report that the academic expectancies of minority students increase and become more unrealistic from the third to the ninth grade. Is it a wise practice to give "social promotions" to children whose accomplishments are clearly substandard? Probably not. In fact, it could be argued that this practice actually perpetuates social inequalities by denying these underachievers the opportunity to repeat a grade and thereby acquire critical academic skills that they will need to do well in the future. But how do children feel about repeating a grade? Does it really help? As we see in Box 14-1, grade retention is a controversial practice that may have either positive or negative effects on retainees, depending on their age, the extent of their deficiencies, their self-esteem, and the amount of support they receive from parents, teachers, and peers.

Effects of School Desegregation on Minority Youth

In 1954 the U.S. Supreme Court issued a landmark decision in *Brown* v. *Board of Education*—one that mandated an end to segregated schooling in the United States. After listening to the testimony of many social scientists, the high court concluded:

> To separate [minority students] from others of similar age and qualifications solely because of race generates a feeling of inferiority as to their status in the community that may affect their hearts and minds in a way unlikely ever to be undone. . . . We conclude that in the field of public education, the doctrine "separate but equal" has no place. Separate educational facilities are inherently unequal.

The *Brown* decision was expected to have at least three positive effects on minority students (in this case, Blacks) and one favorable effect on Whites (Stephan, 1978):

1. For Whites, school desegregation was to lead to more positive attitudes toward Blacks.

BOX 14-1 REPEATING A GRADE: PERSONAL, SOCIAL, AND ACADEMIC CONSEQUENCES

If children do not attain the "minimal competencies" necessary for success in the next grade, they are often required to repeat the work that they have failed to master. Advocates of grade retention argue that repeating a grade is a beneficial experience—one that gives the underachieving child an opportunity to mature both socially and intellectually and to acquire academic skills that are absolutely essential to perform well in the higher grades (Kerzner, 1982). Yet the critics have argued that retained children may often be stigmatized as "different" or even "stupid," an experience that could undermine their self-concepts, their academic expectancies, and their relations with teachers and peers.

For the most part, parents and teachers support grade retention because they believe that the positive aspects of this policy outweigh the negatives (Chase, 1968). Let's now consider the evidence to see whether there is any basis for this claim.

Grade Retention and Academic Achievement

The primary purpose of retaining a child is to allow him or her to acquire important academic skills and thereby do better in school. Yet an examination of the evidence available before 1970 suggests that the policy of holding children back in school was not meeting these objectives. The majority of nonpromoted children performed no better while repeating a grade than they had the first time around. Moreover, children of comparable ability who had been promoted generally outscored retainees on standardized achievement tests (see Plummer, Hazzard-Lineberger, & Graziano, 1984, for review of these data). Yet even the most critical of these early reports acknowledged that about 20% of the retainees were doing better academically after repeating a grade.

The recent literature on grade retention is more encouraging. Nonpromoted children are generally found to make better grades the second time around and to show definite improvements on standardized tests of academic achievement, particularly when they are retained in the lower grades (Ames, 1981; Kerzner, 1982). Retainees are more likely to make good academic progress if (1) their parents support the decision to retain them, (2) they have a positive self-concept before being retained, (3) they have good social skills, and (4) *their academic deficiencies are not too extensive* (Plummer et al., 1984; Sandoval & Hughes, 1981). The last point is important, for it suggests that children who have received several "social promotions" and were not ready for the grade they failed may not profit by repeating it.

Grade Retention and Peer Relations

Do peers stigmatize an older retainee as dumb, incompetent, or otherwise undesirable? Diane Plummer and William Graziano (1987) tried to answer this question by showing second- and fifth-graders photographs of retained and nonretained age mates (whom they did not know) and then asking them who would be liked better, who could give more help with schoolwork, and who would be a better playmate. The results were indeed interesting. On the liking item, a sizable minority of the children (38%) felt that the older, retained child would be liked better than a younger, nonretained classmate. On the academic item, 86% of the second-graders and 66% of the fifth-graders felt that the

---

2. For Blacks, desegregation was to lead to (a) more positive attitudes toward Whites, (b) increases in self-esteem, and (c) increases in academic achievement.

Since the *Brown* decision, several investigators have studied the impact of school desegregation on both Black and White students. Were the early predictions borne out? Let's take a look at the findings.

Has desegregation improved race relations?
As we see in Table 14-1, the data on this issue are mixed. Black prejudice toward Whites was observed to decrease in 50% of the studies, whereas integration led to reduction of White prejudice toward Blacks in only 13% of the studies (Stephan, 1978). However, it is not at all uncommon for both Blacks and Whites in integrated schools to have more negative attitudes toward the other group than their counterparts in *segregated* schools. And this is often true even where integration was achieved voluntarily and without serious incidents (Green & Gerard, 1974; Stephan, 1977).

One reason that school desegregation has not been more successful at improving race relations is that members of various racial and ethnic groups tend to

BOX 14-1 *continued*

older, retained child would be of more assistance with schoolwork. When asked why, they usually stated that the retainee had more experience with such assignments and would know more about them. Finally, more than half (52%) of the second-graders preferred the older, retained child as a playmate, and even 40% of the fifth-graders chose the retainee as a preferred companion. As a cautionary note, it is important to recall that the respondents were evaluating children whom they did not know. Nevertheless, their responses clearly question the notion that a child who has "failed" a grade will automatically be stigmatized as dull, incompetent, or otherwise undesirable.

Grade Retention and Self-Esteem

How do children feel when they fail a grade? It is often assumed that they will be upset and depressed and may begin to lower their academic expectations or to question their self-worth. In fact, some theorists have argued that grade retention can produce a serious loss of self-esteem, which leads to further failure and eventually to feelings of learned helplessness (Johnson, 1981). Do these reactions often occur when a child must repeat a grade?

Apparently not. In one study (Chase, 1968), only 10 of 65 children (15%) showed any emotional discomfort when held back in the first, second, or third grade, and their reactions to being retained were only temporary. However, it could be argued that these retainees were somewhat atypical in that their parents strongly supported the decision to retain them and stated that their children were benefiting from repeating a year at school.

Plummer and Graziano (1987) have recently studied some of the "personal" effects of grade retention in a rural school district in Georgia where a substantial percentage of Black and White students are retained at least once while in elementary school. Second- and fifth-grade retainees and nonretainees were asked to estimate the grades they would receive on their next report card (academic expectancy measure) and to indicate verbally how they viewed themselves on personal and social dimensions such as "lazy," "smart," "popular," "successful," and "honest" (self-esteem measure). The results were clear. With one minor exception (second-grade retainees expected lower grades in reading than their nonretained classmates), retainees did not differ from nonretainees on the academic expectancy measure. Moreover, retainees in both the second and fifth grades actually had more favorable self-concepts than students who had not been retained. We must be cautious in interpreting these results because nearly 40% of the children in this school had been held back at one time or another, so that being a retainee was in no way unusual. Nevertheless, there was little support for the idea that retainees view themselves as less capable of achieving or less "worthy" than nonretainees.

The policy of holding children back to facilitate their eventual academic progress remains highly controversial, and it is possible that alternative strategies such as promoting a child and providing special instruction in areas of deficiency will prove more effective than grade retention—if and when these techniques are tried on a large scale. Nevertheless, it appears that many children can benefit academically from repeating a grade without experiencing poor peer relations or a serious loss of self-esteem.

---

stick together without interacting much with their classmates from other groups. In fact, Neal Finkelstein and Ron Haskins (1983) found that kindergartners who were just entering an integrated school already preferred same-race peers and that these racial cleavages became even stronger over the course of the school year. In other studies, children's preferences for same-race friends have been found to become progressively stronger across grades in integrated schools (see Hartup, 1983). Yet race relations often *improve* when students from different social backgrounds are assigned to work together or choose to participate on multiethnic sports teams (Minuchin

& Shapiro, 1983). Clearly these later observations support Finkelstein and Haskins's (1983) view that "school desegregation will not, by itself, inevitably lead to a destruction of the color barriers that have plagued our society . . . if such barriers are to be reduced, schools will need to design, implement, and monitor programs aimed at facilitating social contacts between blacks and whites" (p. 508).

Has desegregation increased Black children's self-esteem? In his review of the literature, Walter Stephan (1978) found few differences in self-esteem between Black children in segregated and in integrated schools. In fact, none of the 20 studies found that desegregation had had a positive effect on Black self-esteem, and 5 studies (25%) reported that desegregation had had a negative effect. Unfortunately, this research has considered only the short-term effects of desegregation, and it remains to be seen whether the self-concepts of minority children will improve after several years in integrated schools.

Has desegregation increased academic achievement?

Do minority students achieve more in desegregated classrooms? Many of them do, particularly if they begin to attend an integrated school early in their academic careers (Mahan & Mahan, 1970; Stephan, 1978; St. John, 1975). Although the academic gains that result from desegregation are often rather modest, it is worth noting that in only 1 of 34 studies have minority students in integrated classrooms performed at lower levels than their counterparts in segregated schools (Stephan, 1978).

Of course, the effects of desegregation may vary considerably, depending on the child's ability and personality. Are sociable children who make friends easily any more likely to develop favorable attitudes toward students of other races? Will minority students who are high in achievement motivation benefit more from desegregation than those who are apprehensive about competing with Whites? Walter Stephan (1978) suggests that we should now be trying to answer these kinds of questions by studying the effects of desegregation on *individuals* rather than groups. After studying groups, we have some idea what the effects of desegregation are—*but not why they occur*. By looking at how desegregation affects individuals, we may be able to determine the conditions under which different children will react most favorably to multiethnic settings and then use this information to produce more favorable social and academic consequences in our integrated schools.

THE SECOND WORLD OF CHILDHOOD: PEERS AS SOCIALIZATION AGENTS

Most children spend an enormous amount of time and energy playing with other children, and social scientists have long suspected that these peer contacts are important in shaping the conduct and character of each successive generation (Hartup, 1983). Yet it has only been in the past 20 years that developmentalists have begun to focus intensively on peer relations and to chart the many ways that interactions with peers might influence behavior.

Perhaps owing to early research on the behavior of adolescent gangs (see Hartup, 1983), peers have often been characterized as potentially subversive agents who may erode the positive influence of adults and steer the child toward a life of delinquency and antisocial conduct. Indeed, popular novels and films such as *Lord of the Flies* and *A Clockwork Orange* reinforce this point of view.

However, this perspective on peer relations is distorted and unnecessarily negative. Although peers are occasionally "bad influences," they clearly have the potential to affect their playmates in positive ways. Try to imagine what your life would be like if other children had not been available as you were growing up. Would you have acquired the social skills to mix comfortably with others, to cooperate and to engage in socially acceptable forms of competition, or to make appropriate social (or sexual)

TABLE 14-1   Effects of School Desegregation on Prejudice toward Blacks and Whites

Subjects	Number of studies finding increased prejudice	Number of studies finding no change	Number of studies finding decreased prejudice
Blacks (prejudice toward Whites)	5	1	6
Whites (prejudice toward Blacks)	8	5	2

responses to love objects other than your parents? No one can say for sure, but the following letter written by a farmer from the midwestern United States provides a strong clue that interactions with other children may be an important aspect of the socialization process.[2]

Dear Dr. Moore:

I read the report in the Oct. 30 issue of ———— about your study of only children. I am an only child, now 57 years old, and I want to tell you some things about my life. Not only was I an only child, but I grew up in the country where there were no nearby children to play with. My mother didn't want children around. She used to say "I don't want my kid to bother anybody and I don't want nobody's kids bothering me." . . .

From the first year of school, I was teased and made fun of. For example, in about third or fourth grade, I dreaded to get on the school bus and go to school because the other children on the bus called me "Mommy's baby." In about the second grade I heard the boys use a vulgar word. I asked what it meant and they made fun of me. So I learned a lesson—don't ask questions. This can lead to a lot of confusion to hear talk one doesn't understand and not be able to learn what it means. . . .

I never went out with a girl while I was in school—in fact I hardly talked to them. In our school the boys and girls did not play together. Boys were sent to one part of the playground and girls to another. So I didn't learn anything about girls. When we got into high school and boys and girls started dating, I could only listen to their stories about their experiences.

I could tell you a lot more, but the important thing is I have never been married or had any children. I have not been very successful in an occupation or vocation. I believe my troubles are not all due to being an only child . . . but I do believe you are right in recommending playmates for preschool children, and I will add playmates for . . . school agers and not have them strictly supervised by adults. I believe I confirm the experiments with monkeys in being overly timid sometimes and overly aggressive sometimes. Parents of only children should make special efforts to provide playmates for them.

Sincerely yours, _____

If we assume that peers are important agents of socialization, there are a number of questions that remain to be answered. For example, who qualifies as a peer? How do peers influence one another? What is it about peer influence that is unique? What are the consequences (if any) of poor peer relations? Do peers eventually become a more potent source of influence than parents or other adults? Are there cultural differences in the roles that peers play in a child's socialization? These are some of the issues that researchers are currently exploring as they turn in ever-increasing numbers to the study of children's peer groups.

WHO OR WHAT IS A PEER?

Webster's New Collegiate Dictionary defines a peer as "one that is of equal standing with another." Developmentalists also think of peers as "social equals" or as *individuals who, for the moment at least, are operating at similar levels of behavioral complexity* (Lewis & Rosenblum, 1975).

We get some idea of why peer contacts are important by contrasting them to exchanges that occur within the family. A child's interactions with parents and older siblings are rarely equal-status contacts; typically children are placed in a subordinate position by an older member of the family who is trying to teach them something, issuing an order, or otherwise overseeing their activities. By contrast, peers are much less critical and directive, and children are freer to try out new roles, ideas, and behaviors when interacting with someone of similar status. And in so doing, they are likely to learn important lessons about themselves and others—lessons such as "She quits when I don't take turns," "He hits me when I push him," or "Nobody likes a cheater." Many theorists believe that peer contacts are important because they are *equal status* contacts—that is, they teach children to understand and appreciate the perspectives of people *just like themselves* and will thereby contribute to the development of social competencies that are difficult to acquire in the nonegalitarian atmosphere of the home.

Mixed-Age Interactions

According to Hartup (1983), interaction among children of *different* ages is also a critically important context for social and personality development. Although cross-age interactions tend to be somewhat *asymmetrical*, one child (typically the elder) possessing more power or status than the other, it is precisely these asymmetries that may help children to acquire certain social competencies. For example, the presence of younger peers may foster the development of sympathy and compassion, caregiving and prosocial inclinations, teaching skills, and assertiveness in older children. At the same time, younger children may benefit from mixed-age interactions by learning how to seek assistance and how to gracefully defer to the wishes and directives of older, more powerful peers. Moreover, younger children are potentially in a position to acquire many socially and intellectually adaptive patterns of behavior through direct instruction (tutoring) by elder playmates or by observing and imitating the competent behaviors of these "older and wiser" companions.

In their survey of children's social contacts in six cultures, Whiting and Whiting (1975) found that mixed-age interactions do differ in important ways from those among age mates. Nurturant and prosocial behaviors occurred more frequently in mixed-age groups, whereas casually sociable acts (such as conversation and interactive play) as well as antisocial ones (such as aggression) were more likely to occur among age mates. By the time children enter school, they already characterize older peers as more powerful and competent and younger peers as less powerful and competent than themselves (Graziano, Musser, & Brody, 1982). Given these observations, it should not be surprising to find, as Doran French (1984) recently has, that children's preferences for interacting with older, younger, or same-age peers depend on the purpose of that interaction. First- and third-graders clearly preferred age mates to either younger or older children when asked who might be more desirable as a friend. However, older children were preferred to age mates if the child felt the need for sympathy, help, or guidance, whereas younger children were the ones subjects chose if the situation called for them to display compassion or to teach another child what they already knew.

Frequency of Peer Contacts

As you might expect, the amount of contact that children have with peers increases with age. Recently, Sharri Ellis and her colleagues (Ellis, Rogoff, & Cromer, 1981) observed the activities of 436 children aged 2 to 12 as they played in their homes and other locales around the neighborhood. The purpose of this research was to determine how often children interacted with adults, age mates, and other children who differed in age by more than a year. As we see in Figure 14-5, children's exposure to other children increases steadily from infancy through middle childhood, while their contacts with adult companions show a corresponding decrease.

Same-Age versus Mixed-Age Interactions

Since children attend age-graded schools, it seems reasonable to conclude that they would play most often with age mates. However, Ellis et al. (1981) found that they do not! As we see in Figure 14-6, youngsters of all ages spend much less time with age mates than with children who differ in age by more than a year. In another study of children's interactions in a neighborhood setting, Roger Barker and H. F. Wright (1955) found that 65% of peer contacts involved individuals who differed in age by more than 12 months.

Same-Sex versus Mixed-Sex Interactions

In Chapter 12 we noted that preschool children already prefer playmates of their own sex. In their observational study, Ellis et al. found that even 1- to 2-year-olds were playing more often with same-sex companions and that this like-sex bias became increasingly apparent with age. The fact that infants and toddlers play more often with children of their

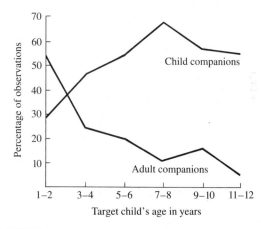

FIGURE 14-5 Developmental changes in children's companionship with adults and other children

own sex probably reflects their parents' idea that boys should be playing with boys and girls with girls. And as children acquire gender stereotypes and sex-typed interests, it is hardly surprising that they would begin to choose same-sex playmates who enjoy the same kind of activities that they do.

What may be most surprising about the naturalistic studies of peer interaction is the sheer amount of contact that children have with one another before they go to school. Even 5–6-year-olds are spending as much leisure time (or more) in the company of children as around adults (Barker & Wright, 1955; Ellis et al., 1981). And what is the "peer group" like? It consists mostly of same-sex children of *different* ages. Now we see why developmentalists define peers as "people who interact at similar levels of behavioral complexity," for only a small percentage of a child's associates are actually age mates.

PHOTO 14-2   Both older and younger children benefit from mixed-age interactions.

PEERS AS PROMOTERS OF SOCIAL COMPETENCE AND PERSONAL ADJUSTMENT

To this point, we have speculated that interactions among children may promote the development of many social and personal competencies that are not easily acquired within the decidedly nonegalitarian parent/child relationship. Is there truly any basis for such a claim? And if so, jut how important are those peer influences? Developmentalists became very interested in these questions after Harry Harlow showed that rhesus monkeys seem to require peer contacts in order to get along with other monkeys. Let's take a closer look.

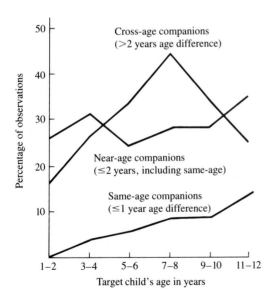

FIGURE 14-6   Developmental changes in children's companionship with children of different ages

Harlow's work with monkeys.   Will youngsters who have little or no contact with peers turn out to be abnormal or maladjusted? To find out, Harry Harlow and his associates (Alexander & Harlow, 1965; Suomi & Harlow, 1975, 1978) raised groups of rhesus monkeys with their mothers and denied them the opportunity to play with their peers. These *"mother only" monkeys* failed to develop normal patterns of social behavior. When finally exposed to age mates, the peer-deprived youngsters preferred to avoid them. On those occasions when they did approach a peer, these social misfits tended to be highly (and inappropriately) aggressive. Moreover, their antisocial tendencies often persisted into adulthood, particularly if they had been denied peer contacts for long periods.

Is peer contact the key to normal social development? Not entirely. In later experiments, Harlow and

PHOTO 14-3 Monkeys raised only with peers form strong mutual attachments and will often attack other monkeys from outside their peer group.

his colleagues separated rhesus monkeys from their mothers and raised them so that they had continuous exposure to their peers. These *"peer only" monkeys* were observed to cling tenaciously to one another and to form strong mutual attachments. Yet their social development was somewhat atypical. Suomi and Harlow (1975) noted: "It is somewhat difficult for a baby monkey to explore its environment with another monkey hanging on for dear life and [when] even the most enthusiastic attempts at play are terminated by a big bearhug" (p. 167). The peer-only monkeys were often disturbed by minor stresses or frustrations, and as adults they became unusually aggressive toward monkeys from outside their peer groups.

And a human parallel. In 1951 Anna Freud and Sophie Dann reported a startling human parallel to Harlow's peer-only monkeys. During the summer of 1945, six 3-year-olds were found living by themselves in a German concentration camp. By the time these children were 12 months old, their parents had been put to death. Although they had received minimal caregiving from a series of inmates who were periodically executed, these children had, in effect, reared themselves.

When rescued at the war's end, the six orphans were flown to a special treatment center in England, where attempts were made to "rehabilitate" them. How did these "peer only" children respond to this treatment? They began by breaking nearly all their toys and damaging their furniture. Moreover, they often reacted with cold indifference or open hostility toward the staff at the center. And like Harlow's monkeys, these children

> had no other wish than to be together and became upset when they were separated . . . , even for short moments. No child would remain upstairs while the others were downstairs. . . . If anything of the kind happened, the single child would constantly ask for the other children, while the group would fret for the missing child. . . .
>
> There was no occasion to urge the children to "take turns"; they did it spontaneously. They were extremely considerate of each other's feelings. . . . At mealtimes handing food to the neighbor was of greater importance than eating oneself [Freud & Dann, 1951, pp. 131–133].

Although these orphans were closely attached to one another and very suspicious of outsiders, they were certainly not psychotic. In fact, they eventually established positive relationships with their adult caregivers and acquired a new language during the first year at the center. The story even has a happy ending, for 35 years later, these orphans were leading effective, productive lives as middle-aged adults. According to Hartup (1983), "No more graphic account exists in the literature to demonstrate resilience in social development and to display that peer interaction can contribute importantly to the socialization of the individual child" (p. 158).

Taken together, Harlow's monkey research and Freud and Dann's observations of their war orphans suggest that parents and peers each contribute something different and perhaps unique to a monkey's (or a child's) social development. Under normal circumstances, parents may provide a sense of *security* that enables their young to explore the environment and discover that other people can be interesting companions. By contrast, contacts with peers seem to promote the development of competent and adaptive patterns of social behavior. Indeed, Harlow's "peer only" monkeys behaved in strange ways as adults only when exposed to strange companions; within their own peer groups, they generally displayed normal patterns of social and sexual behavior (Suomi & Harlow, 1978).

The importance of harmonious peer relations.
Just how important is it that human beings establish and maintain harmonious relations with their peers? Apparently it is very important. Merrill Roff (1961, 1974; Roff, Sells, & Golden, 1972) has collected longitudinal data on a large number of children who were clients at a child guidance center. After tracking these individuals for many years, Roff and his associates found that poor peer relations during childhood (being rejected by many and accepted by few) were a reliable predictor of severe emotional disturbances later in life. Children who had been actively shunned or rejected by their classmates were more likely to be delinquent as adolescents, to receive bad-conduct discharges from the military service, and to display a large number of serious adjustment problems, including neuroses, psychoses, and sexual deviations. A second longitudinal study painted a similar picture: children who had been rejected by their peers in the third grade were more likely than those with good peer relations to be seeking treatment for emotional disturbances 11 years later as young adults (Cowen, Pederson, Babigan, Izzo, & Trost, 1973).

Why might poor peer relations in childhood be good prognostic indicators of later adjustment problems? Perhaps youngsters who are rejected by peers will face later difficulties because they have paid little attention to the values and teachings of the peer group and have simply failed to acquire many socially appropriate patterns of behavior. Indeed, Wyndol Furman and John Masters (1980) found that unpopular 5-year-olds were less likely than their popular classmates to follow rules endorsed by either peers or adults.

Of course, it is unlikely that poor peer relations are entirely responsible for the adjustment problems of an unpopular child. Many unpopular children have shaky interpersonal relations with their parents or live in conflict-ridden homes—experiences that may create their own emotional difficulties while also hindering the child's attempts to establish adequate peer relations (Hetherington, 1981; Lewis, Feiring, McGuffog, & Jaskir, 1984). For example, we know that children who are abused by their parents often attain very low status in the peer group, perhaps owing to their tendency to be highly and inappropriately aggressive with peers (Hoffman-Plotkin & Twentyman, 1984; Main & George, 1985). Moreover, two recent studies have shown that preschoolers with a history of insecure attachments (particularly those who are "anxious and resistant" with their mothers) are likely to be picked on or ignored by peers and to be among the least popular members of a preschool play group (Jacobson & Wille, 1986; LaFreniere & Sroufe, 1985). So bad experiences at home may contribute in a *direct* way to later adjustment problems as well as forecasting the child's future peer relations. But since friendly and harmonious contacts with peers promote the development of adaptive social skills, it would seem that *any* child who fails to establish positive links to the peer group will run a far greater risk of displaying inappropriate and perhaps even pathological patterns of behavior as an adolescent or young adult.

How do children normally secure and maintain good relations with their peers? What factors are most important in determining a child's social standing in the peer group? And what roles might special peers—chums or friends—play in a child's social development? These are the issues we will explore in the pages that follow.

DETERMINANTS OF PEER ACCEPTANCE

Perhaps no other aspect of children's social lives has received more attention than peer acceptance. When we speak of peer acceptance, we are referring to two attributes—a child's *popularity*, or likability, and his or her *status*—a reflection of the child's perceived worth as a contributor to the attainment of group goals (Hartup, 1983). Although these two attributes tend to be positively correlated—popular children enjoy high status, and vice versa—the correlations are often rather modest. Thus, it is possible for a child to be a leader (high status) even though she is not well liked or to be very popular but have only average status in the peer group.

Some determinants of peer acceptance are specific to a particular group or setting. For example, toughness, hostile attitudes toward outgroups, and an ability to handle a motorcycle may make you a valued Hell's Angel, but it is doubtful that these qualities would enhance your standing among the members of your monthly investment club. Clearly, different groups value different attributes, and those who are accepted possess the characteristics that are valued by their peer groups. Nevertheless, there are a number of factors that seem to affect a person's social standing in many kinds of groups, regardless of the age, sex, or sociocultural backgrounds of the members. These are the qualities on which we will focus as we review the determinants of social acceptance in children's groups.

Measuring Children's Standing in the Peer Group

The most common method of assessing a child's status or popularity in the peer group is the *sociometric* test. This procedure requires youngsters to state their preferences for other group members with respect to some definite criterion. If you wanted to measure popularity, for example, you might ask each child to tell you which three peers he especially likes and perhaps to list up to three children he dislikes.[3] This "peer nomination" procedure can even be used to collect social preference data from very young children, who are typically shown photos of their peers and asked to point to those classmates whom they especially like (or dislike). After all the children have been tested in this manner, the investigator can determine the popularity of each child in the group by looking at the number of times the child has been nominated as a "liked" individual or perhaps by counting up the number of these positive nominations and then subtracting the number of negative nominations in which the child has been tabbed as "disliked."

Another method of assessing peer acceptance is to ask children to rate every other member of the peer group on one or more dimensions, such as likability or friendliness. This rating technique is advantageous because (1) it tells the investigator how each group member perceives every other group member and (2) it indicates how each child is perceived by *all* the other members of the group. Moreover, it permits the researcher to identify children who are actively rejected by their peers (rejectees receive very low ratings) without asking raters to explicitly state whom they dislike (Asher & Dodge, 1986).

Although several methods of classifying children's peer acceptance have been used over the years, most investigators agree that there are at least four major categories into which a child might fall:

1. *Sociometric stars*—children who are accepted by a sizable percentage of the peer group and rejected by few (if any) associates.
2. *Amiables or "accepteds"*—these children receive fewer nominations as liked or disliked associates than sociometric stars do, but the clear preponderance of the nominations they receive are *positive* ones.
3. *Isolates or "neglectees"*—these youngsters receive few nominations of any kind. They are neither actively liked nor disliked and are more likely to be ignored by peers.
4. *Rejectees*—these children receive many nominations, the clear majority of which are negative (that is, they are actively disliked). When rating scales are used to assess social acceptance, rejectees receive very low ratings on measures of likability and friendliness.[4]

So we see that there are two categories of children—isolates and rejectees—who are relatively low in peer acceptance. But interestingly enough, it is nowhere near as bad to be ignored by one's peers as it is to be rejected by them. Isolated children whom peers often neglect do not feel as lonely as rejectees (Asher & Wheeler, 1985), and they are much more likely than rejected children to eventually be "accepted" or even achieve the status of sociometric star should they enter a new class or a new play group (Coie & Dodge, 1983; Coie & Kupersmidt, 1983). In addition, it is the rejected child rather than the isolate who faces the greater risk of suffering serious adjustment problems later in life (Cowen et al., 1973; Roff, 1974).

Why do isolates fare better in the long run than their rejected classmates? The answer should become more apparent in the following section as we consider the behavioral strategies that children use to become accepted by peers and see that rejectees often lack many of these basic social skills (see also Box 14-2).

Some Correlates of Peer Acceptance and Rejection

At several points throughout the text, we have discussed factors that seem to contribute to children's popularity or social status. By way of review:

1. *Parenting styles.* Warm, sensitive, and authoritative caregivers tend to raise children who are securely attached and who establish good relations with both adults and peers (Baumrind, 1967; Pastor, 1981; Waters, Wippman, & Sroufe, 1979). Unresponsive caregivers, particularly those who are also permissive, tend to raise children who are hostile and aggressive, while the children of more domineering or authoritarian caregivers are often rather anxious, reserved, and moody around their peers (Baumrind, 1967; MacDonald & Parke, 1984).

2. *Ordinal position effects.* Later-born children who must learn to negotiate with older and more powerful siblings tend to be more popular than first-borns (Miller & Maruyama, 1976).

3. *Cognitive skills.* Both cognitive and social-cognitive skills predict children's peer acceptance. Among groups of third- through eighth-graders, the most popular children are those who have well-developed role-taking skills (Kurdek & Krile, 1982; Pellegrini, 1985), and children who have established intimate friendships score higher on tests of role taking than classmates without close friends (McGuire & Weisz, 1982). There is also a positive relationship between intelligence and peer acceptance: brighter children tend to be the more popular members of many peer groups (Hartup, 1983). Even during the preschool period, popular children score higher than their less popular peers on indicators of cognitive maturity such as mental age (Quay & Jarrett, 1984) and amount of fantasy play (Connolly & Doyle, 1984). Finally, children are often attracted to classmates who do well in school and who have good academic self-concepts (Green, Forehand, Beck, & Vosk, 1980; Hartup, 1983). Indeed, one research team recently provided intensive *academic* skills

training to low-achieving, socially rejected fourth-graders and found that this treatment improved not only the children's reading and math achievement but their social standing as well. One year after the training had ended, these former rejectees were now "accepted" and enjoyed average status in the peer group (Coie & Krehbiel, 1984).

There are at least three additional characteristics that seem to affect children's standing among their peers: their names, their physical attributes, and their patterns of interpersonal behavior.

Names. What's in a name? Apparently quite a lot, in the eyes (or ears) of grade school children. John McDavid and Herbert Harari (1966) asked four groups of 10- to 12-year-olds to rate the attractiveness of a large number of first names. At a later date, the subjects were asked to indicate the three most popular and the three least popular children in their classes. McDavid and Harari found that children with attractive names (for example, Steven, John, Susan, or Kim) were rated as more popular by their peers than children with unusual and less attractive names (for example, Herman or Chastity). And in a later study, Harari and McDavid (1973) found that teachers tend to have more positive achievement expectancies for children with attractive names.

These outcomes, like all correlational findings, must be interpreted with caution. Perhaps having a strange name does handicap children by making them the object of scorn or ridicule. However, we must consider the possibility that parents who give their children unusual names may also encourage unusual behaviors that contribute to the problems that the Myrtles and the Mortimers may have with their peers.

Physical characteristics. Despite the maxim that "beauty is only skin deep," many of us, children included, seem to think otherwise. Although it is difficult to specify exactly what combination of features contributes to facial attractiveness, even 3–5-year-olds can discriminate attractive from unattractive children, and they apparently use the same criteria as adults do when making their judgments

BOX 14-2 WHY REJECTEES REMAIN REJECTED:
A SOCIAL INFORMATION-PROCESSING PERSPECTIVE

In an interesting five-year longitudinal study, John Coie and Kenneth Dodge (1983) found that not all sociometric classifications are equally stable over time. The most popular children in the sample tended to lose some of their very favorable status, although they typically remained "accepted" members of the peer group. And although some isolates or neglectees remained neglected, many showed meaningful *gains* in social acceptance. The one sociometric classification that proved to be highly stable was rejectee: once rejected, children were likely to remain rejected over the long run. As we will see in the text, rejected children typically display patterns of behavior that alienate their peers, and the persistence of these annoying antics does help to explain why rejectees might remain rejected. Yet, there is now reason to suspect that, even if rejectees begin to respond more positively and constructively to their peers, they may find it exceedingly difficult to climb out of the hole they have dug for themselves to become accepted members of the peer group. But why?

Shelley Hymel (1986) has recently proposed that once children achieve a particular sociometric status, this social standing, or reputation, will color other children's impressions of their subsequent behavior. Specifically, Hymel contends that positive acts are likely to be attributed to stable internal causes (that is, the child's good character) if displayed by a *liked* peer but to less stable causes (for example, ulterior motives) if displayed by a child who is *disliked*. Conversely, a negative act is likely to be attributed to unstable causes if displayed by a child who is *liked* (for example, he was just kidding around) but to stable ones if the child is *disliked* (for example, she's mean and nasty). If these information-processing biases exist, it is easy to see why rejected children might remain rejected: their positive acts are likely to be interpreted as having few if any implications for their future behavior and will probably be discounted as unimportant, whereas their negative acts are apt to be perceived as indicative of future conduct and, thus, as a basis for continuing to reject these individuals. But do such interpretive biases exist?

To find out, Hymel had second-, fifth-, and tenth-graders think about situations in which either a liked or a disliked peer had done something positive or negative that had personally affected him or her. Here are some examples of these scenarios:

(Langlois, 1985). Attractive youngsters are often described in more favorable terms (for example, friendlier, more intelligent) than their less attractive playmates by both teachers and other children—even *preschool* children (Adams & Crane, 1980; Langlois, 1985). And when unattractive children do something wrong, they are often judged to be "meaner" or more chronically antisocial than an attractive child who commits the same act (Dion, 1972; Lerner & Lerner, 1977). So it seems that we are often swayed by a pretty face and will act as if whatever is beautiful must be good—or at least not too bad.

Attractive children are generally more popular than their less attractive companions, although a pretty face seems to be more of an asset for girls than for boys (Vaughn & Langlois, 1983). This relationship between facial attractiveness and peer acceptance begins to make some sense when we consider how attractive and unattractive children interact with their peers. Attractive and unattractive 3-year-olds do not yet differ a great deal in the character of their social behaviors during structured play settings. But by age 5, unattractive children are more likely than attractive ones to be active and boisterous during play sessions and to respond more aggressively toward their playmates (Langlois & Downs, 1979). So unattractive children do seem to develop patterns of social interaction that could eventually alienate other children.

Why might this happen? Some theorists have argued that parents, teachers, and other children may contribute to a self-fulfilling prophecy by subtly (or not so subtly) communicating to attractive youngsters that they are smart and are expected to do well in school, behave pleasantly, and achieve good relations with peers. Information of this sort undoubtedly has an effect on children. Attractive youngsters may become progressively more confident, friendly, and outgoing, whereas unattractive children who receive less favorable feedback may suffer a loss of self-

BOX 14-2 *continued*

1. The liked (disliked) peer invites (does not invite) you to a birthday party.
2. The liked (disliked) peer helps you pick up papers you dropped (laughs at you for being so clumsy).

Subjects were then asked to explain why the peer in each scenario had behaved as he or she did.

The results were clear. At all three age levels, subjects attributed *positive* behaviors of the liked peer to relatively stable, personal causes (for example, he invited me because he likes me) but felt that the same behavior displayed by a disliked peer was less stable and often attributable to situational factors (for example, her mother made her invite me). By contrast, *negative* behaviors of liked peers were often attributed to unstable, situational causes (for example, he didn't invite me because he ran out of invitations), whereas the same behaviors displayed by a disliked peer were viewed as reflecting personal motives or dispositions (for example, she's mean; she wanted to make me feel bad). Thus, liked peers are given the benefit of the doubt should they respond negatively to their playmates, a finding that helps to explain why accepted children tend to remain accepted. Conversely, disliked children are assigned personal responsibility for their negative antics without gaining appropriate credit for acts of kindness or compassion that might help them to overcome their bad reputations and low social status.

Surely these results have important implications for interventions aimed at improving the peer acceptance of low-status rejectees. For these youngsters, mere acquisition of social skills and improved social behavior may not be enough if their peers subsequently overlook or discount the implications of these positive social overtures. Perhaps the most effective interventions with extremely unpopular children would be those in which social skills training takes place while the unpopular child is attempting to participate in *prosocial* interactions with peers, so that members of the peer group can plainly see that their unpopular classmate is trying to behave acceptably and they should now be more inclined to support and encourage this kind of behavior. Indeed, Karen Bierman (1986) has recently found that improvements in sociometric status were substantially greater for low-status children who received peer support during social skills training than for those who had lacked such encouragement.

esteem and become more resentful, defiant, and aggressive. This is precisely the way in which the aforementioned stereotypes about physically attractive and unattractive children could become a reality (Langlois & Downs, 1979).

Body build (or physique) is another physical attribute that can affect a child's self-concept and popularity with peers. In one study (Staffieri, 1967), 6–10-year-olds were shown full-length silhouettes of *ectomorphic* (thin, linear), *endomorphic* (soft, rounded, chubby), and *mesomorphic* (athletic and muscular) physiques (see Figure 14-7). After stating which body type they preferred, the children were given a list of adjectives and asked to select those that applied to each body type. Finally, each child listed the names of five classmates who were good friends and three classmates whom he or she didn't like very well.

The results were clear. Not only did children prefer the mesomorphic silhouette, they attributed positive adjectives—for example, *brave*, *strong*, *neat*, and *helpful*—to this figure while assigning much less favorable adjectives to the ectomorphic and endomorphic figures. Among the children themselves, there was a definite relationship between body build and popularity: the mesomorphs in the class turned out to be the most popular children, whereas endomorphic classmates were least popular. Later research with adolescents and adults paints a similar picture—mesomorphs are generally popular individuals who often rise to positions of leadership, whereas ectomorphs and particularly endomorphs tend to be much less popular with their peers (Clausen, 1975; Lerner, 1969).

Finally, there are tremendous individual differences in the age at which children reach puberty, and the timing of this maturational milestone can have important social consequences, at least for males.[5] Longitudinal research conducted at the University of California suggests that early-maturing males tend to

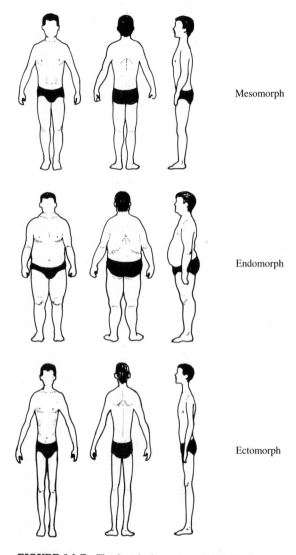

Mesomorph

Endomorph

Ectomorph

FIGURE 14-7 The three body types used in Staffieri's experiment

(Livson & Peskin, 1980; Weatherley, 1964). Finally, it appears that the social advantages associated with early maturation are long-lasting. When retested during their forties, the early maturers from Jones and Bayley's (1950) sample were still more sociable, confident, responsible, and popular with peers than members of the late-maturing group (Jones, 1965).

Why is an early-maturing male in such an advantageous position? Perhaps because adults may react positively to the "adultlike" appearance of an early maturer, affording him privileges and responsibilities normally reserved for older persons. This kind of treatment may promote the sense of poise or self-confidence that enables early maturers to become popular and to assume positions of leadership in the peer group (Eichorn, 1963; Livson & Peskin, 1980). By contrast, if parents, teachers, and peers continue to treat a "boyish looking" late maturer as if he were somehow less worthy of privileges and responsibility, it is easy to see how he could become unsure of himself and feel rejected.

Behavioral characteristics. Although physical characteristics associated with "attractiveness" are meaningful contributors to peer acceptance, even highly attractive children may be very unpopular if playmates consider their conduct inappropriate or antisocial (Langlois & Styczynski, 1979). What behaviors seem to be important in determining a child's standing in the peer group? Shirley Moore (1967) found that popular preschoolers were perceived by their classmates as friendlier, more compliant, and less aggressive than unpopular children. Studies of grade school children find pretty much the same things: popular children are observed to be reasonably calm, outgoing, cooperative, and supportive, whereas neglected children tend to be less talkative and more withdrawn, and extremely unpopular or rejected children can be described as highly active and disruptive braggarts who tend to be snobbish, short-tempered, and aggressive (Coie, Dodge, & Coppotelli, 1982; Coie & Kupersmidt, 1983; Dodge, 1983; French & Wass, 1985).

Do popular children become popular because they are friendly, cooperative, and nonaggressive? Or is it that children become friendlier, more cooperative, and less aggressive after achieving their popularity?

be more poised and confident in social settings and to be overrepresented among pupils who have won athletic honors or student elections. Early maturers were also rated as more attractive, more masculine, less "childish," and less inclined to actively seek others' attention than their later-maturing classmates (Jones & Bayley, 1950). Other investigators report that late-maturing males tend to feel unsure of themselves, socially inadequate, and inferior, and they often express a need for sympathy and understanding

One way to test these competing hypotheses is to place children in play groups with *unfamiliar* peers and then see whether the patterns of behavior they display will predict their eventual status in the peer group. Several studies of this type have been conducted (Coie & Kupersmidt, 1983; Dodge, 1983; Putallaz, 1983), and the results are reasonably consistent: the patterns of behavior that children display do predict the statuses they will achieve with their peers. Children who attain high status in the peer group are quite effective at initiating social interactions and at responding positively to others' bids for attention. Moreover, they first attempt to understand the group's activities and then slowly work their way into the group, so as not to be perceived as pushy, disruptive, and self-serving. By contrast, children who will eventually be rejected by their peers are more likely to force themselves on the group and to insult, threaten, hit, or otherwise mistreat their new playmates—particularly when their intrusive social overtures are not well received. Finally, children who initiate few interactions with their new playmates and who shy away from others' bids for attention are likely to be ignored and neglected.

In sum, children who are accepted by peers tend to be warm and outgoing, and above all, they know how to reward other children. Several kinds of behavior, such as giving attention or approval, cooperating, sharing, asking for information, making useful suggestions, and complying with instructions, will contribute to a child's "rewardingness" and promote (or help to maintain) his or her integration into the peer group. By contrast, selfish, demanding, and aggressive children who are frequently at odds with their playmates are apt to be disliked and rejected, whereas passive youngsters who rarely initiate social contacts run the risk of becoming neglected. Fortunately, both these groups of unpopular children can often be helped to achieve better peer relations through the kinds of social skills training described in Box 7-2.

CHILDREN AND THEIR FRIENDS

As young children become more outgoing and are exposed to a wider variety of peers, they typically form close ties to one or more of their playmates—bonds that we call *friendships*. According to Hartup (1983), true friendships are reciprocal relationships that in some ways resemble the attachments between children and their mothers. In this portion of the chapter, we will first consider how children define friendships and see what they expect from their "special" companions. We will then compare and contrast the social interactions of friends with those of acquaintances and speculate a bit about the role that friends play in a person's social and emotional development.[6]

Children's Conceptions of Friendship

One way to determine what children think about the meaning of friendship is to ask them to tell you (1) what attributes friends should have and (2) what they should be able to expect from a friend. Bigelow (1977; Bigelow & LaGaipa, 1975) tried this approach with Canadian and Scottish first- through eighth-graders and found that children's expectations about friendship progress through three broad stages:

1. *Reward-cost stage.* In this stage, which emerges at about the second or third grade, a friend is a companion who lives nearby, has nice toys, likes to play with me, and plays the way I like to (that is, shares the child's expectations about play activities).

2. *Normative stage.* During grade four or five, shared values and rules become important. Friends are expected to stick up for and be loyal to each other. Friends are also supposed to share possessions, help each other, cooperate, and avoid fighting (Berndt, 1981).

3. *Empathic stage.* Beginning at about the fifth to seventh grade, children begin to see friends as people who share similar interests, who make active attempts to understand each other, and who are willing to self-disclose intimate information (or to listen and respond constructively to the child's own self-disclosures).

Adolescents' expectations about the obligations of friendship represent an extension of this empathic stage, with a little less emphasis on shared interests and a much stronger focus on *reciprocal emotional relations*. For 10- to 11-year-olds, the central obligation of friendship is "to be nice and help each other," whereas 16- to 17-year-olds say that, above all, friends are people whom they can count on for understanding and intimate emotional support (Smollar & Youniss, 1982; Youniss, 1980). So for older adolescents, close friendship seems to imply a unit relation or a "shared identity" in which "me and you" have become a "we" (Hartup, 1983).

Social Interactions between Friends and Acquaintances

Although there is some question whether preschool children form solid, enduring friendships, they do have preferred playmates or "strong associates" (Hinde, Titmus, Easton, & Tamplin, 1985), and they tend to react differently to these youngsters than to mere acquaintances. For example, Masters and Furman (1981) found that nursery-schoolers both give and receive more positive reinforcers (approval, toys, and so forth) when interacting with preferred playmates than with acquaintances, whereas Hinde et al. (1985) noted that punitive or hostile exchanges are more frequent among acquaintances than among strong associates. Strong associates also respond more constructively to strange settings than pairs of unacquainted preschoolers do—suggesting that having a preferred companion seems to reduce a young child's anxiety about uncertain situations and to promote exploration in novel environments (Schwartz, 1972).

Children continue to respond more positively to friends than to nonfriends throughout the grade school years. When 6- to 8-year-olds play a tower-building game under cooperative or competitive guidelines, groups of friends do not necessarily build bigger towers than groups of nonfriends. However, friends are more talkative, pay closer attention to equity rules (for example, "If we take turns, we'll both make more points"), and usually direct their remarks to the group ("Let's do it this way") rather than to each other as individuals ("Put your block over there") (Newcomb, Brady, & Hartup, 1979). Friends don't always agree with each other. But as we noted in Chapter 7, disagreeing friends are more likely than disagreeing acquaintances to fully explain the basis for their conflicting points of view and, thus, provide each other with information that might foster the development of role-taking skills (Nelson

PHOTO 14-4   Sometimes nothing is as reassuring as the affection and encouragement of a friend.

& Aboud, 1985), as well as an ability to compromise.

We have seen that children's conceptions of friendship progress from a somewhat "egocentric" orientation in the early grade school years (that is, friends do what I like to do) to a more "empathic" orientation in later childhood and adolescence (that is, friends should recognize each other's needs and give help or emotional support whenever it is required). These changing views of the obligations of friendship are readily detectable in situations where children must pit their own personal interests against the needs of a friend. Thomas Berndt and his associates (Berndt, Hawkins, & Hoyle, 1986) recently had pairs of fourth-graders and pairs of eighth-graders work on a task in which they could choose to compete (and thereby maximize their own personal outcomes at the expense of the partner) or cooperate (thus enabling both of them to perform the task well). Fourth-graders were observed to compete more with friends than with nonfriends. They tended to view the task as a competitive one and seemed to be especially concerned about the prospect that a close friend would do better and thereby show them up.[7] By contrast, eighth-graders chose to compete more with nonfriends than with friends and were more likely than fourth-graders to say that friends stress equality in their interactions. Clearly, these findings are consistent with the notion that friendships become more other-oriented and mutually supportive as children approach adolescence.

How stable are children's friendships? Friendship networks (that is, the list of *all* individuals the child might nominate as "friends") are not terribly stable over the course of a school year, particularly among younger grade school children. Thomas Berndt and Sally Hoyle (1985) report that first- through fourth-graders typically make more new friends over the course of the year than they lose, whereas eighth-graders are apt to lose more friends than they gain. This latter finding may simply reflect the young adolescent's growing awareness that the obligations of friendship—which now include the exchange of intimate information and the provision of mutual support—are easier to live up to if one selects a smaller circle of very close friends.

Yet there is another side to this "stability" issue. Berndt and his associates (Berndt et al., 1986; Berndt & Hoyle, 1985) find that *"best* friendships" are reasonably stable over the course of a school year, even for first-graders (see Table 14-2). Indeed, it is even possible to predict which pairs of friends will remain friends and which pairs will part company from children's assessments of their friendships at the beginning of a school year: those who remained friendly had earlier rated themselves as more similar to each other and had perceived their relationship as much more intimate than "good friends" had whose friendship eventually dissolved (Berndt et al., 1986; Kandel, 1978).

What Roles Might Friends Play in Social Development?

Do friends play a unique role in a child's social development? Do children who have established adequate peer relations but no close friendships turn out any different from those who have a number of these "special" companions? And might having a close friend or two help to protect a child against the problems associated with having a rejecting parent, being a rejectee in the eyes of most peers, or suffering other stresses such as parental divorce? Unfortunately, no one can answer these questions, for long-term studies of the effects of friendship have yet to be conducted. Nevertheless, the data we have reviewed might permit us to speculate a bit about the roles played by friends as socializing agents.

The fact that children respond more constructively to novel environments in the presence of friends suggests that friendships offer an emotional safety net—a kind of security that not only makes children a little bolder when faced with new challenges but may also make almost any other form of stress (for example, family dissolution, a rejecting parent) a little easier to bear. Indeed, we saw in Chapter 13 that children who respond most constructively to their parents' divorce are those who have the support of friends whose parents are also divorced.

Since friendships are usually described as pleasant or rewarding relationships that are worth preserving, children should be highly motivated to resolve any conflicts with these "special" companions. We've noted that disagreements among friends may foster the development of role-taking skills because friends try harder than acquaintances to fully explain the bases for their conflicting points of view. And given the possibility that one may lose something (or someone) valuable should conflicts remain unresolved, it is likely that squabbles among friends provide an impetus for compromise and cooperation that is simply not present to the same degree in interactions among acquaintances.

Although friendships of all ages are *reciprocal* relationships, we've seen that they are characterized by increasing intimacy and mutuality from middle childhood through adolescence. Could these relatively intense and intimate ties to what are overwhelmingly same-sex companions be necessary for the development of the deep interpersonal sensitivity and commitment so often observed in stable adult love relationships? Harry Stack Sullivan (1953) thought so. Sullivan reported that many of his mentally disturbed patients had failed to form close friendships

TABLE 14-2 Proportions of Best Friendships Remaining Stable over the Course of a School Year

	School grade		
Sex of child	First	Fourth	Eighth
Boys	.52	.77	.73
Girls	.55	.75	.56

when they were young, and he concluded that the close bonds that develop between same-sex friends (or "chums") during preadolescence provide the foundation of caring and compassion that a person needs to establish and maintain intimate love relationships (as well as close friendships) later in life.

So there are good reasons to suspect that close friends and friendships contribute in unique and important ways to social and personality development, and it will be interesting to see whether our speculations pan out in the years ahead as researchers begin to study the long-term implications of having (or not having) friends.

MECHANISMS OF PEER (AND PEER-GROUP) INFLUENCE

To this point, we have seen that it is important for children to establish and maintain good peer relations because they will acquire many competent and adaptive patterns of social behavior through their interactions with peers. And exactly how do peers influence one another? In many of the same ways that parents do—by reinforcing, modeling, and discussing the behaviors and values that they condone.

Peers as Reinforcing Agents

It is easy to see how parents, teachers, and other powerful authority figures are in a position to reward or punish the behavior of children. Yet we might legitimately wonder whether a peer, who shares a similar status with the child, can become an effective agent of reinforcement. Wonder no longer—the evidence is clear: peers are rather potent sources of reinforcement and punishment.

In one study (Wahler, 1967), groups of nursery school children were trained to ignore several of a classmate's social responses and to reinforce others by attending to them. To illustrate the procedure, we will consider the case of Dick, a 5-year-old who frequently threw toys and shouted at his classmates. Two other members of the class were trained to "shape" Dick's behavior by refusing to play with him whenever he made an aggressive response. This particular form of "punishment" brought about a drastic reduction in the frequency of Dick's aggressive behavior and a corresponding increase in the number of

socially appropriate acts, such as playing carefully with the toys. Wahler next instructed the two classmates to reinforce (that is, attend to) Dick's acts of aggression, and the result was a sharp increase in Dick's aggressive activity. Clearly, Dick was modifying his behavior in response to the reinforcements and punishments offered by peers.

Although Wahler's study shows that peers *can* become effective agents of reinforcement, we might wonder whether children *do* reinforce one another to any great extent in their "unprogrammed" day-to-day exchanges on the playground or in the classroom. Michael Lamb and his associates (Lamb, Easterbrooks, & Holden, 1980) hoped to find out by carefully observing how 3- to 5-year-olds reacted when playmates engaged in sex-appropriate or sex-inappropriate (cross-sex) activities. They found that children generally reinforced their companions for sex-appropriate play and were quick to criticize or disrupt a playmate's cross-sex activities. But were these playmates influenced by the treatment they received? Indeed they were. Children who were reinforced for sex-appropriate play tended to keep playing, while those who were punished for sex-inappropriate play usually terminated this activity in less than a minute.

The reinforcers that children provide one another are often subtle or unintentional. For example, if Joey cries or withdraws when Rocky snatches a toy away from him, Joey may be unintentionally *reinforcing* his tormentor's aggressive behavior by allowing Rocky to obtain the toy at little or no cost. If so, Rocky should become more likely to attack Joey in the future. In an observational study of 3–5-year-olds, Gerald Patterson and his associates (Patterson, Littman, & Bricker, 1967) found that the most frequent victims of aggression were those children who often reinforced their attackers by crying, withdrawing, or giving in. And what happens if a victim suddenly begins to "punish" his tormentors by fighting back? Patterson et al. found that this strategy often persuaded the attackers to back off and seek new victims. Of course, victims who learn to repel their tormentors by counterattacking may conclude that aggression is a very rewarding activity and become more aggressive themselves. Indeed, few children remained chronic victims from session to session, and it was not at all unusual for one week's victim to become a later week's victimizer (Patterson et al., 1967).

So peers *are* important sources of social reinforcement. Although we have sampled but three studies from a voluminous literature, the evidence clearly indicates that children's social behaviors are often strengthened, maintained, or virtually eliminated by the favorable or unfavorable reactions they elicit from peers.

Peers as Social Models

Peers influence one another by serving not only as reinforcing and punishing agents but also as social models. For example, children who are afraid of dogs will often overcome their phobic reactions after witnessing a peer (or, better yet, several peers) enjoying themselves while playing with these once-terrifying creatures (Bandura & Menlove, 1968). Among the many other attributes and behaviors that are easily acquired by observing peer models are socially skillful behaviors (Cooke & Apolloni, 1976), achievement behaviors (Sagotsky & Lepper, 1982), moral judgments (Dorr & Fey, 1974), strategies for delaying immediate gratification (Stumphauzer, 1972), and sex-typed attitudes and behaviors (Ruble, Balaban, & Cooper, 1981), to name a few. You may recall that several of these findings were discussed at length in earlier chapters.

Another function that peer models serve is to inform the child how he or she is supposed to behave in different situations. For example, a new child at school may not know whether it is acceptable to visit the water fountain during a study period without first asking the teacher. Yet she will quickly conclude that this behavior is allowed if she sees her classmates doing it.

Finally, children often reach conclusions about their competencies and other personality attributes by comparing their behaviors and accomplishments against those displayed by peers. If a 10-year-old consistently outperforms all her classmates on math tests, she is apt to conclude that she is "smart" or at least "good in math." A 6-year-old who loses every footrace that he has with peers will soon come to think of himself as a slow runner. Because peers are similar in age (and are presumed to be reasonably similar in many other respects), the peer group is the most logical choice for these kinds of social comparisons (see Festinger, 1954; France-Kaatrude & Smith, 1985). It matters little to our "smart" 10-year-old that she knows less math than her teenage sister. And our "snail-like" 6-year-old is not at all comforted by the fact that he can run faster than his 4-year-old brother. In matters of social comparison and self-definition, peers simply have no peer.

Whom do children prefer to imitate? Some peer models will command more attention and are more likely to be imitated than others. For example, youngsters are especially inclined to follow the example of popular children or those who have established friendly relations with them (Hartup, 1983). The age of the model is also important, for kindergartners and grade school children are less likely to imitate the behavior of a younger child than that of an age mate or an older peer (Brody & Stoneman, 1981). And once children acquire gender constancy, at age 5 to 7, they begin to attend more selectively to and would rather imitate models of their own sex (Ruble et al., 1981).

The imitator's effect on the imitated. Do children like to be imitated by their peers? Apparently so. In a recent observational study, Joan Grusec and Rona Abramovitch (1982) found that, when one preschool child imitated another, the model usually reacted very positively to his or her mimic by smiling, laughing, and even imitating the imitator, thereby prolonging a pleasant social interaction. This finding raises an interesting question: Do children learn to imitate their peers as a means of establishing friendly relations or influencing their companions? To find out, Mark Thelen and his associates (Thelen, Miller, Fehrenbach, Frautschi, & Fishbein, 1980) asked some fourth-, fifth-, and sixth-graders to do whatever they could to influence a younger peer to eat some horrible-tasting crackers (social-influence condition). Other children were not asked to influence the behavior of the peer (control condition). Before the crackers were to be eaten, each subject and his or her companion played a game, and the investigators noted how often subjects chose to imitate the strategies of their younger playmates. The results were clear: children who had been told to influence a younger child imitated that child's behavior to a much greater extent than those in the control group did. So it seems that children do like to be imitated and that their imitators know it. And when do children learn to imitate as a means of establishing friendly relations or influencing their playmates? Perhaps as early as age 3, for Steve Dollinger and Melissa Gasser (1981) report that 3–5-year-olds who were instructed to influence a companion reliably chose to imitate the companion's behavior.

Can you imagine a circumstance in which children prefer not to be imitated? Although imitation is generally perceived as a form of flattery, a child who has had a creative idea copied by classmates may be anything but flattered. There is also evidence that children do not like to be imitated by a companion whose status is lower than their own. In one experiment (Thelen & Kirkland, 1976), 8–9-year-olds had solved two problems when they discovered that either an older (high status) or a younger (low status) child was imitating their work. The subjects seemed to enjoy being imitated by the high-status peer, and they were likely to imitate their imitator on later problems. By contrast, children whose efforts had been imitated by the low-status child reported that being imitated was unpleasant, and they often voiced the opinion that their younger imitator had copied their solutions because "he couldn't decide for himself." One implication of these findings is that younger (or other low-status) children may not be very successful at influencing older (or higher-status) associates by imitating their behavior. Indeed, children of higher status may simply consider these imitative responses as additional evidence that their low-status companions are incompetent and perhaps even undesirable as prospective playmates.

The Normative Function of Peer Groups

One of the most important ways that peers influence one another is by forming groups and setting norms that define how group members are supposed to look, think, and act. You may recall from your own childhood that pressures to conform to group norms are often intense and that those who ignore the dictates of their peers risk all sorts of penalties, ranging from simply being labeled a "nerd" to outright rejection. For many youngsters, it is quite an accomplishment to be accepted as "one of the gang" while somehow maintaining respectability in the eyes of parents, teachers, and other important adults.

Characteristics of true "peer groups."   It is difficult to specify the exact age at which group membership becomes important to a child. When social psychologists talk about true "peer groups," they are referring not merely to a collection of playmates but, rather, to a confederation that (1) interacts on a regular basis, (2) defines a sense of belonging, (3) shares implicit or explicit norms that specify how members are supposed to behave, and (4) develops a structure or hierarchal organization that enables the membership to work together toward the accomplishment of shared goals. Older nursery school children do share common interests, assume different roles while playing together, and conform to loosely defined norms or rules of conduct. But the membership of these preschool "play groups" may fluctuate from day to day, and the guidelines to which the children conform are often laid down by adults. The group activities of elementary school children, however, are very different. Members now share norms that *they* have had a hand in creating, and they begin to assume stable roles or "statuses" within the peer society. Moreover, elementary school children clearly identify with their groups; to be a "Brownie," a "Blue Knight," or "one of Smitty's gang" is often a source of great personal pride. So it seems that middle childhood (ages 6–10) is the period when children are assuming membership in what we can call true peer groups.

Under what conditions are a collection of individuals likely to coalesce, forming a true group? Obviously, one prerequisite is that the members of an aggregation be in a position or setting that permits and in some way encourages them to interact regularly. But interaction alone does not necessarily imply the formation of a group. Groups are composed of people who are drawn together by common goals or motives.

The importance of proximity and shared goals to the formation and functioning of children's groups has been demonstrated by Muzafer Sherif and his colleagues (Sherif, Harvey, White, Hood, & Sherif, 1961) in an excellent field experiment known as the "Robber's Cave" study. There were three distinct phases to this classic piece of research, and as we will see in Box 14-3, the results of each phase have taught us important lessons about children's experiences in peer groups.

Conformity to peer pressure. It is often assumed that children become more responsive to peer pressure as they grow older and that adolescence is the period when the peer group has its greatest influence. These assumptions are only partly correct. In highly unfamiliar or ambiguous situations where the appropriate thing to do is not immediately apparent, older adolescents are occasionally found to be more conforming than younger people (Hartup, 1983; Hoving, Hamm, & Galvin, 1969). Yet, if a group of peers is trying to convince a child to partake in questionable conduct or to conform to a judgment that the subject suspects is wrong, there is a curvilinear relationship between age and conformity: children become more conforming between the ages of 6 and 14 but are then less likely to accede to peer pressure from early adolescence onward (Berndt, 1979; Brown, Clasen, & Eicher, 1986; Costanzo & Shaw, 1966). Finally, it is important to note that adolescents are much less likely than younger children to yield to peer influence when the norms or judgments of the peer group are totally lacking in credibility (Hamm, 1970; Hoving et al., 1969). So if a need for peer approval increases as children mature, it seems that this approval motive may often be overridden by a need to be correct!

Age is only one of the many variables that affect a child's willingness to accept influence from peers. For example, children of all ages may find it harder to resist peer pressure in groups with high "group *esprit*" (Sherif, 1956) or in those where virtually everyone endorses the group norms and a potential deviate has little or no prospect of gaining social support for a nonconforming response (Allen & Newtson, 1972; Berenda, 1950). Children are also more likely to yield to their peers if the sources of this influence are older or more competent than they are

(Cohen, Bornstein, & Sherman, 1973; Gelfand, 1962). By contrast, peer pressure from the younger or less competent members of the group is likely to fall on deaf ears. Finally, children of intermediate status conform the most, probably because they hope to become more popular and are trying to improve their status by publicly endorsing the actions and opinions of the peer group (Harvey & Consalvi, 1960).

In sum, we cannot draw any simple conclusions about age trends in conformity, for the patterns that emerge will depend on the type of judgments that children are asked to make, as well as the prestige or competence of the source of influence, the homogeneity of group opinion, and the child's own status within the peer group. But we can say that the stereotype of adolescents as "blind conformists" is a myth, for the evidence we have reviewed indicates that adolescents can easily tolerate differences in opinion when they believe that their own views are correct, and they are more likely than preadolescent children to resist peer pressures in all but the most uncertain situations.

PEER VERSUS ADULT INFLUENCE: THE QUESTION OF CROSS-PRESSURES

Adolescence is often characterized as a stormy period when all children experience "cross-pressures"—severe conflicts between the practices advocated by parents and those favored by peers. How do they react to these conflicting demands? It is commonly assumed that parents and other adults make a stronger impression on the young child but that peers gradually become more influential than parents as children approach adolescence.

Ken Hoving and his associates tested this hypothesis by asking 8-, 10-, 12-, 14-, and 16-year-olds what a child should do in each of ten situations in which parents and peers gave conflicting advice. For example:

> Susan likes music and is trying to decide whether to join the band or the choir. Her *mother and father think* that being in the band would be more fun because the band plays at all the basketball and football games. Susan's *friends think* that she would have more fun in the choir because the choir goes to many different

BOX 14-3   ROBBER'S CAVE: AN EXPERIMENTAL ANALYSIS OF GROUP FORMATION AND INTERGROUP CONFLICT

More than 30 years ago, Muzafer Sherif and his colleagues (Sherif, 1956; Sherif, Harvey, White, Hood, & Sherif, 1961) designed an ingenious field experiment to study the formation and functioning of children's peer groups. The three phases of this experiment and the lessons learned from each are described below.

Phase 1: Group Formation

The 22 subjects who participated in the "Robber's Cave" experiment were 11-year-old boys at a summer camp in Oklahoma. Initially, the campers were divided into two sets and housed in different areas of a large, woodsy preserve. Neither aggregation was aware of the other's presence.

The boys in each aggregation lived closely together and participated in many enjoyable activities such as hiking and crafts, organized games, and the building of "hideouts." To encourage the formation of group structures, camp counselors arranged for the boys to work at tasks requiring them to assume different roles and to coordinate their efforts in order to accomplish shared goals. For example, one evening the boys came to dinner, only to discover that the staff had not prepared the meal. However, the ingredients (for example, raw meat, Kool-Aid, watermelon) were available. Under these circumstances, the hungry boys soon divided the labor: some cooked, others sliced watermelon or mixed drinks, and others either served food or cleaned up. This and other such cooperative activities soon led to the development of cohesive groups. Leaders emerged, individual members assumed different statuses, and each group developed rules or norms to govern its daily activities. The groups even assumed names, becoming the "Eagles" and the "Rattlers."

Let's now summarize this first phase. When previously unacquainted children were thrust together and encouraged to work cooperatively at necessary and/or attractive tasks, they formed cohesive groups, assumed different roles, and developed norms to regulate their interactions and accomplish group goals. But interesting questions remained. For

example, what would happen to "group *esprit*" should the Eagles and Rattlers come in conflict with each other?

Phase 2: Intergroup Conflict

Next, the investigators chose to study intergroup rivalry and its effects on the structure of a peer group. They first arranged for the Eagles and Rattlers to "accidentally" discover each other, and then talked the groups into a series of competitions—baseball games, tugs-of-war, and the like. Prizes were to be awarded to the winners (for example, money, trophies, pocketknives), and the boys practiced intently for the coming events.

Once the competitions began, the investigators were careful to observe the boys' reactions to success and failure. The immediate effect of failure was internal friction, mutual accusation, and blame—in short, decreased group cohesion and a shake-up in the group structure. Thus, when the Rattlers emerged victorious from the first baseball game, Mason (the Eagles' best athlete) threatened to "beat up" certain Eagles if they "didn't try harder" in the future. Craig, the Eagle leader, was eventually deposed for failing to give his all at athletic competition.

As the competitions progressed and boys in each group assumed new statuses, both the Eagles and the Rattlers became more cohesive than ever before. New norms emerged, and increased solidarity within each group was apparent from the hostilities these rival factions displayed toward each other. At first, these exchanges were limited to verbal taunts such as "You're not Eagles, you're pigeons." But after losing a series of contests, the Eagles vented their frustrations by securing the Rattlers' flag and burning it. The Rattlers then lost two consecutive contests, endured the verbal scoffs of the Eagles, and suffered internal disharmony. They finally decided that the Eagles had used unfair tactics in the most recent tug-of-war, and they reacted by staging a raid on the Eagles' cabin, stealing comic books and a pair of jeans belonging to the Eagle leader. The jeans were painted orange and displayed as a flag by the Rattlers.

towns to sing. What do you think Susan will decide to do?

1. Do as her parents say and join the *band*.
2. Do as her friends say and join the *choir*.

Responsiveness to peers increased with age. In other words, the older the subjects, the more likely they

were to discount the advice of parents and favor the opinions of the peer group (Hamm & Hoving, 1971; Utech & Hoving, 1969). Berndt (1979) found a similar pattern of results, noting that peer influence increases most dramatically with age (at least through early adolescence) on matters of *antisocial* conduct.

BOX 14-3   *continued*

Armed with rocks, the Eagles started on a retaliatory raid, but the counselors stopped them before any serious injuries could result.

So the second phase of the experiment revealed that intergroup conflict may bring about changes in the internal structures of rivaling groups, particularly within the group that is placed in a subordinate position by losing. As conflict continues, members of opposing groups develop strong "we versus they" attitudes that help to reestablish a sense of ingroup solidarity and to maintain the group's animosity toward its rivals.

Phase 3: Reducing Intergroup Hostility

Sherif and his associates had created a monster. By the end of phase 2, the Eagles and Rattlers had reached a point at which their contacts with each other invariably resulted in name calling, threats, and fisticuffs. The third phase of the experiment was designed to reduce these hostilities.

It soon became apparent that intergroup conflicts were easier to create than to reduce. One of the first strategies was to bring the boys together in a pleasant, noncompetitive setting—for example, at the movies. This plan failed miserably: the boys used these occasions to call each other names and squabble, and if anything, the hostilities became even more intense. Several other ploys were tried and found ineffective. For example, both groups attended religious services emphasizing cooperation and brotherly love, but they reverted to their rivalrous conduct immediately after the services were over. "Summit" meetings between the two group leaders were not attempted, for it was felt that any concessions made by the leaders would be interpreted by followers as traitorous behavior.

Finally, Sherif et al. devised a strategy that they thought would work. If the two groups were to face common problems that could not be solved by either group working alone, they would be forced to "pull together," and intergroup hostilities should decrease. The counselors then cleverly engineered a series of these common problems, or

"superordinate goals." On one occasion the Eagles and the Rattlers pooled their money to rent an interesting film when it appeared that neither group had the resources to rent it on its own. On another occasion, when everyone was hungry and the camp truck would not start, the boys combined their efforts to get the truck going so that they would have supplies for dinner that night. As a result of these and other cooperative exchanges, the two groups became much less antagonistic toward each other. In fact, friendships developed across group lines, and the Eagles, who had won a monetary prize in the previous athletic competition, ended up using the money to treat their former rivals. Sherif has summarized these results in the following way:

> What our limited experiments have shown is that the possibilities for achieving harmony are greatly enhanced when groups are brought together to work toward common ends. Then favorable information about a disliked group is seen in a new light, and leaders are in a position to take bolder steps toward cooperation. In short, hostility gives way when groups pull together to achieve overriding goals which are real and compelling to all concerned [Sherif, 1956, p. 58].

Surely the results of phase 3 are applicable far beyond the camp setting in which they were obtained. Although feelings have waxed and waned over the years, Americans and Russians typically become much more positive in their perceptions of each other whenever their governments are actively pressing for the attainment of a shared goal—halting the arms race. Perhaps the only way to reduce well-ingrained animosities between groups such as Arabs and Israelis, English and French Canadians, or South African Blacks and Whites is for leaders of these rival factions to identify common problems that must be solved and that neither group is likely to resolve without the other's cooperation. In some cases it will not be easy for opposing forces to identify superordinate goals. But in any case, the search for a common ground will surely prove far less costly in terms of both economic and human resources than a continuation and possible escalation of intense intergroup conflicts.

Similarly, Ed Bixenstine and his colleagues (Bixenstine, DeCorte, & Bixenstine, 1976) found an increase between the ages of 9 and 16 in children's readiness to participate in mischievous acts designed to annoy adults (for example, soaping windows on Halloween).

Situational Determinants of Children's Reactions to Cross-Pressures

Although children become increasingly responsive to peer influence as they mature, there are some situations in which they typically react to cross-pressures by siding with parents rather than peers. *Peers* are likely to be more influential than parents in conflicts involving status norms, friendship choices, or questions of personal and group identity (Brittain, 1963; Hunter, 1985; Sebald & White, 1980). However, adolescents generally prefer the advice of *parents* to that of peers whenever the situation involves scholastic achievement, academic choices, or future aspirations. Perhaps it is fair to say that peers are the primary reference group for questions of the form "Who am I?," whereas the advice of parents, teachers, and other significant adults will carry more weight whenever a teenager grapples with the question "Who am I to be?"

Just How Important Are These Cross-Pressures?

After reviewing much of the available literature, Willard Hartup (1983) concluded that cross-pressures are not nearly so disruptive as they were once thought to be. Adolescents who have established warm relationships with conventional and controlling (that is, nonpermissive) parents seem to experience fewer conflicts of this type (Bixenstine et al., 1976; Brook, Whiteman, & Gordon, 1983). And even when teenagers are at odds with a parent over status issues, privileges, or academic matters, these disagreements do not necessarily make them any more susceptible to peer influence. In fact, Raymond Montemayor (1982) finds that adolescents who argue a lot with their mothers will often react to these conflicts by spending more time alone or with their fathers rather than becoming more involved with peers.

But perhaps the major reason that the cross-pressures "problem" is not a problem for most adolescents is that the values of the peer group are rarely as deviant as people have commonly assumed. Indeed, even though children perceive more peer pressure for deviant or antisocial conduct as they mature, it is important to emphasize that one's friends and associates are more likely to advise *against* or otherwise *discourage* antisocial behavior than to condone it (Brown et al., 1986). And on many issues for which parental and peer norms might seem to be in conflict, the child's behavior is actually a product of *both* parental and peer influences. Consider the fol-

lowing example. Denise Kandel (1973) studied a group of adolescents whose best friends either did or did not smoke marijuana and whose parents either did or did not use psychoactive drugs. Among those teenagers whose parents used drugs but whose friends did not, only 17% were marijuana users. When parents did not use drugs but best friends did, 56% of the adolescents were marijuana users. From these findings, we can conclude that the peer group is more influential than parents over marijuana use. However, the highest rate of marijuana smoking (67%) occurred among teenagers whose parents and peers *both* used psychoactive drugs, and a similar pattern emerges when we look at parental and peer influences on use of alcohol and tobacco (Chassin, Pressin, Sherman, Montello, & McGrew, 1986; Glynn, 1981; Krosnick & Judd, 1982). The implication of these findings is clear: rather than thinking about childhood or adolescent socialization as an issue of parents *versus* peers, we must now determine how parental and peer influences combine to affect developing children.

Some theorists have argued that peers eventually become the primary reference group on issues for which the opinions of an individual's parents and peers are generally *similar* but *varying in extremity* (for example, ideas about an acceptable curfew, appropriate conduct on a date, or access to the family car). Although this conclusion may well be correct, it may also underestimate the full impact of adult influence because the way peers feel about a particular behavior is often an expression of the *average level of parental support* for that behavior among the parents of *all* group members (Siman, 1977). For example, if a 17-year-old stays out with her friends until 11 P.M. when her parents want her in at 10, she may be returning home at a time that her friends' parents think is perfectly acceptable. She is rebellious by her parents' standards but not by those of other parents or the peer group. So parents have an effect on peer-group norms, and an adolescent's response to many issues may depend more on the group atmosphere (that is, the average parental opinion) than on the position of her own parents. The implication is that peer groups may act as a filter for the attitudes and opinions of individual parents, serving to reinterpret these standards as reasonable or unreasonable and thereby exerting a powerful influence on an adolescent's attitudes, values, and behavior.

Cross-Cultural Variations in Peer Influences

We have seen that the peer group plays a very important role in the social and emotional development of American children. However, the United States is often characterized as a rather atypical, youth-oriented culture whose younger constituents (and, indeed, many of their elders) seem obsessed with the notions that "young is beautiful" and that "people over 30 are not to be trusted." This perspective is very different from that of many Oriental cultures, in which children soon learn to respect their elders and to treat the ideas of the aged as "words of wisdom" (Benedict, 1946; DeVos & Hippler, 1969). In many nonindustrialized societies, young boys and girls are routinely assigned chores and responsibilities that restrict their opportunities for play (Leacock, 1971), and children in certain ethnic groups within Western societies may spend little time with peers because they are strongly encouraged to stay at home for family activities (DeVos & Hippler, 1969; Laosa, 1981). So there are reasons to believe that patterns of peer interaction and the nature of peer-group influences may vary considerably from culture to culture.

To date, the most extensive work on peer-group influences in other societies has been conducted by Urie Bronfenbrenner and his colleagues at Cornell University (Bronfenbrenner, 1967; Bronfenbrenner, Devereux, Suci, & Rodgers, 1965; Devereux, 1970). The subjects for these studies were 11–12-year-olds from England, Germany, the Soviet Union, and the United States. The children were asked to respond to a "dilemmas test" that consisted of 30 hypothetical situations, each of which pitted a norm endorsed by adults against peer pressure to deviate from that norm. Here is an example (Bronfenbrenner, 1967, p. 201):

> You and your friends accidentally find a sheet of paper which the teacher must have lost. On this sheet are the questions and answers for a quiz that you are going to have tomorrow. Some of the kids suggest

that you not say anything to the teacher about it, so that all of you can get better marks. What would you really do? Suppose that your friends decide to go ahead. Would you go along with them or refuse?

Refuse to go along with my friends
Absolutely certain   Fairly certain   I guess so
or
Go along with my friends
Absolutely certain   Fairly certain   I guess so

Other dilemmas included situations such as neglecting homework to be with friends, wearing fashions approved by peers but not adults, and collaborating with friends to steal fruit from an orchard marked with "No Trespassing" signs.

Bronfenbrenner found that Russian children showed the greatest resistance to these deviant peer influences. U.S. and German children were more likely to go along with their peers than the Russians were, and English children showed the greatest willingness to take part in peer-sponsored misconduct. In all four cultures, boys showed less conformity to adult norms than girls.

Further analyses revealed that the U.S., English, and German children who spent the most time with their peers were the ones who were most likely to say that they would participate in the deviant activities of the peer group. Yet the amount of contact that a child had with peers was not the only factor that influenced his or her reactions to peer pressure. Both Soviet and American children have a great deal of contact with their peers during the first few years at school. However, these two groups react to examples of peer-sponsored misconduct in very different ways. Consider the following example.

Bronfenbrenner (1967) had Russian and American children take his "dilemmas test" under three conditions: (1) a *neutral* condition in which they were told that their answers would be confidential, (2) an *adult exposure* condition in which they believed that their answers would be seen by parents and teachers, and (3) a *peer exposure* condition in which they were told that their answers would be shown to their classmates. In both cultures, children assigned to the adult-exposure condition were more likely than those in the neutral condition to conform to the socially desirable (adult) norms. However, the peer-exposure condition produced different reactions from the Soviet and the American samples. Soviet children responded as if their answers would be shown to adults—that is, their conformity to adult norms *increased* compared with their classmates in the neutral condition. By contrast, American children became much more willing to conform to the *deviant peer norms* when they were led to believe that classmates would see their answers.

So here are two groups of children, both of whom have a substantial amount of contact with their peers. Yet members of one group (the Americans) often support peer-sponsored misconduct, while members of the second group (the Russians) do not. The reasons for this cultural difference become clearer if we look carefully at how Soviet children are socialized. Bronfenbrenner (1970a) points out that Russian educators use the peer group as an instrument for teaching and continually reinforcing the important sociopolitical values of Soviet society—values such as cooperation, teamwork, and group *esprit*. Children in a typical Russian classroom are divided into teams and encouraged to take part in cooperative, team-oriented activities. These teams frequently test their physical and academic skills against one another in regularly scheduled competitions, and group spirit is strengthened by administering rewards on the basis of team, rather than individual, accomplishments. Not surprisingly, Russian children learn to evaluate the individual in terms of his or her contributions to group goals, and indeed, they are instructed to keep tabs on their teammates, to assist them whenever possible, and to censure those who do not "pull their weight." These lessons are apparently learned at an early age, as we see in the following conversations among third-graders from a Russian school:

"Work more carefully" says Olga to her girlfriend. "See, on account of you our group got behind today. You come to me and we'll work together at home."
Group leader to his classmates: "Today Valodya did the wrong problem. Marsha didn't write neatly and forgot to underline the right words in her lesson. Alyosha had a dirty shirt collar" [Bronfenbrenner, 1970a, p. 60].

In sum, the Soviet peer group is an extension of the adult sociopolitical system, whereas in the United States, children are given a bit more leeway to evolve their own rules, norms, and customs—some of which will inevitably conflict with adult standards. Clearly, the peer group is an important socializing agent for both Russian and American children, and it would be inappropriate to conclude that Russians are less responsive than Americans to peer-group pressure. In fact, the Russian schoolchildren in Bronfenbrenner's (1967) study probably refused to endorse the misconduct of *hypothetical* peers because they expected little if any approval from their *real* classmates for doing so.

SUMMARY

In this chapter we have focused on three extrafamilial agents of socialization: television, schools, and children's peer groups. When television became widely available, children soon began to watch it and spend less time in other leisure activities. Programming on American television is often violent, and there is evidence that a heavy diet of televised violence can instigate antisocial behavior and make children more tolerant of aggression. Television is also an important source of knowledge about people in the outside world. But, unfortunately, the information that children receive is often inaccurate and misleading—frequently consisting of stereotyped portrayals of men, women, and various racial and ethnic groups. Children are also influenced by television commercials, and they may become angry or resentful if a parent refuses to buy a product that they have requested.

Yet the effects of television are not all bad. Children are likely to learn prosocial lessons and to put them into practice after watching acts of kindness on either commercial or educational programs. Parents can help by watching shows such as *Mister Rogers' Neighborhood* with their children and then encouraging them to verbalize or role-play the prosocial lessons they have observed. Educational programs such as *Sesame Street* and *The Electric Company* have been quite successful at fostering basic cognitive skills, particularly when children watch with an adult who discusses the material with them and helps them to apply what they have learned.

By age 6, children are spending several hours of each weekday at school. Schools seem to have two missions: to impart academic knowledge and to teach children how to become "good citizens." Schooling also appears to facilitate cognitive development by teaching children general rules, or intellectual strategies, that help them to solve problems. However, the differences between educated and uneducated people are likely to be small on any intellectual task that does not depend on the use of cognitive strategies that are acquired at school.

Some schools are more "effective" than others at producing positive outcomes such as low absenteeism, an enthusiastic attitude about learning, academic achievement, occupational skills and socially desirable patterns of behavior. Several factors, such as a school's resources, school and class size, and the ways classes and classrooms are organized, have been proposed as possible contributors to effective schooling. It turns out that "effective" schools are those in which the staff works together to achieve well-defined educational objectives. Teachers are helpful and supportive rather than commanding and punitive. The emphasis is on pupils' successes rather than failures, and students receive ample praise and recognition for good work. In short, the effective school environment is a comfortable but businesslike setting in which pupils are motivated to learn.

Traditionally, the task of motivating students has been assigned to classroom instructors. Teacher expectancies may create a self-fulfilling prophecy: students usually do well when teachers expect them to succeed, whereas they tend to fall short of their potential when teachers expect them to do poorly. Teaching style can also affect pupil outcomes. Generally speaking, it appears that an authoritative style is more likely than either authoritarian or permissive instruction to motivate students to do their best. Yet even the authoritative teacher may have to use different instructional techniques with different children in order to "get the most out of" each pupil.

The middle-class bias of most schools may hinder the academic progress of disadvantaged children or those from minority subcultures. Textbooks and other materials tend to portray middle-class values and experiences that may seem irrelevant and uninteresting to these students. Parents of lower-class children are often less knowledgeable about the school system, less involved in school activities, and less likely to encourage their children to excel in the classroom. Middle-class teachers are often more negative in their interactions with lower-class students and do not expect them to do well. All these factors may contribute to the low levels of academic achievement often seen among lower-class and minority populations. It was hoped that school desegregation would help to cure some of these ills. Although minority students often do achieve more in integrated schools, there is little evidence that desegregation has accomplished other important goals such as reducing racial prejudice or raising minority students' self-esteem.

Peer contacts represent a second world for children—a world of equal-status interactions that is very different from the nonegalitarian environment of the home. Contacts with peers increase dramatically with age, and during the preschool or early elementary school years, children are spending at least as much of their leisure time with peers as with adults. The "peer group" consists mainly of *same sex* playmates of *different* ages. Indeed, developmentalists define peers as "those who interact at similar levels of behavioral complexity," because only a small percentage of the child's associates are actually age mates.

Research with monkeys and young children indicates that peer contacts are important for the development of competent and adaptive patterns of social behavior. Children who fail to establish and maintain adequate relations with their peers will run the risk of experiencing any number of severe emotional disturbances later in life. Among the factors that contribute to peer acceptance are secure emotional attachments to parents, physical attributes such as an attractive face, a mesomorphic physique, and early maturation, a popular name, good role-taking skills, and being a later-born child. Popular children are generally friendlier, more supportive, more cooperative, and less aggressive than unpopular children.

Children typically form close ties, or friendships, with one or more members of their play groups. Younger children view a friend as a harmonious playmate, whereas older children and adolescents think of friends as intimate companions who share similar interests and are willing to provide them with emotional support when it is needed. Interactions among friends are more positive and harmonious than those among mere acquaintances, and best friendships tend to be reasonably stable over time. Although the roles that friends play in a child's social development have not been firmly established, it is likely that solid friendships (1) provide a sense of security that enables children to respond more constructively to stresses and challenges, (2) promote the development of role-taking skills and an ability to compromise, and (3) foster the growth of caring and compassionate feelings that are the foundation of intimate love relationships later in life.

Peers influence one another in many of the same ways that parents do—by modeling, reinforcing, and discussing the behaviors and values they condone. During middle childhood, youngsters who pursue similar interests and who work together to accomplish shared goals may coalesce into a group, assume different roles or statuses, and create sets of norms to govern their group-related activities. Intergroup conflict often heightens within-group solidarity but also triggers acts of hostility between groups. Fortunately, these hostilities can be reduced if rivalrous groups work together to achieve common goals.

A variety of factors affect a young person's responsiveness to peer pressures. Children are more likely to accept influence from peers if the source of influence is competent or has high status, if they themselves have intermediate status in the group, or if other members of the group strongly endorse the group norms. Clearly, the stereotype of adolescents as "blind conformists" is a myth, for adolescents can easily tolerate differences of opinion when they believe their own views are correct, and they are more likely than preadolescents to resist peer pressures in all but the most uncertain situations.

Children's reactions to cross-pressures depend on their age and the issue in question. In situations involving status norms, friendship choices, or questions of personal and group identity, children become

increasingly responsive to peers as they mature. But even older children and adolescents prefer the advice of parents to that of peers in situations involving scholastic matters or future aspirations. Cross-pressures are not a major problem for most children, because the values of the peer group tend to be consistent with those of parents and other adults, and the child's behavior is usually a product of both parental and peer influence.

The influence of peer groups may differ somewhat from culture to culture. For example, the Soviet peer group is a mechanism for teaching and maintaining the adult value system, and compliance with adult norms is rather uniform. By contrast, American children are allowed greater freedom to formulate their own rules, norms, and customs, some of which will inevitably conflict with adult standards.

NOTES

1. Indeed, aspects of the "informal curriculum" such as cooperation, fair play, and healthy attitudes toward competition are often emphasized more in *extracurricular* activities than in the classroom. Moreover, we will see later in the chapter that good peer relations are an important contributor to a child's (or adolescent's) personal adjustment and mental health. So there are indeed good reasons for believing that attending a small school may be advantageous if the small-school atmosphere truly encourages students to participate in the structured extracurricular activities with their peers.

2. This letter appears by permission of its author and its recipient, Dr. Shirley G. Moore.

3. The practice of asking children to make "negative" choices by saying whom they dislike is very controversial. Some investigators (for example, Moore, 1967) point out that this procedure contradicts the adult's usual tendency to discourage children from making rejecting statements about their peers, and the feeling is that, if children are allowed to state these negative opinions, they may subsequently behave much more negatively toward associates they dislike. Clearly this is an issue that deserves intensive study. However, early returns with preschool children (see Hayvren & Hymel, 1984) suggest that youngsters who make negative peer nominations are *not* inclined to start criticizing, ridiculing, or responding negatively to the children they have just rejected on the sociometric test.

4. Recently, investigators have found that a small percentage of children in many peer groups seem to fit into none of these four categories. These latter children have

been labeled "controversial" because they are clearly accepted by a sizable number of peers but actively disliked by many others (Bukowski & Newcomb, 1985; Dodge, 1983). Not only do these youngsters display "mixed" popularity, but their social behaviors are highly variable: they may be as prosocially inclined as the most popular youngsters in the group but also high in antisocial activities such as aggressive play and excluding peers from play activities. They are a particularly interesting group because these controversial children do not remain controversial forever. In fact, one study found that nearly 60% of children initially classified as controversial had achieved another status in the peer group over intervals as brief as one month (Newcomb & Bukowski, 1984). Thus, it may be possible to learn a great deal about the origins of peer acceptance by concentrating on these controversial youngsters and determining how they either win over those who initially dislike them and become "accepted" or finally alienate their allies and become "rejectees."

5. Although early-maturing girls are sometimes found to be *less* popular than those who reach puberty late or "on time" (Clausen, 1975; Faust, 1960), this "timing of puberty" effect is not large and does not last very long. Why does it appear at all? Possibly because early-maturing girls perceive more conflicts with parents, who themselves are feeling the strain of now having to closely regulate the behavior of a sexually mature daughter (see Savin-Williams & Small, 1986). This conflictual relation with parents could then color the girl's interactions with peers in ways that temporarily depress her social standing in the peer group.

6. Unfortunately, this discussion must be somewhat speculative in that friendship has not been studied as extensively as it should be. We do know a fair amount about developmental changes in children's conceptions of friendship, but it remains for future research to determine whether having close friends has effects on social development above and beyond those associated with the establishment and maintenance of good peer relations.

7. Of course, this finding does not imply that younger grade-schoolers are always so unresponsive to the needs of close friends. In fact, grade-school children are often more inclined to share possessions with friends than with acquaintances during free-play sessions, and they are generally more willing to assist friends than acquaintances on *noncompetitive* tasks that do not compromise their own self-interests (see Berndt, 1981; Hartup, 1983).

REFERENCES

ADAMS, G. R., & Crane, P. (1980). An assessment of parents' and teachers' expectations of preschool children's social preference for attractive or unattractive children and adults. *Child Development, 51,* 224–231.

ADAMS, R. S., & Biddle, B. J. (1970). *Realities of teaching.* New York: Holt, Rinehart and Winston.

ALEXANDER, B. K., & Harlow, H. F. (1965). Social behavior in juvenile rhesus monkeys subjected to different rearing conditions during the first 6 months of life. *Zoologische Jarbucher Physiologie, 60,* 167–174.

ALLEN, V. L., & Newtson, D. (1972). Development of conformity and independence. *Journal of Personality and Social Psychology, 22,* 18–30.

AMES, L. B. (1981, March). Retention in grade can be a step forward. *Education Digest,* pp. 36–37.

ANDERSON, D. R., Lorch, E. P., Field, D. E., & Sanders, J. (1981). The effects of TV program comprehensibility on preschool children's visual attention to television. *Child Development, 52,* 151–157.

ASHER, S. R., & Dodge, K. A. (1986). Identifying children who are rejected by their peers. *Developmental Psychology, 22,* 444–449.

ASHER, S. R., & Wheeler, V. A. (1985). Children's loneliness: A comparison of rejected and neglected peer status. *Journal of Consulting and Clinical Psychology, 53,* 500–505.

ATKIN, C. (1978). Observation of parent-child interaction in supermarket decision-making. *Journal of Marketing, 42,* 41–45.

BALL, S., & Bogatz, G. (1973). *Reading with television: An evaluation of* The Electric Company. Princeton, NJ: Educational Testing Service.

BANDURA, A., & Menlove, F. L. (1968). Factors determining vicarious extinction of avoidance behavior through symbolic modeling. *Journal of Personality and Social Psychology, 8,* 99–108.

BARCUS, F. E. (1978). *Commercial children's television on weekends and weekday afternoons.* Newtonville, MA: Action for Children's Television.

BARKER, R. G., & Gump, P. V. (1964). *Big school, small school.* Stanford, CA: Stanford University Press.

BARKER, R. G., & Wright, H. F. (1955). *Midwest and its children.* New York: Harper & Row.

BAUMRIND, D. (1967). Child care practices anteceding three patterns of preschool behavior. *Genetic Psychology Monographs, 75,* 43–88.

BAUMRIND, D. (1972). From each according to her ability. *School Review, 80,* 161–197.

BENEDICT, R. (1946). *The chrysanthemum and the sword.* Boston: Houghton Mifflin.

BERENDA, R. W. (1950). *The influence of the group on the judgments of children.* New York: King's Crown Press.

BERNDT, T. J. (1979). Developmental changes in conformity to peers and parents. *Developmental Psychology, 15,* 608–616.

BERNDT, T. J. (1981). Age changes and changes over time in prosocial intentions and behavior between friends. *Developmental Psychology, 17,* 408–416.

BERNDT, T. J., Hawkins, J. A., & Hoyle, S. G. (1986). Changes in friendship during a school year: Effects on children's and adolescents' impressions of friendship and sharing with friends. *Child Development, 57,* 1284–1297.

BERNDT, T. J., & Hoyle, S. G. (1985). Stability and change in childhood and adolescent friendships. *Developmental Psychology, 21,* 1007–1015.

BIERMAN, K. L. (1986). Process of change during social skills training with preadolescents and its relation to treatment outcome. *Child Development, 57,* 230–240.

BIGELOW, B. J. (1977). Children's friendship expectations: A cognitive-developmental study. *Child Development, 48,* 246–253.

BIGELOW, B. J., & LaGaipa, J. J. (1975). Children's written descriptions of friendship: A multidimensional analysis. *Developmental Psychology, 11,* 857–858.

BIXENSTINE, V. C., DeCorte, M. S., & Bixenstine, B. A. (1976). Conformity to peer-sponsored misconduct at four grade levels. *Developmental Psychology, 12,* 226–236.

BOGATZ, G. A., & Ball, S. (1972). *The second year of Sesame Street: A continuing evaluation.* Princeton, NJ: Educational Testing Service.

BOOCOCK, S. S. (1976). Children in contemporary society. In A. Skolnik (Ed.), *Rethinking childhood.* Boston: Little, Brown.

BRITTAIN, C. V. (1963). Adolescent choices and parent-peer cross pressures. *American Sociological Review, 28,* 358–391.

BRODY, G. H., & Stoneman, Z. (1981). Selective imitation of same-age, older, and younger peer models. *Child Development, 52,* 717–720.

BRONFENBRENNER, U. (1967). Response to pressures from peers versus adults in Soviet and American school children. *International Journal of Psychology, 2,* 199–207.

BRONFENBRENNER, U. (1970a). *Two worlds of childhood.* New York: Russell Sage Foundation.

BRONFENBRENNER, U. (1970b). *Who cares for America's children?* Invited address presented at the Conference of the National Association for the Education of Young Children, Washington, DC.

BRONFENBRENNER, U., Devereux, E. C., Suci, G., & Rodgers, R. R. (1965). *Adults and peers as sources of conformity and autonomy.* Paper presented at the Conference for Socialization for Competence, San Juan, PR.

BROOK, J. S., Whiteman, M., & Gordon, A. S. (1983). Stages of drug use in adolescence: Personality, peer, and family correlates. *Developmental Psychology, 19,* 269–277.

BROOKOVER, W., Beady, C., Flood, P., Schweitzer, J., & Wisenbaker, J. (1979). *School social systems and student achievement: Schools can make a difference.* New York: Praeger.

BROPHY, J. E. (1979). Teacher behavior and its effects. *Journal of Educational Psychology, 71,* 733–750.

BROPHY, J. E. (1983). Research on the self-fulfilling prophecy and teacher expectations. *Journal of Educational Psychology, 75,* 631–661.

BROWN, B. B., Clasen, D. R., & Eicher, S. A. (1986). Perceptions of peer pressure, peer conformity dispositions, and self-reported behavior among adolescents. *Developmental Psychology, 22,* 521–530.

BROWN, J. R. (1976). *Children and television.* Beverly Hills, CA: Sage.

BUKOWSKI, W. M., & Newcomb, A. F. (1985). Variability in peer group perceptions: Support for the "controversial" sociometric classification group. *Developmental Psychology, 21,* 1032–1038.

CHASE, J. A. (1968). A study of the impact of grade retention on primary school children. *Journal of Psychology, 70,* 169–177.

CHASSIN, L., Presson, C. C., Sherman, S. J., Montello, D., & McGrew, J. (1986). Changes in peer and parent influence during adolescence: Longitudinal versus cross-sectional perspectives on smoking initiation. *Developmental Psychology, 22,* 327–334.

CLARK, K. B. (1965). *Dark ghetto.* New York: Harper & Row.

CLAUSEN, J. A. (1975). The social meaning of differential physical maturation. In D. Drugastin & G. H. Elder (Eds.), *Adolescence in the life cycle.* New York: Halsted Press.

COHEN, R., Bornstein, R., & Sherman, R. C. (1973). Conformity behavior of children as a function of group makeup and task ambiguity. *Developmental Psychology, 9,* 124–131.

COIE, J. D., & Dodge, K. A. (1983). Continuities and changes in children's social status: A five-year longitudinal study. *Merrill-Palmer Quarterly, 19,* 261–282.

COIE, J. D., Dodge, K. A., & Coppotelli, H. (1982). Dimensions and types of social status: A cross-age perspective. *Developmental Psychology, 18,* 557–570.

COIE, J. D., & Krehbiel, G. (1984). Effects of academic tutoring on the social status of low-achieving, socially rejected children. *Child Development, 55,* 1465–1478.

COIE, J. D., & Kupersmidt, J. B. (1983). A behavioral analysis of emerging social status in boys' groups. *Child Development, 54,* 1400–1416.

COLEMAN, W. T., & Selby, J. J. (1983). *Educating Americans for the 21st century.* Washington, DC: National Science Foundation.

COMMONS, M. L., Richards, F. A., & Kuhn, D. (1982). Systematic and metasystematic reasoning: A case for levels of reasoning beyond Piaget's stage of formal operations. *Child Development, 53,* 1058–1069.

CONNOLLY, J. A., & Doyle, A. (1984). Relation of social fantasy play to social competence in preschoolers. *Developmental Psychology, 20,* 797–806.

COOK, T. D., Appleton, H., Conner, R. F., Shaffer, A., Tabkin, G., & Weber, J. S. (1975). Sesame Street *revisited.* New York: Russell Sage Foundation.

COOKE, T., & Apolloni, T. (1976). Developing positive social-emotional behaviors: A study of training and generalization effects. *Journal of Applied Behavior Analysis, 9,* 65–78.

COPPERMAN, P. (1978). *The literacy hoax.* New York: Morrow.

COSTANZO, P. R., & Shaw, M. E. (1966). Conformity as a function of age level. *Child Development, 37,* 967–975.

COWEN, E. L., Pederson, A., Babigan, H., Izzo, L. D., & Trost, M. A. (1973). Long-term follow-up of early detected vulnerable children. *Journal of Consulting and Clinical Psychology, 41,* 438–446.

DEVEREUX, E. C. (1970). The role of peer group experience in moral development. In J. P. Hill (Ed.), *Minnesota Symposia on Child Psychology* (Vol. 4). Minneapolis: University of Minnesota Press.

DeVOS, G. A., & Hippler, A. A. (1969). Cultural psychology: Comparative studies of human behavior. In G. Lindzey & E. Aronson (Eds.), *Handbook of social psychology* (Vol. 4). Reading, MA: Addison-Wesley.

DION, K. K. (1972). Physical attractiveness and evaluations of children's transgressions. *Journal of Personality and Social Psychology, 24,* 207–213.

DODGE, K. A. (1983). Behavioral antecedents of peer social status. *Child Development, 54,* 1386–1399.

DOLLINGER, S. J., & Gasser, M. (1981). Imitation as social influence. *Journal of Genetic Psychology, 138,* 149–150.

DORR, D., & Fey, S. (1974). Relative power of symbolic adult and peer models in the modification of children's moral choice behavior. *Journal of Personality and Social Psychology, 29,* 335–341.

DWECK, C. S., & Elliott, E. S. (1983). Achievement motivation. In E. M. Hetherington (Ed.), *Handbook of child psychology* (Vol. 4). New York: Wiley.

EDUCATIONAL RESEARCH SERVICE. (1978). *Class size: A summary of research.* Arlington, VA: Author.

EICHORN, D. H. (1963). Biological correlates of behavior. In H. W. Stevenson (Ed.), *Child psychology.* Chicago: University of Chicago Press.

ELLIS, S., Rogoff, B., & Cromer, C. C. (1981). Age segregation in children's social interactions. *Developmental Psychology, 17,* 399–407.

ERON, L. D., Huesmann, L. R., Brice, P., Fischer, P., & Mermelstein, R. (1983). Age trends in the development of aggression, sex-typing, and related television habits. *Developmental Psychology, 19,* 71–77.

FAUST, M. S. (1960). Developmental maturity as a determinant of prestige in adolescent girls. *Child Development, 31,* 173–184.

FESTINGER, L. (1954). A theory of social comparison processes. *Human Relations, 7,* 117–140.

FINKELSTEIN, N. W., & Haskins, R. (1983). Kindergarten children prefer same-color peers. *Child Development, 54,* 502–508.

FRANCE-KAATRUDE, A., & Smith, W. P. (1985). Social comparison, task motivation, and the development of self-evaluative standards in children. *Developmental Psychology, 21,* 1080–1089.

FRENCH, D. C. (1984). Children's knowledge of the social functions of younger, older, and same-age peers. *Child Development, 55,* 1429–1433.

FRENCH, D. C., & Wass, G. A. (1985). Behavioral problems of peer-neglected and peer-rejected elementary-age children: Parent and teacher perspectives. *Child Development, 56,* 246–252.

FREUD, A., & Dann, S. (1951). An experiment in group upbringing. In R. Eisler, A. Freud, H. Hartmann, & E. Kris (Eds.), *The psychoanalytic study of the child* (Vol. 6). New York: International Universities Press.

FRIEDRICH-COFER, L. K., Huston-Stein, A., Kipnis, D. M., Susman, A. J., & Clewett, A. S. (1979). Environmental enhancement of prosocial television content: Effects on interpersonal behavior. *Developmental Psychology, 15,* 637–646.

FULKERSON, K. F., Furr, S., & Brown, D. (1983). Expectations and achievement among third-, sixth-, and ninth-grade black and white males and females. *Developmental Psychology, 19,* 231–236.

FURMAN, W., & Masters, J. C. (1980). Peer interactions, sociometric status, and resistance to deviation in young children. *Developmental*

Psychology, 16, 229–236.

GALST, J. P. (1980). Television food commercials and pronutritional public service announcements as determinants of young children's snack choices. *Child Development, 51,* 935–938.

GELFAND, D. M. (1962). The influence of self-esteem on rate of verbal conditioning and social matching behavior. *Journal of Abnormal and Social Psychology, 65,* 259–265.

GLYNN, T. J. (1981). From family to peer: A review of transitions of influence among drug-using youth. *Journal of Youth and Adolescence, 10,* 363–383.

GOOD, T. L. (1979). Teacher effectiveness in the elementary school: What do we know about it now? *Journal of Teacher Education, 30,* 52–64.

GOOD, T. L., Biddle, B., & Brophy, J. E. (1975). *Teachers make a difference.* New York: Holt, Rinehart and Winston.

GORN, G. J., Goldberg, M. E., & Kanungo, R. N. (1976). The role of educational television in changing the intergroup attitudes of children. *Child Development, 47,* 277–280.

GOTTLIEB, D. (1966). Teaching and students: The views of Negro and white teachers. *Sociology of Education, 37,* 344–353.

GRAVES, S. B. (1975, April). *How to encourage positive racial attitudes.* Paper presented at the biennial meeting of the Society for Research in Child Development, Denver.

GRAZIANO, W. G., Musser, L. M., & Brody, G. H. (1982). *Children's cognitions and preferences regarding younger and older peers.* Unpublished manuscript, University of Georgia.

GREEN, J. A., & Gerard, H. B. (1974). School desegregation and ethnic attitudes. In H. Franklin & J. Sherwood (Eds.), *Integrating the organization.* New York: Free Press.

GREEN, K. D., Forehand, R., Beck, S. J., & Vosk, B. (1980). An assessment of the relationship among measures of children's social competence and children's academic achievement. *Child Development, 51,* 1149–1156.

GRIMES, J. W., & Allinsmith, W. (1961). Compulsivity, anxiety, and school achievement. *Merrill-Palmer Quarterly, 7,* 247–269.

GRUSEC, J. E., & Abramovitch, R. (1982). Imitation of peers and adults in a natural setting: A functional analysis. *Child Development, 53,* 636–642.

HAMM, N. H. (1970). A partial test of a social learning theory of children's conformity. *Journal of Experimental Child Psychology, 9,* 29–42.

HAMM, N. H., & Hoving, K. L. (1971). Conformity in children as a function of grade level, and real versus hypothetical adult and peer models. *Journal of Genetic Psychology, 118,* 253–263.

HARARI, H., & McDavid, J. W. (1973). Teachers' expectations and name stereotypes. *Journal of Educational Psychology, 65,* 222–225.

HARTUP, W. W. (1983). Peer relations. In E. M. Hetherington (Ed.), *Handbook of child psychology* (Vol. 4). New York: Wiley.

HARVEY, O. J., & Consalvi, C. (1960). Status and conformity to pressures in informal groups. *Journal of Abnormal and Social Psychology, 60,* 182–187.

HAYVREN, M., & Hymel, S. (1984). Ethical issues in sociometric testing: The impact of sociometric measures on interactive behavior. *Developmental Psychology, 20,* 844–849.

HETHERINGTON, E. M. (1981). Children and divorce. In R. M. Henderson (Ed.), *Parent-child interaction: Theory, research, and prospects.* Orlando, FL: Academic Press.

HILL, K. T., & Eaton, W. O. (1977). The interaction of test anxiety and success-failure experiences in determining children's arithmetic performances. *Developmental Psychology, 13,* 205–211.

HINDE, R. A., Titmus, G., Easton, D., & Tamplin, A. (1985). Incidence of "friendship" and behavior toward strong associates versus nonassociates in preschoolers. *Child Development, 56,* 234–245.

HOFFMAN-PLOTKIN, D., & Twentyman, C. T. (1984). A multimodal assessment of behavioral and cognitive deficits in abused and neglected children. *Child Development, 55,* 794–802.

HOVING, K. L., Hamm, N., & Galvin, P. (1969). Social influence as a function of stimulus ambiguity at three age levels. *Developmental Psychology, 6,* 631–636.

HUNTER, F. T. (1985). Adolescents' perception of discussions with parents and friends. *Developmental Psychology, 21,* 433–440.

HUSTON, A., & Wright, J. C. (1982). Effects of communications media on children. In C. B. Kopp & J. B. Krakow (Eds.), *The child: Development in a social context.* Reading, MA: Addison-Wesley.

HYMEL, S. (1986). Interpretations of peer behavior: Affective bias in childhood and adolescence. *Child Development, 57,* 431–445.

JACOBSON, J. L., & Wille, D. N. (1986). The influence of attachment pattern on developmental changes in peer interaction from the toddler to the preschool period. *Child Development, 57,* 338–347.

JERSILD, A. T. (1968). *Child psychology.* Englewood Cliffs, NJ: Prentice-Hall.

JOHNSON, D. (1981). Naturally acquired learned helplessness: The relationship of school failure to achievement behavior, attributions, and self-concept. *Journal of Educational Psychology, 73,* 174–180.

JOHNSON, N. (1967). *How to talk back to your television.* Boston: Little, Brown.

JOHNSTON, J., Ettema, J., & Davidson, T. (1980). *An evaluation of "Freestyle": A television series designed to reduce sex-role stereotypes.* Ann Arbor, MI: Institute for Social Research.

JONES, M. C. (1965). Psychological correlates of somatic development. *Child Development, 36,* 899–911.

JONES, M. C., & Bayley, N. (1950). Physical maturing among boys as related to behavior. *Journal of Educational Psychology, 41,* 129–148.

KAGAN, S., & Zahn, G. L. (1975). Field dependence and the school achievement gap between Anglo-American and Mexican-American children. *Journal of Educational Psychology, 67,* 643–650.

KANDEL, D. (1973). Adolescent marijuana use: Role of parents and peers. *Science, 181,* 1067–1070.

KANDEL, D. (1978). Homophily, selection, and socialization in adolescent friendships. *American Journal of Sociology, 84,* 427–436.

KERZNER, R. L. (1982). *The effect of retention on achievement.* Unpublished master's thesis, Kean College.

KROSNICK, J. A., & Judd, C. M. (1982). Transitions in social influence at adolescence: Who induces cigarette smoking. *Developmental Psychology, 18,* 359–368.

KURDEK, L. A., & Krile, D. (1982). A developmental analysis of the relation between peer acceptance and both interpersonal understanding and perceived social self-confidence. *Child Development, 53,* 1485–1491.

LaFRENIERE, P. J., & Sroufe, L. A. (1985). Profiles of peer competence in the preschool: Interrelations between measures, influence of social ecology, and relation to attachment history. *Developmental Psychology, 21,* 56–69.

LAMB, M. E., Easterbrooks, M. A., & Holden, G. W. (1980). Reinforcement and punishment among preschoolers: Characteristics, effects, and correlates. *Child Development, 51,* 1230–1236.

LANGLOIS, J. H. (1985). From the eye of the beholder to behavioral reality: The development of social behaviors and social relations as a function of physical attractiveness. In C. P. Herman (Ed.), *Physical appearance, stigma, and social behavior.* Hillsdale, NJ: Erlbaum.

LANGLOIS, J. H., & Downs, A. C. (1979). Peer relations as a function of physical attractiveness: The eye of the beholder or behavioral reality? *Child Development, 50,* 409–418.

LANGLOIS, J. H., & Styczynski, L. (1979). The effects of physical attractiveness on the behavioral attributions and peer preferences in acquainted children. *International Journal of Behavioral Development, 2,* 325–341.

LAOSA, L. M. (1981). Maternal behavior: Sociocultural diversity in modes of family interaction. In R. W. Henderson (Ed.), *Parent-child interaction: Theory, research, and prospects.* Orlando, FL: Academic Press.

LAOSA, L. M. (1982). School, occupation, culture, and family: The impact of parental schooling on the parent-child relationship. *Journal of Educational Psychology, 74,* 791–827.

LEACOCK, E. (1971, December). At play in African villages. *Natural History,* pp. 60–65.

LERNER, R. M. (1969). The development of stereotyped expectancies of body build relations. *Child Development, 40,* 137–141.

LERNER, R. M., & Lerner, J. (1977). Effects of age, sex, and physical attractiveness on child-peer relations, academic performance, and elementary school adjustment. *Developmental Psychology, 13*, 585–590.

LEWIN, K., Lippitt, R., & White, R. K. (1939). Patterns of aggressive behavior in experimentally created "social climates." *Journal of Social Psychology, 10*, 271–299.

LEWIS, M., Feiring, C., McGuffog, C., & Jaskir, J. (1984). Predicting psychopathology in six-year-olds from early social relations. *Child Development, 55*, 123–136.

LEWIS, M., & Rosenblum, M. A. (1975). *Friendship and peer relations*. New York: Wiley.

LIEBERT, R. M., Sprafkin, J. N., & Davidson, E. S. (1982). *The early window: Effects of television on children and youth*. New York: Pergamon Press.

LIVSON, N., & Peskin, H. (1980). Perspectives on adolescence from longitudinal research. In J. Adelson (Ed.), *Handbook of adolescent psychology*. New York: Wiley.

LYLE, J., & Hoffman, H. R. (1972). Children's use of television and other media. In E. H. Rubinstein, G. A. Comstock, & J. P. Murray (Eds.), *Television in day-to-day life: Patterns of use*. Washington, DC: U.S. Government Printing Office.

MacDONALD, K., & Parke, R. D. (1984). Bridging the gap: Parent-child play interaction and peer interactive competence. *Child Development, 55*, 1265–1277.

MAHAN, A. M., & Mahan, T. W. (1970). Changes in cognitive style: An analysis of the impact of white suburban schools on inner city children. *Integrated Education, 8*, 58–61.

MAIN, M., & George, C. (1985). Responses of abused and disadvantaged toddlers to distress in agemates: A study in the day-care setting. *Developmental Psychology, 21*, 407–412.

MASTERS, J. C., & Furman, W. (1981). Popularity, individual friendship selection, and specific peer interaction among children. *Developmental Psychology, 17*, 344–350.

McDAVID, J. W., & Harari, H. (1966). Stereotyping of names and popularity in grade school children. *Child Development, 37*, 453–459.

McGUIRE, K. D., & Weisz, J. R. (1982). Social cognition and behavioral correlates of preadolescent chumship. *Child Development, 53*, 1478–1484.

MILLER, L. B., & Bizzell, R. P. (1983). Long-term effects of four preschool programs: Sixth, seventh, and eighth grades. *Child Development, 54*, 727–741.

MILLER, N., & Maruyama, G. (1976). Ordinal position and peer popularity. *Journal of Personality and Social Psychology, 33*, 123–131.

MINUCHIN, P. P., & Shapiro, E. K. (1983). The school as a context for social development. In E. M. Hetherington (Ed.), *Handbook of child psychology* (Vol. 4). New York: Wiley.

MONTEMAYOR, R. (1982). The relationship between parent-adolescent conflict and the amount of time adolescents spend alone and with parents and peers. *Child Development, 53*, 1512–1519.

MOORE, S. G. (1967). Correlates of peer acceptance in nursery school children. In W. W. Hartup & N. L. Smothergill (Eds.), *The young child: Reviews of research*. Washington, DC: National Association for the Education of Young Children.

MORGAN, M. (1982). Television and adolescents' sex-role stereotypes: A longitudinal study. *Journal of Personality and Social Psychology, 43*, 947–955.

MURRAY, J. P. (1980). *Television and youth: 25 years of research and controversy*. Boys Town, NE: Boys Town Center for the Study of Youth Development.

NELSON, J., & Aboud, F. E. (1985). The resolution of social conflict among friends. *Child Development, 56*, 1009–1017.

NEWCOMB, A. F., Brady, J. E., & Hartup, W. W. (1979). Friendship and incentive condition as determinants of children's task-oriented social behavior. *Child Development, 50*, 878–881.

NEWCOMB, A. F., & Bukowski, W. M. (1984). A longitudinal study of the utility of social preference and social impact sociometric classification schemes. *Child Development, 55*, 1434–1447.

PAPALIA, D. E., & Olds, S. W. (1979). *A child's world*. New York: McGraw-Hill.

PASTOR, D. L. (1981). The quality of mother-infant attachment and its relationship to toddlers' initial sociability with peers. *Developmental Psychology, 16*, 245–250.

PATTERSON, G. R., Littman, R. A., & Bricker, W. (1967). Assertive behavior in children: A step toward a theory of aggression. *Monographs of the Society for Research in Child Development, 32*(5, Serial No. 113).

PELLEGRINI, D. S. (1985). Social cognition and competence in middle childhood. *Child Development, 56*, 253–264.

PETERSON, P. E., Jeffrey, D. B., Bridgwater, C. A., & Dawson, B. (1984). How pronutritional television programming affects children's dietary habits. *Developmental Psychology, 20*, 55–63.

PETERSON, P. L. (1977). Interactive effects of student anxiety, teacher orientation, and teacher behavior on student achievement and attitude. *Journal of Educational Psychology, 69*, 779–792.

PLUMMER, D. L., & Graziano, W. G. (1987). The impact of grade retention on the social development of elementary school children. *Developmental Psychology, 23*, 267–275.

PLUMMER, D. L., Hazzard-Lineberger, M., & Graziano, W. G. (1984). The academic and social consequences of grade retention: A convergent analysis. In L. Katz (Ed.), *Current topics in early childhood education* (Vol. 6). New York: Ablex.

PRATHER, M. (1969). Project Head Start teacher-pupil-parent interaction study. In E. Grothberg (Ed.), *Review of research 1965 to 1969*. Washington, DC: Project Head Start, Office of Economic Opportunity.

PUTALLAZ, M. (1983). Predicting children's sociometric status from their behavior. *Child Development, 54*, 1417–1426.

QUAY, L. C., & Jarrett, O. S. (1984). Predictors of social acceptance in preschool children. *Developmental Psychology, 20*, 793–796.

REYNOLDS, D., Jones, D., St. Leger, S., & Murgatroyd, S. (1980). School factors and truancy. In L. Hersov & I. Berg (Eds.), *Out of school: Modern perspectives in truancy and school refusal*. Chichester: Wiley.

RIST, R. C. (1970). Student social class and teacher expectations: The self-fulfilling prophecy in ghetto education. *Harvard Educational Review, 40*, 411–451.

ROFF, M. F. (1961). Childhood social interactions and adult bad conduct. *Journal of Abnormal and Social Psychology, 63*, 333–337.

ROFF, M. F. (1974). Childhood antecedents of adult neurosis, severe bad conduct, and psychological health. In D. F. Ricks, A. Thomas, & M. Roff (Eds.), *Life history research in psychopathology* (Vol. 3). Minneapolis: University of Minnesota Press.

ROFF, M. F., Sells, S. B., & Golden, M. M. (1972). *Social adjustment and personality development in children*. Minneapolis: University of Minnesota Press.

ROGOFF, B. (1981). Schooling's influence on memory test performance. *Child Development, 52*, 260–267.

ROSENTHAL, R., & Jacobson, L. (1968). *Pygmalion in the classroom*. New York: Holt, Rinehart and Winston.

ROSENTHAL, T., Underwood, B., & Martin, M. (1969). Assessing classroom incentive practices. *Journal of Educational Psychology, 60*, 370–376.

RUBLE, D. N., Balaban, T., & Cooper, J. (1981). Gender constancy and the effects of sex-typed televised toy commercials. *Child Development, 52*, 667–673.

RUDOLPH, F. (1965). *Essays on early education in the Republic*. Cambridge, MA: Harvard University Press.

RUTTER, M. (1983). School effects on pupil progress: Research findings and policy implications. *Child Development, 54*, 1–29.

RUTTER, M., Maughan, B., Mortimore, P., Ouston, J., & Smith, A. (1979). *Fifteen thousand hours: Secondary schools and their effects on children*. Cambridge, MA: Harvard University Press.

SAGOTSKY, G., & Lepper, M. R. (1982). Generalization of changes in children's preferences for easy or difficult goals induced through peer modeling. *Child Development, 53*, 372–375.

SANDOVAL, J., & Hughes, G. P. (1981). Success in non-promoted first grade children. *Resources in Education* (ERIC Document Reproduction Service No. ED 212 371), 1–204.

SAVIN-WILLIAMS, R. C., & Small, S. A. (1986). The timing of puberty and its relationship to adolescent and parent perceptions of family interactions. *Developmental Psychology, 22*, 342–347.

SCHRAMM, W., Lyle, J., & Parker, E. B. (1961). *Television in the lives of our children.* Stanford, CA: Stanford University Press.

SCHWARTZ, J. C. (1972). Effects of peer familiarity on the behavior of preschoolers in a novel situation. *Journal of Personality and Social Psychology, 24*, 276–284.

SEAVER, W. B. (1973). Effects of naturally induced teacher expectancies. *Journal of Personality and Social Psychology, 28*, 333–342.

SEBALD, H., & White, B. W. (1980). Teenagers' divided reference groups: Uneven alignment with parents and peers. *Adolescence, 15*, 980–984.

SHARP, D., Cole, M., & Lave, C. (1979). Education and cognitive development: The evidence from experimental research. *Monographs of the Society for Research in Child Development, 44*(1–2, Serial No. 178).

SHERIF, M. (1956). Experiments in group conflict. *Scientific American, 195*, 54–58.

SHERIF, M., Harvey, O. J., White, B. J., Hood, W. R., & Sherif, C. W. (1961). *Intergroup conflict and cooperation: The Robber's Cave experiment.* Norman: University of Oklahoma Press.

SIMAN, M. L. (1977). Application of a new model of peer group influence to naturally existing adolescent friendship groups. *Child Development, 48*, 270–274.

SMOLLAR, J., & Youniss, J. (1982). Social development through friendship. In K. H. Rubin & H. S. Ross (Eds.), *Peer relations and social skills in childhood.* New York: Springer-Verlag.

STAFFIERI, J. R. (1967). A study of social stereotype of body image in children. *Journal of Personality and Social Psychology, 7*, 101–104.

STEINBERG, C. S. (1980). *TV facts.* New York: Facts on File.

STEPHAN, W. G. (1977). Cognitive differentiation and intergroup perception. *Sociometry, 40*, 50–58.

STEPHAN, W. G. (1978). School desegregation: An evaluation of the predictions made in *Brown vs. Board of Education. Psychological Bulletin, 85*, 217–238.

ST. JOHN, N. H. (1975). *School desegregation: Outcomes for children.* New York: Wiley.

STONEMAN, Z., & Brody, G. H. (1981). Peers as mediators of television food advertisements aimed at children. *Developmental Psychology, 17*, 853–858.

STUDY: Children with working mothers score lower on tests. (1983, June 26). *Atlanta Journal*, p. 4-A.

STUMPHAUZER, J. S. (1972). Increased delay of gratification in young inmates through imitation of high-delay peer models. *Journal of Personality and Social Psychology, 21*, 10–17.

SULLIVAN, H. S. (1953). *The interpersonal theory of psychiatry.* New York: Norton.

SUOMI, S. J., & Harlow, H. F. (1975). The role and reason of peer relationships in rhesus monkeys. In M. Lewis & L. A. Rosenblum (Eds.), *Friendship and peer relations.* New York: Wiley.

SUOMI, S. J., & Harlow, H. F. (1978). Early experience and social development in rhesus monkeys. In M. E. Lamb (Ed.), *Social and personality development.* New York: Holt, Rinehart and Winston.

THELEN, M. H., & Kirkland, K. D. (1976). On status and being imitated: Effect on reciprocal imitation and attraction. *Journal of Personality and Social Psychology, 33*, 691–697.

THELEN, M. H., Miller, D. J., Fehrenbach, P. A., Frautschi, N. M., & Fishbein, M. D. (1980). Imitation during play as a means of social influence. *Child Development, 51*, 918–920.

THOMAS, N. G., & Berk, L. E. (1981). Effects of school environments on the development of young children's creativity. *Child Development, 52*, 1153–1162.

UTECH, D. A., & Hoving, K. L. (1969). Parent and peers as competing influences in the decisions of children of differing ages. *Journal of Social Psychology, 78*, 267–274.

VAUGHN, B. E., & Langlois, J. H. (1983). Physical attractiveness as a correlate of peer status and social competence in preschool children. *Developmental Psychology, 19*, 561–567.

WAHLER, R. G. (1967). Child-child interactions in five field settings: Some experimental analyses. *Journal of Experimental Child Psychology, 5*, 278–293.

WATERS, E., Wippman, J., & Sroufe, L. A. (1979). Attachment, positive affect, and competence in the peer group: Two studies of construct validation. *Child Development, 50*, 821–829.

WEATHERLEY, D. (1964). Self-perceived rate of physical maturation and personality in late adolescence. *Child Development, 35*, 1197–1210.

WHITING, B. B., & Whiting, J. W. M. (1975). *Children of six cultures.* Cambridge, MA: Harvard University Press.

WRIGHT, J. C., & Huston, A. C. (1983). A matter of form: Potentials of television for young viewers. *American Psychologist, 38*, 835–843.

YOUNISS, J. (1980). *Parents and peers in social development: A Sullivan-Piaget perspective.* Chicago: University of Chicago Press.

NAME INDEX

SUBJECT INDEX

CREDITS

CHAPTER 2. **42,** Figure 2-1 from *Introduction to Behavioral Genetics,* by G. E. McClearn and J. G. DeFries. Copyright 1973 by W. H. Freeman. Reprinted by permission.

CHAPTER 3. **66,** Figure 3-2 adapted from "Influence of Models' Reinforcement Contingencies on the Acquisition of Imitative Responses," by A. Bandura, *Jouranl of Personality and Social Psychology,* 1965, *1,* 589-595. Copyright 1965 by the American Psychological Association. Reprinted by permission.

CHAPTER 5. **118,** Figure 5-1 from "Monographs of the Society for Research in Child Development," by H. R. Shaffer and P. E. Emerson, 1964, *20,* p. 3. Copyright 1964 by The Society for Research in Child Development. Reprinted by permission. **121,** Figure 5-2 from "Affectional Responses in the Infant Monkey," by H. F. Harlow and R. R. Zimmerman, *Science,* 1959, *130,* 421-432. Copyright 1959 by the AAAS. Reprinted by permission. **125,** Figure 5-3 adapted from "Contingent Feedback, Familiarization, and Infant Affect: How a Stranger Becomes a Friend," by M. J. Levitt, *Developmental Psychology,* 1980, *165,* 425-432. Copyright 1980 by the American Psychological Association. Reprinted by permission.

CHAPTER 6. **138,** Table 6-1 from *Patterns of Attachment,* by M. D. S. Ainsworth, M. Blehr, E. Waters, and S. Wall. Copyright © 1978 by Lawrence Erlbaum Association, Inc. Reprinted by permission. **148–149,** Box 601, table adapted from "Security of Infant-Mother-Father and-Metapelet Attachments among Kibbutz-Reared Israeli Children," by A. Sagi, M. E. Lamb, K. S. Lewkowicz, R. Shoham, R. Dvir, and D. Estes. In I. Bretherton and E. Waters (Eds.), "Growing Points of Attachment Theory and Research," 1985, *Monographs of the Society for Research in Child Development, 50,* (Nos. 1-2, Serial No. 209). **155,** Figure 6-1 from "Deprivation Dwarfism," by L. J. Gardner, *Scientific American,* 1972, *227,* 76-82. Copyright © 1972 by Scientific American, Inc. All rights reserved. **158,** Figure 6-2 adapted from "Rehabilitation of Socially Withdrawn Preschool Children through Mixed-Age and Same-Age Socialization," by D. F. Rahe and W. W. Hartup, *Child Development,* 1979, 915-922. © 1979 by The Society for Research in Child Development, Inc. Reprinted by permission.

CHAPTER 7. **171,** Figure 7-1 from "Developmental Perspectives on the Self-System," by S. Harter. In P. H. Mussen (Eds.), *Handbook of Child Psychology,* Vol. 4, *Socialization, Personality and Social Development.* Copyright 1983 by John Wiley & Sons. Reprinted by permission. **172–173,** Box 7-1 from "Cross-Sectional Age Changes in Ego Identity Status during Adolescence," by P. W. Q. Meilman, *Developmental Psychology,* 1979, *15,* 230-231. Copyright 1979 by The American Psychological Association. Reprinted by permission. **175,** Figure 7-2 adapted from "The Development of Person Perception in Childhood and Adolescence: From Behavioral Comparisons to Psychological Constructs to Psychological Comparisons," by C. Barenboim, *Child Development,* 1981, *52,* 129-144. © 1981 by The Society for Research in Child Development. Reprinted by permission. **178,** quotations from "The Process of Causal Attribution," by H. H. Kelley, *American Psychologist,* 1971, *28,* 107-128. Copyright 1973 by the American Psychological Association. Reprinted by permission. **180,** Table 7-1 adapted from "Social-Cognitive Understanding: A Guide to Educational and Clinical Experience," by R. L. Selman. In T. Lickona, (Ed.), *Moral Development and Behavior: Theory, Research, and Social Issues,* 1976, Holt, Rinehart and Winston. **181,** Table 7-2 adapted from "Development of Physical and Social Reasoning in Adolescence," by D. Keating and L. V. Clark, *Developmental Psychology,* 1980, *16,* 23-30. Copyright 1980 by the American Psychological Association. Reprinted by permission.

CHAPTER 8. **201,** Table 8-1 adapted from "Relationships between Achievement Related Motives, Future Orientation, and Academic Performance," by J. O. Raynor, *Journal of Personality and Social Psychology,* 1970, *15,* 23-33. Copyright 1970 by the American Psychological Association. Reprinted by permission. **207,** Table 8-3 adapted from "Reasoning about the Ability of Self and Others," by J. G. Nicholls and A. T. Miller, *Child Development,* 1984, 1990-1999. © 1984 by The Society for Research in Child Development. **209,** Table 8-4 adapted from "Sex Differences in Learned Helplessness II. The Contingencies of Evaluative Feedback in the Classroom, and III. An Experimental Analysis," by C. S. Dweck, S. Davidson, S. Nelson and B. Enna, *Developmental Psychology,* 1978, *14,* 268-276. Copyright 1978 by the American Psychological Association. Reprinted by permission. **210–211,** Box 8-1, figure adapted from "Determinants of Academic Achievement: The Interaction of Children's Achievement Orientations with Skill Area," by B. G. Licht and C. S. Dweck, *Developmental Psychology,* 1984, *20,* 628-636. Copyright 1984 by the American Psychological Association. Reprinted by permission. **215,** Box

8-2, table adapted from "Entrepreneurial Environments and the Emergence of Achievement Motivation in Adolescent Males," by J. H. Turner, *Sociometry*, 1970, *33*, 147-165. Copyright 1970 by the American Sociological Association. Reprinted by permission. **217,** Table 8-6 adapted from "The Relationship between Twelve-Month Home Stimulation and School Achievement," by W. J. van Doorninck, B. M. Caldwell, C. Wright, and W. K. Frankenberg, *Child Development*, 1981, 1080-1083. © 1981 by The Society for Research in Child Development. Reprinted by permission. **220,** Table 8-7 adapted from "The Influence of Discrepancies between Successively Modeled Self-Reward Criteria on the Adoption of a Self-Imposed Standard," by M. J. McMains and R. M. Leiberg, *Journal of Personality and Social Psychology*, 1968, *8*, 166-171. Copyright 1968 by the American Psychological Association.

CHAPTER 9. 238, Box 9-2, figure adapted from "Sex and Aggression: The Influence of Gender Label on the Perception of Aggression in Children," by J. C. Condry and D. F. Ross, *Child Development*, 1985, *56*, 225-233. © 1985 by The Society for Research in Child Development. Reprinted by permission. **242,** Figure 9-1 adapted from "Effects of Frustration, Attack, and Prior Training in Aggressiveness upon Aggressive Behavior," by R. G. Geen, *Journal of Personality and Social Psychology*, 1986, *9*, 316-321. Copyright 1968 by the American Psychological Association. Reprinted by permission. **247,** Figure 9-3 from paper presented by K. A. Dodge at the bienniel meeting of the Society for Research in Child Development, Boston, 1981. **263,** Figure 9-5 adapted from "Effects of Movie Violence on Aggression in a Field Serving as a Function of Group Dominance and Cohesion," by J. P. Leyens, L. Camino, R. D. Parke and L. Berkowitz, *Journal of Personality and Social Psychology*, 1975, *32*, 346-360. Copyright 1975 by the American Psychological Association. Reprinted by permission. **267,** Box 9-3, figure adapted from "Effect of Temporal Separation between Motivation, Aggression, and Consequences: A Developmental Study" by W. A. Collins, *Developmental Psychology*, 1973, *8*, 215-221. Copyright 1973 by the American Psychological Association. Reprinted by permission.

CHAPTER 10. 285, Table 10-1 adapted from "Age Differences in the Behavior of Boys on Three Measures of Altruism," by F. P. Green and F. W. Schneider, *Child Development*, 1974, *45*, 248-251. © 1974 by The Society for Research in Child Development. Reprinted by permission. **290,** Box 10-1, table adapted from "Self-Control and Altruism: Delay of Gratification for Another," by F. H. Kanfer, E. Stifter, and S. J. Morris, *Child Development*, 1981, *47*, 51-61. © 1981 by The Society for Research in Child Development. **291,** Figure 10-2 adapted from "Affect and Altruism," by B. S. Moore, B. Underwood, and L. Rosenhan, *Developmental Psychology*, 1973, *8*, 99-104. Copyright 1973 by the American Psychological Association. Reprinted by permission. **294,** Table 10-2, figure from "Prosocial Development: A Longitudinal Study," by N. Eisenberg, R. Lennon, and K. Roth, *Developmental Psychology*, 1983, *19*, 846-855. Copyright 1983 by the American Psychological Association. Reprinted by permission. **296,** Figure 10-3 adapted from "Effect of Inducing Sadness about Self or Other on Helping Behavior in High and Low-Empathetic Children," by M. A. Barnett, J. A. Howard, E. M. Melton, and G. A. Dino, *Child Development*, 1982, *53*, 920-923. © 1982 by The Society for Research in Child Development. Reprinted by permission. **298,** Figure 10-4 adapted from "Aversive Approval: Interactive Effects of Modeling and Reinforcement on Altruistic Behavior," by E. Midlarsky, J. H. Bryan, and P. Brickman, *Child Develop-*

ment, 1973, *44*, 321-328. © 1981 by The Society for Research in Child Development. Reprinted by permission. **300,** Table 10-3 adapted from "Affect Expressions and Children's Imitative Altruism," by E. Midlarsky and J. H. Bryan, *Journal of Experimental Research in Personality*, 1972, *6*, 195-203. Copyright 1972 by Academic Press, Inc. Adapted by permission. **301,** Figure 10-5 courtesy of Associated Press and UPI. **303,** Box 10-2 adapted from "Positive Socialization via Cooperative Games," by T. D. Orlick, *Developmental Psychology*, 1981, *17*, 426-429. Copyright 1981 by the American Pschological Association. **303,** Box 10-3, table adapted from "Socialization and Situational Influences on Sustained Altruism," by E. G. Clary and J. Miller, *Child Development*, 1986, *57*, 1358-1369. © 1986 by The Society for Research in Child Development.

CHAPTER 11. 321 and **322,** Figures 11-1 and 11-2 adapted from "Factors Influencing Young Children's Use of Motives and Outcomes as Moral Criteria," by S. A. Nelson, *Child Development*, 1980, *51*, 823-829. © 1980 by The Society for Research in Child Development. Reprinted by permission. **328,** Figure 11-3 from "A Longitudinal Study of Moral Judgment," by A. Colby, L. Kohlberg, J. Gibbs, and M. Lieberman, *Monographs of the Society for Research in Child Development*, 1983, *48*, (Nos. 1-2, Serial No. 200), © 1983 by The Society for Research in Child Development. Reprinted by permission. **345,** Table 11-2 adapted from "Contributions of Parents and Peers to Children's Moral Socialization," by G. H. Brody and D. R. Shaffer, *Developmental Psychology*, 1982, *2*, 31-75. Copyright 1982 by the American Psychological Association. **349,** Box 11-5, figure adapted from "Reasoning, Prohibitions, and Motivations for Compliance," by L. Kuczynski, *Developmental Psychology*, 1983, *19*, 126-134. Copyright 1973 by the American Psychological Association.

CHAPTER 12. 359, Table 12-1 adapted from "Sex-Role Stereotypes: A Current Appraisal," by I. K. Broverman, S. R. Vogel, D. M. Broverman, F. E. Clarkson, and P. S. Rosenkrantz, *Journal of Social Issues*, 1972, *28*, 59-78. Copyright 1972 by the Society for the Psychological Study of Social Issues. **360,** Table 12-2 adapted from "A Cross-Cultural Survey of Some Sex Differences in Socialization," by H. Barry III, M. K. Bacon and I. L. Child, *Journal of Abnormal and Social Psychology*, 1957, *55*, 327-332. Copyright 1957 by the American Psychological Association. **367,** Figure 12-1 adapted from "Social Behavior at 33 Months in Same-Sex and Mixed-Sex Dyads," by C. N. Jacklin and E. E. Maccoby, *Child Development*, 1978, *49*, 557-569. © 1978 by The Society for Research in Child Development. Reprinted by permission. **368,** Table 12-5 adapted from "Children, Gender, and Social Structure: An Analysis of the Contents of Letters to Santa Claus," by J. G. Richardson and C. H. Simpson, *Child Development*, 1982, *53*, 429-436. © 1982 by The Society for Research in Child Development. **369,** Figure 12-2 adapted from *Birth to Maturity*, by K. Kagan and H. A. Moss, 1962, John Wiley & Sons, Inc.

CHAPTER 13. 407, Figure 13-1 adapted from "Early Human Experience: A Family Perspective," by J. Belsky, *Developmental Psychology*, 1981, *17*, 3-23. Copyright 1981 by the American Psychological Association. Reprinted by permission. **413,** Table 13-1 adapted from "Child Care Practices Anteceding Three Patterns of Preschool Behavior," by D. Baumrind, *Genetic Psychology Monographs*, 1967, *75*, 43-88. **432,** Figure 13-2 adapted from "Responses of Abused and Disadvantaged Toddlers to Distress in Agemates: A Study in the Day-Care Setting," by M. Main and C. George, *Developmental Psychology*, 1985, *21*, 407-412. Copyright 1985 by the American Psychological Association. Reprinted by permission. **433,** Figure 13-3 adapted from "Child Abuse as Psychopathology: A Sociological Critique and Reformulation," by R. J. Gelles, *American Journal of Orthopsychiatry, 1973, 32,* 611-621.

CHAPTER 14. **444,** Figure 14-1 adapted from *Television and Human Behavior,* by G. Comstock, 1978, Columbia University Press. **449,** Figure 14-2 adapted from Ball and Bogatz, 1970, as presented in R. M. Lieberg, J. N. Sprafkin, and E. S. Davidson, *The Early Window: Effects of Television on Children and Youth,* 1982, Pergamon Press, Inc. **452,** Figure 14-3 adapted from *Fifteen Thousand Hours: Secondary Schools and Their Effects on Children,* by M. Rutter, B. Maughan, P. Mortimer, J. Ouston, and A. Smith, 1979, Harvard University Press. **462,** Table 14-1 from "School Desegregation: An Evaluation of Predictions Made in *Brown v. Board of Education*," by W. G. Stephan, *Psychological Bulletin,* 1978, *85,* 217-238. Copyright 1978 by the American Psychological Association. Reprinted by permission. **464,** Figure 14-5 adapted from "Age Segregation in Children's Social Interactions," by S. Ellis, B. Rogoff, and C. C. Cromer, *Developmental Psychology,* 1981, *17,* 399-407. Copyright 1981 by the American Psychological Association. Reprinted by permission. **465,** Figure 14-6 adapted from "Age Segregation in Children's Social Interactions," by S. Ellis, B. Rogoff, and C. C. Cromer, *Developmental Psychology,* 1981, *17,* 399-407. Copyright 1981 by the American Psychological Association. Reprinted by permission. **475,** Table 14-2 adapted from "Stability and Change in Childhood and Adolescent Friendships," by T. J. Berndt and S. G. Hoyle, *Developmental Psychology,* 1985, *21,* 1007-1015. Copyright 1985 by the American Psychological Association.

PHOTO CREDITS